This book examines the consequences of misspecifications in econometrics for the interpretation and properties of likelihood-based methods of statistical estimation and inference. Professor White first explores the underlying motivation for maximum-likelihood estimation, treats the interpretation of the maximum-likelihood estimator (MLE) for misspecified probability models and gives the conditions under which parameters of interest can be consistently estimated despite misspecification. He then investigates the limiting distribution of the MLE under misspecification, the conditions under which MLE efficiency is not affected despite misspecification and the consequences of misspecification for hypothesis testing and estimating the asymptotic covariance matrix of the parameters. The analysis concludes with an examination of methods by which misspecification problems can be empirically investigated and offers a variety of appropriate tests.

Although the theory presented in the book is motivated by econometric problems, its applicability is by no means restricted to economics. Subject to defined limitations, the theory applies to any scientific context in which statistical analysis is conducted using approximate models.

Econometric Society Monographs No. 22

Estimation, Inference and Specification Analysis

Econometric Society Monographs

Editors:

Jean-Michel Grandmont *Centre d'Études Prospectives d'Économie Mathémtique Appliquées à la Planification, Paris*
Alain Monfort *Institut National de la Statistique et des Études Économiques*

The Econometric Society is an international society for the advancement of economic theory in relation to statistics and mathematics. The Econometric Society Monograph Series is designed to promote the publication of original research contributions of high quality in mathematical economics and theoretical and applied econometrics.

Other titles in the series:

Werner Hildenbrand, Editor *Advances in economic theory*
Werner Hildenbrand, Editor *Advances in econometrics*
G. S. Maddala *Limited-dependent and qualitative variables in econometrics*
Gerard Debreu *Mathematical economics*
Jean-Michel Grandmont *Money and value*
Franklin M. Fisher *Disequilibrium foundations of equilibrium economics*
Bezalel Peleg *Game theoretic analysis of voting in committees*
Roger Bowden and Darrell Turkington *Instrumental variables*
Andreu Mas-Colell *The theory of general economic equilibrium*
James J. Heckman and Burton Singer *Longitudinal analysis of labor market data*
Cheng Hsiao *Analysis of panel data*
Truman F. Bewley, Editor *Advances in economic theory — Fifth World Congress*
Truman F. Bewley, Editor *Advances in econometrics — Fifth World Congress* (Volume I)
Truman F. Bewley, Editor *Advances in econometrics — Fifth World Congress* (Volume II)
Hervé Moulin *Axioms of cooperative decision making*
L. G. Godfrey *Misspecification tests in econometrics*
Tony Lancaster *The econometric analysis of transition data*
Wolfgang Härdle *Applied nonparametric regression*
Alvin E. Roth and Marilda A. Oliveira Sotomayor *Two-sided matching*
Jean-Jacques Laffont, Editor *Advances in economic theory — Sixth World Congress* (Volume 1)
Jean-Jacques Laffont, Editor *Advances in economic theory — Sixth World Congress* (Volume 2)
Christopher A. Sims, Editor *Advances in econometrics — Sixth World Congress* (Volume 1)
Christopher A. Sims, Editor *Advances in econometrics — Sixth World Congress* (Volume 2)

Estimation, Inference and Specification Analysis

HALBERT WHITE
University of California, San Diego

CAMBRIDGE
UNIVERSITY PRESS

Published by the Press Syndicate of the University of Cambridge
The Pitt Building, Trumpington Street, Cambridge CB2 1RP
40 West 20th Street, New York, NY 10011-4211, USA
10 Stamford Road, Oakleigh, Melbourne 3166, Australia

First published 1994

Printed in the United States of America

Library of Congress Cataloging-in-Publication Data

White, Halbert.

Estimation, inference and specification analysis / Halbert White.

p. cm. – (Econometric Society monographs: no. 22)

Includes bibliographical references and indexes.

ISBN 0–521–25280–6

1. Econometric models. I. Title. II. Series.

HB141.W548 1994
330′.01′5195 – dc20 92–30563
CIP

A catalog record for this book is available from the British Library.

ISBN 0–521–25280–6 hardback

To my wife, Kim

The real constitution of things is accustomed to hiding itself.

Heraclitus, *The Cosmic Fragments*

CONTENTS

ACKNOWLEDGMENTS

Work on this monograph began over eleven years ago at the behest of Colin Day, then editorial director of Cambridge University Press. I am deeply grateful to him for his confidence and enthusiasm in my vision of a unified theory of maximum-likelihood estimation under model misspecification, and for his faith that the project would eventually be completed, long after the original timetable for the work had fallen by the wayside. I am pleased to have finally justified his faith. It is my hope that his confidence and enthusiasm will also be justified by this work.

Research on the various parts of this monograph has been conducted in just about every locale to which my academic wanderings have taken me. Work began at the University of Rochester and continued at the University of California San Diego, the Australian National University, North Carolina State University, the Massachusetts Institute of Technology, INSEE and CEPREMAP in Paris and the Oxford Institute of Economics and Statistics, and was finally completed at the University of California San Diego while on sabbatical *in loco* (no pun intended). I wish to express my sincere appreciation to each of these fine institutions for their support. Financial support for this research provided by the National Science Foundation under grants SES81–07552, SES83–00635 and SES85–10637 has been an immeasurable help.

The results obtained and their manner of presentation have been profoundly affected by the inspiration of and interaction with numerous colleagues. For inspiration I thank Jerry Hausman and Frank Fisher of MIT who taught me to think econometrically, and Takeshi Amemiya of Stanford whose work in econometric theory provided me with key insights in the development of the theory that underlies the main results of this work, and whose rigorous and precise approach to econometric theory has provided a high standard I have attempted to emulate. Of the many colleagues from whom I have benefited by discussing with them various aspects of the work presented here, I would like especially to thank Don Andrews, Charles Bates, Larry

Benveniste, Herman Bierens, Richard Carson, Gregory Chow, Paul Churchland, Ian Domowitz, Rob Engle, James Friedman, Ron Gallant, Christian Gourieroux, Clive Granger, A. R. Hall, Peter Hall, Lars Hansen, David Hendry, Alberto Holly, Yongmiao Hong, Chung-Ming Kuan, Mark Machina, Lionel MacKenzie, Graham Mizon, Alain Monfort, Whitney Newey, Adrian Pagan, Peter Phillips, Jean-Francois Richard, Paul Ruud, Eugene Savin, Max Stinchcombe, Quang Vuong, Jon Wellner, Jeff Wooldridge and Ed Zabel. Two anonymous reviewers gave the rough manuscript a very careful and complete reading, and provided numerous helpful suggestions. None of these is to blame if I still haven't got things figured out right. They did their best to straighten me out and for their efforts I am sincerely grateful.

Many people have helped in the preparation of the manuscript. I would especially like to thank Shirl Cicmanec, Leigh Henry, Paula Lindsay, Meredee Byron-O'Brien, Annetta Whiteman, Susan Wiggans and Rose Yamasaki for their skillful and apparently cheerful preparation of a manuscript that might easily have given them nightmares (and probably did, but they were too tactful to tell me).

Finally, I wish to express my deep appreciation to my loving wife Kim, who had no idea that seven months after she married me I was going to spend nearly every lucid moment (and some others) for the next seven months trying to finish this ******* book. After asking, "What happened to all the free time you used to have before we were married?" and hearing my lame explanation that the book was supposed to have been finished five or six years ago, she did not divorce me, but provided more support than any driven theoretical econometrician (or anybody else) has a right to ask. That's why I've dedicated this book to her.

Halbert White
La Jolla, California

CHAPTER 1

Introductory Remarks

The use of sophisticated statistical techniques to estimate the parameters of carefully formulated economic models is today the standard practice in the attempt to learn about and from observed economic phenomena. Of course, this has not always been so. The present state of economic and econometric practice owes a very great deal of its rigor, coherence and elegance to the pioneering work of Frisch, Haavelmo, Tinbergen, Koopmans and Marschak, among others.

Of these pioneers, Haavelmo [1944] is responsible for providing the first comprehensive enunciation of the modern parametric approach to empirical economic analysis in his classic monograph *The Probability Approach in Econometrics*, which appeared as a supplement to *Econometrica*. There Haavelmo persuasively argued that the *ad hoc* correlation analyses and curve fitting techniques then prevalent should be replaced by modern statistical estimation and inference methods applied to carefully formulated probability models. Haavelmo showed how consideration of underlying economic principles, leading to mathematical relations embodying the economic model, together with consideration of difficulties of measurement and observation lead ultimately to a well-formulated parametric probability model. Haavelmo argued that appropriate statistical techniques, such as the method of maximum likelihood, should then be used for purposes of estimation, inference and prediction.

Today, this may appear transparently obvious; but this appearance is in fact merely a measure of the profound effect of the work of Frisch, Haavelmo and their peers. Yet, despite the apparent superiority of this approach over previous *ad hoc* methods and its now nearly universal acceptance, economists have so far largely failed to discover "laws" of economic reality in the same way that physicists have been able to discover "laws" of physical reality. One measure of this failure is that economists are loath to speak of their estimates as estimates of economic "constants" in the same way a physicist speaks of physical constants. Instead, economists speak of "true parameters" or "deep parameters" (Lucas [1976]). The notion of an economic constant seems almost inherently suspect.

It is the premise of this monograph that this failure is not simply a passing characteristic of a discipline still in its infancy and that with the passage of time, adequate theories comparable to those of the physical sciences will be developed. Instead, we claim that because of the exceeding complexity of economic behavior, because of the extreme difficulty of measuring or even properly defining relevant aspects of economic phenomena, and because the economist typically has little or no control over the economic phenomenon under study, economic theory is fundamentally and inherently limited in the degree to which it can describe economic reality or make legitimate falsifiable statements about economic reality. Because the empirical economist must deal with nature in all her complexity, it is optimistic in the extreme to hope or believe that standard parametric economic models or probability models are sufficiently adequate to capture this complexity.

A realistic attitude in such circumstances is that an economic model or a probability model is in fact only a more or less crude approximation to whatever might be the "true" relationships among the observed data, rather than necessarily providing an accurate description of either the actual economic or probabilistic relationships. Consequently, it is necessary to view economic and/or probability models as misspecified to some greater or lesser degree. Once this view is adopted, some serious questions arise.

(1) *Under what conditions can standard parametric statistical techniques such as maximum likelihood be meaningfully applied to estimate the parameters of a misspecified model?*

(2) *What happens if these conditions aren't met?*

(3) *How can one tell if these conditions aren't met?*

The purpose of this monograph is to provide a treatment of these and related issues in a context relevant to much of econometric practice. Because of the central role and wide scope of the method of maximum likelihood in econometrics, our primary focus will be on the use of maximum likelihood techniques to estimate parameters of possibly misspecified models. We follow in the tradition of Cox [1961, 1962], Berk [1966, 1970] and Huber [1967], who first studied maximum likelihood estimation under misspecification of the probability model.

In this book, I examine the consequences of misspecifications ranging from the fundmental to the non-existent for the interpretation and properties of likelihood-based methods of estimation and inference. These consequences lead naturally to specification testing procedures, i.e., statistical methods for detecting the presence of particular or general misspecifications. The term "specification analysis" is credited by Amemiya [1966] to Theil [1961] and refers to examining the consequences for estimation and inference of different sorts of model misspecification. My use of the term specification analysis in the title of this book and elsewhere should be understood as embracing specification testing as well.

The analysis is organized in the following manner. In Chapter 2, we examine the underlying motivation for maximum likelihood estimation. The interpretation of the maximum likelihood estimator (MLE) for misspecified probability models is treated in Chapter 3, and conditions under which parameters of interest can be consistently estimated despite misspecification are given in Chapters 4 and 5. The limiting distribution of the MLE under misspecification is studied in Chapter 6; conditions under which the efficiency of the MLE is not affected despite misspecification are given in Chapter 7; and the consequences of misspecification for hypothesis testing and estimating the asymptotic covariance matrix of the parameters are investigated in Chapter 8. In Chapters 9, 10 and 11 we examine methods by which the possibility of misspecification can be empirically investigated, presenting a variety of tests for misspecification. Chapter 12 contains a summary and some concluding remarks.

The last several years have seen an explosive development in the econometric literature concerned with each of these topics, as the references given in the text should make quite clear. Because of the very broad scope and substantial depth of this literature, it is of course impossible for the present work to encompass any substantial portion of it. My intent here is to provide a theory that embraces and extends only a modest portion of what is presently available, but that can serve both as a springboard for further theoretical development and as a source for potentially useful new empirical methods.

Given recent developments in the literature, many results given here for the first time will not appear surprising; they merely extend results known for the i.i.d case appropriately to the dependent heterogeneous case. Nevertheless, there are a number of specific new developments contained here that deserve mention. For example, we establish consistency of nonlinear quantile estimators with dependent observations in Chapter 5. In Chapter 7 we consider the concepts of weak and super-exogeneity and propose an alternative concept more appropriate in certain contexts. Chapter 9 includes a discussion of Wooldridge's [1990] modified m-test and a construction that permits any specification test to be viewed as a specific classical test. Chapter 10 contains a multitude of potentially useful new specification testing procedures, including a version of the Cox test of non-nested hypotheses applicable with dependent observations, and a useful reformulation of the encompassing principle. Chapter 11 sets out a variety of information matrix tests, and introduces a new test, the cross-information matrix test. Appendix 2 contains a useful new uniform law of large numbers.

The scope of this book is limited not only by its focus on maximum likelihood-type methods, but also by its focus on relatively stable data generating processes. Generally, unit root, trending or explosive processes are ruled out. However, the results are formulated to permit a degree of dependence and heterogeneity in the data generating process not previously available in either the correctly specified or misspecified context. Because economic time-series data appear to exhibit substantial dependence and heterogeneity even after attempts at stabilization, the present theory has at least some claim to relevance in economics.

Although the theory presented here is motivated by problems arising in the statistical analysis of economic phenomena, its applicability is by no means restricted to economics. Subject to the limitations just mentioned, the theory applies to any context in which statistical analysis is conducted using approximate models, such as systems identification (e.g., Ljung [1987]) or learning in artificial neural networks (e.g., Rumelhart and McClelland [1986], White [1989]).

I have attempted to make this book accessible to graduate students well-trained in econometrics or mathematical statistics; it is by no means self-contained. It assumes a knowledge of linear algebra, calculus, probability theory and statistics. Familiarity with the content of *Asymptotic Theory for Econometricians* (White [1984a]) or the equivalent is useful; especially helpful is some familiarity with the texts of Billingsley [1979, 1986], as results given there are relied on heavily throughout this work.

CHAPTER 2

Probability Densities, Likelihood Functions and Quasi-Maximum Likelihood Estimators

In this chapter we provide motivation for the method of maximum likelihood and give conditions ensuring the existence of the quasi-maximum likelihood estimator (QMLE).

2.1 The Data Generation Process

Empirical phenomena are appropriately viewed as the realization of a stochastic process on some suitable probability space. Formally, we state this in the following way.

ASSUMPTION 2.1: The observed data are a realization of a stochastic process $X \equiv \{X_t : \Omega \to \mathbb{R}^v, v \in \mathbb{N}, t = 1, 2, \ldots\}$ on a complete probability space $(\Omega, \mathcal{F}, P_o)$, where $\Omega = \mathbb{R}^{v\infty} \equiv \times_{t=1}^{\infty} \mathbb{R}^v$ and $\mathcal{F} = \mathcal{B}^{v\infty} \equiv \mathcal{B}(\mathbb{R}^{v\infty})$. □

Let ω be a typical element of Ω. As ω ranges over Ω, we have realizations $X_t(\omega)$ ranging over $\mathbb{R}^v$, where v is a finite integer ($\mathbb{N} = \{1, 2, \ldots\}$). The structure of the space Ω is important only to the extent that it allows for sufficiently rich behavior in X_t. For concreteness and convenience, we have chosen $\Omega = \mathbb{R}^{v\infty}$. In this case X_t is the projection operator that selects x_t, the tth coordinate of ω, so that $X_t(\omega) = x_t$. With $\mathcal{F}$ chosen as $\mathcal{B}^{v\infty}$, the Borel σ-field generated by the measurable finite dimensional product cylinders, the projection operators are measurable, so that $X \equiv \{X_t\}$ is a stochastic process on $(\mathbb{R}^{v\infty}, \mathcal{B}^{v\infty}, P_o)$, namely, the *coordinate-variable process* (Billingsley [1979, p. 433]).

In what follows, we shall often partition the $v \times 1$ observation vector X_t as $X_t = (Z'_t, Y'_t)'$, where Y_t is $l \times 1$, so that Z_t is $v - l \times 1$. This is convenient in cases where Y_t is a set of "dependent" variables to be determined (explained, forecasted) at least partly on the basis of other variables Z_t.

The probability measure P_o provides a complete description of the stochastic behavior of the sequence X and can thus be viewed as the "true data generating mechanism." We also call P_o the "data generation process", following Hendry and Richard [1982]. If P_o were known, then one would know all there is to know about the stochastic relationships among the elements of X. Problems of estimation and inference arise precisely because P_o is unknown. If we can observe a realization of the sequence X, it is at least possible that knowledge of P_o could be inferred from X.

From a practical standpoint, we will not have available observations on an entire infinite sequence of realizations. Instead we have a realization x^n of a finite history, $X^n \equiv (X'_1, \ldots, X'_n)'$. We call x^n a *sample of size* n. The stochastic process generating of any sample of size n is completely described by its *distribution*

$$P_o^n(B) \equiv P_o[X^n \in B] \qquad B \in \mathcal{B}^{vn},$$

where $\mathcal{B}^{vn} \equiv \mathcal{B}(\mathbb{R}^{vn})$ is the Borel σ-field generated by the open sets of $\mathbb{R}^{vn} \equiv \times_{t=1}^n \mathbb{R}^v$. Thus, the goal of estimation and inference is to learn about P_o^n using information available in the sample generated by X^n. In this monograph, we focus attention on asymptotics: estimation and inference as n becomes arbitrarily large.

A description of the stochastic behavior of any sample equivalent to that provided by P_o^n is given by its Radon-Nikodým density, under general conditions.

ASSUMPTION 2.2: Let σ-finite measures ν^n on $(\mathbb{R}^{vn}, \mathcal{B}^{vn})$, $n = 1, 2, \ldots$ be given. For each $n = 1, 2, \ldots$, P_o^n is absolutely continuous with respect to ν^n. □

See Appendix 1 for definitions of σ-finiteness, absolute continuity and other measure-theoretic background. When P_o^n is absolutely continuous with respect to ν^n we also say that "ν^n dominates P_o^n."

The Radon-Nikodým theorem implies the existence of the associated densities.

THEOREM 2.1: *Given Assumptions 2.1 and 2.2 there exists a measurable non-negative Radon-Nikodým density $g^n \equiv dP_o^n / d\nu^n$, unique up to a set of ν^n – measure zero, such that*

$$P_o^n(B) = \int_B g^n d\nu^n$$

for all $B \in \mathcal{B}^{vn}$, $n = 1, 2, \ldots$. □

Assumption 2.2 holds trivially by putting $\nu^n = P_o^n$, in which case $g^n(x^n) = 1$ for all x^n in the smallest set $B \in \mathcal{B}^{vn}$ such that $P_o^n(B) = 1$, $n = 1, 2, \ldots$. However, knowledge of P_o is required to make this choice; because knowledge of ν^n will be required to verify certain of our conditions such a choice is not practical. Instead, because we only require that ν^n dominate P_o^n (so that ν^n does not assign zero measure to an event involving X^n having positive probability), a useful choice for ν^n can be based on a knowledge of what values for X^n are possible or have positive probability. This knowledge is usually readily available.

In many cases it is possible to take ν^n to be the product measure $\nu^n = \otimes_{t=1}^n \nu_t$, where ν_t is a σ-finite measure dominating P_{ot}, where $P_{ot}(C) \equiv P_o[X_t \in C]$, $C \in \mathcal{B}^v$.

To illustrate possible choices for ν_t, suppose momentarily that X_t is a scalar. If X_t ranges over the continuum of the real line then ν_t can be chosen as Lebesgue measure, λ. This allows treatment of continuous random variables, and if all the variables are of this kind, then ν^n is a product of Lebesgue measures and g^n is the familiar continuous density function of elementary probability theory.

However, g^n is more generally defined. Suppose that X_t takes on a finite or countable number of distinct values, each with positive probability. This occurs for discrete dependent variables such as those that arise in logit or probit analysis or in Poisson models, as well as for "dummy" explanatory variables. Let D_t be the set of points in $\mathbb{R}$ for which X_t assumes values with positive probability. Then ν_t can be defined as

$$\nu_t(E) = \gamma(E \cap D_t)$$

for any set E in $\mathcal{B}$, where γ is the counting measure, which simply counts the number of points in the set indicated. If all the variables were of this kind, then

$$g^n(x^n) = P_o^n(X_1 = x_1, \ldots, X_n = x_n)$$

for all x^n in $\mathbb{R}^n$.

It is not uncommon to encounter situations in economics in which the dependent or explanatory variables can take values on a continuum but may also have positive probability of assuming a finite or countable number of discrete values. This situation arises in Tobit analysis, where the dependent variable has a positive probability of being observed at zero and may otherwise take any positive value. Defining D_t as above, we can assign an appropriate measure in this case as

$$\nu_t(E) = \gamma(E \cap D_t) + \lambda(E \cap D_t^c)$$

for any E in $\mathcal{B}$, where D_t^c is the complement of D_t in $\mathbb{R}$. When ν^n is a product measure with components of this sort, then g^n has marginal distributions that place mass at points where variables take values with positive probability, and that look like familiar continuous densities elsewhere.

When ν^n is a product measure, there is no need for all of the component measures to be of the same type, and each ν_t may be different to allow for the behavior of the random variable to which it corresponds.

When X_t is not a scalar, ν_t itself can often be constructed as a product measure, say $\nu_t = \otimes_{i=1}^{v} \nu_{ti}$, where ν_{ti} is a σ-finite measure dominating P_{oti}, $P_{oti}(E) \equiv P_o(X_{ti} \in E)$, $E \in \mathcal{B}$. The preceding comments for ν_t now apply to ν_{ti}.

Realistic situations may arise in which the joint probability distribution of X_t is not absolutely continuous with respect to a product measure. For example, consider a labor market in which wages W_t are constrained to lie at or above some minimum wage, $w_{\min}$, and the market clears (labor supply equals labor demand) at an equilibrium wage W_t^e whenever $W_t^e \geq w_{\min}$. Let $X_t = (S_t, D_t, W_t)'$, where S_t is labor supply, D_t is labor demand, and W_t is the wage. Then $P_{ot}(C) = 1$, where C can be taken to be the union of two subsets of half-planes, $C = C_1 \cup C_2$, where $C_1 = \{D_t = S_t,\ W_t > w_{\min},\ D_t \geq 0\}$ and $C_2 = \{S_t \geq D_t,\ W_t = w_{\min},\ D_t \geq 0\}$. In general we may have $P_{ot}(C_1) > 0$ and $P_{ot}(C_2) > 0$. However, if S_t, D_t and W_t are continuously distributed on $[0, \infty)$, $[0, \infty)$ and $(w_{\min}, \infty)$ respectively then the product measure $\nu_t = \nu_{t1} \otimes \nu_{t2} \otimes \nu_{t3}$ where ν_{t1}, ν_{t2} and ν_{t3} are chosen so that the distributions of S_t,D_t and W_t are absolutely continuous with respect to ν_{t1}, ν_{t2},ν_{t3} respectively will satisfy $\nu_t(C_1) = 0$, so that P_{ot} is not absolutely continuous with respect to ν_t.

In this and similar cases, ν_t can be chosen to dominate P_{ot}, but not as a product measure. Similar remarks hold for ν^n and P_o^n. In other cases, absolute continuity with respect to product measures is natural and convenient. We shall note these circumstances as we proceed, but we avoid imposing product measure assumptions across the board because they rule out certain cases that can plausibly occur in realistic applications.

As long as ν^n is properly chosen, Theorem 2.1 ensures the existence of the relevant density function; in particular, it provides an equivalent representation for the true data generation process for samples of size n. Given ν^n, the knowledge of g^n is tantamount to the knowledge of P_o^n, the true data generation process for samples of a given size. Thus, we can attempt to recover P_o^n by using the sample to learn about g^n.

One way to do this is to construct some sort of approximation to g^n based on X^n. For this one needs a criterion by which to evaluate such an approximation. One such criterion is the information criterion introduced by Kullback and Leibler [1951].

DEFINITION 2.2 (*KLIC*)**:** Let $(\Omega, \mathcal{F}, \nu)$ be a measure space, let $g : \Omega \to I\!R^+$ be a measurable function satisfying $\int g \, d\nu < \infty$ and $\int_S g \log g \, d\nu < \infty$, where $S \equiv \{\omega \in \Omega : g(\omega) > 0\}$, and let $f : \Omega \to I\!R^+$ be a measurable function satisfying $\int_S g \log f \, d\nu < \infty$. The *Kullback-Leibler Information Criterion* (KLIC) *is defined as*

$$I\!I(g : f) \equiv \int_S g \log(g/f) \, d\nu . \qquad \square$$

Here and elsewhere, log denotes the natural logarithm.

The KLIC measures the discrepancy or divergence of f from g in a manner formally described by the information inequality, which we now state.

THEOREM 2.3 *(Information Inequality): Let f, g, ν, S, and $I\!I$ be as in Definition 2.2. If $\int_S (g - f) \, d\nu \geq 0$, then $I\!I(g : f) \geq 0$ and $I\!I(g : f) = 0$ if and only if $g = f$ almost everywhere - ν (a.e.$-\nu$) on S.* $\square$

For brevity, we henceforth write $g = f$ for densities $g = f$ *a.e.*$-\nu$ on S. Thus, the KLIC has the essential property that only when two densities f and g coincide (*a.e.* on *S*) does $I\!I(g : f) = 0$. Otherwise $I\!I(g : f) > 0$, so that $I\!I(g : f)$ can serve as a measure of the closeness of f to g, as discussed by Akaike [1973].

Further, the KLIC has a fundamental information-theoretic interpretation, as shown by Renyi [1961, 1970]. If f and g are probability densities, then the KLIC can be interpreted as the surprise experienced on average when we believe that f describes a given phenomenon and we are then informed that in fact the phenomenon is described by g.

The KLIC is not a metric on the space of probability densities (and thus not a measure of goodness of fit in the usual sense) because $I\!I(g : f) \neq I\!I(f : g)$ and because it does not satisfy a triangle inequality. An important and useful metric on this space is ρ, the L_2 distance between $f^{1/2}$ and $g^{1/2}$, defined as

$$\rho^2(g, f) \equiv \int (f^{1/2} - g^{1/2})^2 \, d\nu = 2 - 2 \int (f \, g)^{1/2} \, d\nu .$$

This metric is nicely treated by Pitman [1979] and Le Cam [1986, Ch. 4]. However, it does not easily lend itself to solving the estimation problem directly, because in order to compare the adequacy of two approximations f_1 and f_2 to a given density g, one must know g. This is because

$$\rho^2(g, f_1) - \rho^2(g, f_2) = 2 \int [(f_2/g)^{1/2} - (f_1/g)^{1/2}] g \, d\nu .$$

When g is unknown, as it is in our case, this quantity cannot be evaluated, although it can be estimated with some effort (see Beran [1977]).

In contrast, using the KLIC allows us to avoid this effort in solving the estimation problem. Comparison of the adequacy of two approximations f_1 and f_2 using the KLIC is based on

$$\begin{aligned} \mathbb{I}(g : f_1) - \mathbb{I}(g : f_2) &= \int_S \log(g/f_1) \, g d\nu - \int_S \log(g/f_2) \, g d\nu \\ &= \int_S \log(f_2/f_1) \, g d\nu . \end{aligned}$$

It turns out that this latter quantity can usually be estimated, even though g may be unknown. Using the KLIC therefore leads one to choose the approximation to g for which $\int_S (\log f_i) \, g d\nu$ (or its estimate) is greatest. The KLIC also provides flexibility, in that the approximations considered need not be densities in order for the information inequality to hold.

2.2 Probability Models and Stochastic Specifications

An approximation to g^n can be based on a probability model, defined in the following way.

DEFINITION 2.4 *(Probability Model):* Let $(\Omega, \mathcal{F})$ be a measurable space. A *probability model* is a collection $\mathcal{P}$ of distinct probability measures on $(\Omega, \mathcal{F})$. □

Note that we define the model as a *collection* of probability measures (as does, e.g., Lehmann [1983]). We refer to an element P^o of $\mathcal{P}$ as a "model element." Some authors would refer to P^o as a model, but this is inconvenient for our purposes.

A probability model may or may not be correctly specified. The natural definition of this property is

DEFINITION 2.5 *(Correctly Specified Probability Model):* The probability model $\mathcal{P}$ is *correctly specified for* X if $\mathcal{P}$ contains P_o, the data generating mechanism of Assumption 2.1. Otherwise, $\mathcal{P}$ is misspecified *for* X. □

The only probability model guaranteed to be correctly specified is $\mathcal{P}^*$, the collection of all probability measures on $(\Omega, \mathcal{F})$.

In many cases, it is assumed that P_o belongs to some probability model with elements indexed by a finite dimensional parameter vector, *i.e.* $\mathcal{P} = \{ P_\theta : \theta \in \Theta \subseteq \mathbb{R}^p, p \in \mathbb{N} \}$. We call such a model a *parametric probability model* and write $\mathcal{P} = \{ P_\theta \}$ for brevity. Typically, a parametric probability model $\mathcal{P}$ is a very small subset of $\mathcal{P}^*$. In such cases, misspecification is a serious hazard, if not a foregone conclusion.

Given a parametric probability model, approximations to g^n can be generated in the same way that g^n is itself generated — i.e., as a Radon-Nikodým density.

THEOREM 2.6: *Let $\mathcal{P} = \{ P_\theta \}$ be a parametric probability model. Define P_θ^n as $P_\theta^n(B) \equiv P_\theta[X^n \in B]$, $B \in \mathcal{B}^{vn}$, $n = 1, 2, \ldots, \theta \in \Theta$. Suppose there exists a σ-finite measure η^n on $(\mathbb{R}^{vn}, \mathcal{B}^{vn})$ such that for each θ in Θ, P_θ^n is absolutely continuous with respect to η^n, $n = 1, 2, \ldots$. Then there exists a nonnegative Radon-Nikodým density $f^n(\cdot, \theta) = dP_\theta^n / d\eta^n$ measurable $-\mathcal{B}^{vn}$ for each θ in Θ, $n = 1, 2, \ldots$.* □

In fact, the σ-finite measures η^n can be chosen equal to ν^n whenever this may be convenient. If for all θ P_θ^n is absolutely continuous with respect to any measure $\eta^n \neq \nu^n$, then it follows immediately that P_θ^n is absolutely continuous with respect to $\zeta^n = (\eta^n + \nu^n)/2$. Further, P_o^n is also absolutely continuous with respect to ζ^n. Thus, there is no contradiction or loss of generality in replacing ν^n and η^n with ζ^n in both Assumption 2.2 and Theorem 2.6.

When the conditions of Theorem 2.6 hold, we say that $\mathcal{P}$ is a *regular* (parametric) probability model. We say that the density $f^n(\cdot, \theta)$ is constructed "from the top down" when it is arrived at by first positing a regular parametric probability model $\mathcal{P}$ and then applying Theorem 2.6. The mapping $f^n(x^n, \cdot) : \Theta \to \mathbb{R}^+$ is referred to as the *likelihood function generated by the probability model $\mathcal{P}$ with respect to η^n for the realization x^n*. For brevity, we refer to f^n as the "likelihood function generated by $\mathcal{P}$."

In economics, approximations to g^n are rarely constructed from the top down. They are more often constructed "from the bottom up" in a sense to be made precise shortly. This approach is motivated by the following representation of g^n.

THEOREM 2.7: *Given Assumption 2.1 and 2.2, the densities g^n, $n = 1, 2, \ldots$ can be chosen such that $x^n \in S^n \equiv \{ x^n : g^n(x^n) > 0 \}$ implies $x^{n-1} \in S^{n-1}$ for all x^n in S^n. We refer to densities g^n with this property as "standard". Let $g^1, \ldots, g^n$ be standard densities. Then for all x^n in S^n*

$$\log g^n(x^n) = \sum_{t=1}^{n} \log g_t(x^t),\ n = 1, 2, \ldots,$$

where $g_t(x^t) \equiv g^t(x^t)/g^{t-1}(x^{t-1})$, $t = 2, 3, \ldots$, *and* $g_1(x^1) \equiv g^1(x^1) = g^1(x_1)$. □

Unless otherwise stated, all densities g^n will henceforth be assumed standard.

Often, the function g_t can be interpreted as a conditional density of X_t given X^{t-1} with respect to a measure ν_t. This can be shown to be valid when ν^t can be taken to be the product measure $\nu^t = \nu^{t-1} \otimes \nu_t$, $t = 1, 2, \ldots$. However, even when ν^t cannot be taken to be a product measure in this way, g_t is well defined. We refer to g_t as a "density ratio of X^t given X^{t-1}" to emphasize its similarity to a conditional density. Note that g_t is defined only on S^t in Theorem 2.7. We may define g_t to be any convenient value on the complement $(S^t)^c$.

Let $f_t : \mathbb{R}^{\nu t} \times \Theta \to \mathbb{R}^+$ be used to construct approximations to g_t as $f_t(\cdot, \theta)$, $t = 1, 2, \ldots$. An approximation to g^n can then be constructed "from the bottom up" as

$$f^n(x^n, \theta) \equiv \prod_{t=1}^{n} f_t(x^t, \theta)$$

in a manner analogous to the way in which g^n factors. We call this approximation a "quasi-likelihood" function. An interesting question is under what conditions such an approximation is compatible with a specific probability model. We use the following definition.

DEFINITION 2.8: Let η^n be a measure on $(\mathbb{R}^{\nu n}, \mathcal{B}^{\nu n})$ and let $f^n : \mathbb{R}^{\nu n} \times \Theta \to \mathbb{R}^+$ be measurable $-\mathcal{B}^{\nu n}$ for each θ in Θ, an arbitrary set, $n = 1, 2, \ldots$. For each θ in Θ, define the measure

$$P_\theta^n(B) = \int_B f^n(x^n, \theta)\, d\eta^n(x^n), \qquad B \in \mathcal{B}^{\nu n}.$$

We say that $\{f^n\}$ *generates (the probability model)* $\mathcal{P} = \{P_\theta\}$ *with respect to* $\{\eta^n\}$ if for each θ in Θ there exists a probability measure P_θ on $(\mathbb{R}^{\nu\infty}, \mathcal{B}^{\nu\infty})$ such that for each n the restriction of P_θ to $(\mathbb{R}^{\nu n}, \mathcal{B}^{\nu n})$ is given by P_θ^n, $n = 1, 2, \ldots$. □

When $\{f^n = \Pi_{t=1}^n f_t\}$ generates the probability model $\mathcal{P}$, we say that the probability model is constructed "from the bottom up." A necessary condition for this is given by the following result.

THEOREM 2.9: *Let* $\{\eta_n\}$ *be a sequence of measures on* $(\mathbb{R}^v, \mathcal{B}^v)$, *and define the measures* $\eta^{n+1} = \eta^n \otimes \eta_{n+1}$, $n = 1, 2, \ldots, \eta^1 = \eta_1$. *Let* Θ *be an arbitrary set and suppose that* $f_t : \mathbb{R}^{vt} \times \Theta \rightarrow \mathbb{R}^+$ *is such that* $f_t(\cdot, \theta)$ *is measurable* $-\mathcal{B}^{vt}$ *for each* θ *in* Θ. *Then in order for* $\{f^n = \Pi_{t=1}^n f_t\}$ *to generate a probability model* $\mathcal{P}$ *with respect to* $\{\eta^n\}$, *it is necessary that for each* θ *in* Θ *we have* $\int f_t(x^t, \theta)\, d\eta_t(x_t) = 1$ a.e. - P_θ^{t-1}, $t = 2, 3, \ldots$ and $\int f_1(x_1, \theta)\, d\eta_1(x_1) = 1$. □

In order to generate a probability model, it is therefore necessary that f_t be a conditional density for X_t given X^{t-1} for all θ in Θ, and all t. While this is often perfectly reasonable and natural, this requirement is frequently violated in econometric practice (as, for example, when the stochastic behavior of "exogenous" variables is ignored in the modeling process). Thus, probability models are too narrow a class of approximations to P_o to be generally relevant.

Because of this limitation of probability models, the major focus of our attention throughout this monograph will be on the wider class of *parametric stochastic specifications.*

DEFINITION 2.10 *(Parametric Stochastic Specification):* A *parametric stochastic specification on* $(\Omega, \mathcal{F})$ is a collection $\mathcal{S}$ of sequences of functions $f(\theta) \equiv \{f_t(\cdot, \theta) : \mathbb{R}^{vt} \rightarrow \mathbb{R}^+, t = 1, 2, \ldots\}$ obtained by letting θ range over $\Theta \subseteq \mathbb{R}^p$, $p \in \mathbb{N}$, where for each $t = 1, 2, \ldots$ and each $\theta \in \Theta$, $f_t(\cdot, \theta) : \mathbb{R}^{vt} \rightarrow \mathbb{R}^+$ is measurable $-\mathcal{B}^{vt}$, *i.e.* $\mathcal{S} \equiv \{f(\theta) : \theta \in \Theta\}$. □

For brevity, we shall say that $\mathcal{S} = \{f_t\}$ is a "specification for X" when the conditions of this definition are met. We shall also refer to $f^n = \Pi_{t=1}^n f_t$ as the "quasi-likelihood (specified by $\mathcal{S}$)." We distinguish it from a likelihood function because the quasi-likelihood function need not generate a parametric probability model.

As for probability models, stochastic specifications can be described as correctly specified or misspecified, but because of their greater generality, it is necessary to be precise about the nature of the correctness or incorrectness of a given specification. It is premature to attempt this precision here; we devote the required effort to it in subsequent chapters. It is enough for now to understand that stochastic specifications may be correctly or incorrectly specified to varying degrees.

For our purposes, it is convenient to construct specifications using the following assumption.

ASSUMPTION 2.3: The functions $f_t : \mathbb{R}^{vt} \times \Theta \to \mathbb{R}^+$ are such that $f_t(\cdot, \theta)$ is measurable – $\mathcal{B}^{vt}$ for each θ in Θ, a compact subset of $\mathbb{R}^p$, $p \in \mathbb{N}$, and $f_t(X^t, \cdot)$ is continuous on Θ *a. s.* -P_o, i.e. $f_t(x^t, \cdot)$ is continuous on Θ for all x^t in some $F_t \in \mathcal{B}^{vt}$, $P_o^t[F_t] = 1$, $t = 1, 2, \ldots$. □

The measurability requirement ensures that f_t is a function of at most the the same variables as g_t; the continuity restriction is more a matter of convenience — it could be dispensed with, but at the cost of additional technicalities. Among other things the continuity (*a. s.*) condition rules out situations in which the support of f_t depends on θ in a discontinuous manner.

In many applications, it is convenient or necessary to allow f_t to depend also on n, i.e., to consider double arrays $\{f_{nt} : \mathbb{R}^{vt} \times \Theta \to \mathbb{R}^+, n, t = 1, 2, \ldots\}$. For notational convenience, the possible dependence of f_t on n will be left implicit. Conditions holding for $t = 1, 2, \ldots$ are then to be also understood as holding for $n = 1, 2, \ldots$.

2.3 Existence of the Quasi-Maximum Likelihood Estimator

Given Assumption 2.3 and some additional appropriate conditions, the quasi-likelihood $f^n = \Pi_{t=1}^n f_t$ can be viewed as an approximation to g^n, with adequacy measured by

$$\mathbb{I}(g^n : f^n ; \theta) \equiv \int_{S^n} \left[\log g^n(x^n) / f^n(x^n, \theta)\right] g^n(x^n)\, d\nu^n(x^n).$$

Choosing θ to minimize $\mathbb{I}(g^n : f^n ; \theta)$ is equivalent to choosing θ to maximize

$$\begin{aligned}\bar{L}_n(\theta) &= \int_{S^n} \log f^n(x^n, \theta)\, g^n(x^n)\, d\nu^n(x^n) \\ &= \int_{S^n} \log f^n(x^n, \theta)\, dP_o^n(x^n) \\ &= E(\log f^n(X^n, \theta)) .\end{aligned}$$

When $f^n(x^n, \theta)$ is correctly specified in the sense that $f^n(x^n, \theta_o) = g_n(x^n)$ for a unique vector θ_o in Θ, then choosing θ to maximize $\bar{L}_n(\theta)$ yields θ_o, by the information inequality. This solves the problem of inference, because knowledge of f^n and θ_o is tantamount to knowledge of P_o^n. Apparently, then, choosing θ to maximize $\bar{L}_n(\theta)$ has the essential desirable property that under appropriate conditions, it leads to discovery of the true data generation process.

Unfortunately, θ cannot be chosen in this way because $\bar{L}_n(\theta)$ is an expected value determined by the unknown g^n. However, the problem can often be solved approximately using sample information, in the following way.

Because division by n does not affect the maximizing value of θ, maximizing $\tilde{L}_n(\theta)$ is equivalent to maximizing

$$\bar{L}_n(\theta) \equiv n^{-1} \tilde{L}_n(\theta) = E(n^{-1} \log f^n(X^n, \theta)) .$$

Because $f^n = \Pi_{t=1}^n f_t$, we have

$$n^{-1} \log f^n(X^n, \theta) = n^{-1} \sum_{t=1}^{n} \log f_t(X^t, \theta) .$$

If a law of large numbers applies to the sums on the right above, it follows that for n sufficiently large, $E(n^{-1} \log f^n(X^n, \theta))$ will be well approximated by $L_n(X^n, \theta) \equiv n^{-1} \log f^n(X^n, \theta)$. Hence the value for θ that provides the best approximation to g^n might be well approximated in such cases by the solution $\hat{\theta}_n$ to the problem

$$\text{(2. 1)} \qquad \max_{\theta \in \Theta} \; L_n(X^n, \theta) \equiv n^{-1} \sum_{t=1}^{n} \log f_t(X^t, \theta).$$

The function L_n will be called the *quasi-log-likelihood function*, and a solution $\hat{\theta}_n$ will be called a *quasi-maximum likelihood estimator* (QMLE).

Observe that while the information inequality motivates estimating θ_o by solving (2.1), any number of other considerations might lead one to attempt to estimate θ_o by solving

$$\max_{\theta \in \Theta} \; n^{-1} \sum_{t=1}^{n} q_t(X^t, \theta)$$

for some choice of q_t. Because $\log f_t$ can take either sign, we can simply set $f_t = \exp q_t$ and immediately interpret any such estimation scheme as quasi-maximum likelihood estimation. Proper care must be taken, however, in applying the information inequality.

Nothing so far establishes that a solution to (2.1) exists or what, if any, properties a solution might have. In order to address these issues, we must first take care of a difficulty: Because the support of f^n may depend on θ, f^n may vanish for certain values of θ and x^n even though g^n is positive. This implies that $L_n(X^n, \theta)$ can assume the value $n^{-1} \log 0$ with positive probability. To handle this possibility, we define $\log 0 = -\infty$ and consider the extended real line $\bar{\mathbb{R}} = \mathbb{R} \cup \{-\infty, \infty\}$. We adopt the standard convention that an extended real valued function $f : \Omega \to \bar{\mathbb{R}}$ is measurable - $\mathcal{F}$ if and only if $\{\omega : f(\omega) \in B\} \in \mathcal{F}$ for each B in $\mathcal{B}$ and $\{\omega : f(\omega) = \infty\}$ and $\{\omega : f(\omega) = -\infty\}$ both lie in $\mathcal{F}$.

Because f_t is measurable for each θ in Θ, the sets on which it vanishes are measurable sets. Hence log f_t is a measurable extended real valued function, and therefore so is L_n.

The existence of a QMLE is a consequence of the following result, a modification of a result of Le Cam [1953] and Jennrich [1969].

THEOREM 2.11: *Let* $(\Omega, \mathcal{F})$ *be a measurable space, and let* Θ *be a compact subset of* $\mathbb{R}^p$, $p \in \mathbb{N}$. Let $Q : \Omega \times \Theta \to \overline{\mathbb{R}}$ *be such that* $Q(\cdot, \theta)$ *is measurable for each* θ *in* Θ *and* $Q(\omega, \cdot)$ *is continuous on* Θ *for each* ω *in* $F \in \mathcal{F}$. *Then there exists a function* $\hat{\theta} : \Omega \to \Theta$ *measurable* $- \mathcal{F}$ *such that for all* ω *in* F

$$Q(\omega, \hat{\theta}(\omega)) = \sup_{\theta \in \Theta} Q(\omega, \theta). \qquad \square$$

When Q satisfies the conditions of this result and $P(F) = 1$ we say that "Q is a measurable function continuous on Θ almost surely (*a.s.*)." The existence of a QMLE is ensured by the following result.

THEOREM 2.12: (*Existence 1): Given Assumptions 2.1 and 2.3 and a sequence* $\{\Theta_n\}$ *of compact subsets of* Θ, *for each* $n = 1, 2, \ldots$ *there exists a function* $\hat{\theta}_n : \mathbb{R}^{vn} \to \Theta_n$ *measurable* $- \mathcal{B}^{vn}$ *and a set* $F_n \in \mathcal{B}^{vn}$ *with* $P_o^n(F_n) = 1$ *such that for all* x^n *in* F_n

$$L_n(x^n, \hat{\theta}_n(x^n)) = \max_{\theta \in \Theta_n} L_n(x^n, \theta). \qquad \square$$

When $\hat{\theta}_n$ satisfies the conclusion of this result, we write

$$\hat{\theta}_n = \text{argmax}_{\Theta_n} L_n(X^n, \theta) \quad a.s. - P_o.$$

For now, we are primarily interested in the case for which $\Theta_n = \Theta$ for all n. Dropping this assumption later is useful in treating estimation under sequences of local alternatives.

Thus, a QMLE $\hat{\theta}_n$ exists for each n that, with probability one, maximizes the quasi-log-likelihood. (The set on which $\hat{\theta}_n$ does not necessarily maximize L_n is the set on which L_n is not continuous, so that no maximum need exist.) Although existence of the QMLE is assured here, nothing is said about uniqueness — there may be multiple solutions. Use of the function "argmax" is thus an abuse of notation, but we adopt it for convenience. In what follows, we denote a sequence of QMLE's as $\hat{\theta} \equiv \{\hat{\theta}_n\}$; we shall also refer to $\hat{\theta}$ as a QMLE. We say that "$\mathcal{S}$ generates $\hat{\theta}$" or refer to $\hat{\theta}$ as the QMLE "generated by $\mathcal{S}$."

An important aspect of this result is the measurability of $\hat{\theta}_n$. This establishes that $\hat{\theta}_n$ is a random variable, and therefore has stochastic properties (consistency, asymptotic distribution) that we shall study further in subsequent chapters. Note that $\hat{\theta}_n$ is measurable $-\mathcal{B}^{nv}$, while $\hat{\theta}_n(X^n)$ is measurable $-\mathcal{F}$. For convenience, this latter function will also be denoted $\hat{\theta}_n$ in what follows. The meaning will be clear from the context.

The present result allows treatment of constrained estimation. For example, suppose θ is required to satisfy the restrictions $r(\theta) = 0$, where r is a continuous function on the compact set Θ. Then $\Theta_r \equiv r(\Theta)$ is also a compact set. In this case, Θ is simply replaced by Θ_r in the maximization problem.

Often, the QMLE is sought as the solution to the first order conditions $\nabla L_n(x^n, \theta) = 0$, where ∇ is the gradient operator with respect to θ, so that ∇L_n is a $p \times 1$ vector function. For $\hat{\theta}_n$ to exist as a solution of these equations, ∇L_n must be defined at $\hat{\theta}_n$. For this, it is sufficient to adopt the following assumption.

ASSUMPTION 2.4: $f_t(X^t, \cdot)$ is continuously differentiable on Θ $a.s. - P_o$, i.e. for all x^t in some $F_t \in \mathcal{B}^{vt}$, $P_o^t(F_t) = 1$, $f_t(x^t, \cdot)$ is continuously differentiable on Θ, $t = 1, 2, \ldots$. □

THEOREM 2.13 (*Existence II*): *Given Assumptions 2.1, 2.3 and 2.4, if the QMLE $\hat{\theta}_n$ lies interior to an open subset of Θ a.s.– P_o and $L_n(X^n, \hat{\theta}_n) > -\infty$ a.s. $- P_o$ then $\nabla L_n(X^n, \hat{\theta}_n)$ exists a.s. $- P_o$ and $\nabla L_n(X^n, \hat{\theta}_n) = 0$ a.s. $- P_o$.* □

This result says that when a QMLE exists and the log-likelihood function is differentiable, then an interior QMLE satisfies the first order conditions

$$\nabla L_n(x^n, \theta) = 0 .$$

In other words, at least one solution to these first order conditions exists, given Assumptions 2.1, 2.3 and 2.4, and at least one of these solutions is a QMLE.

The fact that a QMLE can be obtained as a solution to the equations $\nabla L_n(x^n, \theta) = 0$ motivates Huber's [1967] class of m-estimators (maximum likelihood-like estimators), which satisfy conditions of the form

$$n^{-1} \sum_{t=1}^{n} \psi_t (X^t , \hat{\theta}_n) \xrightarrow{a.s.} 0 .$$

The QMLE is obtained by setting

$$\psi_t (x^t , \theta) = \nabla \log f_t(x^t , \theta) = \nabla f_t (x^t , \theta)/f_t (x^t , \theta) .$$

Particular choices for ψ_t will often imply a choice for f_t that satisfies Assumptions 2.3 and 2.4. In particular, if ψ_t admits an antiderivative Ψ_t, then set $f_t = \exp \Psi_t$. However, ψ_t need not have an antiderivative, because e.g. $\partial \psi_{tj}(x^t , \theta) / \partial \theta_i$ need not equal $\partial \psi_{ti}(x^t , \theta) / \partial \theta_j$, where θ_i is the ith component of θ and ψ_{ti} is the ith component of ψ_t. Hence the m-estimators and the QMLE's are closely related, but neither class necessarily contains the other.

2.4 Existence of the Two-Stage Quasi-Maximum Likelihood Estimator

The class of QMLE's can be usefully extended by considering estimators obtained in a two-stage process. Suppose that $\Theta = \mathcal{A} \times \mathcal{B}$ where $\mathcal{A}$ and $\mathcal{B}$ are compact subsets of finite dimensional Euclidean spaces. In many circumstances, it may be convenient to obtain estimates $\hat{\alpha}_n : \mathbb{R}^{vn} \to \mathcal{A}$ in a first stage ($\hat{\alpha}_n$ may or may not be a QMLE) and then obtain $\hat{\beta}_n$ in a second stage by solving the problem

$$(2.2) \qquad \max_{\beta \in \mathcal{B}} \; L_n(X^n , \hat{\alpha}_n , \beta) = n^{-1} \sum_{t=1}^{n} \log f_t(X^t , \hat{\alpha}_n , \beta) .$$

This estimator will be called the *two stage* QMLE (2SQMLE) *generated by* $\mathcal{S} = (\{f_t\} , \{\hat{\alpha}_n\})$. The two stage least squares estimator of Theil [1953] can be viewed as a 2SQMLE, even though it is straightforwardly computed in a single step. The class of 2SQMLE's also includes the two-stage estimators for the selectivity-bias problem of Heckman [1974], as well as Sargan's [1958] Generalized Instrumental Variables Estimator and a class of estimators for simultaneous systems discussed by Hendry [1976].

The existence of the 2SQMLE is proved using the following result.

THEOREM 2.14: *Let* $(\Omega , \mathcal{F})$ *be a measurable space, and let* $\Theta = \mathcal{A} \times \mathcal{B}$ *where* $\mathcal{A}$ *and* $\mathcal{B}$ *are compact subsets of finite dimensional Euclidean spaces. Let* $Q : \Omega \times \mathcal{A} \times \mathcal{B} \to \overline{\mathbb{R}}$ *be such that* $Q(\cdot , \alpha , \beta)$ *is measurable for each* (α , β) *in* $\mathcal{A} \times \mathcal{B}$ *and* $Q(\omega , \cdot , \cdot)$ *is continuous on* $\mathcal{A} \times \mathcal{B}$ *for each* ω *in* $F \in \mathcal{F}$. *Let* $\hat{\alpha} : \Omega \to \mathcal{A}$ *be measurable -* $\mathcal{F}$. *Then*

(i) For each β *in* $\mathcal{B}$, $\tilde{Q}(\cdot, \beta) = Q(\cdot, \hat{\alpha}(\cdot), \beta)$ *is a measurable function on* Ω *and for each* ω *in* F, $\tilde{Q}(\omega, \cdot)$ *is a continuous function on* $\mathcal{B}$;

(ii) There exists a measurable function $\hat{\beta} : \Omega \to \mathcal{B}$ *such that for all* ω *in* F

$$\tilde{Q}(\omega, \hat{\beta}(\omega)) = \sup_{\beta \in \mathcal{B}} \tilde{Q}(\omega, \beta) . \qquad \square$$

Applying this to the 2SQMLE gives the desired result. We use the following assumption.

ASSUMPTION 2.5: $\{\hat{\alpha}_n : \mathbb{R}^{vn} \to \mathcal{A}\}$ is a sequence of measurable functions, where $\mathcal{A}$ is a subset of a finite dimensional Euclidean space. $\square$

THEOREM 2.15: *Given Assumptions 2.1, 2.3 and 2.5, suppose that* $\Theta = \mathcal{A} \times \mathcal{B}$, *where* $\mathcal{A}$ *and* $\mathcal{B}$ *are compact subsets of finite dimensional Euclidean spaces. Let* $\{\mathcal{B}_n\}$ *be a sequence of compact subsets of* $\mathcal{B}$. *Then for each* $n = 1, 2, \ldots$ *there exists a measurable function* $\hat{\beta}_n : \mathbb{R}^{vn} \to \mathcal{B}_n$ *and a set* $F_n \in \mathcal{B}^{vn}$ *with* $P_o^n(F_n) = 1$ *such that for all* x^n *in* F_n

$$L_n(x^n, \hat{\alpha}_n(x^n), \hat{\beta}_n(x^n)) = \max_{\beta \in \mathcal{B}_n} L_n(x^n, \hat{\alpha}_n(x^n), \beta) . \qquad \square$$

This result ensures the measurability of the 2SQMLE, $\hat{\theta}_n = (\hat{\alpha}'_n, \hat{\beta}'_n)'$. As with the QMLE, we are now primarily interested in the case in which $\mathcal{B}_n = \mathcal{B}$ for all n.

A situation sometimes encountered that is not covered by the present result occurs when the parameter space $\mathcal{B}_n$ is dependent on $\hat{\alpha}_n(x^n)$. When x^n is the realization of a random variable, $\mathcal{B}_n$ then becomes random. This case, which can occur under certain cross-equation constraints arising from budget constraints or stability considerations, is considered by Vuong [1984], and a measurability result is given by Stinchcombe and White [1992]. We consider a particular instance of such constraints in Chapter 8.

2.5 Summary

In this chapter we have seen that the phenomenon of interest can be represented equivalently by its probability distribution or by its probability density. Parametric probability models and stochastic specifications provide a collection of functions that can act as approximations to the probability density. The "adequacy" of approximation can be measured by the KLIC, which can be estimated from a sample of data. The parameter vector that minimizes the estimated KLIC is a QMLE $\hat{\theta}_n$. This is a measurable function (i.e., a random variable) under general conditions. The same is also true for the 2SQMLE.

MATHEMATICAL APPENDIX

PROOF OF THEOREM 2.1: Because P_o^n is σ-finite by construction and absolutely continuous with respect to ν^n by Assumption 2.2, the result follows immediately from the Radon-Nikodým theorem (Billingsley [1979, p. 375]); see Appendix 1. □

PROOF OF THEOREM 2.3: Because $\int_S g d\nu < \infty$, we may take $\int_S g\, d\, \nu \leq 1$ without loss of generality. Consequently, $1 \geq \int_S g\, d\, \nu \geq \int_S f\, d\, \nu = \int_S (f/g) g d\nu$. By Jensen's inequality

$$\int_S (f/g) g d\nu \geq \exp \int_S \log(f/g)\, g d\nu$$

given that $\int_S \log(f/g)\, g d\nu < \infty$. Consequently,

$$\log 1 \geq \int_S \log(f/g)\, g d\nu$$

so that our first result holds,

$$\int_S \log(g/f)\, g d\nu \geq 0.$$

To show that $\int_S \log(g/f)\, g d\nu = 0$ if and only if $g = f$ $a.e. - \nu$ on S, we first note that sufficiency of $g = f$ $a.e. - \nu$ on S is obvious. To show necessity, ignore the trivial case $\nu(S) = 0$ and suppose that $\int_S \log(g/f)\, g d\nu = 0$ is true, but that $g = f$ $a.e. - \nu$ on S is false. Then there exists a measurable subset F of S such that $\nu(F) > 0$ and $\omega \in F$ implies $g(\omega) \neq f(\omega)$. Because $g(\omega) > 0$ for $\omega \in S$, $\int_S \log(g/f)\, g d\nu = 0$ is true only if there exist $F_1, F_2 \in \mathcal{F}$ such that $F = F_1 \cup F_2$, $\omega \in F_1$ implies $g(\omega) > f(\omega)$, $\omega \in F_2$ implies $g(\omega) < f(\omega)$ and $\nu(F_1) > 0$, $\nu(F_2) > 0$. Let $F_3 \equiv \{\omega : g(\omega) = f(\omega)\}$ so that $S = F_1 \cup F_2 \cup F_3$. Then

$$\begin{aligned}\int_S (g - f) d\nu &= \int_{F_1} (g - f) d\nu + \int_{F_2} (g - f) d\nu + \int_{F_3} (g - f) d\nu \\ &= \int_{F_1} (g - f) d\nu + \int_{F_2} (g - f) d\nu.\end{aligned}$$

Because $\int_S (g - f) d\nu \geq 0$, it follows that

$$\int_{F_1} (g - f) d\nu \geq \int_{F_2} (f - g) d\nu.$$

Now

$$\int_S \log(g/f)\, g d\nu = \int_{F_1} \log(g/f)\, g d\nu - \int_{F_2} \log(f/g)\, g d\nu.$$

For $\omega \in F_2$, Taylor's theorem gives

$$\log(f/g) = \log 1 + (f/g - 1) - (f/g - 1)^2 / (2\alpha^2), \ \alpha \in (1, f/g)$$
$$< (f/g - 1),$$

so $-\int_{F_2} \log(f/g)\, g d\nu > \int_{F_2} (1 - f/g) g d\nu$. This implies

$$\int_{F_1} \log(g/f)\, g d\nu - \int_{F_2} \log(f/g)\, g d\nu$$
$$> \int_{F_1} \log(g/f)\, g d\nu + \int_{F_2} (g - f) d\nu$$
$$\geq \int_{F_1} \log(g/f)\, g d\nu + \int_{F_1} (f - g) d\nu.$$

For $\omega \in F_1$, Taylor's theorem gives

$$\log(f/g) = \log 1 + (f/g - 1) - (f/g - 1)^2 / (2\alpha^2), \ \alpha \in (f/g, 1)$$
$$< (f/g - 1),$$

so $\int_{F_1} \log(g/f)\, g d\nu = -\int_{F_1} \log(f/g)\, g d\nu > \int_{F_1} (1 - f/g) g d\nu$. Hence

$$\int_{F_1} \log(g/f)\, g d\nu + \int_{F_1} (f - g) d\nu$$
$$> \int_{F_1} (g - f) d\nu + \int_{F_1} (f - g) d\nu = 0.$$

Collecting the preceding inequalities, we obtain $\int_S \log(g/f)\, g d\nu > 0$, a contradiction. Thus $\int_S \log(g/f)\, g d\nu = 0$ implies $g = f\ a.e. - \nu$ on S, and the proof is complete. □

PROOF OF THEOREM 2.6: For each θ in Θ, the proof is identical to that of Theorem 2.1 with P_θ replacing P_o. □

PROOF OF THEOREM 2.7: To show the first result, we use the fact that $0 = P_o^{n-1}[(S^{n-1})^c] = P_o^n[(S^{n-1})^c \times \mathbb{R}^v] = \int_{(S^{n-1})^c \times \mathbb{R}^v} g^n(x^n) d\nu^n(x^n)$. By Bartle [Corollary 4.10, 1966] $g^n(x^n) = 0$ for almost every $(-\nu^n)$ x^n in $(S^{n-1})^c \times \mathbb{R}^v$. Because g^n is unique only up to sets of ν^n-measure zero, we can take g^n such that $g^n(x^n) = 0$ for all x^n in $(S^{n-1})^c \times \mathbb{R}^v$. It follows that $(S^{n-1})^c \times \mathbb{R}^v$ is a subset of $(S^n)^c$, i.e., $x^{n-1} \in (S^{n-1})^c$ implies $x^n \in (S^n)^c$. Equivalently, $x^n \in S^n$ implies $x^{n-1} \in S^{n-1}$.

It follows that when $x^n \in S^n$ we have $x^t \in S^t$, $t = 1, \ldots, n$. Consequently, $g_t(x^t) \equiv g^t(x^t)/g^{t-1}(x^{t-1})$ is defined for $t = 2, \ldots, n$ when $x^n \in S^n$. Appropriate multiplication and division gives

$$g^n(x^n) = [g^n(x^n)/g^{n-1}(x^{n-1})]\,[g^{n-1}(x^{n-1})/g^{n-2}(x^{n-2})] \times \ldots \times g^1(x^1)$$
$$= \prod_{t=1}^{n} g_t(x^t)\,.$$

Taking logarithms gives the result

$$\log g^n(x^n) = \sum_{t=1}^{n} \log g_t(x^t)\,. \qquad \square$$

PROOF OF THEOREM 2.9: Because $\{f^n\}$ generates $\mathcal{P} = \{P_\theta\}$ with respect to $\{\eta^n\}$, we have that for each θ there exists P_θ on $(\Omega, \mathcal{F})$ such that the restriction of P_θ to $(\mathbb{R}^{vn}, \mathcal{B}^{vn})$ is given by

$$P_\theta^n(B) = \int_B f^n(x^n, \theta)\, d\eta^n(x^n),\ B \in \mathcal{B}^{vn},$$

while the restriction to $(\mathbb{R}^{v(n+1)}, \mathcal{B}^{v(n+1)})$ is given by

$$P_\theta^{n+1}(C) = \int_C f^{n+1}(x^{n+1}, \theta)\, d\eta^{n+1}(x^{n+1}) \quad C \in \mathcal{B}^{v(n+1)}\,.$$

Consistency requires $P_\theta^{n+1}(B \times \mathbb{R}^v) = P_\theta^n(B)$ for all $B \in \mathcal{B}^{vn}$; equivalently, for all $B \in \mathcal{B}^{vn}$

$$\int_{B \times \mathbb{R}^v} f^{n+1}(x^{n+1}, \theta)\, d\eta^{n+1}(x^{n+1})$$
$$= \int_B \left[\int_{\mathbb{R}^v} f_{n+1}(x^{n+1}, \theta)\, d\eta_{n+1}(x_{n+1}) \right] f^n(x^n, \theta)\, d\eta^n(x^n)$$
$$= \int_B f^n(x^n, \theta)\, d\eta^n(x^n),$$

where the first equality is from Fubini's theorem (Billingsley [1979, Theorem 18.3]). From the second equality we have

$$\int_B \left[\phi(x^n, \theta) - 1 \right] dP_\theta^n(x^n) = 0\,,$$

with $dP_\theta^n(x^n) = f^n(x^n, \theta)\, d\eta^n(x^n)$ and

$$\phi(x^n, \theta) \equiv \int_{\mathbb{R}^v} f_{n+1}(x^{n+1}, \theta)\, d\eta_{n+1}(x_{n+1})\,.$$

The result follows immediately if we show that $[\phi(X^n, \theta) - 1] = 0$ *a.s.* - P_θ^n. Suppose not. Then there exists $B^* \in \mathcal{B}^{vn}$ for which either $\phi(x^n, \theta) - 1 > 0$ or $\phi(x^n, \theta) - 1 < 0$ when $x^n \in B^*$, such that $P_\theta^n(B^*) > 0$. Then either

$$\int_{B^*} [\phi(x^n, \theta) - 1]\, dP_\theta^n(x^n) > 0$$

or

$$\int_{B^*} [\phi(x^n, \theta) - 1]\, dP_\theta^n(x^n) < 0 .$$

But this contradicts the fact that $\int_B [\phi(x^n, \theta) - 1]\, d\, P_\theta^n(x^n) = 0$ for all $B \in \mathcal{B}^{vn}$. Thus $\phi(X^n, \theta) = 1$ *a.s.* $- P_\theta^n$, and the proof is complete. □

PROOF OF THEOREM 2.11: Identical to that of Lemma 2.1 of Gallant and White [1988], replacing "inf" with "sup". □

PROOF OF THEOREM 2.12: The result follows immediately from Theorem 2.11 because Assumption 2.3 guarantees that L_n satisfies the sufficient conditions. □

PROOF OF THEOREM 2.13: Because $L_n(X^n, \hat{\theta}_n) > -\infty$ *a.s.* $- P_o$, it follows that $f_t(X^t, \hat{\theta}_n) \neq 0$, $t = 1, \ldots, n$, *a.s.* $- P_o$ so that letting $s_t \equiv \nabla f_t / f_t$,

$$s_t(X^t, \hat{\theta}_n) = \nabla f_t(X^t, \hat{\theta}_n)/f_t(X^t, \hat{\theta}_n)\ a.s. - P_{o,}$$

where ∇f_t exists *a.s.* $- P_o$ by Assumption 2.4. It follows that $L_n(X^n, \hat{\theta}_n)$ has a gradient at $\hat{\theta}_n$,

$$\nabla L_n(X^n, \hat{\theta}_n) = n^{-1} \sum_{t=1}^{n} s_t(X^t, \hat{\theta}_n) .$$

Because $\hat{\theta}_n$ maximizes $L_n(X^n, \theta)$ *a.s.* $- P_o$ and is interior to an open subset of Θ *a.s.* $- P_o$, it follows from the multivariate analogue of Theorem 5.8 of Apostol [1957, p. 91] that

$$\nabla L_n(X^n, \hat{\theta}_n) = 0\ a.s. - P_o .$$ □

PROOF OF THEOREM 2.14: (i) For each β in $\mathcal{B}$, $\tilde{Q}(\cdot, \beta) \equiv Q(\cdot, \hat{\alpha}(\cdot), \beta)$ is measurable by Theorem 13.3 of Billingsley [1979]. For each ω in F, $\tilde{Q}(\omega, \cdot)$ is continuous on $\mathcal{B}$ because $Q(\omega, \alpha, \cdot)$ is continuous on $\mathcal{B}$ for each (ω, α) in $F \times \mathcal{A}$.

(ii) The result follows immediately by applying Theorem 2.11 to $\tilde{Q}$. □

PROOF OF THEOREM 2.15: The result follows immediately by applying Theorem 2.14 to $(x^n, \beta) \to L^n(x^n, \hat{\alpha}_n(x^n), \beta)$. □

CHAPTER 3

Consistency of the QMLE

In this chapter we study the behavior of the QMLE $\hat{\theta}_n$ as $n \to \infty$. The heuristic idea is that because $\hat{\theta}_n$ maximizes $L_n(X^n, \theta)$ and $L_n(X^n, \theta)$ tends to $\bar{L}_n(\theta) \equiv E(L_n(X^n, \theta))$, then $\hat{\theta}_n$ should tend to that value of θ, say θ_n^*, that maximizes $\bar{L}_n(\theta)$.

3.1 Stochastic Uniform Convergence and Consistency of the QMLE

The strong law of large numbers ensures under general conditions that for each θ in Θ and any $\varepsilon > 0$ there exists an integer $N(\theta, \varepsilon, \omega)$ and subset $F(\theta)$ of Ω with probability zero such that for all $n > N(\theta, \varepsilon, \omega)$ and $\omega \notin F(\theta)$

$$| L_n(X^n(\omega), \theta) - \bar{L}_n(\theta) | < \varepsilon .$$

In particular, with $\{ \theta_n \}$ a nonstochastic sequence, for given m and all $n > N(\theta_m, \varepsilon, \omega)$ and $\omega \notin F(\theta_m)$

$$| L_n(X^n(\omega), \theta_m) - \bar{L}_n(\theta_m) | < \varepsilon .$$

This reveals a serious inadequacy of the law of large numbers in the present context. Because N depends on θ, it is quite possible that there exists no n such that $n > N(\theta_n, \varepsilon, \omega)$. Even though $L^n(X^n, \theta)$ approaches $\bar{L}_n(\theta)$ for fixed θ, the fact that $\{ \theta_n \}$ is a sequence in Θ makes it possible that $L^n(X^n, \theta_n)$ may never approach $\bar{L}_n(\theta_n)$. This difficulty can be removed by requiring that N not depend on θ.

Another potential difficulty remains, however. This is caused by the dependence of F on θ. One way of avoiding the dependence of F on θ is to consider only events in $F^* = \cup_{\theta \in \Theta} F(\theta)$. However, F^* is a set that may or may not have probability zero. In fact, F^* may not even be a well-defined event (i.e. a measurable set), because in general it is the union of an uncountable number of sets. However, compactness of Θ makes it possible to ensure that the set on which $L_n(X^n, \theta)$ converges to $\bar{L}_n(\theta)$ does not depend on θ and does have probability one.

The following definition of strong uniform convergence provides a structure that will support the heuristic idea given at the outset.

DEFINITION 3.1 (*Strong Uniform Convergence on* Θ)**:** Let $(\Omega, \mathcal{F}, P)$ be a complete probability space, and let Θ be a compact subset of $\mathbb{R}^p$, $p \in \mathbb{N}$. Let $\{Q_n : \Omega \times \Theta \rightarrow \mathbb{R}\}$ be a sequence of random functions continuous on Θ *a.s.*$-P$. Let $\{\bar{Q}_n : \Theta \rightarrow \mathbb{R}\}$ be a sequence of functions. Then $Q_n(\cdot, \theta) - \bar{Q}_n(\theta) \rightarrow 0$ as $n \rightarrow \infty$ *a.s. P uniformly on* Θ if there exists $F \in \mathcal{F}$, $P(F) = 1$ such that given any $\varepsilon > 0$, for each ω in F there exists an integer $N(\omega, \varepsilon) < \infty$ (independent of θ) such that for all $n > N(\omega, \varepsilon)$, $\sup_\Theta | Q_n(\omega, \theta) - \bar{Q}_n(\theta) | < \varepsilon$. □

Similarly, we have the following definition of weak uniform convergence on Θ.

DEFINITION 3.2 (*Weak Uniform Convergence on* Θ)**:** Let $(\Omega, \mathcal{F}, P)$, Θ, Q_n and $\bar{Q}_n$ be as given in Definition 3.1. Then $Q_n(\cdot, \theta) - \bar{Q}_n(\theta) \rightarrow 0$ as $n \rightarrow \infty$ *in probability* $-P$ (*prob* $-P$) *uniformly on* Θ if for any $\varepsilon > 0$ and any $\delta > 0$ there exists an integer $N(\varepsilon, \delta) < \infty$ (independent of θ) such that for all $n > N(\varepsilon, \delta)$

$$P\left[\sup_\Theta | Q_n(\cdot, \theta) - \bar{Q}_n(\theta) | < \varepsilon \right] > 1 - \delta . \qquad \square$$

If Q_n and $\bar{Q}_n$ are vector- or matrix- valued functions, then we use identical terminology to mean that uniform convergence holds element by element.

These particular concepts are by no means the only useful ones in the present context. It is possible to develop a more general theory (e.g. as in White and Wooldridge [1991]), without relying on these notions. We use these concepts for simplicity and concreteness. Note that the assumption of compactness of Θ plays a key role here. Among other things this ensures that the supremum over Θ exists and that the functions $\sup_\Theta | Q_n(\cdot, \theta) - \bar{Q}_n(\theta) |$ are measurable. (See Bierens' [1981, pp. 33–38] excellent monograph for further discussion.)

In our particular application, we often have

$$\begin{aligned} Q_n(\omega, \theta) &= L_n(X^n(\omega), \theta) \\ &= n^{-1} \sum_{t=1}^{n} \log f_t(X^t(\omega), \theta) . \end{aligned}$$

When f and X are such that $L_n(X^n, \theta)$ converges to $\bar{L}_n(\theta)$ as $n \to \infty$ *a.s.* $-P_o$ (*prob* $- P_o$) uniformly on Θ, we say that $\{\log f_t(X^t, \theta)\}$ *obeys the strong (weak) uniform law of large numbers* (ULLN). Primitive conditions on f and X that ensure that $\{\log f_t(X^t, \theta)\}$ satisfies a ULLN are rather generally available. Recent papers by Andrews [1988] and Pötscher and Prucha [1989] provide results that can be used to establish ULLN's in a wide variety of situations. Corollaries of their results are specific results such as those of Le Cam [1953] and Jennrich [1969] ($\log f_t(X^t(\omega), \theta) = \log f_0(X_t(\omega), \theta)$ and X_t i.i.d.); Ranga Rao [1962] and Hansen [1982] ($\log f_t(X^t(\omega), \theta) = \log f_0(X_0(T^t\omega), \theta)$, for T an ergodic measure-preserving transformation, so that $\{X_t = X_0(T^t \cdot)\}$ is stationary and ergodic); Hoadley [1971] ($\log f_t(X^t(\omega), \theta) = \log \tilde{f}_t(X_t(\omega), \theta)$ and X_t independent, not identically distributed); Domowitz and White [1982] and Pötscher and Prucha [1989] ($\log f_t(X^t(\omega), \theta) = \log \tilde{f}_t(X_{t-\tau}(\omega), \cdots, X_t(\omega), \theta)$ and $\{X_t\}$ a mixing process); and Bierens [1982] and Gallant and White [1988] ($\log f_t$ a near epoch dependent function of $\{X_t\}$, a mixing process), among others. Appendix 2 of this monograph contains statements of results for the i.i.d. and stationary ergodic cases, as well as a result for dependent heterogeneous processes derived from recent results of Andrews [1988].

Given the availability of these results and the fact that they span a wide range of situations relevant to econometric practice, we leave the details necessary to treat particular special cases to the interested reader. For our general purposes, it suffices here to adopt uniform convergence as a fundamental assumption.

ASSUMPTION 3.1: (a) For each θ in Θ $E(\log f_t(X^t, \theta))$ exists ai finite, $t = 1, 2, \ldots$;

(b) $E(\log f_t(X^t, \cdot))$ is continuous on Θ, $t = 1, 2, \ldots$; and

(c) $\{\log f_t(X^t, \theta)\}$ obeys the strong (weak) ULLN.

Discussion of conditions that guarantee this assumption in the contex maximum likelihood estimation of misspecified models is given for i observations by White [1982], for mixing processes by White [1984b] ; for near epoch dependent functions of mixing processes by Gallant and Wl [1988]. When f_t depends on both n and t the weak ULLN is more eas satisfied than the strong ULLN.

We noted earlier that $\hat{\theta}_n$ is not guaranteed to maximize $L_n(X^n, \theta)$ uniquely. However, it is convenient to require that $\bar{L}_n(\theta)$ have a unique maximum, so that $\hat{\theta}_n$ is estimating something well defined. Because $\bar{L}_n(\theta)$ explicitly depends upon n, we must ensure that the uniqueness of the maximum of $\bar{L}_n(\theta)$ does not vanish as $n \to \infty$. This could happen if $\bar{L}_n(\theta)$ were a strictly concave function that tended to a constant (flat) function as $n \to \infty$. We rule out such possibilities by requiring that a sequence of maximizers $\theta^* \equiv \{\theta_n^*\}$ of $\{\bar{L}_n(\theta)\}$ be identifiably unique, as defined by Gallant and White [1988].

DEFINITION 3.3 (*Identifiable Uniqueness*): Let $\bar{Q}_n : \Theta \to \bar{\mathbb{R}}$ be continuous on Θ, a compact subset of $\mathbb{R}^p$, $p \in \mathbb{N}$, and let Θ_n be a non-empty compact subset of Θ, $n = 1, 2, \ldots$. Suppose that $\bar{Q}_n(\theta)$ has a maximum on Θ_n at θ_n^*, $n = 1, 2, \ldots$. Let $s_n(\varepsilon)$ be an open sphere in $\mathbb{R}^p$ centered at θ_n^* with fixed radius $\varepsilon > 0$. For each $n = 1, 2, \ldots$ define the neighborhood $\eta_n(\varepsilon) = s_n(\varepsilon) \cap \Theta_n$ with compact complement $\eta_n^c(\varepsilon)$ in Θ_n. The sequence of maximizers $\theta^* \equiv \{\theta_n^*\}$ is said to be *identifiably unique on* $\{\Theta_n\}$ if either for all $\varepsilon > 0$ and all n $\eta_n^c(\varepsilon)$ is empty, or for all $\varepsilon > 0$

$$\limsup_{n \to \infty} \left[\max_{\theta \in \eta_n^c(\varepsilon)} \bar{Q}_n(\theta) - \bar{Q}_n(\theta_n^*) \right] < 0 . \qquad \square$$

For brevity, we shall simply say that θ^* is identifiably unique. Applied to $\bar{L}_n$, this definition ensures that no other value or sequence of values of θ gives values for $\bar{L}_n(\theta)$ that become arbitrarily close to $\bar{L}_n(\theta_n^*)$ as $n \to \infty$. For now we are primarily interested in the case in which $\Theta_n = \Theta$ for all n. Dropping this assumption later allows straightforward treatment of constrained estimation under sequences of local alternatives.

With this background we can state a result that makes rigorous the heuristic ideas outlined at the beginning of this chapter.

THEOREM 3.4: *Let $(\Omega, \mathcal{F}, P)$ be a complete probability space, let Θ be a compact subset of $\mathbb{R}^p$, $p \in \mathbb{N}$ and let $\{\Theta_n\}$ be a sequence of compact subsets of Θ. Let $\{Q_n\}$ be a sequence of random functions continuous on Θ a.s. $-P$ and let $\hat{\theta}_n = \mathrm{argmax}_{\Theta_n} Q_n(\cdot, \theta)$ a.s. $-P$. If $Q_n(\cdot, \theta) - \bar{Q}_n(\theta) \to 0$ as $n \to \infty$ a.s. $-P$ (prob $-P$) uniformly on Θ and if $\{\bar{Q}_n : \Theta \to \bar{\mathbb{R}}\}$ has identifiably unique maximizers θ^* on $\{\Theta_n\}$ then $\hat{\theta}_n - \theta_n^* \to 0$ as $n \to \infty$ a.s. $-P$ (prob $-P$).* $\square$

When the conclusion of this result holds, we say that $\hat{\theta}_n$ *is strongly (weakly) consistent for* θ_n^*.

To apply this result to the QMLE, we impose the following condition.

ASSUMPTION 3.2: $\{\bar{L}_n\}$ has identifiably unique maximizers $\theta^* \equiv \{\theta_n^*\}$ on Θ. □

This condition is the fundamental identification condition in the present context. In particular special cases, there will usually be more primitive assumptions that will guarantee that this holds. For example, when estimating a possibly misspecified linear regression equation by the method of least squares, so that a typical model element is

$$Y_t \mid Z_t \sim N(Z_t^{\prime}\beta, \sigma^2), \qquad t = 1, 2, \ldots,$$

a sufficient condition is that det $[n^{-1} \sum_{t=1}^{n} E(Z_t Z'_t)] \geq \delta > 0$ for all n sufficiently large. With identically distributed $\{Z_t\}$, this reduces to the condition that $E(Z_t Z'_t)$ be nonsingular, so that exact multicollinearity is ruled out.

Often, the Hessian of $L_n(X^n, \cdot)$, denoted $\nabla^2 L_n(X^n, \cdot)$, will exist. (The notation ∇^2 is shorthand for $\nabla' \nabla$ where ∇' is the Jacobian operator.) As in the case of a correctly specified likelihood function (Rothenberg [1973]), the identification condition Assumption 3.2 can then be shown to be related to the negative definiteness of $E(\nabla^2 L_n(X^n, \theta_n^*))$ (uniformly for all n sufficiently large).

The consistency result for the QMLE now follows immediately from Theorem 3.4.

THEOREM 3.5: *Let Assumptions 2.1, 2.3, 3.1 and 3.2 hold, and let $\hat{\theta}$ be generated by $S = \{f_t\}$. Then $\hat{\theta}_n - \theta_n^* \to 0$ as $n \to \infty$ a.s. $-P_o$ (prob $-P_o$).* □

Thus $\hat{\theta}_n$ is generally consistent for θ_n^*, the parameter vector that maximizes $\bar{L}_n(\theta)$ over Θ.

Because the optimand $\bar{L}_n(\theta)$ is indexed by n, so in general must its maximizer θ_n^* depend on n. To investigate the behavior of θ_n^* further, we write

$$\begin{aligned}
\bar{L}_n(\theta) &= E(n^{-1} \log f^n(X^n, \theta)) \\
&= E\left(n^{-1} \sum_{t=1}^{n} \log f_t(X^t, \theta)\right) \\
&= n^{-1} \sum_{t=1}^{n} E(\log f_t(X^t, \theta))
\end{aligned}$$

$$= n^{-1} \sum_{t=1}^{n} \int_{\mathbb{R}^{vt}} \log f_t(x^t, \theta)\, g^t(x^t)\, d\nu^t(x^t) .$$

Thus $\bar{L}_n(\theta)$ is the average of n expectations $E(\log f_t(x^t, \theta))$. The dependence of θ_n^* on n arises because these expectations may be heterogeneous. The last expression reveals that this heterogeneity can arise from two distinct sources: heterogeneity in the approximations f_t or heterogeneity in the true densities g^t. If this heterogeneity is not too severe, then θ_n^* may tend to some limit. Because conditions ensuring such convergence depend on the sequence $\{ g^t \}$, which is both unknown and usually outside the control of the researcher, we do not impose them. The price paid for allowing possibly severe heterogeneity is the dependence of θ_n^* on n.

Regardless of whether or not θ_n^* converges, the expression for $\bar{L}_n$ above shows that θ_n^* depends crucially on both $\{ f_t \}$ and $\{ g^t \}$. Choice of different approximations, say $\{ \tilde{f}_t \}$ will generally (i.e. under misspecification) result in a different solution sequence (and limit, if one exists). Similarly, different data generation processes will generally and naturally lead to different solution sequences (regardless of misspecification).

Because the choice of approximation is under the control of the researcher, the effects on the solution sequence of choosing different approximations can be studied (at least asymptotically) by observing the behavior of the associated QMLE's. Such study is useful in investigating possible misspecification, because although different approximations yield different solution sequences in general (i.e. under misspecification), in the absence of certain kinds of misspecification the solution sequence will be invariant to particular changes in approximation. In Chapter 10 we exploit this fact to obtain Hausman [1978] tests for misspecification.

Unlike the choice of approximation, the data generation process is usually outside the control of the researcher. Nevertheless, the relative effect on the solution sequence of changing the data generation process can in principle be studied by changing the approximation. Specifically, let $\tilde{f}_t(x^t, \theta) = [f_t(x^t, \theta)]^{\phi^t(x^t)}$, where $\phi^t : \mathbb{R}^{vt} \to \mathbb{R}^+$ and $E(\phi^t(X^t)) = \int \phi^t(x^t)\, g^t(x^t)\, d\nu^t(x^t) = 1$. Then

$$\begin{aligned} E(\log \tilde{f}_t(X^t, \theta)) &= \int_{\mathbb{R}^{vt}} \phi^t(x^t) \log f_t(x^t, \theta)\, g^t(x^t)\, d\nu^t(x^t) \\ &= \int_{\mathbb{R}^{vt}} \log f_t(x^t, \theta)\, \tilde{g}^t(x^t)\, d\nu^t(x^t) \\ &\equiv \tilde{E}(\log f_t(X^t, \theta)) \end{aligned}$$

where $\tilde{g}^t = \phi^t g^t$ is a density and $\tilde{E}$ is the associated expectation. Under appropriate conditions (e.g., $\nu^t = \nu^{t-1} \otimes \nu_t$ and provided that $\tilde{g}^t = \int_{R^v} \tilde{g}^{t+1} d\nu_{t+1}$), the sequence $\{ \tilde{g}^t \}$ is a sequence of densities arising from a probability measure, say $\tilde{P}_o \neq P_o$. The solution sequence generated by changing the approximation to $\tilde{f}_t$ from f_t holding g^t constant is thus equivalent to that generated by holding the approximation f_t constant and changing g^t to $\tilde{g}^t$. Modifying the approximation in this way yields "weighted QMLE's" that are of course themselves QMLE's.

An interpretation for θ_n^* in terms of the KLIC can be given under some additional conditions. To ensure that $\mathbb{I}(g^n : f^n ; \theta)$ is not infinite for all θ, we impose the following condition.

ASSUMPTION 3.3: For each $n = 1, 2, \ldots$, $\log g^n(X^n)$ is integrable, i.e. $E \mid \log g^n (X^n) \mid < \infty$. □

The applicability of the information inequality is ensured by the following condition.

ASSUMPTION 3.4: For all θ in Θ, $\int_{S^n} f^n(x^n, \theta)\, d\, \nu^n (x^n) \leq 1$, $n = 1, 2, \ldots$. □

This ensures that $\int_{S^n} (g^n - f^n) d\nu^n \geq 0$ Assumption 3.4 is automatically satisfied when $f^n(x^n, \theta)$ is a probability density with respect to ν^n for each θ, i.e. $\int f^n(x^n, \theta) d\nu^n(x^n) = 1$. Note that Theorem 2.9 is relevant in this case, so that models containing "exogenous" variables generally fail to satisfy Assumption 3.4. We consider such models in subsequent chapters.

Assumptions 3.3 and 3.4 allow us to interpret θ_n^* as the identifiably unique minimizer of the KLIC.

THEOREM 3.6: *(i) Given Assumptions 2.1–2.3, 3.1(a,b), 3.2 and 3.3* $\{ n^{-1} \mathbb{I} (g^n : f^n ; \theta) \}$ *has identifiably unique minimizers* $\{ \theta_n^* \}$.

(ii) Given Assumptions 2.1–2.3, 3.1–3.3, $\hat{\theta}_n$ *is strongly (weakly) consistent for* θ_n^* *as given in (i).*

(iii) Given Assumptions 2.1–2.3, 3.1(a), 3.3 and 3.4, $\mathbb{I} (g^n : f^n ; \theta) \geq 0$, $n = 1, 2, \ldots$. □

When Assumption 3.4 holds the KLIC can be interpreted as a measure of the "surprise" we experience on average if we assume that the true state of the world is described by f^n and it is revealed that in fact g^n describes the world. Theorem 3.6 implies that the QMLE is a consistent estimator for the parameter vector that minimizes our ignorance of the true state of the world. This provides a fairly appealing justification for the method of maximum likelihood in the presence of model misspecification.

3.2 Consistency of the 2SQMLE

Similar consistency results are available for the 2SQMLE, based on the following result.

THEOREM 3.7: *Let* $(\Omega, \mathcal{F})$ *and* $\Theta = \mathcal{A} \times \mathcal{B}$ *be as in Theorem 2.14, and let* P *be a complete probability measure on* $(\Omega, \mathcal{F})$. *Let* $\{Q_n\}$ *be a sequence of measurable functions continuous on* $\Theta = \mathcal{A} \times \mathcal{B}$ *a.s.* $-P$, *and let* $\{\hat{\alpha}_n : \Omega \to \mathcal{A}\}$ *be a sequence of measurable functions such that* $\hat{\alpha}_n - \alpha_n^* \to 0$ *a.s.* $-P$ *(prob* $-P$*) for some nonstochastic sequence* $\{\alpha_n^* \in \mathcal{A}\}$. *Suppose that the sequence* $\{\bar{Q}_n : \Theta \to I\!R\}$ *is continuous on* Θ *uniformly in* n. *If* $Q_n(\cdot, \theta) - \bar{Q}_n(\theta) \to 0$ *as* $n \to \infty$ *a.s.* $-P$ *(prob* $-P$*) uniformly on* Θ *for some sequence* $\{\bar{Q}_n : \Theta \to I\!R\}$, *then* $Q_n(\cdot, \hat{\alpha}_n(\cdot), \beta) - \bar{Q}_n(\alpha_n^*, \beta) \to 0$ *as* $n \to \infty$ *a.s.* $-P$ *(prob* $-P$*) uniformly on* $\mathcal{B}$. □

When $\Theta = \mathcal{A}$, we obtain the following useful result.

COROLLARY 3.8: *Let the conditions of Theorem 3.7 hold with* $\Theta = \mathcal{A}$, *so that* $\hat{\theta}_n - \theta_n^* \to 0$ *a.s.* $-P$ *(prob* $- P$*). Then* $Q_n(\cdot, \hat{\theta}_n) - \bar{Q}_n(\theta_n^*) \to 0$ *as* $n \to \infty$ *a.s.* $-P$ *(prob* $- P$*).* □

This result is used in Theorem 3.12 below and extensively in subsequent chapters.

The result immediately needed for the consistency of the 2SQMLE is

THEOREM 3.9: *Let the conditions of Theorem 3.7 hold, and suppose that* $\{\bar{Q}_n(\alpha_n^*, \beta)\}$ *has identifiably unique maximizers* $\{\beta_n^*\}$ *on* $\{\mathcal{B}_n\}$ *where* $\mathcal{B}_n \subset \mathcal{B}$ *is compact,* $n = 1, 2, \ldots$. *Then* $\hat{\beta}_n - \beta_n^* \to 0$ *as* $n \to \infty$ *a.s.* $-P$ *(prob* $- P$*), where* $\hat{\beta}_n = \text{argmax}_{\mathcal{B}_n} Q_n(\cdot, \hat{\alpha}_n, \beta)$ *a.s.* $- P$. □

The result for the 2SQMLE uses the following additional condition.

ASSUMPTION 3.5: (a) There exists a sequence $\{\hat{\alpha}_n : I\!R^{vn} \to \mathcal{A}\}$ of measurable functions and a nonstochastic sequence $\{\alpha_n^*\}$ on $\mathcal{A}$, a compact subset of a finite dimensional Euclidean space, such that $\hat{\alpha}_n - \alpha_n^* \to 0$ as $n \to \infty$ *a.s.* $-P_o$ (*prob* $- P_o$);

(b) $\{ \bar{L}_n \}$ is continuous on $\Theta = \mathcal{A} \times \mathcal{B}$ uniformly in n where $\mathcal{A}$ and $\mathcal{B}$ are compact subsets of finite dimensional Euclidean spaces; and

(c) $\{ \bar{L}_n(\alpha_n^*, \beta)\}$ has identifiably unique maximizers $\{ \beta_n^* \}$ on $\mathcal{B}$. □

THEOREM 3.10: *Let Assumptions* 2.1, 2.3, 3.1 *and* 3.5 *hold, and let* $\hat{\beta}_n$ *be the 2SQMLE generated by* $\mathcal{S} = (\{ f_t \}, \{ \hat{\alpha}_n \})$. *Then* $\hat{\beta}_n - \beta_n^* \to 0$ *as* $n \to \infty$ *a.s.* $-P_o$ *(prob* $- P_o$*).* □

As with θ_n^*, β_n^* depends on $\{ f_t\}$ and $\{ g^t\}$, as well as (possibly) on α_n^*. An interpretation of β_n^* in terms of the KLIC analogous to that of θ_n^* is also available.

THEOREM 3.11: *(i) Given Assumptions* 2.1–2.3, 3.1 *(a,b),* 3.3 *and* 3.5, $\mathbb{I}\,(g^n : f^n ; \alpha_n^*, \beta)$ *has identifiably unique minimizers* $\{ \beta_n^* \}$:

(ii) Given Assumptions 2.1–2.3, 3.1, 3.3 *and* 3.5, $\hat{\beta}_n$ *is strongly (weakly) consistent for* β_n^* *as given in (i).* □

When $\alpha_n^* \to \alpha_o$, Theorem 3.10 allows us to interpret the 2SQMLE as having the same limit as a QMLE resulting from maximizing $L_n(X^n, \theta)$ subject to the constraint $\alpha = \alpha_o$. For this reason, a study of the limiting properties of 2SQMLE's can often be subsumed in the study of QMLE's. When α_n^* does not converge to some limit, Theorem 3.10 still allows us to interpret the 2SQMLE as having the same limit as a QMLE resulting from maximizing $L_n(X^n, \theta)$ subject to a sequence of constraints on α, i.e. $\{ \alpha = \alpha_n^* \}$. Thus Theorems 3.10 and 3.11 allow us to interpret the stochastic limits of 2SQMLE's as equivalent to the stochastic limits of particular QMLE's.

3.3 Consistency of Estimators Obtained From First Order Conditions

We complete this chapter by studying the properties of estimators obtained as the solution to the first order conditions

$$\nabla L_n(X^n, \theta) = 0 .$$

Our next result is generic and provides conditions under which the value $\hat{\theta}_n$ that maximizes $Q_n(\cdot, \theta)$ is the only consistent solution to the first order conditions $\nabla Q_n(\cdot, \theta) = 0$. This result is essentially that of Foutz [1977].

THEOREM 3.12: *Suppose that the conditions of Theorem 3.4 are satisfied with* $\Theta_n = \Theta$ *for all* n. *Suppose in addition that* $\nabla Q_n(\cdot, \theta)$ *and* $\nabla^2 Q_n(\cdot, \theta)$ *exist and are continuous on* Θ *a.s.* $-P$, *that* $\nabla \bar{Q}_n$ *and* $\nabla^2 \bar{Q}_n$ *exist and are continuous on* Θ *uniformly in* n, *that* $\nabla Q_n(\cdot, \theta) - \nabla \bar{Q}_n(\theta) \to 0$ *and* $\nabla^2 Q_n(\cdot, \theta) - \nabla^2 \bar{Q}_n(\theta) \to 0$ *as* $n \to \infty$ *a.s.* $-P$ *(prob* $-P$*) uniformly on* Θ, *that* $\{\bar{Q}_n(\theta)\}$ *has identifiably unique maximizers* $\{\theta_n^*\}$ *interior to* Θ *uniformly in* n, *that* $|\bar{Q}_n(\theta)| < \Delta$ *for all* θ *in* Θ *and all* $n = 1, 2, \ldots$, *and that* $\{\nabla^2 \bar{Q}_n(\theta_n^*)\}$ *is* $O(1)$ *and negative definite, uniformly in* n.

Then $\hat{\theta}_n = \text{argmax}_\Theta\, Q_n(\cdot, \theta)$ *a.s.* $-P$ *is a solution of the equations* $\nabla Q_n(\cdot, \theta) = 0$ *for all* n *sufficiently large, a.s.* $-P$, $\hat{\theta}_n - \theta_n^* \to 0$ as $n \to \infty$ *a.s.* $-P$ *(prob* $-P$*) and for any sequence* $\{\tilde{\theta}_n\}$ *such that* $\nabla Q_n(\cdot, \tilde{\theta}_n) = 0$ *and* $\tilde{\theta}_n \neq \hat{\theta}_n$ *for all* n *sufficiently large,* $|\tilde{\theta}_n - \theta_n^*| > \varepsilon$ *a.a.n a.s.* $-P$ *for some* $\varepsilon > 0$ $(P[|\tilde{\theta}_n - \theta_n^*| > \varepsilon] \longrightarrow 1$ *as* $n \to \infty$ *for some* $\varepsilon > 0)$. □

The requirement of interiority uniformly in n means that there exists $\varepsilon > 0$ such that for all n sufficiently large (i.e., almost all n, abbreviated $a.a.n$) $\{\theta \in \mathbb{R}^p : |\theta - \theta_n^*| < \varepsilon\} = \{\theta \in \Theta : |\theta - \theta_n^*| < \varepsilon\}$. We say that $\{\nabla^2 \bar{Q}_n(\theta_n^*)\}$ is negative definite uniformly in n whenever $\nabla^2 \bar{Q}_n(\theta_n^*)$ is negative semi-definite for all n and $|\det \nabla^2 \bar{Q}_n(\theta_n^*)| > \varepsilon$ $a.a.n$ for some $\varepsilon > 0$.

When the conditions of this result hold, then there is effectively only one consistent root to the first order conditions asymptotically, and this root is the one that corresponds to a maximum for the objective function $Q_n(\cdot, \theta)$, $a.s. - P$.

We apply this result with $Q_n(\cdot, \theta) = L_n(X^n, \theta)$. We therefore add conditions ensuring that L_n satisfies the appropriate restrictions. The first condition ensures the existence of the second derivatives of L_n.

ASSUMPTION 3.6: $f_t(X^t, \cdot)$ is continuously differentiable of order 2 on Θ $a.s. - P_o$ $t = 1, 2, \ldots$. □

Note that measurability of the derivatives follows from Assumption 2.3 by using the fact that the derivatives are defined as the (measurable) limit of a sequence of (measurable) difference quotients.

Next, we impose the uniform convergence of ∇L_n and $\nabla^2 L_n$ to functions continuous on Θ uniformly in n. The same conditions that ensure the uniform law of large numbers generally guarantee the continuity of the limiting functions (indeed, this continuity is typically used in establishing the ULLN), and an interchange of expectation and derivative. We use the following conditions.

ASSUMPTION 3.7:(a) For all θ in Θ, $\nabla \bar{L}_n(\theta) = E(\nabla L_n(X^n, \theta)) < \infty$, $n = 1, 2, \ldots$;

(b) $E(\nabla L_n(X^n, \cdot))$ is continuous on Θ uniformly in $n = 1, 2, \ldots$;

(c) $\{s_t(X^t, \theta) \equiv \nabla \log f_t(X^t, \theta)\}$ obeys the strong (weak) ULLN. □

Here we introduce the convenient shorthand $s_t = \nabla \log f_t$ to represent the "score" vector of the likelihood.

ASSUMPTION 3.8:(a) For all θ in Θ, $\nabla^2 \bar{L}_n(\theta) = E(\nabla^2 L_n(X^n, \theta)) < \infty$, $n = 1, 2, \ldots$;

(b) $E(\nabla^2 L_n(X^n, \cdot))$ is continuous on Θ uniformly in $n = 1, 2, \ldots$;

(c) $\{\nabla' s_t(X^t, \theta) = \nabla^2 \log f_t(X^t, \theta)\}$ obeys the strong (weak) ULLN. □

The interiority of θ_n^* is imposed directly.

ASSUMPTION 3.2′: The sequence $\{\bar{L}_n(\theta)\}$ is $O(1)$ uniformly on Θ and $\{\bar{L}_n\}$ has identifiably unique maximizers $\{\theta_n^*\}$ interior to Θ uniformly in n. □

For simplicity, we also impose the negative definiteness of $A_n^* \equiv \nabla^2 \bar{L}_n(\theta_n^*)$ directly.

ASSUMPTION 3.9: $\{A_n^*\}$ is $O(1)$ and negative definite uniformly in n. □

The result is:

THEOREM 3.13: *Given Assumptions 2.1, 2.3, 3.1, 3.2′, and 3.6–3.9, let* $\hat{\theta}_n = \text{argmax}_\Theta\, L_n(X^n, \theta)$, $n = 1, 2, \ldots$. *Then* $\nabla L_n(X^n, \hat{\theta}_n) = 0$ *for all n sufficiently large a.s.* $-P_o$, $\hat{\theta}_n - \theta_n^* \to 0$ *as* $n \to \infty$ *a.s.* $-P_o$ *(prob* $-P_o$*), and for any sequence* $\{\tilde{\theta}_n\}$ *such that* $\nabla L_n(X^n, \tilde{\theta}_n) = 0$ *and* $\tilde{\theta}_n \neq \hat{\theta}_n$ *for all n sufficiently large,* $|\tilde{\theta}_n - \theta_n^*| > \varepsilon$ *a.a.n a.s.* $-P_o$ *for some* $\varepsilon > 0$ $(P_o[|\tilde{\theta}_n - \theta_n^*| > \varepsilon] \longrightarrow 1$ *as* $n \to \infty$ *for some* $\varepsilon > 0$*).* □

Thus, the QMLE is (asymptotically) the only solution to the equations $\nabla L_n(X^n, \theta) = 0$ consistent for θ_n^*. If there exists a compact subset $\tilde{\Theta}$ of Θ such that for all n sufficiently large θ_n^* is not contained in $\tilde{\Theta}$, then solutions $\tilde{\theta}_n$ in $\tilde{\Theta}$ to the first order conditions $\nabla L_n(X^n, \theta) = 0$ can be interpreted as estimating $\tilde{\theta}_n^*$ which maximizes $\bar{L}_n(\theta)$ locally, i.e. in $\tilde{\Theta}$, provided the other appropriate conditions are satisfied, and in particular that $\{ \nabla^2 \bar{L}_n(\tilde{\theta}_n^*) \}$ is uniformly negative definite.

3.4 Summary

The results of this chapter establish that the QMLE is generally consistent for a particular parameter vector θ_n^* that depends on the approximations $\{ f_t \}$ and the true densities $\{ g^t \}$. Under appropriate conditions, θ_n^* has optimal information theoretic properties, in that it minimizes the KLIC. A similar interpretation holds for the 2SQMLE.

Whether or not θ_n^* can be given a further interpretation (e.g. an economic interpretation) is another matter. In the next two chapters we consider whether this may be possible, despite the presence of some form of model misspecification.

MATHEMATICAL APPENDIX

The proofs of Theorem 3.4 and of subsequent results make use of the following result:

THEOREM 3.A.1: *Let $\mathcal{X}$ and $\mathcal{X}_n$ be random vectors, $n = 1, 2, \ldots$. $\mathcal{X}_n - \mathcal{X} \to 0$ prob$-P$ if and only if for any subsequence $\{n'\}$ there exists a further subsequence $\{n''\}$ such that $\mathcal{X}_{n''} - \mathcal{X} \to 0$ a.s.$-P$.* □

PROOF: See Lukacs [1975, Theorem 2.4.4] and Bierens [1981, pp. 21–22]. □

Proofs relying on this result will be said to use "the method of subsequences."

PROOF OF THEOREM 3.4: The proof for almost sure convergence is identical to that of Theorem 3.3 of Gallant and White [1988], with $\bar{\mathbb{R}}$ replacing $\mathbb{R}$ and $\bar{\mathcal{B}}$ replacing $\mathcal{B}$.

For convergence in probability, we use the method of subsequences. Hence, the uniform convergence in probability to zero of $Q_n(\cdot, \theta) - \bar{Q}_n(\theta)$ implies that for a given subsequence $\{n'\}$ there exists a further subsequence $\{n''\}$ for which $Q_{n''}(\cdot, \theta) - \bar{Q}_{n''}(\theta) \to 0$ *a.s.*$-P$ uniformly on Θ. Hence, by the proof for strong consistency, there exists a subsequence of $\{\hat{\theta}_{n'} - \theta^*_{n'}\}$ converging to zero *a.s.*$-P$. Because the original choice of subsequence is arbitrary, this holds for every subsequence $\{\hat{\theta}_{n'} - \theta^*_{n'}\}$. Hence, by Theorem 3.A.1, $\hat{\theta}_n - \theta^*_n \to 0$ *prob*$-P$. □

PROOF OF THEOREM 3.5: Assumptions 2.1 and 2.3 ensure that $(\omega, \theta) \to Q_n(\omega, \theta) = L_n(X^n(\omega), \theta)$ satisfies the measurability and continuity requirements of Theorem 3.4, while Assumptions 3.1 and 3.2 ensure the uniform convergence and identifiable uniqueness conditions. The result follows immediately. □

PROOF OF THEOREM 3.6: (i) Given Assumptions 2.1–2.3, 3.1(a) and 3.3, we may write

$$\begin{aligned} \mathbb{I}(g^n : f^n ; \theta) &= E(\log g^n(X^n)/f^n(X^n, \theta)) \\ &= E(\log g^n(X^n)) - E(\log f^n(X^n, \theta)) \end{aligned}$$

$$= E(\log g^n(X^n)) - n\,\bar{L}_n(\theta)$$

so that $n^{-1}\,I\!I\,(g^n : f^n;\theta) = n^{-1}\,E(\log g^n(X^n)) - \bar{L}_n(\theta)$. Because the first term does not depend on θ and is finite for each n given Assumption 3.3, it follows that $n^{-1}\,I\!I\,(g^n : f^n, \theta)$ is minimized when $\bar{L}_n(\theta)$ is maximized. Given Assumptions 3.1(a,b) and 3.2, θ_n^* is the identifiably unique maximizer of $\bar{L}_n$ and is therefore the identifiably unique minimizer of $n^{-1}\,I\!I\,(g^n : f^n;\theta)$.

(ii) The result follows immediately from (i) above and Theorem 3.5.

(iii) Assumptions 2.1–2.3, 3.1(a) and 3.3 ensure the existence and finiteness of $I\!I\,(g^n : f^n;\theta)$. Assumptions 2.3 and 3.4 ensure the applicability of the information inequality (Theorem 2.3) to ensure that $I\!I\,(g^n : f^n;\theta) \geq 0$. □

PROOF OF THEOREM 3.7: Choose $\omega \in F = \{\omega : \hat{\alpha}_n(\omega) - \alpha_n^* \to 0\} \cap \{\omega : Q_n(\omega, \theta) - \bar{Q}_n(\theta) \to 0$ uniformly on $\Theta\}$. By hypothesis $P(F) = 1$. Fix $\varepsilon > 0$. Then $|Q_n(\omega, \hat{\alpha}_n(\omega), \beta) - \bar{Q}_n(\hat{\alpha}_n(\omega), \beta)| < \varepsilon/2$ for all $n \geq N_1(\omega, \varepsilon/2)$ (say) by uniform convergence. Because $\bar{Q}_n$ is continuous on Θ uniformly in n, the fact that $\hat{\alpha}_n(\omega) - \alpha_n^* \to 0$ for ω in F implies that given $\varepsilon > 0$, there exists $\delta(\varepsilon) > 0$ such that for all $n \geq N_2(\omega, \delta(\varepsilon))$, $|\hat{\alpha}_{ni}(\omega) - \alpha_{ni}^*| < \delta(\varepsilon)$, $i = 1, \ldots, q$ and $|\bar{Q}_n(\hat{\alpha}_n(\omega), \beta) - \bar{Q}_n(\alpha_n^*, \beta)| < 6\varepsilon/2$. By the triangle inequality

$$|Q_n(\omega, \hat{\alpha}_n(\omega), \beta) - \bar{Q}_n(\alpha_n^*, \beta)|$$

$$\leq |Q_n(\omega, \hat{\alpha}_n(\omega), \beta) - \bar{Q}_n(\hat{\alpha}_n(\omega), \beta)|$$

$$+ |\bar{Q}_n(\hat{\alpha}_n(\omega), \beta) - \bar{Q}_n(\alpha_n^*, \beta)|$$

$$< \varepsilon$$

for all $n \geq \max[N_1(\omega, \varepsilon/2), N_2(\omega, \delta(\varepsilon))]$. Because this holds for all ω in F and because ε is arbitrary it follows that $Q_n(\cdot, \hat{\alpha}_n, \beta) - \bar{Q}_n(\alpha_n^*, \beta) \to 0$ as $n \to \infty$ *a.s.* $-P$ uniformly on $\mathcal{B}$.

The result for uniform convergence in probability follows by the method of subsequences. □

PROOF OF COROLLARY 3.8: Immediate from Theorem 3.7. Because $\mathcal{B}$ is null, uniformity is irrelevant. □

PROOF OF THEOREM 3.9: We verify the conditions of Theorem 3.4. The choice $\tilde{Q}_n(\cdot, \beta) = Q_n(\cdot, \hat{\alpha}_n(\cdot), \beta)$ is appropriately measurable by Theorem 13.3 of Billingsley [1979, p. 154], and continuity on $\mathcal{B}$ *a.s.* $-P$ follows straightforwardly. The uniform convergence follows from Theorem 3.7, and identifiable uniqueness of β_n^* is assumed. Thus, the conditions of Theorem 3.4 hold, and the result follows. □

PROOF OF THEOREM 3.10: Assumptions 2.1 and 2.3 ensure that $(\omega, \theta) \to Q_n(\omega, \theta) = L_n(X^n(\omega), \theta)$ satisfies the measurability and continuity requirements on Θ, and Assumption 3.1 imposes the uniform convergence requirement. Assumption 3.5(a) ensures that $\hat{\alpha}_n(X^n)$ is appropriately measurable by Theorem 13.3 of Billingsley [1979], and that $\hat{\alpha}_n - \alpha_n^* \to 0$ appropriately. Assumption 3.5(b,c) imposes the uniform continuity and identifiable uniqueness conditions. Thus, Theorem 3.9 applies and the result follows. □

PROOF OF THEOREM 3.11: (i) Given Assumptions 2.1–2.3, 3.1(a,b), 3.3 and 3.5 we may write

$$\mathbb{I}(g^n : f^n ; \alpha_n^*, \beta) = E(\log g^n(X^n)) - n\bar{L}_n(\alpha_n^*, \beta) .$$

Because the first term does not depend on β and because $\log g^n(X^n)$ is integrable for each n by Assumption 3.3, Assumption 3.5(b,c) implies that $n^{-1}\, \mathbb{I}(g^n : f^n ; \alpha_n^*, \beta)$ has identifiably unique minimizers $\{\beta_n^*\}$.

(ii) The additional conditions ensure that $\hat{\beta}_n - \beta_n^* \to 0$ *a.s.* $-P_o$ $(prob - P_o)$ by Theorem 3.9, with β_n^* as given in (i). □

For the next result we define the norm $\| A \|$ of a $p \times p$ matrix A as

$$\| A \| \equiv \sup_{x:\, x'x = 1} (x'Ax)^{1/2}$$

This is often called the operator norm. For a symmetric definite matrix $\| A \|$ is the absolute value of the eigenvalue lying farthest from zero. $\| A \|$ is the radius of a hypersphere that contains any vector Ax for x on the unit hypersphere.

PROOF OF THEOREM 3.12: We follow the argument of Foutz [1977]. Choose ω such that $Q_n(\omega, \cdot)$ is twice continuously differentiable on Θ, $Q_n(\omega, \theta) - \bar{Q}_n(\theta) \to 0$ uniformly on Θ, $\nabla Q_n(\omega, \theta) - \nabla \bar{Q}_n(\theta) \to 0$ uniformly on Θ, and $\nabla^2 Q_n(\omega, \theta) - \nabla^2 \bar{Q}_n(\theta) \to 0$ uniformly on Θ. For any sequence θ^* in Θ it follows from Corollary 3.8 that $\nabla^2 Q_n(\omega, \theta_n^*) - \nabla^2 \bar{Q}_n(\theta_n^*) \to 0$. Because $\{\nabla^2 \bar{Q}_n(\theta_n^*)\}$ is $O(1)$ and uniformly negative definite, it follows from Proposition 2.16 of White [1984a] that $\det \nabla^2 Q_n(\omega, \theta_n^*) - \det \nabla^2 \bar{Q}_n(\theta_n^*) \to 0$. Given the uniform negative definiteness of $\nabla^2 \bar{Q}_n(\theta_n^*)$, it follows that there exists $\delta > 0$ such that $\det \nabla^2 Q_n(\omega, \theta_n^*) < -\delta / 2$ for all n sufficiently large so that the inverse of $\nabla^2 Q_n(\omega, \theta_n^*)$, say $\nabla^2 Q_n(\omega, \theta_n^*)^{-1}$, exists. Let

$$\lambda_n(\omega, \theta_n^*) \equiv 1/(2 \, \| \nabla^2 Q_n(\omega, \theta_n^*)^{-1} \|)$$

$$\bar{\lambda}_n(\theta_n^*) \equiv 1/(2 \, \| \nabla^2 \bar{Q}_n(\theta_n^*)^{-1} \|) .$$

Because $\nabla^2 \bar{Q}_n(\theta_n^*)^{-1}$ is $O(1)$ and uniformly negative definite, it follows that there exist $0 < \delta < \Delta < \infty$ such that $2\delta < \bar{\lambda}_n(\theta_n^*) < \Delta / 2$, and because $\lambda_n(\omega, \theta_n^*) - \bar{\lambda}_n(\theta_n^*) \to 0$ by Proposition 2.16 of White [1984a], it follows that $\delta < \lambda_n(\omega, \theta_n^*) < \Delta$ for all n sufficiently large.

Because $\nabla^2 \bar{Q}_n$ is continuous on Θ uniformly in n, and because $\nabla^2 Q_n(\omega, \theta) - \nabla^2 \bar{Q}_n(\theta) \to 0$ uniformly on Θ, it follows that given any δ, there exists $\eta(\delta) > 0$ such that $\eta(\delta) \downarrow 0$ as $\delta \downarrow 0$ and if $| \theta - \theta_n^* | < \eta$, then $| \nabla^2 Q_n(\omega, \theta) - \nabla^2 Q_n(\omega, \theta_n^*) | < \delta$ for all n sufficiently large. Let $s_n(\eta) = \{\theta \in \Theta : | \theta - \theta^*{}_n | < \eta\}$.

It follows from the inverse function theorem, e.g. Rudin [1964, p. 193], that $\nabla Q_n(\omega, \theta)$ is one-to-one on $s_n(\eta(\delta))$ for δ sufficiently small, say $\delta \le \delta_o$, and that the inverse function ∇Q_n^{-1} is well defined on the image set $\nabla Q_n(\omega, s_n(\eta(\delta)))$. Further, the image set contains the open neighborhood with radius $\lambda_n(\omega, \theta_n^*)\, \eta(\delta)$ around $\nabla Q_n(\omega, \theta_n^*)$, and therefore the open neighborhood with radius $\delta\eta(\delta)$ around $\nabla Q_n(\omega, \theta_n^*)$.

Because $\{\bar{Q}_n(\theta)\}$ has identifiably unique maximizers $\{\theta_n^*\}$, interior to Θ uniformly in n, it follows that $\nabla \bar{Q}_n(\theta_n^*) = 0$. Because $\nabla Q_n(\omega, \theta) - \nabla \bar{Q}_n(\theta) \to 0$ uniformly on Θ, it follows that $\nabla Q_n(\omega, \theta_n^*) - \nabla \bar{Q}_n(\theta_n^*) = \nabla Q_n(\omega, \theta_n^*) - 0 \to 0$. Hence, for all n sufficiently large $| \nabla Q_n(\omega, \theta_n^*) - 0 | < \delta\, \eta(\delta)$, so the image set $\nabla Q_n(\omega, s_n(\eta(\delta)))$ contains the zero vector.

It follows that $\nabla Q_n^{-1}(\omega, 0)$ exists in $s_n(\eta(\delta))$ for all n sufficiently large, and because δ is arbitrary $\nabla Q_n^{-1}(\omega, 0) - \theta_n^* \to 0$. Because $\nabla Q_n(\omega, \theta)$ is one-to-one on $s_n(\eta(\delta_o))$, it follows that any other sequence $\{\tilde{\theta}_n\}$ such that $\nabla Q_n(\omega, \tilde{\theta}_n) = 0$ and $\tilde{\theta}_n \neq \hat{\theta}_n$ for each n sufficiently large must lie outside of $s_n(\eta(\delta_o))$, so that $|\tilde{\theta}_n - \theta_n^*| \geq \varepsilon \equiv \eta(\delta_o)$.

Because this result holds for each ω except on a set of probability zero, it follows that there exists a consistent root of the equations $\nabla Q_n(\omega, \theta) = 0$, and this root is unique, for all n sufficiently large *a.s.*

Because the hypotheses of Theorem 3.4 are satisfied, it follows that $\hat{\theta}_n - \theta_n^* \to 0$ *a.s.* $-P$, where $\hat{\theta}_n$ maximizes $Q_n(\cdot, \theta)$ *a.s.* $-P$. Because θ_n^* is interior to Θ uniformly in n, it follows that $\hat{\theta}_n$ is interior to Θ uniformly in n for all n sufficiently large, *a.s.* $-P$. Because $Q_n(\cdot, \theta) - \bar{Q}_n(\theta) \to 0$ uniformly on Θ *a.s.* $-P$ and because $|\bar{Q}_n(\theta)| < \Delta < \infty$ for all θ in Θ, it follows that $|Q_n(\cdot, \hat{\theta}_n)| < 2\Delta$ *a.s.* $-P$ for all n sufficiently large. Because $\nabla Q_n(\cdot, \theta)$ exists *a.s.* $-P$, it follows that $\nabla Q_n(\cdot, \hat{\theta}_n) = 0$ *a.s.* $-P$ so that $\hat{\theta}_n$ is a root of $\nabla Q_n(\cdot, \theta) = 0$ *a.s.* $-P$ and is consistent. It follows by the uniqueness established above that $\hat{\theta}_n = \nabla Q_n^{-1}(\cdot, 0)$, *a.s.* $-P$.

For the case of convergence in probability, we have that $\hat{\theta}_n - \theta_n^* \to 0$ *prob* $-P$ by Theorem 3.4. Further, the subsequence theorem ensures that given any subsequence $\{n'\}$ there exists a further subsequence $\{n''\}$ such that $((\hat{\theta}_{n''} - \theta_{n''}^*)', Q_{n''}(\cdot, \theta) - \bar{Q}_{n''}(\theta), \nabla' Q_{n''}(\cdot, \theta) - \nabla' \bar{Q}_{n''}(\theta), vech' [\nabla^2 Q_{n''}(\cdot, \theta) - \nabla^2 \bar{Q}_{n''}(\theta)]) \to 0$ *a.s.* $-P$ uniformly on Θ. Apply the foregoing argument to this subsequence, so that there exists a set of probability one such that $\nabla Q_{n''}(\omega, \theta) = 0$ has the unique consistent root $\hat{\theta}_{n''}$ for all n'' sufficiently large and that for any root $\tilde{\theta}_{n''} \neq \hat{\theta}_{n''}$, there exists $\varepsilon > 0$ such that $|\tilde{\theta}_{n''} - \theta_{n''}^*| \geq \varepsilon$ for n'' sufficiently large. Because the subsequence $\{n'\}$ is arbitrary, it follows that for some $\varepsilon > 0$, $P[|\tilde{\theta}_n - \theta_n^*| > \varepsilon] \to 1$. □

PROOF OF THEOREM 3.13: The conditions of Theorem 3.12 are easily verified to hold under the conditions given and the result follows immediately. □

CHAPTER 4

Correctly Specified Models of Density

In the previous chapter, we saw that the QMLE $\hat{\theta}_n$ is consistent for θ_n^*, a parameter vector that minimizes the KLIC. In this chapter, we consider situations in which θ_n^* may be given an interpretation beyond this.

4.1 Specifications Correct in Their Entirety

Recall that in Chapter 2 we defined a probability model as correctly specified if there exists a parameter vector such that the probability model evaluated at that parameter vector corresponds to the data generation process governing the phenomenon of interest. Our definition of a correct parametric stochastic specification is analogous.

DEFINITION 4.1 (*Specification Correct in its Entirety*): The parametric stochastic specification $\mathcal{S} = \{f_t\}$ is *correct in its entirety for X on* Θ *with respect to* $\{\nu^n\}$ if there exists θ_o in Θ such that with $f^n \equiv \Pi_{t=1}^n f_t$, $f^n(x^n, \theta_o) = g^n(x^n)$, for all $x^n \in \mathbb{R}^{\nu n}$, $n = 1, 2, \ldots$. □

For brevity, we say that "$\mathcal{S}$ is correct in its entirety" when this condition holds. In this context, we say that θ_o has a "probability interpretation," i.e., it can be interpreted as the parameter indexing the data generation process within the model specified, so that we can make accurate probability statements about the sequence X using this specification. In this circumstance, a knowledge of θ_o is tantamount to a knowledge of the true data generating mechanism for samples of any size.

In Chapter 2, it was argued heuristically that the MLE should be consistent for θ_o in this circumstance. The first result of this chapter gives specific conditions under which this is true.

THEOREM 4.2: *Given Assumptions 2.1–2.3, 3.1, 3.2 and 3.4, if the specification* $\mathcal{S}$ *is correct in its entirety, then* $\hat{\theta}_n \to \theta_o$ *a.s.* $-P_o$ *(prob* $-P_o$*),* *where $\hat{\theta}_n$ is the QMLE generated by $\mathcal{S}$.* □

In particular, this result ensures the consistency of the MLE for correctly specified models of single equations or systems of equations in contexts allowing for continuous, discrete, censored or truncated variables. Theorem 4.2 is thus a fundamental consistency result for the QMLE.

The present result applies to parametric stochastic specifications rather than to parametric probability models. This is because we do not require f^n to be a density for all θ in Θ, i.e. we allow f^n to integrate to less than unity over $\mathbb{R}^{vn}$ with respect to ν^n. Nevertheless, in order for the specification to be correct in its entirety, it must be a density for at least one element of Θ, namely θ_o. This condition typically fails when "exogenous" variables are present. We treat such cases below.

Theorem 4.2 provides conditions under which the QMLE consistently estimates a quantity that has not only an information theoretic interpretation, but also a probability interpretation, in that θ_o represents the "true parameters" describing the joint probability distribution of X_t, $t = 1, 2, \ldots$, within the context of the given stochastic specification.

We are now in a position to investigate the extent to which such "true parameters" may also be given an economic interpretation. This hinges crucially on the relationship between the correct specification of economic models and of probability models. This relationship is not entirely straightforward.

To appreciate this, we consider a simple example in which the true relation between consumption expenditure e of an individual and her disposable income i is given by

$$e = i^{\delta_o}$$

for $0 < \delta_o < 1$. A correctly specified parametric economic model of this relationship is

(4.1) $$\mathcal{E} \equiv \{e = i^{\alpha} : \alpha \in [0, 1]\} .$$

The nature of economic reality is embodied in the unknown constant δ_o, the income elasticity of consumption, and our goal is to discover this by suitable methods. If we could observe a single individual's income and expenditure without error, then δ_o could be recovered directly as $\delta_o = \log e / \log i$, and we would be done.

In this example, the need for statistical analysis arises if error free observation is not possible. For simplicity, suppose that we attempt to learn about δ_o by taking a random sample of observations from a population of identical individuals (indexed by $t = 1, \ldots, n$) in which income is log-normally distributed with $\log i_t = \mu_o + \upsilon_t$, $\upsilon_t \sim i.i.d.\ N(0, \tau_o^2)$, and that our observations are contaminated by measurement errors in such a way that

$$(4.2) \qquad E_t = \log e_t + \varepsilon_t, \; I_t = \log i_t + \eta_t,$$

where $(\varepsilon_t, \eta_t)' \sim i.i.d.\ N(0, \Sigma_o)$, independently of i_t (hence e_t), where

$$\Sigma_o = \begin{bmatrix} \sigma_{o1}^2 & 0 \\ 0 & \sigma_{o2}^2 \end{bmatrix}.$$

The sampling method and distribution of population attributes, the measurement process, and the economic behavioral relationship combine to give

$$\begin{aligned} E_t &= \delta_o \log i_t + \varepsilon_t \\ &= \delta_o (\mu_o + \upsilon_t) + \varepsilon_t \\ &= \delta_o \mu_o + (\delta_o \upsilon_t + \varepsilon_t) \end{aligned}$$

and

$$I_t = \mu_o + (\upsilon_t + \eta_t), \; t = 1, \ldots, n,$$

so that $(E_t, I_t)'$ is i.i.d. normal with

$$m_o \equiv E[(E_t, I_t)'] = (\delta_o \mu_o, \mu_o)'$$

$$V_o \equiv \text{var}[(E_t, I_t)'] = \begin{bmatrix} \delta_o^2 \tau_o^2 + \sigma_{o1}^2 & \delta_o \tau_o^2 \\ \delta_o \tau_o^2 & \tau_o^2 + \sigma_{o2}^2 \end{bmatrix}.$$

The density associated with this data generating mechanism is therefore

$$g^n(x^n) = (2\pi)^{-n/2} (\det V_o)^{-n/2} \exp\left[-\sum_{t=1}^{n} (x_t - m_o)' V_o^{-1} (x_t - m_o)/2 \right],$$

where x_t is a realization of $(E_t, I_t)'$.

Now suppose we have arrived at a parametric stochastic specification by brilliantly positing the economic model (4.1) and correctly assuming the distribution of income and the measurement relation (4.2) up to some unknown nuisance parameters, and by incorporating the random sampling method to obtain the specification

$$f^n(x^n, \theta) = (2\pi)^{-n/2} (\det V(\theta))^{-n/2} \times \exp\left[-\sum_{t=1}^{n} (x_t - m(\theta))' V(\theta)^{-1} (x_t - m(\theta))/2 \right],$$

where $\theta = (\alpha, \beta, \gamma, \lambda_1, \lambda_2)'$, $m(\theta) = (\alpha\beta, \beta)'$, and

$$V(\theta) = \begin{bmatrix} \alpha^2\gamma^2 + \lambda_1^2 & \alpha\gamma^2 \\ \alpha\gamma^2 & \gamma^2 + \lambda_2^2 \end{bmatrix}.$$

This specification is correct in its entirety for $\{(E_t, I_t)'\}$ because on a suitable choice for Θ there exists $\theta_o = (\alpha_o, \beta_o, \gamma_o, \lambda_{o1}, \lambda_{o2})' = (\delta_o, \mu_o, \tau_o, \sigma_{o1}, \sigma_{o2})'$ such that $m(\theta_o) = m_o$ and $V(\theta_o) = V_o$ so that $f^n(x^n, \theta_o) = g^n(x^n)$ $a.e. - \nu^n$ (where ν^n is the $2n$-fold product of Lebesgue measure). Theorem 4.2 ensures that the MLE $\hat{\theta}_n$ is consistent for θ_o under general regularity conditions. Therefore, our estimate, say $\hat{\alpha}_n$, is consistent for $\alpha_o = \delta_o$, and we can achieve the goal of learning (at least asymptotically) about the income elasticity of consumption expenditure.

In this context, correct specification of the economic model, population distribution and sampling method, and measurement process leads to a situation in which an economic interpretation is valid for the element of θ_o that is of interest. This example thus illustrates the implicit context often assumed for empirical analysis in economics, in which correctness of the stochastic specification supports inferences about economic behavior.

In contrast, consider next what happens if instead of brilliantly positing the model (4.1) we misguidedly adopt the misspecified economic model

$$\tilde{\mathcal{E}} \equiv \{ e = \tilde{\alpha} i : \tilde{\alpha} \in [0, 1] \}. \tag{4.3}$$

If we correctly assume the measurement relation (4.2) and the population distribution of income, let $\alpha = \log \tilde{\alpha}$ and again use symbols $(\beta, \gamma, \lambda_1, \lambda_2)$ in deriving our model, we obtain a model based on the relations

$$\begin{aligned} E_t &= \alpha + \log i_t + \varepsilon_t \\ &= \alpha + (\beta + \upsilon_t) + \varepsilon_t \\ &= (\alpha + \beta) + (\upsilon_t + \varepsilon_t) \end{aligned}$$

and

$$I_t = \beta + (\upsilon_t + \eta_t), \quad t = 1, \ldots, n.$$

Letting $\theta = (\alpha, \beta, \gamma, \lambda_1, \lambda_2)'$ and letting $E_\theta(\cdot)$ and $\text{var}_\theta(\cdot)$ denote expectation and variance when this model is correct with parameter θ, we have

$$\tilde{m}(\theta) = E_\theta((E_t, I_t)') = (\alpha + \beta, \beta)'$$

$$\tilde{V}(\theta) = \text{var}_\theta[(E_t, I_t)'] = \begin{bmatrix} \gamma^2 + \lambda_1^2 & \gamma^2 \\ \gamma^2 & \gamma^2 + \lambda_2^2 \end{bmatrix}.$$

This yields the specification

$$\tilde{f}^n(x^n, \theta)$$
$$= (2\pi)^{-n/2} (\det \tilde{V}(\theta))^{-n/2}$$
$$\times \exp\left[- \sum_{t=1}^{n} (x_t - \tilde{m}(\theta))' \tilde{V}(\theta)^{-1} (x_t - \tilde{m}(\theta))/2 \right].$$

The important feature of this example is that with suitable choice of parameter space Θ, $\{\tilde{f}^n\}$ is in fact *correct in its entirety* despite the fact that it is based on a misspecified economic model (4.3). This is because there exists θ_o in Θ such that $\tilde{m}(\theta_o) = m_o$ and $\tilde{V}(\theta_o) = V_o$. The specific values for the elements of θ_o can be obtained by solving these equations, yielding

$$\alpha_o = \mu_o(\delta_o - 1)$$
$$\beta_o = \mu_o$$
$$\gamma_o = \delta_o^{1/2} \tau_o$$
$$\lambda_{o1} = [\sigma_{o1}^2 + \tau_o^2(\delta_o^2 - \delta_o)]^{1/2}$$
$$\lambda_{o2} = [\sigma_{o2}^2 + (1 - \delta_o)\tau_o^2]^{1/2}.$$

Theorem 4.2 ensures that the MLE $\hat{\theta}_n$ is consistent for θ_o. Although the parameter of interest, α_o, does have an information theoretic interpretation and a probability interpretation, it does *not* have the economic interpretation that the model (4.3) would imply if it were correct. We are not justified in making inferences about the "marginal propensity to consume" based on the QMLE $\hat{\alpha}_n$ for α_o, despite the fact that the stochastic specification is correct in its entirety. Thus, the correctness of a stochastic specification in its entirety is *not* sufficient to ensure the correctness of the underlying parametric economic model. Another way of saying this is that while correct specification of the underlying economic model is part (and *only* part) of a set of sufficient conditions for the correctness of a resulting stochastic specification, it is not a necessary condition. Expressed in terms of the parameters being estimated, the availability of a probability interpretation for θ_o may not imply the availability of an economic interpretation for θ_o or for any of its elements. On the other hand, the lack of a probability interpretation for θ_o *may* signal the lack of an economic interpretation for θ_o. We note that a probability interpretation may be available under conditions weaker than those considered so far. Also, in the next chapter we see that even when a probability interpretation is not available, an interpretation in terms of conditional location or some other conditional attribute may be available. Economic interpretations may or may not be supportable in such situations.

Attribution of economic meaning to parameters estimated by quasi-maximum likelihood methods (or any statistical method for that matter) is therefore fraught with danger. The foregoing discussion suggests a number of useful precautions. Of course, the first is that painstaking care be employed in constructing the stochastic specification $\mathcal{S}$ and its meaningful parameter space Θ, with particular care paid to the possible implications of the failures of specific simplifying assumptions made along the way. The parameters estimated from the resulting model can then serve as a basis for investigating whether or not a probability interpretation can be given, beyond any available information theoretic interpretation. This investigation relies on methods of hypothesis testing and specification analysis to be discussed at length in later chapters.

When the hypothesis that θ_n^* has a probability interpretation is rejected, then generally no economic interpretation is available, and a new specification must be formulated that overcomes the shortcomings of the original. When one fails to reject the hypothesis that θ_n^* has a probability interpretation, then this hypothesis might be viewed as a working hypothesis consistent with the available data. (As with any statistical procedure, absolute proof is unavailable.) Some statistical procedures relevant to these issues are discussed in White [1990]. Entertaining a particular economic interpretation for given parameters as a working hypothesis may in fact require maintaining empirically untestable assumptions. There may be alternative economic models that are observationally equivalent.

Theorem 4.2 provides general conditions sufficient for $\hat{\theta}_n$ to estimate consistently parameters with a probability interpretation. However, these conditions are not necessary — a probability interpretation may well be available even if $\mathcal{S}$ fails to be correctly specified in its entirety, as we now see.

4.2 Specifications Correct for Jointly Dependent Variables

In economics, it is common that the stochastic specification fails to be correct in its entirety for the reason that for no θ_o is $f^n(x^n, \theta_o)$ a density with respect to ν^n, i.e. for all θ in Θ

$$\int f^n(x^n, \theta)\, d\nu^n(x^n) \neq 1 .$$

The reason for this is that effort is often concentrated on constructing a more or less careful parametric specification of the stochastic behavior of a subvector of X_t, say Y_t, conditional on Z_t (with $X_t = (Z_t', Y_t')'$), and possibly on the past history X^{t-1}. The behavior of Z_t is usually not modeled, so that most specifications in econometrics are incomplete approximations to the joint density of $\{X_t\}$. An important question, then, is whether, or, more properly, under what conditions this incompleteness matters.

In classic work originating at the Cowles Commission in the late 1940s and early 1950s Koopmans [1950] showed that if the random disturbances of the structural equations of an econometric model explaining the behavior of the "endogenous" variables, say Y_t, are independent of the remaining observables, say Z_t, then the density of Z_t plays no role in determining the MLE. Koopmans labeled such variables Z_t "exogenous" and concluded "the identifiable parameters . . . can be consistently estimated, by the method of maximum likelihood, i.e. consistently and without bias in large samples, from [the structural] equations only, treating the 'exogenous' variables . . . as if they were fixed in repeated samples" (Koopmans [1950, p. 396]).

On the basis of this finding, the probabilistic behavior of any variables Z_t thought to be independent of the disturbances of the structural equations of an econometric model has simply been ignored in econometric analysis, with few exceptions.

It must be mentioned that the statement that the exogenous variables can be treated as "fixed in repeated samples" is not to be taken literally. The intended meaning of Koopmans' statement is that the distribution of Z_t given X^{t-1} can be ignored in constructing a stochastic specification, as we see below.

Although the concept of exogeneity has a long and distinguished history (e.g. Orcutt [1952], Marschak [1953], Phillips [1956], Sims [1972, 1977], Geweke [1978, 1982], Richard [1979], Engle, Hendry and Richard [1983]), it is actually *irrelevant* for the present treatment of the issue of consistency. The only thing that matters for now is whether certain variables Z_t are ignored in the construction of the stochastic specification. In Chapter 7, we consider the concept of exogeneity as it relates to efficiency.

We proceed by giving a definition of the jointly dependent variables specified by a given stochastic specification $\mathcal{S}$. We first introduce some convenient notation. Recognizing the fact that $f_t(X^t, \theta)$ typically depends only on some subvector of X^t, we let $\ddot{X}^t$ denote the smallest subvector of X^t such that $f_t(X^t, \theta)$ is measurable — $\sigma(\ddot{X}^t)$ for all θ, $t = 1, 2, \ldots$. The dimension of $\ddot{X}^t$ is denoted j_t. $\ddot{X}^t$ can be viewed as containing the variables "included" in the specification for observation t. To emphasize this, we will sometimes abuse notation and write $f_t(\ddot{X}^t, \theta)$ in place of $f_t(X^t, \theta)$. We shall partition $\ddot{X}^t$ as $\ddot{X}^t = (W'_t, Y'_t)'$ for subvectors W_t and Y_t having dimensions k_t and l_t respectively, $j_t = k_t + l_t$. When we wish to emphasize this partition, we will further abuse notation and write $f_t(Y_t, W_t, \theta)$ in place of $f_t(X^t, \theta)$. Realizations of $\ddot{X}^t$, Y_t and W_t will be denoted $\ddot{x}^t$, y_t and w_t respectively.

DEFINITION 4.3: *(Jointly Dependent Variables, Explanatory Variables)*: Given a stochastic specification $\mathcal{S} = \{f_t\}$, suppose there exists a subvector Y_t of both $\ddot{X}^t$ and X_t of dimension $l_t \leq v$ and a measure ζ_t on $(\mathbb{R}^{l_t}, \mathcal{B}^{l_t})$ such that

$$(4.4) \qquad \int_{\mathbb{R}^{l_t}} f_t(y_t, w_t, \theta)\, d\zeta_t(y_t) = 1$$

for all θ in Θ and w_t in $\mathbb{R}^{k_t}$, $k_t \geq 0$, and for no further subvector $\tilde{Y}_t$ of Y_t of dimension $\tilde{l}_t < l_t$ and measure $\tilde{\zeta}_t$ on $(\mathbb{R}^{\tilde{l}_t}, \mathcal{B}^{\tilde{l}_t})$

is it true that

$$\int_{\mathbb{R}^{l_t}} f_t(\tilde{y}_t, \tilde{w}_t, \theta)\, d\,\tilde{z}_t(\tilde{y}_t) = 1$$

for all θ in Θ and $\tilde{w}_t$ in $\mathbb{R}^{\tilde{k}_t}$, $\tilde{k}_t = j_t - \tilde{l}_t$, $\ddot{x}^t = (\tilde{w}'_t, \tilde{y}'_t)'$, $t = 1, 2, \ldots$.

Then $\mathcal{S}$ *specifies (jointly) dependent variables* $Y = \{Y_t\}$ *and explanatory variables* $W = \{W_t\}$ *with respect to* $\{\zeta_t\}$. □

The jointly dependent variables and the explanatory variables are thus solely features of the stochastic specification, and not of the data generation process. The measures ζ_t play a crucial role, in that the dependent variables are those for which f_t can be interpreted as a conditional density of Y_t given W_t with respect to ζ_t for all values of θ. For this reason we refer to (4.4) as the "conditional density condition." When $\mathcal{S}$ specifies dependent variables $Y = \{Y_t\}$ with respect to $\{\zeta_t\}$ we also say that "$\{\zeta_t\}$ generates dependent variables $Y = \{Y_t\}$ in $\mathcal{S}$."

Particular choices for $\{\zeta_t\}$ may generate no dependent variables in $\mathcal{S}$. However, measures ζ_t for which the integral in (4.4) yields a constant depending neither on w_t nor θ (although possibly on t) can generate dependent variables in a modification of $\mathcal{S}$ obtained simply by normalizing (dividing) f_t by this constant. For simplicity and convenience, we assume that such normalizations are carried out whenever necessary.

A further indication of the separation between the data generation process and the dependent and explanatory variables specified by $\mathcal{S}$ with respect to $\{\zeta_t\}$ is that there is not even the requirement that ζ_t dominate the distribution of Y_t. Thus, $\mathcal{S}$ can specify a dependent variable with respect to Lebesgue measure, even though the dependent variable can take on only the values zero or one, as happens when nonlinear least squares is used to estimate the parameters of a probit or logit model for a Bernoulli dependent variable.

To examine the content of Definition 4.3, we consider a simplified version of the bivariate normal model obtained in the income expenditure model above. Suppose, then, that

$$f_t(x^t, \theta) = (2\pi)^{-1} \exp -[(x_{t1} - \mu_1)^2 + (x_{t2} - \mu_2)^2]/2,$$

where $\theta = (\mu_1, \mu_2)'$. First note that f_t depends only on $x_t = (x_{t1}, x_{t2})'$, so that $\ddot{X}_t = X_t$ in this example. The dependent variables can only be X_{t1} and/or X_{t2}. Because f_t is immediately recognized as a bivariate normal density function, the natural choice for ζ_t is $\lambda \otimes \lambda$, Lebesgue measure on $\mathbb{R}^2$. With this choice, we immediately have

$$\int_{\mathbb{R}^2} f_t(x_{t1}, x_{t2}, \theta)\, d\lambda(x_{t1}) d\lambda(x_{t2}) = 1.$$

For this case $\mathcal{S} = \{f_t\}$ apparently specifies jointly dependent variables $\{X_t\}$. However, we must check that no subvector of X_t also satisfies the conditional density condition. Consider X_{t1}. Can we find a measure ζ_t such that

$$\int_{\mathbb{R}} (2\pi)^{-1} \exp - [(x_{t1} - \mu_1)^2 + (x_{t2} - \mu_2)^2]/2\, d\zeta_t(x_{t1}) = 1$$

for all θ in Θ and x_{t2} in $\mathbb{R}$? Now

$$\begin{aligned}
&\int_{\mathbb{R}} (2\pi)^{-1} \exp - [(x_{t1} - \mu_1)^2 + (x_{t2} - \mu_2)^2]/2\, d\zeta_t(x_{t1}) \\
&= (2\pi)^{-1/2} \exp[-(x_{t2} - \mu_2)^2/2] \\
&\quad \times \int_{\mathbb{R}} (2\pi)^{-1/2} \exp[-(x_{t1} - \mu_1)^2/2] d\zeta_t(x_{t1}) \\
&= (2\pi)^{-1/2} \exp[-(x_{t2} - \mu_2)^2/2]\, c(\mu_1)
\end{aligned}$$

with $c(\mu_1) \equiv \int_{\mathbb{R}} (2\pi)^{-1/2} \exp[-(x_{t1} - \mu_1)^2/2]\, d\, \zeta_t\, (x_{t1})$. Because c cannot depend on x_{t2}, there is no way to choose ζ_t to obtain $\int_{\mathbb{R}} f_t(x_{t1}, x_{t2}, \theta)\, d\, \zeta_t\, (x_{t1}) = 1$ (or constant) for all $\theta \in \Theta$ and x_{t2}. The situation is identical for X_{t2}. Consequently, $\mathcal{S}$ does indeed specify jointly dependent variables $\{X_t\}$. Note that W_t is null in this case.

Next suppose that the specification is further simplified to

$$f_t(x^t, \theta) = (2\pi)^{-1/2} \exp - (x_{t1} - \theta\, x_{t2})^2/2\,,$$

which obviously implies that the QMLE is obtained from the least squares regression of X_{t1} on X_{t2}. To verify that X_{t1} is indeed the dependent variable, we first note that as before $\ddot{X}^t = X_t$, so X_{t1} and/or X_{t2} may be the dependent variable(s). Consider X_{t1}, and take $\zeta_t = \lambda$, Lebesgue measure on $\mathbb{R}$. We have

$$\int_{\mathbb{R}} (2\pi)^{-1/2} \exp[-(x_{t1} - \theta\, x_{t2})^2/2] d\, \lambda\, (x_{t1}) = 1$$

for all θ in Θ and x_{t2}, so that the conditional density condition holds for X_{t1}. Next consider X_{t2}, again with $\zeta_t = \lambda$. We have

$$\begin{aligned}
&\int_{\mathbb{R}} (2\pi)^{-1/2} \exp[-(x_{t1} - \theta\, x_{t2})^2/2] d\, \lambda(x_{t2}) \\
&= \int_{\mathbb{R}} (2\pi)^{-1/2} \exp[-\theta^2 (x_{t2} - x_{t1}/\theta)^2/2] d\, \lambda(x_{t2}) \\
&= \theta^{-1}\,,
\end{aligned}$$

using the fact that $\int_{\mathbb{R}} \theta(2\pi)^{-1/2} \exp[-\theta^2 (x_{t2} - x_{t1}/\theta)^2/2] d\, \lambda(x_{t2}) = 1$. Unless $\Theta = \{1\}$, the conditional density condition fails for x_{t2}. Other choices for ζ_t potentially introduce x_{t1} into the expression for $\int_{\mathbb{R}} f_t(x_t, \theta)\, d\, \zeta_t\, (x_{t2})$, so X_{t2} cannot be a dependent variable, but is instead the explanatory variable, $W_t = X_{t2}$.

To appreciate the effect of the second part of Definition 4.3, consider what happens if we take $\zeta_t = \lambda \otimes \upsilon$, where υ is uniform measure on (0, 1). Then

$$\begin{aligned}
&\int_{\mathbb{R}^2} f_t(x_t, \theta)\, d\, \zeta_t(x_t) \\
&= \int_{\mathbb{R}} \left[\int_{\mathbb{R}} (2\pi)^{-1/2} \exp[-(x_{t1} - \theta\, x_{t2})^2/2] d\, \lambda(x_{t1}) \right] d\, \upsilon\, (x_{t2}) \\
&= \int_{\mathbb{R}} d\, \upsilon\, (x_{t2}) \\
&= 1\,,
\end{aligned}$$

so that the conditional density condition holds for $\lambda \otimes \upsilon$. However, we already know that X_{t1} and $\zeta_t = \lambda$ also satisfy the conditional density condition, so the second part of Definition 4.3 is violated, ruling out the possibility that $\mathcal{S}$ specifies dependent variables $\{X_t\}$ with respect to $\{\lambda \otimes \upsilon\}$.

These examples show that Definition 4.3 delivers the expected answers in the familiar case of linear regression, and illustrate the role played by each part of the definition. The definition also applies in less obvious situations unrelated to regression analysis.

We introduce some additional notation and provide some additional discussion of nomenclature. When $\mathcal{S}$ specifies dependent variables $Y = \{Y_t\}$, we partition X_t as $X_t = (Z'_t, Y'_t)'$. The variables Z_t can correspond to variables usually thought of as "exogenous", but in fact Z_t could contain more. This possibility arises when the stochastic specification is that appropriate for implementation of the method of limited information maximum likelihood (LIML), as proposed by Anderson and Rubin [1949]. In LIML estimation, interest attaches only to parameters that appear in some subset of the equations of a structural econometric model. A stochastic specification appropriate to this situation yields jointly dependent variables Y_t corresponding to the "included endogenous" variables in the equation subset of interest, and Z_t contains the "exogenous" variables as well as variables appearing in the other equations. These other variables are referred to as "excluded endogenous" because f_t does not depend on these elements of Z_t. It is necessary to include them in X_t because f_t may well depend on lagged values of such "excluded endogenous" variables.

Thus, in full information maximum likelihood (FIML) contexts, Z_t corresponds to the variables assumed to be "exogenous" while in LIML contexts Z_t comprises variables assumed to be either "exogenous" or "excluded endogenous." Because of the possibilities for confusion, we shall not rely on the "exogenous/endogenous" nomenclature.

It is also convenient to define $\tilde{X}^{t-1} \equiv (X'_1, \ldots, X'_{t-1}, Z'_t)'$, which we refer to as the *predetermined variables specified by $\mathcal{S}$ with respect to $\{\zeta_t\}$*. The qualification of the preceding paragraph makes this usage fully appropriate only in FIML-like contexts, but for simplicity we shall leave this qualification implicit. The elements of W_t are a subset of those of $\tilde{X}^{t-1}$, so the explanatory variables can also be thought of as the "included predetermined variables". As is true for dependent and explanatory variables, the nomenclature "predetermined variables" refers only to the stochastic specification and does not refer to any aspect of the data generation process.

Whenever $\mathcal{S}$ specifies dependent and explanatory variables Y and W we can consider f_t as an approximation to the true conditional density (more generally, density ratio) of Y_t given W_t, defined below. We impose the following assumption.

ASSUMPTION 4.1: Let a partition of $\ddot{X}^t$ ($j_t \times 1$) be given as $\ddot{X}^t = (W'_t, Y'_t)'$ where Y_t ($l_t \times 1$) is also a subvector of X_t, $t = 1, 2, \ldots$. Let $\ddot{\nu}^t$ and $\ddot{\nu}_t$ be given σ-finite measures on $(\mathbb{R}^{j_t}, \mathcal{B}^{j_t})$ and $(\mathbb{R}^{k_t}, \mathcal{B}^{k_t})$ respectively, $k_t = j_t - l_t \geq 0$, $t = 1, 2, \ldots$. Then the distribution of $\ddot{X}^t$, denoted $\ddot{P}_o^t$, and the distribution of W_t, denoted $\ddot{P}_{ot}$, are absolutely continuous with respect to $\ddot{\nu}^t$ and $\ddot{\nu}_t$ respectively, $t = 1, 2, \ldots$. □

Note that the partition of $\ddot{X}^t$ is arbitrary for now. In Assumption 4.3, we relate the partition to $\mathcal{S}$.

Given Assumption 4.1, it follows from the Radon-Nikodým theorem that there exist measurable density functions $\ddot{g}^t \equiv d\ddot{P}_o^t / d\ddot{\nu}^t$ and $\ddot{g}_t \equiv d\ddot{P}_{ot} / d\ddot{\nu}_t$, $t = 1, 2, \ldots$ for $\ddot{X}^t$ and W_t respectively. We denote the density ratio of Y_t given W_t as h_t, defined as

$$h_t(y_t, w_t) = \ddot{g}^t(y_t, w_t) / \ddot{g}_t(w_t) \qquad y_t \in \mathbb{R}^{l_t},\ w_t \in \mathbb{R}^{k_t}.$$

If $E(\log h_t(Y_t, W_t))$ exists, we can define the average Kullback-Leibler information of h_t relative to f_t as

$$\mathcal{I}_n(\{h_t : f_t\}; \theta) \equiv n^{-1} \sum_{t=1}^{n} \mathbb{I}(h_t : f_t; \theta),$$

where $\mathbb{I}(h_t : f_t; \theta) = E(\log h_t(Y_t, W_t) / f_t(Y_t, W_t, \theta))$. Note that when $Y_t = X_t$ and $W_t = X^{t-1}$ we have $\mathcal{I}_n(\{h_t : f_t\}; \theta) = n^{-1}\, \mathbb{I}(g^n : f^n; \theta)$ (use Theorem 2.7), but this equality does not hold in general.

A result analogous to Theorem 3.6 holds under appropriate conditions. To ensure the finiteness of $\mathcal{I}_n$ we impose an analog of Assumption 3.3.

ASSUMPTION 4.2: For each $t = 1, 2, \ldots$, $E\,|\log h_t(Y_t, W_t)| < \infty$. □

ASSUMPTION 4.3: Let $\mathcal{S}$ specify dependent variables $Y = \{Y_t\}$ and explanatory variables $W = \{W_t\}$ with respect to a given sequence $\{\zeta_t\}$ such that Assumption 4.1 holds for the induced partition $\ddot{X}^t = (W'_t, Y'_t)'$, $t = 1, 2, \ldots$. Then for all θ in Θ

$$(4.5) \qquad \int_{\ddot{S}^t} f_t(y_t, w_t, \theta)\, \ddot{g}_t(w_t)\, d\ddot{\nu}^t(y_t, w_t) \leq 1, \quad t = 1, 2, \ldots,$$

where $\ddot{S}^t \equiv \{\ddot{x}^t \in \mathbb{R}^{j_t} : \ddot{g}^t(\ddot{x}^t) > 0\}$. □

Condition (4.5) follows immediately from the joint dependence of Y_t whenever we can take $\ddot{\nu}^t = \ddot{\nu}_t \otimes \zeta_t$, because

$$\int_{\ddot{S}^t} f_t(y_t, w_t, \theta)\, \ddot{g}_t(w_t)\, d\,\ddot{\nu}^t(y_t, w_t)$$
$$= \int_{\ddot{S}^t} f_t(y_t, w_t, \theta)\, \ddot{g}_t(w_t)\, d\,\zeta_t(y_t)\, d\,\ddot{\nu}_t(w_t)$$
$$\leq \int_{\ddot{S}_t \times I\!R^{l_t}} f_t(y_t, w_t, \theta)\, \ddot{g}_t(w_t)\, d\,\zeta_t(y_t)\, d\,\ddot{\nu}_t(w_t)$$
$$= \int_{\ddot{S}_t} [\int_{I\!R^{l_t}} f_t(y_t, w_t, \theta)\, d\,\zeta_t(y_t)]\, \ddot{g}_t(w_t)\, d\,\ddot{\nu}_t(w_t)$$
$$= \int_{\ddot{S}_t} \ddot{g}_t(w_t)\, d\,\ddot{\nu}_t(w_t) = 1 \qquad \text{for all } \theta \in \Theta.$$

The inequality holds because f_t and $\ddot{g}_t$ are non-negative, and $\ddot{S}^t \subset \ddot{S}_t \times I\!R^{l_t}$, $\ddot{S}_t \equiv \{ w_t \in I\!R^{k_t} : \ddot{g}_t(w_t) > 0 \}$, given that we may take $\ddot{g}^t$ to be such that $(w'_t, y'_t)' \in \ddot{S}_t$ implies $w_t \in \ddot{S}_t$ (as in the proof of Theorem 2.7).

Because Assumption 4.3 plays a fundamental role in several results to follow, being able to take $\ddot{\nu}^t = \ddot{\nu}_t \otimes \zeta_t$ provides a key benefit from achieving direct contact between reality ($\ddot{\nu}^t$ and $\ddot{\nu}_t$) and the modeling process (ζ_t). However, the information inequality applies and conveys useful information even in cases where this direct contact is absent, but the weaker condition (4.5) nevertheless holds.

The analog of Theorem 3.6 is

THEOREM 4.4: *(i) Given Assumptions 2.1, 2.3, 3.1(a,b), 3.2, 4.1 and 4.2,* $\{ \Gamma_n(\{ h_t : f_t \} ; \theta) \}$ *has identifiably unique minimizers* $\{ \theta^*_n \}$.

(ii) Given Assumptions 2.1, 2.3, 3.1, 3.2, 4.1 and 4.2, $\hat{\theta}_n$ *is strongly (weakly) consistent for* θ^*_n *as given in (i).*

(iii) Given Assumptions 2.1, 2.3, 3.1(a), 4.2 and 4.3, $\Gamma_n(\{ h_t : f_t \} ; \theta) \geq 0$*, for all* θ *in* Θ, $n = 1, 2, \ldots$. □

Note that results (i) and (ii) hold for any partition of $\ddot{X}^t$ satisfying Assumptions 4.1 and 4.2. The role of Y_t as jointly dependent variables comes into play only in (iii) when the information inequality is used to establish the non-negativity of Γ_n.

Thus, θ_{n*} can retain its information theoretic interpretation even when f^n is specified incompletely, as when the stochastic behavior of certain variables Z_t is ignored in constructing f^n. The information theoretic interpretation now relates to how well f_t acts as an approximation to h_t, the density ratio of the dependent variables Y_t given the explanatory variables W_t .

A result analogous to Theorem 4.2 holds when f_t is correctly specified in the sense of the following definition.

DEFINITION 4.5 (*Specification Correct for* $\{Y_t \mid W_t\}$): Let $\mathcal{S}$ specify dependent variables Y and explanatory variables W. Then $\mathcal{S}$ is *correct for* $\{Y_t \mid W_t\}$ *on* Θ *with respect to* $\{\ddot{v}^t, \ddot{v}_t\}$ if there exists θ_o in Θ such that $f_t(x^t, \theta_o) = h_t(y_t, w_t)$, for all x^t in $\mathbb{R}^{vt}$, $t = 1, 2, \ldots$. □

For brevity we say that "$\mathcal{S}$ is correct for $\{Y_t \mid W_t\}$" when this condition holds. When the value θ_o is of particular importance, we shall say that "$\mathcal{S}$ is correctly specified for $\{Y_t \mid W_t\}$ at θ_o."

The following analog to Theorem 4.2 generalizes a result due to Levine [1983].

THEOREM 4.6: *Given Assumptions 2.1, 2.3, 3.1, 3.2, and 4.3, if the specification* $\mathcal{S}$ *is correct for* $\{Y_t \mid W_t\}$ *then* $\hat{\theta}_n \to \theta_o$ *a.s.* $-P_o$ (*prob* $-P_o$), *where* $\hat{\theta}_n$ *is the QMLE generated by* $\mathcal{S}$. □

This result provides a rigorous background against which to interpret Koopmans' statement about treating the "exogenous" variables as if they were "fixed in repeated samples." From this result we see that we can ignore modeling a subset of X_t, namely Z_t, and still obtain consistent estimates of the probabilistically meaningful θ_o, provided that we correctly model the conditional distribution of the jointly dependent variables Y_t given the remaining included variables, W_t. However, because of the possibilities for dynamic misspecification, to which we next turn our attention, the probabilistically meaningful θ_o may or may not be the object that is of most interest to the investigator.

Theorem 4.6 contains a number of interesting and important special cases. For example when $W_t = \tilde{X}^{t-1}$ (so that the specification takes complete account of the dynamic structure of X), we have a time-series analog of Andersen's [1970] consistency result for conditional maximum likelihood estimators of correctly specified models with i.i.d. observations.

The present result contains more, however, because it provides conditions under which the dynamic structure of X can be partially or completely ignored without affecting the ability of the QMLE to estimate consistently probabilistically meaningful parameters θ_o. In order to be explicit about the implications of Theorem 4.6 in this regard, it is helpful to introduce the notion of Granger-causality (Granger [1969], Granger and Newbold [1986]).

DEFINITION 4.7 (*Granger-Causality*): For $t = 1, 2, \ldots$ partition X_t as $(Z'_t, Y'_t)'$, define $\tilde{X}^{t-1} = (X'^{t-1}, Z'_t)'$ and let W_t be a given subvector of $\tilde{X}^{t-1}$. Let V_t contain all the elements of $\tilde{X}^{t-1}$ not included in W_t so that

$\sigma(X^t) = \sigma(Y_t) \vee \sigma(W_t) \vee \sigma(V_t)$. We say that V_t *does not Granger-cause* Y_t *with respect to* $\tilde{X}^{t-1}$ if $P_o[Y_t \in B \mid \tilde{X}^{t-1}] = P_o[Y_t \in B \mid W_t]$ for all $B \in \mathcal{B}^{l_t}$, where $P_o[\,\cdot \mid W_t]$ denotes the conditional probability distribution relative to the σ-field $\sigma(W_t)$ and similarly for $\tilde{X}^{t-1}$.

We say that $V = \{ V_t \}$ *does not Granger-cause* $Y = \{ Y_t \}$ *in* $X = \{ X_t \}$ if V_t does not Granger-cause Y_t with respect to $\tilde{X}^{t-1}$, $t = 1, 2, \ldots$. □

Granger-causality is thus a property of the data generation process. With it, we can define the concept of dynamic misspecification.

DEFINITION 4.8 (*Dynamic Misspecification*): Let $\mathcal{S}$ specify dependent variables Y and explanatory variables W. For this choice of Y and W, define V as in Definition 4.7. We say that $\mathcal{S}$ is *not subject to dynamic misspecification* if V does not Granger-cause Y in X. Otherwise, we say that $\mathcal{S}$ is *subject to dynamic misspecification.* □

When $\mathcal{S}$ is correctly specified for $\{ Y_t \mid W_t \}$ and is not subject to dynamic misspecification, we shall say that $\mathcal{S}$ is "correctly specified for $\{ Y_t \mid \tilde{X}^{t-1} \}$" without requiring $\sigma(W_t) = \sigma(\tilde{X}^{t-1})$. Dynamic misspecification occurs when the stochastic specification omits variables Granger-causing the jointly dependent variables. Expressed in terms of conditional densities, dynamic misspecification occurs when for all θ $f_t(X^t, \theta)$ is measurable with respect to a smaller σ-field than the smallest σ-field with respect to which the density ratio of Y_t given $\tilde{X}^{t-1}$, denoted $h_t(Y_t, \tilde{X}^{t-1})$ (or $h_t(X^t)$), is measurable. (When $\ddot{X}^t = X^t$ and $W_t = \tilde{X}^{t-1}$ we have $\ddot{v}^t = v^t$ and we let $\tilde{v}^{t-1}$ correspond to $\ddot{v}_t$.)

For example, suppose that a random scalar X_t is generated by the AR(2) process

$$X_t = a_o X_{t-1} + b_o X_{t-2} + \varepsilon_t \, ,$$

where ε_t is *i.i.d.* $N(0, \sigma_\varepsilon^2)$ $t = 1, 2, \ldots$. Suppose for convenience that the roots of the characteristic polynomial lie outside the unit circle, so that $\{X_t\}$ is a stationary process. Then

$$h_t(x^t) = (2\pi)^{-1/2} \sigma_\varepsilon^{-1} \exp[-(x_t - a_o\, x_{t-1} - b_o\, x_{t-2})^2 / 2\sigma_\varepsilon^2], \quad t = 1, 2, \ldots .$$

However, suppose that an AR(1) model is specified with typical element

$$X_t = \alpha X_{t-1} + \eta_t \qquad \alpha \in [-1, 1],$$

where η_t is $i.i.d.$ $N(0, \gamma^2)$, $\gamma > 0$, $t = 1, 2, \ldots$. Then

$$f_t(x^t, \theta) = (2\pi)^{-1/2} \gamma^{-1} \exp[-(x_t - \alpha x_{t-1})^2 / 2\gamma^2].$$

This model is subject to dynamic misspecification because h_t depends on x_{t-2}, x_{t-1} and x_t, while f_t depends only on x_{t-1} and x_t. The dependence on x_{t-2} has been ignored, and a dynamic misspecification thereby committed.

Despite the dynamic misspecification, we may still have $\{f_t\}$ correct for $\{Y_t \mid W_t\}$. In the present AR(1) example $Y_t = X_t$ and $W_t = X_{t-1}$ with respect to $\{\zeta_t = \lambda\}$. The AR(2) data generation process implies that (X_t, X_{t-1}) has a joint normal distribution with mean zero and

$$\text{var}\,[(X_t, X_{t-1})'] = \begin{bmatrix} \sigma_o^2 & \rho_o \sigma_o^2 \\ \rho_o \sigma_o^2 & \sigma_o^2 \end{bmatrix}, \qquad t = 1, 2, \ldots,$$

with $\rho_o = a_o / (1 - b_o)$ and $\sigma_o^2 = \sigma_\varepsilon^2 / (1 + a_o^2 - b_o^2 - 2a_o \rho_o)$. This implies that the distribution of X_t given X_{t-1} is $N(\rho_o X_{t-1}, \sigma_o^2(1 - \rho_o^2))$, i.e.

$$h_t(y_t, w_t) = (2\pi)^{-1/2}[\sigma_o^2(1 - \rho_o^2)]^{-1/2} \exp[-(x_t - \rho_o x_{t-1})^2 / 2\sigma_o^2(1 - \rho_o^2)].$$

Because there exists $\theta_o = (\alpha_o, \gamma_o)' = (\rho_o, \sigma_o(1 - \rho_o^2)^{1/2})'$ for which $f_t(x^t, \theta_o) = h_t(y_t, w_t)$, Definition 4.5 is satisfied, so that $\{f_t\}$ is indeed a correct specification for $\{Y_t \mid W_t\}$, i.e. $\{X_t \mid X_{t-1}\}$ in the present case. Despite the dynamic misspecification, Theorem 4.6 ensures that $\hat{\theta}_n$ is consistent for $\theta_o = (\alpha_o, \gamma_o)'$. It is in this sense that $\hat{\theta}_n$ is consistent for parameters with a probability interpretation; however, any economic interpretation that might have attached to a_o is not shared by α_o unless there is in fact no dynamic misspecification, i.e. $b_o = 0$.

There are circumstances in which dynamic misspecification need not destroy a possible economic interpretation for particular parameters. Robinson [1982], Gourieroux, Monfort and Trognon [1985], and Poirier and Ruud [1988] consider Tobit and probit models in which dynamic misspecifications occur as a result of neglected serial correlation (i.e. the underlying errors of the data generation process exhibit serial correlation but the observations are treated as if they were independent). Their results, which are corollaries of Theorem 4.6, show that consistent estimation of parameters of interest is possible despite such dynamic misspecification. It must be noted that the correctness of underlying normality assumptions plays an essential role in these particular cases.

In other cases, failure of distributional assumptions is not as serious a problem. As is well known, estimating the parameters of a linear regression model with no lagged dependent variables by ordinary least squares (the QMLE under a normality assumption) neglecting the effects of serially correlated error terms (and thus committing a dynamic misspecification) does not render the least squares estimator inconsistent. Furthermore, the failure of the normality assumption is not crucial in this case. Such situations are examined in some detail in the following chapter.

An immediate and obvious corollary of Theorem 4.6 is that when $\mathcal{S}$ is correctly specified for $\{Y_t \mid \tilde{X}^{t-1}\}$, then $\hat{\theta}_n$ is consistent for θ_o such that $f_t(x^t, \theta_o) = h_t(x^t)$. Despite the correctness of $\mathcal{S}$ for $\{Y_t \mid \tilde{X}^{t-1}\}$, there is still no guarantee that θ_o has some desired economic interpretation.

To see this, consider the expenditure/income example of the previous section with data generation process as in (4.2). Suppose we (erroneously) assume the absence of measurement error in observing income, and suppose we extend the model for expenditure by allowing for the presence of a constant, so that

$$(4.6) \qquad E_t = \beta + \alpha I_t + \varepsilon_t$$

with $\varepsilon_t \sim N(0, \gamma^2)$ forms the basis for the specification

$$f_t(X^t, \theta) = (2\pi)^{-1/2}\, \gamma^{-1} \exp[-(E_t - \beta - \alpha I_t)^2 / 2\gamma^2]\,,$$

with $\theta = (\alpha, \beta, \gamma)'$. The joint normality of E_t and I_t implies that in fact

$$E_t \mid I_t \sim N(M_t, v_o^2)$$

$$M_t = \delta_o\, \mu_o\, \sigma_{o2}^2 / (\tau_o^2 + \sigma_{o2}^2) + [\delta_o\, \tau_o^2 / (\tau_o^2 + \sigma_{o2}^2)]\, I_t$$

$$v_o^2 = (\delta_o^2\, \tau_o^2 + \sigma_{o1}^2)\, (\delta_o\, \tau_o^2\, \sigma_{o2}^2 + \sigma_{o1}^2\, \tau_o^2 + \sigma_{o1}^2\, \sigma_{o2}^2)$$

$$\times [\, (\delta_o \tau_o^2 + \sigma_{o1}^2)(\tau_o^2 + \sigma_{o2}^2)\,].$$

It follows that $\{ f_t \}$ is correct for $\{ E_t \mid I_t \}$ because $f_t(X^t, \theta_o) = h_t(Y_t, W_t)$ for all t with $\theta_o = (\alpha_o, \beta_o, \gamma_o)'$,

$$\alpha_o = \delta_o \tau_o^2 / (\tau_o^2 + \sigma_{o2}^2)$$

$$\beta_o = \delta_o \mu_o \sigma_{o2}^2 / (\tau_o^2 + \sigma_{o2}^2)$$

$$\gamma_o = v_o \, .$$

Furthermore, because of independence, there is no dynamic misspecification so that $\mathcal{S}$ is correct for $\{Y_t \mid \tilde{X}^{t-1}\}$. Theorem 4.6 ensures that we can consistently estimate α_o by $\hat{\alpha}_n$. However, the absence of dynamic misspecification still does not permit us to interpret α_o as the income elasticity of consumption. A necessary and sufficient condition for this is that $\sigma_{o2} = 0$, i.e. that there is in fact no error in the measurement of income. We see here the familiar "downward bias" in α_o that the presence of measurement error induces in the QMLE (least squares in this context).

4.3 Summary

Theorems 4.2 and 4.6 provide general conditions under which the QMLE is consistent for a parameter vector θ_o with a meaningful probability interpretation. Generally, when $\mathcal{S}$ is correctly specified θ_o can be interpreted as the "true parameter vector" for the density ratio (e.g. conditional density) of the dependent variables given the explanatory variables. This is true despite the possible presence of dynamic misspecification. Our examples illustrate that the correct specification of an underlying economic model is by itself neither necessary nor sufficient for the correctness of a resulting stochastic specification in this sense. The measurement process, the sampling process and the characteristics of the sampled population all play important roles. It is therefore essential that the stochastic specification be constructed from the economic model with care at each stage, with particular attention paid to the consequences of the failure of assumptions made about the behavioral model, the measurement process, the sampling process and the characteristics of the sampled population. This care will then provide useful insight into whether θ_o can be given a meaningful economic interpretation consistent with an underlying model of economic behavior.

While the results of this chapter show that certain aspects of the joint distribution of $\{ X_t \}$ can be ignored or misspecified without adversely affecting the ability of the QMLE to estimate parameters θ_o with a probability interpretation, these conditions nevertheless demand a great deal in the way of correct distributional assumptions for the dependent variables. In our income/expenditure examples, non-normality of the measurement errors and/or the distribution of log i_t would imply that $\mathcal{S} = \{ f_t \}$ fails to be correctly specified. Yet it is well known that such failure of distributional assumptions need not have adverse consequences. We consider this kind of misspecification in the next chapter.

MATHEMATICAL APPENDIX

PROOF OF THEOREM 4.2: Given Assumptions 2.1–2.3, 3.1, 3.2, 3.4 and correct specification, Theorem 3.6 ensures $\{\mathbb{I}(g^n: f^n; \theta)\}$ has identifiably unique minimizers $\{\theta_n^*\}$. By the information inequality $\mathbb{I}(g^n : f^n; \theta_o) = 0$ given the correctness of $\{f^n\}$ so that θ_o minimizes $\mathbb{I}(g^n : f^n; \theta)$. The identifiable uniqueness of $\{\theta_n^*\}$ implies that we may take $\theta_n^* = \theta_o$. □

PROOF OF THEOREM 4.4:(i) As in the proof of Theorem 3.6, we have $\mathcal{I}_n(\{h_t : f_t\}; \theta) = n^{-1}\sum_{t=1}^{n} E(\log h_t(Y_t, W_t)) - \bar{L}_n(\theta)$, given Assumptions 2.1, 2.3, 3.1(a), 4.1 and 4.2. Because the first term does not depend on θ and $\bar{L}_n$ has identifiably unique maximizers $\{\theta_n^*\}$ given in addition Assumptions 3.1(b) and 3.2, the result follows.

(ii) Assumptions 2.1, 2.3, 3.1 and 3.2 ensure that $\hat{\theta}_n - \theta_n^* \to 0$ a.s. $-P_o$(prob $- P_o$) by Theorem 3.5. The interpretation for θ_n^* holds under the additional Assumptions 4.1 and 4.2 by (i).

(iii) By definition

$$\begin{aligned}\mathbb{I}(h_t : f_t; \theta) &= E(\log h_t(Y_t, W_t)/f_t(Y_t, W_t, \theta)) \\ &= \int_{\ddot{S}^t} \log h_t(\ddot{x}^t)/f_t(\ddot{x}^t, \theta) \quad \ddot{g}^t(\ddot{x}^t)\, d\, \ddot{v}^t(\ddot{x}^t) \\ &= \int_{\ddot{S}^t} \log \ddot{g}^t(\ddot{x}^t)/[f_t(\ddot{x}^t, \theta)\, \ddot{g}_t(w_t)] \quad \ddot{g}_t(\ddot{x}^t)\, d\, \ddot{v}^t(\ddot{x}^t)\end{aligned}$$

under Assumptions 2.1, 2.3, 3.1(a), 4.2 and 4.3. Inequality (4.5) of Assumption 4.3 guarantees that the Information Inequality (Theorem 2.3) applies to yield $\mathbb{I}(h_t : f_t; \theta) \geq 0$. Hence $\mathcal{I}_n(\{h_t : f_t\}; \theta) \geq 0$ also. □

PROOF OF THEOREM 4.6: Because $\mathcal{S}$ is correct for $\{Y_t \mid W_t\}$ on Θ, we have for $\theta_o \in \Theta$ that $f_t(y_t, w_t, \theta_o) = h_t(y_t, w_t)$, implying that $f_t(y_t, w_t, \theta_o)\ddot{g}_t(w_t) = \ddot{g}^t(\ddot{x}^t)$. Given Assumption 4.3 and correct specification, we have that Assumption 3.1 suffices for Assumption 4.2; the Information Inequality thus applies as in the proof of Theorem 4.4(iii). Because $f_t(y_t, w_t, \theta_o)\ddot{g}_t(w_t) = \ddot{g}^t(\ddot{x}^t)$ we have that $\mathbb{I}(h_t: f_t; \theta_o) = 0$ $t = 1, 2, \ldots,$ and $\mathcal{I}_n(\{h_t : f_t\}; \theta_o) = 0$ so that θ_o minimizes $\mathcal{I}_n$. The identifiable uniqueness of $\{\theta_n^*\}$ implies that we may take $\theta_n^* = \theta_o$. The consistency of $\hat{\theta}_n$ follows from Theorem 4.4(ii). □

CHAPTER 5

Correctly Specified Models of Conditional Expectation

Often, a complete specification of a model for a particular conditional density is unavailable, either because the theory describing the relationship between the variables of interest lacks sufficient power to describe the density of interest, or because interest only attaches to certain aspects of the conditional density. Usually, both these reasons underlie the way in which a particular specification is formulated. In this chapter we explore the consequences for the QMLE of ignoring or misspecifying features of the true conditional density that are not of direct interest.

5.1 Conditional Expectations and the Linear Exponential Family

Typically, interest in economics attaches to a fairly limited range of attributes of the conditional density, such as the conditional mean or the conditional variance. Because the conditional variance can be represented as the difference between the conditional mean of the square of the random variable of interest and the square of the conditional mean of that variable, we focus in this section on the properties of the QMLE as an estimator of the parameters of the conditional mean of Y_t given W_t. Specifically, we seek to answer the question, "Under what conditions will the QMLE provide a consistent estimate of the true parameters of a correctly specified model of the conditional mean despite misspecification of other aspects of the conditional distribution?" We also consider the issue of interpreting the QMLE when the model of the conditional mean is misspecified.

We specify a model for the conditional mean of Y_t given W_t (an *expectational* or *locational model*) as a collection of sequences

$$\mathcal{M} \equiv \{ \mu(\theta) : \theta \in \Theta \} , \mu(\theta) = \{ \mu_t(\cdot , \theta) : \mathbb{R}^{k_t} \to \mathbb{R}^l \} .$$

We impose the following formal conditions on μ_t.

ASSUMPTION 5.1: The functions $\mu_t : \mathbb{R}^{k_t} \times \Theta \to \mathbb{R}^l$ are such that for each θ in Θ, a compact subset of $\mathbb{R}^p$, $\mu_t(\cdot, \theta)$ is measurable $-\mathcal{B}^{k_t}$, and $\mu_t(W_t, \cdot)$ is continuous on Θ, $a.s.-P_o$, $t = 1, 2, \ldots$ for a given choice of explanatory variables $W = \{W_t\}$. □

A specification f_t is often constructed as $f_t(X^t, \theta) = \exp \phi_t(Y_t, \mu_t(W_t, \theta))$, where ϕ_t is such that f_t has appropriate properties. The most common method for estimating the parameters of μ_t is the method of least squares. This estimator results from specifying μ_t and choosing ϕ_t in the following way.

ASSUMPTION 5.2: For $t = 1, 2, \ldots$, the specification f_t is given by $f_t(X^t, \theta) = \exp \phi_t(Y_t, \mu_t(W_t, \theta))$ where $\phi_t(y, \mu) = -(l/2) \log 2\pi - (y - \mu)'(y - \mu)/2$. □

This specification is equivalent to the model having typical elements for which

$$Y_t \mid W_t \sim N(\mu_t(W_t, \theta), I_l), \quad t = 1, 2, \ldots .$$

Note that the conditional covariance matrix here is specified to be the identity matrix. A more general specification is that

$$Y_t \mid W_t \sim N(\mu_t(W_t, \theta), D_t) \qquad t = 1, 2, \ldots,$$

where $\{D_t\}$ is a sequence of "known" conditional covariance matrices measurable-$\sigma(W_t)$. We say that D_t is "known" to reflect the fact that we are not concerned here with estimating D_t. We treat estimation of D_t in Chapter 6.

This model can be re-written in a manner consistent with Assumption 5.2 by defining

$$Y_t^* \equiv D_t^{-1/2} Y_t$$

and

$$\mu_t^*(W_t, \theta) \equiv D_t^{-1/2} \mu_t(W_t, \theta)$$

so that the model is based on

$$Y_t^* \mid W_t \sim N(\mu_t^*(W_t, \theta), I_l) .$$

The QMLE for this model is the weighted least-squares estimator with weights $D_t^{-1/2}$.

Returning to the specifications of Assumption 5.2, it is readily verified that the QMLE $\hat{\theta}$ generated by $\mathcal{S}$ is identical to the nonlinear least squares (NLS) estimator, which solves the problem

$$\min_{\theta \in \Theta} n^{-1} \sum_{t=1}^{n} (Y_t - \mu_t(W_t, \theta))'(Y_t - \mu_t(W_t, \theta)) .$$

Application of Theorem 3.5 immediately yields the following result.

THEOREM 5.1: *Given Assumption 2.1, let* $\mathcal{S} = \{f_t\}$ *for* f_t *as specified in Assumptions 5.1 and 5.2 and let* $\hat{\theta}$ *be the QMLE generated by* $\mathcal{S}$. *If Assumptions 3.1 and 3.2 also hold then* $\hat{\theta}_n - \theta_n^* \to 0$ *as* $n \to \infty$ $a.s.-P_o$ $(prob - P_o)$ *where* θ_n^* *minimizes*

$$(5.1) \qquad n^{-1} \sum_{t=1}^{n} tr\ E([Y_t - \mu_t(W_t, \theta)]\,[Y_t - \mu_t(W_t, \theta)]') ,$$

the average value of the trace of the mean squared error matrix for $\mu_t(W_t, \theta)$ *as a predictor of* Y_t. *Furthermore, if* $E \mid Y_t \mid < \infty$, θ_n^* *minimizes*

$$(5.2) \qquad n^{-1} \sum_{t=1}^{n} tr\ E([E(Y_t \mid W_t) - \mu_t(W_t, \theta)] \times [E(Y_t \mid W_t) - \mu_t(W_t, \theta)]') .$$

□

In other words, $\hat{\theta}_n$ is a consistent estimator for θ_n^*, the parameter vector that provides the best mean squared error of prediction in the sense of equation (5.1). Whether or not this parameter value is useful in forecasting Y_t given W_t as $\mu_t(W_t, \theta_n^*)$ depends on the appropriateness of the objective function (5.1) for evaluating the error of a particular forecast. If X is a strictly stationary process, (5.1) may be quite appropriate. Otherwise, θ_n^* may be less helpful in forecasting because the distribution describing the relationship between Y_t and W_t in a particular time period may be quite different from the average relationship that (5.1) is measuring. Note that different values of θ_n^* may well be obtained for different choices of D_t implicit here. Different selections for the "weighting" matrices D_t may affect the usefulness of θ_n^* in forming predictions for specific time periods. In particular, any choice for $\{D_t\}$ that removes the dependence of (5.1) on n may be particularly useful in forecasting contexts.

Equation (5.2) measures the adequacy of $\mu_t(W_t, \theta)$ as an approximation to the true conditional expectation, $E(Y_t \mid W_t)$. The theorem guarantees that

$\mu_t(W_t, \theta_n^*)$ is the best possible approximation to $E(Y_t \mid W_t)$ in the mean squared error sense of (5.2). Again, different choices for D_t may affect the way in which this approximation is evaluated.

A detailed treatment of the properties of the QMLE under Assumption 5.2 is given by Domowitz and White [1982] for the case of mixing sequences $\{X_t\}$. White [1981] considers the case of i.i.d. observations.

We use the following definition for a correctly specified model of the conditional mean.

DEFINITION 5.2 (*Specification Correct for* $\{E(Y_t \mid W_t)\}$): The expectational model $\mathcal{M}$ is *correctly specified for* $\{E(Y_t \mid W_t)\}$ *on* Θ if $E \mid Y_t \mid < \infty$ and there exists θ_o in Θ such that

$$\mu_t(W_t, \theta_o) = E(Y_t \mid W_t) \qquad a.s. - P_o, \; t = 1, 2, \ldots . \qquad \square$$

When Definition 5.2 holds, θ_o no longer necessarily has a probability interpretation, but does have a "location" interpretation.

An immediate corollary to Theorem 5.1 is the following.

COROLLARY 5.3: *Given Assumption 2.1, let* $\mathcal{S} = \{f_t\}$ *for* f_t *as specified in Assumptions 5.1 and 5.2, and let* $\hat{\theta}$ *be the QMLE generated by* $\mathcal{S}$. *If Assumptions 3.1 and 3.2 also hold and if* $\mathcal{M}$ *is correctly specified for* $\{E(Y_t \mid W_t)\}$ *on* Θ, *then* $\hat{\theta}_n \to \theta_o$ *a.s.*$-P_o$ *(prob* $- P_o$*)*. $\square$

In other words, the QMLE corresponding to the NLS estimator is consistent for the true parameters of the conditional expectation, regardless of whether or not Y_t is distributed conditionally as normal. When $\mathcal{M}$ is correct for $\{E(Y_t \mid W_t)\}$ but $\mathcal{S} = \{f_t(X^t, \theta) = \exp \phi_t(Y_t, \mu_t(W_t, \theta))\}$ is not correct for $\{Y_t \mid W_t\}$ (e.g. Y_t is not conditionally normal) we say that $\mathcal{S}$ suffers from *distributional misspecification*. The present result shows that distributional misspecification does not affect the ability of NLS to estimate parameters of the conditional mean consistently.

The range of situations covered by Theorem 5.1 and Corollary 5.2 is fairly broad, and includes most of the least-squares-based procedures in econometrics for both single equations and systems of equations. The present results cover equations that are linear or nonlinear in the parameters, with or without cross-equation constraints (such as those arising from overidentifying structural restrictions or from rational expectations models), in situations in which appropriate or inappropriate transformations to "correct" for serial correlation (e.g. pseudo-differencing) or heteroskedasticity (as implied by particular choices for D_t) have been made.

Two-stage least-squares-based procedures such as those of Heckman [1974] for the selectivity bias problem or for dealing with limited dependent variables are also covered by considering the appropriate 2SQMLE.

The multivariate normal density specified in Assumption 5.2 is a special case of a more general family of densities that Gourieroux, Monfort and Trognon [1984] have shown to have useful properties in estimating the parameters of the conditional mean. This family is a reparameterization of the multivariate linear exponential family defined by Bildikar and Patil [1968]. It yields the following specifications.

ASSUMPTION 5.3: (a) The specification f_t is given by $f_t(X^t, \theta) = \exp \phi_t(Y_t, \mu_t(W_t, \theta))$ with $\phi_t(y, \mu) = a_t(\mu) + b_t(y) + y' c_t(\mu)$, where $a_t : \mathbb{R}^l \to \mathbb{R}$ is continuous, $b_t : \mathbb{R}^l \to \mathbb{R}$ is measurable-$\mathcal{B}^l$, and $c_t : \mathbb{R}^l \to \mathbb{R}^l$ is continuous and one-to-one $t = 1, 2, \ldots$;

(b) The functions a_t, b_t and c_t in (a) are such that for a given σ-finite measure ζ_t on $(\mathbb{R}^l, \mathcal{B}^l)$,

$$\int_{\mathbb{R}^l} \exp \phi_t(y, \mu)\, d\zeta_t(y) = 1$$

$$\int_{\mathbb{R}^l} y \exp \phi_t(y, \mu)\, d\zeta_t(y) = \mu, \qquad t = 1, 2, \ldots,$$

for all μ in $\mathbb{M}_t \equiv \{ \mu_t(w, \theta) : w \in S_{W_t}, \theta \in \Theta \} \subset \mathbb{R}^l$, where S_{W_t} is the support of W_t, $t = 1, 2, \ldots$ □

The restriction in Assumption 5.3(b) that $\exp \phi_t$ be a density with respect to ζ_t and that μ be the mean of this density entails (given differentiability) the restriction that $[\nabla_\mu c_t(\mu)]\, \mu = - \nabla_\mu a_t(\mu)$, where ∇_μ is the gradient operator with respect to μ.

The multivariate normal density just considered occurs as the special case in which

$$a_t(\mu) = -\mu'\mu/2$$

$$b_t(y) = -(y'y + l \cdot \log 2\pi)/2$$

$$c_t(\mu) = \mu\,.$$

Other special cases include the Bernoulli, binomial, Poisson, negative binomial, hypergeometric, and logarithmic series densities (e.g. Johnson and Kotz [1970]) and their multivariate generalizations such as the multinomial and negative multinomial, as well as the gamma (including χ^2), Pareto, and Weibull distributions. In each of the cases mentioned, there may be either some parameters that must be assumed known, or some transformation of the dependent variable that (e.g. taking the logarithm) may be needed in order to obtain a representation as a linear exponential density.

Note that the measure ζ_t in Assumption 5.3 need not dominate the distribution of Y_t.

Application of Theorem 3.5 yields the following generalization of Theorem 5.1.

THEOREM 5.4: *Given Assumption 2.1, suppose $\mathcal{S} = \{f_t\}$ for f_t as given in Assumptions 5.1 and 5.3(a) and let $\hat{\theta}$ be the QMLE generated by $\mathcal{S}$. If Assumptions 3.1 and 3.2 also hold, then $\hat{\theta}_n - \theta_n^* \to 0$ as $n \to \infty$ a.s. $-P_o$ ($prob - P_o$), where θ_n^* maximizes*

$$(5.3) \qquad n^{-1} \sum_{t=1}^{n} E[a_t(\mu_t(W_t, \theta)) + Y_t' c_t(\mu_t(W_t, \theta))]$$

$$= n^{-1} \sum_{t=1}^{n} E[a_t(\mu_t(W_t, \theta)) + E(Y_t' \mid W_t) c_t(\mu_t(W_t, \theta))],$$

where the equality holds provided that $E \mid Y_t \mid < \infty$. □

It is less easy to provide a heuristic interpretation of (5.3) than to provide one comparable to that given (5.1) and (5.2). Nevertheless, specific choices for a_t and c_t often yield useful insights as illustrated by an example to be given shortly.

The fact that $\hat{\theta}_n$ provides a consistent estimator for the parameters of a correctly specified model for the conditional expectation of Y_t given W_t follows with the imposition of Assumption 5.3(b).

COROLLARY 5.5: *Given Assumption 2.1, suppose $\mathcal{S} = \{f_t\}$ for f_t as given in Assumptions 5.1 and 5.3 and let $\hat{\theta}$ be the QMLE generated by $\mathcal{S}$. If Assumptions 3.1 and 3.2 also hold, and if $\mathcal{M}$ is correctly specified for $\{E(Y_t \mid W_t)\}$ on Θ, then $\hat{\theta}_n \to \theta_o$ a.s. $- P_o$ ($prob - P_o$).* □

In other words, the QMLE obtained by specifying the log-likelihood to be a member of the linear exponential family is consistent for the true parameter value of a correctly specified model of the conditional expectation, regardless of whether or not the true underlying density is in the linear exponential family (provided of course that the specified regularity conditions hold). This result was obtained by Gourieroux, Monfort and Trognon [1984] for a model satisfying the regularity conditions of Burguete, Gallant and Souza [1982]. Those conditions require the explanatory variables to be fixed or "strictly exogenous" and the "errors" $\varepsilon_t \equiv Y_t - E(Y_t \mid W_t)$ to be independent and identically distributed. Corollary 5.5 shows that the result of Gourieroux, Monfort and Trognon extends to dynamic models with serially correlated and/or heteroskedastic errors.

An example that provides useful insight is the simple case in which $Y_t \mid W_t$ has the Bernoulli distribution with parameter $p_t^o = E(Y_t \mid W_t)$. Let $p_t(\theta) \equiv \mu_t(W_t, \theta)$ be the specified parametric approximation to p_t^o. Different choices for μ_t can yield a QMLE corresponding to such estimators as the probit or logit estimators. In this case

$$a_t(p) = \log(1-p)$$

$$c_t(p) = \log p/(1-p) .$$

Simple algebra shows that (5.3) can be written

$$(5.4) \qquad n^{-1} \sum_{t=1}^{n} E\,[(1-p_t^o) \log\,[1-p_t(\theta)] + p_t^o \log p_t(\theta)] .$$

This quantity is maximized by choosing $\theta = \theta_o$ when the conditional mean is correctly specified. The maximized value then has the form

$$n^{-1} \sum_{t=1}^{n} E\,[(1-p_t^o) \log\,[1-p_t^o] + p_t^o \log p_t^o] .$$

Each of the summands in this expression is the opposite of the *entropy* of the distribution of Y_t given W_t (e.g. see Theil [1971, pp. 636–638]), a measure of the expected information content contained in a message that $Y_t = 1$ when W_t is known.

When there is no θ_o value in Θ for which $p_t(\theta_o) = p_t^o$, the value θ_n^* that maximizes (5.3) gives the value that makes (5.4) closest to the opposite of the average expected entropy. In other words, θ_n^* is chosen so as to yield the least average surprise when we learn that $Y_t = 1$ given that our model is $p_t(\theta) = \mu_t(W_t, \theta)$.

According to Corollary 5.5, a specification based on the linear exponential family is sufficient for consistent estimation of the true parameters of a correctly specified model of $E(Y_t \mid W_t)$. Gourieroux, Monfort and Trognon [1984] show that in their framework a specification based on the linear exponential family is also necessary in a sense. This is true in the present framework as well.

To obtain this result in the present framework, we add appropriate conditions. First, we formally state the general way in which the specification is built up from μ_t.

ASSUMPTION 5.4: The specification f_t is given by $f_t(x^t, \theta) = \exp$

$\phi_t(y_t, \mu_t(w_t, \theta))$, where $\phi_t : \mathbb{R}^l \times \mathbb{R}^l \to \mathbb{R}$ is such that $\phi_t(\cdot, \mu) : \mathbb{R}^l \to \mathbb{R}$ is measurable-$\mathcal{B}^l$ for each μ in $\mathbb{R}^l$, and $\phi_t(y, \cdot) : \mathbb{R}^l \to \mathbb{R}$ is continuous on $\mathbb{R}^l$, $t = 1, 2, \ldots$. □

Next, we impose a differentiability condition.

ASSUMPTION 5.5: For each $t = 1, 2, \ldots$, $\phi_t(y, \cdot) : \mathbb{R}^l \to \mathbb{R}$ is continuously differentiable on $\mathbb{M}_t$, and $\mu_t(W_t, \cdot)$ is continuously differentiable on Θ *a.s.*$-P_o$. □

The desired result is the following.

THEOREM 5.6: *Let f_t satisfy the conditions of Assumption 5.4, and suppose further that for some measure ζ_t*

$$\int_{\mathbb{R}^l} \exp \phi_t(y, \mu)\, d\zeta_t(y) = 1$$

and

$$\int_{\mathbb{R}^l} y \exp \phi_t(y, \mu)\, d\zeta_t(y) = \mu$$

for all μ in a given set $\mathbb{M}_t \subset \mathbb{R}^l$, $t = 1, 2, \ldots$. Suppose that for any probability measure P_o such that Assumptions 2.1, 3.1, 3.2′, 3.7(a), 5.1, 5.4 and 5.5 hold we have that $\theta_n^* = \theta_o$, $n = 1, 2, \ldots$ when $\mu_t(W_t, \theta_o) = E(Y_t/W_t)$ a.s. $-P_o$ for θ_o in Θ, the closure of an open connected set such that $\mu_t(W_t, \theta) \in \mathbb{M}_t$ a.s.$-P_o$ for all θ in Θ.

Then Assumption 5.3 holds, i.e. f_t is a member of the linear exponential family, $t = 1, 2, \ldots$. □

In other words, if we seek a specification that will deliver consistent estimates of the true parameters of a correctly specified model of the conditional mean regardless of the properties of P_o (beyond minimal regularity conditions) then we must choose the linear exponential specification. This result is not precisely a converse to Corollary 5.5. We have imposed differentiability (Assumption 5.5) as well as interiority of θ_n^* (Assumption 3.2′). Moreover, for consistent estimation of θ_o it is only necessary that $\theta_n^* \to \theta_o$, rather than $\theta_n^* = \theta_o$, $n = 1, 2, \ldots$. For this reason, it is possible to estimate θ_o consistently even when the specified model is not a member of the linear exponential family for some indices t. Generally, however, the number of such cases will have to constitute a vanishingly small proportion of the sample. Otherwise, it can be shown that inconsistency will result. Bearing this minor qualification in mind, we can speak loosely of the fact that the linear exponential family is essentially the only family that allows consistent estimation of the parameter of the conditional mean regardless of the true probability law P_o.

Our results so far demonstrate that when $\mathcal{M}$ is correct for $\{E(Y_t \mid W_t)\}$ it is generally possible to estimate locationally meaningful parameters. Ruud [1983, 1986] discusses conditions under which it is still possible to estimate consistently parameters of interest when $\mathcal{M}$ is not correct for $\{E(Y_t \mid W_t)\}$. In particular, for the Bernoulli example discussed above Ruud shows that under certain conditions on the distribution of W_t it is possible to estimate parameters of interest consistently, at least up to a factor of proportionality, even when the model for the conditional mean of the Bernoulli distribution has been misspecified. This implies, for example, that parameters of interest can be consistently estimated up to a factor of proportionality when a logit model has been erroneously estimated in place of a probit model. This kind of result has been noted in other contexts as well, such as in estimating the parameters of the Tobit model, as found by Goldberger [1981] and Greene [1981]. We refer the interested reader to Ruud [1983, 1986].

5.2 Specifications Admitting Residuals

Although the linear exponential specification is the only one guaranteed to deliver consistent estimates of the true parameters of a correctly specified model of the conditional mean regardless of distributional misspecification, other families may yield consistent estimates if P_o is further restricted. To investigate this possibility, we consider specifications admitting residuals, defined in the following way.

DEFINITION 5.7 (*Specification Admitting Residuals*): Let $\mathcal{S} = \{f_t\}$ specify dependent variables Y and explanatory variables W with respect to $\{\zeta_t\}$, and suppose $\{\mu_t\}$ satisfies Assumption 5.1. Then $\mathcal{S}$ *admits residuals* $\{u_t(\theta) \equiv Y_t - \mu_t(W_t, \theta)\}$ if $f_t(X^t, \theta) = \exp q_t(u_t(\theta), W_t)$ where $q_t : \mathbb{R}^l \times \mathbb{R}^{k_t} \to \mathbb{R}$ is such that $q_t(\cdot, w_t)$ is continuous on $\mathbb{R}^l$ for each w_t in $\mathbb{R}^{k_t}$ and $q_t(u, \cdot)$ is measurable-$\mathcal{B}^{k_t}$ for each u in $\mathbb{R}^l$. □

Our primary focus will be on a rather limited (but still fairly interesting) subclass of such specifications. For notational convenience, we let $|u_t(\theta)|$ denote the $l \times 1$ vector with elements $|u_{ti}(\theta)|$, $i = 1, \ldots, l$ in what follows.

The specifications to be treated here satisfy the following assumption.

ASSUMPTION 5.6:(a) The specification f_t is given by $f_t(X^t, \theta) = \exp - \xi_t(\mid u_t(\theta) \mid)$, where ξ_t is a continuous nondecreasing proper convex function on $\times_{i=1}^{l} [0, \infty]$, $t = 1, 2, \ldots$;

(b) There exists an $l \times 1$ subgradient $\Delta \xi_t$ of ξ_t such that for each θ in Θ, $\Delta\xi_t(\mid u_t(\theta) \mid)$ is measurable-$\sigma(Y_t, W_t)$; and $E(\Delta \xi_t(\mid Y_t - E(Y_t \mid W_t) \mid) < \infty$, $t = 1, 2, \ldots$. □

The subgradient operator Δ is as defined by Rockafeller [1970, p. 215].

Assumption 5.6 requires the specified quasi-log-likelihood function to be a sufficiently well-behaved function of the absolute value of the residual, $u_t(\theta)$. The conditions placed on the behavior of ξ_t are that it be non-decreasing, i.e. that the log-likelihood does not increase as the residual increases in absolute value, and that it be a proper convex function. The convex function ξ_t is proper if $\xi_t(v) > -\infty$ for at least one v and $\xi_t(v) < +\infty$ for every real v (see Rockafellar [1970, pp. 24, 307]). In the present context, this requirement causes no loss of generality.

When $l = 1$ (the case of a single dependent variable), the least squares estimator is obtained by setting $\xi_t(v) = v^2/2$. The least absolute deviations estimator is obtained for $\xi_t(v) = v$. The general L_p-norm estimators are obtained by setting $\xi_t(v) = v^p / p$, and these are convex provided $p \geq 1$. When $l > 1$, multivariate analogs of the L_p-estimator can be obtained by setting $\xi_t(v) = \Sigma_{i=1}^{l} v_i^p / p$. A wide variety of other univariate and multivariate estimators are allowed by Assumption 5.6, such as a class of estimators due to Huber [1964] for which with $l = 1$

$$
\begin{aligned}
\xi(v) &= v^2/2 \quad \text{if} \quad v < c \\
&= cv \quad \text{if} \quad v \geq c\,.
\end{aligned}
$$

The general result with $\mathcal{M}$ misspecified for $\{E(Y_t \mid W_t)\}$ is the following.

THEOREM 5.8: *Given Assumption 2.1, let $\mathcal{S} = \{f_t\}$ for f_t as specified in Assumptions 5.1 and 5.6 and let $\hat{\theta}$ be the QMLE generated by $\mathcal{S}$. If Assumptions 3.1 and 3.2 also hold, then $\hat{\theta}_n - \theta_n^* \to 0$ as $n \to \infty$ a.s. $-P_o$ (prob $-P_o$), where θ_n^* maximizes*

$$
-n^{-1} \sum_{t=1}^{n} E(\xi_t(\mid u_t(\theta) \mid))\,. \qquad \square
$$

Equivalently θ_n^* minimizes the average expected value of a specific function (ξ_t) of the absolute residual. When the conditional mean is correctly specified, a consistency result holds under the following symmetry assumption.

ASSUMPTION 5.7: For any Borel set B in $\mathcal{B}^l, P_o\ [Y_t - E(Y_t \mid W_t) \in B \mid W_t] = P_o\,[E(Y_t \mid W_t) - Y_t \in B \mid W_t]\,, t = 1, 2, \ldots$. □

An immediate implication of this assumption is that the conditional mean, $E\,(Y_t \mid W_t)$, is identical to the conditional median, say $M\,(Y_t \mid W_t)$, for each $t = 1, 2, \ldots$.

COROLLARY 5.9: *Given Assumption 2.1, let $\mathcal{S} = \{f_t\}$ for f_t as specified in Assumptions 5.1 and 5.6, and let $\hat{\theta}$ be the QMLE generated by $\mathcal{S}$. If Assumptions 3.1, 3.2 and 5.7 also hold, and if $\mathcal{M}$ is correctly specified for $\{E\,(Y_t \mid W_t)\}$ on Θ, then $\hat{\theta}_n \to \theta_o$ a.s. $-P_o$ (prob $-P_o$).* □

Although the symmetry assumption is quite convenient, it is not always necessary. For example, symmetry is completely unnecessary in the case of the least squares estimator. For the multivariate LAD estimator ($\xi_t(v) = \Sigma_{i=1}^{l}$ v_i) failure of the symmetry assumption results in the possible failure of the consistency of the parameters estimated for the parameters of a correctly specified model of the conditional mean, but has no effect whatsoever on the ability of the LAD estimator to estimate consistently the parameters of a correctly specified model of the conditional median.

Note that *joint* symmetry is required by Assumption 5.7. If one only has marginal symmetry, the consistency result of Corollary 5.9 still holds provided the ith subgradient of ξ_t does not depend on v_j, $i \neq j$, as is true for the objective functions $\xi_t(v) = \Sigma_{i=1}^{l}\ v_i^p \,/\, p$.

Convexity is not necessary for consistency. Many consistent estimators are available that result from a choice for ξ_t that violates the convexity assumption, for example, the (Q)MLE based on the Cauchy distribution. Besides consistency, many of these estimators have other desirable properties, such as a lack of sensitivity to certain kinds of gross outliers, as well as high efficiency. Estimators with these properties are said to be "robust." Conditions ensuring consistency, as well as cases in which inconsistency occurs are discussed by Freedman and Diaconis [1982].

In some circumstances, a more general notion of residual is considered. A general model treated in econometrics is the "implicit nonlinear simultaneous equations model" (Amemiya [1977]). This model arises when it is assumed that the data generation process satisfies a set of implicit nonlinear simultaneous equations such that for some $\theta_o \in \Theta$

$$u_t(Y_t, W_t, \theta_o)|W_t \sim N(0, D_t) \qquad t = 1, 2, \ldots,$$

where now $u_t : \mathbb{R}^l \times \mathbb{R}^{k_t} \times \Theta \to \mathbb{R}^l$. Treating θ_o as unknown, and (for simplicity) taking D_t to be "known" leads to a specification of the form

$$\begin{aligned}\log f_t(Y_t, W_t, \theta) = &- (l/2) \log 2\pi - 1/2 \log \det D_t \\ &+ \log |\det \nabla_y u_t(Y_t, W_t, \theta)| \\ &- u_t(Y_t, W_t, \theta)' D_t^{-1} u_t(Y_t, W_t, \theta)/2,\end{aligned}$$

where $\nabla_y u_t$ denotes the $l \times l$ gradient of u_t with respect to its first argument. The term $\log |\det \nabla_y u_t|$ arises from the standard change-of-variable formula (e.g. Billingsley [1979, Theorem 17.2]); in the foregoing ("explicit") case with $u_t(Y_t, W_t, \theta) = Y_t - \mu_t(W_t, \theta)$ we have $\nabla_y u_t = I_l$ so that $\log |\det \nabla_y u_t| = 0$.

Application of Theorem 4.6 to the implicit specification f_t above yields the consistency for θ_o of the (Q)MLE generated by $\mathcal{S} = \{f_t\}$ when $\mathcal{S}$ is correctly specified for $\{Y_t | W_t\}$. Amemiya [1977, p. 955] points out that the validity of the normality assumption is "crucial" for the consistency of the (Q)MLE for θ_o. Although Phillips [1982] presents some examples in which consistency for θ_o is retained even in the presence of non-normality, these examples rely on the existence of a highly specific relationship between the specific non-normal distribution underlying the data generation process and the specific form of $\nabla_\theta u_t$. In an unpublished note, White [1980a] shows that the normal distribution is essentially the only continuous distribution that guarantees consistency of this QMLE regardless of the specific form of $\nabla_\theta u_t$.

The reason for this is that a characterization of the normal distribution ensures that only for the normal distribution is it true that

$$\begin{aligned}E(\nabla_\theta \log f_t(X^t, \theta_o)) &= E(\nabla_\theta \log |\det \nabla_y u_t(Y_t, W_t, \theta_o)|) \\ &- E(\nabla_\theta u_t(Y_t, W_t, \theta_o) D_t^{-1} u_t(Y_t, W_t, \theta_o)) = 0\end{aligned}$$

regardless of the specific form of $\nabla_\theta u_t$. In the present context, then, non-normality generally implies $\nabla_\theta \bar{L}_n(\theta_o) = n^{-1} \Sigma_{t=1}^n E(\nabla_\theta \log f_t(X^t, \theta_o)) \neq 0$ so that θ_o cannot maximize $\bar{L}_n(\theta)$ and we cannot have $\hat{\theta}_n \to \theta_o$ $a.s. -P_o$ $(prob - P_o)$. In other words, distributional misspecification generally leads to the inconsistency of the normal QMLE generated by the implicit nonlinear simultaneous equations model. Similar results may hold generally for implicit models based on other distributional assumptions.

5.3 Correct Specification of Conditional Attributes

Techniques essentially identical to those used to establish the consistency of a given QMLE for the parameters of a correctly specified model of the conditional mean can be used to establish analogous results when interest focuses on some other aspect of the conditional distribution, such as the conditional median or a particular conditional quantile of Y_t given W_t. We shall let α denote any attribute functional of interest, so that $\alpha(Y_t \mid W_t)$ is some $\sigma(W_t)$–measurable $l \times 1$ function of the conditional distribution of Y_t given W_t. For example, we could set $\alpha = E$ so that $\alpha(Y_t \mid W_t) = E(Y_t \mid W_t)$; or we could set $\alpha = M$ so that $\alpha(Y_t \mid W_t) = M(Y_t \mid W_t)$, the conditional median. The appropriate definition for a correctly specified model of an arbitrary conditional attribute is the following.

DEFINITION 5.10 (*Specification Correct for* $\alpha(Y_t \mid W_t)$): Let $\{\alpha(Y_t \mid W_t)\}$ be a sequence of well-defined attributes of Y_t given W_t. The model $\mathcal{M} = \{\mu_t\}$ is *correctly specified for* $\{\alpha(Y_t \mid W_t)\}$ *on* Θ if there exists θ_o in Θ such that

$$\mu_t(W_t, \theta_o) = \alpha(Y_t \mid W_t) \qquad a.s.-P_o \quad t = 1, 2, \ldots . \qquad \square$$

COROLLARY 5.11: *Given Assumptions 2.1, let $\mathcal{S} = \{f_t\}$ for f_t as specified in Assumptions 5.1 and 5.4 and let $\hat{\theta}$ be the QMLE generated by $\mathcal{S}$. If Assumptions 3.1 and 3.2 also hold, if $\mathcal{M}$ is correctly specified for $\{\alpha(Y_t \mid W_t)\}$ on Θ, and if*

$$(5.5) \qquad E(\phi_t(Y_t, \mu_t(W_t, \theta))) \leq E(\phi_t(Y_t, \alpha(Y_t \mid W_t)) \quad t = 1, 2, \ldots$$

for all θ in Θ, then $\hat{\theta}_n \to \theta_o$ as $n \to \infty$, $a.s.-P_o$ $(prob - P_o)$. $\square$

For example, this result ensures the consistency of the nonlinear LAD estimator for the parameters of the conditional median without the symmetry assumption by setting $\alpha(Y_t \mid W_t) = M(Y_t \mid W_t)$ (take Y_t a scalar for simplicity), and

$$\phi_t(Y_t, \mu_t(W_t, \theta)) = -\mid Y_t - \mu_t(W_t, \theta) \mid .$$

This estimator is treated by Oberhofer [1982] in the i.i.d case, and is a special case of a regression quantile estimator such as that proposed for the linear model by Koenker and Bassett [1978].

To investigate the regression quantile estimator, let $\alpha(Y_t \mid W_t)$ be the qth quantile of the distribution of Y_t given W_t, say $Q_q(Y_t \mid W_t)$, where for $0 < q < 1$

$$q = P_o\,[Y_t < Q_q\,(Y_t \mid W_t) \mid W_t]\,.$$

An appropriate choice for ϕ_t in this context is given by the following assumption.

ASSUMPTION 5.8: The specification f_t is given by $f_t(X^t, \theta) = \exp \phi_t(Y_t, \mu_t(W_t, \theta))$, where $\phi_t : \mathbb{R} \times \mathbb{R} \to \mathbb{R}$ and

$$\phi_t(y, \mu) = -\mid y - \mu \mid (q\ 1[y \geq \mu] + (1 - q)1[y < \mu]),$$

where $1[\,\cdot\,]$ is the indicator function for the specified event, $t = 1, 2, \ldots$ □

A consistency result for the quantile estimator is

COROLLARY 5.12: *Given Assumption 2.1, let $\mathcal{S} = \{f_t\}$ for f_t as specified in Assumptions 5.1 and 5.8 and let $\hat{\theta}$ be the QMLE generated by $\mathcal{S}$. If Assumptions 3.1 and 3.2 also hold and if $\mathcal{M}$ is correctly specified for $\{Q_q\,(Y_t \mid W_t)\}$ on Θ, then $\hat{\theta}_n \to \theta_o$ as $n \to \infty$, a.s. $-P_o$ (prob $- P_o$).* □

This result thus establishes an analog of Koenker and Bassett's [1978] consistency result for nonlinear models of regression quantiles in a dynamic context allowing for the possibility of dynamic misspecification.

Another useful way to exploit Corollary 5.11 is to let Y_t be a vector containing l replications of a single dependent variable, e.g. $Y_t = (\tilde{Y}_t, \tilde{Y}_t)'$ and let $\alpha\,(Y_t \mid W_t)$ be a vector containing l different functionals of the conditional distribution of Y_t given W_t, e.g. $\alpha\,(Y_t \mid W_t) = (E\,(\tilde{Y}_t \mid W_t),\, M(\tilde{Y}_t \mid W_t))'$. One could then obtain consistent estimates of the parameters of the conditional mean and conditional median of $\tilde{Y}_t$ by solving a single optimization problem. This approach can be useful in the context of testing for misspecifications that would invalidate a desired probability or economic interpretation.

5.4 The Method of Moments

Recognizing the inability of economic theory to deliver a complete specification of the conditional density appropriate for modeling a given economic phenomenon, many researchers avoid doing so. Instead, because they believe that theory or introspection provides sufficient information to specify correctly models of certain conditional moments of the phenomenon of interest, they make use of estimation methods that rely only on the conditional moment models believed to be correctly specified. These "method of moments" estimators, given elegant and general treatment in econometrics by Hansen [1982], are based on the assumption that for a given set of conditioning variables W_t and some θ_o in Θ it is true that

$$E(\psi_t(X^t, \theta_o) \mid W_t) = 0, \qquad t = 1, 2, \ldots,$$

where $\psi_t : \mathbb{R}^{vt} \times \Theta \to \mathbb{R}^q$, $q \in \mathbb{N}$ (say). Note that W_t may be null (i.e., $\sigma(W_t) = \{\varnothing, \Omega\}$) in which case the expectation is unconditional. For example, if it is believed that $\mathcal{M} = \{\mu_t\}$ is correctly specified for $\{E(Y_t \mid W_t)\}$, then for any measurable function $a_t : \mathbb{R}^{k_t} \to \mathbb{R}^{q \times l}$, there exists θ_o in Θ such that

$$E(a_t(W_t)(Y_t - \mu_t(W_t, \theta_o)) \mid W_t) = 0 \qquad t = 1, 2, \ldots .$$

In this situation, we have $\psi_t(X^t, \theta) = a_t(W_t)(Y_t - \mu_t(W_t, \theta))$.

The law of iterated expectations implies that $E(\psi_t(X^t, \theta_o)) = 0$ also, so that

$$n^{-1} \sum_{t=1}^{n} E(\psi_t(X^t, \theta_o)) = 0.$$

For any θ in Θ, the average expectation $n^{-1} \sum_{t=1}^{n} E(\psi_t(X^t, \theta))$ can be estimated by the sample average

$$n^{-1} \sum_{t=1}^{n} \psi_t(X^t, \theta).$$

Method of moments estimation proceeds by finding $\hat{\theta}_n$ for which $n^{-1} \sum_{t=1}^{n} \psi_t(X^t, \hat{\theta}_n)$ is as close to zero as possible. If $q = p$, then we are essentially back to the case of Huber's (1964) m-estimators discussed in Chapter 2, as $\hat{\theta}_n$ can usually be chosen so that $n^{-1} \sum_{t=1}^{n} \psi_t(X^t, \hat{\theta}_n) = 0$ or $n^{-1} \sum_{t=1}^{n} \psi_t(X^t, \hat{\theta}_n) \to 0 \ a.s. - P_o$. When $q > p$, such a $\hat{\theta}_n$ need not exist, as there are more equations (q) than unknowns (p). The standard procedure is to choose $\hat{\theta}_n$ to solve the problem

$$\min_{\theta \in \Theta} \ (n^{-1} \sum_{t=1}^{n} \psi_t(X^t, \theta))' \hat{V}_n^- (n^{-1} \sum_{t=1}^{n} \psi_t(X^t, \theta)),$$

where $\hat{V}_n$ is some appropriately chosen positive semi-definite symmetric $q \times q$ matrix. The minimand is the square of a weighted Euclidian distance of $n^{-1} \sum_{t=1}^{n} \psi_t(X^t, \theta)$ from zero.

General theory for such estimators can be found in Hansen [1982], Bates and White [1985, 1988] and Gallant and White [1988]. The latter reference provides a treatment of the case in which the moment conditions are misspecified in the sense that for no sequence $\{\theta_n^*\}$ is it true that $n^{-1} \sum_{t=1}^{n} E(\psi_t(X^t, \theta_n^*)) \to 0$ as $n \to \infty$. We refer the interested reader to Gallant and White [1988] for details, as the method of moments estimator is not a quasi-maximum likelihood estimator of the form given primary consideration here.

There is, however, a sense in which method of moments estimation can be understood as a form of QMLE. The central limit theorem (see Chapter 6) ensures under general conditions that $V_n^{o^{-1/2}} n^{-1/2} \sum_{t=1}^{n} \psi_t(X^t, \theta_o)$ is distributed approximately as multivariate standard normal, $N(0, I_q)$, where $V_n^o = \text{var}(n^{-1/2} \sum_{t=1}^{n} \psi_t(X^t, \theta_o))$, provided this is sufficiently well behaved.

This fact suggests specification of a model with a typical element

$$V_n^{o^{-1/2}} n^{-1/2} \sum_{t=1}^{n} \psi_t(X^t, \theta) \sim N(0, I_q),$$

which results in a specification of the form

$$f^n(X^t, \theta) =$$

$$(2\pi)^{-q/2} [\det V_n^o]^{-/2} \exp - [(n^{-1/2} \sum_{t=1}^{n} \psi_t(X^t, \theta))' V_n^{o^{-1}} (n^{-1/2} \sum_{t=1}^{n} \psi_t(X^t, \theta))]/2,$$

so that the QMLE solves

$$\max_{\theta \in \Theta} \ \log f^n(X^t, \theta) = -(q/2) \log 2\pi$$

$$-(1/2) \log \det V_n^o \ (n^{-1/2} \sum_{t=1}^{n} \psi_t(X^t, \theta))' V_n^{o^{-1}} \ (n^{-1/2} \sum_{t=1}^{n} \psi_t(X^t, \theta))/2 .$$

If $\hat{V}_n = V_n^o$, then this yields the method of moments estimator defined above. In practice, V_n^o is usually unknown, but can be estimated in a previous stage, as $\hat{V}_n$, say. The elements of $\hat{V}_n$ correspond to the elements of $\hat{\alpha}_n$ in our treatment of the two stage QMLE. Thus, the method of moments estimator corresponds to the 2SQMLE solving the problem

$$\max_{\theta \in \Theta} - (q/2) \log 2\pi - (n^{-1/2} \sum_{t=1}^{n} \psi_t(X^t, \theta))' \hat{V}_n^{-} (n^{-1/2} \sum_{t=1}^{n} \psi_t(X^t, \theta))/2 .$$

With f^n in this form we cannot write $f^n = \Pi_{t=1}^n f_t$ for f_t satisfying the conditions of our earlier results for the QMLE. Nevertheless, existence and consistency results for both the correctly and incorrectly specified cases follow from Theorems 2.15 and 3.7. Details are given in Hansen [1982], Bates and White [1985, 1988] and Gallant and White [1988]. In particular, when moment conditions are correctly specified (e.g. $E(\psi_t(X^t, \theta_o)) = 0$, $t = 1, 2, \ldots$ for some $\theta_o \in \Theta$), it follows under general conditions that $\hat{\theta}_n \rightarrow \theta_o$ $a.s.-P_o$.

Viewing method of moments estimators as QMLE's in this way suggests some interesting possibilities. Although we do not pursue further implications here, we note that obtaining more accurate asymptotic approximations to the distribution of $V_n^{o^{-1/2}} n^{-1/2} \sum_{t=1}^n \psi_t(X^t, \theta_o)$ (e.g. via Edgeworth expansions) will suggest alternative method of moments estimators that can be obtained from a QMLE based on a model such that $V_n^{o^{-1/2}} n^{-1/2} \sum_{t=1}^n \psi_t(X^t, \theta)$ has the improved asymptotic approximation as its joint distribution. The resulting method of moments estimators could conceivably have improved second or higher order asymptotic efficiency properties relative to standard method of moments estimators under correct specification.

5.5 Summary

The results of this chapter show that quasi-maximum likelihood methods can be used to estimate consistently parameters that have a location or attribute interpretation, regardless of distributional misspecification. The linear exponential family has the fundamental property that it is essentially the only family having the property that when used with a location model as the basis for quasi-maximum likelihood estimation, it delivers consistent estimates of the parameters of a correctly specified model of the conditional expectation of Y_t given W_t, regardless of distributional misspecification. Other families deliver such estimates under some restrictions on the data generation process, such as conditional symmetry. In general, choice of the quasi-likelihood function determines what aspect or attribute of the true conditional distribution is approximated by a model of conditional location.

MATHEMATICAL APPENDIX

PROOF OF THEOREM 5.1: Given Assumption 5.2, for each μ in $\mathbb{R}^l$, $\phi_t(\cdot, \mu)$ is measurable-$\mathcal{B}^l$ and for each y in $\mathbb{R}^l$, $\phi_t(y, \cdot)$ is continuous on $\mathbb{R}^l$. It follows from Theorem 13.3 of Billingsley [1979] that for each θ in Θ, $x^t \to \log f_t(x^t, \theta) = \phi_t(y_t, \mu_t(w_t, \theta))$ is measurable-$\mathcal{B}^{vt}$. Further, $\log f_t(X^t, \cdot) = \phi_t(Y_t, \mu_t(W_t, \cdot))$ is continuous on Θ $a.s.-P_o$, given in addition Assumption 5.1. As exp $(\cdot)$ is a continuous function, it follows that Assumption 2.3 holds for $f_t = \exp \phi_t$.

Because Assumptions 2.1, 3.1 and 3.2 are also in force, it follows from Theorem 3.5 that $\hat{\theta}_n - \theta_n^* \to 0$ as $n \to \infty$ $a.s.-P_o$ $(prob - P_o)$, where θ_n^* maximizes $\bar{L}_n(\theta)$ which, given Assumption 5.2, is of the form

$$\bar{L}_n(\theta) = -\frac{1}{2}\, l \cdot \log 2\pi$$
$$-\frac{1}{2} n^{-1} \sum_{t=1}^{n} E\,[(Y_t - \mu_t(W_t, \theta))'(Y_t - \mu_t(W_t, \theta))]\,.$$

Now

$$E\,[(Y_t - \mu_t(W_t, \theta))'(Y_t - \mu_t(W_t, \theta))]$$
$$= E\,[tr\,(Y_t - \mu_t(W_t, \theta))\,(Y_t - \mu_t(W_t, \theta))']$$
$$= tr\; E\,[(Y_t - \mu_t(W_t, \theta))\,(Y_t - \mu_t(W_t, \theta))']\,,$$

so the maximum of $\bar{L}_n$ occurs when

$$n^{-1} \sum_{t=1}^{n} E\,[(Y_t - \mu_t(W_t, \theta))'(Y_t - \mu_t(W_t, \theta))]$$
$$= n^{-1} \sum_{t=1}^{n} tr\; E\,[(Y_t - \mu_t(W_t, \theta))\,(Y_t - \mu_t(W_t, \theta))']$$

is minimized, establishing (5.1).

Adding and subtracting $E\,(Y_t \mid W_t)$, which exists $a.s.$ and is finite given that $E \mid Y_t \mid < \infty$, gives

$$E\,[(Y_t - \mu_t(W_t, \theta))\,(Y_t - \mu_t(W_t, \theta))']$$
$$= E\,[(Y_t - E(Y_t \mid W_t) + E\,(Y_t \mid W_t) - \mu_t(W_t, \theta))$$
$$(Y_t - E(Y_t \mid W_t) + E(Y_t \mid W_t) - \mu_t(W_t, \theta))']$$
$$= E\,[(Y_t - E\,(Y_t \mid W_t))\,(Y_t - E\,(Y_t \mid W_t))']$$

$$+ E[(Y_t - E(Y_t \mid W_t))(E(Y_t \mid W_t) - \mu_t(W_t, \theta))']$$
$$+ E[(E(Y_t \mid W_t) - \mu_t(W_t, \theta))(Y_t - E(Y_t \mid W_t))']$$
$$+ E[(E(Y_t \mid W_t) - \mu_t(W_t, \theta))(E(Y_t \mid W_t) - \mu_t(W_t, \theta))']$$
$$= E[(Y_t - E(Y_t \mid W_t))(Y_t - E(Y_t \mid W_t))']$$
$$+ E[(E(Y_t \mid W_t) - \mu_t(W_t, \theta))(E(Y_t \mid W_t) - \mu_t(W_t, \theta))']$$

because

$$\begin{aligned} E[(Y_t - E(Y_t \mid W_t))(E(Y_t \mid W_t) - \mu_t(W_t, \theta))'] &= E[E((Y_t - E(Y_t \mid W_t)) \\ &\quad \times (E(Y_t \mid W_t) - \mu_t(W_t, \theta))' \mid W_t)] \\ &= E[E(Y_t \mid W_t)(E(Y_t \mid W_t) - \mu_t(W_t, \theta))' \\ &\quad - E(Y_t \mid W_t)(E(Y_t \mid W_t) - \mu_t(W_t, \theta))'] \\ &= 0 . \end{aligned}$$

Hence

$$\begin{aligned} n^{-1} \sum_{t=1}^{n} tr\, E[(Y_t - \mu_t(W_t, \theta))(Y_t - \mu_t(W_t, \theta))'] &= n^{-1} \sum_{t=1}^{n} tr\, E[(Y_t - E(Y_t \mid W_t))(Y_t - E(Y_t \mid W_t))'] \\ &\quad + n^{-1} \sum_{t=1}^{n} tr\, E[(E(Y_t \mid W_t) - \mu_t(W_t, \theta))(E(Y_t \mid W_t) - \mu_t(W_t, \theta))'] . \end{aligned}$$

Because the first term doesn't depend on θ, the minimum occurs when the second term is minimized, establishing (5.2). □

PROOF OF COROLLARY 5.3: By Theorem 5.1, θ_n^* minimizes

$$n^{-1} \sum_{t=1}^{n} tr\, E[(E(Y_t \mid W_t) - \mu_t(W_t, \theta))(E(Y_t \mid W_t) - \mu_t(W_t, \theta))'],$$

a nonnegative scalar. With correct specification this nonnegative quantity equals zero and is therefore minimized at θ_o. As θ_n^* is identifiably unique, it follows that we may take $\theta_n^* = \theta_o$, $n = 1, 2, \ldots$. □

PROOF OF THEOREM 5.4: As in the proof of Theorem 5.1, Assumptions 5.1 and 5.3(a) ensure that Assumption 2.3 holds. Because Assumptions 2.1, 3.1 and 3.2 are also in force, it follows from Theorem 3.5 that

$\hat{\theta}_n - \theta_n^* \xrightarrow{a.s.} 0$ where θ_n^* maximizes $\bar{L}_n(\theta)$, which, given Assumption 5.3(a) is of the form

$$\bar{L}_n(\theta) = n^{-1} \sum_{t=1}^{n} E\,[a_t(\mu_t(W_t\,,\theta)) + b_t(Y_t) + Y_t'\,c_t(\mu_t(W_t\,,\theta))]$$

$$= n^{-1} \sum_{t=1}^{n} E\,(b_t(Y_t)) + n^{-1} \sum_{t=1}^{n} E\,[a_t(\mu_t(W_t\,,\theta)) + Y_t' c_t(\mu_t(W_t\,,\theta))]\,.$$

Because the first term does not depend on θ, $\bar{L}_n(\theta)$ is maximized when

$$n^{-1} \sum_{t=1}^{n} E\,[a_t(\mu_t(W_t\,,\theta)) + Y_t' c_t(\mu_t(W_t\,,\theta))]$$

is maximized, establishing the right hand side of (5.3).

Given that $E\,|\,Y_t\,| < \infty$, $E\,(Y_t \mid W_t)$ exists $a.s.$ and the law of iterated expectations applies to yield

$$E\,[a_t(\mu_t(W_t\,,\theta)) + Y_t'\,c_t(\mu_t(W_t\,,\theta))]$$
$$= E\,[\,E(a_t(\mu_t(W_t\,,\theta)) + Y_t'\,c_t(\mu_t(W_t\,,\theta)) \mid W_t)]$$
$$= E\,[a_t(\mu_t(W_t\,,\theta)) + E\,(Y_t' \mid W_t) c_t(\mu_t(W_t\,,\theta))]$$

so that

$$n^{-1} \sum_{t=1}^{n} E\,[a_t(\mu_t(W_t\,,\theta)) + Y_t'\,c_t(\mu_t(W_t\,,\theta))]$$

$$= n^{-1} \sum_{t=1}^{n} E\,[a_t(\mu_t(W_t\,,\theta)) + E\,(Y_t' \mid W_t) c_t(\mu_t(W_t\,,\theta))]\,. \qquad \square$$

PROOF OF COROLLARY 5.5: We use the approach of Gourieroux, Monfort and Trognon [1984], and show that for $t = 1, 2, \ldots$ and all θ in Θ

$$a_t(\mu_t(W_t\,,\theta)) + E\,(Y_t' \mid W_t) c_t(\mu_t(W_t\,,\theta))$$
$$\leq a_t(\mu_t(W_t\,,\theta_o)) + E\,(Y_t' \mid W_t) c_t(\mu_t(W_t\,,\theta_o)) \qquad a.s. - P_o$$

under correct specification. The result then follows directly from Theorem 5.4. Let

$$d_t(y\,,\mu) = \exp\,[a_t(\mu) + b_t(y) + y'\,c_t(\mu)]\,.$$

Given Assumption 5.3(b), it follows from the information inequality that

$$\int_{\mathbb{R}^l} \log\,[d_t(y\,,\mu_o) / d_t\,(y\,,\mu)]\; d_t(y\,,\mu_o)\; d\,\zeta_t(y)$$

$$= \int_{\mathbb{R}^l} [a_t(\mu_o) + b_t(y) + y' c_t(\mu_o) - a_t(\mu) - b_t(y) \\ - y' c_t(\mu)] \, d_t(y, \mu_o) d\, \zeta_t(y) \geq 0$$

for each (μ_o, μ) in $\mathbb{M}_t \times \mathbb{M}_t \subset \mathbb{R}^l \times \mathbb{R}^l$. Given Assumption 5.3(b), it follows from this that

$$a_t(\mu_o) + \mu_o' c_t(\mu_o) - a_t(\mu) - \mu_o' c_t(\mu) \geq 0$$

or

$$a_t(\mu) + \mu_o' c_t(\mu) \leq a_t(\mu_o) + \mu_o' c_t(\mu_o)$$

for each (μ_o, μ) in $\mathbb{M}_t \times \mathbb{M}_t$. Given Assumption 5.3(b), $\mu_t(W_t, \theta) \in \mathbb{M}_t$ for all θ in Θ $a.s.-P_o$. Therefore, with correct specification, we have

$$E(Y_t \mid W_t) = \mu_t(W_t, \theta_o) \in \mathbb{M}_t, \quad t = 1, 2, \ldots, a.s. - P_o .$$

It follows that for $t = 1, 2, \ldots$ and all θ in Θ

$$a_t(\mu_t(W_t, \theta)) + E(Y_t' \mid W_t) \, c_t(\mu_t(W_t, \theta)) \\ \leq a_t(\mu_t(W_t, \theta_o)) + E(Y_t' \mid W_t) \, c_t(\mu_t(W_t, \theta_o)) \qquad a.s. - P_o$$

under correct specification, as was to be shown. Hence θ_o maximizes

$$n^{-1} \sum_{t=1}^{n} E(a_t[\mu_t(W_t, \theta)] + E(Y_t' \mid W_t) \, c_t[\mu_t(W_t, \theta)]) .$$

But θ_n^* is the identifiably unique maximizer of this quantity, so we may take $\theta_n^* = \theta_o$ for all $n = 1, 2, \ldots$. It follows from Theorem 5.4 that $\hat{\theta}_n \to \theta_o$ $a.s.-P_o$ $(prob - P_o)$. □

PROOF OF THEOREM 5.6: This proof is adapted from Gourieroux, Monfort and Trognon [1984]. It suffices to show that the conclusion holds for P_o such that Y_t is i.i.d. with $E(Y_t) = \theta_o$. For now set $l = 1$ so that Y_t is a scalar.

Because $\theta_n^* = \theta_o$ is the identifiably unique maximizer of $\bar{L}_n(\theta)$, interior to Θ, it follows that $\nabla \bar{L}_n(\theta_o) = 0$. In particular, let $-\infty < y_1 < \theta_o < y_2 < \infty$ and suppose that $P_o[Y_t = y_1] = p_o$ and $P_o[Y_t = y_2] = 1 - p_o$. Then

$$\theta_o = p_o \, y_1 + (1 - p_o) \, y_2$$

and

$$\bar{L}_n(\theta) = p_o \, n^{-1} \sum_{t=1}^{n} \log f_t(y_1, \theta) + (1 - p_o) \, n^{-1} \sum_{t=1}^{n} \log f_t(y_2, \theta)$$

so

$$\nabla \bar{L}_n(\theta_o) = p_o \, n^{-1} \sum_{t=1}^{n} \nabla \log f_t(y_1, \theta_o) + (1 - p_o) \, n^{-1} \sum_{t=1}^{n} \nabla \log f_t(y_2, \theta_o) = 0 \, .$$

Because $p_o = (y_2 - \theta_o)/(y_2 - y_1)$ it follows that

$$(y_2 - \theta_o) \, n^{-1} \sum_{t=1}^{n} \nabla \log f_t(y_1, \theta_o) + (\theta_o - y_1) \, n^{-1} \sum_{t=1}^{n} \nabla \log f_t(y_2, \theta_o) = 0$$

for all $y_1 < \theta_o$ and all $y_2 > \theta_o$.

Now fix y_1. It follows that for all $y_2 > \theta_o$

$$n^{-1} \sum_{t=1}^{n} \nabla \log f_t(y_2, \theta_o) = (y_2 - \theta_o) \left[n^{-1} \sum_{t=1}^{n} \nabla \log f_t(y_1, \theta_o)/(y_1 - \theta_o) \right] .$$

Because this relation must hold for any choice of $y_1 < \theta_o$ and for each $n = 1, 2, \ldots$ it follows that

$$\nabla \log f_t(y_2, \theta_o) = (y_2 - \theta_o) \, \phi_{2t}(\theta_o) ,$$

where $\phi_{2t}(\theta_o) = \nabla \log f_t(y_1, \theta_o)/(y_1 - \theta_o)$ depends only on θ_o. Fixing y_2, a similar argument establishes that

$$\nabla \log f_t(y_1, \theta_o) = (y_1 - \theta_o) \, \phi_{1t}(\theta_o) ,$$

where $\phi_{1t}(\theta_o) = \nabla \log f_t(y_2, \theta_o)/(y_2 - \theta_o)$ depends only on θ_o. Substituting these facts we find that

$$(y_2 - \theta_o) \, n^{-1} \sum_{t=1}^{n} \nabla \log f_t(y_1, \theta_o) + (\theta_o - y_1) \, n^{-1} \sum_{t=1}^{n} \nabla \log f_t(y_2, \theta_o) = (y_2 - \theta_o)(y_1 - \theta_o) \, n^{-1} \sum_{t=1}^{n} \phi_{1t}(\theta_o)$$

$$- (y_1 - \theta_o)(y_2 - \theta_o)\, n^{-1} \sum_{t=1}^{n} \phi_{2t}(\theta_o)$$
$$= 0\,,$$

or

$$n^{-1} \sum_{t=1}^{n} \phi_{1t}(\theta_o) = n^{-1} \sum_{t=1}^{n} \phi_{2t}(\theta_o)\,.$$

Because this equation must hold for $n = 1, 2, \ldots$ it follows that $\phi_{1t}\,(\theta_o) = \phi_{2t}(\theta_o) = \phi_t(\theta_o)$, say, $t = 1, 2, \ldots$. Hence

$$\nabla \log f_t(y\,, \theta_o) = (y - \theta_o)\, \phi_t(\theta_o)\,.$$

The result that

$$\log f_t(y\,, \theta_o) = a_t(\theta_o) + b_t(y) + y\; c_t(\theta_o)\,, \quad t = 1, 2, \ldots$$

follows by integrating both sides of the differential equation above with respect to θ in the interior of Θ, a connected set, and extending to Θ using the continuity of $\log f_t\,(y, \cdot\,)$ on Θ.

For the case $l > 1$ a similar proof is available, in which masses $p_1\,, \ldots, p_{l+1}$ are placed at points $y_1\,, \ldots, y_{l+1}$ so that $\Sigma_{i=1}^{l+1}\, p_i y_i = \theta_o$. □

PROOF OF THEOREM 5.8: Given Assumptions 5.1 and 5.6(a), it follows that Assumption 2.3 holds. As Assumptions 2.1, 3.1 and 3.2 are in force, it follows from Theorem 3.5 that $\hat{\theta}_n - \theta_n^* \to 0$ as $n \to \infty$ $a.s.-P_o(\,prob - P_o)$ where θ_n^* maximizes

$$\bar{L}_n(\theta) = n^{-1} \sum_{t=1}^{n} E(\log f_t(X^t\,,\ \theta))$$
$$= -\, n^{-1} \sum_{t=1}^{n} E(\,\xi_t(\,|\, u_t(\theta)\,|\,))\,.$$

□

PROOF OF COROLLARY 5.9: The result follows by showing that $\theta_n^* = \theta_o$ given Assumptions 5.6 and 5.7 with correct specification. For this, it suffices to show that

$$E(\log f_t(X^t\,, \theta)) \le E(\log f_t(X^t\,, \theta_o)) \qquad t = 1, 2, \ldots\,,$$

for all θ in Θ.

Recall that $u_{ti}(\theta) \equiv Y_{ti} - \mu_{ti}(W_t\,, \theta)\,, i = 1, \ldots, l$, and that $|\,u_t(\theta)\,|$ is the $l \times 1$ vector with elements $|\,u_{ti}(\theta)\,|$. Given Assumption 5.6, it suffices to show that

$$E[\,\xi_t(\,|\,u_t(\theta)\,|\,)] \geq E[\,\xi_t(\,|\,u_t(\theta_o)\,|\,)] \qquad t = 1, 2, \ldots,$$

for all θ in Θ. Because ξ_t is a proper convex function, it follows from Theorem 23.4 of Rockafellar [1970] that there exists a subgradient $\Delta\,\xi_t$ with elements $\Delta\,\xi_{ti}$, $i = 1, \ldots, l$ such that

$$\xi_t(\,|u_t(\theta)|\,) \geq \xi_t(\,|u_t(\theta_o)|\,) + \sum_{i=1}^{l} \Delta\,\xi_{ti}(\,|u_t(\theta_o)|\,)\,(\,|u_{ti}(\theta)| - |u_{ti}(\theta_o)|\,)\,.$$

Further, the absolute value function is a proper convex function with (measurable) subgradient $\Delta\,|u_{ti}(\theta_o)| = 1_{[u_{ti}(\theta_o) > 0]} - 1_{[u_{ti}(\theta_o) < 0]}$, so that

$$|u_{ti}(\theta)| - |u_{ti}(\theta_o)| \geq \Delta\,|u_{ti}(\theta_o)\,|\,(u_{ti}(\theta) - u_{ti}(\theta_o))$$
$$= \Delta\,|u_{ti}(\theta_o)|\,(\,\mu_{ti}(W_t\,,\theta_o) - \mu_{ti}(W_t\,,\theta))\,.$$

Because ξ_t is nondecreasing, $\Delta\,\xi_{ti} \geq 0$. Therefore

$$\xi_t(|u_t(\theta)|) \geq \xi_t(|u_t(\theta_o)|) + \sum_{i=1}^{l} \Delta\,\xi_{ti}(\,|u_t(\theta_o)\,|\,)\,\Delta\,|u_{ti}(\theta_o)\,|\,(\mu_{ti}(W_t\,,\theta_o) - \mu_{ti}(W_t\,,\theta))\,.$$

The result now follows by showing that for $i = 1, \ldots, l$

$$E(\Delta\,\xi_{ti}(\,|u_t(\theta_o)\,|)\,\Delta\,|u_{ti}(\theta_o)\,|\,[\mu_{ti}(W_t\,,\theta_o) - \mu_{ti}(W_t\,,\theta)]) = 0\,,$$

which implies the desired conclusion, i.e.

$$E(\xi_t(\,|u_t(\theta)\,|)) \geq E(\xi_t(\,|u_t(\theta_o)\,|))\,.$$

We apply the law of iterated expectations, and write

$$E(\Delta\,\xi_{ti}(\,|u_t(\theta_o)\,|)\,\Delta\,|u_{ti}(\theta_o)\,|\,[\,\mu_{ti}(W_t\,,\theta_o) - \mu_{ti}(W_t\,,\theta)])$$
$$= E(E[\Delta\,\xi_{ti}(\,|u_t(\theta_o)\,|)\,\Delta\,|u_{ti}(\theta_o)\,|\,(\,\mu_{ti}(W_t\,,\theta_o) - \mu_{ti}(W_t\,,\theta))\,|\,W_t])$$
$$= E(E[\Delta\,\xi_{ti}(\,|u_t(\theta_o)\,|)\,\Delta|u_{ti}(\theta_o)||W_t]\,\{\,\mu_{ti}(W_t\,,\theta_o) - \mu_{ti}(W_t\,,\theta)\})\,.$$

It follows from the symmetry imposed in Assumption 5.7 that

$$E[\Delta\,\xi_{ti}(\,|u_t(\theta_o)\,|)\,\Delta\,|u_{ti}(\theta_o)\,|\,|\,W_t] = 0$$

because

$$\Delta\,\xi_{ti}(\,|u_t(\theta_o)\,|)\,\Delta\,|u_{ti}(\theta_o)\,|$$
$$= \Delta\,\xi_{ti}(\,|u_t(\theta_o)\,|)\,1_{[u_{ti}(\theta_o) > 0]} - \Delta\,\xi_{ti}(\,|u_t(\theta_o)\,|)\,1_{[u_{ti}(\theta_o) < 0]}$$
$$= \Delta\,\xi_{ti}(\,|u_t(\theta_o)\,|)\,1_{[u_{ti}(\theta_o) > 0]} - \Delta\,\xi_{ti}(\,|-u_t(\theta_o)\,|)\;\;1_{[-u_{ti}(\theta_o) > 0]}$$

so that

$$E[\Delta\, \xi_{ti}(\,|u_t(\theta_o)|)\, \Delta\, |u_{ti}(\theta_o)|\, |\, W_t]$$
$$= E[\Delta\, \xi_{ti}(\,|u_t(\theta_o)|)\, 1_{[u_{ti}(\theta_o) > 0]}\, |\, W_t]$$
$$- E[\Delta\, \xi_{ti}(\,|-u_t(\theta_o)|)\, 1_{[-u_{ti}(\theta_o) > 0]}\, |\, W_t]\,.$$

The symmetry imposed in Assumption 5.7 ensures that the conditional distribution of $-u_t(\theta_o)$ is identical to that of $u_t(\theta_o)$, implying

$$E[\Delta\, \xi_{ti}(\,|u_t(\theta_o)|)\, 1_{[u_{ti}(\theta_o) > 0]}\, |\, W_t]$$
$$= E[\Delta\, \xi_{ti}(\,|-u_t(\theta_o)|)\, 1_{[-u_{ti}(\theta_o) > 0]}\, |\, W_t]\,,$$

and because this expectation is finite given Assumption 5.6(b),

$$E[\Delta\, \xi_{ti}(\,|u_t(\theta_o)|)\, \Delta\, |u_{ti}(\theta_o)|\, |\, W_t] = 0\,.$$

It now follows that

$$E(\Delta\, \xi_{ti}(\,|u_t(\theta_o)|)\, \Delta\, |u_{ti}(\theta_o)|\, [\, \mu_{ti}(W_t\,, \theta_o) - \mu_{ti}(W_t\,, \theta)]) = 0$$

and the proof is complete. □

PROOF OF COROLLARY 5.11: Given Assumption 2.1, 3.1, 3.2, 5.1 and 5.4, it follows from Theorem 3.5 that $\hat{\theta}_n - \theta_n^* \longrightarrow 0$ as $n \to \infty$ $a.s.-P_o$ $(prob - P_o)$ where θ_n^* maximizes

$$\bar{L}_n(\theta) = n^{-1} \sum_{t=1}^{n} E(\phi_t(Y_t\,,\ \mu_t(W_t\,,\ \theta)))\,.$$

By assumption, for $t = 1, 2, \ldots$ and for all θ in Θ

$$E(\phi_t(Y_t\,, \mu_t(W_t\,, \theta))) \le E(\phi_t(Y_t\,,\ \alpha(Y_t\,|\,W_t)))$$

and because $\mathcal{M}$ is correctly specified

$$E(\phi_t(Y_t\,, \mu_t(W_t\,, \theta)) \le E(\phi_t(Y_t\,, \mu_t(W_t\,, \theta_o)))\,.$$

It follows immediately that $\bar{L}_n(\theta) \le \bar{L}_n(\theta_o)$ so that $\theta_n^* = \theta_o$ for all $n = 1, 2, \ldots$. Thus $\hat{\theta}_n \to \theta_o$ as $n \to \infty$ $a.s.-P_o$ $(prob - P_o)$. □

PROOF OF COROLLARY 5.12: We verify the conditions of Corollary 5.11. First we verify that Assumption 5.4 holds. For each μ, $\phi_t(\,\cdot\,, \mu)$ is clearly measurable-$\mathcal{B}^1$, as it is a product of a measurable function and the sum of two measurable indicator functions. Further, for given y_o, say, ϕ_t is a continuous transformation of the "check" function, which attains a maximum at $\mu = y_o$. This function is clearly continuous in μ for arbitrary $y_o \in \mathbb{R}$, so that Assumption 5.4 holds.

It remains to verify condition (5.5). Because of correct specification, we have that $\mu_t(W_t, \theta_o) = Q_q(Y_t \mid W_t)$, so it suffices to verify that for all $\theta \in \Theta$

$$E[\phi_t(Y_t, \mu_t(W_t, \theta))] \leq E[\phi_t(Y_t, \mu_t(W_t, \theta_o))] \ , t = 1, 2, \ldots .$$

Now ϕ_t can be written in terms of $u_t(\theta) \equiv Y_t - \mu_t(W_t, \theta)$ as $\phi_t(Y_t, \mu_t(W_t, \theta)) = - c_t(u_t(\theta))$, where

$$c_t(u) = \mid u \mid (q \ 1[u \geq 0] + (1 - q) \ 1[u < 0]).$$

It is readily verified that c_t is a proper convex function of u, with (measurable) subgradient $\Delta \ c_t(u) = q \ 1[u \geq 0] - (1 - q) \ 1[u < 0]$. Hence

$$\begin{aligned} c_t(u_t(\theta)) - c_t(u_t(\theta_o)) &\geq \Delta \ c_t(u_t(\theta_o)) \ (u_t(\theta) - u_t(\theta_o)) \\ &= q \ 1[Y_t \geq \mu_t(W_t, \theta_o)] - (1 - q) \ 1[Y_t < \mu_t(W_t, \theta_o)]) \\ &\qquad \times (\mu(W_t, \theta_o) - \mu(W_t, \theta)) \ . \end{aligned}$$

By the law of iterated expectations,

$$\begin{aligned} E[c_t(u_t(\theta)) - c_t(u_t(\theta_o))] &= E(E[c_t(u_t(\theta)) - c_t(u_t(\theta_o)) \mid W_t]) \\ &\geq E[E(q \ 1[Y_t \geq \mu_t(W_t, \theta_o)] - (1 - q) \ 1[Y_t < \mu_t(W_t, \theta_o)] \mid W_t) \\ &\qquad \times (\mu_t(W_t, \theta_o) - \mu_t(W_t, \theta))] \\ &= E([q \ (1 - q) - (1 - q) \ q] \ [\mu_t(W_t, \theta_o) - \mu_t(W_t, \theta)]) \\ &= 0 \ . \end{aligned}$$

Hence for all θ in Θ

$$E[c_t(u_t(\theta))] \geq E[c_t(u_t(\theta_o))]$$

or

$$E[\phi_t(Y_t, \mu_t(W_t, \theta))] \leq E[\phi_t(Y_t, \mu_t(W_t, \theta_o))]$$

$t = 1, 2, \ldots$, and the proof is complete. □

CHAPTER 6

The Asymptotic Distribution of the QMLE and the Information Matrix Equality

In this chapter, we study the consequences of possible misspecification for the asymptotic distribution of the QMLE and the 2SQMLE, paying particular attention to the form of the asymptotic covariance matrix implied by different kinds of misspecification.

6.1 Asymptotic Normality of the QMLE

For cases in which an estimator is obtained by solving a sufficiently smooth optimization problem, the heuristics underlying the results we seek are straightforward. In particular, if an estimator $\hat{\theta}_n$ maximizes $Q_n(\,\cdot\,, \theta)$ interior to Θ, we have

$$\nabla Q_n(\,\cdot\,, \hat{\theta}_n) = 0 \,.$$

Letting $\nabla \hat{Q}_n \equiv \nabla Q_n(\,\cdot\,, \hat{\theta}_n)$, $\nabla Q_n^* \equiv \nabla Q_n(\,\cdot\,, \theta_n^*)$, and taking a mean value expansion around θ_n^* gives

$$\nabla \hat{Q}_n = \nabla Q_n^* + \nabla^2 \ddot{Q}_n \, (\hat{\theta}_n - \theta_n^*) \,,$$

where each row of the Hessian $\nabla^2 \ddot{Q}_n$ is evaluated at a (different) mean value $\ddot{\theta}_n$ lying between $\hat{\theta}_n$ and θ_n^*. Solving for $\hat{\theta}_n - \theta_n^*$ gives $\hat{\theta}_n - \theta_n^* = -(\nabla^2 \ddot{Q}_n)^{-1} \; \nabla Q_n^*$.

With suitable regularity conditions, $\nabla^2 \ddot{Q}_n^{-1} (= (\nabla^2 \ddot{Q}_n)^{-1})$ will converge in probability to some limit depending on θ_n^*, say A_n^{*-1}, and, when suitably normalized, ∇Q_n^* will have a limiting distribution, often the normal distribution. For cases in which explosive behavior of random quantities is ruled out, a suitable normalization is to multiply by $\sqrt{n}$. This gives

$$\sqrt{n}(\hat{\theta}_n - \theta_n^*) = - A_n^{*-1} \sqrt{n} \nabla Q_n^* + o_P(1) ,$$

so that $\sqrt{n}(\hat{\theta}_n - \theta_n^*)$ has the same distribution as $- A_n^{*-1} \sqrt{n} \nabla Q_n^*$ asymptotically.

The results of this section follow from a theorem of Domowitz and White [1982] based on a rigorous version of this argument. In order to state this theorem and subsequent results, we make use of the following definition of the asymptotic normality of a sequence of random vectors.

DEFINITION 6.1 (*Asymptotic Normality*): Let $\{\mathcal{Z}_n\}$ be a sequence of random $p \times 1$ vectors, let $\{\mu_n\}$ be a nonstochastic $O(1)$ sequence of $p \times 1$ vectors, and let $\{V_n\}$ be a nonstochastic $O(1)$ sequence of symmetric positive semi-definite $p \times p$ matrices. Then $\mathcal{Z}_n$ is *distributed asymptotically as* $N(\mu_n, V_n)$, denoted $\mathcal{Z}_n \overset{A}{\sim} N(\mu_n, V_n)$ if

$$E(\exp[i a' \mathcal{Z}_n]) - \exp[i a' \mu_n - a' V_n a / 2] \to 0 \text{ as } n \to \infty$$

uniformly for a in compact subsets of $\mathbb{R}^p$, with $i \equiv \sqrt{-1}$. □

When the conditions of Definition 6.1 hold and $\{V_n\}$ is uniformly positive definite, then $V_n^{-1/2} (\mathcal{Z}_n - \mu_n) \overset{A}{\sim} N(0, I_p)$, where $V_n^{-1/2}$ is such that $V_n^{-1/2} V_n V_n^{-1/2'} = I_p$. For the applications of interest in this chapter, we will have $\mu_n = 0$. Sequences $\{\mu_n\} = O(1)$ are useful in later chapters.

Our version of the result of Domowitz and White is as follows.

THEOREM 6.2: *Let $(\Omega, \mathcal{F}, P)$ be a complete probability space, let Θ be a compact subset of $\mathbb{R}^p$ ($p \in \mathbb{N}$) with non-empty interior and let $Q_n : \Omega \times \Theta \to \mathbb{R}$ be a random function continuously differentiable of order 2 on Θ, a.s.−P, $n = 1, 2, \ldots$. Let $\hat{\theta}_n : \Omega \to \Theta$ be measurable−$\mathcal{F}$, $n = 1, 2, \ldots$ such that $\hat{\theta}_n = \text{argmax}_\Theta\, Q_n(\cdot, \theta)$ a.s.−P and $\hat{\theta}_n - \theta_n^* \to 0$ as $n \to \infty$ prob − P, where $\{\theta_n^*\}$ is interior to Θ uniformly in n. Suppose there exists a nonstochastic sequence of $p \times p$ matrices $\{B_n^*\}$ that is $O(1)$ and uniformly positive definite such that*

$$B_n^{*-1/2} \sqrt{n} \nabla Q_n^* \overset{A}{\sim} N(0, I_p) ,$$

where $\nabla Q_n^* \equiv \nabla Q_n(\cdot, \theta_n^*)$. *If there exists a sequence* $\{A_n : \Theta \to \mathbb{R}^{p \times p}\}$ *such that* $\{A_n\}$ *is continuous on* Θ *uniformly in* n, $\nabla^2 Q_n(\cdot, \theta) - A_n(\theta) \to 0$ *as* $n \to \infty$ *prob* $-P$ *uniformly on* Θ *and* $\{A_n^* \equiv A_n(\theta_n^*)\}$ *is* $O(1)$ *and uniformly non-singular (i.e.* $|\det A_n^*| \geq \delta > 0$ *a.a. n), then*

$$\sqrt{n}\,(\hat{\theta}_n - \theta_n^*) = -A_n^{*-1}\sqrt{n}\,\nabla Q_n^* + o_P(1), \text{ and}$$

$$B_n^{*-1/2} A_n^* \sqrt{n}\,(\hat{\theta}_n - \theta_n^*) \overset{A}{\sim} N(0, I_p). \qquad \square$$

It is easy to see that this result applies to the QMLE by choosing

$$Q_n(\omega, \theta) = L_n(X^n(\omega), \theta),$$

provided that L_n satisfies appropriate regularity conditions. The measurability condition is weak, and holds given Assumption 2.3. The requirement that $Q_n(\cdot, \theta)$ be continuously differentiable of order 2 on Θ, $a.s.-P$ is less weak, as it immediately rules out non-smooth objective functions, such as those generating the LAD or quantile estimators. While these can be handled in the context of misspecified dynamic models (as in Wooldridge [1986]), we adopt differentiability here for convenience and simplicity. In the present case, Assumption 3.6 already ensures that $L_n(X^n, \theta)$ has the specified differentiability properties.

The existence and consistency theorems ensure that the QMLE $\hat{\theta}_n$ and its limit θ_n^* behave as Theorem 6.2 requires, with the exception of the uniform interiority condition. But this is already imposed in Assumption 3.2′. To apply Theorem 6.2, it remains to establish the existence of matrices A_n^* and B_n^* with the desired properties. Now Assumptions 3.8 and 3.9 guarantee that the choice $A_n(\theta) \equiv \nabla^2 \bar{L}_n(\theta) = E(\nabla^2 L_n(X^n, \theta))$ has the desired properties, so we only need to ensure that $B_n^{*-1/2}\sqrt{n}\,\nabla Q_n^* \overset{A}{\sim} N(0, I_p)$.

For this, we use the following definition.

DEFINITION 6.3: Let $\{U_{nt}\}$ be a double array of random $p \times 1$ vectors. Then $\{U_{nt}\}$ *obeys the central limit theorem with covariance matrix* $\{V_n\}$ if for each n and t, $E(U_{nt}' U_{nt}) < \infty$, and

$$V_n^{-1/2} \sum_{t=1}^{n} [U_{nt} - E(U_{nt})] \overset{A}{\sim} N(0, I_p),$$

where $V_n \equiv \text{var}\,(\Sigma_{t=1}^n U_{nt})$ is finite and positive definite. □

By defining $\tilde{U}_{nt} = V_n^{-1/2}\, U_{nt}$, we could avoid explicit mention of V_n. However, in our application V_n will be of particular interest, so we explicitly include it here. Typically, the asymptotic behavior of $\sqrt{n}(\hat{\theta}_n - \theta_n^*)$ is established by finding matrices C_n^*, V_n and double arrays $\{U_{nt}\}$ such that

$$C_n^{*-1/2}\sqrt{n}(\hat{\theta}_n - \theta_n^*) - V_n^{-1/2} \sum_{t=1}^{n} [U_{nt} - E(U_{nt})] \to 0 \;\; prob - P_o$$

so that when $\{U_{nt}\}$ obeys the central limit theorem, $\sqrt{n}(\hat{\theta}_n - \theta_n^*)$ is distributed asymptotically as normal. When $C_n^{*-1/2}\sqrt{n}(\hat{\theta}_n - \theta_n^*) \overset{A}{\sim} N(0, I_p)$, we say that C_n^* is the *asymptotic covariance matrix* of $\hat{\theta}_n$, denoted avar $(\hat{\theta}_n) = C_n^*$.

We ensure that Theorem 6.2 applies by adding the following assumption.

ASSUMPTION 6.1: The double array $\{n^{-1/2}\, s_t^* \equiv n^{-1/2}\, \nabla \log f_t(X^t, \theta_n^*)\}$ obeys the central limit theorem with covariance matrix $\{B_n^*\}$, where $\{B_n^*\}$ is $O(1)$ and uniformly positive definite. □

As usual, we suppress the subscript n in defining s_t^*. With this condition, we have that

$$\begin{aligned} B_n^{*-1/2} &\sum_{t=1}^{n} [n^{-1/2}\, s_t^* - E(n^{-1/2}\, s_t^*)] \\ &= B_n^{*-1/2}\sqrt{n}\,\nabla L_n^* - B_n^{*-1/2}\sqrt{n}\,E(\nabla L_n^*) \\ &= B_n^{*-1/2}\sqrt{n}\,\nabla L_n^* \overset{A}{\sim} N(0, I_p)\,, \end{aligned}$$

with $\nabla L_n^* \equiv \nabla L_n(X^n, \theta_n^*)$, where the last and crucial equality follows because Assumption 3.7(a) and the interiority of θ_n^* imply $E(\nabla L_n^*) = \nabla \bar{L}_n^* = 0$. It is important to note that in general

$$E(s_t^*) \neq 0\,.$$

We see later that this fact has important implications for estimating the asymptotic covariance matrix of the QMLE.

We state Assumption 6.1 in this general form rather than placing more primitive conditions on $\{f_t\}$ and $\{X_t\}$ because just as in the case of the ULLN, there exists a variety of central limit results which can be used to obtain primitive conditions guaranteeing Assumption 6.1. These include the

Lindeberg-Feller CLT ($\{X_t\}$ independent), the Gordin [1969] CLT ($f_t = f_o$, $\theta_n^* = \theta_o$, $\{X_t\}$ stationary and ergodic), the Domowitz and White [1982] CLT (f_t a function of a finite number of lags of $\{X_t\}$, a mixing process) and the Wooldridge [1986] CLT (f_t a near epoch dependent function of $\{X_t\}$, a mixing process). White [1982] discusses application of the Lindeberg-Levy CLT to ensure Assumption 6.1; White [1984a] uses the Domowitz and White[1982] CLT; and Gallant and White [1988] use CLT's of Wooldridge [1986]. Appendix 3 of this monograph contains several of these results.

Our asymptotic distribution result for the QMLE can now be given.

THEOREM 6.4 (*QMLE Asymptotic Normality*): *Given Assumptions 2.1, 2.3, 3.1, 3.2′, 3.6, 3.7(a), 3.8, 3.9 and 6.1,*

$$\sqrt{n}\,(\hat{\theta}_n - \theta_n^*) = -\,A_n^{*-1}\,\sqrt{n}\,\nabla\,L_n^* + o_{P_o}(1)$$

and

$$B_n^{*-1/2}\,A_n^*\,\sqrt{n}\,(\hat{\theta}_n - \theta_n^*) \overset{A}{\sim} N(0\,,\,I_p)\,,$$

where $A_n^* \equiv \nabla^2\,\bar{L}_n(\theta_n^*) = E(\nabla^2\,L_n^*)$ *and* $B_n^* \equiv \mathrm{var}[n^{-1/2}\,\Sigma_{t=1}^n\,s_t^*]$, *so that avar* $\hat{\theta}_n = A_n^{*-1}\,B_n^*\,A_n^{*-1}$. □

This result provides the fundamental basis for subsequent results concerning efficiency, hypothesis testing and specification testing properties of the QMLE. A similar result is available for the 2SQMLE, but we defer treatment of that case until later.

6.2 Specification Effects for the Asymptotic Covariance Matrix

In this section we consider the implications of various misspecifications for the asymptotic covariance matrix of the QMLE, $A_n^{*-1}\,B_n^*\,A_n^{*-1}$. We first consider general specifications $\mathcal{S}$ and then specialize to specifications $\mathcal{M}$ used in conjunction with the linear exponential family.

6.2.a General Specifications

First, consider the case in which $\mathcal{S}$ is correct in its entirety for X. We have previously seen that $\theta_n^* = \theta_o$ for all $n = 1, 2, \ldots$. Thus

$$A_n^* = A_n^o \equiv E(n^{-1} \nabla^2 \log f^{\,n}(X^n, \theta_o))$$

$$B_n^* = B_n^o \equiv \mathrm{var}(n^{-1/2} \nabla \log f^{\,n}(X^n, \theta_o)) .$$

Because $E(\nabla L_n(X^n, \theta_o)) = \nabla \bar{L}_n^o \equiv \nabla \bar{L}_n(\theta_o) = 0$, we have

$$B_n^o = E(n^{-1} \nabla \log f^{\,n}(X^n, \theta_o) \nabla' \log f^{\,n}(X^n, \theta_o)) .$$

Under some mild regularity conditions, much more can be said. Specifically, when $f^{\,n}$ is a density for all θ we have

$$\int_{S_\theta^n} f^n(x^n, \theta) \; d\nu^n(x^n) = 1 ,$$

where S_θ^n is the support of $f^n(x^n, \theta)$, $S_\theta^n \equiv \{x^n : \; f^n(x^n, \theta) > 0\}$. Therefore

$$\nabla \int_{S_\theta^n} f^n(x^n, \theta) \; d\nu^n(x^n) = 0$$

and

$$\nabla^2 \int_{S_\theta^n} f^n(x^n, \theta) \, d\nu^n(x^n) = 0 .$$

The following assumption formally imposes the requirement that the derivatives and integrals above can be interchanged.

ASSUMPTION 6.2:(a) For all θ in *int* Θ

$$\int_{S_\theta^n} \nabla f^n(x^n, \theta) \, d\nu^n(x^n) = 0 , \qquad n = 1, 2, \ldots ;$$

(b) For all θ in *int* Θ

$$\int_{S_\theta^n} \nabla^2 f^n(x^n, \theta) \, d\nu^n(x^n) = 0 , \qquad n = 1, 2, \ldots .$$

□

This assumption is directly verifiable from the specification, and is commonly imposed in treatment of the method of maximum likelihood.

Given Assumption 6.2 and letting $s^n \equiv \nabla \log f^n$, the fact that $\nabla f^n(x^n, \theta) = s^n(x^n, \theta) f^n(x^n, \theta)$ on S_θ^n implies that for all θ in *int* Θ

$$\int_{S_\theta^n} s^n(x^n, \theta)\, f^n(x^n, \theta)\, d\nu^n(x^n) = 0\,,$$

and

$$\int_{S_\theta^n} [\nabla' s^n(x^n, \theta) + s^n(x^n, \theta)\, s^n(x^n, \theta)'\,]\, f^n(x^n, \theta)\, d\nu^n(x^n) = 0\,.$$

When f^n is correct in its entirety and we evaluate these expressions at θ_o we have

$$\int_{S_{\theta_o}^n} s^n(x^n, \theta_o) f^n(x^n, \theta_o)\, d\nu^n(x^n) = E(s^n(X^n, \theta_o)) = 0$$

and

$$\int_{S_{\theta_o}^n} [\nabla' s^n(x^n, \theta_o) + s^n(x^n, \theta_o)\, s^n(x^n, \theta_o)'\,]\, f^n(x^n, \theta_o)\, d\nu^n(x^n)$$

$$= E(\nabla' s^n(X^n, \theta_o)) + E(s^n(X^n, \theta_o) s^n(X^n, \theta_o)'\,)$$

$$= 0\,.$$

The first result is one we have already seen, but the second is new, and implies that

$$A_n^o = -\, B_n^o\,, \qquad n = 1, 2, \ldots\,.$$

This result is called the *information matrix equality* because it establishes the equality of the expected value of the Hessian of the log-likelihood evaluated at the true parameter θ_o with the opposite of the *Fisher information matrix*, B_n^o.

Formally, the result is the following.

THEOREM 6.5: *(i) Given Assumptions 2.1-2.3, 3.1(a,b), 3.2, 3.4, 3.6 and 6.2, if S is correct in its entirety at* $\theta_o \in$ *int* Θ, *then* $\theta_n^* = \theta_o$ *and*

$$A_n^o = -\, B_n^o\,, \quad n = 1, 2, \ldots\,.$$

(ii) If Assumptions 3.1(c), 3.7(a), 3.8 and 6.1 also hold, then the conclusions of Theorem 6.4 hold with

$$\text{avar}\, \hat\theta_n = -\, A_n^{o\,-1} = B_n^{o\,-1}\,.$$

□

This result underlies the usual techniques for estimating avar $\hat{\theta}_n$, as it suffices simply to estimate $-A_n^{o\,-1}$ or $B_n^{o\,-1}$. Of course, failure of the specification to be correct in its entirety will imply that such techniques may lead to inconsistent estimators for avar $\hat{\theta}_n$, and consequently to faulty inferences, as we see in Chapter 8.

The information matrix equality also has implications for estimator efficiency, as we shall see in Chapter 7, and provides a useful basis for specification testing, as we see in Chapter 11.

Although we have just noted that the information matrix equality may fail when the specification is not correct in its entirety, this is not always the case. Consider the situation in which $\mathcal{S}$ is correctly specified for $\{Y_t \mid W_t\}$ with respect to $\{\ddot{\mathrm{v}}^t, \ddot{\mathrm{v}}_t\}$ and $\ddot{\mathrm{v}}^t = \ddot{\mathrm{v}}_t \otimes \zeta_t$. When $f_t(x^t, \theta)$ is a conditional density with respect to ζ_t for all θ in Θ we have

$$\int_{S_{\theta,t}} f_t(x^t, \theta)\, d\zeta_t(y_t) = 1\ ,$$

where $S_{\theta,t} = \{y_t : f_t(x^t, \theta) > 0\}$. Note that $S_{\theta,t}$ now depends implicitly on w_t. For given w_t, we have

$$\nabla \int_{S_{\theta,t}} f_t(x^t, \theta)\, d\zeta_t(y_t) = 0$$

and

$$\nabla^2 \int_{S_{\theta,t}} f_t(x^t, \theta)\, d\zeta_t(y_t) = 0\ .$$

The following assumption formally imposes the requirement that these derivatives and integrals can be interchanged.

ASSUMPTION 6.3:(a) For all θ in *int* Θ

$$\int_{S_{\theta,t}} \nabla f_t(y_t, w_t, \theta)\, d\zeta_t(y_t) = 0 \qquad a.e.-\ddot{\mathrm{v}}_t,\ t = 1, 2, \ldots\ ;$$

(b) For all θ in *int* Θ

$$\int_{S_{\theta,t}} \nabla^2 f_t(y_t, w_t, \theta)\, d\zeta_t(y_t) = 0 \qquad a.e.-\ddot{\mathrm{v}}_t,\ t = 1, 2, \ldots . \qquad \square$$

As before, this condition can be verified directly from the specification. Using the fact that $\nabla f_t(y_t, w_t, \theta) = s_t(y_t, w_t, \theta) f_t(y_t, w_t, \theta)$ on $S_{\theta,t}$ one can show that with correct specification, setting $\theta = \theta_o$ and $s_t^o \equiv$

$s_t(Y_t, W_t, \theta_o)$ gives

$$\int_{S_{\theta_o,t}} s_t(y_t, W_t, \theta_o) f_t(y_t, W_t, \theta_o)\, d\zeta_t(y_t)$$
$$= E(s_t^o \mid W_t) = 0 \quad a.s.-P_o\,.$$

In the absence of dynamic misspecification, $E(s_t^o \mid W_t) = E(s_t^o \mid \tilde{X}^{t-1})$. In this case, $\{s_t^o, \tilde{\mathcal{F}}^t\}$ $(\tilde{\mathcal{F}}^{t-1} \equiv \sigma(\tilde{X}^{t-1}))$ is a martingale difference sequence, so that s_t^o is uncorrelated with its past values. We then have

$$B_n^* = B_n^o \equiv \text{var}(n^{-1/2} \sum_{t=1}^{n} s_t^o)$$
$$= n^{-1} \sum_{t=1}^{n} E(s_t^o\, s_t^{o\prime}) \equiv \bar{B}_n^o\,.$$

When $\mathcal{S}$ is correct for $\{Y_t \mid W_t\}$ it follows from Assumption 6.3(b) that

$$\int_{S_{\theta_o,t}} [\, \nabla' s_t(y_t, W_t, \theta_o) + s_t(y_t, W_t, \theta_o)\, s_t(y_t, W_t, \theta_o)' \,]$$
$$\times f_t(y_t, W_t, \theta_o)\, d\zeta_t(y_t)$$
$$= E[(\nabla' s_t^o + s_t^o\, s_t^{o\prime}) \mid W_t] = 0 \qquad a.s.-P_o\,.$$

The law of iterated expectations gives

$$E(\nabla' s_t^o) + E(s_t^o\, s_t^{o\prime}) = 0\,,$$

so that even with dynamic misspecification

$$A_n^o = n^{-1} \sum_{t=1}^{n} E(\nabla' s_t^o)$$
$$= -\, n^{-1} \sum_{t=1}^{n} E(s_t^o\, s_t^{o\prime})\,.$$
$$= -\, \bar{B}_n^o\,.$$

The absence of dynamic misspecification implies $B_n^o = \bar{B}_n^o$ which then yields the information matrix equality

$$A_n^o = -\, B_n^o\,.$$

Furthermore, in the absence of dynamic misspecification

$$E[\nabla' s_t^o + s_t^o\, s_t^{o\prime} \mid W_t] = E[\nabla' s_t^o + s_t^o\, s_t^{o\prime} \mid \tilde{X}^{t-1}]$$
$$= 0 \qquad a.s.-P_o$$

so that $\{\nabla' s_t^o + s_t^o\, s_t^{o\prime}, \tilde{\mathcal{F}}^t\}$ is a martingale difference sequence. This establishes the following information matrix equality result.

THEOREM 6.6: *Given Assumptions 2.1, 2.3, 3.1(a,b), 3.2, 3.6, 4.3 and 6.3, if $\mathcal{S}$ is correct for $\{Y_t \mid W_t\}$ at $\theta_o \in int\, \Theta$ with respect to $\{\ddot{\nu}^t, \ddot{\nu}_t\}$, $\ddot{\nu}^t = \ddot{\nu}_t \otimes \zeta_t$, then $\theta_n^* = \theta_o$ for all $n = 1, 2, \ldots$, $E(s_t^o \mid W_t) = 0$, $E(\nabla' s_t^o + s_t^o\, s_t^{o\prime} \mid W_t) = 0$, and*

$$A_n^o = -\, n^{-1} \sum_{t=1}^{n} E(s_t^o\, s_t^{o\prime}) = -\, \bar{B}_n^o\,, \quad n = 1, 2, \ldots .$$

If in addition there is no dynamic misspecification, then $\{s_t^o, \tilde{\mathcal{F}}^t\}$ and $\{\nabla' s_t^o + s_t^o\, s_t^{o\prime}, \tilde{\mathcal{F}}^t\}$ are martingale difference sequences, so that

$$B_n^o = \bar{B}_n^o \quad \text{and} \quad A_n^o = -\, B_n^o\,.$$

If Assumptions 3.1(c), 3.7(a), 3.8, and 6.1 also hold, then the conclusions of Theorem 6.4 hold with

$$\text{avar}\; \hat{\theta}_n = -\, A_n^{o\,-1} = B_n^{o\,-1}\,. \qquad \square$$

This result shows that by itself, correct specification of $\mathcal{S}$ for $\{Y_t \mid W_t\}$ is not enough for the information matrix equality. The presence of dynamic misspecification causes s_t^o to be autocorrelated, which means that B_n^o must take these correlations into account, thus generally differing from $-A_n^o$. Consequently, dynamic misspecification generally destroys the information matrix equality, invalidating inferences based on estimates of avar $\hat{\theta}_n$ that exploit the information matrix equality as we see in Chapter 8 and affecting the efficiency of the estimator as we see in Chapter 7. The martingale difference property of s_t^o provides a basis for testing for the absence of dynamic misspecification, as we see in Chapter 11.

As the theorem establishes, the information matrix equality does hold in the absence of dynamic misspecification and when $\mathcal{S}$ is correctly specified for $\{Y_t \mid W_t\}$.

Now suppose that we have the absence of dynamic misspecification, but that $\mathcal{S}$ is not correctly specified for $\{Y_t \mid W_t\}$. In this case we have

$$B_n^* = \text{var}\,[n^{-1/2} \sum_{t=1}^{n} s_t^*]$$

and we also have that

$$E(s_t^* \mid W_t) = E(s_t^* \mid \tilde{X}^{t-1})$$

because of the absence of dynamic misspecification. However, there is nothing to guarantee that these expectations are zero. Thus, even with the absence of dynamic misspecification, s_t^* may exhibit autocorrelation as a consequence of the failure of the specification to adequately capture the dependence of Y_t on elements of W_t that exhibit time dependence. Nor is there any necessary relationship between A_n^* and B_n^* in this case. By itself, the absence of dynamic misspecification is of little relevance in ensuring the validity of the information matrix equality. Expressed differently, the failure of s_t^* to be a martingale difference sequence does not by itself signal the presence of dynamic misspecification.

6.2.b *Linear Exponential Specifications*

Now suppose that we have the model $\mathcal{M}$ correctly specified for $\{E(Y_t \mid W_t)\}$ and that f_t is a member of the linear exponential family (i.e. Assumption 5.3 holds). To investigate the properties of the asymptotic covariance matrix of the QMLE in this case, we strengthen Assumption 5.3 to permit the differentiation of a_t and c_t.

ASSUMPTION 5.3′: Assumption 5.3 holds, and a_t and c_t are continuously differentiable of order 2 on $int\, \mathbb{M}_t$, $t = 1, 2, \ldots$. □

The following result, similar to Properties 1 and 3 of Gourieroux, Monfort and Trognon [1984], establishes some useful features of the linear exponential family.

LEMMA 6.7: *(i) Given Assumption 5.3′*

$$\int \nabla_\mu \exp \phi_t(y, \mu)\, d\zeta_t(y) = 0$$

and $\nabla_\mu \, a_t(\mu) = -(\nabla_\mu \, c_t(\mu))\, \mu$ *for* $\mu \in int\, \mathbb{M}_t$, $t = 1, 2, \ldots$;

(ii) Further,

$$\int \nabla^2_\mu \exp \phi_t(y, \mu)\, d\zeta_t(y) = 0$$

and $\nabla_\mu \, c_t(\mu) = \nabla_\mu{}' c_t(\mu) = D_t(\mu)^{-1}$ *for all* $\mu \in int\, \mathbb{M}_t$, *where*

$$D_t(\mu) \equiv \int (y-\mu)\,(y-\mu)' \exp \phi_t(y, \mu)\, d\zeta_t(y), \quad t = 1, 2, \ldots . \qquad \square$$

This result shows that conditions analogous to those of Assumption 6.3 automatically hold for the linear exponential family, as well as establishing the useful equalities $\nabla_\mu \, a_t = -(\nabla_\mu \, c_t)\, \mu$ and $\nabla_\mu \, c_t = D_t^{-1}$ where D_t is the covariance matrix "built into" the linear exponential specification.

Given the differentiability of a_t and c_t, we can obtain an expression for s_t, provided that μ_t is suitably differentiable. We impose the following condition.

ASSUMPTION 6.4: For $t = 1, 2, \ldots$, the functions $\mu_t(W_t, \cdot)$ are continuously differentiable of order 2 on Θ, $a.s.-P_o$. $\square$

Putting $\nabla_\mu \, a_t = -(\nabla_\mu \, c_t)\, \mu$, we have

$$\underset{p \times 1}{s_t(X^t, \theta)} = \underset{p \times l}{\nabla_\theta \, \mu_t(W_t, \theta)}\; \underset{l \times l}{\nabla_\mu \, c_t(\mu_t(W_t, \theta))}\; \underset{l \times 1}{(Y_t - \mu_t(W_t, \theta))}.$$

An interesting and useful feature of this result is that the score s_t is expressed as a linear transformation of the "generalized residual" $u_t(\theta) \equiv Y_t - \mu_t(W_t, \theta)$, where the $p \times l$ transformation matrix does not depend on Y_t. The matrix $\nabla_\mu \, c_t = D_t^{-1}$ "adjusts for" contemporaneous correlation in $Y_t - \mu_t$, while $\nabla_\theta \, \mu_t$ acts as a matrix of "instrumental variables."

This form for s_t motivates the following definition of specifications admitting generalized residuals and generalized instruments.

DEFINITION 6.8 (*Specification Admitting Generalized Residuals and Generalized Instruments*): Let $\mathcal{S} = \{f_t\}$ specify dependent variables Y and explanatory variables W. Given Assumption 2.1, suppose that Assumptions 2.3 and 2.4 hold. Then $\mathcal{S}$ *admits generalized residuals* $u = \{u_t\}$ *and generalized instruments* $i = \{i_t\}$ if there exist functions $u_t : \mathbb{R}^l \times \mathbb{R}^{k_t} \times \Theta \to \mathbb{R}^l$ and $i_t : \mathbb{R}^{k_t} \times \Theta \to \mathbb{R}^{p \times l}$ such that

$$\underset{p\times 1}{s_t}(Y_t, W_t, \theta) = \underset{p\times l}{i_t}(W_t, \theta)\, \underset{l\times 1}{u_t}(Y_t, W_t, \theta),$$

where for each θ in Θ $u_t(\cdot, \cdot, \theta)$ and $i_t(\cdot, \theta)$ are measurable-$\mathcal{B}^l \otimes \mathcal{B}^{k_t}$ and-$\mathcal{B}^{k_t}$ respectively and $u_t(Y_t, W_t, \cdot)$ and $i_t(W_t, \cdot)$ are continuous on Θ, $a.s.-P_o$, $t = 1, 2, \ldots$. □

For the linear exponential case, we may set

$$u_t(Y_t, W_t, \theta) = Y_t - \mu_t(W_t, \theta)$$

$$i_t(W_t, \theta) = \nabla_\theta\, \mu_t(W_t, \theta)\, \nabla_\mu\, c_t(\, \mu_t(W_t, \theta)) .$$

Alternatively, we could set

$$u_t(Y_t, W_t, \theta) = [\, \nabla_\mu\, c_t(\, \mu_t(W_t, \theta))]^{1/2}\, (Y_t - \mu_t(W_t, \theta))$$

$$i_t(W_t, \theta) = \nabla_\theta\, \mu_t(W_t, \theta)\, [\, \nabla_\mu\, c_t(\, \mu_t(W_t, \theta))]^{1/2} .$$

The appropriate choice is dictated by convenience in any particular context.

Because the linear exponential case is the primary case of a specification admitting generalized residuals and generalized instruments, the role played by the present definition is primarily that of establishing a convenient nomenclature. This definition coincides with that of the generalized residuals considered by Cox and Snell [1968].

When $\mathcal{M}$ is correctly specified for $\{E(Y_t \mid W_t)\}$, we have $\mu_t(W_t, \theta_o) = E(Y_t \mid W_t)$ $a.s.-P_o$, so that with s_t as above

$$\begin{aligned} E(s_t^o \mid W_t) &= \nabla_\theta\, \mu_t^o\ \ \nabla_\mu\, c_t^o\ E(u_t^o \mid W_t) \\ &= 0 \qquad a.s.-P_o , \end{aligned}$$

with $u_t^o \equiv u_t(\theta_o)$, $\nabla_\mu\, c_t^o \equiv \nabla_\mu\, c_t(\mu_t(W_t, \theta_o))$, $\nabla_\theta\, \mu_t^o \equiv \nabla_\theta\, \mu_t(W_t, \theta_o)$. Without dynamic misspecification,

$$E(s_t^o \mid W_t) = E(s_t^o \mid \tilde{X}^{t-1}) = 0 \qquad a.s.-P_o$$

so that $\{s_t^o, \tilde{\mathcal{F}}^t\}$ is a martingale difference sequence. This implies that in the absence of dynamic misspecification

$$B_n^* = B_n^o = n^{-1} \sum_{t=1}^{n} E(s_t^o \, s_t^{o\prime})$$

$$= n^{-1} \sum_{t=1}^{n} E(\nabla_\theta \, \mu_t^o \, \nabla_\mu \, c_t^o \, \Sigma_t^o \, \nabla_\mu' \, c_t^o \, \nabla_\theta' \, \mu_t^o)$$

$$= n^{-1} \sum_{t=1}^{n} E(\nabla_\theta \, \mu_t^o \, D_t^{o\,-1} \, \Sigma_t^o \, D_t^{o\,-1} \, \nabla_\theta' \, \mu_t^o) \, ,$$

where $\Sigma_t^o \equiv E(u_t^o \, u_t^{o\prime} \mid W_t)$ is the actual conditional covariance matrix of Y_t given W_t, and $D_t^o = D_t(\,\mu_t(W_t\,,\,\theta_o))$ is the conditional covariance "built into" the chosen specification. No particular relationship between Σ_t^o and D_t^o need exist.

To obtain an expression for A_n^*, we use the fact that

$$A_n^* = A_n^o = n^{-1} \sum_{t=1}^{n} E(\nabla' s_t^o) \, .$$

Straightforward algebra gives

$$E(\nabla' s_t^o \mid W_t) = -\, \nabla_\theta \, \mu_t^o \, \nabla_\mu \, c_t^o \, \nabla_\theta' \, \mu_t^o$$

$$= -\, \nabla_\theta \, \mu_t^o \, D_t^{o\,-1} \, \nabla_\theta' \, \mu_t^o$$

with correct specification. This leads us to a dynamic version of some interesting results of Gourieroux, Monfort and Trognon [1984].

THEOREM 6.9: *Given Assumptions 2.1, 5.1, 6.4 and 5.3′, if $\mathcal{M}$ is correct for $\{E(Y_t \mid W_t)\}$, and $f_t(X^t\,,\,\theta) = \exp \phi_t(Y_t\,,\,\mu_t(W_t\,,\,\theta))$, $t = 1, 2, \ldots$, then θ_n^* $= \theta_o$ for all $n = 1, 2, \ldots$, $E(s_t^o \mid W_t) = 0$ for all $t = 1, 2, \ldots$ and*

$$A_n^o = -\, n^{-1} \sum_{t=1}^{n} E(\nabla_\theta \, \mu_t^o \, D_t^{o\,-1} \, \nabla_\theta' \, \mu_t^o) \, , \qquad n = 1, 2, \ldots \, .$$

If in addition there is no dynamic misspecification, then $\{s_t^o = \nabla_\theta \, \mu_t^o \, \nabla_\mu \, c_t^o \, u_t^o \, , \, \tilde{\mathcal{F}}^t\}$ is a martingale difference sequence, and

$$B_n^o = n^{-1} \sum_{t=1}^{n} E(\nabla_\theta \, \mu_t^o \, D_t^{o\,-1} \, \Sigma_t^o \, D_t^{o\,-1} \, \nabla_\theta' \, \mu_t^o) \, .$$

Further if $\Sigma_t^o = D_t^o$, then $E(\nabla' s_t^o + s_t^o \, s_t^{o\prime} \mid W_t) = 0$ regardless of dynamic misspecification. If there is no dynamic misspecification then $\{\nabla' s_t^o + s_t^o \, s_t^{o\prime}\,,$ $\tilde{\mathcal{F}}^t\}$ is a martingale difference sequence, with

$$\nabla' s_t^o = [\, u_t^{o\prime} \nabla'_\mu c_t^o \otimes I_p \,] \, \nabla_\theta^2 \mu_t^o \; +$$

$$[\, u_t^{o\prime} \otimes \nabla_\theta \mu_t^o \,] \nabla_\mu^2 c_t^o \, \nabla'_\theta \mu_t^o - \nabla_\theta \mu_t^o \, \nabla_\mu c_t^o \, \nabla'_\theta \mu_t^o \, ,$$

and therefore

$$A_n^o = - \, B_n^o \, .$$

Here $\nabla_\mu^2 c_t^o$ *and* $\nabla_\theta^2 \mu_t^o$ *denote the* $l^2 \times l$ and $lp \times p$ *Hessian matrices of* c_t *and* μ_t *evaluated at* θ_o. *(We follow the conventions of Magnus and Neudecker [1988, p. 114].) If Assumptions 3.1, 3.2′, 3.7(a), 3.8 and 6.1 also hold, then the conclusions of Theorem 6.4 hold, with*

$$\text{avar } \hat{\theta}_n = - \, A_n^{o\,-1} = B_n^{o\,-1} \, . \qquad \square$$

This result shows that the correctness of $\mathcal{M}$ for $\{E(Y_t \mid W_t)\}$ and the absence of dynamic misspecification are not by themselves enough to guarantee that the information matrix equality holds. We further need that $\Sigma_t^o = D_t^o$, which is a condition requiring that the conditional variance of Y_t be compatible with that of the member of the linear exponential family chosen for purposes of estimation. When $\Sigma_t^o \neq D_t^o$ we have a form of neglected heteroskedasticity.

In particular cases, this compatibility may be achieved by appropriate choice of certain nuisance parameters. We explore this issue further when we consider the behavior of the 2SQMLE.

At this point, it is helpful to give a brief summary of the results obtained so far. We have seen in general that under appropriate regularity conditions, the QMLE $\hat{\theta}_n$ has the normal distribution asymptotically, centered at θ_n^* and with

$$\text{avar } \hat{\theta}_n = A_n^{*-1} \, B_n^* \, A_n^{*-1} \, .$$

With entirely correct specification and appropriate regularity conditions, the form of the asymptotic covariance matrix simplifies due to the validity of the information matrix equality. Even without entirely correct specification, we have seen that the information matrix equality holds, provided that the specification is not subject to dynamic misspecification and either that $\mathcal{S}$ is correct for $\{Y_t \mid W_t\}$ or that $\mathcal{M}$ is correct for $\{E(Y_t \mid W_t)\}$ with $\Sigma_t^o = D_t^o$, i.e. one also knows (or perhaps can correctly specify a model of) the conditional variance. The information matrix equality may hold in other particular cases;

conditions under which this is true should be part of the investigation of the properties of any particular model. In fact, whether or not the information matrix equality holds can be investigated empirically. We devote Chapter 11 to examining specification tests based on empirical analysis of the validity of the information matrix equality.

6.3 Asymptotic Normality of the 2SQMLE

Now we consider the asymptotic distribution for the 2SQMLE. In general, a two stage estimator $\hat{\beta}_n$ is obtained by solving the problem

$$\max_{\beta \in \mathcal{B}} \quad Q_{2n}(\cdot, \hat{\alpha}_n, \beta),$$

where $\hat{\alpha}_n$ is some estimator obtained in a prior first stage. The joint distribution of $\hat{\theta}_n{}' = (\hat{\alpha}_n{}', \hat{\beta}_n{}')$ is conveniently obtained if we suppose that $\hat{\alpha}_n$ is also obtained by solving an optimization problem, say

$$\max_{\alpha \in \mathcal{A}} \quad Q_{1n}(\cdot, \alpha).$$

With sufficient smoothness, if $\hat{\alpha}_n$ is interior to $\mathcal{A}$ and $\hat{\beta}_n$ is interior to $\mathcal{B}$, then

$$\underset{q \times 1}{\nabla_\alpha Q_{1n}(\cdot, \hat{\alpha}_n) = 0}$$

$$\underset{r \times 1}{\nabla_\beta Q_{2n}(\cdot, \hat{B}_n) = 0}$$

Letting $\hat{s}_n \equiv s_n(\cdot, \hat{\theta}_n) = (\nabla_\alpha' Q_{1n}(\cdot, \hat{\alpha}_n), \nabla_\beta' Q_{2n}(\cdot, \hat{\alpha}_n, \hat{\beta}_n))'$ we have that $\hat{s}_n = 0$, and a heuristic argument identical to that at the outset of this chapter with s_n replacing ∇Q_n yields

$$\sqrt{n}(\hat{\theta}_n - \theta_n^*) = -A_n^{*-1} \sqrt{n}\, s_n^* + o_{P_o}(1),$$

where A_n^* is the probability limit for $\nabla_\theta' \ddot{s}_n$, the $p \times p$ Jacobian of s_n with rows evaluated at suitable mean values. Thus, $\sqrt{n}\,(\hat{\theta}_n - \theta_n^*)$ will have the same distribution as $-A_n^{*-1} \sqrt{n}\, s_n^*$ asymptotically, analogous to the previous case.

The following result is based on a rigorous development of this argument and is the basis for our asymptotic normality results for the 2SQMLE. It contains Theorem 6.2 as a corollary, and is in fact a general result guaranteeing asymptotic normality for m-estimators.

THEOREM 6.10: *Let $(\Omega, \mathcal{F}, P)$ be a complete probability space, let Θ be a compact subset of $\mathbb{R}^p$, $p \in \mathbb{N}$, and let $\psi_n : \Omega \times \Theta \longrightarrow \mathbb{R}^p$ be such that $\psi_n(\cdot, \theta)$ is measurable - $\mathcal{F}$ for each θ in Θ, and $\psi_n(\omega, \cdot)$ is continuously differentiable on Θ a.s.$-P$, $n = 1, 2, \ldots$. Let $\hat{\theta}_n : \Omega \longrightarrow \Theta$ be measurable $-\mathcal{F}$, $n = 1, 2, \ldots$ such that $\hat{\theta}_n - \theta_n^* \longrightarrow 0$ prob $- P$ as $n \longrightarrow \infty$, where $\{\theta_n^*\}$ is interior to Θ uniformly in n, and $\sqrt{n}\, \hat{\psi}_n \equiv \sqrt{n}\, \psi_n(\cdot, \hat{\theta}_n) \longrightarrow 0$ prob $- P$. Suppose there exists a sequence of $p \times p$ matrices $\{B_n^*\}$ that is $O(1)$ and uniformly positive definite such that*

$$B_n^{*-1/2} \sqrt{n}\, \psi_n^* \overset{A}{\sim} N(0, I_p),$$

where $\psi_n^* \equiv \psi_n(\cdot, \theta_n^*)$. If there exists a sequence $\{A_n : \Theta \longrightarrow \mathbb{R}^{p \times p}\}$ such that $\{A_n\}$ is continuous on Θ uniformly in n, $\nabla' \psi_n(\cdot, \theta) - A_n(\theta) \longrightarrow 0$ prob $- P$ as $n \longrightarrow \infty$ uniformly on Θ and $\{A_n^* \equiv A_n(\theta_n^*)\}$ is $O(1)$ and uniformly nonsingular, then

$$\sqrt{n}\, (\hat{\theta}_n - \theta_n^*) = - A_n^{*-1} \sqrt{n}\, \psi_n^* + o_P(1)$$

and

$$B_n^{*-1/2} A_n^* \sqrt{n}(\hat{\theta}_n - \theta_n^*) \overset{A}{\sim} N(0, I_p). \qquad \square$$

Obviously, this result contains Theorem 6.2 as the special case in which $\nabla Q_n = \psi_n$. The present result is more flexible, as ψ_n need not be the gradient of a particular objective function, but may instead be the gradient from several different optimization problems (as with the 2SQMLE); it may also represent linear combinations of a number of arbitrary "moments" thought to have zero expectation, as in the case of generalized method of moments (GMM) estimators discussed in section 5.4.

In our specific application, we have

$$\psi_n(\omega, \theta)' = (\nabla'_\alpha L_{1n}(X^n(\omega), \alpha), \nabla'_\beta L_{2n}(X^n(\omega), \hat{\alpha}_n(\omega), \beta)),$$

where $\hat{\alpha}_n$ solves the problem

$$\max_{\alpha \in \mathcal{A}} \quad L_{1n}(X^n, \alpha)$$

and $\hat{\beta}_n$ solves the problem

$$\max_{\beta \in \mathcal{B}} \quad L_{2n}(X^n, \hat{\alpha}_n, \beta).$$

We have added the subscripts 1 and 2 to the quasi-log-likelihood functions to distinguish between the first and second stage optimization problems. To obtain the desired result, we shall assume that the underlying specifications f_{1t} and f_{2t} satisfy conditions appropriate for applying the consistency theorems (Theorems 3.5 and 3.10 respectively), as well as interiority (Assumption 3.2′) and Assumptions 3.6-3.9, which ensure the existence and appropriate convergence of required derivatives.

The only remaining requirement is to ensure that $B_n^{*-1/2} \sqrt{n}\ \psi_n^* \overset{A}{\sim} N(0, I_p)$. We impose the following condition.

ASSUMPTION 6.5: The double array $\{(n^{-1/2} s_{1t}^{*\prime}, n^{-1/2} s_{2t}^{*\prime})' \equiv (n^{-1/2}\ \nabla'_\alpha \log f_{1t}(X^t, \alpha_n^*), n^{-1/2}\ \nabla'_\beta \log f_{2t}(X^t, \theta_n^*))'\}$ obeys the central limit theorem with covariance matrix $\{B_n^*\}$, where $\{B_n^*\}$ is $O(1)$ and uniformly positive definite. □

As in the previous case, we have sufficient structure to ensure that $E(\psi_n^*) = 0$.

We write $\nabla_{\alpha\alpha}$ for $\nabla'_\alpha(\nabla_\alpha)$, $\nabla_{\beta\beta}$ for $\nabla'_\beta(\nabla_\beta)$ and $\nabla_{\alpha\beta}$ for $\nabla'_\alpha(\nabla_\beta)$ in our next result. The asymptotic distribution result for the 2SQMLE is the following:

THEOREM 6.11 (*2SQMLE Asymptotic Normality I*): *Given Assumptions 2.1, 2.3, 3.1, 3.6, 3.7(a), 3.8, 3.9 and 6.5 for $\{f_{1t}\}$ and $\{f_{2t}\}$ with 3.2′ holding for $\bar{L}_{1n}(X^n, \alpha)$ and $\bar{L}_{2n}(X^n, \alpha_n^*, \beta)$ we have*

$$\sqrt{n}(\hat{\theta}_n - \theta_n^*) = - A_n^{*-1} \sqrt{n}\, \psi_n^* + o_{P_o}(1)$$

and

$$B_n^{*-1/2} A_n^* \sqrt{n}\, (\hat{\theta}_n - \theta_n^*) \overset{A}{\sim} N(0, I_p),$$

where $\psi_n^{*\prime} = (\nabla'_\alpha L_{1n}(X^n, \alpha_n^*), \nabla'_\beta L_{2n}(X^n, \alpha_n^*, \beta_n^*))$,

$$A_n^* = \begin{bmatrix} \nabla_{\alpha\alpha} \bar{L}_{1n}(\alpha_n^*) & 0 \\ \nabla_{\alpha\beta} \bar{L}_{2n}(\theta_n^*) & \nabla_{\beta\beta} \bar{L}_{2n}(\theta_n^*) \end{bmatrix}$$

and

$$B_n^* \equiv \text{var}\, [n^{-1/2} \sum_{t=1}^{n} (s_{1t}^{*\prime}, s_{2t}^{*\prime})']$$

so that

$$\text{avar}\, \hat{\theta}_n = A_n^{*-1} B_n^* A_n^{*-1\prime}.$$

In particular,

$$\text{avar}\, \hat{\alpha}_n = A_{11n}^{*-1} B_{11n}^* A_{11n}^{*-1},$$

and

$$\begin{aligned} \text{avar}\, \hat{\beta}_n &= A_{22n}^{*-1} B_{22n}^* A_{22n}^{*-1} \\ &- A_{22n}^{*-1} A_{21n}^* A_{11n}^{*-1} B_{12n}^* A_{22n}^{*-1} - A_{22n}^{*-1} B_{21n}^* A_{11n}^{*-1} A_{21n}^{*\prime} A_{22n}^{*-1} \\ &+ A_{22n}^{*-1} A_{21n}^* A_{11n}^{*-1} B_{11n}^* A_{11n}^{*-1} A_{21n}^{*\prime} A_{22n}^{*-1}, \end{aligned}$$

with $A_{11n}^* \equiv \nabla_{\alpha\alpha} \bar{L}_{1n}(\alpha_n^*)$, $A_{21n}^* \equiv \nabla_{\alpha\beta} \bar{L}_{2n}(\theta_n^*)$, $A_{22n}^* \equiv \nabla_{\beta\beta} \bar{L}_{2n}(\theta_n^*)$, *and we partition* B_n^* *conformably as*

$$B_n^* = \begin{bmatrix} B_{11n}^* & B_{12n}^* \\ B_{21n}^* & B_{22n}^* \end{bmatrix}. \qquad \square$$

As we should expect, the result shows that the first stage estimator $\hat{\alpha}_n$ has asymptotic variance given by Theorem 6.4, while $\hat{\beta}_n$ has a much more complicated asymptotic covariance matrix than it would have if α_n^* were not estimated, but simply replaced $\hat{\alpha}_n$ in forming the 2SQMLE. In the latter case, one can show that

$$\text{avar } \tilde{\beta}_n = A_{22n}^{*-1} \, B_{22n}^* \, A_{22n}^{*-1} ,$$

where $\tilde{\beta}_n \equiv \text{argmax}_{\mathcal{B}} \; L_{2n}(X^n, \alpha_n^*, \beta) \; a.s.-P_o$. Straightforward algebra shows that the difference avar $\hat{\beta}_n$ − avar $\tilde{\beta}_n$ is a positive semi-definite matrix. This difference is therefore the additional dispersion in the asymptotic distribution of $\hat{\beta}_n$ introduced by the estimation of $\hat{\alpha}_n$.

Although information matrix equalities of the form $A_{22n}^* = -B_{22n}^*$ can still hold with appropriately correct specifications, the presence of terms in avar $\hat{\beta}_n$ involving A_{21n}^* prevents simplifications in avar $\hat{\beta}_n$ analogous to those seen earlier for avar $\hat{\theta}_n$.

An important special case occurs when $A_{21n}^* \equiv \nabla_{\alpha\beta} \bar{L}_{2n}^* = 0$, implying that avar $\tilde{\beta}_n$ = avar $\hat{\beta}_n$. In this case, the estimation of $\hat{\alpha}_n$ has no effect on the asymptotic distribution of $\hat{\beta}_n$. This case is commonly referred to as a situation in which the "information matrix is block diagonal." In fact, we see that it is instead the block diagonality of the Hessian $\nabla_\theta^{\,2} \bar{L}_{2n}^*$ that is important. The information matrix equality need not hold in the present context, so that the block diagonality of the information matrix is not implied by that of $\nabla_\theta^2 \bar{L}_{2n}^*$.

Because the behavior of $\hat{\beta}_n$ is isolated from that of $\hat{\alpha}_n$ by this block diagonality, it is possible to state a simpler result for the 2SQMLE which does not require placing as much structure on $\hat{\alpha}_n$. We impose

ASSUMPTION 6.6: $\{\hat{\alpha}_n : \Omega \to \mathbb{R}^q\}$ is a sequence of functions measurable-$\mathcal{F}$ such that $\{\sqrt{n}(\hat{\alpha}_n - \alpha_n^*)\}$ is $O_{P_o}(1)$ for some real valued sequence $\{\alpha_n^*\}$. □

Block-diagonality of $\nabla^2 \bar{L}_{2n}^*$ allows us to obtain the following simpler result for the 2SQMLE.

THEOREM 6.12 (*2SQMLE Asymptotic Normality II*): *Given Assumption 2.1, let Assumption 6.6 hold for $\hat{\alpha}_n$, and suppose that Assumptions 2.3, 3.1, 3.6, 3.7(a), 3.8 and 3.9 hold for $\{f_{2t}\}$, that Assumption 3.2′ holds for*

$\{L_{2n}(X^n, \alpha_n^*, \beta)\}$, *and that Assumption 6.1 holds for* $\{n^{-1/2} \nabla_\beta \log f_{2t}(X^t, \theta_n^*)\}$. *If* $\nabla_{\alpha\beta} \bar{L}_{2n}^* = 0$, *then*

$$\sqrt{n}(\hat{\beta}_n - \beta_n^*) = - A_{22n}^{*-1} \sqrt{n} \nabla_\beta L_{2n}^* + o_{P_o}(1)$$

and

$$B_{22n}^{*-1/2} A_{22n}^* \sqrt{n}(\hat{\beta}_n - \beta_n^*) \overset{A}{\sim} N(0, I_p),$$

where

$$A_{22n}^* \equiv \nabla_{\beta\beta} \bar{L}_{2n}^* = E(\nabla_{\beta\beta} L_{2n}(X^n, \alpha_n^*, \beta_n^*)),$$

and

$$B_{22n}^* \equiv \text{var}\, [n^{-1/2} \sum_{t=1}^{n} \nabla_\beta \log f_{2t}(X^t, \alpha_n^*, \beta_n^*)],$$

so that

$$\text{avar}\, \hat{\beta}_n = A_{22n}^{*-1} B_{22n}^* A_{22n}^{*-1}. \qquad \square$$

This result is entirely parallel to Theorem 6.4 for $\hat{\theta}_n$. With $\nabla_{\alpha\beta} \bar{L}_{2n}^* = 0$ and Assumption 6.6 holding, we see that avar $\hat{\beta}_n$ coincides with avar $\tilde{\beta}_n$, so that estimation of $\hat{\alpha}_n$ no longer complicates avar $\hat{\beta}_n$. We can act essentially as if α_n^* were known.

Versions of Theorem 6.5, 6.6 and 6.9 continue to hold if, when $\theta'_o = (\alpha'_o, \beta'_o)$, we have that $\alpha_n^* = \alpha_o$. We specifically consider a version of Theorem 6.9 for a family of linear exponential densities extended by the inclusion of a nuisance parameter, as discussed in Gourieroux, Monfort and Trognon [1984]. Such parameters occur naturally in such families as the normal and gamma, acting essentially as scaling parameters. In the normal case, it is the covariance matrix itself that acts as a nuisance parameter.

The extension of the linear exponential family of interest here is given in the following assumption.

ASSUMPTION 6.7: For $t = 1, 2, \ldots$

$$\phi_t(y, \mu, \kappa) = a_t(\mu, \kappa) + b_t(y, \kappa) + y' c_t(\mu, \kappa),$$

where $a_t : \mathbb{M}_t \times \mathbb{K}_t \to \mathbb{R}$ is continuously differentiable of order 2 on

$int\,(\mathbb{M}_t \times \mathbb{K}_t)$, $\mathbb{M}_t \subseteq \mathbb{R}^l$, $\mathbb{K}_t \subseteq \mathbb{R}^{l \times l}$; $b_t : \mathbb{R}^l \times \mathbb{K}_t \to \mathbb{R}$ is such that $b_t(\,\cdot\,, \kappa) : \mathbb{R}^l \to \mathbb{R}$ is measurable–$\mathcal{B}^l / \mathcal{B}$ for each κ in $\mathbb{K}_t$ and $b_t(y, \cdot\,) : \mathbb{K}_t \to \mathbb{R}$ is continuous on $\mathbb{K}_t$ $a.s.-P_o$; $c_t : \mathbb{M}_t \times \mathbb{K}_t \to \mathbb{R}^l$ is continuously differentiable of order 2 on $int\,(\mathbb{M}_t \times \mathbb{K}_t)$, $\nabla_\mu\, c_t(\mu, \kappa)$ is nonsingular for each $(\mu, \kappa) \in int\,(\mathbb{M}_t \times \mathbb{K}_t)$, and for each $\mu \in int\,\mathbb{M}_t$, $\nabla_\mu\, c_t(\mu, \cdot\,) : \mathbb{K}_t \to \mathbb{R}^{l \times l}$ is one-to-one.

Further, for a given σ-finite measure ζ_t, the functions a_t, b_t and c_t satisfy

$$\int_{\mathbb{R}^l} \exp \phi_t(y, \mu, \kappa)\, d\zeta_t(y) = 1$$

and

$$\int_{\mathbb{R}^l} y \exp \phi_t(y, \mu, \kappa)\, d\zeta_t(y) = \mu$$

for all (μ, κ) in $\mathbb{M}_t \times \mathbb{K}_t$, $t = 1, 2, \ldots$. □

The parameters κ are the nuisance parameters here. By assumption, they do not affect the mean μ; moreover, Lemma 6.7 holds with Assumption 6.7 replacing Assumption 5.3′. This implies that $\nabla_\mu\, a_t(\mu, \kappa) = -[\nabla_\mu\, c_t(\mu, \kappa)]\,\mu$ and $\nabla_\mu\, c_t(\mu, \kappa)^{-1} = D_t(\mu, \kappa)$ for all $(\mu, \kappa) \in int\,(\mathbb{M}_t \times \mathbb{K}_t)$, where

$$D_t(\mu, \kappa) \equiv \int (y - \mu)\,(y - \mu)' \exp \phi_t(y, \mu, \kappa)\, d\zeta_t(y)\,.$$

Because $\nabla_\mu\, c_t(\mu, \cdot\,)$ is one-to-one with inverse function $\nabla_\mu\, c_t^{-1}(\mu, \cdot)$, say, any desired value for $D_t(\mu, \kappa)$, say D_t^o, can be achieved by setting

$$\kappa = \nabla_\mu\, c_t^{-1}(\mu, D_t^{o\,-1})\,.$$

Two-stage estimation procedures arise naturally in the present context when the appropriate value for D_t^o is unknown, but there exists a model based on $v_t(W_t, \gamma)$ (say) such that $D_t^o = v_t(W_t, \gamma_o)$. Then the choice

$$\kappa_t(W_t, \alpha) = \nabla_\mu\, c_t^{-1}(\mu_t(W_t, \delta), v_t(W_t, \gamma)^{-1})$$

with $\alpha' = (\gamma', \delta')$ can be used to ensure the desired value for D_t by replacing α with a consistent first stage estimator, say $\hat{\alpha}_n$. Note that here $\delta \in \mathcal{B}$, but we wish to emphasize that the estimator $\hat{\delta}_n$ is obtained independently of $\hat{\beta}_n$.

Formally, we impose conditions on κ_t analogous to those imposed on μ_t.

ASSUMPTION 6.8: The functions $\kappa_t : \mathbb{R}^{k_t} \times \mathcal{A} \longrightarrow \mathbb{R}^{l \times l}$ are such that for each α in $\mathcal{A}$, a compact set of $\mathbb{R}^q$, $\kappa_t(\cdot, \alpha)$ is measurable$-\mathcal{B}^{k_t}$, and $\kappa_t(W_t, \cdot)$ is continuously differentiable of order 2 on $\mathcal{A}$, $a.s.-P_o$. □

Given some first stage estimator $\hat{\alpha}_n$, the second stage estimator $\hat{\beta}_n$ solves the problem

$$\max_{\beta \in \mathcal{B}} \; n^{-1} \sum_{t=1}^{n} [a_t(\mu_t(W_t, \beta), \kappa_t(W_t, \hat{\alpha}_n)) + Y_t' \, c_t(\mu_t(W_t, \beta), \kappa_t(W_t, \hat{\alpha}_n))]$$

$$\equiv L_{2n}(X^n, \hat{\alpha}_n, \beta) .$$

Note that the term involving b_t has been omitted as it does not depend on β. Thus

$$\nabla_\beta L_{2n}(X^n, \alpha, \beta)$$

$$= n^{-1} \sum_{t=1}^{n} \nabla_\beta \mu_t(W_t, \beta) \nabla_\mu a_t(\mu_t(W_t, \beta), \kappa_t(W_t, \alpha))$$

$$+ \nabla_\beta \mu_t(W_t, \beta) \nabla_\mu c_t(\mu_t(W_t, \beta), \kappa_t(W_t, \alpha)) Y_t .$$

Because $\nabla_\mu a_t = -[\nabla_\mu c_t] \mu_t$ as before, it follows that

$$\nabla_\beta L_{2n}(X^n, \alpha, \beta)$$

$$= n^{-1} \sum_{t=1}^{n} \nabla_\beta \mu_t(W_t, \beta) \nabla_\mu c_t(\mu_t(W_t, \beta), \kappa_t(W_t, \alpha)) \times (Y_t - \mu_t(W_t, \beta)) .$$

Now

$$\nabla_{\alpha\beta} L_{2n}(X^n, \alpha, \beta)$$

$$= n^{-1} \sum_{t=1}^{n} \nabla'_\alpha [\nabla_\beta \mu_t(W_t, \beta) \nabla_\mu c_t(\mu_t(W_t, \beta), \kappa_t(W_t, \alpha))]$$

$$\times (Y_t - \mu_t(W_t, \beta)) .$$

When $\mathcal{M}$ is correctly specified for $\{E(Y_t \mid W_t)\}$, we have that $\hat{\beta}_n \rightarrow \beta_o$ $prob - P_o$ regardless of $\{\alpha_n^*\}$, so that

$$\nabla_{\alpha\beta} \bar{L}_{2n}(\theta_n^*) = E(\nabla_{\alpha\beta} L_{2n}(X^n, \alpha_n^*, \beta_o))$$

$$= n^{-1} \sum_{t=1}^{n} E(\nabla'_\alpha [\nabla_\beta \mu_t(W_t, \beta_o) \nabla_\mu c_t(\mu_t(W_t, \beta_o), \kappa_t(W_t, \alpha_n^*))]$$

$$\times (Y_t - \mu_t(W_t, \beta_o)))$$

$$= n^{-1} \sum_{t=1}^{n} E(\nabla'_\alpha [\nabla_\beta \mu_t(W_t, \beta_o) \nabla_\mu c_t(\mu_t(W_t, \beta_o), \kappa_t(W_t, \alpha_n^*))]$$

$$\times E(Y_t - \mu_t(W_t, \beta_o) \mid W_t))$$

$$= 0 .$$

Thus, because of block diagonality, Theorem 6.12 gives

$$\text{avar } \hat{\beta}_n = A_{22n}^{*-1} B_{22n}^* A_{22n}^{*-1} ,$$

where

$$A_{22n}^* = - n^{-1} \sum_{t=1}^{n} E(\nabla_\beta \mu_t^o D_t^{*-1} \nabla'_\beta \mu_t^o)$$

analogous to Theorem 6.9, where

$$D_t^* \equiv D_t(\mu_t(W_t, \beta_o), \kappa_t(W_t, \alpha_n^*))$$

and

$$B_{22n}^* = n^{-1} \sum_{t=1}^{n} E(\nabla_\beta \mu_t^o D_t^{*-1} \Sigma_t^o D_t^{*-1} \nabla'_\beta \mu_t^o)$$

with Σ_t^o defined as before. If we have that $D_t^* = \Sigma_t^o$, then it follows that

$$A_{22n}^o = - B_{22n}^o ,$$

where A_{22n}^o denotes A_{22n}^* with $(\alpha_n^{*\prime}, \beta_o')'$ replacing θ_n^* and B_{22n}^o defined similarly. As we saw above, this can be guaranteed by proper choice of κ_t, given that one is able to correctly specify a model for Σ_t^o.

This discussion can be formally summarized in the following way.

THEOREM 6.13: *Given Assumptions 2.1, 5.1, 6.4, 6.7 and 6.8, suppose that for all* θ *in* $\Theta \equiv \mathcal{A} \times \mathcal{B}$, $P_o\, [\mu_t\,(W_t\,,\beta) \in int\, \mathbb{M}_t\,,\ \kappa_t\,(W_t\,,\alpha) \in int\, \mathbb{K}_t] = 1\ , t = 1, 2, \ldots.$

(i) If $\mathcal{M}$ *is correct for* $\{E(Y_t \mid W_t)\}$ *on* Θ, *then* $\beta_n^* = \beta_o$ *and*

$$A_{22n}^* = -\, n^{-1} \sum_{t=1}^{n} E(\nabla_\beta\, \mu_t^o\, D_t^{*\,-1}\, \nabla'_\beta\, \mu_t^o\,),\ n = 1, 2, \ldots,$$

where for arbitrary α_n^*

$$D_t^* \equiv D_t(\,\mu_t(W_t\,,\beta_o)\,,\ \kappa_t(W_t\,,\alpha_n^*\,))\ .$$

(ii) If in addition there is no dynamic misspecification, then $\{\nabla_\beta \log f_t(X^t\,,\alpha_n^*\,,\beta_o)\,,\ \tilde{\mathcal{F}}^t\}$ *is a martingale difference sequence, and*

$$B_{22n}^* = n^{-1} \sum_{t=1}^{n} E(\nabla_\beta\, \mu_t^o\, D_t^{*\,-1}\, \Sigma_t^o\, D_t^{*\,-1}\, \nabla'_\beta\, \mu_t^o\,)\ .$$

(iii) If κ_t *and* $\alpha_n^* = \alpha_o$ *are such that* $\Sigma_t^o = D_t^o$, *then* $\{\nabla' s_t^o + s_t^o\, s_t^{o\prime}\ ,\ \tilde{\mathcal{F}}^t\}$ *is a martingale difference sequence,* $A_{22n}^* = A_{22n}^o\,,\ B_{22n}^* = B_{22n}^o$ *and*

$$A_{22n}^o = -\, B_{22n}^o\ .$$

(iv) Given the conditions at the outset and those of (i) and (ii), suppose that Assumption 6.6 holds for $\hat{\alpha}_n$ *with* α_n^* *arbitrary, Assumptions 3.1, 3.7(a), 3.8, and 3.9 hold for* $\{f_{2t}\}$, *Assumption 3.2′ holds for* $\{L_{2n}(X^n\,,\alpha_n^*\,,\beta\,)\}$ *and Assumption 6.1 holds for* $\{n^{-1/2}\, \nabla_\beta \log f_{2t}\,(X^t\,,\alpha_n^*\,,\beta_o)\}$. *Then*

$$\sqrt{n}(\hat{\beta}_n - \beta_o\,) = -\, A_{22n}^{*\,-1}\, \sqrt{n}\, \nabla_\beta\, L_{2n}(X^n\,,\alpha_n^*\,,\beta_o) + o_{P_o}(1)$$

and

$$B_{22n}^{*-1/2}\, A_{22n}^*\, \sqrt{n}(\hat{\beta}_n - \beta_o\,) \overset{A}{\sim} N(0\,, I_p)\,,$$

with A_{22n}^* *and* B_{22n}^* *as given above.*

(v) If κ_t *and* $\alpha_n^* = \alpha_o$ *are such that* $\Sigma_t^o = D_t^o$, *then*

$$\text{avar}\ \hat{\beta}_n = -\, A_{22n}^{o\,-1} = B_{22n}^{o\,-1}\ . \qquad \square$$

From (i) and (ii) it follows that linear exponential QMLE's have the same asymptotic distributions as specific nonlinear weighted least squares estimators, a result obtained in a non-dynamic setting by Charnes, Frome and Yu [1976]. (Indeed these estimators are asymptotically equivalent.) This result also establishes properties in a dynamic context for the "Quasi-Generalized Pseudo-Maximum likelihood estimator" (QGPMLE) proposed by Gourieroux, Monfort and Trognon [1984]. The essential feature of the present result is that by properly choosing the nuisance parameters, it is in principle possible to guarantee the validity of the information matrix equality with all that this subsequently implies for efficiency, inference, and specification testing. Essentially, this entails correctly specifying models for the conditional mean as well as the conditional variance of the dependent variables.

This version of the result for the QGPMLE provides a rigorous justification for time series versions of such estimators as Zellner's seemingly unrelated regressions estimator (SURE) (Zellner [1962]) and three stage least squares (3SLS) (Zellner and Theil [1962]), as well as for particular two stage ARCH estimators (Engle [1982a]). It also extends the validity of an estimator based on the gamma distribution proposed by Gourieroux, Monfort and Trognon [1984] to the dynamic context.

An interesting feature of the present result is that when κ_t and $\alpha_n^* = \alpha_o$ are such that the information matrix equality holds, then avar $\hat{\beta}_n$ does not depend on which member of the linear exponential family is used to obtain the estimator, as it depends only on $\nabla_\beta \mu_t^o$ and Σ_t^o. For example, the probit estimator arises from models based on the assumption that

$$Y_t \mid \tilde{\mathcal{F}}^{t-1} \sim B(\mu_t(W_t, \beta) = \Phi(W_t' \beta)),$$

where $B(p)$ is the Bernoulli distribution with parameter p and Φ is the unit cumulative normal distribution function. The Bernoulli distribution is a member of the linear exponential family, and the foregoing theory establishes that the probit estimator $\hat{\beta}_n$ obtained by maximizing

$$L_n(X^n, \beta) \equiv n^{-1} \sum_{t=1}^{n} (1 - Y_t) \log [1 - \Phi(W'_t \beta)] + Y_t \log [\Phi(W'_t \beta)]$$

has

$$\text{avar } \hat{\beta}_n = [\, n^{-1} \sum_{t=1}^{n} E(\phi(W'_t \beta_o)^2 W_t \Sigma_t^{o\,-1} W'_t)\,]^{-1},$$

where ϕ in this context represents the unit normal density function and

$\Sigma_t^{o\,-1} = [\Phi(W'_t\,\beta_o)\,(1 - \Phi(W'_t\,\beta_o))]^{-1}$.

Alternatively, a two step estimator with identical asymptotic variance can be constructed in the following way. First, obtain $\hat{\alpha}_n$ by solving the problem

$$\max_{\alpha \in \mathcal{A}} \; L_{1n}(X^n, \alpha) \equiv -n^{-1} \sum_{t=1}^{n} [Y_t - \Phi(W'_t\,\alpha)]^2 .$$

This yields $\hat{\alpha}_n$ such that $\hat{\alpha}_n \to \beta_o$ $prob - P_o$, provided $\beta_o \in \mathcal{A}$. Second, obtain $\tilde{\beta}_n$ by solving the nonlinear weighted least squares problem

$$\max_{\beta \in \mathcal{B}} \; L_{2n}(X^n, \hat{\alpha}_n, \beta)$$

$$\equiv -n^{-1} \sum_{t=1}^{n} [Y_t - \Phi(W'_t\,\beta)]^2\,[\Phi(W'_t\,\hat{\alpha}_n)\,(1 - \Phi(W'_t\,\hat{\alpha}_n))]^{-1} .$$

This QMLE is based on a choice for ψ_t satisfying Assumption 6.7, and with proper regularity conditions, Theorem 6.13 implies that

$$\text{avar}\;\tilde{\beta}_n = [\,n^{-1} \sum_{t=1}^{n} E(\phi(W'_t\,\beta_o)^2\,W_t\,\Sigma_t^{o\,-1} W'_t\,)\,]^{-1} ,$$

which is identical to that for the probit estimator. For further discussion see Gourieroux, Monfort and Trognon [1984].

6.4 Summary

In this chapter, we see that under some regularity conditions, the QMLE is distributed asymptotically as normal, despite the possible presence of misspecification. However, both the centering and scaling used in obtaining the asymptotic normality result are affected by misspecification. Centering is affected, because one must center around θ_n^*; scaling is affected because the form of the asymptotic covariance matrix is determined by the extent of the misspecification.

In the complete absence of misspecification, we have the information matrix equality holding. The presence of dynamic misspecification invalidates the information matrix equality, as does the presence of neglected heterogeneity. These results also hold for 2SQMLE's obtained from the linear exponential family.

MATHEMATICAL APPENDIX

PROOF OF THEOREM 6.2: We first consider the properties of the sequence $\{\sqrt{n}(\hat{\theta}_n - \theta_n^*)\}$. Let $\{n'\}$ index an arbitrary subsequence $\{\sqrt{n'}(\hat{\theta}_{n'} - \theta_{n'}^*)\}$. Let $F_1 \in \mathcal{F}$ be the set with $P(F_1) = 1$ on which $\hat{\theta}_n(\omega) = \text{argmax}_\Theta Q_n(\omega, \theta)$ and $Q_n(\omega, \cdot)$ is continuously differentiable of order 2 on Θ, $n = 1, 2, \ldots$. For $\omega \notin F_1$, define $\nabla Q_n(\omega, \theta) \equiv 0$, $\nabla^2 Q_n(\omega, \theta) \equiv 0$ for all $\theta \in \Theta$.

By assumption, $\hat{\theta}_n - \theta_n^* \longrightarrow 0$ *prob* $- P$ and $\nabla^2 Q_n(\cdot, \theta) - A_n(\theta) \longrightarrow 0$ *prob* $- P$ uniformly on Θ. By the subsequence theorem, the arbitrary subsequence $\{\hat{\theta}_{n'} - \theta_{n'}^*, \nabla^2 Q_{n'}(\cdot, \theta) - A_{n'}(\theta)\}$ contains a further subsequence, say $\{\hat{\theta}_{n''} - \theta_{n''}^*, \nabla^2 Q_{n''}(\cdot, \theta) - A_{n''}(\theta)\}$ converging almost surely to zero (uniformly on Θ). Let $F_2 \in \mathcal{F}$ be the set with $P(F_2) = 1$ for which this convergence occurs. Define $F = F_1 \cap F_2$ so that $P(F) = 1$.

Because $\{\theta_n^*\}$ is interior to Θ uniformly in n, there exists $\varepsilon > 0$ such that $\bar{\eta}_n(\varepsilon) \equiv \{\theta \in \mathbb{R}^p : |\theta - \theta_n^*| \leq \varepsilon/2\}$ is interior to Θ $a.a.n$. By construction, $\bar{\eta}_n(\varepsilon)$ is a compact convex set; further $\hat{\theta}_{n''}(\omega) \in \bar{\eta}_{n''}(\varepsilon)$ $a.a.n''$ for $\omega \in F$ by consistency. For ω in F, $\hat{\theta}_{n''}$ maximizes $Q_{n''}$ interior to Θ $a.a.n''$ so that

$$\nabla Q_{n''}(\omega, \hat{\theta}_{n''}(\omega)) = 0 \qquad a.a.\ n''.$$

By the mean value theorem of Jennrich [1969, Lemma 3] there exist measurable functions $\ddot{\theta}_{n''}^i : \Omega \rightarrow \bar{\eta}_{n''}(\varepsilon)$, $i = 1, \ldots, p$ lying on the segment connecting $\hat{\theta}_{n''}$ and $\theta_{n''}^*$ such that

$$\nabla \hat{Q}_{n''} = \nabla Q_{n''}^* + \nabla^2 \ddot{Q}_{n''} (\hat{\theta}_{n''} - \theta_{n''}^*) \qquad a.a.\ n'',$$

where $\nabla^2 \ddot{Q}_{n''}$ is the $p \times p$ Hessian matrix $\nabla^2 Q_{n''}(\omega, \theta)$ with i th row evaluated at $\ddot{\theta}_{n''}^i$. Because $\nabla \hat{Q}_{n''} = 0$ $a.a.\ n''$, we have

$$\nabla^2 \ddot{Q}_{n''}(\hat{\theta}_{n''} - \theta_{n''}^*) = -\nabla Q_{n''}^* \ a.a.\ n''.$$

The uniform convergence of $\nabla^2 Q_{n''}(\omega, \theta) - A_{n''}(\theta)$ and the convergence of $\ddot{\theta}_{n''}^i - \theta_{n''}^*$ to zero on F together imply by Corollary 3.8 and Proposition 2.16 of White [1984a] that for $a.a.n''$ $|\det \nabla^2 \ddot{Q}_{n''} - \det A_{n''}^*| < \delta/2$, so that $|\det \nabla^2 \ddot{Q}_{n''}| > \delta/2$ $a.a.n$ and $\nabla^2 \ddot{Q}_{n''}$ is nonsingular $a.a.\ n''$.

Therefore, on F

$$\hat{\theta}_{n''} - \theta^*_{n''} = - \nabla^2 \ddot{Q}^{-1}_{n''} \nabla Q^*_{n''} \qquad a.a.\ n'' .$$

Multiplying by $\sqrt{n''}$ and adding and subtracting appropriately gives, for ω in F

$$\sqrt{n''}(\hat{\theta}_{n''} - \theta^*_{n''}) = - A^{*-1}_{n''} \sqrt{n''} \nabla Q^*_{n''}$$
$$+ (A^{*-1}_{n''} - \nabla^2 \ddot{Q}^{-1}_{n''}) B^{*1/2}_{n''} B^{*-1/2}_{n''} \sqrt{n''} \nabla Q^*_{n''} \qquad a.a.\ n'' .$$

Now $B^{*-1/2}_n \sqrt{n} \nabla Q^*_n$ and therefore $B^{*-1/2}_{n''} \sqrt{n''} \nabla Q^*_{n''}$ converges in distribution and is therefore $O_P(1)$, while

$$(A^{*-1}_{n''} - \nabla^2 \ddot{Q}^{-1}_{n''}) B^{*1/2}_{n''} = o_P(1)$$

given $B^*_n = O(1)$ and $A^*_{n''} - \nabla^2 \ddot{Q}_{n''} \to 0\ a.s.-P$ It follows that $(A^{*-1}_{n''} - \nabla^2 \ddot{Q}^{-1}_{n''}) \sqrt{n''} \nabla Q^*_{n''} = o_P(1)$.

Applying the subsequence theorem to the subsequence indexed by $\{n''\}$, it follows that there exists a further subsequence indexed by $\{n'''\}$ such that

$$(A^{*-1}_{n'''} - \nabla^2 \ddot{Q}^{-1}_{n'''}) \sqrt{n'''} \nabla Q^*_{n'''} \longrightarrow 0 \qquad a.s.-P .$$

Therefore

$$\sqrt{n'''}(\hat{\theta}_{n'''} - \theta^*_{n'''} + A^{*-1}_{n'''} \sqrt{n'''} \nabla Q^*_{n'''}) \longrightarrow 0 \qquad a.s.-P .$$

Because this is true for an arbitrary subsequence $\{n'\}$, it therefore follows from the subsequence theorem that

$$\sqrt{n}(\hat{\theta}_n - \theta^*_n) = - A^{*-1}_n \sqrt{n} \nabla Q^*_n + o_P(1) .$$

Because $\{B^{*-1/2}_n A^*_n\}$ is $O(1)$ given the conditions imposed on $\{B^*_n\}$ and $\{A^*_n\}$, it follows that

$$B^{*-1/2}_n A^*_n \sqrt{n} (\hat{\theta}_n - \theta^*_n) = - B^{*-1/2}_n \sqrt{n} \nabla Q^*_n + o_P(1) .$$

Because $B^{*-1/2}_n \sqrt{n} \nabla Q^*_n \overset{A}{\sim} N(0, I_p)$, it follows by the Asymptotic

Equivalence Lemma (White [1984a, Lemma 4.7]) that

$$B_n^{*-1/2} A_n^* \sqrt{n}(\hat{\theta}_n - \theta_n^*) \overset{A}{\sim} N(0, I_p) . \qquad \square$$

PROOF OF THEOREM 6.4: We verify the conditions of Theorem 6.2. By Assumption 2.1, $(\Omega, \mathcal{F}, P_o)$ has the required properties, while Assumptions 2.3 and 3.6 ensure that

$$Q_n(\omega, \theta) = L_n(X^n(\omega), \theta) = n^{-1} \sum_{t=1}^{n} \log f_t(X^t(\omega), \theta)$$

satisfies the required measurability and differentiability requirements. Theorem 2.12 ensures that $\hat{\theta}_n(X^n) = \text{argmax}_\Theta \ L_n(X^n, \theta) \ a.s.-P_o$ is measurable, given Assumptions 2.1 and 2.3, and Theorem 3.5 ensures that $\hat{\theta}_n - \theta_n^* \longrightarrow 0 \ prob - P_o$ given Assumptions 2.1, 2.3, 3.1 and 3.2′, with θ_n^* interior to Θ uniformly in n given Assumption 3.2′.

Assumption 6.1 ensures that

$$B_n^{*-1/2} n^{-1/2} \sum_{t=1}^{n} [s_t^* - E(s_t^*)] \overset{A}{\sim} N(0, I_p) ,$$

where $\{B_n^* \equiv \text{var}\,(n^{-1/2} \Sigma_{t=1}^n s_t^*)\}$ is $O(1)$ and uniformly positive definite. Now

$$B_n^{*-1/2} n^{-1/2} \sum_{t=1}^{n} E(s_t^*) = B_n^{*-1/2} n^{1/2} E(\nabla L_n(X^n, \theta_n^*))$$
$$= B_n^{*-1/2} n^{1/2} \nabla \bar{L}_n^* ,$$

given Assumption 3.7(a). Because θ_n^* minimizes $\bar{L}_n(\theta)$ interior to Θ, we have $\nabla \bar{L}_n^* = 0$. Therefore

$$B_n^{*-1/2} \sqrt{n} \nabla L_n^* = B_n^{*-1/2} n^{-1/2} \sum_{t=1}^{n} s_t^* \overset{A}{\sim} N(0, I_p) .$$

Given Assumption 3.8, we have that

$$\nabla^2 L_n(X^n, \theta) - \nabla^2 \bar{L}_n(\theta) \longrightarrow 0 \quad prob - P_o \quad \text{as } n \longrightarrow \infty$$

uniformly on Θ, so that $\nabla^2 \bar{L}_n(\theta)$ corresponds to $A_n(\theta)$. Assumption 3.9 ensures that $\{A_n^* \equiv \nabla^2 \bar{L}_n(\theta_n^*)\}$ is $O(1)$ and uniformly negative definite.

Thus, the conditions of Theorem 6.2 hold, implying that

$$\sqrt{n}(\hat{\theta}_n - \theta_n^*) = - A_n^{*-1} \sqrt{n}\, \nabla L_n^* + o_{P_o}(1)$$

and that

$$B_n^{*-1/2} A_n^* \sqrt{n}(\hat{\theta}_n - \theta_n^*) \overset{A}{\sim} N(0, I_p) . \qquad \square$$

PROOF OF THEOREM 6.5: The proof of the first result is given in the text. The second result follows immediately from Theorem 6.4, with $\theta_n^* = \theta_o$ for all $n = 1, 2, \ldots$. □

PROOF OF THEOREM 6.6: The proof of the first result is given in the text. The second result follows immediately from Theorem 6.4, with $\theta_n^* = \theta_o$ for all $n = 1, 2, \ldots$. □

PROOF OF LEMMA 6.7: (i) Letting $d_t(y, \mu) = \exp \phi_t(y, \mu)$ we have

$$\int d_t(y, \mu)\, d\, \zeta_t(y) = 1$$

so that

$$\nabla_\mu \int d_t(y, \mu)\, d\, \zeta_t(y) = 0 .$$

Consequently, it suffices to show that

$$\nabla_\mu \int d_t(y, \mu)\, d\, \zeta_t(y) = \int \nabla_\mu\, d_t(y, \mu)\, d\, \zeta_t(y)$$

because if so, we have

$$\begin{aligned}\int \nabla_\mu\, d_t(y, \mu)\, d\, \zeta_t(y) &= \int (\nabla_\mu\, a_t(\mu) + [\nabla_\mu\, c_t(\mu)]\, y)\, d_t(y, \mu)\, d\, \zeta_t(y) \\ &= 0\end{aligned}$$

and Assumption 5.3′ immediately implies

$$\nabla_\mu\, a_t(\mu) + [\nabla_\mu\, c_t(\mu)]\,\mu = 0\,,$$

establishing the desired result.

To show that

$$\nabla_\mu \int d_t(y\,,\mu)\, d\,\zeta_t(y) = \int \nabla_\mu\, d_t(y\,,\mu)\, d\,\zeta_t(y)$$

we use a vector generalization of Theorem 16.8(ii) of Billingsley [1979].

By Assumption 5.3′, $d_t(y\,,\mu)$ is a measurable function of y for each μ in $\mathbb{M}_t$, and for each y in $\mathbb{R}^l$, $d_t(y\,,\mu)$ has gradient $\nabla_\mu\, d_t(y\,,\mu)$ on *int* $\mathbb{M}_t$. The result follows by showing that for each $\mu_o \in$ *int* $\mathbb{M}_t$, there exist integrable dominating functions $D_{ti}(y\,,\mu_o) \geq |\partial d_t(y\,,\mu)/\partial\mu_i|$ for all μ in some open neighborhood of μ_o, $i = 1, \ldots, l$.

Thus, consider the neighborhood $\mathbb{M}_o(\varepsilon) \equiv \{\, \mu \in \mathbb{R}^l : |\mu - \mu_o| < \varepsilon\}$. For μ_o in *int* $\mathbb{M}_t$, there exists $\varepsilon > 0$ sufficiently small that $\mathbb{M}_o(\varepsilon) \subset \mathbb{M}_t$. The compact neighborhood $\bar{\mathbb{M}}_o(\varepsilon/2) = \{\, \mu \in \mathbb{R}^l : |\mu - \mu_o| \leq \varepsilon/2\}$ also lies in $\mathbb{M}_t$. We show that $\partial d_t(y\,,\mu)/\partial\mu_i$ is dominated on this neighborhood and therefore on $\mathbb{M}_o(\varepsilon/2)$ by an integrable function. Now

$$\begin{aligned} &|\partial d_t(y\,,\mu)/\partial\mu_i| \\ &\quad = |\partial a_t(\mu)/\partial\mu_i + \sum_{j=1}^{l} y_j \partial\, c_{tj}(\mu)/\partial\mu_i|\, d_t(y\,,\mu) \\ &\quad \leq [\,|\partial a_t(\mu)/\partial\mu_i| + \sum_{j=1}^{l} |y_j|\, |\partial c_{tj}(\mu)/\partial\mu_i|\,]\, d_t(y\,,\mu)\,. \end{aligned}$$

Because $|\partial a_t(\mu)/\partial\mu_i|$ and $|\partial c_{tj}(\mu)/\partial\mu_i|$, $j = 1, \ldots, l$ are finite continuous functions on the compact neighborhood $\bar{\mathbb{M}}_o(\varepsilon/2)$, they attain a finite maximum on $\bar{\mathbb{M}}_o(\varepsilon/2)$, implying the existence of $\Delta < \infty$ such that $|\partial a_t(\mu)/\partial\mu_i| \leq \Delta$, $|\partial c_{tj}(\mu)/\partial\mu_i| \leq \Delta$ for all μ in $\bar{\mathbb{M}}_o(\varepsilon/2)$. Therefore for all such μ

$$|\partial d_t(y\,,\mu)/\partial\mu_i| \leq (\Delta + \Delta \sum_{j=1}^{l} |y_j|)\, d_t(y\,,\mu)\,.$$

As shown in the proof of Corollary 5.5, for all $\mu\,,\mu_o$ in $\mathbb{M}_t \times \mathbb{M}_t$

$$a_t(\mu) + \mu'_o\, c_t(\mu) \leq a_t(\mu_o) + \mu'_o\, c_t(\mu_o)\,.$$

Therefore for all μ in $\bar{\mathbb{M}}_o(\varepsilon/2)$

$$d_t(y\,,\mu) = \exp\,[a_t(\mu) + b_t(y) + y' c_t(\mu)]$$

$$= \exp\,[a_t(\mu) + b_t(y) + \mu'_o c_t(\mu)]\, \exp\,[(y-\mu_o)'\, c_t(\mu)]$$

$$\le \exp\,[a_t(\mu_o) + b_t(y) + \mu'_o\, c_t(\mu_o)]\, \exp\,[(y-\mu_o)'\, c_t(\mu)]$$

$$= \exp\,[a_t(\mu_o) + b_t(y) + y'\, c_t(\mu_o)]\, \exp\,[(y-\mu_o)'\,(c_t(\mu) - c_t(\mu_o))]$$

$$= d_t(y\,,\mu_o)\, \exp\,[y'(c_t(\mu) - c_t(\mu_o))]\, \exp\,[-\,\mu'_o\,(c_t(\mu) - c_t(\mu_o))]\ .$$

Because $\exp\,[-\,\mu'_o\,(c_t(\mu) - c_t(\mu_o))]$ is a continuous function of μ on the compact set $\bar{M}_o(\varepsilon/2)$, we can choose Δ so that $\exp\,[-\,\mu'_o\ (c_t(\mu) - c_t(\mu_o))] < \Delta$. Further

$$\exp\,[y'\,(c_t(\mu) - c_t(\mu_o))] = \exp\,[\ \sum_{j=1}^{l}\ y_j\,(c_{tj}(\mu) - c_{tj}(\mu_o))]$$

$$\le \exp\,[\ \sum_{j=1}^{l}\ |y_j|\,|c_{tj}(\mu) - c_{tj}(\mu_o)|]\ .$$

Because $|c_{tj}(\mu) - c_{tj}(\mu_o)|$, $j = 1, \ldots, l$ are continuous in μ on $\bar{M}_o(\varepsilon/2)$, we can choose Δ so that $|c_{tj}(\mu) - c_{tj}(\mu_o)| < \Delta$ for all $\mu \in \bar{M}_o(\varepsilon/2)$, $j = 1\,, \ldots, l$. Collecting these inequalities gives

$$|\partial d_t(y\,,\mu)/\partial \mu_i| \le (\Delta + \Delta \sum_{j=1}^{l} |y_j|)\ \Delta\ (\exp \Delta \sum_{j=1}^{l} |y_j|)\ d_t(y\,,\mu_o)$$

$$= \Delta^2 \exp\,(\Delta \sum_{j=1}^{l} |y_j|)\ d_t(y\,,\mu_o)$$

$$+\,\Delta^2 \sum_{j=1}^{l} |y_j| \exp\,(\Delta \sum_{j=1}^{l} |y_j|)\ d_t(y\,,\mu_o)$$

$$\equiv D_{ti}(y\,,\mu_o)\ .$$

Observe that Δ can be chosen to ensure that the same dominating function is valid for all $i = 1, \ldots, l$. The result follows by showing that $D_{ti}(y\,,\mu_o)$ is integrable. Now

$$\int D_{ti}(y\,,\mu_o)\ d\,\zeta_t(y)$$

$$= \Delta^2 \int \exp\,(\Delta \sum_{j=1}^{l} |y_j|)\ d_t(y\,,\mu_o)\ d\,\zeta_t(y)$$

$$+\,\Delta^2 \int \sum_{j=1}^{l} |y_j| \exp\,(\Delta \sum_{j=1}^{l} |y_j|)\ d_t(y\,,\mu_o)\ d\,\zeta_t(y)$$

$$= \Delta^2 \int_0^\infty \exp(\Delta\tau)\, d\, F(\tau) + \Delta^2 \int_0^\infty \tau \exp(\Delta\,\tau)\, d\, F(\tau)\,,$$

where $F(\tau)$ is the cumulative distribution function of the random variable $T \equiv \Sigma_{j=1}^{l} |Y_j|$, when the joint distribution of $Y = (Y_1, \ldots, Y_j)$ has density $d_t(y, \mu_o)$ with respect to ζ_t. The first term is the Laplace Transform of $F(\tau)$, $\int_0^\infty \exp(-s\tau)\, d\, F(\tau)$, evaluated at $s = -\Delta$. It follows from Corollary 2.1 of Widder [1946, p. 39] that this integral converges (is finite), as it converges for all s in the complex plane. Further, the Laplace transform is analytic (Theorem 5a of Widder [1946, p. 57]) so that

$$-\int_0^\infty \tau \exp[-s\tau]\, d\, F(\tau)$$

converges for all s in the complex plane, and in particular at $s = -\Delta$. Therefore

$$\int D_{ti}(y, \mu_o)\, d\, \zeta_t(y) < \infty\,,$$

and the proof is complete.

(ii) For this result, it suffices to show that

$$\nabla_\mu^2 \int d_t(y, \mu)\, d\, \zeta_t(y) = \int \nabla_\mu^2\, d_t(y, \mu)\, d\, \zeta_t(y)\,,$$

because if so,

$$\int \nabla_\mu^2\, d_t(y, \mu)\, d\, \zeta_t(y) = 0\,.$$

Suppose for the moment that this is so. Given that $\nabla_\mu\, a_t = -\nabla_\mu\, c_t(\mu)\mu$ as established in (i) and writing the Jacobian of a matrix function $\phi(\mu)$ as $\nabla'_\mu \phi(\mu)$ we have

$$\begin{aligned}
\nabla_\mu^2\, d_t(y, \mu) &= \nabla'_\mu(\nabla_\mu\, d_t(y, \mu)) \\
&= \nabla'_\mu\, [\nabla_\mu\, c_t(\mu)\, (y - \mu)\, d_t(y, \mu)] \\
&= \nabla'_\mu\, [\nabla_\mu\, c_t(\mu)\, (y - \mu)\,]\, d_t(y, \mu) + \nabla_\mu\, c_t(\mu)\, (y - \mu)\, \nabla'_\mu\, d_t(y, \mu) \\
&= [(y - \mu)' \otimes I_l]\, \nabla'_\mu(\nabla_\mu\, c_t(\mu))\, d_t(y, \mu) - \nabla_\mu\, c_t(\mu)\, d_t(y, \mu)
\end{aligned}$$

$$+ \nabla_\mu c_t(\mu)\,(y-\mu)\,(y-\mu)'\,\nabla'_\mu c_t(\mu)\, d_t(y,\mu)\,.$$

Therefore

$$\begin{aligned}\int \nabla^2_\mu d_t(y,\mu)\, d\,\eta_t(y) &= -\nabla_\mu c_t(\mu) + \nabla_\mu c_t(\mu)\, D_t(\mu)\, \nabla'_\mu c_t(\mu)\\ &= 0\,.\end{aligned}$$

The requirement that c_t be one-to-one on $I\!M_t$ and the differentiability of c_t imply that $\nabla_\mu c_t(\mu)$ is nonsingular for all μ in *int* $I\!M_t$. Therefore

$$\nabla_\mu c_t(\mu)\, D_t(\mu)\, \nabla'_\mu\; c_t(\mu) = \nabla_\mu c_t(\mu)$$

implies

$$D_t(\mu)\, \nabla'_\mu c_t(\mu) = I_l$$

or

$$\nabla'_\mu c_t(\mu) = D_t(\mu)^{-1}\,,$$

as desired. The symmetry of $D_t(\mu)$ implies that of $\nabla_\mu c_t(\mu)$.

The proof that

$$\nabla^2_\mu \int d_t(y,\mu)\, d\,\zeta_t(y) = \int \nabla^2_\mu d_t(y,\mu)\, d\,\zeta_t(y)$$

is obtained by writing

$$\begin{aligned}\nabla^2_\mu \int d_t(y,\mu)\, d\zeta_t(y) &= \nabla'_\mu[\nabla_\mu \int d_t(y,\mu)\, d\zeta_t(y)]\\ &= \nabla'_\mu \int \nabla_\mu d_t(y,\mu)\, d\,\zeta_t(y)\end{aligned}$$

and using arguments similar to those in (i) to establish that

$$\nabla'_\mu \int \nabla_\mu d_t(y,\mu)\, d\,\zeta_t(y) = \int \nabla^2_\mu d_t(y,\mu)\, d\zeta_t(y)\,.$$

We omit the tedious details. □

PROOF OF THEOREM 6.9: The proof of the result for $\{s_t^o, \tilde{\mathcal{F}}^t\}$ and B_n^o is given in the text. The results for A_n^o and $\{\nabla' s_t^o + s_t^o\, s_t^{o\prime}, \tilde{\mathcal{F}}^t\}$ follow from differentiation with respect to θ of

$$\underset{p\times 1}{s_t(x^t, \theta)} = \underset{p\times l}{\nabla_\theta\, \mu_t(v_t, \theta)}\ \underset{l\times l}{\nabla_\mu\, c_t(\mu_t(w_t, \theta))}\ \underset{l\times 1}{(y_t - \mu_t(w_t, \theta))}\,.$$

Tedious but straightforward algebra yields

$$\underset{p\times p}{\nabla'_\theta\, s_t} = \underset{p\times lp}{[u'_t\, \nabla_\mu\, c_t \otimes I_p]}\ \underset{lp\times p}{\nabla_\theta^2\, \mu_t}$$

$$+ \underset{p\times l^2}{[u'_t \otimes \nabla_\theta\, \mu_t]}\ \underset{l^2\times l}{\nabla_\mu^2\, c_t}\ \underset{l\times p}{\nabla'_\theta\, \mu_t} - \underset{p\times p}{\nabla_\theta\, \mu_t \nabla_\mu\, c_t\, \nabla'_\theta\, \mu_t}\,.$$

Because $E(u_t^o \mid W_t) = 0$, it follows that

$$E(\nabla'_\theta\, s_t^o \mid W_t) = -\nabla_\theta\, \mu_t^o\, \nabla_\mu\, c_t^o\, \nabla'_\theta\, \mu_t^o\,,$$

as all terms involving u_t^o vanish. Using Lemma 6.7 gives

$$A_n^o = n^{-1} \sum_{t=1}^{n} E(\nabla' s_t^o) = n^{-1} \sum_{t=1}^{n} E[E(\nabla'_\theta s_t^o \mid W_t)]$$
$$= -n^{-1} \sum_{t=1}^{n} E(\nabla_\theta\, \mu_t^o\, D_t^{o\,-1}\, \nabla'_\theta\, \mu_t^o)\,.$$

In the absence of dynamic misspecification,

$$E(\nabla'_\theta\, s_t^o + s_t^o\, s_t^{o\prime} \mid W_t) = E(\nabla'_\theta\, s_t^o + s_t^o\, s_t^{o\prime} \mid \tilde{X}^{t-1})$$
$$= -\nabla_\theta\, \mu_t^o\, D_t^{o\,-1}\, \nabla'_\theta\, \mu_t^o + \nabla_\theta\, \mu_t^o\, D_t^{o\,-1}\, \Sigma_t^o\, D_t^{o\,-1}\, \nabla'_\theta\, \mu_t^o\,.$$

When $\Sigma_t^o = D_t^o$, then the two terms above cancel, so that

$$E(\nabla'_\theta\, s_t^o + s_t^o\, s_t^{o\prime} \mid \tilde{X}^{t-1}) = 0 \qquad a.s.-P_o\,.$$

Because $\nabla'_\theta\, s_t^o + s_t^o\, s_t^{o\prime}$ is measurable–$\tilde{\mathcal{F}}^t$, it follows that $\{\nabla'_\theta\, s_t^o + s_t^o\, s_t^{o\prime}, \tilde{\mathcal{F}}^t\}$ is a martingale difference sequence. Furthermore, $E(\nabla'_\theta\, s_t^o) = -\, E(s_t^o\, s_t^{o\prime})$ implies

$$A_n^o = -\, B_n^o\ .$$

The final result follows immediately from Theorem 6.4. □

PROOF OF THEOREM 6.10: We use an argument similar to that of Theorem 6.2, and consider the properties of the sequence $\{\sqrt{n}(\hat{\theta}_n - \theta_n^*)\}$. Let $\{n'\}$ index an arbitrary subsequence of $\{n\}$. Let $F_1 \in \mathcal{F}$ be the set with $P(F_1) = 1$ on which $\psi_n(\omega, \cdot)$ is continuously differentiable on Θ, $n = 1, 2, \ldots$.

By assumption, $\hat{\theta}_n - \theta_n^* \longrightarrow 0\ prob - P$, $\sqrt{n}\ \psi_n(\cdot, \hat{\theta}_n) \longrightarrow 0\ prob - P$ and $\nabla'\ \psi_n(\cdot, \theta) - A_n(\theta) \longrightarrow 0\ prob - P$ uniformly on Θ. By the subsequence theorem, the arbitrary subsequence $\{\hat{\theta}_{n'} - \theta_{n'}^*, \sqrt{n'}\ \psi_{n'}(\cdot, \hat{\theta}_{n'}), \nabla'\ \psi_{n'}(\cdot, \theta) - A_{n'}(\theta)\}$ contains a further subsequence, say $\{\hat{\theta}_{n''} - \theta_{n''}^*, \sqrt{n''}\ \psi_{n''}(\cdot, \hat{\theta}_{n''}), \nabla'\ \psi_{n''}(\cdot, \theta) - A_{n''}(\theta)\}$ converging almost surely to zero (uniformly on Θ). Let $F_2 \in \mathcal{F}$ be the set with $P(F_2) = 1$ on which this convergence occurs. Define $F = F_1 \cap F_2$, so that $P(F) = 1$.

By the same argument as in Theorem 6.2 there exist compact convex neighborhoods $\bar{\eta}_n(\varepsilon)$ such that $\hat{\theta}_{n''}(\omega) \in \bar{\eta}_{n''}(\varepsilon)\ a.a.\ n''$ for $\omega \in F$. By the mean value theorem of Jennrich [1969, Lemma 3],

$$\sqrt{n''}\ \hat{\psi}_{n''} = \sqrt{n''}\ \psi_{n''}^* + \sqrt{n''}\ \nabla'\ \ddot{\psi}_{n''}(\hat{\theta}_{n''} - \theta_{n''}^*) \qquad a.a.\ n''\ ,$$

where $\hat{\psi}_n \equiv \psi_n(\omega, \hat{\theta}_n)$ and $\nabla'\ \ddot{\psi}_{n''}$ is the $p \times p$ Jacobian of $\psi_{n''}$ with ith row evaluated at $\ddot{\theta}_{n''}^i$. Rearranging yields

$$\nabla'\ \ddot{\psi}_{n''}\ \sqrt{n''}(\hat{\theta}_{n''} - \theta_{n''}^*) = -\ \sqrt{n''}\ \psi_{n''}^* + \sqrt{n''}\ \hat{\psi}_{n''} \qquad a.a.\ n''\ .$$

The uniform convergence of $\nabla'\ \psi_{n''}(\omega, \theta) - A_{n''}(\theta)$ and the convergence of $\ddot{\theta}_{n''}^i - \theta_{n''}^*$ to zero $a.s.-P$ (i.e. on F) imply by Corollary 3.8 and Proposition 2.16 of White [1984a] that for $a.a.\ n''$ $|\,det\ \nabla'\ \ddot{\psi}_{n''} - \det A_{n''}^*\,| < \delta/2$, so that $|\det \nabla'\ \ddot{\psi}_{n''}| > \delta/2\ a.a.\ n''$ and $\nabla'\ \ddot{\psi}_{n''}$ is therefore nonsingular $a.a.\ n''$. The fact that $\{A_n^*\}$ is $O(1)$ then implies that $\{\nabla'\ \ddot{\psi}_{n''}^{-1}\}$ is $O_{a.s.}(1)$. Therefore, for ω in F

$$\sqrt{n''}(\hat{\theta}_{n''} - \theta_{n''}^*) = -\ \nabla'\ \ddot{\psi}_{n''}^{-1}\ \sqrt{n''}\ \psi_{n''}^* + \nabla'\ \ddot{\psi}_{n''}^{-1}\ \sqrt{n''}\ \hat{\psi}_{n''}\ \ a.a.\ n''$$

$$= - A_{n''}^{*-1} \sqrt{n''}\, \psi_{n''}^{*} + \nabla' \ddot{\psi}_{n''}^{-1} \sqrt{n''}\, \hat{\psi}_{n''}$$
$$- (\nabla' \ddot{\psi}_{n''}^{-1} - A_{n''}^{*-1})\, B_{n''}^{*1/2} B_{n''}^{*-1/2} \sqrt{n''}\, \psi_{n''}^{*} \qquad a.a.\ n'' .$$

Because $\nabla' \ddot{\psi}_{n''}^{-1}$ is $O_{a.s.}(1)$ and $\sqrt{n''}\, \hat{\psi}_{n''}$ is $o_{a.s.}(1)$, the second term above vanishes almost surely, while the third term is $o_P(1)$, by the argument of Theorem 6.2. Applying the subsequence theorem to the subsequence indexed by $\{n''\}$, it follows that there exists a further subsequence indexed by $\{n'''\}$ such that

$$(\nabla' \ddot{\psi}_{n'''}^{-1} - A_{n'''}^{*-1})\sqrt{n'''}\, \psi_{n'''}^{*} \longrightarrow 0 \qquad a.s.-P .$$

Hence,

$$\sqrt{n'''}\, (\hat{\theta}_{n'''} - \theta_{n'''}^{*}) + A_{n'''}^{*-1} \sqrt{n'''}\, \psi_{n'''}^{*} \longrightarrow 0 \qquad a.s.-P.$$

Because this is true for an arbitrary subsequence $\{n'\}$ it follows from the subsequence theorem that

$$\sqrt{n}\, (\hat{\theta}_n - \theta_n^{*}) = - A_n^{*-1} \sqrt{n}\, \psi_n^{*} + o_P(1) .$$

The final result follows by argument identical to that of Theorem 6.2. □

PROOF OF THEOREM 6.11: We verify the conditions of Theorem 6.10 for $\psi_n(\omega, \theta) \equiv (\nabla_\alpha L_{1n}(X^n(\omega), \alpha)', \nabla_\beta L_{2n}(X^n(\omega), \alpha_n^{*}, \beta)')$.

Assumption 2.1 specifies that $(\Omega, \mathcal{F}, P_o)$ is a complete probability space, and $\Theta = \mathcal{A} \times \mathcal{B}$ is compact given Assumption 2.3. Assumptions 2.3 and 3.6 ensure that $\psi_n(\omega, \theta)$ is defined on $F \in \mathcal{F}$, $P_o(F) = 1$, and we extend ψ_n to be defined on Ω by setting $\psi_n(\omega, \theta) = 0$, $\nabla \psi_n(\omega, \theta) = 0$ for all $\theta \in \Theta, \omega \in F^c$. For each θ in Θ, $\psi_n(\cdot, \theta)$ is measurable-$\mathbb{F}$ given Assumptions 2.3 and 3.6. Assumption 3.6 also acts to ensure that $\nabla \psi_n(\omega, \cdot)$ is continuously differentiable on Θ. The Existence Theorems 2.11 and 2.12 ensure the measurability of $\hat{\theta}_n = (\hat{\alpha}'_n, \hat{\beta}'_n)'$ given Assumptions 2.1 and 2.3, and the Consistency Theorems 3.5 and 3.10 ensure that $\hat{\theta}_n - \theta_n^{*} \longrightarrow 0$ *prob* $- P_o$ under Assumptions 2.1, 2.3, 3.1 and 3.2′. Assumption 3.2′ guarantees that $\{\theta_n^{*\prime} = (\alpha_n^{*\prime}, \beta_n^{*\prime})\}$ is interior to Θ uniformly in n. We verify that $\sqrt{n}\, \hat{\psi}_n \longrightarrow 0$ *prob* $- P_o$ below.

Assumption 6.5 ensures that

$$B_n^{*-1/2} \sqrt{n}\, [\psi_n^{*} - E(\psi_n^{*})] \overset{A}{\sim} N(0, I_p) ,$$

while the interiority of α_n^* and β_n^* maximizing $\bar{L}_{1n}(\alpha)$ and $\bar{L}_{2n}(\alpha_n^*, \beta)$ respectively ensures that

$$(\nabla_\alpha \bar{L}_{1n}(\alpha_n^*)', \nabla_\beta \bar{L}_{2n}(\alpha_n^*, \beta_n^*)')$$
$$= E(\nabla_\alpha L_{1n}(\alpha_n^*)', \nabla_\beta L_{2n}(\alpha_n^*, \beta_n^*)') = E(\psi_n^{*\prime}) = 0 ,$$

where the first equality is ensured by Assumption 3.7(a). Thus

$$B_n^{*-1/2} \sqrt{n}\, \psi_n^* \overset{A}{\sim} N(0, I_p) .$$

Assumption 3.8 ensures that $\nabla' \psi_n(\cdot, \theta) - A_n(\theta) \longrightarrow 0$ $prob - P_o$ uniformly on Θ, where $A_n(\theta) \equiv E(\nabla' \psi_n(\cdot, \theta))$ is continuous on Θ uniformly in n. By Assumption 3.9 $\{A_n^*\}$ is $O(1)$. The uniform negative definiteness of A_n^* is implied by Assumption 3.9, as

$$\det A_n^* = \det A_{11n}^* \cdot \det A_{22n}^* < -\delta^2/4$$

for some $\delta > 0$ and all n sufficiently large.

It remains to verify that $\sqrt{n}\, \hat{\psi}_n \to 0$ $prob - P_o$. Now $\hat{\alpha}_n =$ argmax$_{\mathcal{A}}$ $L_{1n}(X^n, \alpha)$ $a.s.$ $-P_o$, while $\hat{\beta}_n =$ argmax$_{\mathcal{B}}$ $L_{2n}(X^n, \alpha_n^*, \beta)$ $a.s.-P_o$. Because α_n^* and β_n^* are interior to $\mathcal{A}$ and $\mathcal{B}$ respectively uniformly in n, argument identical to that in Theorem 6.2 establishes that for any arbitrary subsequence $\{\sqrt{n'}\, \hat{\psi}_{n'}\}$ there exists a further subsequence $\{\sqrt{n''}\, \hat{\psi}_{n''}\}$ such that $\sqrt{n''}\, \hat{\psi}_{n''} = 0$ $a.a.\ n''$, $a.s.-P_o$. It follows that $\sqrt{n}\, \hat{\psi}_n \to 0$ $prob - P_o$. Therefore the conditions of Theorem 6.10 hold implying that

$$\sqrt{n}(\hat{\theta}_n - \theta_n^*) = - A_n^{*-1} \sqrt{n}\, \psi_n^* + o_{P_o}(1)$$

and

$$B_n^{*-1/2} A_n^* \sqrt{n}(\hat{\theta}_n - \theta_n^*) \overset{A}{\sim} N(0, I_p) .$$

The specific form for A_n^* follows because by Assumption 3.8(a) $E(\nabla_{\alpha\alpha} L_{1n}(X^n, \alpha_n^*)) = \nabla_{\alpha\alpha} \bar{L}_{1n}(\alpha_n^*)$, $E(\nabla_{\alpha\beta} L_{2n}(X^n, \alpha_n^*, \beta_n^*)) = \nabla_{\alpha\beta} \bar{L}_{2n}(\theta_n^*)$ and $E(\nabla_{\beta\beta} L_{2n}(X^n, \alpha_n^*, \beta_n^*)) = \nabla_{\beta\beta} \bar{L}_{2n}(\theta_n^*)$. The expressions for avar $\hat{\alpha}_n$ and avar $\hat{B}_n$ follow by application of the formula for the partitioned inverse. □

PROOF OF THEOREM 6.12: We verify the conditions of Theorem 6.10 with $\Theta \equiv \mathcal{B}$, and with

$$\psi_n(\omega, \beta) \equiv \nabla_\beta L_{2n}(X^n(\omega), \alpha_n^*, \beta).$$

Straightforward modification of the argument for Theorem 6.11 establishes that all the required conditions are ensured by the assumptions given, with the exception of the condition that $\sqrt{n}\,\hat{\psi}_n = o_{P_o}(1)$. Now

$$\sqrt{n}\,\hat{\psi}_n \equiv \nabla_\beta L_{2n}(X^n, \alpha_n^*, \hat{\beta}_n).$$

Arguments similar to those in the proof of Theorem 6.2 establish that there exist convex compact neighborhoods $\bar{\eta}_n(\varepsilon) \equiv \{\theta \in I\!R^p : |\theta - \theta_n^*| \leq \varepsilon/2\}$ such that for any subsequence $\{\sqrt{n'}\,\hat{\psi}_{n'}\}$ of $\{\sqrt{n}\,\hat{\psi}_n\}$, the corresponding subsequence $\{\hat{\theta}_{n'} - \theta_{n'}^*, \nabla_{\alpha\beta} L_{2n'}(X^{n'}, \theta) - \nabla_{\alpha\beta} \bar{L}_{2n'}(\theta)\}$ contains a further subsequence $\{\hat{\theta}_{n''} - \theta_{n''}^*, \nabla_{\alpha\beta} L_{2n''}(X^{n''}, \theta) - \nabla_{\alpha\beta} \bar{L}_{2n''}(\theta)\}$ such that $\hat{\alpha}_{n''}$ lies in $\bar{\eta}_{\alpha n''}(\varepsilon) \equiv \bar{\eta}_{n''}(\varepsilon) \cap \mathcal{A}$ and $\hat{B}_{n''}$ lies in $\bar{\eta}_{\beta n''}(\varepsilon) \equiv \eta_{n''}(\varepsilon) \cap \mathcal{B}$. By construction, $\bar{\eta}_{\alpha n''}(\varepsilon)$ and $\bar{\eta}_{\beta n''}(\varepsilon)$ lie wholly interior to $\mathcal{A}$ and $\mathcal{B}$ respectively and are convex compact sets. Because $\hat{\beta}_{n''}$ therefore maximizes $L_{2n''}(X^{n''}, \hat{\alpha}_{n''}, \beta)$ interior to $\mathcal{B}$ $a.a.\ n''$ we have

$$\nabla_\beta L_{2n''}(X^{n''}, \hat{\alpha}_{n''}, \hat{\beta}_{n''}) = 0 \qquad a.a.\ n'',\ a.s.-P_o.$$

By the mean value theorem of Jennrich [1969, Lemma 3] there exist measurable functions $\ddot{\alpha}_{n''}^{\,i} : \Omega \rightarrow \bar{\eta}_{\alpha n''}(\varepsilon)$, $i = 1, \ldots, q$ lying on the segment connecting $\alpha_{n''}^*$ and $\hat{\alpha}_{n''}$ such that

$$\begin{aligned}\nabla_\beta L_{2n''}(X^{n''}, \alpha_{n''}^*, \hat{\beta}_{n''}) &= \nabla_\beta L_{2n''}(X^{n''}, \hat{\alpha}_{n''}, \hat{\beta}_{n''}) \\ &\quad + \nabla_{\alpha\beta} \ddot{L}_{2n''}(\hat{\alpha}_{n''} - \alpha_{n''}^*),\ a.a.\ n'',\ a.s.-P_o,\end{aligned}$$

where $\nabla_{\alpha\beta} \ddot{L}_{2n''}$ is the indicated $r \times q$ submatrix of the Hessian with i th row evaluated at $\ddot{\alpha}_n^i$. Equivalently,

$$\begin{aligned}\sqrt{n''}\,\hat{\psi}_{n''} &= \sqrt{n''}\,\nabla_\beta L_{2n''}(X^{n''}, \hat{\alpha}_{n''}, \hat{\beta}_{n''}) \\ &\quad + \nabla_{\alpha\beta} \ddot{L}_{2n''} \sqrt{n''}\,(\hat{\alpha}_{n''} - \alpha_{n''}^*)\ \ a.a.\ n'',\ a.s.-P_o.\end{aligned}$$

Because $\nabla_\beta L_{2n''}(X^{n''}, \hat{\alpha}_{n''}, \hat{\beta}_{n''}) = 0 \;\; a.a.\, n'' \;\; a.s.-P_o$, the first term vanishes almost surely. By Assumption 6.6, $\sqrt{n}\,(\hat{\alpha}_n - \alpha^*_n)$ is $O_{P_o}(1)$, as must be $\sqrt{n''}(\hat{\alpha}_{n''} - \alpha^*_{n''})$. By Corollary 3.8, we have that $\nabla_{\alpha\beta}\, \ddot{L}_{2n''} - \nabla_{\alpha\beta}\, \bar{L}_{2n''}(\theta^*_{n''}) \longrightarrow 0 \;\; a.s.-P_o$. But $\nabla_{\alpha\beta}\, \bar{L}^*_{2n''} \equiv \nabla_{\alpha\beta}\, \bar{L}_{2n''}(\theta^*_{n''}) = 0$ by assumption, so that $\nabla_{\alpha\beta}\, \ddot{L}_{2n} \longrightarrow 0 \;\; a.s - P_o$. This implies that $\nabla_{\alpha\beta}\, \ddot{L}_{2n''}\, \sqrt{n''}\,(\hat{\alpha}_{n''} - \alpha^*_{n''})$ is $o_{P_o}(1)$, so that there exists a further subsequence indexed by $\{n'''\}$ for which $\nabla_{\alpha\beta}\, \ddot{L}_{2n'''}\, \sqrt{n'''}(\hat{\alpha}_{n'''} - \alpha^*_{n'''}) \longrightarrow 0 \;\; a.s.-P_o$. Thus

$$\sqrt{n'''}\;\hat{\psi}_{n'''} \longrightarrow 0 \qquad a.s.-P_o\,,$$

which, by the subsequence theorem, implies $\sqrt{n}\;\hat{\psi}_n \longrightarrow 0 \;\; prob - P_o$ because $\{\sqrt{n'}\;\hat{\psi}_{n'}\}$ was arbitrary.

The conditions of Theorem 6.10 therefore hold, so that

$$\sqrt{n}(\hat{\beta}_n - \beta^*_n) = -\, A^{*\,-1}_{22n}\, \sqrt{n}\, \nabla_\beta\, L^*_{2n} + o_{P_o}(1)$$

and

$$B^{*-1/2}_{22n}\, A^*_{22n}\, \sqrt{n}(\hat{\beta}_n - \beta^*_n) \overset{A}{\sim} N(0, I_p)\,. \qquad \square$$

PROOF OF THEOREM 6.13: (i) The expression for A^*_{22n} is derived in the text. Given Assumption 6.7

$$E(\nabla_\beta \log f_t(X^t, \alpha^*_n, \beta_o) \mid W_t) = \nabla_\beta\, \mu^o_t\, \nabla_\mu\, c_t(\mu^o_t, \kappa^*_t)\, E(u^o_t \mid W_t) = 0$$

where $\kappa^*_t \equiv \kappa_t(W_t, \alpha^*_n)$. In the absence of dynamic misspecification

$$E(\nabla_\beta \log f_t(X^t, \alpha^*_n, \beta_o) \mid W_t) = E(\nabla_\beta \log f_t(X^t, \alpha^*_n, \beta_o) | \tilde{X}^{t-1}) = 0\,.$$

Because $\nabla_\beta \log f_t(X^t, \alpha^*_n, \beta_o)$ is measurable $- \tilde{\mathcal{F}}^t$, $\{\nabla_\beta \log f_t(X^t, \alpha^*_n, \beta_o),\; \tilde{\mathcal{F}}^t\}$ is a martingale difference sequence. The expression for B^*_{22n} is derived in the text.

The additional conditions ensure that Theorem 6.12 applies, and (ii), (iii), (iv) and (v) follow straightforwardly. □

CHAPTER 7

Asymptotic Efficiency

In earlier chapters we have seen that under general conditions the QMLE tends stochastically to θ_n^*, a parameter vector that minimizes the average Kullback-Leibler distance of the specification f_t from h_t, the conditional density ratio of the dependent variables Y_t given the explanatory variables W_t. In Chapter 6, we saw that the QMLE has a normal distribution asymptotically under general conditions, centered at θ_n^* and with a particular covariance matrix.

In many cases, it is possible to construct a variety of such well behaved estimators for some sequence $\theta^* \equiv \{\theta_n^*\}$. (Such estimators may or may not be QMLE's as defined here.) This is essentially always true in situations for which it is possible to construct a model that is correctly specified at least to some extent. Given this possibility, it is important to have some appropriate means of comparing the relative performance of alternative estimators for θ^*, and to ask whether there is a way of estimating θ^* that is "best" in this appropriate sense under specific conditions.

The purpose of this chapter is to address these issues. We first consider asymptotic efficiency for models correctly specified in their entirety, using an approach of Bahadur [1964]. We then consider the relation between efficiency and exogeneity, and efficient estimation using linear exponential models.

7.1 Asymptotic Efficiency for Correctly Specified Models

7.1.a Asymptotic Efficiency of Unconstrained Estimators

So far, we have been primarily concerned with the behavior of particular estimators given a specific unknown data generating mechanism, P_o. In choosing a "best" estimator, consideration must now be given to the behavior of a class of estimators (a "choice set") in relation to a collection of relevant data generating mechanisms (a probability model, as defined in Chapter 2).

Given a probability model, there is typically associated with it a parameter of interest. For example, in the probability model $\mathcal{P} = \{P_\theta : \theta \in \Theta\}$, the parameter vector θ (or some function of it, e.g. a subvector) is usually the object of interest. The following formal definition of parameters of interest is sufficient for consideration of models correctly specified to some extent.

DEFINITION 7.1 (*Parameters of Interest*): Let $(\Omega, \mathcal{F})$ be a measurable space, and let $\mathcal{R}$ be a given collection $\{P^o\}$ of probability measures (a probability model) on $(\Omega, \mathcal{F})$. Let $\Theta \subset \mathbb{R}^p$ be given. The *parameters of interest* are defined by a mapping $\mathcal{T}: \mathcal{R} \to \Theta$. □

Given parameters of interest, we can specify the following class of estimators relevant to the problem of choosing a best estimator.

DEFINITION 7.2 (*Consistent Asymptotically Normal Class*): Given $(\Omega, \mathcal{F})$ and $\Theta \subset \mathbb{R}^p$, let $\mathcal{R}$ be a probability model, and let $\mathcal{T}: \mathcal{R} \to \Theta$. A collection of estimators $\mathcal{E}(\mathcal{R}, \mathcal{T})$ is a *consistent asymptotically normal* (CAN) *class for $\mathcal{T}$ on $\mathcal{R}$* if each element $\hat{\theta}$ of $\mathcal{E}(\mathcal{R}, \mathcal{T})$ is a sequence $\hat{\theta} = \{\hat{\theta}_n : \Omega \to \Theta\}$ of functions measurable - $\mathcal{F}$ such that for each P^o in $\mathcal{R}$ there exists a nonstochastic bounded sequence $\{C_n^o\}$ of $p \times p$ symmetric positive semidefinite matrices such that

$$\sqrt{n}\,(\hat{\theta}_n - \theta^o) \overset{A^o}{\sim} N(0, C_n^o),$$

where $\theta^o = \mathcal{T}(P^o)$ and $\overset{A^o}{\sim}$ denotes asymptotic distribution under P^o. □

Thus, a CAN estimator is consistent and asymptotically normal for the parameters of interest regardless of which member of $\mathcal{R}$ may have generated the data. A CAN class $\mathcal{E}(\mathcal{R}, \mathcal{T})$ is a collection of such estimators.

Because $\hat{\theta}_n - \theta^o = n^{-1/2}[\sqrt{n}\,(\hat{\theta}_n - \theta^o)]$ we have

$$E^o(\exp[i\,a'(\hat{\theta}_n - \theta^o)]) = E^o(\exp[i\,a_n'\sqrt{n}\,(\hat{\theta}_n - \theta^o)]),$$

where $a_n = n^{-1/2}\,a$. By Definition 6.1, uniform convergence with a in compact subsets of $\mathbb{R}^p$ implies that

$$E^o(\exp[i\, a' (\hat{\theta}_n - \theta^o)]) - \exp[-a_n{}' \, C_n^o \, a_n / 2] \longrightarrow 0 \,.$$

But

$$\exp[-a_n' \, C_n^o \, a_n / 2] = \exp[-n^{-1} \, a' \, C_n^o \, a / 2] \longrightarrow 1$$

given that C_n^o is bounded. By the inversion theorem for characteristic functions, this implies that $\hat{\theta}_n - \theta^o \to 0$ *prob* $- P^o$. This justifies use of the word "consistent" in the definition.

Use of the normalization $\sqrt{n}$ is appropriate in our context; however, in some circumstances involving trends (e.g. Weiss [1971, 1973]) other choices are warranted. These are beyond the scope of our analysis.

Note that both $\mathcal{R}$ and $\mathcal{T}$ play important roles in determining the estimators comprising the class. To see this, let $\mathcal{R}$ be the class of probability measures generating i.i.d. scalar sequences $\{X_t\}$ such that $E^o \mid X_1 \mid < \infty$ for each P^o in $\mathcal{R}$. If $\mathcal{T}(P^o) = med^o \; X_1$ where med^o denotes median under P^o, then the least absolute deviations estimator may lie in $\mathcal{E}(\mathcal{R}, \mathcal{T})$, but not the least squares estimator. This is because least squares fails to be consistent for $med^o \; X_1$ for asymmetric distributions generally. On the other hand, if $\mathcal{T}(P^o) = E^o(X_1)$, then least squares may lie in $\mathcal{E}(\mathcal{R}, \mathcal{T})$, but not least absolute deviations, as this is inconsistent for $E^o(X_1)$ generally.

Now fix $\mathcal{T}(P^o) = E^o(X_1)$, and consider what happens as $\mathcal{R}$ varies. If $\mathcal{R}$ includes only symmetric distributions, then both least squares and least absolute deviations may be in $\mathcal{E}(\mathcal{R}, \mathcal{T})$. However, if $\mathcal{R}$ includes asymmetric distributions, then $\mathcal{E}(\mathcal{R}, \mathcal{T})$ may contain least squares, but not least absolute deviations.

In addition, $\mathcal{R}$ may be required to satisfy a number of more or less restrictive regularity conditions, in order to ensure the existence of asymptotically normal estimators.

From a general point of view, it is in fact arbitrary and restrictive to limit attention to asymptotically normal estimators. Consideration of more general classes of estimators for the case of correctly specified models is given elegant and general treatment by Ibragimov and Has'minskii [1981]. We restrict attention to the asymptotically normal case here for simplicity.

Given that we restrict attention to CAN classes of estimators, we need a criterion by which to measure the "goodness" of each estimator in the class. Heuristically, the "closer" an estimator $\hat{\theta}_n$ is to θ^o (on average) the better. In the study of finite sample behavior of estimators a common measure of "goodness" is the mean squared error of $\hat{\theta}_n$ for θ^o, $E^o([\hat{\theta}_n - \theta^o]^2)$. When $\hat{\theta}_n$ is unbiased for θ^o, this becomes the variance, $\text{var}^o \; \hat{\theta}_n = E^o([\hat{\theta}_n - \theta^o]^2)$.

In the finite sample context, the famous Cramér-Rao theorem (Rao

[1945], Cramér [1946]; also credited to Frechet [1943] and Darmois [1945]) gives a lower bound for the variance achievable by an unbiased estimator for particular parameters of interest. It is well known that under appropriate regularity conditions an estimator achieving the Cramér-Rao lower bound must be the maximum likelihood estimator. When closeness of $\hat{\theta}_n$ to θ^o is measured by mean squared error and the MLE is unbiased, the MLE is thus "efficient" among unbiased estimators.

Analogous results in an asymptotic context are more subtle. Le Cam [1953] credits J.L. Hodges with the estimator

$$\begin{aligned}\tilde{X}_n &\equiv \bar{X}_n \quad | \bar{X}_n | \geq n^{-1/4} \\ &\equiv 0 \quad | \bar{X}_n | < n^{-1}/4 ,\end{aligned}$$

where $\bar{X}_n$ is the mean of a sample of random variables $\{X_t\}$ independent and identically distributed as $N(\theta, 1)$. It is readily verified that both $\bar{X}_n$ (the MLE) and $\tilde{X}_n$ are CAN with avar $^o\ \bar{X}_n = 1$ for all θ^o, but with avar $^o\ \tilde{X}_n = 1$ for $\theta^o \neq 0$ and avar $^o\ \tilde{X}_n = 0$ for $\theta^o = 0$. The estimator $\tilde{X}_n$ is therefore said to be "superefficient" in the sense that it has asymptotic variance less than or equal to that of the MLE for all relevant θ^o with strict inequality for (at least) one value of θ^o.

The existence of superefficient estimators implies that a straightforward asymptotic analogue of the Cramér-Rao bound is not available in a CAN class without additional restrictions. Rao [1963] shows that if attention is restricted to consistent *uniformly* asymptotically normal (CUAN) estimators (that is, CAN estimators for which the convergence to normality is uniform in compact subsets of *int* Θ), then an asymptotic Cramér-Rao bound is available. Uniformity is a reasonable requirement insofar as it helps ensure that attempts to improve the concentration of an estimator (measured for example by mean squared error) for one particular parameter value do not lead to deterioration for other parameter values. The Hodges estimator obtains superefficiency at the cost of uniformity.

Bahadur (1964) establishes an asymptotic Cramér-Rao bound under somewhat weaker conditions. Here we follow Bahadur's approach, and obtain analogous results. We do not use the weakest of Bahadur's conditions. However, the results hold in fairly general stochastic settings. We use the following definition.

DEFINITION 7.3 (*Locally Asymptotically Normal Family*): Given $(\Omega, \mathcal{F})$, let $\mathcal{P}$ be a regular (parametric) probability model (see Theorem 2.6). Then

$\mathcal{P}$ is a *locally asymptotically normal* (LAN) family if for each $\theta^o \in int\ \Theta$ there exists a sequence $\{I_n^o\}$ that is $O(1)$ and uniformly positive definite such that for any sequence $\{a_n\}$, $a_n \in \mathbb{R}^p$, for which $a_n{}' I_n^o a_n = 1$,

$$K_n^o \equiv n[L_n(X^n, \theta_n^o) - L_n(X^n, \theta^o)] + 1/2 \overset{A^o}{\sim} N(0, 1),$$

where $\theta_n^o \equiv \theta^o + n^{-1/2} a_n$, $L_n(X^n, \theta) \equiv n^{-1} \log f^n(X^n, \theta)$, $f^n(\cdot, \theta) \equiv dP_\theta^n / d\nu^n$ and $\overset{A^o}{\sim}$ denotes convergence in distribution under P_{θ^o}. □

The local asymptotic normality concept was introduced by Le Cam [1960]. To see what this requires in the present context, use Taylor's theorem to write

$$L_n(X^n, \theta_n^o) = L_n(X^n, \theta^o) + \nabla' L_n(X^n, \theta^o)(\theta_n^o - \theta^o)$$
$$+ (\theta_n^o - \theta^o)' \nabla^2 \ddot{L}_n (\theta_n^o - \theta^o)/2,$$

where $\nabla^2 \ddot{L}_n$ is the Hessian of L_n with rows evaluated at values lying on the segment connecting θ_n^o and θ^o. Because $\theta_n^o - \theta^o = n^{-1/2} a_n$, we get

$$n[L_n(X^n, \theta_n^o) - L_n(X^n, \theta^o)] + a_n{}' I_n^o a_n/2$$
$$= n^{1/2} \nabla' L_n(X^n, \theta^o) a_n + a_n{}' I_n^o a_n/2 + a_n{}' \nabla^2 \ddot{L}_n a_n/2$$
$$= a_n{}'[n^{-1/2} \sum_{t=1}^{n} s_t^o] + a_n{}'(\nabla^2 \ddot{L}_n + I_n^o) a_n/2,$$

with $s_t^o \equiv s_t(X^t, \theta^o)$. Typically, a central limit theorem will ensure that the first term satisfies $(a_n{}' I_n^o a_n)^{-1/2} a_n{}' [n^{-1/2} \sum_{t=1}^n s_t^o] \overset{A^o}{\sim} N(0, 1)$, where $I_n^o \equiv \text{var}^o [n^{1/2} \nabla L_n(X^n, \theta^o)]$. A uniform law of large numbers and Corollary 3.8 will ensure that $\nabla^2 \ddot{L}_n - E^o(\nabla^2 L_n(X^n, \theta^o)) = o_{P_{\theta^o}}(1)$. The information matrix equality plays the crucial role of ensuring that $I_n^o = -E^o(\nabla^2 L_n(X^n, \theta^o))$, so that the second term vanishes in probability. Setting $a'_n I_n^o a_n = 1$ then permits us to obtain the following result.

THEOREM 7.4: *Let $\mathcal{P}$ be a regular probability model, and for each θ in*

Θ, let $f_t(x^t, \theta)$ be the conditional density guaranteed by Theorem 2.6. For this choice of f_t suppose that for each θ^o in int Θ when $P_o = P_{\theta^o}$ in Assumption 2.1, we have that Assumptions 2.3, 3.1(a,b), 3.2, 3.6, 3.7(a), 3.8 and 6.1 hold. If Assumption 6.2 also holds, then $\mathcal{P}$ is a LAN family. □

Thus, the model has the LAN property if each element P_θ in an appropriate set satisfies regularity conditions similar to those that ensure consistency and asymptotic normality of the MLE for models correctly specified in their entirety.

Models satisfying this LAN property are the probability models that are relevant to our treatment of asymptotic efficiency. Following Bahadur [1964], we further restrict attention to estimators that satisfy the condition given by the following definition.

DEFINITION 7.5 (*Regular Consistent Asymptotically Normal Class*): Let $\mathcal{P}$ be a LAN family, and let $\mathcal{T}: \mathcal{P} \longrightarrow \Theta$ be defined so that $\mathcal{T}(P_\theta) = \theta$. The class $\mathcal{E}(\mathcal{P}, \mathcal{T})$ is a *regular consistent asymptotically normal* class (RCAN) of estimators for $\mathcal{T}$ on $\mathcal{P}$ if $\mathcal{E}(\mathcal{P}, \mathcal{T})$ is a CAN class for $\mathcal{T}$ on $\mathcal{P}$ and for any $\tilde{\theta} = \{\tilde{\theta}_n\} \in \mathcal{E}(\mathcal{P}, \mathcal{T})$

$$P_\theta^n [b' \tilde{\theta}_n \geq b'\theta] \longrightarrow 1/2 \quad \text{as} \quad n \rightarrow \infty$$

uniformly on *int* Θ for any $b \in \mathbb{R}^p$, $b'b = 1$. □

The regularity condition $P_\theta^n[b' \tilde{\theta}_n \geq b'\theta] \longrightarrow 1/2$ uniformly is one considered by Bahadur [1964]; it requires that $b'\tilde{\theta}_n$ be asymptotically median-unbiased uniformly on *int* Θ for arbitrary $b \in \mathbb{R}^p$. Uniform asymptotic normality is sufficient for this. We use the generic term "regular" rather than "uniform" to distinguish between these cases. Bahadur's [1964] results utilize a condition which is "a little weaker" than that of Definition 7.5 (Bahadur [1964, p. 1545]), namely that $\liminf_{n\to\infty} P_{\theta_n^o}^n (b'\tilde{\theta}_n < b'\theta_n^o) \leq 1/2$. This condition delivers the conclusion that the asymptotic Cramér-Rao bound holds except on a set of measure zero in *int* Θ, provided that asymptotic variances converge. We adopt the stronger condition to handle cases in which asymptotic variances need not converge due to heterogeneity. We also obtain the stronger conclusion that the bound holds everywhere in *int* Θ. Formally, we have the following Bahadur-type asymptotic Cramér-Rao bound.

THEOREM 7.6: *Let $\mathcal{E}(\mathcal{P}, \mathcal{T})$ be a RCAN class with $\mathcal{T}(\mathcal{P}) = \Theta$. For any*

$\tilde{\theta} = \{\tilde{\theta}_n\} \in \mathcal{E}(\mathcal{P}, \mathcal{T})$ with $C_n^o \equiv \text{avar}\,^o\, \tilde{\theta}_n$ under $P_{\theta^o} \in \mathcal{P}, \theta^o \in$ int Θ, it follows that for each θ^o in int Θ, C_n^o is uniformly positive definite and for all n sufficiently large

$$C_n^o - I_n^{o-1}$$

is positive semi-definite. □

This result gives content to the following definition of asymptotic efficiency for RCAN estimators.

DEFINITION 7.7 (*Asymptotic Efficiency*): Let $\mathcal{E}(\mathcal{P}, \mathcal{T})$ be a RCAN class with $\mathcal{T}(\mathcal{P}) = \Theta$, and let $\hat{\theta}$ and $\tilde{\theta}$ be elements of $\mathcal{E}(\mathcal{P}, \mathcal{T})$. The estimator $\hat{\theta}$ is *asymptotically efficient relative to* $\tilde{\theta}$ in $\mathcal{E}(\mathcal{P}, \mathcal{T})$ if for all $\lambda \in \mathbb{R}^p$, $\lambda'\lambda = 1$,

$$\liminf_{n\to\infty} \lambda'[\text{avar}\,^o\, \tilde{\theta}_n - \text{avar}\,^o\, \hat{\theta}_n]\, \lambda \geq 0$$

for all P_{θ^o} in $\mathcal{P}$, $\theta^o \in$ *int* Θ.

The estimator $\hat{\theta}$ is *asymptotically efficient in* $\mathcal{E}(\mathcal{P}, \mathcal{T})$ if it is asymptotically efficient relative to all $\tilde{\theta} \in \mathcal{E}(\mathcal{P}, \mathcal{T})$. □

Given Definition 7.7, Theorem 7.6 can be used to ensure the existence of an asymptotically efficient estimator and to verify whether a particular element of $\mathcal{E}(\mathcal{P}, \mathcal{T})$ is asymptotically efficient by comparing $\text{avar}\,^o\, \tilde{\theta}_n$ to I_n^{o-1}. If $\text{avar}\,^o\, \tilde{\theta}_n - I_n^{o-1} \to 0$ as $n \to \infty$ then $\tilde{\theta}$ is asymptotically efficient in $\mathcal{E}(\mathcal{P}, \mathcal{T})$. Note that this definition makes no reference to the actual data generation process P_o, but only to the elements of the model $\mathcal{P}$.

It is a familiar result that the maximum likelihood estimator is asymptotically efficient under general conditions (Roussas [1972], Ibragimov and Has'minskii [1981]). An efficiency result for the MLE in the present (restricted) context follows immediately from Theorem 7.6.

THEOREM 7.8: *Let the conditions of Theorem 7.4 and Assumption 3.1(c) hold with $\mathcal{T}(\mathcal{P}) = \Theta$. Suppose that the MLE $\hat{\theta}$ generated by $\mathcal{S} = \{f^n = \Pi_{t=1}^n f_t\}$ belongs to the RCAN class $\mathcal{E}(\mathcal{P}, \mathcal{T})$. Then*

(i) $\hat{\theta}$ is asymptotically efficient in $\mathcal{E}(\mathcal{P}, \mathcal{T})$;

(ii) if $\mathcal{S}$ is correctly specified in its entirety, then $\hat{\theta}$ attains the minimum asymptotic variance bound, i.e. $\text{avar}\, \hat{\theta}_n = I_n^{o-1}$. □

This result follows immediately by showing that avar $^o\,\hat{\theta}_n = I_n^{o-1}$. In applications, the challenge is to show that the MLE is RCAN. Because conditions ensuring this depend upon the specific stochastic properties of X_t, we do not discuss such conditions here. However, uniform asymptotic normality suffices for our notion of regularity. Uniform versions of the central limit theorems discussed in Appendix 3 can be proved using, e.g., results of Parzen [1954].

Note the distinction made in stating the conclusion of this theorem between the asymptotic efficiency of the MLE and its attainment of the minimum asymptotic variance bound. In standard treatment of the efficiency problem it is implicitly assumed that the model is correctly specified. Here, we do not make this assumption implicit. Thus, we distinguish between asymptotic efficiency as a property of an element of a class of estimators *without* reference to P_o, and the attainment of the minimum asymptotic variance bound which is meaningful only *with* reference to the data generating process P_o. If P_o does not belong to $\mathcal{P}$, the MLE associated with $\mathcal{P}$ is no longer necessarily consistent (as we have seen earlier) nor does it necessarily attain the minimum asymptotic variance bound. We explore this further in the following section. For now we note that the contrapositive of (ii) (i.e., if $\hat{\theta}$ does not attain the minimum asymptotic variance bound, then P_o does not belong to $\mathcal{P}$) is useful in investigating the issue of model misspecification. Again, examination of the validity of the information matrix equality is helpful in this regard. We pursue this further in Chapter 11.

Bearing the distinction between asymptotic efficiency and the attainment of the minimum asymptotic variance bound in mind, we shall sometimes also refer to the latter property as "efficiency" for the sake of brevity. The meaning will be clear from the context.

The maximum likelihood estimator is by no means the only asymptotically efficient estimator. A computationally convenient alternative is the *two-step estimator* (Le Cam [1956])

$$\ddot{\theta}_n = \tilde{\theta}_n - \tilde{A}_n^- \nabla L_n(X^n, \tilde{\theta}_n),$$

where $\tilde{\theta}_n$ is any CAN estimator and $\tilde{A}_n - E^o(\nabla^2 L_n(X^n, \theta^o)) \to 0$ $prob - P^o$. Formally, we have the following result:

THEOREM 7.9: *Let the conditions of Theorem 7.4 and Assumption 3.1(c) hold with $\mathcal{T}(\mathcal{P}) = \Theta$. Let $\tilde{\theta} = \{\tilde{\theta}_n\}$ be an estimator such that for each θ^o in* *int* Θ, $\sqrt{n}\,(\tilde{\theta}_n - \theta^o)$ *is* $O_{P_{\theta^o}}(1)$, *and let* $\{\tilde{A}_n\}$ *be a sequence of stochastic matrices such that for each* θ^o *in int* Θ, $\tilde{A}_n - E^o\,(\nabla^2 L_n(X^n, \theta^o)) \to 0$ *prob* $-\, P_{\theta^o}$. *Define*

$$\ddot{\theta}_n = \tilde{\theta}_n - \tilde{A}_n^- \,\nabla\, L_n(X^n, \tilde{\theta}_n),$$

where $\tilde{A}_n^-$ *is a generalized inverse of* $\tilde{A}_n$. *Let* $\hat{\theta}$ *be the MLE generated by* $\mathcal{P}$. *Then*

(*i*) *for each* θ^o *in int* Θ, $\sqrt{n}\,(\ddot{\theta}_n - \hat{\theta}_n) \to 0$ *prob* $-\, P_{\theta^o}$;

(*ii*) *if* $\ddot{\theta}$ *belongs to the RCAN class* $\mathcal{E}(\mathcal{P}, \mathcal{T})$, *then* $\ddot{\theta}$ *is asymptotically efficient in* $\mathcal{E}(\mathcal{P}, \mathcal{T})$;

(*iii*) *if* $\mathcal{S} = \{f^n\}$ *is correctly specified in its entirety, then* $\ddot{\theta}$ *attains the minimum asymptotic variance bound.* □

This efficiency result is a version of a result originally due to Le Cam [1956]. It affords the potential for considerably simplified computation of an efficient estimator.

7.1.b *Asymptotic Efficiency of Constrained Estimators*

In many cases, the parameters of interest may be known to satisfy certain constraints. One way of expressing such constraints is to write them as

$$\theta = d(\gamma)$$

for some known function $d : \Gamma \to \Theta$, $\Gamma \subset \mathbb{R}^c$, $c \leq p$. A prominent example of this situation in econometrics is the case of simultaneous systems of linear equations with (over)-identifying restrictions. In this case θ corresponds to the parameters of the reduced form, γ corresponds to the structural parameters, and d specifies explicitly the relation between them.

As discussed by Rothenberg [1973], there are other essentially equivalent ways of representing such constraints. The representation $\theta = d(\gamma)$ is the most convenient one here.

With such constraints available, the problem of interest is to find appropriate asymptotic efficiency bounds for θ as well as for γ. Finding such bounds for γ is a straightforward task given Theorem 7.6. Essentially, it suffices to ensure that appropriate regularity conditions hold with respect to the restricted probability model $\tilde{\mathcal{P}} = \{P_{d(\gamma)} : \gamma \in \Gamma\} \subset \mathcal{P}$. This involves putting appropriate conditions on the likelihood functions

$$\tilde{f}^{\,n}(X^n, \gamma) \equiv f^n(X^n, d(\gamma)) .$$

The following condition on d is useful in this regard.

ASSUMPTION 7.1: Let Γ be a compact subset of $\mathbb{R}^c$, $c \le p$, and let $d : \Gamma \to \Theta$ be a twice continuously differentiable injective mapping (i.e. $\gamma_1 \ne \gamma_2$ implies $d(\gamma_1) \ne d(\gamma_2)$). □

We define the $p \times c$ Jacobian matrix $D \equiv [\partial d_i / \partial \gamma_j,\ i = 1, \ldots, p;\ j = 1, \ldots, c]$. Because d is injective, D (a function of γ) has full column rank c everywhere in Γ. We have the following result.

THEOREM 7.10: *Let $\mathcal{P} = \{P_\theta : \theta \in \Theta\}$ be a regular probability model, and for each θ in Θ, let $f_t(x^t, \theta)$ be the conditional density guaranteed by Theorem 2.7. Given Assumption 7.1 and this choice for f_t, suppose that for each γ^o in int Γ when $P_o = P_{d(\gamma^o)}$ in Assumption 2.1, we have that Assumptions 2.3, 3.1, 3.2, 3.6, 3.7, 3.8 and 6.1 hold. Suppose Assumption 6.2 also holds.*

(i) Let $\tilde{\mathcal{P}} = \{P_{d(\gamma)} : \gamma \in \Gamma\}$ with $\tilde{\mathcal{T}}(\tilde{\mathcal{P}}) = \Gamma$, and let $\mathcal{E}(\tilde{\mathcal{P}}, \tilde{\mathcal{T}})$ be a RCAN class. For any $\tilde{\gamma} = \{\tilde{\gamma}_n\} \in \mathcal{E}(\tilde{\mathcal{P}}, \tilde{\mathcal{T}})$ with $\tilde{C}_n^o \equiv \text{avar}^{\,o}(\tilde{\gamma}_n - \gamma^o)$ under $P_{d(\gamma^o)} \in \tilde{\mathcal{P}}$, $\gamma^o \in$ int Γ, it follows that $\tilde{C}_n^o$ is uniformly positive definite for each γ^o in int Γ, and for all n sufficiently large

$$\tilde{C}_n^o - \tilde{I}_n^{o-1}$$

is positive semi-definite, where $\tilde{I}_n^o \equiv D^{o\prime} I_n^o D^o$, $D^o \equiv D(\gamma^o)$.

(ii) If the MLE $\hat{\gamma} = \{\hat{\gamma}_n\}$ generated by $\tilde{\mathcal{S}} = \{\tilde{f}_n\}$ belongs to $\mathcal{E}(\tilde{\mathcal{P}}, \tilde{\mathcal{T}})$, then $\hat{\gamma}$ is asymptotically efficient in $\mathcal{E}(\tilde{\mathcal{P}}, \tilde{\mathcal{T}})$.

(iii) If $\tilde{\mathcal{S}}$ is correctly specified in its entirety, then $\hat{\gamma}$ attains the minimum asymptotic variance bound. □

Thus, the asymptotically efficient estimator is again the MLE, $\hat{\gamma}$. Now however, the efficiency bound is expressed in terms of the information matrix of the unconstrained MLE for θ (cf. Rothenberg [1973, Ch. 2.5]).

Given any CAN estimator $\tilde{\gamma}$ for γ, a CAN for θ is given by $\{\tilde{\theta}_n = d(\tilde{\gamma}_n)\}$. This follows by taking a mean value expansion of $d(\tilde{\gamma}_n)$ around γ^o to obtain

$$\tilde{\theta}_n = d(\gamma^o) + \ddot{D}_n(\tilde{\gamma}_n - \gamma^o),$$

where $\ddot{D}_n$ is the Jacobian D with rows evaluated at mean values lying between $\tilde{\gamma}_n$ and γ^o. Because $d(\gamma^o) = \theta^o$,

$$\begin{aligned}\sqrt{n}\,(\tilde{\theta}_n - \theta^o) &= \ddot{D}_n \sqrt{n}\,(\tilde{\gamma}_n - \gamma^o) \\ &= D^o \sqrt{n}\,(\tilde{\gamma}_n - \gamma^o) + (\ddot{D}_n - D^o)\sqrt{n}\,(\tilde{\gamma}_n - \gamma^o) \\ &= D^o \sqrt{n}\,(\tilde{\gamma}_n - \gamma^o) + o_{P_{\theta^o}}(1).\end{aligned}$$

The last term vanishes in probability because $\sqrt{n}\,(\tilde{\gamma}_n - \gamma^o)$ is bounded in probability and $\ddot{D}_n - D^o$ vanishes in probability given the consistency of $\tilde{\gamma}_n$ and the continuity of D. It follows that $\sqrt{n}\,(\tilde{\theta}_n - \theta^o)$ has the same asymptotic distribution as $D^o \sqrt{n}\,(\tilde{\gamma}_n - \gamma^o)$; when $\sqrt{n}\,(\tilde{\gamma}_n - \gamma^o) \overset{A^o}{\sim} N(0, \tilde{C}^o_n)$, we have

$$\sqrt{n}\,(\tilde{\theta}_n - \theta^o) \overset{A^o}{\sim} N(0, D^o\, \tilde{C}^o_n\, D^{o\prime}).$$

Observe that $D^o\, \tilde{C}^o_n\, D^{o\prime}$ is a $p \times p$ matrix with rank $c \le p$. When $c < p$, this asymptotic covariance matrix is singular. It follows that even if $\tilde{\gamma}$ belongs to a RCAN class $\mathcal{E}(\tilde{\mathcal{P}}, \tilde{\mathcal{T}})$, $\tilde{\theta}$ cannot belong to a RCAN class when $c < p$ because of this singular covariance matrix. Nevertheless, when $\tilde{\theta}$ is constructed in this way from $\tilde{\gamma}$ belonging to a RCAN class, it is possible to give an efficiency bound for $\tilde{\theta}$.

THEOREM 7.11: *(i) Let the conditions of Theorem 7.10 hold, with $\mathcal{E}(\tilde{\mathcal{P}}, \tilde{\mathcal{T}})$ a RCAN class. Define the class*

$$\mathcal{E}(\tilde{\mathcal{P}}, d(\tilde{\mathcal{T}})) \equiv \{\tilde{\theta} = \{\tilde{\theta}_n\} : \tilde{\theta}_n = d(\tilde{\gamma}_n),\, n = 1, 2, \ldots,\, \tilde{\gamma} \in \mathcal{E}(\tilde{\mathcal{P}}, \tilde{\mathcal{T}})\}.$$

Then $\mathcal{E}(\tilde{\mathcal{P}}, d(\tilde{\mathcal{T}}))$ is a CAN class, and for each γ^o in int Γ and each $\tilde{\theta} \in \mathcal{E}(\tilde{\mathcal{P}}, d(\tilde{\mathcal{T}}))$

$$\text{avar}^{\,o}\, \tilde{\theta}_n - D^o (D^{o\prime}\, I^o_n\, D^o)^{-1}\, D^{o\prime}$$

is positive semi-definite.

(ii) If the constrained MLE $\hat{\theta} = d(\hat{\gamma})$ *belongs to* $\mathcal{E}(\tilde{\mathcal{P}}, d(\tilde{\mathcal{T}}))$, *then for each* γ^o *in int* Γ, $\text{avar}^{\,o}\, \hat{\theta}_n = D^o\,(D^{o\prime}\, I_n^o\, D^o\,)^{-1}\, D^{o\prime}$.

(iii) If $\tilde{\mathcal{S}}$ *is correctly specified in its entirety, then* $\hat{\theta}$ *attains the minimum asymptotic variance bound, i.e.* $\text{avar}\, \hat{\theta}_n = D^o\,(D^{o\prime}\, I_n^o\, D^o\,)^{-1}\, D^{o\prime}$. □

Thus, the estimator for θ^o with smallest asymptotic variance is the constrained MLE. By comparing the bound given by this result to that of Theorem 7.6, we can evaluate the improvement in efficiency afforded by the constraints $\theta = d(\gamma)$. The difference between the bounds is

$$I_n^{o-1} - D^o\,(D^{o\prime}\, I_n^o\, D^o\,)^{-1}\, D^{o\prime}$$

$$= I_n^{o-1/2}\left[I_p - I_n^{o\,1/2}\, D^o(D^{o\prime}\, I_n^{o\,1/2}\, I_n^{o\,1/2}\, D^o\,)^{-1}\, D^{o\prime}\, I_n^{o\,1/2}\right] I_n^{o-1/2},$$

where $I_n^{o\,1/2}$ is the symmetric (nonsingular) matrix square root of I_n^o. Setting $G_n^o = I_n^{o\,1/2}\, D^o$, we see that

$$I_n^{o^{-1}} - D^o(D^{o\prime}\, I_n^o\, D^o\,)^{-1}\, D^{o\prime}$$

$$= I_n^{o-1/2}\left[I_p - G_n^o(G_n^{o\prime}\, G_n^o)^{-1}\, G_n^{o\prime}\right] I_n^{o-1/2},$$

which, because of the idempotent matrix in square brackets, is a positive semi-definite matrix (cf. Rothenberg [1973, Ch. 2.5]). In the special case in which $c = p$, we see that in fact the efficiency bound is unaffected, so that (locally) invertible transformations have no effect on efficiency. However, when $c < p$ efficiency gains do emerge.

These results give a simple and reasonably satisfactory account of the issue of asymptotic efficiency for asymptotically normal estimators given the availability of models correctly specified in their entirety. We now turn to a consideration of the implications of various kinds of misspecification.

7.2 Efficiency and Exogeneity

In Chapter 4, we considered the effects of two related forms of possible misspecification. The first arises when for no θ_o in Θ is $f^n(x^n, \theta_o)$ a density with respect to ν^n. This usually results when certain variables are treated as "exogenous." We saw in Chapter 4 that if $\mathcal{S}$ is correct for $\{Y_t \mid \tilde{X}^{t-1}\}$ on Θ, then the QMLE is consistent for θ_o such that $f_t(x^t, \theta_o) = h_t(x^t)$, $t = 1, 2, \ldots$ (recall that h_t is the "true" conditional density ratio of Y_t given $\tilde{X}^{t-1}$), and in Chapter 6 we saw conditions ensuring the asymptotic normality of the QMLE and the validity of the information matrix equality in this case. The other form of misspecification considered in Chapter 4 arises from a possibly incomplete dynamic specification in which one models $\{Y_t \mid W_t\}$ instead of $\{Y_t \mid \tilde{X}^{t-1}\}$. Consideration of simple examples shows that dynamic misspecifications can adversely affect the information matrix equality and the efficiency of the QMLE, as in the case of linear regression (OLS) applied to a model for which the DGP implies serially correlated errors. The only case in which efficiency is potentially unaffected generally by modeling $\{Y_t \mid W_t\}$ instead of $\{Y_t \mid \tilde{X}^{t-1}\}$ is when the conditional distributions of $Y_t \mid W_t$ and $Y_t \mid \tilde{X}^{t-1}$ coincide, that is, in the absence of dynamic misspecification. Accordingly, we consider in this section the efficiency effects of treating certain variables as exogenous, in the absence of dynamic misspecification.

As we have seen, asymptotic efficiency is a property of an estimator relative to a class of estimators that have particular properties under any data generation process in some relevant family of probability measures. For simplicity, in this section we dispense with the formalism of varying the data generation process; instead we focus on the behavior of particular estimators under the given data generation process P_o of Assumption 2.1 when it is assumed to lie in some LAN family $\mathcal{P}$. With appropriate additional assumptions, the QMLE's considered here are RCAN, so that the asymptotic efficiency theory of the preceding section applies. We content ourselves with examining how the asymptotic covariance matrix of the QMLE compares to that of a relevant MLE for given P_o; that is, we focus on attainment of the minimum asymptotic variance bound. The reader can undertake the exercise of letting P_o vary over $\mathcal{P}$ to provide formal conditions under which asymptotic efficiency relations hold.

We compare the asymptotic covariance matrix of the QMLE generated by the specification $\mathcal{S} = \{f_t\}$ correct for $\{Y_t \mid \tilde{X}^{t-1}\}$ with that of the MLE obtained from a model that does not ignore the distribution of Z_t given X^{t-1}. If the two asymptotic covariance matrices are the same, then we will not lose information relevant to asymptotic inference and confidence interval statements by ignoring the distribution of Z_t given X^{t-1}.

Engle, Hendry and Richard [1983] (EHR) relate notions of "weak exogeneity" and "strong exogeneity" to this issue. It turns out, however, that these notions are not entirely satisfactory for the present discussion, for reasons to be discussed shortly. Instead, we introduce a related concept that is directly relevant here.

DEFINITION 7.12 (*Informational Exogeneity*): Let $\mathcal{S} = \{f_t\}$ specify dependent variables Y and explanatory variables W with respect to $\{\zeta_t\}$ and suppose $\mathcal{S}$ is correctly specified for $\{Y_t \mid \tilde{X}^{t-1}\}$ at $\theta_o \in int\, \Theta$ with respect to $\{\nu^t, \tilde{\nu}^{t-1}\}$, where $\tilde{\nu}^{t-1}$ dominates $\tilde{P}_o^{\,t-1}$, the distribution of $\tilde{X}^{t-1} = (X^{t-1\prime}, Z_t{}')'$, $t = 1, 2, \ldots$. Let $\tilde{\mathcal{S}} = \{\tilde{f}(\theta) : \theta \in \Theta\}$ specify dependent variables $Z = \{Z_t\}$ and explanatory variables $\tilde{W} = \{\tilde{W}_t\}$ and let $\tilde{\mathcal{S}}$ be correctly specified for $\{Z_t \mid X^{t-1}\}$ at θ_o with respect to $\{\tilde{\nu}^{t-1}, \nu^{t-1}\}$.

We say that $\{Z_t \mid X^{t-1}\}$ is *informationally exogenous* for θ_o if for any specification $\tilde{\mathcal{S}}$ as just described, $\nabla_\theta \tilde{f}_t\, (\tilde{x}^{t-1},\ \theta_o) = 0\ \ a.e. - \ \tilde{\nu}^{t-1}$, $t = 1, 2, \ldots$. □

Thus, informational exogeneity is a property of a data generation process relative to a correctly specified model. The justification for this nomenclature is provided by the following result.

THEOREM 7.13: *Let $\mathcal{S}$ and $\tilde{\mathcal{S}}$ be as in Definition 7.12, and define $\mathcal{S}^* \equiv \{f_t \cdot \tilde{f}_t\}$. Then*

(i) $\mathcal{S}^*$ is correct for $\{X_t \mid X^{t-1}\}$ at θ_o with respect to $\{\nu^t, \nu^{t-1}\}$.

Suppose in addition that all the conditions of Theorem 6.6 hold for $\mathcal{S}$; that Assumptions 2.3, 3.1, 3.6, 3.7(a), 3.8, 4.2, 4.3 and 6.3 hold for $\tilde{\mathcal{S}}$; that $\nu^n = \nu^{n-1} \otimes \nu_n$ in Assumption 2.2 with ν_n and ζ_n such that $\nu_n = \zeta_n \otimes \tilde{\zeta}_n$ (and with $\tilde{\nu}^{n-1} = \nu^{n-1} \otimes \tilde{\zeta}_n$), $n = 1, 2, \ldots$; and that Assumption 3.3 holds. Let $\hat{\theta}$ denote the QMLE generated by $\mathcal{S}$ and let $\hat{\theta}^*$ denote the QMLE generated by $\mathcal{S}^*$.

(ii) If $\{Z_t \mid X^{t-1}\}$ is informationally exogenous for θ_o, then the conditions of Theorem 6.5 hold for $\mathcal{S}^*$ and in addition avar $\hat{\theta}_n$ = avar $\hat{\theta}_n^*$ for all such $\tilde{\mathcal{S}}$.

(iii) Suppose that Assumption 6.1 holds for $f_t^* = f_t \cdot \tilde{f}_t$. Then the conditions of Theorem 6.5 hold for $\mathcal{S}^*$ and avar $\hat{\theta}_n$ − avar $\hat{\theta}_n^*$ is positive semi-definite for all n. If in addition each of the sequences $\{\bar{B}_n^o \equiv n^{-1} \sum_{t=1}^n E\,(s_t^o\, s_t^{o\prime})\}$ and $\{\tilde{B}_n^o \equiv n^{-1} \sum_{t=1}^n E\,(\tilde{s}_t^o\, \tilde{s}_t^{o\prime})\}$ converge (with $s_t^o \equiv \nabla f_t\,(X^t, \theta_o)$, $\tilde{s}_t^o \equiv \nabla \tilde{f}_t\,(\tilde{X}^{t-1}, \theta_o)$), and if for some $\lambda \in I\!R^p$, $\lambda' \lambda = 1$, $\lim \lambda' \tilde{B}_n^o \lambda > 0$, so that $\{Z_t \mid X^{t-1}\}$ is not informationally exogenous for θ_o, then there exists $\tilde{\lambda} \in I\!R^p$, $\tilde{\lambda}' \tilde{\lambda} = 1$ such that $\lim \tilde{\lambda}'$ (avar $\hat{\theta}_n$ - avar $\hat{\theta}_n^*$) $\tilde{\lambda} > 0$. □

The result of (ii) says that when $\{Z_t \mid X^{t-1}\}$ is informationally exogenous for θ_o, then failing to model $\{Z_t \mid X^{t-1}\}$ leads to no information loss in estimating θ_o, as measured by the asymptotic covariance matrix. Result (iii) provides a form of converse, by establishing that when $\{Z_t \mid X^{t-1}\}$ is not informationally exogenous, insofar as $\lim \lambda' \tilde{B}_n^o \lambda > 0$ for some unit vector λ, then an appropriate MLE is superior to a QMLE that fails to model $\{Z_t \mid X^{t-1}\}$. The assumed convergence of $\{\bar{B}_n^o\}$ and $\{\tilde{B}_n^o\}$ is a stronger condition than we typically impose. Extreme heterogeneity leading to nonconvergence can be accommodated by replacing the conditions of convergence and $\lim \lambda' \tilde{B}_n^o \lambda > 0$ with the condition that $\liminf_n \lambda' \tilde{B}_n^o \lambda > 0$ for an appropriate collection of unit vectors λ; however, we avoid making this explicit to avoid getting bogged down in technicalities.

To appreciate the usefulness of the present concept as well as the way in which it relates to earlier definitions of exogeneity, we compare informational exogeneity to the notions of weak- and super-exogeneity proposed in the influential work of Engle, Hendry and Richard [1983].

EHR adapt a definition of Florens and Mouchart [1980] to define Z_t as "*weakly exogenous* over the sample period for [parameters of interest] ψ" if a (correctly specified) model $f_t^*(x^t, \lambda)$ for $X_t \mid X^{t-1}$ can be factored as

$$f_t^*(X^t, \lambda) = f_t(X^t, \lambda_1) \cdot \tilde{f}_t(\tilde{X}^{t-1}, \lambda_2),$$

where f_t is a (correctly specified) model of $Y_t \mid \tilde{X}^{t-1}$ and $\tilde{f}_t$ is a (correctly specified) model of $Z_t \mid X^{t-1}$, for variation free λ_1 and λ_2, i.e. $(\lambda_1, \lambda_2) \in \Lambda = \Lambda_1 \times \Lambda_2$, with ψ (corresponding to our θ) solely a function of λ_1 (EHR, Definitions 2.4 and 2.5), $t = 1, 2, \ldots, n$.

The requirement that f_t and $\tilde{f}_t$ be correctly specified is implicit in EHR, but it is useful to be explicit about this. Otherwise, the condition has nothing to say about the stochastic behavior of $X_t \mid X^{t-1}$ but only about how this behavior is modeled. Note that weak exogeneity applies to situations in which one has available a sequence of correctly specified models for $X_t \mid X^{t-1}$. In contrast, informational exogeneity applies to situations in which one has available a correctly specified model for the sequence $\{Y_t \mid \tilde{X}^{t-1}\}$.

EHR give an example of $X_t = (Y_t, Z_t)'$ distributed as i.i.d. bivariate normal $N(\mu_o, \sigma_o)$, $\mu_o = (\mu_{o1}, \mu_{o2})'$, $\sigma_o = [\sigma_{oij}]$, so that $Y_t \mid Z_t \sim N(\alpha_o + \beta_o Z_t, v_o^2)$, where $\beta_o = \sigma_{o12} / \sigma_{o22}$, $\alpha_o = \mu_{o1} - \beta_o \mu_{o2}$ and $v_o^2 = \sigma_{o11} - \sigma_{o12}^2 / \sigma_{o22}$. The two equation model having typical element

$$Y_t = \alpha + \beta Z_t + \varepsilon_{1t}$$

$$Z_t = \mu_2 + \varepsilon_{2t} ,$$

with $\varepsilon_t = (\varepsilon_{1t}, \varepsilon_{2t})'$ jointly normal such that $E(\varepsilon_t) = 0$, $\text{var}\, \varepsilon_{1t} = v^2$, $\text{cov}\, (\varepsilon_{1t}, \varepsilon_{2t}) = 0$, $\text{var}\, \varepsilon_{2t} = \sigma_{22}$, is correctly specified for this DGP, and it is straightforward to verify that Z_t is weakly exogenous for $(\alpha_o, \beta_o, v_o^2)$ for any sample size n.

Similarly, because of the correct specification of a model for $\{Y_t \mid \tilde{X}^{t-1}\}$ based on the first of these equations, it is straightforward to verify that $Z_t \mid X^{t-1}$ is informationally exogenous for $(\alpha_o, \beta_o, v_o^2)$ in this situation. Note that the concept of informational exogeneity does not require explicit consideration of a model for $Z_t \mid X^{t-1}$ and its associated nuisance parameters. Nevertheless, this consideration is often helpful. The present example illustrates a situation in which weak exogeneity is sufficient for informational exogeneity.

A situation in which weak exogeneity is not sufficient for informational exogeneity arises when there is a regime change or intervention of the sort considered by EHR, but Z_t is not "super exogenous." Regime changes amount simply to changes in the marginal distribution of Z_t. If Z_t is weakly exogenous and if in addition such changes leave the conditional distribution of $Y_t \mid Z_t$ unchanged, then Z_t is said to be "super exogenous" (EHR, Definitions 2.7, 2.8 and 2.9).

To see what can happen, for the bivariate normal example just given, consider a regime change in which σ_{o22} increases at some point. If the other values μ_o, σ_{o11} and σ_{o12} are unaffected, then the values for $\beta_o = \sigma_{o12} / \sigma_{o22}$, $\alpha_o = \mu_{o1} - \beta_o \mu_{o2}$ and $v_o^2 = \sigma_{o11} - \sigma_{o12}^2 / \sigma_{o22}$ change, so that Z_t is not super exogenous, despite its weak exogeneity.

Although the concept of informational exogeneity is explicitly formulated to apply in the face of regime changes, it is defined only in situations in which a correct parametric specification for the sequence $\{Y_t \mid \tilde{X}^{t-1}\}$ is available, i.e. there are constants θ_o such that $f_t(x^t, \theta_o) = h_t(x^t)$, $t = 1, 2, \ldots$. In the regime change under consideration and in the absence of super exogeneity, a model that ignored the regime change would not have such a θ_o available and would thus be misspecified for $\{Y_t \mid \tilde{X}^{t-1}\}$. Because of misspecification, the notion of informational exogeneity would not be defined, despite the presence of weak exogeneity.

On the other hand, a correctly specified model that explicitly takes account of regime changes can possess informationally exogenous variables even in the absence of super exogeneity, precisely because of the absence of misspecification for $\{Y_t \mid \tilde{X}^{t-1}\}$.

If Z_t is weakly exogenous and if under a regime change μ_o, σ_{o11} and

σ_{o12} adjust to keep β_o , α_o and ν_o^2 constant, then Z_t is super exogenous. With super exogeneity, a model ignoring regime changes is no longer misspecified, and informational exogeneity can be straightforwardly verified for a model ignoring regime changes.

The concept of informational exogeneity is thus closely related to the concepts of weak and super exogeneity. However, because of its explicit relation to correctly specified models for the sequence $\{Y_t \mid \tilde{X}^{t-1}\}$ rather than to a sequence of correctly specified models for $X_t \mid X^{t-1}$, the concept allows attention first to be focused on the issue of correct specification to whatever degree and then on the issue of efficiency, rather than intermingling them as the concepts of weak and super exogeneity do.

The concept of super exogeneity is further related by EHR to issues of policy analysis, the idea being that when certain variables are super exogenous, then the parameters of a correctly specified model conditioning on super exogenous variables can be estimated consistently regardless of possible regime changes. It follows that the effects of policy interventions can be legitimately studied using the model at hand evaluated at the estimated parameters.

Although it takes us slightly afield of our present concern with issues of estimation efficiency, it is appropriate here to introduce and briefly discuss a notion weaker than super exogeneity relevant to policy analysis. Just as super exogeneity unnecessarily intermingles issues of correct model specification and estimator efficiency, it also unnecessarily intermingles issues of correct model specification and policy analysis. The following concept permits separation of these issues.

DEFINITION 7.14 (*Conditional Invariance*): Let $h_t(y_t, w_t) = \ddot{g}^t(y_t, w_t) / \ddot{g}_t(w_t)$ be the density ratio of $Y_t \mid W_t$, $t = 1, 2, \ldots$. Then $\{Y_t \mid W_t\}$ is *(nontrivially) conditionally invariant* if $\{W_t\}$ is a heterogeneous process and h_t is time independent, i.e. $h_t = h_1$, $t = 2, 3, \ldots$. □

Conditional invariance is a property of the data generating process, defined without regard to any model, unlike super exogeneity. The definition rules out consideration of cases in which $\{Z_t\}$ is stationary, as this would trivially imply that h_t is time independent.

Conditional invariance can be viewed as a form of necessary condition for examining the effects on Y_t of policy changes (changes in the distribution of W_t), because if $\{Y_t \mid W_t\}$ is not conditionally invariant, then changing the distribution of W_t may change the relationship between Y_t and W_t in unpredictable ways. In this situation, even a correctly specified model of the old relationship is likely to be of little value in describing the behavior of Y_t under the new regime.

By itself, conditional invariance cannot be sufficient for analysis of arbitrary policy interventions because it pertains only to the invariance of h_t in the presence of regime changes compatible with the underlying data generating process, rather than invariance of h_t in the presence of arbitrary changes in the distribution of $\{W_t\}$. In any case, one can only subject the former invariance to empirical tests.

Thus, a correctly specified model for conditionally invariant $\{Y_t \mid W_t\}$ can be used to analyze policy interventions compatible with the underlying data generating process. However, correct specification of a model of $\{Y_t \mid W_t\}$ is not a necessary condition for analyzing the effects of such interventions. The possibility of legitimate policy analysis using a misspecified model for conditionally invariant $\{Y_t \mid W_t\}$ arises because a misspecified model can still be used to make approximate statements about the (invariant) probability distribution of Y_t given W_t. As we saw in Chapters 3 to 5, θ^* will depend on the joint distribution of $\{W_t\}$, so weighted QMLE estimation may be used to obtain a value of θ^* relevant to the distribution of $\{W_t\}$ to be achieved by the policy intervention. Use of an appropriately weighted QMLE with the misspecified model can then deliver potentially useful approximate probability statements about Y_t given W_t under the intervention. Similar considerations pertain to invariance of $\{E(Y_t \mid W_t)\}$.

Further discussion of these possibilities will take us too far afield of our main concerns in this chapter, so we shall be content with these brief remarks. However, our discussion here suggests that the notions of informational exogeneity and conditional invariance may be useful alternatives to the notions of weak and super exogeneity, especially when model specification is in doubt.

7.3 Minimum Variance Estimation in Linear Exponential Families

In Chapter 5, we considered the consequences for consistency of distributional misspecifications in which a model of conditional expectation was nevertheless correctly specified. We saw there that a QMLE generated by a member of the linear exponential family is the only QMLE guaranteed to be consistent and asymptotically normal for the parameters of the conditional expectation regardless of the underlying data generation process (Theorem 5.6).

Given the results of Theorems 7.8 and 7.11, it is clear that linear exponential QMLE's will generally be less efficient than an appropriate MLE obtained from a model correctly specified in its entirety. Nevertheless, it is useful to see if we can find a linear exponential QMLE that has smaller asymptotic covariance than any other. Such an estimator would be preferred asymptotically if one were to limit attention to linear exponential QMLE's. The following result extends to the dynamic case an efficiency result for the QGPMLE (quasi-generalized pseudo-MLE) given by Gourieroux, Monfort and Trognon [1984].

THEOREM 7.15: *Suppose the conditions of Theorem 6.13(iv) hold with associated estimator* $\hat{\beta} = \{\hat{\beta}_n\}$, *and let* $\hat{\beta}^* = \{\hat{\beta}_n^*\}$ *be an estimator obtained by choosing* $\{\kappa_t\}$ *and* $\{\alpha_n^*\}$ *so that the conditions of Theorem 6.13(iv) hold, i.e.* $D_t^* = \Sigma_t^o$. *Then* avar $\hat{\beta}_n$ − avar $\hat{\beta}_n^*$ *is positive semi-definite for all n.* □

A familiar choice for an estimator that satisfies the conditions of Theorem 6.13(iv) is the nonlinear generalized least squares (NLGLS) estimator, which solves the problem

$$\min_{\beta \in B} n^{-1} \sum_{t=1}^{n} [Y_t - \mu_t(W_t, \beta)]' \hat{\Sigma}_t^{-1} [Y_t - \mu_t(W_t, \beta)] ,$$

where $\hat{\Sigma}_t^{-1} = \kappa_t(W_t, \hat{\alpha}_n)$ is such that $\Sigma_t^{o\,-1} = \kappa_t(W_t, \alpha_o)$. This implements a linear exponential family estimator with $a_t(\mu, \kappa) = \mu' \kappa \mu / 2$ and $c_t(\mu, \kappa) = \kappa \mu$. For this choice, $D_t(\mu, \kappa) = \kappa^{-1}$.

A computationally convenient estimator asymptotically equivalent to the NLGLS estimator is a two step estimator analogous to that of Theorem 7.9. This estimator takes the form

$$\ddot{\beta}_n = \tilde{\beta}_n - \tilde{A}_{22n}^{-} \nabla_\beta L_{2n}(X^n, \hat{\alpha}_n, \tilde{\beta}_n) ,$$

where

$$\tilde{A}_{22n} \equiv n^{-1} \sum_{t=1}^{n} \nabla_\beta \mu_t(W_t, \tilde{\beta}_n) \hat{\Sigma}_t^{-1} \nabla_\beta' \mu_t(W_t, \tilde{\beta}_n) ,$$

$$\nabla_\beta L_{2n}(X^n, \hat{\alpha}_n, \tilde{\beta}_n) \equiv n^{-1} \sum_{t=1}^{n} \nabla_\beta \mu_t(W_t, \tilde{\beta}_n) \hat{\Sigma}_t^{-1} (Y_t - \mu_t(W_t, \tilde{\beta}_n)),$$

and $\tilde{\beta}_n$ is a consistent estimator for β_o such that $\sqrt{n}(\tilde{\beta}_n - \beta_o)$ is $O_{P_o}(1)$, *e.g.*, the nonlinear least squares estimator.

Thus, asymptotically efficient estimators for any member of the linear exponential family can be obtained by nonlinear least squares, followed by one step of a weighted nonlinear least squares iteration. Of course, this efficiency depends on $\mathcal{M} = \{\mu_t\}$ being correctly specified for $\{E(Y_t \mid \tilde{X}^{t-1})\}$, (no dynamic misspecification), and choice of κ_t so that $\{\kappa_t^{-1}\}$ is correctly specified for $\{\text{var}(Y_t \mid \tilde{X}^{t-1})\}$.

We again emphasize that for an asymptotic efficiency result to obtain, the result of Theorem 7.15 must be shown to hold for all P^o in some suitable family and for all $\hat{\beta}$ in an appropriate class of estimators. We have avoided this formalism here for simplicity. As given, the result pertains only to what happens under P_o. However, an appropriate formal framework for asymptotic efficiency is given by Bates and White [1990]. An appropriate probability model $\mathcal{P}$ is

$$\mathcal{P} = \{P_\theta : E_\theta(Y_t \mid \tilde{X}^{t-1}) = \mu_t(W_t, \beta),\ \text{var}_\theta(Y_t \mid \tilde{X}^{t-1}) = V_t(W_t, \gamma),$$
$$\theta = (\beta', \gamma')' \in \Theta, \Theta = \mathcal{B} \times \Gamma\}$$

and an appropriate class of estimators is the class of two-stage linear exponential family estimators and their two-step equivalents.

The result of Theorem 7.15 can be extended to establish that the NLGLS estimator is asymptotically efficient in the regular consistent asymptotically normal indexed class of estimators treated by Theorem 6.13. This is a relatively limited form of efficiency result.

7.4 Summary

In this chapter we have seen that the minimum asymptotic variance bound can be attained in the face of incomplete specifications, such as those ignoring informationally exogenous and Granger non-causal variables, or, as just considered, distributional aspects beyond the second moment. Numerous examples can be given to show that dynamic misspecification may adversely affect consistency, and if not consistency, then attainment of the asymptotic variance bound. Implicit in Theorem 7.15 is the implication that neglected heteroskedasticity may also adversely affect attainment of the asymptotic variance bound. In every case considered, the attainment or not of the minimum asymptotic variance bound can be traced back to the validity of the information matrix equality, which we investigated at length in the previous chapter.

We have not addressed the issue of whether there is some sense in which a QMLE for an arbitrarily misspecified model may or may not be asymptotically efficient. For such an investigation to be meaningful, we must have a way to extend the definition of parameters of interest to arbitrarily misspecified models, which generally yield estimators not consistent for parameters of interest in the usual sense. One way to achieve this extension is to allow a given specification to determine the parameters of interest by simply defining them to be the sequence $\theta^* = \{\theta_n^*\}$. One may then investigate the properties of alternative estimators that yield the same sequence θ^* under P as does a given specification, regardless of which P in some appropriate collection generates the data. This approach has recently been taken by Vuong [1986] for i.i.d. observations using finite sample techniques related to the classical treatment of the Cramér-Rao bound. It appears possible to extend Vuong's approach to the dependent heterogeneous case in a large sample context. We do not pursue this extension here.

An alternative approach to the question of asymptotic efficiency in estimation with an arbitrarily misspecified model is taken by Beran [1980]. Beran considers the "parameters of interest" in the arbitrary misspecified case to be the distribution of the sample, P_o^n, which is estimated by $P_{\hat{\theta}_n}^n$, where $\{P_\theta^n : \theta \in \Theta\}$ is the parametric model for a sample of size n, and $\hat{\theta}_n$ is some estimator, e.g. a QMLE. Beran considers the risk $E_{P_o^n}(w[\,\rho(P_{\hat{\theta}_n}^n,\ P_o^n)])$, where w is a nonnegative monotone increasing function of the metric ρ on the set of all probability measures, under a sequence $\{P_o^n\}$ which is not too far from $\{P_\theta^n\}$, and obtains asymptotic lower bounds on the minimax risk. Beran's analysis treats the i.i.d. case, taking ρ to be the Hellinger metric discussed in Chapter 2. The results generalize the classical Cramér-Rao bound in an insightful way.

Beran's approach is elegant and appealing. Extending his results to dependent heterogeneous processes would yield asymptotic efficiency results directly relevant to the problem of estimation of arbitrarily misspecified models in the context treated here. Unfortunately, this extension is beyond the scope of our treatment, and must be left to other work.

MATHEMATICAL APPENDIX

PROOF OF THEOREM 7.4: Choose $\theta^o \in int\,\Theta$ and $\{a_n\}$ such that $a_n{}'\, I_n^o\, a_n = 1$. Define $\theta_n^o = \theta^o + n^{-1/2}\, a_n$. Given Assumption 3.6 (differentiability of order 2 on Θ $a.s.-P_{\theta^o}$), the interiority of θ^o, and the boundedness of a_n, Taylor's theorem yields

$$L_n(X^n, \theta_n^o) = L_n(X^n, \theta^o) + \nabla' L_n(X^n, \theta^o)\,(\theta_n^o - \theta^o)$$

$$+ (\theta_n^o - \theta^o)'\, \nabla^2\, \ddot{L}_n (\theta_n^o - \theta^o)/2\,,$$

where $\nabla^2\, \ddot{L}_n$ is the $p \times p$ Hessian with rows evaluated at values lying on the segment connecting θ_n^o and θ^o. Substituting for θ_n^o, we have

$$n\, L_n(X^n, \theta_n^o) - n\, L_n(X^n, \theta^o) + a_n{}'\, I_n^o\, a_n/2$$

$$= n^{1/2}\, \nabla' L_n(X^n, \theta^o)\, a_n + a_n{}'\, I_n^o\, a_n/2 + a_a{}'\, \nabla^2\, \ddot{L}_n\, a_n/2\,.$$

$$= a_n{}'\, n^{-1/2} \sum_{t=1}^{n} s_t^o + a_n{}'(I_n^o + \nabla^2\, \ddot{L}_n\,)a_n\,/2\,.$$

Given Assumption 6.1 we have that $n^{-1/2} s_t^*$ obeys the central limit theorem with covariance matrix B_n^*. By Theorem 3.6, Assumptions 2.1-2.3, 3.1(a,b), 3.2, 3.4, and the correct specification of $\mathcal{S}$ imply that $\theta_n^* = \theta^o$, so that in fact $n^{-1/2}\, s_t^o$ obeys the central limit theorem with asymptotic covariance matrix B_n^o, say, where B_n^o is $O(1)$ and uniformly positive definite. Further, from Theorem 6.5(i), Assumption 6.2 then implies $A_n^o = -\,B_n^o$, where $A_n^o \equiv E^o(\nabla^2\, L_n(X^n, \theta^o))$.

Setting $I_n^o = B_n^o$ and using the fact that $a_n{}'\, I_n^o\, a_n = 1$, we have that

$$K_n \equiv (a_n{}'\, I_n^o\, a_n)^{-1/2}\, [n\, L_n(X^n, \theta_n^o) - n\, L_n(X^n, \theta^o) + a_n{}'\, I_n^o\, a_n/2]$$

$$= (a_n{}'\, B_n^o\, a_n)^{-1/2}\, a_n{}'\, n^{-1/2} \sum_{t=1}^{n} s_t^o + (a'_n\, B_n^o\, a_n)^{-1/2}\, a'_n(B_n^o + \nabla^2\, \ddot{L}_n\,)a_n/2\,.$$

Given Assumption 6.1 and the fact that $E(s_t^o) = 0$ given Assumption 3.7(a), the first term above converges in distribution to $N(0,\, 1)$ by Corollary 4.24 of White [1984a] so that the result follows from the asymptotic equivalence lemma (e.g. White [1984a, Lemma 4.7]) provided that

$$(a'_n\, B_n^o\, a_n)^{-1/2}\, a'_n(B_n^o + \nabla^2\, \ddot{L}_n\,)a_n/2 \to 0 \qquad prob - P_{\theta^o}\,.$$

Now $(a'_n\, B_n^o\, a_n)^{-1/2} = 1$ and $\nabla^2\, L_n$ obeys the (weak) uniform law of large numbers by Assumption 3.8. It follows from Corollary 3.8 that $\nabla^2\, \ddot{L}_n - A_n^o \to 0\ prob - P_{\theta^o}$. But $A_n^o = -\,B_n^o$, so that $B_n^o + \nabla^2\, \ddot{L}_n \to 0\ \ prob - P_{\theta^o}$. The desired convergence to zero in probability follows immediately, given the boundedness of a_n.

Because a_n and θ^o are arbitrary, we have shown that $\mathcal{P}$ satisfies the conditions of Definition 7.3, and is therefore a LAN family. □

The proof of Theorem 7.6 requires the following lemma.

LEMMA 7.A.1: Let $f_n : \mathbb{R} \to \mathbb{R}$ be measurable, $n = 1, 2, \ldots$ and suppose that $\mathcal{X}_n \overset{A}{\sim} \mathcal{X} : \Omega \to \mathbb{R}$, a random variable on the complete probability space $(\Omega\, , \mathcal{F}\, , P)$. Suppose that the set of discontinuities of f_n, denoted D_n, is a countable set such that f_n is continuous on D^c, the complement of $D \equiv \cup_{n=1}^{\infty} D_n$, uniformly in n and that $P[\,\mathcal{X} \in D] = 0$.

Suppose also that $\{f_n(\,\mathcal{X}_n)\}$ and $\{f_n(\,\mathcal{X}\,)\}$ are uniformly integrable. Then $E(f_n(\mathcal{X}_n)) - E(f_n(\,\mathcal{X}\,)) \to 0$. □

PROOF: By the Skorohod Representation Theorem (29.6, Billingsley [1979]) there exist a probability space $(\tilde{\Omega}\, , \tilde{\mathcal{F}}\, , \tilde{P})$ and random variables $\tilde{X}_n : \tilde{\Omega} \to \mathbb{R}$ and $\tilde{X} : \tilde{\Omega} \to \mathbb{R}$ having distributions identical to those of $\mathcal{X}_n$ and $\mathcal{X}$, such that $\tilde{X}_n(\tilde{\omega}) \to \tilde{X}(\tilde{\omega})$ for all $\tilde{\omega}$ in $\tilde{\Omega}$. Because $P[\mathcal{X} \in D] = 0$, there exits $\tilde{F} = [\tilde{\omega} : \tilde{X}(\tilde{\omega}) \in D] \in \tilde{\mathcal{F}}$ such that $\tilde{P}(\tilde{F}) = 0$. Choose $\tilde{\omega} \in \tilde{F}^c$. Because f_n is continuous uniformly in n on D^c, given $\varepsilon > 0$ there exists δ such that for $|\, x - x_o\,| < \delta$

$$|\, f_n(x) - f_n(x_o)\,| < \varepsilon$$

for all $x_o \in D^c$. Because $\tilde{X}_n \to \tilde{X}$, for given δ there exists $N(\tilde{\omega}\, , \delta)$, such that $|\tilde{X}_n(\tilde{\omega}) - \tilde{X}(\tilde{\omega})\,| < \delta$ for all $n > N(\tilde{\omega}\, , \delta)$. Thus, given ε there exists $N(\tilde{\omega}\, , \delta(\varepsilon))$ such that $|\, f_n(\tilde{X}_n(\tilde{\omega})) - f_n(\tilde{X}(\tilde{\omega}))\,| < \varepsilon$, for all $n > N(\tilde{\omega}\, , \delta(\varepsilon))$, $\tilde{\omega} \in \tilde{F}^c$, $\tilde{P}(\tilde{F}^c\,) = 1$. Thus $f_n(\tilde{X}_n) - f_n(\tilde{X}) \to 0\ a.s. -\tilde{P}$. Given that $f_n(\mathcal{X}_n)$ and $f_n(\mathcal{X})$ are uniformly integrable, it follows that $f_n(\tilde{X}_n)$ and $f_n(\tilde{X})$ are uniformly integrable. Therefore by Theorem 16.13 of Billingsley [1979] $\tilde{E}(f_n(\tilde{X}_n) - f_n(\tilde{X})) \to 0$. But because $\tilde{X}_n$ and $\tilde{X}$ have the same distribution as $\mathcal{X}_n$ and $\mathcal{X}$ it follows that $E(f_n(\mathcal{X}_n)) - E(f_n(\mathcal{X})) \to 0$. □

PROOF OF THEOREM 7.6: We follow the approach of Bahadur [1964]. Choose $\theta^o \in int\ \Theta$ and for now suppose that $\{C_n^o\}$ is uniformly positive definite. For any $\{a_n\}$, $a_n{}'\ I_n^o\ a_n = 1$, let $\mathcal{C}_n = \{x^n : K_n^o \geq k\}$ where $k \in \mathbb{R}$. Now $P_{\theta^o}^n(\mathcal{C}_n) = E^o(1[K_n^o \geq k])$ and $K_n^o \overset{A^o}{\sim} \mathcal{Z} \sim N(0, 1)$ by assumption. The functions $f(\cdot) = 1[\cdot \geq k]$ are measurable with a single discontinuity at k, which has measure zero under $N(0, 1)$. It follows from Theorem 25.7 of Billingsley [1979] that $P_{\theta^o}^n(\mathcal{C}_n) \to 1 - \Phi(k)$ as $n \to \infty$.

Next we show that $P_{\theta_n^o}^n(\mathcal{C}_n) \to 1 - \Phi(k-1)$ as $n \to \infty$. Now

$$1 - P_{\theta_n^o}^n(\mathcal{C}_n) = \int_{\mathcal{C}_n^c} f^n(x^n, \theta_n^o)\, d\nu^n(x^n)$$

$$= \int_{\mathcal{C}_n^c} \exp n[L_n(x^n, \theta_n^o) - L_n(x^n, \theta^o)]\, dP_{\theta^o}^n(x^n)$$

$$= \int_{\mathcal{C}_n^c} \exp[K_n^o - 1/2]\, dP_{\theta^o}^n$$

$$= \exp(-1/2)\, E^o(1[K_n^o < k] \exp K_n^o)\,.$$

It follows from Theorem 25.7 of Billingsley [1979] that

$$\exp(-1/2)\, E^o(1[K_n^o < k] \exp K_n^o)$$

$$\to \exp(-1/2) \int_{-\infty}^{k} \exp z \cdot \exp(-z^2/2)\,(2\pi)^{-1/2}\, dz$$

$$= \int_{-\infty}^{k} \exp[-(z-1)^2/2]\,(2\pi)^{-1/2}\, dz$$

$$= \Phi(k-1)\,,$$

so that $P_{\theta_n^o}^n(\mathcal{C}_n) \to 1 - \Phi(k-1)$.

For arbitrary $\varepsilon > 0$, set $k = 1 + \varepsilon$. Then $P_{\theta_n^o}^n(\mathcal{C}_n) \to 1 - \Phi(\varepsilon)$, which implies $\limsup_{n\to\infty} P_{\theta_n^o}^n(\mathcal{C}_n) < 1/2$. Choose b arbitrarily and for notational convenience, write

$$\mathcal{D}_n \equiv \{x^n : b'\,\tilde{\theta}_n \geq b'\,\theta_n^o\}\,.$$

By assumption $P^n_\theta[b'\tilde{\theta}_n \geq b'\theta] \to 1/2$ as $n \to \infty$ uniformly on *int* Θ. Hence $P^n_{\theta^o_n}[\mathcal{D}_n] \to 1/2$ as $n \to \infty$. Consequently, for all n sufficiently large

$$P^n_{\theta^o_n}(\mathcal{D}_n) > P^n_{\theta^o_n}(\mathcal{C}_n) .$$

For each n regard $\mathcal{C}_n$ and $\mathcal{D}_n$ as alternative critical regions for testing $b'\theta^o$ against $b'\theta^o_n$. Because $\mathcal{C}_n$ is an optimum critical region by the Neyman-Pearson [1933] lemma, the inequality above implies

$$P^n_{\theta^o}(\mathcal{D}_n) > P^n_{\theta^o}(\mathcal{C}_n)$$

for all n sufficiently large. Now

$$\begin{aligned} P^n_{\theta^o}(\mathcal{D}_n) &= P^n_{\theta^o}[b'\tilde{\theta}_n \geq b'\theta^o_n] \\ &= P^n_{\theta^o}[b'\tilde{\theta}_n \geq b'\theta^o + b'a_n n^{-1/2}] \\ &= P^n_{\theta^o}[n^{1/2}b'(\tilde{\theta}_n - \theta^o) \geq b'a_n] \\ &= P^n_{\theta^o}[n^{1/2}b'(\tilde{\theta}_n - \theta^o)/(b'C^o_n b)^{1/2} \geq b'a_n/(b'C^o_n b')^{1/2}] , \end{aligned}$$

given the uniform positive definiteness of C^o_n. It follows from the asymptotic normality of $n^{1/2}(\tilde{\theta}_n - \theta^o)$ under P_{θ^o} and Lemma 7.A.1 that

$$P^n_{\theta^o}(\mathcal{D}_n) - [1 - \Phi(b'a_n/(b'C^o_n b)^{1/2})] \to 0 .$$

Because $P^n_{\theta^o}(\mathcal{C}_n) - [1 - \Phi(k)] \to 0$, the inequality $P^n_{\theta^o}(\mathcal{D}_n) > P^n_{\theta^o}(\mathcal{C}_n)$ implies that

$$1 - \Phi(b'a_n/(b'C^o_n b)^{1/2}) \geq 1 - \Phi(k) .$$

With $k = 1 + \varepsilon$ for arbitrary $\varepsilon > 0$ and all a_n such that $a'_n I^o_n a_n = 1$, it follows that for all n sufficiently large

$$1 \geq b'a_n/(b'C^o_n b)^{1/2}$$

or

$$b' C_n^o b \geq (b' a_n)^2 .$$

Maximization of $(b' a_n)^2$ with respect to a_n subject to $a'_n I_n^o a_n = 1$ can be verified to occur with $a_n = I_n^{o-1} b / (b' I_n^{o-1} b)^{1/2}$, so that

$$b' C_n^o b \geq b' I_n^{o-1} b .$$

Because b is arbitrary, it follows that $C_n^o - I_n^{o-1}$ is positive semi-definite for all n sufficiently large.

Now drop the requirement that $\{C_n^o\}$ is positive definite uniformly in n. Define $\tilde{\theta}_n^* = \tilde{\theta}_n + \varepsilon\, n^{-1/2}\, \mathcal{Z}\, 1[\theta = \theta^o]$ where $\varepsilon > 0$ is an arbitrary constant scalar and $\mathcal{Z} \sim N(0, I_p)$ independent of $\{X_t\}$. It follows that

$$\sqrt{n}\, (\tilde{\theta}_n^* - \theta) \overset{A^o}{\sim} N(0, C_n(\theta) + \varepsilon^2\, 1[\theta = \theta^o] I_p)$$

for each θ in *int* Θ. In particular, $C_n^* \equiv C_n^o + \varepsilon^2 I_p$ is now uniformly positive definite. Furthermore, for any $b \in \mathbb{R}^p$, $b'b = 1$, $P_\theta^n [b' \tilde{\theta}_n^* \geq b' \theta] \to 1/2$ as $n \to \infty$ uniformly on Θ, because for $\theta \neq \theta^o$, $\theta \in$ *int* Θ, $P_\theta^n [b' \tilde{\theta}_n^* \geq b'\theta] = P_\theta^n [b' \tilde{\theta}_n \geq b'\theta]$, so regularity ensures that given $\varepsilon > 0$ there exists $N_1(\varepsilon)$ such that $| P_\theta^n [b' \tilde{\theta}_n^* \geq b' \theta] - 1/2 | < \varepsilon$ for all $\theta \in$ *int* Θ, $\theta \neq \theta^o$ and for all $n > N_1(\varepsilon)$, while for θ^o, asymptotic normality ensures that given $\varepsilon > 0$ there exists $N_2(\varepsilon)$ such that

$$| P_{\theta^o}^n [b' \tilde{\theta}_n^* \geq b' \theta^o] - \Phi(0 / [b' C_n^o b + \varepsilon^2]) |$$

$$= | P_{\theta^o}^n [b' \tilde{\theta}_n^* \geq b' \theta^o] - 1/2 | < \varepsilon$$

for all $n > N_2(\varepsilon)$. Hence, given $\varepsilon > 0$

$$| P_\theta^n [b' \tilde{\theta}_n^* \geq b' \theta] - 1/2 | < \varepsilon$$

for all $n > \max(N_1(\varepsilon), N_2(\varepsilon))$ for all θ in *int* Θ.

It follows from the argument above that $C_n^* - I_n^{o-1}$ is positive semi-definite for all n sufficiently large, i.e. $C_n^o + \varepsilon^2 I_p - I_n^{o-1}$ is positive semi-definite. Because I_n^{o-1} is uniformly positive definite and because ε is arbitrary, it follows that C_n^o is also uniformly positive definite.

Because θ^o is arbitrary, the above result holds everywhere in *int* Θ, and the proof is complete. □

PROOF OF THEOREM 7.8: (i) It suffices to show that $\text{avar}^o\,\hat{\theta}_n = I_n^{o-1}$ for each θ^o in *int* Θ. This follows directly from Theorem 6.5 under the conditions of Theorem 7.4 and Assumption 3.1(c), with $B_n^o = I_n^o$.

(ii) This follows immediately from (i) when $P_o \in \mathcal{P}$. □

PROOF OF THEOREM 7.9: (i) By definition

$$\ddot{\theta}_n = \tilde{\theta}_n - \tilde{A}_n^- \nabla L_n(X^n, \tilde{\theta}_n) .$$

Fix θ^o in *int* Θ, and choose an arbitrary subsequence $\{n'\}$. Because $\tilde{A}_n - E^o(\nabla^2 L_n(X^n, \theta^o)) \to 0$ *prob* $-P_{\theta^o}$, there exists a further subsequence $\{n''\}$ such that $\tilde{A}_{n''} - E^o(\nabla^2 L_{n''}(X^{n''}, \theta^o)) \to 0$ *a.s.*–P_{θ^o}. It follows that for all n'' sufficiently large $\tilde{A}_{n''}$ is nonsingular, *a.s.*–P_{θ^o}, given (inter alia) Assumptions 6.1 and 6.2, which ensure the (uniform) nonsingularity of $E^o(\nabla^2 L_{n''}(X^{n''}, \theta^o))$. Thus consider

$$\ddot{\theta}_{n''} = \tilde{\theta}_{n''} - \tilde{A}_{n''}^{-1} \nabla L_{n''}(X^{n''}, \tilde{\theta}_{n''}) .$$

A mean value expansion of $\nabla L_{n''}$ around $\hat{\theta}_{n''}$ gives

$$\ddot{\theta}_{n''} = \tilde{\theta}_{n''} - \tilde{A}_{n''}^{-1} \nabla L_{n''}(X^{n''}, \hat{\theta}_{n''}) - \tilde{A}_{n''}^{-1} \nabla^2 \ddot{L}_{n''} (\tilde{\theta}_{n''} - \hat{\theta}_{n''}) .$$

Therefore, for given θ^o

$$\sqrt{n''}\,(\ddot{\theta}_{n''} - \hat{\theta}_{n''}) = -\sqrt{n''}\,\tilde{A}_{n''}^{-1} \nabla L_{n''}(X^{n''}, \hat{\theta}_{n''})$$
$$+ (\tilde{A}_{n''}^{-1} \nabla^2 \ddot{L}_{n''} - I_p) \sqrt{n''}\,(\hat{\theta}_{n''} - \theta^o)$$
$$+ (I_p - \tilde{A}_{n''}^{-1} \nabla^2 \ddot{L}_{n''}) \sqrt{n''}\,(\tilde{\theta}_{n''} - \theta^o) .$$

Given Assumption 6.1, $\tilde{A}_{n''}^{-1}$ is bounded *a.s.*–P_{θ^o}, and $\sqrt{n''}\,\nabla L_{n''}(X^{n''}, \hat{\theta}_{n''})$ vanishes *a.s.*–P_{θ^o}, as in the proof of Theorem 6.2. Thus

$-\sqrt{n''}\,\tilde{A}_{n''}^{-1}\,\nabla L_{n''}\,(X^{n''}, \hat{\theta}_{n''})$ vanishes $a.s.-P_{\theta^o}$. Further, the second and third terms vanish in probability because $\sqrt{n''}\,(\hat{\theta}_{n''} - \theta^o)$ and $\sqrt{n''}\,(\tilde{\theta}_{n''} - \theta^o)$ are bounded in probability and because $\tilde{A}_{n''}^{-1}\,\nabla^2\,\ddot{L}_{n''} \to I_p\ prob-P_{\theta^o}$. Hence $\sqrt{n''}\,(\ddot{\theta}_{n''} - \hat{\theta}_{n''})$ vanishes in probability. It follows that there exists a further subsequence $\{n'''\}$ such that $\sqrt{n'''}\,(\ddot{\theta}_{n'''} - \hat{\theta}_{n''})$ vanishes almost surely. Because $\{n'\}$ is arbitrary, it follows from the subsequence theorem that $\sqrt{n}(\ddot{\theta}_n - \hat{\theta}_n) \to 0\ prob-P_{\theta^o}$. Because θ^o is arbitrary, this holds for all θ^o in $int\ \Theta$.

(ii) It follows from the asymptotic equivalence lemma that $\text{avar}^o\ \ddot{\theta}_n = \text{avar}^o\ \hat{\theta}_n$ for all θ^o in $int\ \Theta$. If $\ddot{\theta}$ is RCAN, it follows that $\ddot{\theta}$ is asymptotically efficient in $\mathcal{E}(\mathcal{P}, \mathcal{T})$.

(iii) This follows immediately from (ii) when $P_o \in \mathcal{P}$. □

PROOF OF THEOREM 7.10:(i) We verify the conditions of Theorems 7.4 and 7.6 for $\mathcal{E}(\tilde{\mathcal{P}}, \tilde{\mathcal{T}})$. Because $\mathcal{P}$ is a regular parametric probability model, it follows immediately that $\tilde{\mathcal{P}} \subset \mathcal{P}$ is a regular parametric probability model. Choose γ^o in $int\ \Gamma$ and set $P_o = \tilde{P}_{\gamma^o} = P_{d(\gamma^o)}$ in Assumption 2.1. Given Assumptions 2.3 and 7.1 (continuity), Assumption 2.3 holds for $\tilde{f}_t(\cdot, \gamma) = f_t(\cdot, d(\gamma))$. Assumptions 3.1 and 7.1 (continuity), ensure that Assumption 3.1 holds for $\log \tilde{f}_t(X^t, \gamma) = \log f_t(X_t, d(\gamma))$, while Assumptions 3.2 and 7.1 (injection) ensure that Assumption 3.2 holds for $\{E^o(\log \tilde{f}_n(X^n, \gamma))\}$ with identifiably unique maximizers γ^o. Assumptions 3.6 and 7.1 (continuous differentiability of order 2) ensure that Assumption 3.6 holds for $\tilde{f}_t$, while Assumptions 3.7(a) and 7.1 (continuous differentiability) ensure that

$$\begin{aligned} E^o(\nabla_\gamma \tilde{L}_n(X^n, \gamma)) &= E^o(D(\gamma)'\,\nabla_\theta L_n(X^n, d(\gamma))) \\ &= D(\gamma)'\,\nabla_\theta\,E^o(L_n(X^n, d(\gamma))) \\ &= \nabla_\gamma\,E^o(\tilde{L}_n(X^n, \gamma)), \end{aligned}$$

so that Assumption 3.7(a) holds for $\tilde{L}_n = n^{-1} \log \tilde{f}_n$. Similarly Assumptions 3.8 and 7.1 (continuous differentiability of order 2) ensure that Assumption 3.8 holds for $\tilde{L}_n$: the argument for 3.8(a) is analogous to that for 3.7(a); the continuity of $E^o(\nabla_\gamma^2 \tilde{L}_n(X^n, \gamma))$ uniformly in n required by 3.8(b) follows by writing

$$\begin{aligned} \nabla_\gamma^2 \tilde{L}_n(X^n, \gamma) = {} & D(\gamma)'\,\nabla_\theta^2 L_n(X^n, d(\gamma))\,D(\gamma) \\ & + [\nabla_\theta' L_n(X^n, d(\gamma)) \otimes I_c]\,\nabla_\gamma^2 d(\gamma), \end{aligned}$$

where $\nabla_\gamma^2 d(\gamma) = [\nabla^2 d_1(\gamma)', \ldots, \nabla^2 d_r(\gamma)']'$ is a $cp \times c$ matrix, invoking the continuity of D and $\nabla_\gamma^2 d$ ensured by Assumption 7.1, and the continuity uniformly in n of $E^o(\nabla_\theta^2 L_n(X^n, \theta))$ and $E^o(\nabla_\theta L_n(X^n, \theta))$ ensured by Assumptions 3.7(b) and 3.8(b); and the validity of the ULLN required of $\nabla_\gamma^2 \log \tilde{f}_t$ by 3.8(c) follows because

$$\nabla_\gamma^2 \log \tilde{f}_t(X^t, \gamma) = D(\gamma)' \nabla_\theta^2 \log f_t(X^t, d(\gamma)) D(\gamma)$$

$$+ [\nabla_\theta' \log f_t(X^t, d(\gamma)) \otimes I_c] \nabla_\gamma^2 d(\gamma)$$

with $\nabla_\theta^2 \log f_t$ and $\nabla_\theta \log f_t$ satisfying the ULLN by Assumption 3.8(c) and 3.7(c), and D and $\nabla_\gamma^2 d$ continuous on the compact set Γ.

Assumptions 6.1 and 7.1 (injection) ensure that Assumption 6.1 holds for $\nabla_\gamma \log \tilde{f}_t(X^t, \gamma^o) = D(\gamma^o)' \nabla_\theta \log f_t(X^t, d(\gamma^o))$, with $\tilde{B}_n^o = D^{o\prime} B_n^o D^o$. Because D^o is finite (D is a real valued function continuous on a compact set) with full rank, and B_n^o is $O(1)$ and uniformly positive definite it follows that $\tilde{B}_n^o$ is $O(1)$ and uniformly positive definite.

Because γ^o is arbitrary, the conditions just established hold for all γ^o in *int* Γ.

Assumption 6.2 and Assumption 7.1 (continuous differentiability of order 2; $\gamma \in$ *int* Γ implies $\theta \in$ *int* Θ) ensure that

$$\int_{\tilde{S}_\gamma^n} \nabla_\gamma \tilde{f}^n(x^n, \gamma)\, dv^n(x^n)$$

$$= [\int_{S_{d(\gamma)}^n} D(\gamma)' \nabla_\theta f^n(x^n, d(\gamma))\, dv^n(x^n)] = 0$$

and

$$\int_{\tilde{S}_\gamma^n} \nabla_\gamma^2 \tilde{f}^n(x^n, \gamma)\, dv^n(x^n)$$

$$= D(\gamma)' [\int_{S_{d(\gamma)}^n} \nabla_\theta^2 f^n(x^n, d(\gamma))\, dv^n(x^n)] D(\gamma)$$

$$+ [\int_{S_{d(\gamma)}^n} \nabla_\theta' f^n(x^n, d(\gamma))\, dv^n(x^n) \otimes I_c] \nabla_\gamma^2 d(\gamma)$$

$$= 0 .$$

Thus, the conditions of Theorem 7.4 hold, so that $\tilde{\mathcal{P}}$ is a LAN family, with $\tilde{I}_n^o = D^{o\prime} B_n^o D^o$.

The result of (i) now follows immediately from Theorem 7.6.

(ii) This follows immediately from Theorem 7.8, as does (iii). □

PROOF OF THEOREM 7.11:(i) In the text, it is shown that for arbitrary γ^o in *int* Γ,

$$\sqrt{n}\,(\tilde{\theta}_n - \theta^o) \overset{A^o}{\sim} N(0, D^o\, \tilde{C}_n^o\, D^{o\prime})\,.$$

It follows immediately that $\mathcal{E}(\tilde{\mathcal{P}}, d(\tilde{\mathcal{T}}))$ is a CAN class. For each γ^o in *int* Γ, by Theorem 7.10 $\tilde{C}_n^o - (D^{o\prime}\, I_n^o\, D^o)^{-1}$ is p.s.d. Therefore

$$\begin{aligned} &D^o\, \tilde{C}_n^o\, D^{o\prime} - D^o\,(D^{o\prime}\, I_n^o\, D^o)^{-1}\, D^{o\prime} \\ &= \text{avar}^o\, \tilde{\theta}_n - D^o\,(D^{o\prime}\, I_n^o\, D^o)^{-1}\, D^{o\prime} \end{aligned}$$

is p.s.d. for each γ^o in *int* Γ.

(ii) This follows immediately from Theorem 7.10(ii).

(iii) This follows immediately from Theorem 7.10(iii). □

PROOF OF THEOREM 7.13:(i) Because $\mathcal{S}$ is correct for $\{ Y_t \mid \tilde{X}^{t-1} \}$ we have $f_t\,(x^t, \theta_o) = h_t(\,y^t, \tilde{x}^{t-1})$ (defined in Chapter 4 as the density ratio of Y_t given $\tilde{X}^{t-1}$ with respect to $\{ \nu^t, \tilde{\nu}^{t-1}\}$) and because $\tilde{\mathcal{S}}$ is correct for $\{ Z_t \mid X^{t-1}\}$ at θ_o we have $\tilde{f}_t\,(\tilde{x}^{t-1}, \theta_o) = \tilde{h}_t\,(z_t, x^{t-1})$, the density ratio of Z_t given X^{t-1} with respect to $\{\tilde{\nu}^{t-1}, \nu^{t-1}\}$. Thus $f_t(x^t, \theta_o) \cdot \tilde{f}_t(\tilde{x}^{t-1}, \theta_o) = h_t(y_t, \tilde{x}^{t-1}) \cdot \tilde{h}_t(z_t, x^{t-1}) = [\,g_t(x_t)/\tilde{g}_t\,(\tilde{x}^{t-1})] \times [\,\tilde{g}_t\,(\tilde{x}^{t-1}) \,/\, g_{t-1}\,(x^{t-1})] = g_t(x^t)/g_{t-1}\,(x^{t-1})$. It follows that $\mathcal{S}^* = \{f_t \cdot \tilde{f}_t\}$ is correctly specified for $\{ X_t \mid X^{t-1}\}$ on Θ with respect to $\{ \nu^t, \nu^{t-1}\}$.

(ii) We verify the conditions of Theorem 6.5 for $\mathcal{S}^*$. Assumptions 2.1 and 2.2 are maintained implicitly in Definition 7.12. Assumption 2.3 holds for $f_t^* = f_t \cdot \tilde{f}_t$ as it holds individually for f_t and $\tilde{f}_t$, and measurability and continuity are preserved under multiplication.

Now $\log f_t^* = \log f_t + \log \tilde{f}_t$, so $\{ \log f_t^* \}$ is easily seen to satisfy Assumptions 3.1(a) and 3.1(b) given that $\log f_t$ and $\log \tilde{f}_t$ do. Further,

$$\sup_{\theta \in \Theta} \left| \, n^{-1} \textstyle\sum_{t=1}^{nr} \log f_t^*\,(X^t, \theta)) \right|$$

$$= \sup_{\theta\in\Theta} | n^{-1} \textstyle\sum_{t=1}^{n} [\log f_t(X^t, \theta) - E(\log f_t(X^t, \theta))]$$

$$+ n^{-1} \textstyle\sum_{t=1}^{n} [\log \tilde{f}_t(\tilde{X}^{t-1}, \theta) - E(\log \tilde{f}_t(\tilde{X}^{t-1}, \theta))] |$$

$$\leq \sup_{\theta\in\Theta} | n^{-1} \textstyle\sum_{t=1}^{n} \log f_t(X^t, \theta) - E(\log f_t(X^t, \theta)) |$$

$$+ \sup_{\theta\in\Theta} | n^{-1} \textstyle\sum_{t=1}^{n} \log \tilde{f}_t(\tilde{X}^{t-1}, \theta) - E(\log \tilde{f}_t(\tilde{X}^{t-1}, \theta)) |$$

From this we see that $\{ \log f_t^* \}$ satisfies the uniform law of large numbers given that $\{ \log f_t \}$ and $\{ \log \tilde{f}_t \}$ both do, verifying Assumption 3.1(c).

For Assumption 3.2′ it suffices that

$$L_n^*(\theta) \equiv n^{-1} \sum_{t=1}^{n} E(\log f_t(X^t, \theta)) + n^{-1} \sum_{t=1}^{n} E(\log \tilde{f}_t(\tilde{X}^{t-1}, \theta))$$

has identifiably unique maximizer θ_o interior to Θ. Assumptions 2.1, 2.3, 3.1(a,b), 3.2 and 4.3 for $\mathcal{S}$ and correct specification ensure by Theorem 4.4 that $n^{-1} \sum_{t=1}^{n} E(\log f_t(X^t, \theta))$ has identifiably unique maximizer θ_o. Assumptions 2.1, 2.3, 3.1(a), 4.2 and 4.3 for $\tilde{\mathcal{S}}$ ensure by Theorem 4.4(iii) that

$$n^{-1} \sum_{t=1}^{n} E(\log \tilde{f}_t(\tilde{X}^{t-1}, \theta)) \leq n^{-1} \sum_{t=1}^{n} E(\log \tilde{f}_t(\tilde{X}^{t-1}, \theta_o))$$

given that $\tilde{\mathcal{S}}$ is correctly specified for $\{ Z_t \mid X^{t-1} \}$ at θ_o. It follows that $L_n^*(\theta)$ has identifiably unique maximizer θ_o, interior to Θ by assumption.

Assumption 3.3 is imposed directly. To verify Assumption 3.4 we observe that because $\mathcal{S}$ specifies dependent variables Y and explanatory variables W with $\{ \ddot{v}^t = \ddot{v}_t \otimes \zeta_t \}$ (as in Theorem 6.6) and because $\tilde{\mathcal{S}}$ specifies dependent variables Z and explanatory variables $\tilde{W}$ with $\{ \tilde{v}^{t-1} = \tilde{v}_t \otimes \tilde{\zeta}_t \}$, we have

$$\int_{\mathbb{R}^v} f_t^*(x^t, \theta)\, d\zeta_t(y_t)\, d\tilde{\zeta}_t(z_t)$$

$$= \int_{\mathbb{R}^{v-l}} [\int_{\mathbb{R}^l} f_t(y_t, w_t, \theta)\, d\zeta_t(y_t)]\, \tilde{f}_t(z_t, \tilde{w}_t, \theta)\, d\tilde{\zeta}_t(z_t)$$

$$= \int_{\mathbb{R}^{v-l}} \tilde{f}_t(z_t, \tilde{w}_t, \theta)\, d\tilde{\zeta}_t(z_t) = 1, \qquad t = 1, 2, \ldots .$$

Consequently, with $f^{*n} = \Pi_{t=1}^{n} f_t^*$

$$\int_{S^n} f^{*n}(x^n, \theta)\, d v^n(x_n)$$

$$= \int_{\mathbb{R}^{v n}} f^{*n}(x^n, \theta)\, d\nu^n(x^n)$$

$$= \int_{\mathbb{R}^{v\,n-v}} [\int_{\mathbb{R}^v} f_n^*(x^n, \theta)\, d\nu_n(x_n)]\, f^{*\,n-1}(x^{n-1}, \theta)\, d\nu^{n-1}(x^{n-1})$$

$$= \int_{\mathbb{R}^{v\,n-v}} f^{*\,n-1}(x^{n-1}, \theta)\, d\nu^{n-1}(x^{n-1}) \qquad n = 2, 3, \ldots$$

given that $\nu^n = \nu^{n-1} \otimes \nu_n$ and $\nu_n = \zeta_n \otimes \tilde{\zeta}_n$. Because $f^{*1} = f_1^*$, it follows that $\int_{S^n} f^{*\,n}(x^n, \theta)\, d\nu^n(x^n) = 1$, verifying Assumption 3.4.

Assumption 3.6 holds for f_t^* given that it holds for f_t and $\tilde{f}_t$ individually. Assumption 3.7(a) also holds for $\mathcal{S}^*$ given that it holds for $\mathcal{S}$ and $\tilde{\mathcal{S}}$ individually, as does Assumption 3.8.

Assumption 6.1 requires that the central limit theorem hold for $\{ n^{-1/2} s_t^*(X^t, \theta_o) = n^{-1/2} s_t(X^t, \theta_o) + n^{-1/2} \tilde{s}_t(\tilde{X}^{t-1}, \theta_o) \}$, $\tilde{s}_t \equiv \nabla \log \tilde{f}_t$. However, the assumption that $\{ Z_t \mid X^{t-1} \}$ is informationally exogenous for θ_o implies

$$\tilde{s}_t(\tilde{X}^{t-1}, \theta_o) = \nabla_\theta \tilde{f}_t(\tilde{X}^{t-1}, \theta_o) / \tilde{f}_t(\tilde{X}^{t-1}, \theta_o) = 0 \quad a.s.-P_o\,.$$

Thus, Assumption 6.1 for $\mathcal{S}$ ensures Assumption 6.1 for $\mathcal{S}^*$.

Finally, we apply induction to verify Assumption 6.2. We give the argument explicitly only for Assumption 6.2(a). The argument for Assumption 6.2(b) is analogous. Now $\nabla f^{*\,n} = \nabla f_n^*\, f^{*i\,n-1} + f_n^* \nabla f^{*\,n-1}$, so

$$\int_{S_\theta^{*n}} \nabla f^{*n}(x^n, \theta)\, d\nu^n(x^n)$$

$$= \int_{S_\theta^{*n}} \nabla f_n^*(x^n, \theta)\, f^{*\,n-1}(x^{n-1}, \theta)\, d\nu_n(x_n)\, d\nu^{n-1}(x^{n-1})$$

$$+ \int_{S_\theta^{*n}} f_n^*(x^n, \theta) \nabla f^{*\,n-1}(x^{n-1}, \theta)\, d\nu_n(x_n)\, d\nu^{n-1}(x^{n-1})$$

$$= \int_{S_\theta^{*\,n-1}} [\int_{S_{n,\theta}^*} \nabla f_n^*(x^n, \theta)\, d\nu_n(x_n)]\, f^{*n-1}(x^{n-1}, \theta)\, d\nu^{n-1}(x^{n-1})$$

$$+ \int_{S_\theta^{*n-1}} [\int_{S_{n,\theta}^*} f_n^*(x^n, \theta)\, d\nu_n(x_n)]\, \nabla f^{*\,n-1}(x^{n-1}, \theta)\, d\nu^{n-1}(x^{n-1}).$$

The results above establish that $\int_{S_{n,\theta}^*} f_n^*(x^n, \theta)\, d\nu_n(x_n) = 1$, and by the induction hypothesis $\int_{S_\theta^{*n-1}} \nabla f^{*n-1}(x^{n-1}, \theta)\, d\nu^{n-1}(x^{n-1}) = 0$. Consequently, the second term of the above sum vanishes. The first term also vanishes, provided that $\int_{S_{n,\theta}^*} \nabla f_n^*(x^n, \theta)\, d\nu_n(x_n) = 0 \quad a.e. - \nu^{n-1}$. Now $\nabla f_n^* = \nabla f_n \cdot \tilde{f}_n + f_n \cdot \nabla \tilde{f}_n$. As above,

$$
\begin{aligned}
&\int_{S_{n,\theta}^*} \nabla f_n^*(x^n, \theta)\, d\nu_n(x_n) \\
&= \int_{S_{n,\theta}^*} \nabla f_n(x^n, \theta)\, \tilde{f}_n(\tilde{x}^{n-1}, \theta)\, d\zeta_n(y_n)\, d\tilde{\zeta}_n(z_n) \\
&\quad + \int_{S_{n,\theta}^*} f_n(x^n, \theta)\, \nabla \tilde{f}_n(\tilde{x}^{n-1}, \theta)\, d\zeta_n(y_n)\, d\tilde{\zeta}_n(z_n) \\
&= \int_{\tilde{S}_{n,\theta}} \left[\int_{S_{n,\theta}} \nabla f_n(x^n, \theta)\, d\zeta_n(y_n)\right] \tilde{f}_n(\tilde{x}^{n-1}, \theta)\, d\tilde{\zeta}_n(z_n) \\
&\quad + \int_{\tilde{S}_{n,\theta}} \left[\int_{S_{n,\theta}} f_n(x^n, \theta)\, d\zeta_n(y_n)\right] \nabla \tilde{f}_n(\tilde{x}^{n-1}, \theta)\, d\tilde{\zeta}_n(z_n).
\end{aligned}
$$

The first term of this sum vanishes $a.e. - \nu^{n-1}$, as Assumption 6.3(a) holds for $\mathcal{S}$, and the second term vanishes $a.e. - \nu^{n-1}$ as Assumption 6.3(a) holds for $\tilde{\mathcal{S}}$. It follows by induction that $\int_{S_\theta^{*n}} \nabla f^{*n}(x^n, \theta)\, d\nu_n(x^n) = 0$ for all n, provided that $\int_{S_\theta^{*1}} f^{*1}(x^1, \theta)\, d\nu^1(x^1) = 0$. But $x^1 = x_1$ and $f^{*1} = f_1^*$ and the logic above establish this, so Assumption 6.2(a) holds. The argument for Assumption 6.2(b) is similar, so the conditions of Theorem 6.5 hold for $\mathcal{S}^*$ as claimed.

We apply Theorem 6.5 to $\mathcal{S}^*$ to infer that avar $\hat{\theta}_n^* = -[E(\nabla^2 L_n^*(X^n, \theta_o))]^{-1}$, where $\nabla^2 L_n^*(X^n, \theta_o) = \nabla^2 L_n(X^n, \theta_o) + \nabla^2 \tilde{L}_n(X^n, \theta_o)$, with $\nabla^2 \tilde{L}_n(X^n, \theta_o) \equiv n^{-1} \sum_{t=1}^n \nabla^2 \log \tilde{f}_t(\tilde{X}^{t-1}, \theta_o)$. Under the conditions of Theorem 6.6 for $\mathcal{S}$, it follows that avar $\hat{\theta}_n = -[E(\nabla^2 L_n(X^n, \theta_o))]^{-1}$. The result of (ii) follows by showing that $E(\nabla^2 \tilde{L}_n(X^n, \theta_o)) = 0$.

Given Assumption 6.3 for $\tilde{f}_t$, we have that

$$
\begin{aligned}
&E(\nabla^2 \log \tilde{f}_t(\tilde{X}^{t-1}, \theta_o)) = \\
&- E[\nabla \log \tilde{f}_t(\tilde{X}^{t-1}, \theta_o)\, \nabla' \log \tilde{f}_t(\tilde{X}^{t-1}, \theta_o)].
\end{aligned}
$$

(See the discussion following Assumption 6.3.) Because $\{Z_t \mid X^{t-1}\}$ is informationally exogenous for θ_o, $\nabla \log \tilde{f}_t(\tilde{X}^{t-1}, \theta_o) = 0$ $a.s.-P_o$, from which it follows that

$$E(\nabla^2 \log \tilde{f}_t(\tilde{X}^{r\,t-1}, \theta_o)) = 0\,,$$

so that

$$E(\nabla^2 \tilde{L}_n(X^n, \theta_o)) = 0\,,$$

as desired. Because $\{\tilde{f}_t\}$ is arbitrary, the proof of (ii) is complete.

(iii) By argument identical to that of (ii), we establish that the conditions of Theorem 6.5 hold except that now we assume directly that Assumption 6.1 holds for $\{n^{-1/2}\, s_t^*(X^t, \theta_o)\}$. Applying Theorem 6.5, we again have avar $\hat{\theta}_n^* = -[E(\nabla^2 L_n^*(X^n, \theta_o))]^{-1}$, and because the conditions of Theorem 6.6 hold for $\mathcal{S}$, we have avar $\hat{\theta}_n = -[E(\nabla^2 L_n(X^n, \theta_o))]^{-1}$. Now

$$\text{avar}\, \hat{\theta}_n - \text{avar}\, \hat{\theta}_n^* = [E(\nabla^2 L_n^*(X, \theta_o))]^{-1} - [E(\nabla^2 L_n(X^n, \theta_o))]^{-1}$$

is positive semi-definite if and only if

$$E(\nabla^2 L_n(X^n, \theta_o)) - E(\nabla^2 L_n^*(X^n, \theta_o))$$

$$= -E(\nabla^2 \tilde{L}_n(X^n, \theta_o))$$

is positive semi-definite (e.g., White [1984a, Proposition 4.44]). Given Assumption 6.3 for $\tilde{f}_t$, we have that

$$-E(\nabla^2 \log \tilde{f}_t(\tilde{X}^{t-1}, \theta_o))$$

$$= E[\nabla \log \tilde{f}_t(\tilde{X}^{t-1}, \theta_o)\, \nabla' \log \tilde{f}_t\, (\tilde{X}^{t-1}, \theta_o)]$$

so that

$$-E(\nabla^2 \tilde{L}_n(X^n, \theta_o))$$

$$= n^{-1} \sum_{t=1}^{n} E[(\nabla \log \tilde{f}_t(\tilde{X}^{t-1}, \theta_o)\, \nabla' \log \tilde{f}_t(\tilde{X}^{t-1}, \theta_o)]$$

$$\equiv \tilde{B}_n^o$$

is positive semi-definite (p.s.d.) for all n as claimed.

To establish the existence of $\tilde{\lambda} \in \mathbb{R}^p$ such that $\tilde{\lambda}'\tilde{\lambda} = 1$ and $\lim \tilde{\lambda}'$ (avar $\hat{\theta}_n$ − avar $\hat{\theta}_n^*$) $\tilde{\lambda} > 0$ given that $\lim \lambda' \tilde{B}_n^o \lambda > 0$, we give a proof by contradiction. Thus, suppose that for all $\tilde{\lambda} \in \mathbb{R}^p$, $\tilde{\lambda}'\tilde{\lambda} = 1$, we have $\lim \tilde{\lambda}'$ (avar $\hat{\theta}_n$ −

avar $\hat{\theta}_n^*)\ \tilde{\lambda} \leq 0$. Because avar $\hat{\theta}_n$ - avar $\hat{\theta}_n^*$ is p.s.d. as just established, we have $\lim \tilde{\lambda}'$ (avar $\hat{\theta}_n$ - avar $\hat{\theta}_n^*)\ \tilde{\lambda} = 0$ for all $\tilde{\lambda}$. It follows that avar $\hat{\theta}_n$ - avar $\hat{\theta}_n^* = [E(\nabla^2\ L_n^*\ (X,\ \theta_o))]^{-1} - E[\nabla^2\ L_n\ (X^n,\ \theta_o)]^{-1} = \bar{B}_n^{o-1} - (\bar{B}_n^o + \tilde{B}_n^o)^{-1} \rightarrow 0$, where the second equality is a consequence of the information matrix equality. Because $\{\bar{B}_n^o\}$ and $\{\tilde{B}_n^o\}$ both are assumed to converge and $\{\bar{B}_n^o\}$ and $\{\bar{B}_n^o + \tilde{B}_n^o\}$ are (uniformly) positive definite given Assumption 6.1, it follows that $\bar{B}_n^o + \tilde{B}_n^o - \bar{B}_n^o = \tilde{B}_n^o \rightarrow 0$ also. But this implies $\lambda'\ \tilde{B}_n^o\ \lambda \rightarrow 0$ as $n \rightarrow \infty$ for all $\lambda \in I\!R^p$, $\lambda'\lambda = 1$, a contradiction. □

PROOF OF THEOREM 7.15: In light of Theorem 2.3 of Bates and White [1990], it suffices to show that

$$A_{22n}^* \equiv E(\nabla_{\beta\beta}\ L_{2n}\ (X^n\ , \alpha_n^*\ , \beta_o)) = n^{-1} \textstyle\sum_{t=1}^n E(\nabla_\beta\ \mu_t^o\ D_t^{*-1}\ \nabla_\beta{}'\ \mu_t^o)$$

satisfies

$$A_{22n}^* \equiv \text{cov}[n^{1/2}\ \nabla_\beta\ L_{2n}\ (X^n\ , \alpha_n^*\ , \beta_o)\ , n^{1/2}\ \nabla_\beta\ \tilde{L}_{2n}\ (X^n\ , \alpha_o\ , \beta_o)]\ ,$$

where $\nabla_\beta\ \tilde{L}_{2n}\ (X^n\ , \alpha_o\ , \beta_o) = n^{-1} \sum_{t=1}^n \nabla_\beta\ \mu_t^o\ \Sigma_t^{o-1}(Y_t - \mu_t^o)$. Now

$$\text{cov}\ [n^{1/2}\ \nabla_\beta\ L_{2n}(X^n\ , \alpha_n^*\ , \beta_o)\ , n^{1/2}\ \nabla_\beta\ \tilde{L}_{2n}\ (X^n\ , \alpha_o\ , \beta_o)]$$

$$= E[n\ \nabla_\beta\ L_{2n}(X^n\ , \alpha_n^*\ , \beta_o)\ \nabla'_\beta\ \tilde{L}_{2n}\ (X^n\ , \alpha_o\ , \beta_o)]$$

$$= n^{-1} \sum_{t=1}^{n} E(\nabla_\beta\ \mu_t^o\ D_t^{*-1}\ (Y_t - \mu_t^o\ )(Y_t - \mu_t^o\ )'\ \Sigma_t^{o-1}\ \nabla'_\beta\ \mu_t^o)\ ,$$

where the equalities follow by the martingale difference property of $Y_t - \mu_t^o$. By the law of iterated expectations

$$E(\nabla_\beta\ \mu_t^o\ D_t^{*-1}\ (Y_t - \mu_t^o\ )\ (Y_t - \mu_t^o\ )'\ \Sigma_t^{o-1}\ \nabla'_\beta\ \mu_t^o)$$

$$= E[E(\nabla_\beta\ \mu_t^o\ D_t^{*-1}\ (Y_t - \mu_t^o\ )(Y_t - \mu_t^o\ )'\ \Sigma_t^{o-1}\ \nabla'_\beta\ \mu_t^o\ |\ W_t)]$$

$$= E[\nabla_\beta \mu_t^o D_t^{*-1} E[(Y_t - \mu_t^o)(Y_t - \mu_t^o)' \mid W_t] \Sigma_t^{o-1} \nabla'_\beta \mu_t^o]$$

$$= E(\nabla_\beta \mu_t^o D_t^{*-1} \nabla'_\beta \mu_t^o) .$$

The last equality follows because $\Sigma_t^o \equiv E[(Y_t - \mu_t^o)(Y_t - \mu_t^o)' \mid W_t]$. Therefore

$$\text{cov}[n^{1/2} \nabla_\beta L_{2n}(X^n, \alpha_n^*, \beta_o), n^{1/2} \nabla_\beta \tilde{L}_{2n}(X^n, \alpha_o, \beta_o)]$$

$$= n^{-1} \sum_{t=1}^{n} E(\nabla_\beta \mu_t^o D_t^{*-1} \nabla_\beta' \mu_t^o)$$

$$= A_{22n}^* ,$$

and the proof is complete. □

CHAPTER 8

Hypothesis Testing and Asymptotic Covariance Matrix Estimation

Despite the possibility that the model underlying a particular estimation procedure is misspecified, we may still want to draw inferences about particular parameters of interest, either because the misspecification does not affect our ability to estimate particular parameters of interest θ_o consistently, or because we are directly interested in the parameters of the optimal approximation, θ_n^*.

In the classical situation, hypotheses about the "true parameters" θ_o of a correctly specified model are usually expressed as a set of restrictions on the parameters, embodied in a set of (possibly nonlinear) equations such as

$$H_o: \ r(\theta_o) = 0 \, ,$$

where $r : \Theta \to \mathbb{R}^q$, $q \leq p$. An alternative hypothesis that is frequently of interest is

$$H_a: \ r(\theta_o) \neq 0 \, .$$

Hypothesis tests are conducted by constructing an appropriate test statistic and using the known distributional properties of the test statistic to decide whether or not the test statistic takes on a value plausible under H_o. If θ_o is estimated by the method of maximum likelihood, then three classical test statistics are available: the Wald [1943], Lagrange multiplier (Rao [1947], Aitchison and Silvey [1958]) and likelihood ratio (Neyman and Pearson [1933]) statistics. Even if the method of maximum likelihood is not used, analogs of these test statistics are usually available. The purpose of this chapter is to study the properties of these statistics and their analogs and the resulting tests under particular forms of misspecification. As we see below, it is the effect of the misspecification on the form of the asymptotic covariance matrix and on the possibility of consistently estimating the asymptotic covariance matrix that determines the properties of these tests.

8.1 Hypothesis Testing with the QMLE

8.1.a The Null Hypothesis and Its Interpretation

In the presence of misspecification, θ_o is no longer necessarily defined. It is therefore necessary to reformulate H_o in a way that is meaningful regardless of misspecification. Under misspecification, the role of θ_o is played by $\theta_n^*(P_o)$, where the dependence of θ_n^* on P_o (which we examined in Chapter 3) is now made explicit.

The dependence of θ_n^* on n may necessitate the dependence of the hypothesized restrictions on n; it is also possible that the restrictions hypothesized may hold only in some appropriate limit. In recognition of these possibilities, we consider a null hypothesis of the form

$$H_o: \sqrt{n}\, r_n^* \equiv \sqrt{n}\, r_n(\theta_n^*(P_o)) \to 0 \quad \text{as} \quad n \to \infty .$$

The appearance of $\sqrt{n}$ in this formulation of H_o governs the rate at which r_n^* approaches zero in a manner consistent with asymptotic normality results applicable in the present context.

When the model $\mathcal{P} = \{P_\theta : \theta \in \Theta\}$ is correctly specified, a classical test of $H_o : r(\theta_o) = 0$ against $H_a : r(\theta_o) \neq 0$ is equivalent to a test of $H'_o : P_o \in \mathcal{P}_o$ against $H'_a : P_o \in \mathcal{P} - \mathcal{P}_o$, where $\mathcal{P}_o = \{P_\theta : r(\theta) = 0 , \theta \in \Theta\}$. It is insightful to express $H_o : \sqrt{n}\, r_n^* \to 0$ equivalently as $P_o \in \mathcal{P}_o$ for some appropriate model $\mathcal{P}_o$ in a manner analogous to that appropriate for the case of a correctly specified model. We use the following definition.

DEFINITION 8.1 (*Null Model*): Let $r = \{r_n : \Theta \to I\!R^q\}$, $q \leq p$, be a given sequence of functions. The *null model associated with* r , denoted $\mathcal{P}_o(r)$, is the collection of all probability measures P^o on $(\Omega , \mathcal{F})$ such that when Assumption 2.1 holds with $P_o = P^o$, Assumptions 2.3 and 3.2 hold and $\sqrt{n} r_n(\theta_n^*(P^o)) \to 0$. □

We invoke Assumptions 2.3 and 3.2 in this definition to ensure that θ_n^* is well defined; in other contexts, different conditions will suffice to define θ_n^*.

Testing $H_o : \sqrt{n} r_n^* \to 0$ against $H_a : H_o$ *is false* is therefore equivalent to testing $H_o' : P_o \in \mathcal{P}_o$ against the alternative $H_a' : P_o \notin \mathcal{P}_o$. Here and wherever convenient we suppress the dependence of $\mathcal{P}_o$ on r, and simply refer to $\mathcal{P}_o$ as the "null model."

This definition allows us to draw useful distinctions between hypothesis testing in the context of correctly specified models, and hypothesis testing in the context of potentially misspecified models. In the classical situation, the null hypothesis is much more restricted: in the strictest sense, failure to reject the null hypothesis is interpreted as a consequence of empirical evidence (embodied by the test statistic) consistent with P_o belonging to $\mathcal{P}_o = \{P_\theta : r(\theta) = 0\}$, i.e. consistent with the hypothesis that $\mathcal{P}_o$ is correctly specified in its entirety. At the other extreme is the interpretation entailed by Definition 8.1, namely that failure to reject the null hypothesis is a consequence of empirical evidence consistent with P_o belonging to the null model associated with r, $\mathcal{P}_o(r)$, which includes $\mathcal{P}_o$ and much more besides, as $\mathcal{P}_o$ may be misspecified to greater or lesser extent without necessarily invalidating $\sqrt{n} r_n(\theta_n^*(P_o)) \to 0$. Intermediate to these two extremes is an interpretation in which failure to reject the null hypothesis is interpreted as a consequence of evidence consistent with the correctness to some extent of a given specification that imposes the restrictions tested, e.g. $\mathcal{M}_o = \{\mu(\theta) : r(\theta) = 0\}$.

The distinction between the classical interpretation and that adopted here is made complete by considering the interpretation of rejection of the null hypothesis. Interpreted strictly, the classical approach continues to maintain the correctness of $\mathcal{P} = \{P_\theta : \theta \in \Theta\}$ in its entirety even when $\mathcal{P}_o$ is rejected. With the present approach, rejection of $\mathcal{P}_o$ is interpreted as evidence simply that P_o does not belong to $\mathcal{P}_o$, i.e. it belongs to the complement of $\mathcal{P}_o$ in the set of all probability measures on $(\Omega, \mathcal{F})$. This interpretation is that associated with the notion of "pure significance testing." The intermediate interpretation of the null hypothesis considered above supports a classical interpretation in the face of rejection in which one maintains the correctness of the underlying specification, say $\mathcal{M} = \{\mu(\theta), \theta \in \Theta\}$; it also supports a significance testing interpretation in the face of rejection, in which one concludes that P_o does not belong to a probability model compatible with $\mathcal{M}_o = \{\mu(\theta) : r(\theta) = 0\}$, without making any commitment as to whether or not $\mathcal{M}$ is correctly specified.

There are other ways to impose the restrictions comprising the null hypothesis. In Chapter 7, we considered the efficiency effects of restrictions of the form $\theta = d(\gamma)$, for a known function $d : \Gamma \to \Theta$, $\Gamma \subset \mathbb{R}^c$, $c \le p$. It is not uncommon for hypotheses to be formulated in a similar manner as $\theta_o = d(\gamma_o)$, for some (typically unknown) parameter vector $\gamma_o \in \Gamma$. Given a QMLE $\hat{\theta}_n$ and an estimate of γ_o, say $\hat{\gamma}_n$, a test of $\theta_o = d(\gamma_o)$ can be based on $\hat{\theta}_n - d(\hat{\gamma}_n)$. In the present setting an analog of such a null hypothesis would be H_o: $\sqrt{n}\,(\theta_n^* - d_n(\gamma_n^*)) \to 0$, for some sequence $\{d_n : \Gamma \to \Theta\}$. However, for simplicity in our theoretical treatment, we do not explicitly consider hypotheses expressed in this way. Instead, we treat them implicitly by assuming that $\{d_n\}$ is sufficiently well behaved that the restrictions $\sqrt{n}(\theta_n^* - d_n(\gamma_n^*)) \to 0$ can be equivalently represented as $\sqrt{n}\, r_n^* \to 0$. This is indeed true under mild restrictions on $\{d_n\}$.

To see why this is so, consider the simpler situation in which it is hypothesized that $\theta_o = d(\gamma_o)$. Let $d = (d_1{}', d_2{}')'$, where $d_1 : \Gamma \to \mathcal{A}$, $\mathcal{A} \subset \mathbb{R}^c$, and $d_2 : \Gamma \to \mathcal{B}$, $\mathcal{B} \subset \mathbb{R}^{p-c}$, $\Theta = \mathcal{A} \times \mathcal{B}$, with d_1 a continuously differentiable function with nonsingular Jacobian $\nabla_\gamma{}' d_1(\gamma_o)$. Then the inverse function theorem (e.g., Rudin [1964, p. 193]) guarantees the existence of a continuously differentiable inverse of d_1, say d_1^{-1}, such that $\gamma = d_1^{-1}(\alpha)$ in some open neighborhood of α_o. Thus

$$\theta_o - d(\gamma_o) = \begin{bmatrix} \alpha_o - d_1\,(d_1^{-1}(\alpha_o)) \\ \\ \beta_o - d_2\,(d_1^{-1}(\alpha_o)) \end{bmatrix}.$$

The equation $\alpha_o - d_1(d_1^{-1}(\alpha_o)) = 0$ provides no restriction on α_o, because $\alpha - d_1(d_1^{-1}(\alpha)) = 0$ for all α in the neighborhood of α_o. However, restrictions are imposed by the function $r(\theta_o) = \beta_o - d_2(d_1^{-1}(\alpha_o)) = 0$. (Here r is $(p-c) \times 1$ so that $q = p - c$.) The situation is entirely analogous when $\sqrt{n}\,(\theta_n^* - d_n(\gamma_n^*)) \to 0$ instead of $\theta_o = d(\gamma_o)$. However, the argument is complicated somewhat by the need to account properly for the dependence of the relevant functions on n.

A more general form of hypothesis is treated by Gourieroux and Monfort [1985], who consider restrictions of the form H_o: $b(\theta_o, \gamma_o) = 0$, where $b : \Theta \times \Gamma \to \mathbb{R}^q$, $\Gamma \subset \mathbb{R}^c$, $\Theta \subset \mathbb{R}^p$, $c \le q \le p$. With $b(\theta_o, \gamma_o) = \theta_o - d(\gamma_o) = 0$, we have the immediately preceding case. In applications, the ability to cast H_o in the implicit form $b(\theta_o, \gamma_o) = 0$ may be especially convenient, as Gourieroux and Monfort [1985] discuss. An analog of H_o relevant to the present case is H_o: $\sqrt{n}\, b_n(\theta_n^*, \gamma_n^*) \to 0$. Again, we will not treat this case explicitly, but we suppose instead that $\{b_n\}$ is sufficiently well behaved that $\sqrt{n}\, b_n(\theta_n^*, \gamma_n^*) \to 0$ can be represented as $\sqrt{n}\, r_n(\theta_n^*) \to 0$.

To see what is involved, we consider $b(\theta_o, \gamma_o) = 0$. Let $b = (b_1{}', b_2{}')'$, where $b_1 : \Theta \times \Gamma \to \mathbb{R}^c$, $b_2 : \Theta \times \Gamma \to \mathbb{R}^{q-c}$. The implicit function theorem ensures the existence of a continuously differentiable function e on a neighborhood of θ_o such that $\gamma_o = e(\theta_o)$ and $b_1(\theta, e(\theta)) = 0$, provided that

b_1 is continuously differentiable in θ and γ and that the Jacobian $\nabla_\gamma' b_1$ has full rank at γ_o. When this is true, the restrictions are embodied by $r(\theta_o) = b(\theta_o, e(\theta_o)) = 0$. (Again r is $q \times 1$.) Arguments for $\{b_n\}$ and $\{r_n\}$ are more tedious, but straightforward.

Thus, restricting attention to a null hypothesis of the form $H_o : \sqrt{n}\, r_n^* \to 0$ results in little loss of generality for the theory that follows.

8.1.b Some Preliminary Results on Convergence in Distribution

The asymptotic properties of each of the tests considered here are obtained by exploiting the asymptotic normality of the QMLE established in Chapter 6. In particular, the classical test statistics and their analogs are studied by showing that they converge in distribution to quadratic forms in normal random variables. The following version of a result of Baldessari [1969] describes the distribution of such quadratic forms.

LEMMA 8.2: *Suppose $\mathcal{Z} \sim N(\mu, V)$ where $\mathcal{Z}$ and μ are $q \times 1$, and V is a symmetric positive definite $q \times q$ matrix. Let K be a real symmetric $q \times q$ matrix. Then*

$$\mathcal{Z}' K \mathcal{Z} \sim N_2(\mu, V; K) \equiv \sum_{i=1}^{c} \lambda_i \chi^2(m_i, \xi_i),$$

where λ_i, $i = 1, \ldots, c$ are the distinct eigenvalues of $V^{1/2} K V^{1/2}$, with $V^{1/2}$ the symmetric positive definite matrix square root of V; $\chi^2(m, \xi)$ is the noncentral chi-square distribution with degrees of freedom m and noncentrality parameter ξ, and $\chi^2(m_i, \xi_i)$ are mutually independent, $i = 1, \ldots, c$; m_i is the multiplicity of λ_i, $\sum_{i=1}^{c} m_i = q$; and

$$\xi_i = \mu' V^{1/2} G B_i G' V^{1/2} \mu, \quad i = 1, \ldots, c,$$

where G is a $q \times q$ orthonormal matrix containing the eigenvectors of $V^{1/2} K V^{1/2}$ and B_i is the $q \times q$ diagonal matrix which has diagonal element 1 where $G'(V^{1/2} K V^{1/2})G$ has diagonal element λ_i and zero otherwise. □

Because we will refer frequently to such quadratic forms, we have introduced the convenient notation $N_2(\mu, V; K)$. An immediate corollary of this result is that $N_2(0, V; V^{-1}) = \chi^2(q, 0) \equiv \chi_q^2$.

This fact underlies and motivates construction of the standard Wald, Lagrange multiplier and likelihood ratio tests. For example, the Wald test for $H_o : r(\theta_o) = 0$ is based on the statistic $\hat{r}_n = r(\hat{\theta}_n)$. Under the conditions of Theorem 6.4, when $r(\theta_o) = 0$ it can be shown that $\sqrt{n}\hat{r}_n$ has the asymptotic distribution $N(0, -R^o A_n^{o-1} R^{o\prime})$, where $R^o = \nabla' r(\theta_o)$. Given an estimator for $R^o A_n^{o-1} R^{o\prime}$, say $\hat{R}_n \hat{A}_n^- \hat{R}_n{}'$, it is natural to consider

$$\mathcal{W}_n = -n\hat{r}_n{}' [\hat{R}_n \hat{A}_n^- \hat{R}_n{}']^- \hat{r}_n$$

as the basis for a test of H_o against $H_a : r(\theta_o) \neq 0$. We expect that under appropriate conditions $\mathcal{W}_n \overset{A}{\sim} \chi_q^2$ under H_o.

This is indeed the case, as we see in the next subsection. However, misspecification may result in the inconsistency of the covariance matrix estimator used to form the test statistic, so it is important to have available theoretical tools that apply despite such misspecification. One difficulty created by the possible inconsistency of the asymptotic covariance matrix estimator is that the distribution of the associated test statistic need not converge (i.e., there is no limiting distribution in the usual sense), even under H_o. Nevertheless, it is often still possible to show that the distribution of the test statistics of interest gets close to a known distribution (depending on n) that can be used to make probability statements. It is this use that makes the limiting distribution of interest in the standard case. For this reason, we extend the definition of asymptotic distribution in the following way.

DEFINITION 8.3 (*Asymptotic Distribution*): Let $\{\mathcal{X}_n\}$ and $\{\mathcal{Z}_n\}$ be sequences of random variables with distribution functions $F_n(x) = P[\mathcal{X}_n \leq x]$, $G_n(x) = P[\mathcal{Z}_n \leq x]$. Let $\mathcal{D}_n$ be the set of discontinuities of G_n, and define $\mathcal{D} \equiv \cup_{n=1}^{\infty} \mathcal{D}_n$. Then *$\mathcal{X}_n$ is distributed asymptotically as $\mathcal{Z}_n$*, denoted $\mathcal{X}_n \overset{A}{\sim} \mathcal{Z}_n$, if for each $x \in \mathcal{D}^c$ $F_n(x) - G_n(x) \to 0$ as $n \to \infty$. □

Thus, the distribution of $\mathcal{Z}_n$, when known, can be used to make asymptotically valid statements about the distribution of $\mathcal{X}_n$. When $G_n = G$ for all n, the definition reduces to the standard definition of convergence in distribution. It is also straightforward to show that our earlier definition for $\mathcal{X}_n \overset{A}{\sim} N(\mu_n, V_n)$ is compatible with Definition 8.3 (in the scalar case $G_n(x) = \Phi((x - \mu_n)/V_n^{1/2})$). Note that for this definition $\mathcal{X}_n$ and $\mathcal{Z}_n$ need not be defined on the same probability space.

The following result is useful in establishing that $\mathcal{X}_n \overset{A}{\sim} \mathcal{Z}_n$ in particular instances.

PROPOSITION 8.4: *(i) Suppose that* $\mathcal{X}_n \overset{A}{\sim} \mathcal{Z}_n$ *and that* $G_n(x) \equiv P[\mathcal{Z}_n \le x]$ *is continuous in x uniformly in n. Let* $F_n(x) \equiv P[\mathcal{X}_n \le x]$. *Then for each* $x \in \mathbb{R}$ *and any* $\varepsilon > 0$, *there exist* $N(\varepsilon) < \infty$ *and* $\delta(\varepsilon) > 0$ *(possibly depending on x) such that for all* $n > N(\varepsilon)$

$$F_n(x + \delta(\varepsilon)) - F_n(x - \delta(\varepsilon)) < \varepsilon.$$

(ii) Suppose that $\mathcal{X}_n - \mathcal{Z}_n \to 0$ *prob-P, and that given* $x \in \mathbb{R}$ *and any* $\varepsilon > 0$ *there exist* $N(\varepsilon) < \infty$ *and* $\delta(\varepsilon) > 0$ *such that for all* $n > N(\varepsilon)$, $G_n(x + \delta(\varepsilon)) - G_n(x - \delta(\varepsilon)) < \varepsilon$. *Then* $F_n(x) - G_n(x) \to 0$. *If this holds for each* $x \in \mathcal{D}^c$, *then* $\mathcal{X}_n \overset{A}{\sim} \mathcal{Z}_n$.

(iii) Suppose that $\mathcal{X}_n - \mathcal{Z}_n \to 0$ *prob* $- P$, *and that* $\mathcal{Z}_n \overset{A}{\sim} \mathcal{Y}_n$, *where* $H_n(x) \equiv P[\mathcal{Y}_n \le x]$ *is continuous in x uniformly in n. Then* $\mathcal{X}_n \overset{A}{\sim} \mathcal{Y}_n$. □

Result (iii) is an extension of the familiar asymptotic equivalence lemma (e.g. White [1984a, Lemma 4.7]). We also make use of the following result for convergence to a multivariate normal distribution.

PROPOSITION 8.5: *Suppose* $\mathcal{X}_n - \mathcal{Z}_n \to 0$ *prob* $- P$, *and that* $\mathcal{Z}_n \overset{A}{\sim} N(\mu_n, V_n)$, *where* $\{\mu_n\}$, $\{V_n\}$ *are* $O(1)$ *and* $\{V_n\}$ *is uniformly positive definite. Then* $\mathcal{X}_n \overset{A}{\sim} N(\mu_n, V_n)$. □

We now have available definitions and results that allow statement and proof of a theorem on the asymptotic distribution of quadratic forms of asymptotically normal random variables. The following result underlies all our subsequent results on the asymptotic distributions of test statistics.

THEOREM 8.6: *Suppose that* $\mathcal{X}_n \overset{A}{\sim} N(\mu_n, V_n)$ *and that* $\hat{K}_n - K_n \to 0$ *prob* $- P$, *where* $\mathcal{X}_n$ *and* μ_n *are* $q \times 1$ *vectors with* $\{\mu_n\} = O(1)$, *and* V_n, $\hat{K}_n$ *and* K_n *are symmetric* $q \times q$ *matrices with* $\{V_n\}$, $\{K_n\}$ $O(1)$ *and uniformly positive definite. Then*

$$\mathcal{X}_n' \hat{K}_n^{-} \mathcal{X}_n \overset{A}{\sim} N_2(\mu_n, V_n ; K_n^{-1}).$$

Furthermore, if $\mu_n = 0$ *and* $K_n = V_n$*, then*

$$\mathcal{X}_n{}'\hat{K}_n^- \mathcal{X}_n \overset{A}{\sim} \chi_q. \qquad \square$$

In our applications, $\mathcal{X}_n$ will be an appropriate function of $\hat{\theta}_n$, and $\hat{K}_n$ will be some (not necessarily consistent) estimator of the asymptotic covariance matrix of this function.

8.1.c Behavior of Test Statistics Under the Null Hypothesis

We consider the properties of tests based on the following statistics:

$$\begin{aligned}
\mathcal{W}_n &\equiv n\,\hat{r}_n{}'(\hat{R}_n\,\hat{C}_n\,\hat{R}_n{}')^-\,\hat{r}_n \\
\mathcal{LM}_n &\equiv n\,\nabla'\tilde{L}_n\,\nabla^2\tilde{L}_n^-\,\tilde{R}_n{}'(\tilde{R}_n\,\tilde{C}_n\,\tilde{R}_n{}')^-\,\tilde{R}_n\,\nabla^2\tilde{L}_n^-\,\nabla\tilde{L}_n \\
\mathcal{LR}_n &\equiv -2n\,(\tilde{L}_n - \hat{L}_n) \\
\mathcal{H}_n &\equiv n(\tilde{\theta}_n - \hat{\theta}_n)'\,\hat{R}_n{}'\,(\hat{R}_n\,\hat{C}_n\,\hat{R}_n{}')^-\,\hat{R}_n\,(\tilde{\theta}_n - \hat{\theta}_n)
\end{aligned}$$

where $\hat{r}_n \equiv r_n(\hat{\theta}_n)$, $\hat{R}_n \equiv R_n(\hat{\theta}_n)$ with $\hat{\theta}_n$ the QMLE as before; $\nabla\tilde{L}_n \equiv \nabla L_n(X^n, \tilde{\theta}_n)$, $\tilde{R}_n = R_n(\tilde{\theta}_n)$, with $\tilde{\theta}_n$ the constrained QMLE obtained as the solution to the problem $\max_{\theta\in\Theta} L_n(X^n, \theta)$ *s.t.* $r_n(\theta) = 0$; $\tilde{L}_n \equiv L_n(X^n, \tilde{\theta}_n)$ and $\hat{L}_n \equiv L_n(X^n, \hat{\theta}_n)$; and $\hat{C}_n$ and $\tilde{C}_n$ are estimators of the asymptotic covariance matrix of $(\hat{\theta}_n - \theta_n^*)$.

For now we consider only statistics based on the QMLE and the constrained QMLE. We defer treatment of statistics based on the 2SQMLE, although the analysis is quite similar.

Before stating results describing the properties of these test statistics under the null hypothesis, we give a brief discussion of the motivation for each.

The statistic $\mathcal{W}_n$ is an analog of the classical Wald [1943] statistic; it is based on a direct comparison of $\hat{r}_n$ to zero, the limiting value of r_n^* under H_o. Heuristically, the form of the test statistic is obtained by using a mean value expansion and the fact that $\sqrt{n}\,r_n^* \to 0$ under H_o to write

$$\begin{aligned}
\sqrt{n}\,\hat{r}_n &= \sqrt{n}\,r_n^* + R_n^*\,\sqrt{n}(\hat{\theta}_n - \theta_n^*) + o_{P_o}(1) \\
&= R_n^*\,\sqrt{n}(\hat{\theta}_n - \theta_n^*) + o_{P_o}(1)\,.
\end{aligned}$$

Theorem 6.4 then guarantees that $\sqrt{n}\,\hat{r}_n \overset{A}{\sim} N(0,\, R_n^*\, A_n^{*-1}\, B_n^*\, A_n^{*-1}\, R_n^{*\prime})$ given H_o. When $\hat{C}_n$ is consistent for $A_n^{*-1}\, B_n^*\, A_n^{*\prime}$, we generally have $\mathcal{W}_n \overset{A}{\sim} \chi_q^2$ under H_o, as we see shortly. Classical versions of $\mathcal{W}_n$ use a choice of $\hat{C}_n$ motivated by the validity of the information matrix equality.

The form given for the $\mathcal{LM}_n$ statistic is obtained by reasoning entirely analogous to that of Aitchison and Silvey [1958], except that $\tilde{C}_n$ is free to be chosen here. Consider the Lagrangian $\mathcal{L}_n(\theta, \lambda)$ associated with the problem $\max_{\theta\in\Theta} L_n(X^n, \theta)$ *s.t.* $r_n(\theta) = 0$,

$$\mathcal{L}_n(\theta, \lambda) = L_n(X^n, \theta) + \lambda' r_n(\theta)\ .$$

Tedious algebra shows that when $\sqrt{n}\, r_n^* \to 0$,

$$\sqrt{n}\,\tilde{\lambda}_n = [R_n^*\, A_n^{*-1}\, R_n^{*\prime}]^{-1}\, R_n^*\, \sqrt{n}(\hat{\theta}_n - \theta_n^*) + o_{P_o}(1)$$

(cf. Gourieroux and Monfort [1985, eq. (25)]), where $\tilde{\lambda}_n$ is the solution in λ to the saddle point conditions for $\mathcal{L}_n$. Thus

$$\sqrt{n}\,\tilde{\lambda}_n \overset{A}{\sim} N(0,\, [R_n^*\, A_n^{*-1}\, R_n^{*\prime}]^{-1}\, R_n^*\, A_n^{*-1}\, B_n^*\, A_n^{*-1}\, R_n^{*\prime}[R_n^*\, A_n^{*-1}\, R_n^{*\prime}]^{-1})$$

given H_o and the conditions of Theorem 6.4. Theorem 8.6 suggests that given $\tilde{C}_n$ consistent for $A_n^{*-1}\, B_n^*\, A_n^{*-1}$, we have under H_o that

$$n\,\tilde{\lambda}_n'\, \tilde{R}_n\, \nabla^2 \tilde{L}_n^-\, \tilde{R}_n'\, (\tilde{R}_n\, \tilde{C}_n\, \tilde{R}_n')^-\, \tilde{R}_n\, \nabla^2 \tilde{L}_n^-\, \tilde{R}_n'\, \tilde{\lambda}_n \overset{A}{\sim} \chi_q^2\ .$$

Essentially, this statistic tests the hypothesis that $\lambda_n^* \to 0$, where $\tilde{\lambda}_n - \lambda_n^* \to 0$ *prob* $- P_o$. The explicit form for $\mathcal{LM}_n$ given earlier comes from the saddle point conditions

$$\nabla'_\theta\, \mathcal{L}_n(\tilde{\theta}_n, \tilde{\lambda}_n) = \nabla'\, L_n(X^n, \tilde{\theta}_n) + \tilde{\lambda}_n'\, R_n(\tilde{\theta}_n) = 0$$

so that $\nabla' \tilde{L}_n = -\,\tilde{\lambda}_n'\, \tilde{R}_n$.

The likelihood ratio statistic was shown by Neyman and Pearson [1933] to yield hypothesis tests with specific optimality properties. When the model is correctly specified, $\mathcal{LR}_n$ is well known to have the χ^2_q distribution asymptotically (e.g. Rao [1973, pp. 418–419]) under the null hypothesis. The demonstration of this is based on an application of Taylor's theorem to $\tilde{L}_n$.

The statistic $\mathcal{H}_n$ can be viewed as a version of a particular Hausman [1978] test in which we compare the efficient constrained (Q)MLE $\tilde{\theta}_n$ to an inefficient but consistent (Q)MLE $\hat{\theta}_n$. The asymptotic distribution of $\sqrt{n}(\tilde{\theta}_n - \hat{\theta}_n)$ is degenerate, but that of $R_n^* \sqrt{n}(\tilde{\theta}_n - \hat{\theta}_n)$, which forms the basis for the test, is not. We note in passing that $\hat{R}_n$ and $\hat{C}_n$ can be replaced by $\tilde{R}_n$ and $\tilde{C}_n$ in forming $\mathcal{H}_n$ without affecting any of the results obtained below. We leave this possibility implicit for notational simplicity. In fact $\hat{\theta}_n$ or $\tilde{\theta}_n$ can be replaced by any estimator consistent for θ_n^* under H_o in forming $\hat{R}_n$ and $\hat{C}_n$ or $\tilde{R}_n$ and $\tilde{C}_n$ for use in constructing $\mathcal{W}_n$, $\mathcal{LM}_n$ or $\mathcal{H}_n$ without affecting the validity of the following results. We also leave this possibility implicit for notational convenience.

The statistics $\mathcal{LM}_n$, $\mathcal{LR}_n$ and $\mathcal{H}_n$ require results describing the asymptotic properties of the constrained estimator $\tilde{\theta}_n$. Existence follows directly from Theorem 2.14.

THEOREM 8.7: *Let $\{r_n : \Theta \to \mathbb{R}^q\}$ be a sequence of continuous functions, and suppose that the set $\Theta_n \equiv \{\theta \in \Theta : r_n(\theta) = 0\}$ is non-empty, $n = 1, 2, \ldots$. Given Assumption 2.1 and 2.3 for each $n = 1, 2, \ldots$ there exists a function $\tilde{\theta}_n : \mathbb{R}^{vn} \to \Theta_n$ measurable-$\mathcal{B}^{vn}$ and a set $F_n \in \mathcal{B}^{vn}$ with $P_o^n(F_n) = 1$ such that for all x^n in F_n,*

$$L_n(x^n, \tilde{\theta}_n(x^n)) = \max_{\theta \in \Theta_n} L_n(x^n, \theta) . \qquad \square$$

The following condition, analogous to Assumption CN of Gallant and White [1988], is instrumental in obtaining the desired consistency result for $\tilde{\theta}_n$ under the null hypothesis. It essentially extends the functions r_n in such a way that appropriate inversions can be carried out.

ASSUMPTION 8.1(a): The sequence $\{r_n : \Theta \to \mathbb{R}^q\}$ has elements continuous on Θ uniformly in n;

(b) $\Theta_n \equiv \{\theta \in \Theta : r_n(\theta) = 0\}$ is non-empty, $n = 1, 2, \ldots$;

(c) $\sup_n \sup_\Theta | r_n(\theta) | < \infty$ and when $q = p$, let r_n be one-to-one with inverse r_n^{-1} on $M_n \equiv \{\rho \in \mathbb{R}^p : \rho = r_n(\theta), \theta \in \Theta\}$ such that the extension of r_n^{-1} to $M = \cup_{n=1}^\infty M_n$ is continuous uniformly in n.

For $q < p$, suppose there exist functions $e_n : \Theta \to \mathbb{R}^{p-q}$ continuous on Θ uniformly in n such that $\sup_n \sup_\Theta | e_n(\theta) | < \infty$, and the mapping $\psi_n = (e_n', r_n')'$, $\psi_n : \Theta \to \mathbb{R}^p$ has inverse ψ_n^{-1} on $M_n \equiv \{(\gamma, \rho) : \gamma = e_n(\theta), \rho = r_n(\theta), \theta \in \Theta\}$ such that the extension of ψ_n^{-1} to $M \equiv \Gamma \times R$, $\Gamma \equiv \cup_{n=1}^\infty \Gamma_n$, $R = \cup_{n=1}^\infty R_n$, $\Gamma_n \equiv \{\gamma : \gamma = e_n(\theta), \theta \in \Theta\}$, $R_n \equiv \{\rho : \rho = r_n(\theta), \theta \in \Theta\}$, is continuous uniformly in n. □

THEOREM 8.8: *(i) Given Assumptions 2.1, 2.3, 3.2 ′, 3.5(b) and 8.1, suppose that $r_n^* \to 0$. Let θ_n^o be a solution to the problem*

$$\max_\Theta \bar{L}_n(\theta) \;\; s.t. \;\; r_n(\theta) = 0, \quad n = 1, 2, \ldots .$$

Then $\bar{L}_n(\theta_n^o) - \bar{L}_n(\theta_n^*) \to 0$ and $\theta_n^o - \theta_n^* \to 0$.

(ii) If Assumption 3.1 also holds, then $\tilde{\theta}_n - \theta_n^o \to 0 \; a.s.-P_o \; (prob - P_o)$ and $\tilde{\theta}_n - \theta_n^* \to 0 \; a.s.-P_o \; (prob - P_o)$. □

This consistency result exploits the validity of the constraints by using the assumption that $r_n^* \to 0$. Dropping this condition is appropriate under the global alternative; we examine this in Theorem 8.12 below.

Imposing the following differentiability condition on r_n makes it possible to give a fundamental result from which the desired results on the behavior of $\mathcal{W}_n$, $\mathcal{LM}_n$, $\mathcal{LR}_n$ and $\mathcal{H}_n$ follow straightforwardly.

ASSUMPTION 8.2: The sequence $\{r_n : \Theta \to \mathbb{R}^q\}$ has elements continuously differentiable on Θ uniformly in n, such that $\{R_n^* = \nabla' r_n(\theta_n^*)\}$ is $O(1)$ and has full row rank q, uniformly in n. □

THEOREM 8.9: *Given the conditions of Theorem 6.4 and Assumption 8.2, suppose that $\{\sqrt{n}\, r_n^*\}$ is $O(1)$. Then*

$$(i) \;\; \sqrt{n}\, \hat{r}_n = \sqrt{n}\, r_n^* + R_n^* \sqrt{n}(\hat{\theta}_n - \theta_n^*) + o_{P_o}(1) \;\; and$$

$$\sqrt{n}\, \hat{r}_n \overset{A}{\sim} N(\sqrt{n}\, r_n^*, R_n^* A_n^{*-1} B_n^* A_n^{*-1} R_n^{*\prime}) .$$

If Assumption 8.1 also holds, then

(ii) $-\sqrt{n}\,\tilde{R}_n\,\nabla^2\,\tilde{L}_n^-\,\nabla\,\tilde{L}_n = \sqrt{n}\,r_n^* + R_n^*\,\sqrt{n}(\hat{\theta}_n - \theta_n^*) + o_{P_o}(1)$ *and*

$$-\sqrt{n}\,\tilde{R}_n\,\nabla^2\,\tilde{L}_n^-\,\nabla\,\tilde{L}_n \overset{A}{\sim} N(\sqrt{n}\,r_n^*,\ R_n^*\,A_n^{*-1}\,B_n^*\,A_n^{*-1}\,R_n^{*\prime})\,;$$

(iii) $\sqrt{n}(\hat{\theta}_n - \tilde{\theta}_n) = -\,A_n^{*-1}\,R_n^{*\prime}(R_n^*\,A_n^{*-1}\,R_n^{*\prime})^{-1}\,\sqrt{n}\,r_n^*$
$-\,A_n^{*-1}\,R_n^{*\prime}(R_n^*\,A_n^{*-1}\,R_n^{*\prime})^{-1}\,R_n^*\,\sqrt{n}(\hat{\theta}_n - \theta_n^*) + o_{P_o}(1)$;

(iv) $\hat{R}_n\,\sqrt{n}(\hat{\theta}_n - \tilde{\theta}_n) = -\,\sqrt{n}\,r_n^* - R_n^*\,\sqrt{n}(\hat{\theta}_n - \theta_n^*) + o_{P_o}(1)$ *and*

$$R_n^*\,\sqrt{n}(\hat{\theta}_n - \tilde{\theta}_n) \overset{A}{\sim} N(-\sqrt{n}\,r_n^*,\ R_n^*\,A_n^{*-1}\,B_n^*\,A_n^{*-1}\,R_n^{*\prime}).$$ □

Application of Theorem 8.6 under H_o immediately yields the following theorem on the behavior of $\mathcal{W}_n$, $\mathcal{LM}_n$, $\mathcal{LR}_n$ and $\mathcal{H}_n$.

THEOREM 8.10: *Given the conditions of Theorem 6.4 and Assumption 8.2, suppose that* $\sqrt{n}r_n^* \to 0$ *, i.e.* $P_o \in \mathcal{P}_o$*, where* $\mathcal{P}_o$ *is the null model. Let* $\{C_n^*\}$ *be a* $O(1)$ *and uniformly positive definite sequence of symmetric* $p \times p$ *matrices, and let* $\{\hat{C}_n\}$, $\{\tilde{C}_n\}$ *be sequences of measurable positive semi-definite symmetric* $p \times p$ *matrices.*

(i) *If* $\hat{C}_n - C_n^* \to 0$ *prob* $- P_o$*, then*

$$\mathcal{W}_n \overset{A}{\sim} N_2(0,\ R_n^*\,A_n^{*-1}\,B_n^*\,A_n^{*-1}\,R_n^{*\prime};\ [R_n^*\,C_n^*\,R_n^{*\prime}]^{-1})\,.$$

If in addition $C_n^* = A_n^{*-1}\,B_n^*\,A_n^{*-1}$*, then* $\mathcal{W}_n \overset{A}{\sim} \chi_q^2$.

Suppose Assumption 8.1 also holds.

(ii) If $\tilde{C}_n - C_n^* \to 0$ *prob* $- P_o$*, then*

$$\mathcal{LM}_n \overset{A}{\sim} N_2(0,\ R_n^*\,A_n^{*-1}\,B_n^*\,A_n^{*-1}\,R_n^{*\prime};\ [R_n^*\,C_n^*\,R_n^{*\prime}]^{-1})\,.$$

If in addition $C_n^* = A_n^{*-1}\,B_n^*\,A_n^{*-1}$*, then* $\mathcal{LM}_n \overset{A}{\sim} \chi_q^2$.

(iii) $\mathcal{LR}_n \overset{A}{\sim} N_2(0,\ R_n^*\,A_n^{*-1}\,B_n^*\,A_n^{*-1}\,R_n^{*\prime};\ -[R_n^*\,A_n^{*-1}\,R_n^{*\prime}]^{-1})$.

If in addition $A_n^* + B_n^* \to 0$*, then* $\mathcal{LR}_n \overset{A}{\sim} \chi_q^2$.

(iv) If $\hat{C}_n - C_n^* \to 0$ *prob* $- P_o$ *, then*

$$\mathcal{H}_n \overset{A}{\sim} N_2(0, R_n^* A_n^{*-1} B_n^* A_n^{*-1} R_n^{*\prime};\ [R_n^* C_n^* R_n^{*\prime}]^{-1}).$$

If in addition $C_n^* = A_n^{*-1} B_n^* A_n^{*-1}$, *then* $\mathcal{H}_n \overset{A}{\sim} \chi_q^2$. □

This result supports construction of tests of H_o of known asymptotic size, despite the possible presence of misspecification, provided that it is possible to choose $\hat{C}_n$ or $\tilde{C}_n$ to be consistent for $A_n^{*-1} B_n^* A_n^{*-1}$. When this can be done, an asymptotically valid critical value for a test of size α using $\mathcal{W}_n$, $\mathcal{LM}_n$ or $\mathcal{H}_n$ is given by $\chi^2_{q,1-\alpha}$, the $1-\alpha$ percentile of the χ_q^2 distribution. Thus one would reject H_o at level α asymptotically if $\mathcal{W}_n > \chi_{q,1-\alpha}$ ($\mathcal{LM}_n > \chi^2_{q,1-\alpha}$, $\mathcal{H}_n > \chi^2_{q,1-\alpha}$).

Result (iii) in principle permits construction of a valid asymptotic critical value for $\mathcal{LR}_n$ when the information matrix equality fails ($A_n^* + B_n^* \not\to 0$), but for this we must still have a consistent estimator for $A_n^{*-1} B_n^* A_n^{*-1}$ and carry out some rather laborious computations. A test of proper size is more easily obtained from $\mathcal{W}_n$, $\mathcal{LM}_n$ or $\mathcal{H}_n$.

Another way of stating the result of (iii) is that failure of the information matrix equality invalidates the standard χ^2 test based on the $\mathcal{LR}_n$ statistic (Foutz and Srivastava [1977], Kent [1982]). When the information matrix equality holds, as investigated at length in Chapter 6, the $\mathcal{LR}_n$ statistic can be used as a χ^2 statistic, as can computationally simpler versions of $\mathcal{W}_n$, $\mathcal{LM}_n$, or $\mathcal{H}_n$. We explore this issue further below.

We emphasize that the presence of misspecification may make it impossible to achieve $C_n^* = A_n^{*-1} B_n^* A_n^{*-1}$. Theorem 8.10 gives the distributions of $\mathcal{W}_n$, $\mathcal{LM}_n$, $\mathcal{LR}_n$ and $\mathcal{H}_n$ in this case as well. However, it may be impossible to construct a test of proper size when $A_n^{*-1} B_n^* A_n^{*-1}$ cannot be consistently estimated. Thus, depending on the extent and nature of the misspecification, it may or may not be possible to conduct valid inference asymptotically. To investigate this issue, we consider in Section 8.3 the conditions under which the asymptotic covariance matrix $A_n^{*-1} B_n^* A_n^{*-1}$ possesses consistent estimators.

8.1.d Behavior of Test Statistics under Local Alternatives

Now we consider the behavior of $\mathcal{W}_n$, $\mathcal{LM}_n$, $\mathcal{LR}_n$ and $\mathcal{H}_n$ when instead of $\sqrt{n} r_n^* \to 0$ we have $\{\sqrt{n} r_n^*\} = O(1)$. This case allows analysis of our test statistics under a form of local alternative, and therefore supports investigation of local power properties of the associated test procedures. We define the model for the local alternative in the following way.

DEFINITION 8.11 (*Locally Alternative Model*): Let $r = \{r_n : \Theta \rightarrow \mathbb{R}^q\}$ be a given sequence of functions. The *locally alternative model associated with r*, denoted $\mathcal{P}_a(r)$, is the collection of all probability measures P^o on $(\Omega, \mathcal{F})$ such that when Assumption 2.1 holds with $P_o = P^o$, Assumptions 2.3 and 3.2 hold and $\{\sqrt{n} r_n(\theta_n^*(P^o))\}$ is $O(1)$. □

As with $\mathcal{P}_o$, we often drop explicit reference to r, and simply refer to the locally alternative model $\mathcal{P}_a$.

In the literature on the behavior of testing procedures under local alternatives, the standard approach is to subject the data generating mechanism to a drift (Neyman [1937], Le Cam and Lehmann [1974]), while holding H_o fixed. Thus, in the classical setting one studies tests of, say, $H_o\colon\ \theta_o = 0$ under a sequence of alternatives, for example $H_{a,n}\colon\ \theta_o = n^{-1/2}$. Associated with $H_{a,n}$ is a sequence of probability measures $P_{o,n}$ with associated parameter of interest $\theta_{o,n} = n^{-1/2}$, so that a different data generation process is supposed to give rise to each sample of size $n = 1, 2, \ldots$.

Such an approach allows relatively straightforward analysis in the case of correctly specified models, particularly with i.i.d. observations. However, replacing P_o with a sequence $\{P_{o,n}\}$ in the present possibly misspecified, dependent context creates a host of technical difficulties. Formulating $\mathcal{P}_a$ in the manner of Definition 8.11 makes it possible to avoid these difficulties completely, using a method previously exploited by Gallant and Jorgenson [1979] and Gallant and White [1988]. Instead of replacing P_o with a sequence $\{P_{o,n}\}$, we hold P_o fixed and take advantage of the flexibility afforded by our choice of constraint, $r_n^* \rightarrow 0$. The problem is posed in such a way that Theorem 8.9 can be applied immediately.

Theorem 8.10 gives results under H_o, that is, when $P_o \in \mathcal{P}_o$. To extend this result to local alternatives, we now assume that $P_o \in \mathcal{P}_a$. To see what this entails, suppose that $\theta_o = 0$ describes the data generation process, and suppose that the model is estimated under the constraints $r_n(\theta) \equiv \theta - n^{-1/2} = 0$, $n = 1, 2, \ldots$. Thus $H_o\colon\ \sqrt{n}\, r_n^* \rightarrow 0$ becomes $\sqrt{n}\, \theta_n^* \rightarrow 1$. However, when in fact $\theta_n^* = \theta_o = 0$ we have $\sqrt{n}\, r_n(\theta_o) = \sqrt{n}\, \theta_o - 1 = -1$, which is $O(1)$, so that for this choice of r_n, $P_o \in \mathcal{P}_a$. Note that regardless of whether $P_o \in \mathcal{P}_o$ or $P_o \in \mathcal{P}_a$ we have $r_n^* \rightarrow 0$, and it is in this sense that $H_a : \{\sqrt{n} r_n^*\} = O(1)$ constitutes a local alternative to H_o. Essentially the restrictions r_n are being chosen in such a way as to accommodate the data generation process (at a sufficiently slow rate), in contrast to the classical approach in which a sequence of data generation processes is chosen in such a way as to accommodate the hypothesized restriction. Both approaches are technical artifices that deliver the same conclusions. Our choice of approach is dictated by its convenience. The result for the behavior of $\mathcal{W}_n$, $\mathcal{LM}_n$, $\mathcal{LR}_n$ and $\mathcal{H}_n$ under the local alternative H_a in the presence of misspecification is as follows.

THEOREM 8.12: *Given the conditions of Theorem 6.4 and Assumption 8.2, suppose that $\{\sqrt{n} r_n^*\} = O(1)$, i.e. $P_o \in \mathcal{P}_a$, the locally alternative model. Let $\{C_n^*\}$ be a $O(1)$ and uniformly positive definite sequence of symmetric $p \times p$ matrices, and let $\{\hat{C}_n\}$, $\{\tilde{C}_n\}$ be sequences of measurable positive semi-definite symmetric $p \times p$ matrices.*

(i) If $\hat{C}_n - C_n^* \to 0$ prob $- P_o$, then

$$\mathcal{W}_n \overset{A}{\sim} N_2(\sqrt{n}\, r_n^*,\, R_n^*\, A_n^{*-1}\, B_n^*\, A_n^{*-1}\, R_n^{*\prime};\, [R_n^*\, C_n^*\, R_n^{*\prime}]^{-1}) .$$

If in addition $C_n^* = A_n^{*-1}\, B_n^*\, A_n^{*-1}$, then $\mathcal{W}_n \overset{A}{\sim} \chi^2(q, \xi_n)$ with

$$\xi_n \equiv n\, r_n^{*\prime} [R_n^*\, A_n^{*-1}\, B_n^*\, A_n^{*-1}\, R_n^{*\prime}]^{-1}\, r_n^* .$$

Suppose Assumption 8.1 also holds.

(ii) If $\tilde{C}_n - C_n^* \to 0$ prob $- P_o$, then

$$\mathcal{LM}_n \overset{A}{\sim} N_2(\sqrt{n}\, r_n^*,\, R_n^*\, A_n^{*-1}\, B_n^*\, A_n^{*-1}\, R_n^{*\prime};\, [R_n^*\, C_n^*\, R_n^{*\prime}]^{-1}) .$$

If in addition $C_n^* = A_n^{*-1}\, B_n^*\, A_n^{*-1}$, then $\mathcal{LM}_n \overset{A}{\sim} \chi^2(q, \xi_n)$.

(iii) $\mathcal{LR}_n \overset{A}{\sim} N_2(\sqrt{n}\, r_n^*,\, R_n^*\, A_n^{*-1}\, B_n^*\, A_n^{*-1}\, R_n^{*\prime};\, -[R_n^*\, A_n^{*-1}\, R_n^{*\prime}]^{-1})$.

If in addition $A_n^* + B_n^* \to 0$, then $\mathcal{LR}_n \overset{A}{\sim} \chi^2(q, \xi_n)$.

(iv) If $\hat{C}_n - C_n^* \to 0$ *prob* $- P_o$, *then*

$$\mathcal{H}_n \overset{A}{\sim} N_2(\sqrt{n}\, r_n^*,\, R_n^*\, A_n^{*-1}\, B_n^*\, A_n^{*-1}\, R_n^{*\prime};\, [R_n^*\, C_n^*\, R_n^{*\prime}]^{-1})\,.$$

If in addition $C_n^* = A_n^{*-1}\, B_n^*\, A_n^{*-1}$, *then* $\mathcal{H}_n \overset{A}{\sim} \chi^2(q, \xi_n)$. □

Note that Theorem 8.10 is a straightforward corollary of this result. We see that $\mathcal{W}_n$, $\mathcal{LM}_n$ and $\mathcal{H}_n$ all have the same distribution asymptotically under H_a (and H_o). In fact, $\mathcal{W}_n - \mathcal{LM}_n$, $\mathcal{W}_n - \mathcal{H}_n$ and $\mathcal{LM}_n - \mathcal{H}_n$ all converge to zero in probability under H_a. When $A_n^* + B_n^* \to 0$, then we also have $\mathcal{W}_n - \mathcal{LR}_n$, $\mathcal{LM}_n - \mathcal{LR}_n$, $\mathcal{H}_n - \mathcal{LR}_n$ converging to zero in probability. Consequently, a choice among these statistics must be made on the basis of finite sample performance and/or computational convenience.

It is straightforward to show that the asymptotic local power of a test based on the $\chi^2(q, \xi)$ distribution is increasing in ξ. Therefore, a test with maximal local power asymptotically is obtained by choosing $\hat{\theta}_n$ in such a way as to make $A_n^{*-1}\, B_n^*\, A_n^{*-1}$ as small as possible. In the context of correct specification to some extent, this is accomplished by basing the test on an efficient estimator $\hat{\theta}_n$. The results of the previous chapter are relevant in this regard.

8.1.e Behavior of Test Statistics Under the Global Alternative

To complete this section, we consider the behavior of $\mathcal{W}_n$, $\mathcal{LM}_n$, $\mathcal{LR}_n$ and $\mathcal{H}_n$ when P_o belongs to neither $\mathcal{P}_o$ nor $\mathcal{P}_a$, but belongs instead to a form of global alternative. To study this case, we do not need as much structure as in the previous sections. We rely on the following result.

THEOREM 8.13: *Let* $(\Omega, \mathcal{F}, P)$ *be a complete probability space, and let* $\mathcal{X}_n : \Omega \to \mathbb{R}^q$ *and* $\hat{K}_n : \Omega \to \mathbb{R}^{q \times q}$, $q \in \mathbb{N}$ *be measurable functions,* $n = 1, 2, \ldots,$ *such that* $\hat{K}_n$ *is symmetric and* $\hat{K}_n - K_n \to 0$ *prob-P, where* $\{K_n\}$ *is a O (1) and uniformly positive definite sequence of nonstochastic symmetric* $q \times q$ *matrices.*

If for some $\varepsilon > 0$, $P[\mathcal{X}_n'\mathcal{X}_n / n > \varepsilon] \to 1$, *then for any nonstochastic scalar sequence* $\{k_n\} = o(n)$, $P[\mathcal{X}_n'\, \hat{K}_n^- \mathcal{X}_n > k_n] \to 1$. □

The random variables $\mathcal{X}_n$ and $\hat{K}_n$ play the same roles in this result as they do in Theorem 8.6. There, however, the conditions imposed ensured that for all $\varepsilon > 0$, $P[\mathcal{X}_n{}' \mathcal{X}_n / n > \varepsilon] \to 0$, as $\mathcal{X}_n{}' \mathcal{X}_n$ is $O_P(1)$. The present result applies when $\mathcal{X}_n{}'\mathcal{X}_n$ is no longer $O_P(1)$.

To see how Theorem 8.13 applies in the present context, consider the case of the Wald statistic $\mathcal{W}_n = n\hat{r}_n{}'(\hat{R}_n\hat{C}_n\hat{R}_n{}')^{-}\hat{r}_n$. Clearly $\hat{K}_n$ corresponds to $\hat{R}_n\hat{C}_n\hat{R}'_n$, while $\mathcal{X}_n$ corresponds to $\sqrt{n}\hat{r}_n$. The crucial condition of Theorem 8.13 is that for some $\varepsilon_o > 0$, $P_o[\hat{r}_n{}'\hat{r}_n > \varepsilon_o] \to 1$. Because $\hat{r}_n - r_n^* \to 0$ *prob* $- P_o$ in general, it follows that when $r_n^{*\prime}r_n^* > 2\,\varepsilon_o$ for all n sufficiently large

$$\begin{aligned} P_o[\hat{r}_n{}'\hat{r}_n > \varepsilon_o] &\geq P_o[\hat{r}_n{}'\hat{r}_n - r_n^{*\prime}r_n^* > -\varepsilon_o] \\ &\geq P_o[|\hat{r}_n{}'\hat{r}_n - r_n^{*\prime}r_n^*| < \varepsilon_o] \\ &\to 1. \end{aligned}$$

From Theorem 8.13, we have in particular that for any constant $k \in \mathbb{R}$, $P_o[\mathcal{W}_n > k] \to 1$, i.e. the Wald test is a *consistent* test of H_o, because the probability of rejecting H_o tends to one as $n \to \infty$ when P_o belongs to the global alternative defined by the property $r_n^{*\prime}r_n^* > 2\,\varepsilon_o$ for all n sufficiently large, regardless of the critical value chosen for the test. In fact, the result is stronger than this because we can have a sequence of critical values $k_n \to \infty$ for which consistency is maintained (provided $\{k_n\} = o(n)$).

In order to use Theorem 8.13, we adopt the following definition of the globally alternative model associated with r.

DEFINITION 8.14 (*Globally Alternative Model*): Let $r = \{r_n : \Theta \to \mathbb{R}^q\}$ be a given sequence of functions. The *globally alternative model associated with* r, denoted $\mathcal{P}_A(r)$, is the collection of all probability measures P^o on $(\Omega, \mathcal{F})$ such that when Assumption 2.1 holds with $P_o = P^o$, Assumptions 2.3 and 3.2 hold and there exist $\varepsilon^o > 0$ and $N^o \in \mathbb{N}$ such that $r_n(\theta_n^*(P^o))'\, r_n(\theta_n^*(P^o)) > \varepsilon^o$ for all $n > N^o$. □

Note that ε^o and N^o have superscripts indicating that they may depend on P^o. Also note that $\mathcal{P}_o$, $\mathcal{P}_a$ and $\mathcal{P}_A$ do not exhaust all possibilities, because we can have $r_{n'}^* = 0$ for some subsequence $\{n'\}$ without $P_o \in \mathcal{P}_o$ or $P_o \in \mathcal{P}_a$ holding. Cases falling in this latter category are outside the scope of our treatment; as they are somewhat pathological, we do not give them further consideration.

To obtain results for the properties of tests based on $\mathcal{LM}_n$, $\mathcal{LR}_n$ and $\mathcal{H}_n$ under the global alternative, we need a result that describes the behavior of the QMLE when the (incorrect) constraints $r_n(\theta) = 0$ are binding asymptotically. We use the following condition:

ASSUMPTION 8.3: $\{\bar{L}_n\}$ has identifiably unique maximizers $\theta^o \equiv \{\theta_n^o\}$ on $\{\Theta_n\}$, $\Theta_n = \{\theta \in \Theta : r_n(\theta) = 0\}$. □

We have the following analog of Theorem 8.8.

THEOREM 8.15: *(i) Given Assumptions 2.1, 2.3, 3.2 and 8.1 (a,b) suppose that for some $\varepsilon_o > 0$ and $N_o \in \mathbb{N}$, $r_n^{*\prime} r_n^* > \varepsilon_o$ for all $n > N_o$. Let θ_n^o be a solution to the problem*

$$\max_{\theta\in\Theta} \bar{L}_n(\theta) \ s.t. \ r_n(\theta) = 0\,, \quad n = 1, 2, \ldots .$$

Then there exists $\delta_o > 0$ such that $|\theta_n^* - \theta_n^o| > \delta_o$ (where $|\cdot|$ is any norm on $\mathbb{R}^p$) for all n sufficiently large.

(ii) If Assumptions 3.1 and 8.3 also hold, then $\tilde{\theta}_n - \theta_n^o \to 0$ $a.s. - P_o$ ($prob - P_o$) and there exists $\delta_o > 0$ such that $|\tilde{\theta}_n - \theta_n^*| > \delta_o/2$ $a.a.n$ $a.s. - P_o$ $(P_o[|\tilde{\theta}_n - \theta_n^*| > \delta_o/2] \to 1)$. □

Thus, the imposition of incorrect constraints leads to a constrained estimator inconsistent for θ_n^*, as for example when common factor restrictions are incorrectly imposed in time series regression by modeling the error of a (dynamically misspecified) regression as AR (1). To treat the $\mathcal{LM}_n$ statistic in the present context, we use the following condition.

ASSUMPTION 8.4: (a) $\{R_n^o = \nabla' r_n(\theta_n^o)\}$ is $O(1)$ and has full row rank q uniformly in n;

(b) $\{\nabla^2 \bar{L}_n^o = \nabla^2 \bar{L}_n(\theta_n^o)\}$ is $O(1)$ and negative definite uniformly in n. □

We can now give a result describing the behavior of the $\mathcal{W}_n$, $\mathcal{LM}_n$, $\mathcal{LR}_n$ and $\mathcal{H}_n$ statistics under the global alternative.

THEOREM 8.16: *Given the conditions of Theorem 3.5 and Assumption*

8.1(a), suppose that there exist $\varepsilon_o > 0$ *and* $N_o \in I\!N$ *such that* $r_n^{*\prime} r_n^* > \varepsilon_o$ *for all* $n > N_o$, i.e. $P_o \in \mathcal{P}_A$, *the globally alternative model. Let* $\{C_n^*\}$ *and* $\{C_n^o\}$ *be O (1) and uniformly positive definite sequences of symmetric* $p \times p$ *matrices, let* $\{\hat{C}_n\}$ *and* $\{\tilde{C}_n\}$ *be sequences of measurable positive semi-definite symmetric* $p \times p$ *matrices and let* $\{k_n\} = o(n)$.

(i) If $\hat{C}_n - C_n^* \to 0$ *prob* $- P_o$ *and Assumption 8.2 holds, then* $P_o[\mathcal{W}_n > k_n] \to 1$.

Suppose Assumptions 8.1(b) and 8.3 also hold.

(ii) If $\tilde{C}_n - C_n^o \to 0$ *prob* $- P_o$, *if Assumptions 3.6–3.8 and 8.4 also hold, and if for all* $n > N_o$ *we have* $\nabla' \bar{L}_n^o\, \nabla^2\, \bar{L}_n^{o\,-1}\, R_n^{o\prime}\, R_n^o\, \nabla^2\, \bar{L}_n^{o\,-1} \nabla \bar{L}_n^o >$ ε_o, *then* $P_o[\mathcal{LM}_n > k_n] \to 1$, *with* $\nabla \bar{L}_n^o \equiv \nabla \bar{L}_n(\theta_n^o)$.

(iii) If Assumption 3.5(b) also holds, then $P_o[\mathcal{LR}_n > k_n] \to 1$.

(iv) If $\hat{C}_n - C_n^* \to 0$ *prob* $- P_o$, *Assumption 8.2 holds, and if for all* $n > N_o$, $(\theta_n^o - \theta_n^*)' R_n^{*\prime} R_n^* (\theta_n^o - \theta_n^*) > \varepsilon_o$, *then* $P_o[\mathcal{H}_n > k_n] \to 1$. □

Thus, under appropriate conditions, consistent tests against $r_n^* \to 0$ can be based on $\mathcal{W}_n$, $\mathcal{LM}_n$, $\mathcal{LR}_n$ or $\mathcal{H}_n$. Note that the $\mathcal{LM}_n$ and $\mathcal{H}_n$ statistics require additional conditions to ensure consistency. For the $\mathcal{LM}_n$ statistic, consistency fails when θ_n^o is a critical point for $\bar{L}_n$, $a.a.n$; for the $\mathcal{H}_n$ statistic, consistency fails when $\theta_n^o - \theta_n^*$ lies in the column null space of R_n^*, $a.a.n$.

8.2 Hypothesis Testing with the 2SQMLE

The situation for the 2SQMLE is particularly straightforward when the restrictions involve only β (the parameters estimated in the second stage) and when $\nabla_{\alpha\beta}\, \bar{L}_{2n}^* = 0$ (the case treated in Theorem 6.12). The results of sections 8.1.c - 8.1.e translate directly, with minor changes in notation and substitution of appropriate conditions. For this case, we replace $r_n\colon \Theta \to I\!R^q$ with $r_n\colon \mathcal{B} \to I\!R^q$ and Θ_n with $\mathcal{B}_n \equiv \{\beta \in \mathcal{B}\colon r_n(\beta) = 0\}$. Existence of a constrained estimator $\tilde{\beta}_n$ follows directly from Theorem 2.15. Assumption 8.1 is modified by replacing Θ with $\mathcal{B}$ and Θ_n with $\mathcal{B}_n$. Consistency of $\tilde{\beta}_n$ for β_n^* and for β_n^o, the solution to $\max_{\beta \in \mathcal{B}} \bar{L}_{2n}(\alpha_n^*, \beta)$ *s.t.* $r_n(\beta) = 0$, follows by arguments analogous to those of Theorem 8.8. Assumption 8.2 is modified by replacing Θ with $\mathcal{B}$ and defining $R_n^* = \nabla' r_n(\beta_n^*)$. The conclusions of Theorem 8.9 hold with $\hat{r}_n = r_n(\hat{\beta}_n)$, $r_n^* = r_n(\beta_n^*)$, $\tilde{r}_n = r_n(\tilde{\beta}_n)$, $\tilde{R}_n = R_n(\tilde{\beta}_n)$, $\nabla \tilde{L}_n = \nabla_\beta\, L_{2n}(X^n, \hat{\alpha}_n, \tilde{\beta}_n)$, $\nabla^2 \tilde{L}_n = \nabla_{\beta\beta}\, L_{2n}(X^n, \hat{\alpha}_n, \tilde{\beta}_n)$, with $\hat{\theta}_n$ and $\tilde{\theta}_n$

replaced with $\hat{\beta}_n$ and $\tilde{\beta}_n$, and with A_n^* and B_n^* replaced with A_{22n}^* and B_{22n}^*, given the conditions of Theorem 6.12, and the modifications of Assumptions 8.1 and 8.2. Theorems 8.10 and 8.12 hold with these identical substitutions (and corresponding modifications in constructing $\mathcal{W}_n$, $\mathcal{LM}_n$, $\mathcal{LR}_n$ and $\mathcal{H}_n$). Assumption 8.3 holds with $\bar{L}_{2n}$ in place of $\bar{L}_n$, and Theorem 8.15 translates directly with Assumption 3.5 replacing Assumption 3.2. Assumption 8.4 is modified by setting $R_n^o = \nabla_\beta' r_n(\beta_n^o)$ and $\nabla^2 \bar{L}_n^o = \nabla_{\beta\beta} \bar{L}_{2n}(\beta_n^o)$. Theorem 8.16 then translates directly, with the conditions of Theorem 3.10 replacing those of Theorem 3.5. Thus, when $\nabla_{\alpha\beta}\, \bar{L}_{2n}^* = 0$ and there are no restrictions between α and β the results for the 2SQMLE are essentially identical to those for the QMLE.

The results remain similar for 2SQMLE's for which $\nabla_{\alpha\beta}\, \bar{L}_{2n}^* \neq 0$ or when there are restrictions between α and β, but some additional details arise that must be explicitly treated. We define $\mathcal{W}_n$, $\mathcal{LM}_n$, $\mathcal{LR}_n$ and $\mathcal{H}_n$ as given originally, but with the QMLE $\hat{\theta}_n$ replaced by the 2SQMLE $\hat{\theta}_n' = (\hat{\alpha}_n', \hat{\beta}_n')$ and with the constrained QMLE replaced by the constrained 2SQMLE, denoted $\tilde{\theta}_n' = (\hat{\alpha}_n', \tilde{\beta}_n')$ where $\hat{\alpha}_n$ is the first stage estimator and $\tilde{\beta}_n$ is the constrained second stage estimator, which is now defined as the solution to the problem

$$\max_{\beta \in \mathcal{B}} L_{2n}(X^n, \hat{\alpha}_n, \beta) \quad s.t. \quad r_n(\hat{\alpha}_n, \beta) = 0 \,.$$

The appearance of $\hat{\alpha}_n$ in the constraint equations renders Theorem 2.15 inapplicable. To establish the existence of a measurable constrained 2SQMLE, we use a theorem of Debreu [1967]. To apply this result, we require the following condition.

ASSUMPTION 8.5: With $\Theta = \mathcal{A} \times \mathcal{B}$ for $\mathcal{A}$ and $\mathcal{B}$ compact subsets of finite dimensional Euclidean spaces, for each α in $\mathcal{A}$ there is a β in $\mathcal{B}$ such that $r_n(\alpha, \beta) = 0$, where $r_n : \Theta \to \mathbb{R}^q$ is continuous on Θ, $n = 1, 2, \ldots$. □

This is a reasonable requirement in the present context, as it ensures the existence of a solution to the constrained estimation problem regardless of ω. We apply Debreu's [1967] Theorem 4.5 to ensure that the resulting constrained 2SQMLE is measurable. The following result is similar to theorems of Border [1984] and Stinchcombe and White [1992].

THEOREM 8.17: *Let $\hat{\alpha}_n : \mathbb{R}^{vn} \to \mathcal{A}$ be measurable $n = 1, 2, \ldots$. Given Assumptions 2.1, 2.3 and 8.5, for each $n = 1, 2, \ldots$ there exists a measurable* *function* $\tilde{\beta}_n: \mathbb{R}^{vn} \to \mathcal{B}$ *and a set* $F_n \in \mathcal{B}^{vn}$ *with* $P_o^n(F_n) = 1$ *such that for all* x^n *in* F_n

$$L_{2n}(x^n, \hat{\alpha}_n(x^n), \tilde{\beta}_n(x^n)) = \max_{\beta \in \hat{\mathcal{B}}_n(x^n)} L_{2n}(x^n, \hat{\alpha}_n(x^n), \beta),$$

where $\hat{\mathcal{B}}_n(x^n) \equiv \{\beta \in \mathcal{B}: r_n(\hat{\alpha}_n(x^n), \beta) = 0\}$. □

A consistency result analogous to that of Theorem 8.8 holds under the conditions of the following result.

THEOREM 8.18: *(i) Given Assumptions 2.1, 2.3, 8.1, 8.5 and 3.5 with* $\theta_n^{*\prime} = (\alpha_n^{*\prime}, \beta_n^{*\prime})$ *interior to* Θ *uniformly in n, suppose that* $r_n^* \to 0$. *Let* β_n^o *be a solution to the problem*

$$\max_{\mathcal{B}} \bar{L}_{2n}(\alpha_n^*, \beta) \quad s.t. \quad r_n(\alpha_n^*, \beta) = 0, \quad n = 1, 2, \ldots .$$

Then $\bar{L}_{2n}(\alpha_n^*, \beta_n^o) - \bar{L}_{2n}(\alpha_n^*, \beta_n^*) \to 0$ *and* $\theta_n^o - \theta_n^* \to 0$, *with* $\theta_n^{o\prime} \equiv (\alpha_n^{*\prime}, \beta_n^{o\prime})$.

(ii) If Assumption 3.1 also holds, then $\tilde{\theta}_n - \theta_n^o \to 0$ *a.s.*$-P_o$ *(prob*$-P_o$*) and* $\tilde{\theta}_n - \theta_n^* \to$ *a.s.*$-P_o$ *(prob*$-P_o$*) with* $\tilde{\theta}_n' \equiv (\hat{\alpha}_n', \tilde{\beta}_n')$. □

Theorem 8.9 translates in the following way.

THEOREM 8.19: *Given the conditions of Theorem 6.11 and Assumption 8.2, suppose that* $\{\sqrt{n}\, r_n^*\}$ *is* $O(1)$. *Then 8.9(i) holds with* $A_n^{*-1} B_n^* A_n^{*-1}$ *replaced by* $A_n^{*-1} B_n^* A_n^{*-1\prime}$ *as given in Theorem 6.11. If Assumptions 8.1 and 8.5 also hold, then 8.9(ii), (iii) and (iv) hold, with the identical replacement.* □

Theorems 8.10 and 8.12 translate analogously. We state only the translation of Theorem 8.12, as it contains that of 8.10 as a special case.

THEOREM 8.20: *Given the conditions of Theorem 6.11 and Assumption 8.2, suppose that* $\{\sqrt{n r_n^*}\} = O(1)$, $(P_o \in \mathcal{P}_a)$, *and let* $\{C_n^*\}$, $\{\hat{C}_n\}$ *and*

$\{\tilde{C}_n\}$ be as given in Theorem 8.12. Then 8.12(i) holds with $A_n^{*-1}\ B_n^*\ A_n^{*-1}$ replaced with $A_n^{*-1}\ B_n^*\ A_n^{*-1\prime}$ as defined in Theorem 6.11. If Assumptions 8.1 and 8.5 also hold, then 8.12(ii), (iii) and (iv) hold, with the identical replacement. □

A translation of Theorem 8.15 is as follows.

THEOREM 8.21: *(i): Given Assumptions 2.1, 2.3, 3.5, and 8.1 (a,b), suppose that for some $\varepsilon_o > 0$ and $N_o \in I\!N$, $r_n^{*\prime} r_n^* > \varepsilon_o$ for all $n > N_o$. Let β_n^o be a solution to the problem*

$$\max_{\beta \in \mathcal{B}} \bar{L}_{2n}(\alpha_n^*, \beta) \;\; s.t. \;\; r_n(\alpha_n^*, \beta) = 0 \quad , n = 1, 2, \ldots \;\; .$$

Then there exists $\delta_o > 0$ such that $|\beta_n^* - \beta_n^o| > \delta_o$ a.a.n, which then implies $|\theta_n^* - \theta_n^o| > \delta_o$ a.a.n.

(ii) If Assumptions 3.1, 8.3 and 8.5 also hold, then $\tilde{\theta}_n - \theta_n^o \to 0$ a.s. $- P_o$ ($prob - P_o$), and there exists $\delta_o > 0$ such that $|\tilde{\theta}_n - \theta_n^o| > \delta_o/2$ a.a.n a.s. $- P_o$ ($P_o[|\tilde{\theta}_n - \theta_n^*| > \delta_o/2] \to 1$). □

The translation of Theorem 8.16 requires modifying Assumption 8.4(b) so that

$$\nabla^2 \bar{L}_n^o = \begin{bmatrix} \nabla_{\alpha\alpha} \bar{L}_{1n}(\alpha_n^*) & 0 \\ \nabla_{\alpha\beta} \bar{L}_{2n}(\theta_n^o) & \nabla_{\beta\beta} \bar{L}_{2n}(\theta_n^o) \end{bmatrix} .$$

With this modification understood, we have the following translation of Theorem 8.16:

THEOREM 8.22: *Given the conditions of Theorem 3.10 and Assumption 8.1(a), suppose that there exist $\varepsilon_o > 0$ and $N_o \in I\!N$ such that $r_n^{*\prime} r_n^* > \varepsilon_o$ for all $n > N_o$, i.e. $P_o \in \mathcal{P}_A$, and let $\{C_n^*\}$, $\{C_n^o\}$, $\{\hat{C}_n\}$ and $\{\tilde{C}_n\}$ be as given in Theorem 8.16. Then 8.16(i) holds given Assumption 8.2. If Assumptions 8.1(b), 8.3 and 8.5 also hold, then 8.16 (ii) holds (with Assumptions 3.6–3.8* *holding for both* $\{f_{1t}\}$ *and* $\{f_{2t}\}$ *and 8.4 holding), 8.16(iii) holds (with Assumption 3.5(b) holding), and 8.16(iv) holds (with Assumption 8.2 holding).* □

Thus, results for the 2SQMLE are entirely analogous to those for the QMLE.

8.3 Asymptotic Covariance Matrix Estimation

All of the foregoing results indicate that inference is most conveniently conducted when $\hat{C}_n - C_n^* \longrightarrow 0$ *prob* $-P_o$ with $C_n^* = A_n^{*-1} B_n^* A_n^{*-1\prime}$, because the χ_q^2 distribution can then be used to construct appropriate critical regions. We now consider the implications of misspecification for achieving this. The analysis splits conveniently into two cases: the case in which the information matrix equality holds ($A_n^* + B_n^* \to 0$) and the case in which it doesn't.

First, we consider the case in which the information matrix equality holds.

THEOREM 8.23: *Given Assumptions 2.1, 2.3, 3.2, 3.6, 3.8(a) and 3.9, suppose that* $A_n^* + B_n^* \to 0$, $B_n^* \equiv \text{var}(\sqrt{n}\, \nabla L_n^*)$. *If* $\hat{A}_n - A_n^* \to 0$ *a.s.*$-P_o$ *(prob*$-P_o$*), then* $-\hat{A}_n^- - A_n^{*-1} B_n^* A_n^{*-1} \to 0$ *a.s.*$-P_o$ *(prob*$-P_o$*).* □

Thus, when the information matrix equality holds and a consistent estimator $\hat{A}_n$ for A_n^* is available, the choice $\hat{C}_n = -\hat{A}_n^-$ has the desired property that $\hat{C}_n - C_n^* \to 0$ *prob* $-P_o$, $C_n^* = A_n^{*-1} B_n^* A_n^{*-1}$.

Consistent estimators for A_n^* are available under general conditions, regardless of misspecification. The following result justifies the use of two common estimators.

THEOREM 8.24:*(i) Given Assumptions 2.1, 2.3, 3.1, 3.2, 3.6 and 3.8,*

$$\hat{A}_n - A_n^* \to 0 \quad a.s.-P_o \quad (prob-P_o)\,,$$

where, letting $\nabla^2 \log \hat{f}_t \equiv \nabla^2 \log f_t(X^t, \hat{\theta}_n)$,

$$\hat{A}_n \equiv n^{-1} \sum_{t=1}^{n} \nabla^2 \log \hat{f}_t\,.$$

(ii)(a) Given Assumptions 2.1, 2.3, 3.1, 3.6, 3.8, 8.1(a,b) and 8.3,

$$\tilde{A}_n - A_n^o \to 0 \quad a.s. - P_o \ \ (prob - P_o),$$

where $A_n^o = \nabla^2 \bar{L}_n(\theta_n^o)$, *and letting* $\nabla^2 \log \tilde{f}_t \equiv \nabla^2 \log f_t(X^t, \tilde{\theta}_n)$,

$$\tilde{A}_n \equiv n^{-1} \sum_{t=1}^{n} \nabla^2 \log \tilde{f}_t .$$

(b) If in addition Assumptions 3.2′, 3.5(b) and 8.1(c) hold, Assumption 8.3 is dropped, and $r_n^* \to 0$, *then* $\tilde{A}_n - A_n^* \to 0 \ \ a.s. - P_o$ ($prob - P_o$). □

This result follows immediately from Corollary 3.8. The conditions stated ensure that the QMLE $\hat{\theta}_n$ and the constrained QMLE $\tilde{\theta}_n$ are consistent for θ_n^* and θ_n^o respectively. Any appropriately consistent estimator can be used in place of $\hat{\theta}_n$ or $\tilde{\theta}_n$ without affecting the conclusion. The estimator $\hat{A}_n$ is used in forming the classical Wald statistic, $\mathcal{W}_n$, while $\tilde{A}_n$ is used in forming the classical Lagrange multiplier statistic. Either $\hat{A}_n$ or $\tilde{A}_n$ may be used in forming $\mathcal{H}_n$.

The fact that the information matrix equality is imposed in Theorem 8.23 is thus crucial to the validity of the classical test statistics. When the information matrix equality is violated, we generally have only the results of Theorem 8.23, so that $-\hat{A}_n^- + A_n^{*-1} \to 0$ $prob - P_o$, implying that

$$\mathcal{W}_n \overset{A}{\sim} N_2(0, R_n^* A_n^{*-1} B_n^* A_n^{*-1} R_n^*; - [R_n^* A_n^{*-1} R_n^*]^{-1})$$

and that inferences based on the χ_q^2 distribution are invalid. A similar result holds for the $\mathcal{LM}_n$ and $\mathcal{H}_n$ statistics. Thus, when the information matrix equality fails, the classical Wald, classical Lagrange-multiplier, Hausman, and (as we saw previously) likelihood ratio tests do not have the χ_q^2 distribution asymptotically, and hypothesis tests based on the χ_q^2 distribution do not have the correct (nominal) size asymptotically.

The situation here is precisely the generalization of the fact that the usual least squares parameter covariance estimator leads to faulty inferences in the presence of neglected serial correlation or (conditional or unconditional) heteroskedasticity.

For this reason, it is of paramount importance in applications to verify the validity of the information matrix equality. The results of Chapter 6 provide theoretical conditions under which the information matrix equality holds. However, the validity of the information matrix equality is in fact an empirically refutable hypothesis. In Chapter 11 we provide specific procedures for testing the validity of the information matrix equality.

Analogs of Theorems 8.23 and 8.24 are straightforwardly available for cases involving the 2SQMLE. When $r_n : \mathcal{B} \to \mathbb{R}^q$ and $\nabla_{\alpha\beta} L_{2n}^* = 0$, the results hold under analogous conditions with A_{22n}^* and B_{22n}^* replacing A_n^* and B_n^*, $\nabla^2 \log f_{2t}$ replacing $\nabla^2 \log f_t$ and $\hat{\theta}_n{}' = (\hat{\alpha}_n{}', \hat{\beta}_n{}')$, $\tilde{\theta}_n{}' = (\hat{\alpha}_n{}', \tilde{\beta}_n{}')$. In the general case, A_n^* and B_n^* are as defined in Theorem 6.11 and $\nabla^2 \log f_t$ is replaced by

$$\begin{bmatrix} \nabla_{\alpha\alpha} \log f_{1t} & 0 \\ \nabla_{\alpha\beta} \log f_{2t} & \nabla_{\beta\beta} \log f_{2t} \end{bmatrix}.$$

The information matrix equality is generally possible only when $\nabla_{\alpha\beta} \bar{L}_{2n}^* \to 0$. For brevity, we content ourselves with only this informal discussion of results for the general 2SQMLE.

When the information matrix equality holds, it is also possible to obtain a consistent estimator of $A_n^{*-1} B_n^* A_n^{*-1}$ by estimating B_n^{*-1} instead of $-A_n^{*-1}$. We define

$$\bar{B}_n(\theta) \equiv n^{-1} \sum_{t=1}^{n} E[s_t(X^t, \theta)\, s_t(X^t, \theta)'] .$$

THEOREM 8.25: *(i) Given Assumptions 2.1, 2.3, 3.2, 3.6, 3.8, and 3.9, suppose that* $A_n^* + \bar{B}_n^* \to 0$, *so that* $\{\bar{B}_n^* \equiv \bar{B}_n(\theta_n^*)\}$ *is* $O(1)$ *and uniformly positive definite. If* $\hat{B}_n - \bar{B}_n^* \to 0$ *a.s.–*P_o *(prob–*P_o*), then* $\hat{B}_n^- - A_n^{*-1} \bar{B}_n^* A_n^{*-1} \to 0$ *a.s.–*P_o *(prob–*P_o*).*

(ii) If in addition $\{s_t^*, \mathcal{F}^t\}$ *is a martingale difference sequence, then*

$$\bar{B}_n^* = B_n^* \equiv \mathrm{var}(\sqrt{n}\, \nabla L_n^*),$$

so that $\hat{B}_n^- - A_n^{*-1} B_n^* A_n^{*-1} \to 0$ *a.s.–*P_o *(prob–*P_o*).* □

The requirement that $\{s_t^*, \mathcal{F}^t\}$ be a martingale difference sequence is of considerable importance. Without it, the full information matrix equality need not hold. We discuss this requirement somewhat further below.

Under the conditions of Theorem 8.25, it suffices to obtain a consistent estimator for $\bar{B}_n^*$. As with A_n^*, consistent estimators are available despite the presence of misspecification. We make use of the following assumption.

ASSUMPTION 8.6: (a) The elements of $\bar{B}_n(\cdot)$ are finite and continuous on Θ uniformly in $n = 1, 2, \ldots$;

(b) The elements of $\{s_t(X^t, \theta)s_t(X^t, \theta)'\}$ obey the strong (weak) ULLN. □

THEOREM 8.26: *(i) Given Assumptions 2.1, 2.3, 2.4, 3.1, 3.2, and 8.6*

$$\hat{B}_n - \bar{B}_n^* \to 0 \qquad a.s. - P_o \quad (prob - P_o),$$

where $\hat{B}_n = n^{-1} \sum_{t=1}^n \hat{s}_t \, \hat{s}_t'$, $\hat{s}_t \equiv s_t(X^t, \hat{\theta}_n)$.

(ii)(a) Given Assumptions 2.1, 2.3, 2.4, 3.1, 8.1 (a,b), 8.3 and 8.6

$$\tilde{B}_n - \bar{B}_n^o \to 0 \quad a.s. - P_o \quad (prob - P_o),$$

where $\bar{B}_n^o = E(n^{-1} \sum_{t=1}^n s_t(X^t, \theta_n^o)s_t(X^t, \theta_n^o)')$, *and letting* $\tilde{s}_t = s_t(X^t, \tilde{\theta}_n)$,

$$\tilde{B}_n = n^{-1} \sum_{t=1}^{n} \tilde{s}_t \tilde{s}_t'.$$

(b) If in addition Assumptions 3.2 ′, and 3.5 (b) and 8.1(c) hold, Assumption 8.3 is dropped, and $r_n^* \to 0$, *then* $\tilde{B}_n - \bar{B}_n^* \to 0$ $a.s. - P_o$ $(prob - P_o)$. □

Test statistics based on $\hat{B}_n$ or $\tilde{B}_n$ are computationally convenient, as they do not require evaluation of second derivatives. Computer algorithms that make use of the Berndt, Hall, Hall, Hausman [1974] method for maximizing L_n will frequently provide asymptotic standard errors and test statistics based on $\hat{B}_n$ or $\tilde{B}_n$.

All of the warnings earlier raised regarding the use of $\hat{A}_n$ or $\tilde{A}_n$ apply equally to use of $\hat{B}_n$ or $\tilde{B}_n$. We emphasize the crucial role played by the martingale difference requirement on $\{s_t^*, \mathcal{F}^t\}$. Checking this martingale difference condition is an important aspect of verifying the information matrix equality. The martingale difference assumption generally fails in the presence of dynamic misspecification. It may also fail even with independent observations, as we see below. (The reason is that we may have $E(s_t^*) \neq 0$.) In Chapter 11, we provide specific methods for checking the martingale difference condition.

Analogous results for the 2SQMLE are straightforwardly available. Again, we provide only an informal discussion. When $r_n : \mathcal{B} \to \mathbb{R}^q$, and $\nabla_{\alpha\beta} \bar{L}_{2n}^* = 0$, the results hold under analogous conditions with A_n^* and $\bar{B}_n^*$ replaced by A_{22n}^* and $\bar{B}_{22n}^*$, where the latter matrix is defined with s_{2t} replacing s_t, and with $\hat{\theta}_n' = (\hat{\alpha}_n', \hat{\beta}_n')$, $\tilde{\theta}_n' = (\hat{\alpha}_n', \tilde{\beta}_n')$, $\theta_n^{*\prime} = (\alpha_n^{*\prime}, \beta_n^{*\prime})$, $\theta_n^{o\prime} = (\alpha_n^{*\prime}, \beta_n^{o\prime})$. In the general case, A_n^* and B_n^* are as defined in Theorem 6.11 and s_t is replaced by $(s_{1t}', s_{2t}')'$.

The results of Theorems 8.23 to 8.26 thus justify the choices $\hat{C}_n = -\hat{A}_n^-$ or $\hat{B}_n^-$, $\tilde{C}_n = -\tilde{A}_n^-$ or $\tilde{B}_n^-$ in constructing asymptotic χ_q^2 statistics under fairly restrictive conditions. Earlier results establishing that these conditions hold are Theorem 6.6 which assumes that $\mathcal{S}$ is correct for $\{Y_t \mid W_t\}$ and that there is no dynamic misspecification (i.e. $\mathcal{S}$ is correct for $\{Y_t | \tilde{X}^{t-1}\}$), and Theorems 6.9 and 6.13, which assume that $\mathcal{M}$ is correctly specified for $\{E(Y_t \mid W_t)\}$, there is no dynamic misspecification, and (a correct model of) the conditional variance of Y_t given W_t is known. When these conditions fail, the information matrix equality also generally fails, and the classical test statistics fail to have the χ_q^2 distribution asymptotically.

Now consider the case in which $A_n^* + B_n^* \nrightarrow 0$. We require an estimator for $A_n^{*-1} B_n^* A_n^{*-1}$. It is natural to attempt to estimate this with $\hat{A}_n^{-1} \hat{B}_n \hat{A}_n^{-1}$, where $\hat{A}_n - A_n^* \to 0$ $prob - P_o$ and $\hat{B}_n - B_n^* \to 0$ $prob - P_o$. Theorem 8.24 gives general conditions ensuring a consistent estimator for A_n^*. The challenge is to find a consistent estimator for $B_n^* \equiv \text{var}(\sqrt{n}\, \nabla L_n^*)$. Theorem 8.26 gives a consistent estimator for $\bar{B}_n^*$. We again exploit a martingale difference condition to obtain a somewhat more general result.

THEOREM 8.27: *(i) Given Assumptions 2.1, 2.3, 2.4, 3.1, 3.2, and 8.6, suppose that $\{s_t^* - E(s_t^*), \mathcal{F}^t\}$ is a martingale difference sequence. Then*

$$\hat{B}_n - (B_n^* + U_n^*) \to 0 \qquad a.s. - P_o \quad (prob - P_o),$$

where $U_n^* = n^{-1} \sum_{t=1}^n E(s_t^*)\, E(s_t^{*\prime})$.

If $U_n^* \to 0$ *also, then* $\hat{B}_n - B_n^* \to 0$ *a.s.* $-P_o$ (*prob* $- P_o$).

(ii)(a) Given Assumptions 2.1, 2.3, 2.4, 3.1, 8.1(a,b), 8.3 and 8.6, suppose that $\{s_t^o - E(s_t^o), \mathcal{F}^t\}$ $(s_t^o \equiv s_t(X^t, \theta_n^o))$ *is a martingale difference sequence. Then*

$$\tilde{B}_n - (B_n^o + U_n^o) \to 0 \;\; a.s. - P_o \;\; (prob - P_o)\,,$$

where $U_n^o = n^{-1} \sum_{t=1}^{n} E(s_t^o) E(s_t^{o\prime})$.

If $U_n^o \to 0$ *also, then* $\tilde{B}_n - B_n^o \to 0$ *a.s.* $- P_o$ (*prob* $- P_o$).

(b) If in addition Assumptions 3.2′, 3.5(b) and 8.1(c) hold, Assumption 8.3 is dropped and $r_n^* \to 0$, *and if* $\{s_t^* - E(s_t^*), \mathcal{F}^t\}$ *is a martingale difference sequence, then*

$$\tilde{B}_n - (B_n^* - U_n^*) \to 0 \;\; a.s. - P_o \; (prob - P_o).$$

If $U_n^* \to 0$ *also, then* $\tilde{B}_n - B_n^* \to 0$ *a.s.* $- P_o$ (*prob* $- P_o$). □

Combining these results with those of Theorem 8.24 gives the following general result for covariance matrix estimation in the presence of misspecification.

COROLLARY 8.28: *(i) Suppose the conditions of Theorems 8.24(i) and 8.27(i) hold. Then*

$$\hat{A}_n^- \, \hat{B}_n \, \hat{A}_n^- - A_n^{*-1} (B_n^* + U_n^*) A_n^{*-1} \to 0 \qquad a.s. - P_o \quad (prob - P_o)\,.$$

If $U_n^* \to 0$ *also, then*

$$\hat{A}_n^- \, \hat{B}_n \, \hat{A}_n^- - A_n^{*-1} \, B_n^* \, A_n^{*-1} \to 0 \qquad a.s. - P_o \quad (prob - P_o)\,.$$

(ii) (a) Suppose the conditions of Theorems 8.24(ii.a) and 8.27(ii.a) hold. Then

$$\tilde{A}_n^- \, \tilde{B}_n \tilde{A}_n^- - A_n^{o-1} (B_n^o + U_n^o) A_n^{o-1} \to 0 \quad a.s. - P_o \quad (prob - P_o)\,.$$

If $U_n^o \to 0$ *also, then*

$$\tilde{A}_n^- \tilde{B}_n \tilde{A}_n^- - A_n^{o\,-1} B_n^o A_n^{o\,-1} \rightarrow 0 \quad a.s.-P_o \quad (prob-P_o).$$

(b) Suppose the conditions of Theorems 8.24(ii.b) and 8.27 (ii.b) hold. Then

$$\tilde{A}_n^- \tilde{B}_n \tilde{A}_n^- - A_n^{*\,-1}(B_n^* + U_n^*)A_n^{*\,-1} \rightarrow 0 \quad a.s.-P_o \quad (prob-P_o).$$

If $U_n^* \rightarrow 0$ *also, then*

$$\tilde{A}_n^- \tilde{B}_n \tilde{A}_n^- - A_n^{*\,-1} B_n^* A_n^{*\,-1} \rightarrow 0 \quad a.s.-P_o \quad (prob-P_o). \qquad \square$$

There are two features of this result that dictate caution in using the χ_q^2 distribution to find critical values for $\mathcal{W}_n$, $\mathcal{LM}_n$ or $\mathcal{H}_n$ constructed using $\hat{C}_n = \hat{A}_n^{-1} \hat{B}_n \hat{A}_n^{-1}$ or $\tilde{C}_n = \tilde{A}_n^{-1} \tilde{B}_n \tilde{A}_n^{-1}$. The first is the requirement that $\{s_t^* - E(s_t^*),\ \mathcal{F}^t\}$ be a martingale difference sequence; the second is the requirement that $U_n^* \rightarrow 0$.

Theorems 6.9 and 6.13 provide conditions under which these requirements are satisfied. Specifically, it is assumed there that $\mathcal{M}$ is correctly specified for $\{E(Y_t \mid W_t)\}$, and that there is no dynamic misspecification (i.e. $\mathcal{M}$ is correctly specified for $\{E(Y_t \mid \tilde{X}^{t-1})\}$). Generally, either dynamic misspecification or misspecification of $\mathcal{M}$ for $\{E(Y_t \mid W_t)\}$ will lead to the failure of $\{s_t^* - E(s_t^*),\ \mathcal{F}^t\}$ to be a martingale difference sequence, and thus to the failure of $\hat{B}_n$ ($\tilde{B}_n$) to estimate B_n^* consistently. (Instead, $\hat{B}_n - \overline{B}_n^* \rightarrow 0$ or $\tilde{B}_n - \overline{B}_n^* \rightarrow 0$, $B_n^* - \overline{B}_n^* \nrightarrow 0$.) Thus the presence of dynamic misspecification and/or misspecification of $\mathcal{M}$ generally invalidate $\hat{A}_n^{-1} \hat{B}_n \hat{A}_n^{-1}$ and $\tilde{A}_n^{-1} \tilde{B}_n \tilde{A}_n^{-1}$ as consistent estimators for $A_n^* B_n^* A_n^{*-1}$, invalidating the use of critical values based on the χ_q^2 distribution.

It is interesting to examine in more detail what happens when $\{X_t\}$ is an independent sequence. In this case, dynamic misspecification is ruled out, so that $\{s_t^* - E(s_t^*), \mathcal{F}^t\}$ is guaranteed to be a martingale difference sequence, regardless of any form of misspecification. The difficulty created by misspecification for covariance matrix estimation is the possible failure of $U_n^* \rightarrow 0$. As noted by Chow [1981], in the presence of heterogeneous (i.e. not identically distributed) observations, misspecification of $\mathcal{S}$ for $\{Y_t \mid Z_t\}$ or $\mathcal{M}$ for $\{E(Y_t \mid Z_t)\}$ generally implies $E(s_t^*) \neq 0$, even though $n^{-1} \sum_{t=1}^n E(s_t^*) = 0$. When this occurs, it is generally not possible to obtain a consistent estimator for $A_n^{*-1} B_n^* A_n^{*-1}$, but only for $A_n^{*-1} (B_n^* + U_n^*) A_n^{*-1}$ due to the failure of U_n^* to vanish. Consequently, we have for example that

$$\mathcal{W}_n \overset{A}{\sim} N_2(0,\ R_n^*\ A_n^{*-1}\ B_n^*\ A_n^{*-1}\ R_n^{*\prime};\ [R_n^*\ A_n^{*-1}\ (B_n^* + U_n^*)A_n^{*-1}\ R_n^{*\prime}]^{-1}).$$

The χ_q^2 distribution does not give correct critical values for $\mathcal{W}_n$. Nevertheless, it can be used to construct conservative size α critical values (i.e. values that yield a test with size less than a specified level α) using $\chi^2_{q,\,1-\alpha}$, as $\mathcal{W}_n$ tends to be too small relative to the χ_q^2 distribution in this case.

When $\{X_t\}$ is independent and identically distributed, and when $f_t(\cdot\,,\ \theta) = f_0(\cdot\,,\theta)$ for all t (the model embodies no regime changes), then $\theta_n^* = \theta_0^*$, say, and $s_t^* \equiv s_t(X^t\,,\theta_n^*) = \nabla \log f_0(X_t\,,\theta_0^*)$. Because $n^{-1}\ \sum_{t=1}^n E(s_t^*) = 0$ and $E(s_t^*)$ is the same for all n and t, we have $E(s_t^*) = 0$, so that $U_n^* = 0$. In this special case $\hat{A}_n\ \hat{B}_n\ \hat{A}_n^{-1}$ does consistently estimate $A_n^{*-1}\ B_n^*\ A_n^{*-1}$ in the presence of arbitrary misspecification. This is the case treated by White [1982].

Now consider the consequences of $\{s_t^* - E(s_t^*),\ \mathcal{F}^t\}$ failing to be a martingale difference sequence as a consequence of dynamic misspecification and/or the misspecification of $\mathcal{S}$ for $\{Y_t \mid W_t\}$ or $\mathcal{M}$ for $\{E(Y_t \mid W_t)\}$. This is the general case of misspecification in a time-series context. Now

$$\begin{aligned}
B_n^* &= \operatorname{var}(\sqrt{n}\ \nabla\ L_n^*) \\
&= \operatorname{var}(n^{-1/2} \sum_{t=1}^n s_t^*) \\
&= n^{-1} \sum_{t=1}^n E(s_t^*\ s_t^{*\prime}) + n^{-1} \sum_{\tau=1}^{n-1} \sum_{t=\tau+1}^{n} [E(s_t^*\ s_{t-\tau}^{*\prime}) + E(s_{t-\tau}^*\ s_t^{*\prime})] \\
&= \bar{B}_n^* + \ddot{B}_n^*,
\end{aligned}$$

where we let $\ddot{B}_n^* \equiv B_n^* - \bar{B}_n^*$ with $\bar{B}_n^*$ as previously defined. The difficulties associated with this case arise from the presence of $\ddot{B}_n^*$, which vanishes when $\{s_t^*\,,\mathcal{F}^t\}$ is a martingale difference sequence, but generally not otherwise. We see that $\ddot{B}_n$ contains $n-1$ terms, each of which must be adequately estimated. With only n observations, this is not possible without some further conditions.

Domowitz and White [1982] proposed an estimator for this situation in which mixing properties of the underlying process $\{X_t\}$ are exploited to allow terms with large τ to be neglected. An improved version of the Domowitz and White estimator was given by Newey and West [1987]. The

Newey and West estimator is guaranteed to be positive semi-definite, a property not possessed by the Domowitz and White estimator. Newey and West also corrected an error in the technical conditions of Domowitz and White. Gallant and White [1988] have established the consistency of a generalized version of the Newey and West estimator under conditions permitting misspecification and requiring $\{X_t\}$ to be a near epoch dependent function of an underlying mixing process. Andrews [1991] provides an estimator consistent for $\ddot{B}_n^*$ in the absence of misspecification that eliminates having to specify the "truncation lag", a nuisance parameter on which the foregoing estimators all depend.

We shall not concern ourselves here with the rather intricate details that arise in proper treatment of this general case, but refer the interested reader to Chapter 6 of Gallant and White [1988] and to Andrews [1991]. Gallant and White treat estimators of the form

$$(8.1) \qquad \hat{B}_n \equiv w_{n0}\, n^{-1} \sum_{t=1}^{n} \hat{s}_t\, \hat{s}_t{}' + n^{-1} \sum_{\tau=1}^{\lambda_n} w_{n\tau} \sum_{t=\tau+1}^{n} [\hat{s}_t\, \hat{s}_{t-\tau}{}' + \hat{s}_{t-\tau}\, \hat{s}_t{}']$$

$$\tilde{B}_n \equiv w_{n0}\, n^{-1} \sum_{t=1}^{n} \tilde{s}_t\, \tilde{s}_t{}' + n^{-1} \sum_{\tau=1}^{\lambda_n} w_{n\tau} \sum_{t=\tau+1}^{n} [\tilde{s}_t\, \tilde{s}_{t-\tau}{}' + \tilde{s}_{t-\tau}\, \tilde{s}_t{}'],$$

where $\lambda_n = o(n^{1/4})$, $\lambda_n \to \infty$ as $n \to \infty$, and

$$w_{n\tau} = \sum_{t=\tau+1}^{\lambda_n+1} a_{nt}\, a_{n,t-\tau}$$

for any triangular array $\{a_{nt}\}$, $n = 1, 2, \ldots,\ t = 1, \ldots, \lambda_n + 1$ such that $|w_{n\tau}| \le \Delta < \infty$, $n = 1, 2, \ldots,\ \tau = 0, \ldots, \lambda_n$ and for each τ, $w_{n\tau} \to 1$ as $n \to \infty$. Gallant and White provide conditions under which

$$\hat{B}_n - (B_n^* + U_n^*) \longrightarrow 0 \ \ prob - P_o$$

and

$$\tilde{B}_n - (B_n^* + U_n^*) \longrightarrow 0 \ \ prob - P_o\,,$$

where now

$$U_n^* = w_{n0}\, n^{-1} \sum_{t=1}^{n} E(s_t^*)\, E(s_t^{*\prime})$$
$$+ n^{-1} \sum_{\tau=1}^{\lambda_n} w_{n\tau} \sum_{t=\tau+1}^{n} [E(s_t^*)\, E(s_{t-\tau}^{*\prime}) + E(s_{t-\tau}^*)\, E(s_t^{*\prime})]\,.$$

Unfortunately, while it can be shown that U_n^* is positive semi-definite, there is in general nothing to ensure that $\{U_n^*\}$ is $O(1)$. Thus, it may happen that $\hat{A}_n^{-1}\, \hat{B}_n\, \hat{A}_n^{-1} \to \infty$ in the presence of arbitrary misspecification.

Circumstances under which $U_n^* = 0$ (so that $A_n^{*-1}\, B_n^*\, A_n^{*-1}$ can be consistently estimated) arise when $\mathcal{S}$ is correct for $\{Y_t \mid W_t\}$ and Assumption 6.3(a) holds, or when $\mathcal{M}$ is correct for $\{E(Y_t \mid W_t)\}$; in either case, only dynamic misspecification is present. It also happens that $U_n^* = 0$ in the presence of arbitrary misspecification when $\{X_t\}$ is stationary and the model incorporates no regime changes. Although Theorem 8.10 supports the use of the χ_q^2 distribution for conducting inferences based on $\hat{C}_n = \hat{A}_n^{-1}\, \hat{B}_n\, \hat{A}_n^{-1}$ or $\tilde{C}_n = \tilde{A}_n^{-1}\, \tilde{B}_n\, \tilde{A}_n^{-1}$ in these cases, there is only modest evidence available on how well $\hat{B}_n$ or $\tilde{B}_n$ actually perform in finite samples as estimators of B_n^* in samples of realistic size. For this reason, it may be worthwhile to devote considerable effort to obtaining a specification for which $\{s_t^* - E(s_t^*),\, \mathcal{F}^t\}$ is a martingale difference sequence (or nearly so), rather than attempting to mitigate whatever damage might have been done by a dynamic misspecification by using the estimators of Gallant and White [1988] or Andrews [1991].

Entirely analogous results hold for the 2SQMLE; we leave the details of the general case to the reader. However, it is useful to provide explicit formulae for some covariance matrix estimators relevant to the estimation of the exponential family models of Assumption 6.7. Recall that Theorem 6.13 establishes that

$$B_{22n}^{*-1/2}\, A_{22n}^*\, \sqrt{n}\, (\hat{\beta}_n - \beta_o) \overset{A}{\sim} N(0, I)$$

when $\mathcal{M}$ is correct for $\{E(Y_t \mid W_t)\}$, where

$$A_{22n}^* = -\, n^{-1} \sum_{t=1}^{n} E(\nabla_\beta\, \mu_t^o\, D_t^{*-1}\, \nabla_\beta{}'\, \mu_t^o)\, .$$

In the further absence of dynamic misspecification,

$$B_{22n}^* = n^{-1} \sum_{t=1}^{n} E(\nabla_\beta\, \mu_t^o\, D_t^{*-1}\, \Sigma_t^o\, D_t^{*-1}\, \nabla_\beta{}'\, \mu_t^o)\, .$$

The estimators discussed earlier are of course available, but because of the complicated form of $\nabla^2 \log f_t$ (see Theorem 6.9), the estimator based on $\nabla^2 \log \hat{f}_t$ is extremely cumbersome. Instead, one may exploit the correct specification of $\mathcal{M}$ to neglect terms that vanish in expectation when estimating A^*_{22n}. Such an estimator is

$$\hat{A}_{22n} = -\, n^{-1} \sum_{t=1}^{n} \nabla_\beta\, \hat{\mu}_t\, \hat{D}_t^{-1}\, \nabla_\beta{}'\, \hat{\mu}_t \,,$$

where $\nabla_\beta\, \hat{\mu}_t \equiv \nabla_\beta\, \mu_t(W_t\,, \hat{\beta}_n)$, $\hat{D}_t \equiv D_t(\,\mu_t(W_t\,, \hat{\beta}_n),\ \kappa_t(W_t\,, \hat{\alpha}_n))$. The natural estimator for B^*_{22n} is

$$\hat{B}_{22n} = n^{-1} \sum_{t=1}^{n} \nabla_\beta\, \hat{\mu}_t\, \hat{D}_t^{-1}\, (Y_t - \hat{\mu}_t)\, (Y_t - \hat{\mu}_t)'\, \hat{D}_t^{-1}\, \nabla_\beta{}'\, \hat{\mu}_t \,.$$

The choice $\hat{C}_n = \hat{A}^-_{22n}\, \hat{B}_{22n}\, \hat{A}^-_{22n}$ is then the generalization of the heteroskedasticity-consistent covariance matrix estimator of White [1980b]. In the case of the constrained 2SQMLE, $\tilde{\beta}_n$ replaces $\hat{\beta}_n$. Convergence of $\hat{A}_{22n}$ to A^*_{22n} and of $\hat{B}_{22n}$ to B^*_{22n} is ensured essentially by the consistency of $\hat{\beta}_n$ or $\tilde{\beta}_n$ for β_o and of $\hat{\alpha}_n$ for α^*_n, and by conditions that guarantee that the uniform law of large numbers holds for $\nabla_\beta\, \mu_t\, D_t^{-1}\, \nabla_\beta{}'\, \mu_t$ and for $\nabla_\beta\, \mu_t\, D_t^{-1}\, (Y_t - \mu_t)\, (Y_t - \mu_t)'\, D_t^{-1}\, \nabla_\beta{}'\, \mu_t$.

We emphasize that the usefulness of $\hat{C}_n = \hat{A}^-_{22n}\, \hat{B}_{22n}\, \hat{A}^-_{22n}$ in the present context is crucially dependent upon the validity of the expressions given for A^*_{22n} and B^*_{22n}. If $\mathcal{M}$ is misspecified, then terms neglected in obtaining the expression above for A^*_{22n} do not vanish, and $\hat{A}_{22n}$ is then generally inconsistent for $E(\nabla_{\beta\beta}\, L^*_n\,)$. The validity of the expression for B^*_{22n} not only requires the correct specification of $\mathcal{M}$, but also the absence of dynamic misspecification. If only dynamic misspecification is present, then a consistent estimator is available. However, if $\mathcal{M}$ is misspecified and the observations are heterogeneous and/or the model embodies regime changes, then the consistent estimators need not exist. The results of the following chapters contain results useful in detecting such misspecifications.

8.4 Summary

In this chapter, we have seen how the null hypothesis in a given testing context may be interpreted in a manner consistent with the presence of misspecification. We also saw how misspecification affects the properties of the classical test statistics, adversely affecting their size. Tests of proper size can be obtained by using asymptotic covariance matrix estimators consistent in the presence of misspecification to construct analogs of the classical statistics. Such misspecification-consistent covariance matrix estimators are not always available; they may fail to exist in the case of a misspecified model of a heterogeneous dependent process.

MATHEMATICAL APPENDIX

PROOF OF LEMMA 8.2: Let $\mathcal{Y} = V^{-1/2}\, \mathcal{Z}$, so that $\mathcal{Y} \sim N(V^{-1/2}\, \mu, I_q)$. It follows immediately from Theorem 1 of Baldessari [1969] that

$$\mathcal{Z}'\, K\, \mathcal{Z} = \mathcal{Y}'\, V^{1/2}\, K\, V^{1/2}\, \mathcal{Y}$$

$$\sim \sum_{i=1}^{c} \lambda_i\, \chi^2\, (m_i\,, \xi_i\,)$$

for λ_i , m_i and ξ_i as defined in the text. □

PROOF OF PROPOSITION 8.4: (i) Choose $x \in \mathbb{R}$ and $\varepsilon > 0$. For all $\delta > 0$, the triangle inequality implies

$$| F_n(x+\delta) - F_n(x-\delta) | \le | F_n(x+\delta) - G_n(x+\delta) |$$

$$+ | G_n(x+\delta) - G_n(x-\delta) | + | G_n(x-\delta) - F_n(x-\delta) | .$$

Because G_n is assumed continuous in x uniformly in n, it follows that for all n, there exists $\delta_x(\varepsilon)$ such that

$$| G_n(x+\delta_x(\varepsilon)) - G_n(x-\delta_x(\varepsilon)) | < \varepsilon .$$

Because $\mathcal{X}_n \overset{A}{\sim} \mathcal{Z}_n$, it follows that there exist finite integers $N_1(x+\delta_x(\varepsilon)\,, \varepsilon)$ and $N_2(x-\delta_x(\varepsilon)\,, \varepsilon)$ such that for all $n > N_o(x\,, \varepsilon) \equiv \max\, [N_1(x+\delta_x(\varepsilon), \varepsilon), N_2(x-\delta_x(\varepsilon), \varepsilon)]$

$$| F_n(x+\delta_x(\varepsilon)) - G_n(x+\delta_x(\varepsilon)) | < \varepsilon$$

and

$$| F_n(x-\delta_x(\varepsilon)) - G_n(x-\delta_x(\varepsilon)) | < \varepsilon .$$

Hence for all $n > N_o(x\,, \varepsilon)$

$$F_n(x + \delta_x(\varepsilon)) - F_n(x - \delta_x(\varepsilon)) < 3\,\varepsilon\,.$$

The result follows upon setting $N(\varepsilon) \equiv N_o(x, \varepsilon/3)$, $\delta(\varepsilon) = \delta_x(\varepsilon/3)$.

(ii) Fix x. The events $\mathcal{Z}_n > x + \delta$ and $|\mathcal{X}_n - \mathcal{Z}_n| \leq \delta$ imply $\mathcal{X}_n > x$ for any $\delta > 0$. By the implication rule (Lukacs [1975, p.7])

$$P[\mathcal{X}_n \leq x] \leq P[\mathcal{Z}_n \leq x + \delta\,] + P[|\mathcal{X}_n - \mathcal{Z}_n| > \delta\,],$$

so that

$$P[\mathcal{X}_n \leq x] - P[\mathcal{Z}_n \leq x\,] \leq P[x < \mathcal{Z}_n \leq x + \delta\,] + P[|\mathcal{X}_n - \mathcal{Z}_n| > \delta\,]\,,$$

that is,

$$F_n(x) - G_n(x) \leq (G_n(x + \delta) - G_n(x)) + P[|\mathcal{X}_n - \mathcal{Z}_n| > \delta\,]\,.$$

Given $\varepsilon > 0$, there exist $N_1(\varepsilon) < \infty$ and $\delta(\varepsilon) > 0$ such that $G_n\ (x + \delta\ (\varepsilon)) - G_n(x) < \varepsilon$ for $n > N_1(\varepsilon)$. Because $\mathcal{X}_n - \mathcal{Z}_n \to 0$ *prob* $-\ P$, it also follows that there exists $N_2(\varepsilon, \delta(\varepsilon)) < \infty$ such that for all $n > N_2(\varepsilon, \delta(\varepsilon))$, $P[|\mathcal{X}_n - \mathcal{Z}_n| > \delta(\varepsilon)] < \varepsilon$. Hence for all $n > N_o(\varepsilon) = \max[N_1(\varepsilon), N_2(\varepsilon, \delta(\varepsilon))]$ we have

$$F_n(x) - G_n(x) \leq 2\,\varepsilon\,.$$

Similarly, the events $\mathcal{Z}_n \leq x - \delta$ and $|\mathcal{X}_n - \mathcal{Z}_n| \leq \delta$ imply $\mathcal{X}_n \leq x$ for any δ. Analogous reasoning to that above establishes that

$$G_n(x) - F_n(x) \leq 2\,\varepsilon$$

for $n > N_o(\varepsilon)$. Because $\varepsilon > 0$ is arbitrary, it follows that $F_n(x) - G_n(x) \to 0$ as $n \to \infty$. If this is true for each $x \in \mathcal{D}^c$, then it follows by Definition 8.3 that $\mathcal{X}_n \overset{A}{\sim} \mathcal{Z}_n$.

(iii) We assume $\mathcal{X}_n - \mathcal{Z}_n \to 0$ *prob* $-\ P$, and because $\mathcal{Z}_n \overset{A}{\sim} \mathcal{Y}_n$, where $H_n(x) \equiv P[\mathcal{Y}_n \geq x]$ is continuous in x uniformly in n, it follows from (i) that the conditions of (ii) hold for G_n for each $x \in \mathbb{R}$. Thus $F_n(x) - G_n(x) \to 0$. Because $G_n(x) - H_n(x) \to 0$, we have $F_n(x) - H_n(x) \to 0$ for each $x \in \mathbb{R}$, i.e. $\mathcal{X}_n \overset{A}{\sim} \mathcal{Y}_n$. □

PROOF OF PROPOSITION 8.5: Because $\mathcal{X}_n - \mathcal{Z}_n \to 0$ $prob-P$ and $\{\mu_n\}$, $\{V_n^{-1}\}$ are $O(1)$, we have $V_n^{-1/2}(\mathcal{X}_n - \mathcal{Z}_n) = V_n^{-1/2}(\mathcal{X}_n - \mu_n) - V_n^{-1/2}(\mathcal{Z}_n - \mu_n) \to 0$ $prob-P$. Because $\mathcal{Z}_n \overset{A}{\sim} N(\mu_n, V_n)$, it follows that $V_n^{-1/2}(\mathcal{Z}_n - \mu_n) \overset{A}{\sim} N(0, I)$. By the asymptotic equivalence lemma (White [1984a, Lemma 4.7]), we have $V_n^{-1/2}(\mathcal{X}_n - \mu_n) \overset{A}{\sim} N(0, I)$, i.e. $\mathcal{X}_n \overset{A}{\sim} N(\mu_n, V_n)$. □

PROOF OF THEOREM 8.6: First, consider

$$\mathcal{X}_n' \hat{K}_n^- \mathcal{X}_n - \mathcal{X}_n' K_n^{-1} \mathcal{X}_n = \mathcal{X}_n'(\hat{K}_n^- - K_n^{-1})\,\mathcal{X}_n .$$

Because $\mathcal{X}_n = O_P(1)$ given that $\mathcal{X}_n \overset{A}{\sim} N(\mu_n, V_n)$, $\{\mu_n\}$, $\{V_n\} = O(1)$, it follows that $\mathcal{X}_n'(\hat{K}_n^- - K_n^{-1})\mathcal{X}_n \to 0$ $prob-P$, provided that $\hat{K}_n^- - K_n^{-1} \to 0$ $prob-P$.

Now $\hat{K}_n - K_n \to 0$ $prob-P$ by assumption. Given any subsequence $\{n'\}$ it follows that there exists a further subsequence $\{n''\}$ such that $\hat{K}_{n''} - K_{n''} \to 0$ $a.s.-P$. It follows that for all n'' sufficiently large $\hat{K}_{n''}$ is nonsingular $a.s.-P$ (given the uniform positive definiteness of K_n) and that $\hat{K}_{n''}^- - K_{n''}^{-1} \to 0$ $a.s.-P$. Because $\{n'\}$ is arbitrary, we have $\hat{K}_n^- - K_n^{-1} \to 0$ $prob-P$. Therefore $\mathcal{X}_n'(\hat{K}_n^- - K_n^{-1})\,\mathcal{X}_n \to 0$ $prob-P$.

The result follows from Proposition 8.4(iii) if $\mathcal{X}_n' K_n^{-1} \mathcal{X}_n \overset{A}{\sim} N_2(\mu_n, V_n; K_n^{-1})$. Because $\mathcal{X}_n \overset{A}{\sim} N(\mu_n, V_n)$, we have $\mathcal{Y}_n = V_n^{-1/2}\mathcal{X}_n - V_n^{-1/2}\mu_n \overset{A}{\sim} N(0, I_q)$. It follows from the Skorohod representation theorem (e.g. Billingsley [1979, Theorem 29.6]) that there exist random variables $\mathcal{Z}_n$ with distribution identical to that of $\mathcal{Y}_n$ such that $\mathcal{Z}_n - \mathcal{Z} \to 0$, where $\mathcal{Z} \sim N(0, I_q)$. Hence,

$$P[\mathcal{X}_n' K_n^{-1} \mathcal{X}_n \le x] = P[(\mu_n + V_n^{1/2}\mathcal{Y}_n)' K_n^{-1} (\mu_n + V_n^{1/2}\mathcal{Y}_n) \le x]$$

$$= P[(\mu_n + V_n^{1/2}\mathcal{Z}_n)' K_n^{-1} (\mu_n + V_n^{1/2}\mathcal{Z}_n) \le x] .$$

The fact that $\mathcal{Z}_n - \mathcal{Z} \to 0$ implies that

$$(\mu_n + V_n^{1/2}\,\mathcal{Z}_n)'\,K_n^{-1}(\mu_n + V_n^{1/2}\,\mathcal{Z}_n) - (\mu_n + V_n^{1/2}\,\mathcal{Z})'\,K_n^{-1}(\mu_n + V_n^{1/2}\,\mathcal{Z}) \to 0\,.$$

The distribution of the second term is $N_2(\mu_n\,, V_n\,; K_n^{-1})$ by Lemma 8.2. It follows from Proposition 8.4(ii) that

$$P[(\mu_n + V_n^{1/2}\,\mathcal{Z}_n)'\,K_n^{-1}(\mu_n + V_n^{1/2}\,\mathcal{Z}_n) \le x] - P[(\mu_n + V_n^{1/2}\,\mathcal{Z})'\,K_n^{-1}\,(\mu_n + V_n^{1/2}\,\mathcal{Z}) \le x] \to 0\,.$$

Therefore $\mathcal{X}_n{}'\,K_n^{-1}\,\mathcal{X}_n \overset{A}{\sim} N_2(\mu_n\,, V_n\,; K_n^{-1})$, and the proof is complete. □

PROOF OF THEOREM 8.7: Because r_n is continuous and Θ is compact, it follows that Θ_n is compact. The remaining conditions of Theorem 2.14 are satisfied given Assumptions 2.1 and 2.3, so the result follows. □

PROOF OF THEOREM 8.8: (i) We modify the argument of Lemma 7.1 of Gallant and White [1988]. First suppose $p = q$. Because Θ_n is non-empty, it follows that the zero p-vector belongs to M_n, for each $n = 1, 2, \ldots$. We also have $r_n^* \in M_n$. Hence $r_n^{-1}(r_n^*) - r_n^{-1}(0) = \theta_n^* - \theta_n^o$ for all $n = 1, 2, \ldots$, and because r_n^{-1} is continuous on M uniformly in n, the fact that $r_n^* \to 0$ implies $r_n^{-1}(r_n^*) - r_n^{-1}(0) = \theta_n^* - \theta_n^o \to 0$. The continuity of $\bar{L}_n$ on Θ uniformly in n imposed by Assumption 3.5(b) now ensures that $\bar{L}_n(\theta_n^*) - \bar{L}_n(\theta_n^o) \to 0$.

Now suppose $q < p$. Let $\varepsilon > 0$ be given. Given Assumption 3.2′ there exists $N_0 \in \mathbb{N}$ such that

$$\delta(\varepsilon) = \inf_{n>N_0}\,\inf_{|\theta-\theta_n^*|>\varepsilon}\,|\bar{L}_n(\theta) - \bar{L}_n^*\,| > 0\,.$$

We have $r_n(\theta_n^o) = 0$, $r_n^* = r_n(\theta_n^*)$; put $e_n^o = e_n(\theta_n^o)$ and $e_n^* = e_n(\theta_n^*)$. Given $\sup_n \sup_\Theta |\,r_n(\theta)\,| < \infty$, $\sup_n \sup_\Theta |\,e_n(\theta)\,| < \infty$, it follows that M is compact. Because M is compact, ψ_n^{-1} is uniformly continuous on M uniformly in n so that $r_n^* \to 0$ implies

$$\sup_\Gamma |\,\psi_n^{-1}(\gamma, r_n^*) - \psi_n^{-1}(\gamma, 0)\,| \longrightarrow 0\,.$$

In particular, putting $\theta_n^\# = \psi_n^{-1}(e_n^*\,, 0)$ (note that $\theta_n^\#$ need not belong to Θ) and $\theta_n^* = \psi_n^{-1}(e_n^*\,, r_n^*)$, we have $\theta_n^* - \theta_n^\# \to 0$. Because θ_n^* is interior to Θ uniformly in n given Assumption 3.2′, it follows that for all $n > N_1$, say,

$\theta_n^\# \in \Theta$. This implies that $(e_n(\theta_n^\#), r_n(\theta_n^\#))$ belongs to M_n so that $\psi_n(\theta_n^\#) = (e_n^*, 0)$, i.e. $r_n(\theta_n^\#) = 0$. Because $\bar{L}_n$ is continuous on Θ uniformly in n, there exits N_2 such that $|\theta - \theta_n^*| < \eta(\delta)$ implies

$$|\bar{L}_n(\theta) - \bar{L}_n(\theta_n^*)| < \delta$$

for all $n > N_2$. Choose N_3 large enough so that $|\theta_n^* - \theta_n^\#| < \eta(\delta(\varepsilon))$ for all $n > N_3$. Because $r_n(\theta_n^\#) = 0$ we have $\bar{L}_n(\theta_n^o) \geq \bar{L}_n(\theta_n^\#)$ for $n > N_1$, as θ_n^o maximizes $\bar{L}_n$ on Θ_n. For $n > \max(N_0, N_1, N_2, N_3)$ we have

$$\bar{L}_n(\theta_n^o) \geq \bar{L}_n(\theta_n^\#) > \bar{L}_n(\theta_n^*) - \delta(\varepsilon) .$$

But this implies $|\bar{L}_n(\theta_n^o) - \bar{L}_n(\theta_n^*)| < \delta(\varepsilon)$, so that $|\theta_n^o - \theta_n^*| < \varepsilon$. Because ε is arbitrary, the first result follows.

(ii) Fix $\varepsilon > 0$. Given Assumption 3.2′, there exists $N_0 \in \mathbb{N}$ such that

$$\delta(\varepsilon) = \inf_{n>N_0} \inf_{|\theta-\theta_n^*|>\varepsilon} |\bar{L}_n(\theta) - \bar{L}_n^*| > 0 .$$

Given Assumption 3.1, there exists $N_1 \in \mathbb{N}$ such that for $n > N_1$

$$L_n(X^n, \theta_n^o) > \bar{L}_n(\theta_n^o) - \delta(\varepsilon)/3 \qquad a.s.-P_o .$$

Because $L_n(X^n, \tilde{\theta}_n) \geq L_n(X^n, \theta_n^o)$ $a.s.-P_o$, we have

$$L_n(X^n, \tilde{\theta}_n) > \bar{L}_n(\theta_n^o) - \delta(\varepsilon)/3 \qquad a.s.-P_o .$$

Given Assumption 3.1, there exists $N_2 \in \mathbb{N}$ such that for $n > N_2$

$$\bar{L}_n(\tilde{\theta}_n) > L_n(X^n, \tilde{\theta}_n) - \delta(\varepsilon)/3 \qquad a.s.-P_o$$

so that $\bar{L}_n(\tilde{\theta}_n) > \bar{L}_n(\theta_n^o) - 2\delta(\varepsilon)/3$ $a.s.-P_o$. Part (i) establishes that there exists $N_3 \in \mathbb{N}$ such that for $n > N_3$, $\bar{L}_n(\theta_n^o) > \bar{L}_n(\theta_n^*) - \delta(\varepsilon)/3$, so that for $n > \max(N_0, N_1, N_2, N_3)$

$$\bar{L}_n(\tilde{\theta}_n) > \bar{L}_n(\theta_n^*) - \delta(\varepsilon) \qquad a.s.-P_o\,.$$

Thus $|\tilde{\theta}_n - \theta_n^*| < \varepsilon$ $a.s.-P_o$. Because ε is arbitrary, we have $\tilde{\theta}_n - \theta_n^* \to 0$ $a.s.-P_o$. Because $\theta_n^o - \theta_n^* \to 0$, we also have $\tilde{\theta}_n - \theta_n^o \to 0$ $a.s.-P_o$.

Results for convergence in probability follow by the method of subsequences. □

PROOF OF THEOREM 8.9: (i) Because $\hat{\theta}_n - \theta_n^* \to 0$ $prob - P_o$, for any subsequence $\{n'\}$ there exists a further subsequence $\{n''\}$ such that $\hat{\theta}_{n''} - \theta_{n''}^* \to 0$ $a.s.-P_o$. Hence, for all n'' sufficiently large, $\hat{\theta}_{n''}$ lies interior to a convex compact neighborhood of $\theta_{n''}^*$, which is interior to Θ uniformly in n'' given Assumption 3.2′. A mean value expansion of $\hat{r}_{n''} \equiv r_{n''}(\hat{\theta}_{n''})$ around $\theta_{n''}^*$ then gives

$$\sqrt{n''}\,\hat{r}_{n''} = \sqrt{n''}\,r_{n''}^* + \ddot{R}_{n''}\sqrt{n''}\,(\hat{\theta}_{n''} - \theta_{n''}^*) \qquad a.s.-P_o\,,$$

where $\ddot{R}_{n''}$ has rows evaluated at mean values lying between $\hat{\theta}_{n''}$ and $\theta_{n''}^*$. Adding and subtracting $R_{n''}^*\sqrt{n''}\,(\hat{\theta}_{n''} - \theta_{n''}^*)$ gives

$$\sqrt{n''}\,\hat{r}_{n''} = \sqrt{n''}\,r_{n''}^* + R_{n''}^*\sqrt{n''}\,(\hat{\theta}_{n''} - \theta_{n''}^*)$$
$$+ (\ddot{R}_{n''} - R_{n''}^*)\sqrt{n''}\,(\hat{\theta}_{n''} - \theta_{n''}^*)\ a.s.-P_o\,.$$

It follows from Theorem 6.4 that $\sqrt{n''}\,(\hat{\theta}_{n''} - \theta_{n''}^*)$ is $O_{P_o}(1)$, while $\ddot{R}_{n''} - R_{n''}^* \to 0$ $a.s.-P_o$ follows given $\hat{\theta}_{n''} - \theta_{n''}^* \to 0$ $a.s.-P_o$ and the continuity of R_n on the compact set Θ uniformly in n. Hence $(\ddot{R}_{n''} - R_{n''}^*)\sqrt{n''}$ $(\hat{\theta}_{n''} - \theta_{n''}^*) = o_{P_o}(1)$, so that there exists a further subsequence $\{n'''\}$ such that

$$\sqrt{n'''}\,\hat{r}_{n'''} - \sqrt{n'''}\,r_{n'''}^* - R_{n'''}^*\sqrt{n'''}\,(\hat{\theta}_{n'''} - \theta_{n'''}^*) \to 0 \qquad a.s.-P_o\,.$$

Because $\{n'\}$ is arbitrary, it follows from the subsequence theorem that

$$\sqrt{n}\,\hat{r}_n - \sqrt{n}\,r_n^* - R_n^*\sqrt{n}\,(\hat{\theta}_n - \theta_n^*) \longrightarrow 0\ prob - P_o\,.$$

Because $\{\sqrt{n}\, r_n^*\}$ and $\{R_n^*\}$ are $O(1)$, it follows from Proposition 8.5 and Theorem 6.4 that

$$\sqrt{n}\, \hat{r}_n \overset{A}{\sim} N(\sqrt{n}\, r_n^*, R_n^* A_n^{*-1} B_n^* A_n^{*-1} R_n^{*\prime}) .$$

(ii) By Theorem 8.7 we have that $\tilde{\theta}_n = \text{argmax}_{\Theta_n} L_n(X^n, \theta)$ $a.s.-P_o$ and by Theorem 8.8(ii) we have that $\tilde{\theta}_n - \theta_n^* \to 0$ $prob - P_o$. Given any subsequence $\{n'\}$, there then exists a further subsequence $\{n''\}$ such that $\tilde{\theta}_{n''} - \theta_{n''}^* \to 0$ $a.s.-P_o$. Hence, for all $n > N_1 \in I\!N$, say, $\tilde{\theta}_{n''}$ lies in a convex compact neighborhood of $\theta_{n''}^*$, so that $\tilde{\theta}_{n''} \in int\, \Theta$ $a.s.-P_o$ given the interiority of θ_n^* uniformly in n ensured by Assumption 3.2′. Because $\tilde{\theta}_{n''}$ is the constrained maximizer of $L_{n''}(X^{n''}, \theta)$, it follows that $L_{n''}(X^{n''}, \theta) \le L_{n''}(X^{n''}, \tilde{\theta}_{n''})$ $a.s.-P_o$ for all $\theta \in (int\, \Theta) \cap \Theta_{n''}$. Now the continuity of R_n uniformly in n, the full row rank of R_n^* uniformly in n and the fact that $\tilde{\theta}_{n''} - \theta_{n''}^* \to 0$ $a.s.-P_o$ ensure that $\tilde{R}_{n''} \equiv R_{n''}(\tilde{\theta}_{n''})$ has full row rank for all $n'' > N_2 \in I\!N$, say, $a.s.-P_o$. It follows from Lagrange's Theorem (e.g. Bartle [1976, Theorem 42.7]) that there exists $\tilde{\lambda}_{n''} \in I\!R^q$ such that for $n'' > \max(N_1, N_2)$

$$-\nabla \tilde{L}_{n''} = \tilde{R}_{n''}{}' \tilde{\lambda}_{n''} \qquad a.s.-P_o .$$

Applying the mean value theorem for random functions (Jennrich [1969, Lemma 3]) to $\nabla \tilde{L}_{n''}$, and applying the mean value theorem to $\tilde{r}_{n''} = 0$ gives

$$\nabla L_{n''}^* + \nabla^2 \ddot{L}_{n''}(\tilde{\theta}_{n''} - \theta_{n''}^*) + \tilde{R}_{n''}{}' \tilde{\lambda}_{n''} = 0 \qquad a.s.-P_o$$

$$r_{n''}^* + \ddot{R}_{n''}(\tilde{\theta}_{n''} - \theta_{n''}^*) = 0 \qquad a.s.-P_o .$$

where the rows of $\nabla^2 \ddot{L}_{n''}$ and $\ddot{R}_{n''}$ are evaluated at mean values lying between $\tilde{\theta}_{n''}$ and $\theta_{n''}^*$.

Because $\sqrt{n}(\hat{\theta}_n - \theta_n^*) = -A_n^{*-1} \sqrt{n}\, \nabla L_n^* + o_{P_o}(1)$ by Theorem 6.4, it follows that $\{n''\}$ can be chosen so that

$$(8.A.1) \quad -A_{n''}^* \sqrt{n''}(\hat{\theta}_{n''} - \theta_{n''}^*) + \nabla^2 \ddot{L}_{n''} \sqrt{n''}(\tilde{\theta}_{n''} - \theta_{n''}^*)$$

$$+ \tilde{R}_{n''}{}' \sqrt{n''}\, \tilde{\lambda}_{n''} \to 0 \ a.s.-P_o .$$

Because $\nabla^2 \ddot{L}_{n''}$ is nonsingular *a.s.* $- P_o$ for all n'' sufficiently large, given Assumptions 3.8, 3.9 and $\tilde{\theta}_{n''} - \theta^*_{n''} \to 0$ *a.s.* $- P_o$ it follows that

$$\sqrt{n''}\,(\tilde{\theta}_{n''} - \theta^*_{n''}) = \nabla^2 \ddot{L}^{-1}_{n''}\, A^*_{n''}\, \sqrt{n''}\,(\hat{\theta}_{n''} - \theta^*_{n''})$$

$$- \nabla^2 \ddot{L}^{-1}_{n''}\, \tilde{R}'_{n''}\, \sqrt{n''}\, \tilde{\lambda}_{n''} + o_{\text{a.s.}}(1)\,.$$

Substituting this into the expansion for $\tilde{r}_{n''}$ gives

$$\ddot{R}_{n''}\, \nabla^2 \ddot{L}^{-1}_{n''}\, A^*_n\, \sqrt{n''}\,(\hat{\theta}_{n''} - \theta^*_{n''}) - \ddot{R}_{n''}\, \nabla^2 \ddot{L}^{-1}_{n''}\, \tilde{R}'_{n''}\, \sqrt{n''}\, \tilde{\lambda}_{n''}$$

$$= - \sqrt{n''}\, r^*_{n''} + o_{\text{a.s.}}(1)\,.$$

Because R^*_n has full row rank uniformly in n and because $\tilde{\theta}_{n''} - \theta^*_{n''} \to 0$ $a.s.-P_o$, it follows that $\ddot{R}_{n''}\, \nabla^2 \ddot{L}^{-1}_{n''}\, \tilde{R}'_{n''}$ has full rank for n sufficiently large $a.s.-P_o$, and is therefore invertible. Consequently

$$\sqrt{n''}\, \tilde{\lambda}_{n''} = (\ddot{R}_{n''}\, \nabla^2 \ddot{L}^{-1}_{n''}\, \tilde{R}'_{n''})^{-1} \sqrt{n''}\, r^*_{n''}$$

$$+ (\ddot{R}_{n''}\, \nabla^2 \ddot{L}^{-1}_{n''}\, \tilde{R}'_{n''})^{-1}\, \ddot{R}_{n''}\, \nabla^2 \ddot{L}^{-1}_{n''}\, A^*_{n''}\, \sqrt{n''}\,(\hat{\theta}_{n''} - \theta^*_{n''}) + o_{a.s.}(1)\,.$$

Because $\{\sqrt{n''}\, r^*_{n''}\}$ is $O(1)$, $\ddot{R}_{n''} - R^*_{n''} \to 0$ $a.s.-P_o$, $\tilde{R}_{n''} - R^*_{n''} \to 0$ $a.s.-P_o$, $\nabla^2 \ddot{L}^{-1}_{n''} - A^{*-1}_{n''} \to 0$ $a.s.-P_o$ and because $\sqrt{n''}\,(\hat{\theta}_{n''} - \theta^*_{n''})$ is $O_{P_o}(1)$, it follows that

$$(8.A.2) \quad \sqrt{n''}\, \tilde{\lambda}_{n''} - (R^*_{n''}\, A^{*-1}_{n''}\, R^{*\prime}_{n''})^{-1} \sqrt{n''}\, r^*_{n''}$$

$$- (R^*_{n''}\, A^{*-1}_{n''}\, R^{*\prime}_{n''})^{-1}\, R^*_{n''}\, \sqrt{n''}\,(\hat{\theta}_{n''} - \theta^*_{n''})$$

$$\to 0 \qquad prob - P_o\,.$$

Therefore there exists a further subsequence $\{n'''\}$ such that

$$\sqrt{n'''}\, \tilde{\lambda}_{n'''} - (R^*_{n'''}\, A^{*-1}_{n'''}\, R^{*\prime}_{n'''})^{-1} \sqrt{n'''}\, r^*_{n'''}$$

$$- (R^*_{n'''}\, A^{*-1}_{n'''}\, R^{*\prime}_{n'''})^{-1}\, R^*_{n'''}\, \sqrt{n'''}\,(\hat{\theta}_{n'''} - \theta^*_{n'''})$$

$$\to 0 \quad a.s.-P_o\,.$$

Because $\tilde{R}_{n''} \nabla^2 \tilde{L}_{n''}^{-1} \tilde{R}'_{n''} - R^*_{n''} A^{*-1}_{n''} R^{*\prime}_{n''} \to 0$ $a.s.{-}P_o$ and $\nabla \tilde{L}_{n''} = - \tilde{R}'_{n''} \tilde{\lambda}_{n''}$, we have

$$\sqrt{n'''}\, \tilde{R}_{n'''} \nabla^2 \tilde{L}_{n'''}^{-1} \nabla \tilde{L}_{n'''} + \sqrt{n'''}\, r^*_{n'''}$$
$$+ R^*_{n'''} \sqrt{n'''}\, (\hat{\theta}_{n'''} - \theta^*_{n'''})$$
$$\to 0 \quad a.s.{-}P_o .$$

From this, it follows from the subsequence theorem that

$$\sqrt{n}\, \tilde{R}_n \nabla^2 \tilde{L}_n^{-} \nabla \tilde{L}_n + \sqrt{n}\, r^*_n + R^*_n \sqrt{n} (\hat{\theta}_n - \theta^*_n) \longrightarrow 0 \ prob - P_o .$$

Because $\{\sqrt{n}\, r^*_n\}$ and $\{R^*_n\}$ are $O(1)$, it follows from Proposition 8.5 and Theorem 6.4 that

$$\sqrt{n}\, \tilde{R}_n \nabla^2 \tilde{L}_n^{-} \nabla \tilde{L}_n \overset{A}{\sim} N(-\sqrt{n}\, r^*_n , R^*_n A^{*-1}_n B^*_n A^{*-1}_n R^{*\prime}_n) .$$

(iii) It follows from (8.A.1) that

$$\sqrt{n''}\, (\tilde{\theta}_{n''} - \theta^*_{n''}) - \nabla^2 \ddot{L}_{n''}^{-1} A^*_{n''} \sqrt{n''}\, (\hat{\theta}_{n''} - \theta^*_{n''})$$
$$+ \nabla^2 \ddot{L}_{n''}^{-1} \tilde{R}'_{n''} \sqrt{n''}\, \tilde{\lambda}_{n''}$$
$$= \sqrt{n''}\, (\tilde{\theta}_{n''} - \hat{\theta}_{n''}) - (\nabla^2 \ddot{L}_{n''}^{-1} A^*_{n''} - I_p) \sqrt{n''}\, (\hat{\theta}_{n''} - \theta^*_{n''})$$
$$+ \nabla^2 \ddot{L}_{n''}^{-1} \tilde{R}'_{n''} \sqrt{n''}\, \tilde{\lambda}_{n''}$$
$$\to 0 \quad a.s.{-}P_o .$$

Because $\nabla^2 \ddot{L}_{n''}^{-1} A^*_{n''} \to I_p$ $a.s.{-}P_o$, $\sqrt{n''}\, (\hat{\theta}_{n''} - \theta^*_{n''})$ is $O_{P_o}(1)$, and $\tilde{R}_{n''} - R^*_{n''} \to 0$ $a.s.{-}P_o$, and given (8.A.2), it follows that there exists a further subsequence $\{n'''\}$ such that

$$\sqrt{n'''}\, (\tilde{\theta}_{n'''} - \hat{\theta}_{n'''}) + A^{*-1}_{n'''} R^{*\prime}_{n'''} [(R^*_{n'''} A^{*-1}_{n'''} R^{*\prime}_{n'''})^{-1} \sqrt{n'''}\, r^*_{n'''}$$
$$+ (R^*_{n'''} A^{*-1}_{n'''} R^{*\prime}_{n'''})^{-1} R^*_{n'''} \sqrt{n'''}\, (\hat{\theta}_{n'''} - \theta^*_{n'''})]$$
$$\to 0 \quad a.s.{-}P_o .$$

Therefore, it follows from the subsequence theorem that

$$\sqrt{n}(\tilde{\theta}_n - \hat{\theta}_n) + A_n^{*-1} R_n^{*\prime}[(R_n^* A_n^{*-1} R_n^{*\prime})^{-1} \sqrt{n}\, r_n^*$$

$$+ (R_n^* A_n^{*-1} R_n^{*\prime})^{-1} R_n^* \sqrt{n}(\hat{\theta}_n - \theta_n^*)] = o_{P_o}(1)\,.$$

(iv) Because $\{R_n^*\}$ is $O(1)$, we also have

$$R_n^* \sqrt{n}(\tilde{\theta}_n - \hat{\theta}_n) + \sqrt{n}\, r_n^* + R_n^* \sqrt{n}(\hat{\theta}_n - \theta_n^*) \longrightarrow 0 \ prob - P_o\,.$$

Again, it follows from Proposition 8.5 and Theorem 6.4 that

$$R_n^* \sqrt{n}(\tilde{\theta}_n - \hat{\theta}_n) \overset{A}{\sim} N(-\sqrt{n}\, r_n^*,\, R_n^* A_n^{*-1} B_n^* A_n^{*-1} R_n^{*\prime})\,. \qquad \square$$

PROOF OF THEOREM 8.10: (i) We apply Theorem 8.6 with $\mathcal{X}_n = \sqrt{n}\,\hat{r}_n$, $\hat{K}_n = \hat{R}_n \hat{C}_n \hat{R}_n'$, $K_n = R_n^* C_n^* R_n^{*\prime}$ and $V_n = R_n^* A_n^{*-1} B_n^* A_n^{*-1} R_n^{*\prime}$. Given Assumption 8.2 and the conditions of Theorem 6.4, this choice for $\{V_n\}$ is $O(1)$ and uniformly positive definite. Because $\{C_n^*\}$ is $O(1)$ and uniformly positive definite and $\{R_n^*\}$ is $O(1)$ with full row rank q uniformly in n, it follows that this choice of $\{K_n\}$ is $O(1)$ and uniformly positive definite. The matrix V_n is symmetric by construction, and $\hat{C}_n$ and C_n^* are symmetric by assumption. Further, the facts that $\hat{\theta}_n - \theta_n^* \to 0 \ prob - P_o$, $\hat{C}_n - C_n^* \to 0 \ prob - P_o$ and the continuity of R_n on Θ uniformly in n ensure that $\hat{K}_n - K_n \to 0 \ prob - P_o$ for this choice of $\hat{K}_n$ and K_n. Applying Theorems 8.6 and 8.9(i) with $\mathcal{X}_n = \sqrt{n}\,\hat{r}_n$ and letting $\sqrt{n}\, r_n^* \to 0$ now gives

$$\mathcal{W}_n \overset{A}{\sim} N_2(0,\, R_n^* A_n^{*-1} B_n^* A_n^{*-1} R_n^{*\prime};\ [R_n^* C_n^* R_n^{*\prime}]^{-1})\,.$$

When $C_n^* = A_n^{*-1} B_n^* A_n^{*-1}$, we immediately have $\mathcal{W}_n \overset{A}{\sim} \chi_q^2$.

(ii) The proof is identical to that of (i) with

$$\mathcal{X}_n = -\sqrt{n}\,\tilde{R}_n \nabla^2 \tilde{L}_n^- \nabla \tilde{L}_n\,,\ \hat{K}_n = \tilde{R}_n \tilde{C}_n \tilde{R}_n'\,.$$

(iii) A two term mean value expansion of $\tilde{L}_n$ around $\hat{L}_n$ yields

$$\mathcal{LR}_n = -\,2n\,(\bar{L}_n - \hat{L}_n)$$
$$= -\,n(\tilde{\theta}_n - \hat{\theta}_n)'\,A_n^*\,(\tilde{\theta}_n - \hat{\theta}_n) + o_{P_o}(1)\,.$$

From Theorem 8.9(iii) we have that

$$\sqrt{n}\,(\hat{\theta}_n - \tilde{\theta}_n) = -\,A_n^{*-1}\,R_n^{*\prime}(R_n^*\,A_n^{*-1}\,R_n^{*\prime})^{-1}\,\sqrt{n}\,r_n^*$$
$$-\,A_n^{*-1}\,R_n^{*\prime}(R_n^*\,A_n^{*-1}\,R_n^{*\prime})^{-1}\,R_n^*\,\sqrt{n}\,(\hat{\theta}_n - \theta_n^*) + o_{P_o}(1)\,.$$

Letting $\sqrt{n}\,r_n^* \rightarrow 0$, we have

$$\mathcal{LR}_n = -\,n\,(\hat{\theta}_n - \theta_n^*)'\,R_n^{*\prime}\,[R_n^*\,A_n^{*-1}\,R_n^{*\prime}]^{-1}\,R_n^*\,(\hat{\theta}_n - \theta_n^*) + o_{P_o}(1)\,.$$

It now follows from Theorem 6.4, Theorem 8.6 and Proposition 8.4(iii) that $\mathcal{LR}_n \overset{A}{\sim} N_2(0,\,R_n^*\,A_n^{*-1}\,B_n^*\,A_n^{*-1}\,R_n^{*\prime};\,-\,[R_n^*\,A_n^{*-1}\,R_n^{*\prime}]^{-1})\,.$

(iv) The proof is identical to that of (i) with

$$\mathcal{X}_n = \hat{R}_n\,\sqrt{n}\,(\hat{\theta}_n - \tilde{\theta}_n)\,,\ \hat{K}_n = \hat{R}_n\,\hat{C}_n\,\hat{R}_n'\,.$$ □

PROOF OF THEOREM 8.12: Identical to that of Theorem 8.10, except that $\{\sqrt{n}\,r_n^*\} = O(1)$ instead of $\sqrt{n}\,r_n^* \rightarrow 0$. Note that $\{\sqrt{n}\,r_n^*\} = O(1)$ implies $r_n^* \rightarrow 0$. □

PROOF OF THEOREM 8.13: By assumption there exists $\varepsilon > 0$ such that $P_o[\mathcal{X}_n'\,\mathcal{X}_n/n > \varepsilon] = E(1[\mathcal{X}_n'\,\mathcal{X}_n/n > \varepsilon]) \rightarrow 1$. Because $1[\mathcal{X}_n'\,\mathcal{X}_n/n > \varepsilon] - 1 \le 0$, it follows that $E(1[\mathcal{X}_n'\,\mathcal{X}_n/n > \varepsilon] - 1) = -\,E\,|\,1[\mathcal{X}_n'\,\mathcal{X}_n/n > \varepsilon] - 1\,| \rightarrow 0$, which implies $1[\mathcal{X}_n'\,\mathcal{X}_n/n > \varepsilon] \rightarrow 1$ $prob - P_o$. Because $\hat{K}_n - K_n \rightarrow 0$ $prob - P_o$ and $\{K_n\}$ is $O(1)$ and uniformly positive definite, it follows that $\hat{\lambda}_n - \lambda_n \rightarrow 0$ $prob - P_o$, where $\hat{\lambda}_n$ and λ_n are the minimum eigenvalues of $\hat{K}_n^-$ and K_n^{-1} respectively, with $\lambda_n > \eta > 0$, *a.a.n.*

Given any subsequence $\{n'\}$, it follows from the subsequence theorem that there exists a further subsequence $\{n''\}$ such that $1[\mathcal{X}_{n''}'\,\mathcal{X}_{n''}/n'' > \varepsilon] - 1 \rightarrow 0$ $a.s. - P_o$ and $\hat{\lambda}_{n''} - \lambda_{n''} \rightarrow 0$ $a.s. - P_o$. Because $\mathcal{X}_{n''}'\,\mathcal{X}_{n''}\,\hat{\lambda}_{n''} > k_{n''}$ implies $\mathcal{X}_{n''}'\hat{K}_{n''}^-\mathcal{X}_{n''} > k_{n''}$ it follows that

$$1[\mathcal{X}_{n''}'\hat{K}_{n''}^{-}\mathcal{X}_{n''} > k_{n''}] \geq 1[\mathcal{X}_{n''}'\,\mathcal{X}_{n''}\,\hat{\lambda}_{n''} > k_{n''}].$$

Because $\hat{\lambda}_{n''} - \lambda_{n''} \to 0 \quad a.s.-P_o$ and $\lambda_{n''} > \eta > 0$, it follows that $\hat{\lambda}_{n''} > \eta/2 \quad a.a.n'' \quad a.s.-P_o$. Consequently

$$1[\mathcal{X}_{n''}'\,\hat{K}_{n''}^{-}\,\mathcal{X}_{n''} > k_{n''}] \geq 1[\mathcal{X}_{n''}'\,\mathcal{X}_{n''}\,\eta/2 > k_{n''}] \quad a.a.n'' \quad a.s.-P_o\,.$$

Because $\{k_{n''}\} = o(n'')$, we have $\varepsilon > 2k_{n''}/(\eta n'')$ $a.a.n''$. Because $\mathcal{X}_{n''}\,\mathcal{X}_{n''}/n'' > \varepsilon$ implies $\mathcal{X}_{n''}\,\mathcal{X}_{n''}/n'' > 2k_{n''}/(\eta n'')$, or equivalently $\mathcal{X}_{n''}'\,\mathcal{X}_{n''}\,\eta/2 > k_{n''}$, we have

$$1[\mathcal{X}_{n''}'\,\hat{K}_{n''}^{-}\,\mathcal{X}_{n''} > k_{n''}] \geq 1[\mathcal{X}_{n''}'\,\mathcal{X}_{n''}/n'' > \varepsilon] \quad a.a.n'' \quad a.s.-P_o\,.$$

Because $1[\mathcal{X}_{n''}'\,\mathcal{X}_{n''}/n'' > \varepsilon] \to 1 \; a.s.-P_o$ and $1 \geq 1[\mathcal{X}_{n''}'\,\hat{K}_{n''}^{-}\,\mathcal{X}_{n''} > k_{n''}]$, it follows that $1[\mathcal{X}_{n''}'\,\hat{K}_{n''}^{-}\,\mathcal{X}_{n''} > k_{n''}] \to 1 \; a.s.-P_o$. Because $\{n'\}$ is arbitrary, it follows from the subsequence theorem that $1[\mathcal{X}_n'\,\hat{K}_n^{-}\,\mathcal{X}_n > k_n] \to 1$ $prob-P_o$. Because $1[\mathcal{X}_n'\hat{K}_n^{-}\;\mathcal{X}_n > k_n]$ is bounded, it is uniformly integrable, so that $P_o[\mathcal{X}_n'\,\hat{K}_n^{-}\,\mathcal{X}_n > k_n] = E(1[\mathcal{X}_n'\,\hat{K}_n^{-}\,\mathcal{X}_n > k_n]) \to 1$ by Theorem 25.12 of Billingsley [1979]. □

PROOF OF THEOREM 8.15: (i) Suppose that the conclusion is false, so that given any $N \in \mathbb{N}$ and $\delta > 0$ there exists $n > N$ such that $|\theta_n^* - \theta_n^o| < \delta$. Because r_n is continuous on Θ uniformly in n by Assumption 8.1(a), given any $\varepsilon > 0$ there exists $\delta(\varepsilon)$ such that for any $\theta_1, \theta_2 \in \Theta$, $|\theta_1 - \theta_2| < \delta(\varepsilon)$,

$$|r_n(\theta_1)'r_n(\theta_1) - r_n(\theta_2)'r_n(\theta_2)| < \varepsilon, \quad n = 1, 2, \ldots .$$

Pick arbitrary $N \in \mathbb{N}$ and $\varepsilon > 0$, and choose $n > N$ so that $|\theta_n^* - \theta_n^o| < \delta(\varepsilon)$, for $\delta(\varepsilon)$ as just given. Then $|r_n^{*\prime}\,r_n^* - r_n^{o\prime}\,r_n^o| < \varepsilon$, $r_n^o \equiv r_n(\theta_n^o) = 0$, so that $r_n^{*\prime}\,r_n^* < \varepsilon$. Because ε and N are arbitrary, this contradicts the assumption that for some $\varepsilon_o > 0$, $r_n^{*\prime}\,r_n^* > \varepsilon_o$ for all $n > N_o$, and the result follows.

(ii) The proof that $\tilde{\theta}_n - \theta_n^o \to 0 \quad a.s.-P_o \; (prob-P_o)$ is identical to that of Theorem 3.5, with $\{\theta_n^o\}$ replacing $\{\theta_n^*\}$ in application of Theorem 3.4. By the triangle inequality $|a| \geq |a+b| - |b|$, so that

$$|\tilde{\theta}_n - \theta_n^*| \geq |\theta_n^o - \theta_n^*| - |\tilde{\theta}_n - \theta_n^o| .$$

From (i), we have that $|\theta_n^o - \theta_n^*| > \delta_o$ *a.a.n* for some $\delta_o > 0$, and we have just established that $\tilde{\theta}_n - \theta_n^o \to 0 \quad a.s. - P_o$ so that $|\tilde{\theta}_n - \theta_n^o| < \delta_o/2$ $a.a.n \ a.s. - P_o$. Consequently, $|\tilde{\theta}_n - \theta_n^*| > \delta_o/2 \quad a.a.n \ a.s. - P_o$. The results for convergence in probability follow similarly, and the proof is complete. □

PROOF OF THEOREM 8.16 : We apply Theorem 8.13.

(i) Assumption 8.1(a) ensures that r_n is continuous on Θ uniformly in n, and the conditions of Theorem 3.5 ensure that $\hat{\theta}_n - \theta_n^* \to 0 \quad prob - P_o$. It follows from Corollary 3.8 that $\hat{r}_n - r_n^* \to 0 \quad prob - P_o$, from which it follows that $\hat{r}_n'\hat{r}_n - r_n^{*\prime}r_n^* \to 0 \quad prob - P_o$ (e.g. Proposition 2.30 White [1984a]).

Because the events $|\hat{r}_{ni}'\hat{r}_n - r_n^{*\prime}r_n^*| < \varepsilon_o/2$ and $r_n^{*\prime}r_n^* > \varepsilon_o$ imply $\hat{r}_n'\hat{r}_n > \varepsilon_o/2$, it follows from the implication rule that

$$P_o[\hat{r}_n'\hat{r}_n \leq \varepsilon_o/2] \leq P_o[|\hat{r}_n'\hat{r}_n - r_n^{*\prime}r_n^*| \geq \varepsilon_o/2] + P_o[r_n^{*\prime}r_n^* \leq \varepsilon_o]$$

$$\to 0 \ \text{ as } \ n \to \infty,$$

as $|\hat{r}_n'\hat{r}_n - r_n^{*\prime}r_n^*| \to 0 \quad prob - P_o$ and $P_o[r_n^{*\prime}r_n^* \leq \varepsilon_o] = 0 \quad a.a.n.$ Taking the complement, we obtain $P_o[\hat{r}_n'\hat{r}_n > \varepsilon_o/2] \to 1$.

Given the conditions on $\hat{C}_n$ and C_n^* together with Assumption 8.2 and the conditions of Theorem 3.5, it follows from Corollary 3.8 that $\hat{R}_n - R_n^* \to 0$ $prob - P_o$ and that $\hat{R}_n\hat{C}_n\hat{R}_n' - R_n^*C_n^*R_n^{*\prime} \to 0 \quad prob - P_o$ (Proposition 2.30 of White [1984a]). Assumption 8.2 and the properties of C_n^* ensure that $\{R_n^*C_n^*R_n^{*\prime}\}$ is $O(1)$ and uniformly positive definite. Consequently, the conditions of Theorem 8.13 hold with

$$\mathcal{X}_n = \sqrt{n}\hat{r}_n , \hat{K}_n = \hat{R}_n\hat{C}_n\hat{R}_n' , K_n = R_n^*C_n^*R_n^{*\prime},$$

so that for $\{k_n\} = o(n)$

$$P_o[\mathcal{W}_n > k_n] = P_o[n\hat{r}_n'(\hat{R}_n\hat{C}_n\hat{R}_n')^- r_n > k_n] \to 1.$$

(ii) The argument is analogous to that of (i), except that $\hat{r}_n$ is replaced by $\tilde{R}_n \nabla^2 \tilde{L}_n^- \nabla \tilde{L}_n$, r_n^* is replaced by $R_n^o \nabla^2 \bar{L}_n^{o-1} \nabla \bar{L}_n^o$, $\hat{R}_n \hat{C}_n \hat{R}_n'$ is replaced by $\tilde{R}_n \tilde{C}_n \tilde{R}_n'$, and $R_n^* C_n^* R_n^{*\prime}$ is replaced by $R_n^o C_n^o R_n^{o\prime}$. The assumptions of Theorem 8.15, Assumptions 3.6, 3.7, 3.8 and 8.4 ensure that $\tilde{R}_n \nabla^2 \tilde{L}_n^- \nabla \tilde{L}_n - R_n^o \nabla^2 \bar{L}_n^{o-1} \nabla \bar{L}_n^o \to 0 \;\; prob - P_o$ via Corollary 3.8 and Proposition 2.30 of White [1984a]. The assumptions of Theorem 8.15 and Assumption 8.4(a) ensure that $\tilde{R}_n \tilde{C}_n \tilde{R}_n' - R_n^o C_n^o R_n^{o\prime} \to 0 \;\; prob - P_o$, where $\{R_n^o C_n^o R_n^{o\prime}\}$ is $O(1)$ and uniformly positive definite.

(iii) Given Assumption 3.2 and $|\theta_n^* - \theta_n^o| > \delta_o \;\; a.a.n$ as established in Theorem 8.15, it follows that there exists $\varepsilon_o > 0$ such that $\bar{L}_n^* - \bar{L}_n^o > \varepsilon_o$ $a.a.n$, with $\bar{L}_n^o \equiv \bar{L}_n(\theta_n^o)$. Given $\hat{\theta}_n - \theta_n^* \to 0 \;\; prob - P_o$ and $\tilde{\theta}_n - \theta_n^o \to 0 \;\; prob - P_o$ (Theorems 3.5 and 8.15(ii)), it follows from Corollary 3.8 that $\hat{L}_n - \bar{L}_n^* \to 0 \;\; prob - P_o$ and $\tilde{L}_n - \bar{L}_n^o \to 0 \;\; prob - P_o$, given Assumption 3.5(b). The events $\bar{L}_n^* - \bar{L}_n^o > \varepsilon_o \;\, a.a.n$, $|\hat{L}_n - \bar{L}_n^*| < \varepsilon_o/4$ and $|\tilde{L}_n - \bar{L}_n^o| < \varepsilon_o/4$ imply $\hat{L}_n - \tilde{L}_n > \varepsilon_o/2$. It follows from the implication rule that

$$P_o[\hat{L}_n - \tilde{L}_n \le \varepsilon_o/2] \le P_o[|\hat{L}_n - \bar{L}_n^*| \ge \varepsilon_o/4]$$
$$+ P_o[|\tilde{L}_n - \bar{L}_n^o| \ge \varepsilon/4] + P_o[\bar{L}_n^* - \bar{L}_n^o \le \varepsilon_o] \to 0$$

so that $P_o[\hat{L}_n - \tilde{L}_n > \varepsilon_o/2] \to 1$. For $\{k_n\} = o(n)$ we have $\varepsilon_o > k_n/n$ $a.a.n.$ When $\varepsilon_o > k_n/n$, we have $P_o[\hat{L}_n - \tilde{L}_n > \varepsilon_o/2] \le P_o[\hat{L}_n - \tilde{L}_n > k_n/2n]$ so that

$$P_o[\mathcal{LR}_n > k_n] = P_o[2n(\hat{L}_n - \tilde{L}_n) > k_n] \to 1.$$

(iv) The argument is analogous to that of (i), except that $\hat{r}_n$ is replaced by $\hat{R}_n(\tilde{\theta}_n - \hat{\theta}_n)$ and r_n^* is replaced by $R_n^*(\theta_n^o - \theta_n^*)$. The assumptions of Theorems 3.5 and 8.15 and Assumption 8.2 ensure that $\hat{R}_n(\tilde{\theta}_n - \hat{\theta}_n) - R_n^*(\theta_n^o - \theta_n^*) \to 0 \;\; prob - P_o$ via Corollary 3.8 and Proposition 2.30 of White [1984a]. □

PROOF OF THEOREM 8.17: We verify the conditions of Debreu's [1967] Theorem 4.5. Our correspondence $\hat{\mathcal{B}}_n$ corresponds to Debreu's ϕ: $\mathbb{R}^{vn} \to \mathbb{B}(\mathcal{B})$. Assumption 2.1 ensures that $(\Omega, \mathcal{F}, P_o)$ is complete. It follows that the projection of this space to $(\mathbb{R}^{vn}, \mathcal{F}_n, P_o^n)$ is also complete. Completeness of $(\mathbb{R}^{vn}, \mathcal{F}_n, P_o^n)$ allows us to take $\mathcal{F}_n = \mathcal{F}_n^*$ (Debreu's notation for the completion (Lebesque extension)). Because $\mathcal{B}$ is a compact subset of a Euclidean space, it is a complete separable metric space, as Debreu requires.

We must first show that $\hat{\mathcal{B}}_n$ is an $\mathcal{F}_n$-measurable compact-valued correspondence. Because $\hat{\alpha}_n : \Omega \to \mathcal{A}$, it suffices for compactness to show that for each α in $\mathcal{A}$, the cross-section of $\Theta_n \equiv \{\theta \in \Theta : r_n(\theta) = 0\}$ at α, denoted $\Theta_n(\alpha) \equiv \{\beta \in \mathcal{B} : (\alpha, \beta) \in \Theta_n\}$, is compact. Now the continuity of r_n on Θ, a compact set, ensures that Θ_n is compact. Because $\Theta_n(\alpha)$ is a subset of Θ_n, a compact set, it will suffice to show that $\Theta_n(\alpha)$ is closed. Let β_m be any convergent sequence in $\Theta_n(\alpha)$, with $\beta_m \to \beta^o$ (say). Then by continuity $r_n(\alpha, \beta_m) \to r_n(\alpha, \beta^o)$. But $r_n(\alpha, \beta_m) = 0$ $m = 1, 2, \ldots$, so that $r_n(\alpha, \beta^o) = 0$. Thus $\beta^o \in \Theta_n(\alpha)$, so that $\Theta_n(\alpha)$ is closed. It follows that $\hat{\mathcal{B}}_n$ is compact-valued.

To show that $\hat{\mathcal{B}}_n$ is measurable-$\mathcal{F}_n$, we note that the graph of $\Theta_n(\alpha)$ is the pre-image of r and is therefore closed and consequently measurable-$\mathcal{B}(\mathcal{A} \times \mathcal{B})$. The function $\hat{\alpha}_n : \mathbb{R}^{vn} \to \mathcal{A}$ is measurable-$\mathcal{F}_n$ by assumption. It follows from Klein and Thompson [1984, Proposition 6.3.4] that the composition $\hat{\mathcal{B}}_n(x^n) = \Theta_n(\hat{\alpha}_n(x^n))$ is measurable-$\mathcal{F}_n$.

Next we establish that $L_{2n}(x^n, \hat{\alpha}_n(x^n), \beta)$ is measurable- $\mathcal{B}(\mathcal{F}_n^* \times \mathcal{B}(\mathcal{B}))$ and upper semi-continuous on $\hat{\mathcal{B}}_n(x_n)$ for each x_n in $\mathbb{R}^{vn}$. Given Assumptions 2.3 and 8.5 we have that $L_{2n}(x^n, \hat{\alpha}_n(x^n), \beta)$ is in fact continuous on $\hat{\mathcal{B}}_n(x^n)$ for each x^n in $\mathbb{R}^{vn}$. Measurability of L_{2n} follows given Assumptions 2.1, 2.3 and 8.5 from Lemma 2.15 of Stinchcombe and White [1992], which establishes the measurability of L_{2n} with respect to $\mathcal{B}(\mathcal{F}_n^* \times \mathcal{B}(\mathcal{A}) \times \mathcal{B}(\mathcal{B}))$, and then from Theorem 13.1 of Billingsley [1979].

It now follows from Debreu's [1967] Theorem 4.5 that the set $\{\beta \in \hat{\mathcal{B}}_n(x^n) : L_{2n}(x^n, \hat{\alpha}_n(x^n), \beta) =$
$\in \hat{\mathcal{B}}_n(x^n)\ L_{2n}(x^n, \hat{\alpha}_n(x^n), \beta)\}$ is measurable. The existence of the measurable function $\tilde{\beta}_n$ now follows directly from the measurable selection theorem (e.g., Hildenbrand [1974, p. 54]). □

PROOF OF THEOREM 8.18: (i) The proof is identical to that of Theorem 8.8(i), except that $\Theta_n \equiv \{(\alpha, \beta) : \alpha = \alpha_n^*, r_n(\alpha_n^*, \beta) = 0\}$ and when $q < p$ we begin by defining

$$\delta(\varepsilon) = \inf_{n > N_0} \inf_{|\beta - \beta_n^*| > \varepsilon} |\bar{L}_{2n}(\alpha_n^*, \beta) - \bar{L}_{2n}^*| > 0,$$

and we choose N_2 so that $|\beta - \beta_n^*| < \eta(\delta)$ implies $|\bar{L}_{2n}(\alpha_n^*, \beta) -$

$\bar{L}_{2n}(\theta_n^*) | < \delta$. The argument supports the conclusion that $| \beta_n^o - \beta_n^* | < \varepsilon$ so that $\beta_n^o - \beta_n^* \to 0$. It follows trivially that $\theta_n^o - \theta_n^* \to 0$.

(ii) The argument is identical to that of 8.8(ii) except that $\delta(\varepsilon)$ is defined as in (i), and we replace $\tilde{\theta}_n$ in 8.8(ii) by $(\alpha_n^{*\prime}, \tilde{\beta}_n')'$. The argument supports the conclusion that $\tilde{\beta}_n - \beta_n^* \to 0$ $a.s.-P_o$ $(prob-P_o)$, hence by (i) $\tilde{\beta}_n - \beta_n^o \to 0$ $a.s.-P_o$ $(prob-P_o)$. Assumption 3.5(a) guarantees that $\hat{\alpha}_n - \alpha_n^* \to 0$ $a.s.-P_o$ $(prob-P_o)$, so that $\tilde{\theta}_n' = (\hat{\alpha}_n', \tilde{\beta}_n')$ satisfies $\tilde{\theta}_n - \theta_n^o \to 0$ $a.s.-P_o$ $(prob-P_o)$. □

PROOF OF THEOREM 8.19: The proof is identical to that of Theorem 8.9, except that Theorem 6.11 is invoked instead of Theorem 6.4, and Theorems 8.17 and 8.18 ensure the existence and consistency of $\tilde{\theta}_n$ instead of Theorems 8.7 and 8.8. □

PROOF OF THEOREM 8.20: The proof is identical to that of Theorem 8.12 except that Theorem 8.19 is invoked instead of Theorem 8.9 and Theorem 6.11 is invoked instead of Theorem 6.4. □

PROOF OF THEOREM 8.21: (i) The argument is identical to that of Theorem 8.15(i) with $\Theta = \mathcal{A} \times \mathcal{B}$, $\theta_n^{*\prime} = (\alpha_n^{*\prime}, \beta_n^{*\prime})$, $\theta_n^{o\prime} = (\alpha_n^{*\prime}, \beta_n^{o\prime})$.

(ii) The argument is identical to that of Theorem 8.15 (ii), with the modification of (i). □

PROOF OF THEOREM 8.22: The argument is identical to that of Theorem 8.16, except that Theorem 8.21 is used in place of Theorem 8.15. □

PROOF OF THEOREM 8.23: If $A_n^* + B_n^* \to 0$, we have $-A_n^{*-1} A_n^* A_n^{*-1} - A_n^{*-1} B_n^* A_n^{*-1} = -A_n^{*-1} - A_n^{*-1} B_n^* A_n^{*-1} \to 0$, given that $\{A_n^*\}$ and $\{A_n^{*-1}\}$ are $O(1)$ by Assumption 3.9. Because $\hat{A}_n - A_n^* \to 0$ $a.s.-P_o$, we have that $\hat{A}_n$ is nonsingular for all n sufficiently large $a.s.-P_o$, so that $\hat{A}_n^- = \hat{A}_n^{-1}$. Because A_n^* is negative definite uniformly in n, we have $\hat{A}_n^- - A_n^{*-1} \to 0$ $a.s.-P_o$. It then follows immediately that $-\hat{A}_n^- - A_n^{*-1} B_n^* A_n^{*-1} \to 0$ $a.s.-P_o$. The argument for convergence in probability follows by the method of subsequences. □

PROOF OF THEOREM 8.24: (i) The result follows directly from Corollary 3.8. Assumptions 2.1, 2.3, 3.1 and 3.2 ensure that $\hat{\theta}_n - \theta_n^* \to 0$ $a.s.-P_o$ $(prob-P_o)$ by Theorem 3.5. Assumptions 2.1, 2.3 and 3.6 ensure that $n^{-1} \sum_{t=1}^{n} \nabla^2 \log f_t(X^t, \theta)$ satisfies the needed measurability and continuity conditions, and Assumption 3.8 ensures that $n^{-1} \sum_{t=1}^{n} \nabla^2 \log f_t(X^t, \theta) - \nabla^2 \bar{L}_n(\theta) \to 0$ $a.s.-P_o$ $(prob-P_o)$ uniformly on Θ, with $\{\nabla^2 \bar{L}_n\}$ continuous on Θ uniformly in n. Thus the conditions of Corollary 3.8 hold and the result follows.

(ii) The proof is identical to (i) except that in part (b) Theorem 8.8 ensures $\tilde{\theta}_n - \theta_n^* \to 0$ $a.s.-P_o$ $(prob-P_o)$. □

PROOF OF THEOREM 8.25: (i) Because $A_n^* + \bar{B}_n^* \to 0$ and $\{A_n^*\}$, $\{A_n^{*-1}\}$, $\{\bar{B}_n^*\}$, $\{\bar{B}_n^{*-1}\}$ are $O(1)$ it follows that $A_n^{*-1} + \bar{B}_n^{*-1} \to 0$. As in the proof of Theorem 8.23, $-A_n^{*-1} - A_n^{*-1} \bar{B}_n^* A_n^{*-1} \to 0$. It follows that $\bar{B}_n^{*-1} - A_n^{*-1} \bar{B}_n^* A_n^{*-1} \to 0$. The remainder of the proof is analogous to that of Theorem 8.23 with $\hat{B}_n$ replacing $\hat{A}_n$, so that $\hat{B}_n^- - A_n^{*-1} \bar{B}_n^* A_n^{*-1} \to 0$ $a.s.-P_o$ $(prob-P_o)$.

(ii) By definition $B_n^* \equiv \mathrm{var}(\sqrt{n}\, \nabla L_n^*) = \mathrm{var}(n^{-1/2} \sum_{t=1}^{n} s_t^*)$. If $\{s_t^*, \mathcal{F}^t\}$ is a martingale difference sequence then

$$\mathrm{var}(n^{-1/2} \sum_{t=1}^{n} s_t^*) = n^{-1} \sum_{t=1}^{n} E(s_t^* s_t^{*\prime}) = \bar{B}_n^* .$$

Thus $B_n^* = \bar{B}_n^*$, and the result follows immediately. □

PROOF OF THEOREM 8.26: The proof is analogous to that of Theorem 8.24 with $s_t s_t'$ replacing $\nabla^2 \log f_t$ and with $\bar{B}_n$ replacing $\nabla^2 \bar{L}_n$. Assumption 8.6 is invoked instead of Assumption 3.8. Because differentiability of first order only is required, Assumption 2.4 replaces Assumption 3.6. □

PROOF OF THEOREM 8.27: (i) If $\{s_t^* - E(s_t^*), \mathcal{F}^t\}$ is a martingale difference sequence, then $B_n^* = \mathrm{var}(\sqrt{n}\, \nabla L_n^*) = \mathrm{var}\,[n^{-1/2} \sum_{t=1}^{n} s_t^* - E(s_t^*)] = n^{-1} \sum_{t=1}^{n} E(s_t^* s_t^{*\prime}) - n^{-1} \sum_{t=1}^{n} E(s_t^*) E(s_t^{*\prime}) = \bar{B}_n^* - U_n^*$. Hence $\bar{B}_n^* = B_n^* + U_n^*$. The argument of Theorem 8.26 applies to yield $\hat{B}_n - \bar{B}_n^* \to 0$ $a.s.-P_o$ $(prob-P_o)$, i.e., $\hat{B}_n - (B_n^* + U_n^*) \to 0$ $a.s.-P_o$ $(prob-P_o)$. If $U_n^* \to 0$ then it follows immediately that $\hat{B}_n - B_n^* \to 0$ $a.s.-P_o$ $(prob-P_o)$.

(ii) The arguments for $\tilde{B}_n$ are analogous. □

PROOF OF COROLLARY 8.28: (i) From Theorem 8.24(i) it follows that $\hat{A}_n - A_n^* \to 0$ $a.s.-P_o$ $(prob-P_o)$. Given Assumption 3.9 we have

$\hat{A}_n^- - A_n^{*-1} \to 0$ $a.s.-P_o$ $(prob-P_o)$. From Theorem 8.19(i) we have $\hat{B}_n - (B_n^* + U_n^*) \to 0$ $a.s.-P_o$ $(prob-P_o)$. Because $\{A_n^{*-1}\}$ and $\{\bar{B}_n^* = B_n^* + U_n^*\}$ are $O(1)$, it follows from Proposition 2.16 or Proposition 2.30 of White [1984a] that $\hat{A}_n^- \hat{B}_n \hat{A}_n^- - A_n^{*-1} (B_n^* + U_n^*) A_n^{*-1} \to 0$ $a.s.-P_o$ $(prob-P_o)$. (ii) The argument for $\tilde{B}_n$ is analogous. □

CHAPTER 9

Specification Testing Via m-Tests

In earlier chapters we have considered at some length the consequences of correct specification and misspecification. In this chapter, we consider statistical methods for detecting the presence of misspecification.

Specific methods for detecting misspecification are based on the contrasting consequences of correct specification and misspecification. For example, when a model is correctly specified there are usually numerous consistent estimators for the parameters of interest (e.g., ordinary least squares and weighted least squares). If the model is correctly specified, these different estimators should have similar values asymptotically. If these values are not sufficiently similar, then the model is not correctly specified. This reasoning forms the basis for the Hausman [1978] test, a special case of which we encountered in the previous chapter. Such tests have power because of the divergence of alternative estimators under misspecification. As another example, correct specification implies the validity of the information matrix equality. If estimators for $-A_n^*$ and B_n^* are not sufficiently similar, then one has empirical evidence against the validity of the information matrix equality and thus against the correctness of the model specification. This reasoning forms the basis for the information matrix tests (White [1982, 1987]). Such tests have power because of the failure of the information matrix equality under misspecification.

In fact, there is an extremely wide range of such specification testing procedures, all of which operate by testing the empirical validity of some particular consequence of correct specification. In this chapter we provide some general theory for these tests. In the next chapter we examine a number of useful special cases in detail, specifically, the Lagrange multiplier test, Newey's [1985] conditional moment test, the Hausman [1978] test, Cox's [1961, 1962] test of non-nested hypotheses, and the encompassing tests of Mizon [1984] and Mizon and Richard [1986].

Our analysis is greatly simplified by exploiting a framework for specification testing proposed independently by Newey [1985] and Tauchen

[1985], in which all of the tests just mentioned can be embedded as special cases. We also provide results that establish a previously missing link between specification tests and the classical hypothesis tests of the previous chapter. These results show that the tests of Newey and Tauchen can be viewed as specific forms of Lagrange-multiplier tests for specific restrictions in a specific parametric model related to the model forming the basis for a given specification test. This highlights the similarities of and differences between specification testing and classical hypothesis testing.

9.1 The m-Testing Framework

The general specification testing framework of Newey and Tauchen is based on the fact that when $\mathcal{S}$ or $\mathcal{M}$ is correctly specified, there are typically a multitude of functions $m_t : \mathbb{R}^{vt} \times \Theta \to \mathbb{R}^q$ such that

$$E(m_t(X^t, \theta_o)) = 0, \qquad t = 1, 2, \ldots .$$

For example, we have from Theorem 6.9 that when $\mathcal{M}$ is correct for $\{E(Y_t \mid \tilde{X}^{t-1})\}$ and Assumption 5.3′ holds (*inter alia*), then $E(s_t^o \mid \tilde{X}^{t-1}) = E(\nabla_\theta \mu_t^o \nabla_\mu c_t^o u_t^o \mid \tilde{X}^{t-1}) = 0$. It follows that

$$E(s_t^o\, s_{t-1}^{o\prime}) = E(\nabla_\theta \mu_t^o \nabla_\mu c_t^o u_t^o u_{t-1}^{o\prime} \nabla'_\mu c_{t-1}^o \nabla'_\theta \mu_{t-1}^o) = 0,$$

because $E(s_t^o\, s_{t-1}^{o\prime}) = E(E(s_t^o\, s_{t-1}^{o\prime} \mid \tilde{X}^{t-1})) = E(E(s_t^o \mid \tilde{X}^{t-1})\, s_{t-1}^{o\prime}) = 0$. In this case $m_t = vec\; s_t\, s_{t-1}'$, and $E(m_t(X^t, \theta_o)) = 0$ is a consequence of correct specification. We formalize these notions using the following definitions.

DEFINITION 9.1 (*Compatible Model, Model Explicitly Tested*): (i) The probability model $\mathcal{P}_{\mathcal{S}}$ ($\mathcal{P}_{\mathcal{M}}$) *compatible* with a given specification $\mathcal{S}$ ($\mathcal{M}$) is the collection of all probability measures P^o such that $\mathcal{S}$ is correctly specified for $\{Y_t \mid W_t\}$ under P^o ($\mathcal{M}$ is correctly specified for $\{E^o(Y_t \mid W_t)\}$).

(ii) Let Θ and Π be subsets of finite dimensional Euclidean spaces and let $m = \{m_t : \mathbb{R}^{vt} \times \Theta \times \Pi\}$ be a sequence of measurable functions. The *model explicitly tested by* m, denoted $\mathcal{P}_{\mathcal{S}}^e(m)$ ($\mathcal{P}_{\mathcal{M}}^e(m)$), is the subset of $\mathcal{P}_{\mathcal{S}}$ ($\mathcal{P}_{\mathcal{M}}$) for which $m_t(X^t, \theta, \pi)$ is integrable $-P^o$ and $E^o(m_t(X^t, \theta^o, \pi)) = 0$, $t = 1, 2, \ldots$, for all π in Π. □

The parameters π appearing in the second part of this definition provide useful flexibility in the treatment to follow — they can be thought of as "nuisance" parameters. We examine their role in detail subsequently. We refer to the functions m_t as the "indicators" for the model explicitly tested.

For example, the specification $\mathcal{M} = \{ \mu_t(W_t, \theta) \}$ has compatible probability model $\mathcal{P}_{\mathcal{M}} = \{P^o : E^o(Y_t \mid W_t) = \mu_t(W_t, \theta^o), \theta^o \in \Theta \}$. With indicators $m_t = vec\ s_t\ s_{t-1}'$, the model explicitly tested by m, $\mathcal{P}^e_{\mathcal{M}}(m)$, includes that subset of $\mathcal{P}_{\mathcal{M}}$ for which $E^o(Y_t \mid W_t) = E^o(Y_t \mid \tilde{X}^{t-1})$, because for each such P^o,

$$
\begin{aligned}
E^o(m_t(X^t, \theta^o)) &= E^o(vec\ s_t(X^t, \theta^o)\ s_{t-1}(X^{t-1}, \theta^o)') \\
&= 0 \qquad\qquad t = 1, 2, \ldots .
\end{aligned}
$$

If P_o belongs to this particular subset of $\mathcal{P}^e_{\mathcal{M}}(m)$, then not only is $\mathcal{M}$ correctly specified for $\{E(Y_t \mid W_t)\}$ but there is no dynamic misspecification, because $\mathcal{M}$ is also correctly specified for $\{E(Y_t \mid \tilde{X}^{t-1})\}$. Note, however, that $\mathcal{P}^e_{\mathcal{M}}(m)$ may include more than those P^o for which $E^o(Y_t \mid W_t) = E^o(Y_t \mid \tilde{X}^{t-1})$, so that absence of dynamic misspecification is not guaranteed by $P_o \in \mathcal{P}^e_{\mathcal{M}}(m)$.

In this example, $\mathcal{P}^e_{\mathcal{M}}(m)$ is a proper subset of $\mathcal{P}_{\mathcal{M}}$. Although this is often the case, there are choices of m for which $\mathcal{P}^e_{\mathcal{M}}(m)$ and $\mathcal{P}_{\mathcal{M}}$ coincide; Bierens' [1990] version of the m-test is an example of such a choice for m. See also Stinchcombe and White [1993].

These concepts allow us to make clear the sense in which any test of $P_o \in \mathcal{P}^e_{\mathcal{M}}(m)(m)$ is a specification test. If one has statistical evidence that $P_o \in \mathcal{P}^e_{\mathcal{M}}(m)$, then because $\mathcal{P}^e_{\mathcal{M}}(m)$ is a subset of $\mathcal{P}_{\mathcal{M}}$, one has evidence that $P_o \in \mathcal{P}_{\mathcal{M}}$, i.e. that $\mathcal{M}$ is correctly specified (for $\{E(Y_t \mid W_t)\}$). If one has statistical evidence that $P_o \notin \mathcal{P}^e_{\mathcal{M}}(m)$, then certainly one has evidence that $\mathcal{P}^e_{\mathcal{M}}(m)$ is misspecified; however, unless $\mathcal{P}^e_{\mathcal{M}}(m) = \mathcal{P}_{\mathcal{M}}$, we cannot know whether or not $\mathcal{M}$ is misspecified for $\{E(Y_t|W_t)\}$ without further testing.

Any statistical test of the hypothesis that $P_o \in \mathcal{P}^e_{\mathcal{M}}(m)$ (or of the related hypothesis $\mathcal{P}^u_o(m)$ to be given shortly) is a form of m-test. The statistics to be presented in this and the following chapters are convenient statistics for testing $P_o \in \mathcal{P}^e_{\mathcal{M}}(m)$. We emphasize that they are by no means the only way in which m-tests can or should be implemented, and that the scope of m-testing is not limited to the particular statistics discussed here.

Bearing this caveat in mind, we consider tests of $P_o \in \mathcal{P}^e_{\mathcal{M}}(m)$ based on the convenient statistic

$$\hat{M}_n = n^{-1} \sum_{t=1}^{n} \hat{m}_t , \qquad \hat{m}_t \equiv m_t(X^t , \hat{\theta}_n , \hat{\pi}_n) ,$$

where $\hat{\theta}_n$ is a convenient estimator such as the QMLE or 2SQMLE and $\hat{\pi}_n$ is a nuisance parameter estimator. Generally, $\hat{M}_n - \bar{M}_n^* \to 0 \; prob - P_o$, where $\bar{M}_n^* \equiv n^{-1} \sum_{t=1}^{n} E(m_t^*)$, $m_t^* \equiv m_t(X^t , \theta_n^* , \pi_n^*)$, for an appropriate sequence $\{(\theta_n^* , \pi_n^*)\}$. When $P_o \in \mathcal{P}_{\mathcal{M}}^e(m)$ we have $\bar{M}_n^* = 0$, so that $\hat{M}_n$ should be close to zero. If $\hat{M}_n$ is far from zero, we have statistical evidence of misspecification ($P_o \notin \mathcal{P}_{\mathcal{M}}^e(m)$). The question of how far from zero $\hat{M}_n$ must be in order to constitute statistical evidence of misspecification is resolved by exploiting its asymptotic distribution. Under general conditions, this distribution is multivariate normal with a consistently estimatable covariance matrix. As in the previous chapter, quadratic forms in $\hat{M}_n$ can be constructed with known asymptotic distributions.

Our first result is a generic result that allows statement of general results for m-tests analogous to Theorem 3.2 of White [1987].

THEOREM 9.2: *(i) Let the conditions of Theorem 6.10 hold, and suppose there exist: (1) a sequence $\{\hat{\pi}_n : \Omega \to \Pi\}$ of measurable functions, where Π is a compact subset of finite dimensional Euclidean space; (2) a nonstochastic sequence $\{\pi_n^* \in \Pi\}$ such that $\hat{\pi}_n - \pi_n^* \to 0 \; prob - P$; and (3) a sequence of measurable functions $\{m_t : \Omega \times \Theta \times \Pi \to \mathbb{R}^q\}$ such that with $\hat{M}_n \equiv n^{-1} \sum_{t=1}^{n} m_t(\cdot , \hat{\theta}_n , \hat{\pi}_n)$, $M_n^* \equiv n^{-1} \sum_{t=1}^{n} m_t(\cdot , \theta_n^* , \pi_n^*)$ we have*

$$\sqrt{n}\, \hat{M}_n = \sqrt{n}\, M_n^* - G_n^* \sqrt{n}(\hat{\theta}_n - \theta_n^*) + o_P(1)$$

for some $O(1)$ nonstochastic sequence of $q \times p$ matrices $\{G_n^*\}$. Then

$$\sqrt{n}\, \hat{M}_n = \sqrt{n}(M_n^* + G_n^* A_n^{*-1} \psi_n^*) + o_P(1) ,$$

with A_n^* and ψ_n^* as defined in Theorem 6.10.

(ii) If in addition $\sqrt{n}(M_n^* + G_n^* A_n^{*-1} \psi_n^*) \overset{A}{\sim} N(a_n^* , V_n^*)$, $V_n^* \equiv \mathrm{var}\, [\sqrt{n}(M_n^* + G_n^* A_n^{*-1} \psi_n^*)]$, where $\{a_n^*\}$ and $\{V_n^*\}$ are $O(1)$ and $\{V_n^*\}$ is uniformly positive definite, then $\sqrt{n}\, \hat{M}_n \overset{A}{\sim} N(a_n^* , V_n^*)$.

(iii) Suppose also that $\hat{J}_n - J_n^* \to 0$ *prob* $- P$, *where* $\{\hat{J}_n\}$ *is a sequence of random positive semi-definite symmetric* $q \times q$ *matrices and* $\{J_n^*\}$ *is a nonstochastic sequence of uniformly positive definite* $O(1)$ *symmetric* $q \times q$ *matrices. Then*

$$n\, \hat{M}_n'\, \hat{J}_n^-\, \hat{M}_n \overset{A}{\sim} N_2(a_n^*, V_n^*; J_n^{*-1})\,.$$

In particular, if $J_n^* = V_n^*$ *and* $a_n^* \to 0$, *then*

$$n\, \hat{M}_n'\, \hat{J}_n^-\, \hat{M}_n \overset{A}{\sim} \chi_q^2\,.$$

□

The conditions of this result hold when (something like) a mean value expansion of $\hat{M}_n$ can be taken around (θ_n^*, π_n^*). The terms resulting from the presence of π are required to vanish by the conditions of the theorem. These terms may vanish for different reasons in different contexts, as the examples of the next chapter demonstrate. It is also possible that $G_n^* = 0$ but we do not require this.

Note that in the statement of this generic result, $m_t(\cdot, \theta, \pi)$ is a function on Ω, while in our previous discussion it was a function on $\mathbb{R}^{vt}$. In what follows, we revert to $m_t(\cdot, \theta, \pi)$ being a function on $\mathbb{R}^{vt}$.

To state results justifying the m-tests of Newey and Tauchen in a general dynamic setting when $\hat{\theta}_n$ is a QMLE or a 2SQMLE, we impose the following conditions on the moment functions underlying the m-test.

ASSUMPTION 9.1: (a) The functions $m_t: \mathbb{R}^{vt} \times \Theta \times \Pi \to \mathbb{R}^q$, where Θ and Π are compact subsets of finite dimensional Euclidean spaces, are such that $m_t(\cdot, \theta, \pi)$ is measurable - $\mathcal{B}^{vt}$ for each (θ, π) in $\Theta \times \Pi$ and $m_t(X^t, \cdot, \cdot)$ is continuous on $\Theta \times \Pi$ $a.s. - P_o$; and (b) for each π in Π, $m_t(X^t, \cdot, \pi)$ is continuously differentiable on Θ *a.s.* $- P_o$, $t = 1, 2, \ldots$. □

ASSUMPTION 9.2: (a) There exists a measurable sequence $\{\hat{\pi}_n : \Omega \to \Pi\}$;
(b) There exists a nonstochastic $O(1)$ sequence $\{\pi_n^*\}$, $\pi_n^* \in \Pi$, $n = 1, 2, \ldots$, such that $\hat{\pi}_n - \pi_n^* \to 0$ *prob* $- P_o$. □

These conditions ensure that the relevant conditions of Theorem 9.2(i) hold for m_t. Note that here $m_t(X^t(\omega), \theta, \pi)$ corresponds to $m_t(\omega, \theta, \pi)$ of Theorem 9.2.

Just as $\{s_t\}$ may implicitly represent a doubly indexed array $\{s_{nt}\}$, the functions $\{m_t\}$ may also implicitly represent a doubly indexed array $\{m_{nt}\}$ provided that conditions holding (uniformly) for $t = 1, 2, \ldots$ also hold for $n = 1, 2, \ldots$. We leave dependence on n implicit for notational convenience, although applications will often require this dependence.

The conditions of part (ii) of Theorem 9.2 determine the cases under which we shall be able easily to determine the size and local power properties of tests based on $\hat{M}_n$. The model explicitly tested based on m, $\mathcal{P}_a^u$, is not sufficiently restrictive in this regard, as it in no way imposes restrictions sufficient to ensure asymptotic normality of $\sqrt{n}(M_n^* + G_n^* A_n^{*-1} \psi_n^*)$. On the other hand, $\mathcal{P}_a^u$ does not necessarily include certain probability measures P^o for which $E^o(\sqrt{n}\, M_n^*) \to 0$. Tests based on $\hat{M}_n$ have power equal to size for such alternatives. Because of these limitations, $P_o \in \mathcal{P}_a^u$ cannot form the fundamental null hypothesis for the specification tests considered here. Instead, we make use of the following definition of the probability model underlying the (specification) test, analogous to that of White [1987, Definition 3.1].

DEFINITION 9.3 (*Model Underlying the Test*): The *model underlying the specification test based on indicators* $m = \{m_t\}$ *and* (2S)QMLE $\hat{\theta}$ is defined as the collection $\mathcal{P}_o^u(m)$ of all probability measures P^o such that: (i) when $P_o = P^o$ in Assumption 2.1, the conditions of Theorem 6.4 or 6.11 hold for the specification(s) generating $\hat{\theta}$, Assumptions 9.1 and 9.2 hold, $\nabla_\theta m_t(X^t, \theta_n^*, \pi_n^*)$ is integrable $- P^o$, uniformly in t, $n = 1, 2, \ldots$, and letting $\hat{M}_n \equiv n^{-1} \sum_{t=1}^n m_t(X^t, \hat{\theta}_n, \hat{\pi}_n)$, $M_n^* \equiv n^{-1} \sum_{t=1}^n m_t(X^t, \theta_n^*, \pi_n^*)$ and $\nabla_\theta \bar{M}_n^* \equiv n^{-1} \sum_{t=1}^n E^o(\nabla_\theta m_t(X^t, \theta_n^*, \pi_n^*))$, we have that

$$\sqrt{n}\, \hat{M}_n = \sqrt{n}\, M_n^* + \nabla'_\theta \bar{M}_n^* \sqrt{n}(\hat{\theta}_n - \theta_n^*) + o_{P^o}(1) \; ; \quad \text{and}$$

(ii) there exists a nonstochastic sequence $\{V_n^* \equiv \operatorname{var}^o [\sqrt{n}\, (M_n^* - \nabla'_\theta \bar{M}_n^* A_n^{*-1} s_n^*)]\}$ $O(1)$ and uniformly positive definite such that

$$\sqrt{n}\,(M_n^* - \nabla'_\theta \bar{M}_n^* A_n^{*-1} s_n^*) \overset{A^o}{\sim} N(0, V_n^*) \, ,$$

where A_n^* and s_n^* are as given in Theorem 6.4 or 6.11. □

Note that s_n^* replaces ψ_n^* because we now refer explicitly to a (2S) QMLE.

For brevity, we refer to $\mathcal{P}_o^u(m)$ as "the model underlying the test." When convenient, we drop explicit reference to m, and refer simply to $\mathcal{P}_o^u$. This model has two essential features: first, the randomness of $\hat{\pi}_n$ makes no contribution to the asymptotic distribution of $\sqrt{n}\,\hat{M}_n$ (essentially without loss of generality, because otherwise $\hat{\pi}_n$ can be absorbed into $\hat{\theta}_n$); and second, $\sqrt{n}(M_n^* - \nabla_\theta' \bar{M}_n^* A_n^{*-1} s_n^*)$ is distributed asymptotically as normal with mean *zero*. It is the mean zero property that allows $P_o \in \mathcal{P}_o^u$ to be interpreted as a meaningful null hypothesis for our specification tests. Given Assumptions 9.1 and 9.2, the model underlying the test thus includes all elements of the model explicitly tested for which the regularity conditions of Theorem 9.2 hold, as well as measures P^o for which $E^o(\sqrt{n}\,M_n^*) \to 0$.

Note that this definition is formulated so as to apply explicitly to the QMLE or 2SQMLE. This is for our convenience in the present context. The estimator $\hat{\theta}$ can generally be any estimator satisfying the conditions of Theorem 6.10. It is a useful fact that the specification(s) generating $\hat{\theta}$ may or may not be related to the specification explicitly tested by m.

The local alternatives to the specification test are given by the next definition.

DEFINITION 9.4 (*Local Alternative to the Model Underlying the Test*): The *local alternative to the model underlying the specification test based on indicators m and* (2S)QMLE $\hat{\theta}$ is defined as the collection $\mathcal{P}_a^u(m)$ of all probability measures P^o such that: (i) condition 9.3 (i) holds; and (ii) for $\{V_n^*\}$ as in 9.3(ii) and a nonstochastic $O(1)$ sequence $\{a_n^*\}$

$$\sqrt{n}\,(M_n^* - \nabla_\theta' \bar{M}_n^* A_n^{*-1} s_n^*) \overset{A^o}{\sim} N(a_n^*, V_n^*)\,. \qquad □$$

Generally, we have $a_n^* = E^o(\sqrt{n}\,M_n^*)$. The drift implicit in this definition can be achieved in a manner analogous to that used in the previous chapter by choosing double arrays $\{m_{nt}\}$ (and $\{f_{nt}\}$ when appropriate) in such a way that $E(\sqrt{n}\,M_n^*) = a_n^*$ is $O(1)$. For brevity, we refer to $\mathcal{P}_a^u$ as "the local alternative."

We can now state the following general result for specification tests in a dynamic context based on the (2S)QMLE.

THEOREM 9.5: *Let* $\{\hat{J}_n : \Omega \to \mathbb{R}^{q\times q}\}$ *be a measurable sequence of symmetric positive semi-definite matrices, and suppose that* $\{J_n^*\}$ *is a non-stochastic sequence of symmetric* $q \times q$ *matrices such that* $\{J_n^*\}$ *is* $O(1)$ *and uniformly positive definite and* $\hat{J}_n - J_n^* \to 0$ *prob* $- P_o$.

If $P_o \in \mathcal{P}_a^u$, then $\sqrt{n}\,\hat{M}_n \overset{A}{\sim} N(a_n^*, V_n^*)$ *and*

$$\mathcal{M}_n \equiv n\,\hat{M}_n{}'\,\hat{J}_n^-\,\hat{M}_n \overset{A}{\sim} N_2(a_n^*, V_n^*\,;\, J_n^{*-1})\,.$$

If in addition $P_o \in \mathcal{P}_o^u$ *and* $J_n^* = V_n^*$, *then* $\mathcal{M}_n \equiv n\,\hat{M}_n{}'\,\hat{J}_n^-\,\hat{M}_n \overset{A}{\sim} \chi_q^2$. □

Theorem 9.5 characterizes the asymptotic distribution of the $\mathcal{M}_n$ statistic of Newey and Tauchen in a general context under both null and local alternative hypotheses, regardless of whether or not $\hat{J}_n$ is a consistent estimator for V_n^*. When $\hat{J}_n$ is consistent for V_n^*, then the χ_q^2 distribution can be used to construct a specification test of any desired size asymptotically. Specifically, one rejects $H_o:\ P_o \in \mathcal{P}_o^u$ in favor of $P_o \notin \mathcal{P}_o^u$ at the α significance level if $\mathcal{M}_n > \chi^2_{q,\,1-\alpha}$.

In contrast to the hypotheses considered in the previous chapter in which one tested non-stochastic constraints on $\hat{\theta}_n$, the present approach can be interpreted as testing stochastic constraints on $\hat{\theta}_n$. The results of the previous chapter hold with $m_{nt} = r_n$ for all t.

Compared to classical hypothesis tests in which $H_o:\ P_o \in \tilde{\mathcal{P}}_o, \tilde{\mathcal{P}}_o = \{P_\theta : \theta \in \Theta_o \subset \Theta\}$, the present null hypothesis includes much more in the way of "implicit" null hypotheses, while also recognizing alternatives beyond the classical alternatives $\tilde{\mathcal{P}}_a = \tilde{\mathcal{P}} - \tilde{\mathcal{P}}_o, \tilde{\mathcal{P}} = \{P_\theta : \theta \in \Theta\}$.

Although Theorem 9.5 describes the behavior of the $\mathcal{M}_n$ statistic under the null hypothesis and local alternatives, it does not say what happens under global alternatives. The relevant global alternatives are described by the following definition.

DEFINITION 9.6 (*Global Alternative to the Model Underlying the Test*)**:** The *global alternative to the model underlying the specification test based on indicators m and* (2S)QMLE $\hat{\theta}$ is defined as the collection $\mathcal{P}_A^u(m)$ of all probability measures P^o such that when $P_o = P^o$ in Assumption 2.1, the conditions of Theorem 3.5 or 3.10 hold for the specification(s) generating $\hat{\theta}$, Assumptions 9.1(a) and 9.2 hold, and for some $\varepsilon^o > 0$ and $N^o \in \mathbb{N}$ we have $\bar{M}_n^{*\prime} \bar{M}_n^* > \varepsilon^o$ for all $n > N^o$. □

This is not the most general definition of the global alternative that could be formulated in the present context. We adopt it because it insightfully relates the global alternative explicitly to the readily interpretable condition

$$\bar{M}_n^{*\prime} \bar{M}_n^* > \varepsilon^o > 0 \qquad a.a.\ n.$$

The global alternative thus contains any probability measure P^o for which any element of $\bar{M}_n^* = n^{-1} \sum_{t=1}^n E(m_t^*)$ is eventually bounded away from zero by some (arbitrarily small) amount.

For simplicity we refer to $\mathcal{P}_A^u(m)$ as the "global alternative," and sometimes drop explicit reference to m. The following condition allows us to describe the behavior of m-tests under the global alternative.

ASSUMPTION 9.3: (a) The elements of $\bar{M}_n$, $\bar{M}_n = n^{-1} \sum_{t=1}^n E(m_t(X^t, \cdot, \cdot))$, are finite and continuous on $\Theta \times \Pi$ uniformly in $n = 1, 2, \ldots$;

(b) The elements of $\{m_t(X^t, \theta, \pi)\}$ obey the weak ULLN. □

THEOREM 9.7: *Let $\hat{J}_n$ and J_n^* be as in Theorem 9.5. If $P_o \in \mathcal{P}_A^u$ and Assumption 9.3 holds, then for $\{k_n\} = o(n)$, $P_o[\mathcal{M}_n > k_n] \to 1$.* □

Thus, m-tests are generally consistent tests against any element of $\mathcal{P}_A^u$. Although it is possible to have $\bar{M}_n^* \not\to 0$ without having $\bar{M}_n^{*\prime} \bar{M}_n^* > \varepsilon_o$ *a.a. n*, we refer heuristically to this consistency by saying that m-tests are "sensitive to departures from $\bar{M}_n^* \to 0$."

As in the previous chapter, the ability to obtain a consistent covariance matrix estimator $\hat{J}_n$ is essential to constructing specification tests of known size. In many cases, fairly simple estimators for V_n^* are consistent. However, the conditions under which this consistency obtains require further restrictions on the elements of $\mathcal{P}_o^u$. For convenience in stating subsequent results, we adopt the following definition.

DEFINITION 9.8 (*Model Implicitly Tested*)**:** Let $\mathcal{P}_o^u(m)$ be the model underlying the test. For a given sequence $\hat{J} = \{\hat{J}_n : \Omega \to \mathbb{R}^{q \times q}\}$ of measurable symmetric positive semi-definite matrices, let $\mathcal{P}_o^i(m)$ be the subset of $\mathcal{P}_o^u(m)$ for which $\hat{J}_n - V_n^* \to 0$ *prob* $- P^o$, $P^o \in \mathcal{P}_o^u(m)$. We call $\mathcal{P}_o^i(m)$ the *model implicitly tested using $\hat{J}$.* □

Thus $\mathcal{P}_o^i(m)$ is simply the model within which $\mathcal{M}_n$ has the χ_q^2 distribution asymptotically. Different choices for $\hat{J}_n$ will lead to different models implicitly tested. Because the choice for $\hat{J}_n$ will always be clear from the context, we do not explicitly indicate the dependence of $\mathcal{P}_o^i$ on $\hat{J}_n$. As we see next, computationally simple estimators $\hat{J}_n$ often yield rather narrow models implicitly tested. Achieving a broad model implicitly tested may require use of fairly complicated estimators $\hat{J}_n$. As in the preceding chapter, Theorem 9.5 provides the appropriate asymptotic distribution regardless of whether or not $J_n^* = V_n^*$.

The most general case occurs when $\{ m_t^* - \nabla_\theta' \bar{M}_n^* A_n^{*-1} s_t^*, \mathcal{F}^t \}$ is not necessarily a martingale difference sequence. A potentially useful estimator for V_n^* can be constructed in this case by replacing $\hat{s}_t$ in equation (8.1) by

$$\hat{\xi}_t \equiv \hat{m}_t - \nabla_\theta' \hat{M}_n \hat{A}_n^- \hat{s}_t ,$$

where $\nabla_\theta \hat{M}_n = n^{-1} \sum_{t=1}^n \nabla_\theta m_t(X^t, \hat{\theta}_n, \hat{\pi}_n)$ and $\hat{A}_n$ is a consistent estimator of A_n^*. For simplicity, we have suppressed the n subscript in $\hat{\chi}_t$. In this case $\hat{J}_n$ can be taken to be of the form

$$\hat{J}_n = w_{n0}\, n^{-1} \sum_{t=1}^{n} \hat{\xi}_t \hat{\xi}_t' + n^{-1} \sum_{\tau=1}^{\lambda_n} w_{n\tau} \sum_{t=\tau+1}^{n} [\hat{\xi}_t \hat{\xi}_{t-\tau}' + \hat{\xi}_{t-\tau} \hat{\xi}_t']$$

where λ_n and $\{ w_{n\tau} \}$ are as described in Chapter 8. Regularity conditions under which such an estimator is consistent can be obtained by methods analogous to those used by Gallant and White [1988, Chapter 7]. We do not pursue them here.

More tractable estimators for V_n^* are often available. When $\nabla_\theta \bar{M}_n^* \to 0$ and $\{ m_t^*, \mathcal{F}^t \}$ is a martingale difference sequence under $P_o \in \mathcal{P}_o^u$ we may use the estimator

$$\hat{K}_n \equiv n^{-1} \sum_{t=1}^{n} \hat{m}_t \hat{m}_t' .$$

The consistency of this estimator for $K_n^* \equiv n^{-1} \sum_{t=1}^n E(m_t^* m_t^{*\prime})$ is ensured by the following condition.

ASSUMPTION 9.4: (a) The elements of $K_n, K_n = E[n^{-1} \sum_{t=1}^n m_t$

$(X^t, \cdot, \cdot) m_t(X^t, \cdot, \cdot)']$, are finite and continuous on $\Theta \times \Pi$ uniformly in $n = 1, 2, \ldots$;

(b) The elements of $\{ m_t(X^t, \theta, \pi)\, m_t(X^t, \theta, \pi)' \}$ obey the weak ULLN. □

COROLLARY 9.9: *(i) Given the conditions of Theorem 2.12 or 2.15, and Assumptions 9.1(a) and 9.2(a), $\{\hat{K}_n = n^{-1} \sum_{t=1}^{n} \hat{m}_t\, \hat{m}_t'\}$ is a measurable sequence of symmetric positive semi-definite matrices.*

(ii) If in addition the conditions of Theorem 3.5 or 3.10 hold, and Assumptions 9.2(b) and 9.4 hold, then $\hat{K}_n - K_n^* \to 0$ prob $- P_o$, $K_n^* \equiv n^{-1} \sum_{t=1}^{n} E(m_t^*\, m_t^{*\prime})$. Further, $\{K_n^*\}$ is $O(1)$.

(iii) If in addition Assumption 9.1(b) holds, $\{K_n^*\}$ is uniformly positive definite, and $P_o \in \mathcal{P}_a^u$, then $\mathcal{M}_n = n\, \hat{M}_n'\, \hat{K}_n^-\, \hat{M}_n \overset{A}{\sim} N_2(a_n^*, V_n^*; K_n^{*-1})$, and if $P_o \in \mathcal{P}_o^i$, the model implicitly tested using $\hat{K}_n$, then $\mathcal{M}_n \overset{A}{\sim} \chi_q^2$.

In particular, $\mathcal{P}_o^i$ includes all elements of $\mathcal{P}_o^u$ for which $\{m_t^*, \mathcal{F}^t\}$ is a martingale difference sequence and either $\{\nabla_\theta\, m_t^*, \mathcal{F}^t\}$ is a martingale difference sequence, or $\nabla_\theta\, \bar{M}_n^* = 0$.

(iv) If $P_o \in \mathcal{P}_A^u$ and, in addition to the conditions of (i) and (ii), $\{K_n^*\}$ is uniformly positive definite and Assumption 9.3 holds, then for $\{k_n\} = o(n)$, $P_o[\mathcal{M}_n > k_n] \to 1$. □

In the present case, the statistic $\mathcal{M}_n = n\, \hat{M}_n'\, \hat{K}_n^-\, \hat{M}_n$ can be very simply computed as nR^2, where R^2 is the (uncentered, i.e., constant unadjusted) squared multiple correlation coefficient (e.g. Theil [1971, p. 164]) from the artificial regression of the constant unity on the explanatory variables $\hat{m}_t'$ (the estimated indicators). According to (iii), when $P_o \in \mathcal{P}_o^i$, then $nR^2 \overset{A}{\sim} \chi_q^2$, so that an m-test of size α can be conducted by rejecting H_o: $P_o \in \mathcal{P}_o^i$ whenever $nR^2 > \chi^2_{q,1-\alpha}$. This test has local power properties fully characterized by (iii); by (iv), it is consistent against any element of $\mathcal{P}_A^u$.

The condition that $\nabla_\theta\, \bar{M}_n^* = 0$ is not uncommon in applications, but will not always hold. Using a clever approach due to Wooldridge [1990], the indicators $\{ m_t \}$ can often be modified to ensure that this condition does hold for the modified indicators. We consider this modification below. However, because Wooldridge's approach does not apply universally, it is important to know what happens when $\nabla_\theta\, \bar{M}_n^* \nrightarrow 0$. A leading case when $\nabla_\theta\, \bar{M}_n^* \nrightarrow 0$ is that $\{m_t^* - \nabla_\theta'\, \bar{M}_n^*\, A_n^{*-1}\, s_t^*, \mathcal{F}^t\}$ is a martingale difference sequence under $P_o \in \mathcal{P}_a^u$. A useful estimator for this case is

$$\hat{J}_n = n^{-1} \sum_{t=1}^{n} \hat{\xi}_t \, \hat{\xi}_t{}' .$$

The consistency of this estimator is ensured with the aid of the following conditions.

ASSUMPTION 9.5: (a) The elements of $\nabla_\theta \bar{M}_n$, $\nabla_\theta \bar{M}_n \equiv n^{-1} \Sigma_{t=1}^{n} E\,(\nabla_\theta m_t\,(X^t, \cdot, \cdot))$, are finite and continuous on $\Theta \times \Pi$ uniformly in $n = 1, 2, \ldots$;

(b) The elements of $\{\nabla_\theta m_t\,(X^t, \theta, \pi)\}$ obey the weak ULLN. □

ASSUMPTION 9.6: (a) The elements of G_n, $G_n = E\,[n^{-1} \sum_{t=1}^{n} m_t(X^t, \cdot, \cdot)\, s_t(X^t, \cdot)']$, are finite and continuous on $\Theta \times \Pi$ uniformly in $n = 1, 2, \ldots$;

(b) The elements of $\{m_t(X^t, \theta, \pi)\, s_t(X^t, \theta)'\}$ obey the weak ULLN. □

COROLLARY 9.10: *(i) Given the conditions of Theorem 2.12 or 2.15 and Assumptions 3.6, 9.1 and 9.2(a), $\{\hat{J}_n = n^{-1} \sum_{t=1}^{n} \hat{\xi}_t \, \hat{\xi}_t{}'\}$ is a measurable sequence of symmetric positive semi-definite matrices.*

(ii) If in addition the conditions of Theorem 3.5 or 3.10 and Assumptions 3.8, 3.9, 8.6, 9.2(b), 9.4, 9.5 and 9.6 hold then $\hat{J}_n - J_n^* \to 0$ prob $- P_o$ where

$$J_n^* = K_n^* - \nabla_\theta' \bar{M}_n^* \, A_n^{*-1} \, G_n^{*\prime} - G_n^* \, A_n^{*-1\prime} \, \nabla_\theta \bar{M}_n^*$$

$$+ \nabla_\theta' \bar{M}_n^* \, A_n^{*-1} \, \bar{B}_n^* \, A_n^{*-1\prime} \, \nabla_\theta \bar{M}_n^*$$

with $G_n^* \equiv n^{-1} \sum_{t=1}^{n} E(m_t^* \, s_t^{*\prime})$. Further, $\{J_n^*\}$ is $O(1)$.

(iii) Suppose in addition $\{J_n^*\}$ is uniformly positive definite and $P_o \in \mathcal{P}_a^u$. Then

(a) Letting $\mathcal{M}_n = n\hat{M}_n' \, \hat{J}_n^- \, \hat{M}_n$, $\mathcal{M}_n \overset{A}{\sim} N_2(a_n^*, V_n^*; J_n^{*-1})$, and if $P_o \in \mathcal{P}_o^i$, then $\mathcal{M}_n \overset{A}{\sim} \chi_q^2$, where $\mathcal{P}_o^i$ is the model implicitly tested using $\hat{J}_n$ as given in (i).

(b) Letting $\mathcal{M}_n' = nR^2$, where R^2 is the (constant unadjusted) squared multiple correlation coefficient from the regression of the constant unity on the explanatory variables $\hat{\xi}_t{}'$, it follows that $\mathcal{M}_n' - \mathcal{M}_n \to 0$ prob $- P_o$, so that $\mathcal{M}_n' \overset{A}{\sim} N_2(a_n^*, V_n^*; J_n^{*-1})$, and if $P_o \in \mathcal{P}_o^i$, then $\mathcal{M}_n' \overset{A}{\sim} \chi_q^2$.

In particular, $\mathcal{P}_o^i$ *includes all elements of* $\mathcal{P}_o^u$ *for which* $\{ m_t^* - \nabla_\theta' \bar{M}_n^* A_n^{*-1} s_t^*, \mathcal{F}^t \}$ *is a martingale difference sequence.*

(iv) If $P_o \in \mathcal{P}_A^u$ *and, in addition to the conditions of (i) and (ii),* $\{J_n^*\}$ *is uniformly positive definite and Assumption 9.3 holds, then for* $\{k_n\} = o(n)$, $P_o[\mathcal{M}_n > k_n] \to 1$. *If in addition Assumption 3.2′ holds for the QMLE or Assumption 3.2′ holds for* $\bar{L}_{1n}(\alpha)$ *and* $\bar{L}_{2n}(\alpha_n^*, \beta)$ *for the 2SQMLE, then* $P_o[\mathcal{M}_n' > k_n] \to 1$. □

Because $\{ s_t^*, \mathcal{F}^t \}$ is a martingale difference sequence when $\mathcal{S}$ or $\mathcal{M}$ is correctly specified for $\{ Y_t \mid \tilde{X}^{t-1} \}$ or $\{ E(Y_t \mid \tilde{X}^{t-1}) \}$ respectively (so that dynamic misspecification is absent), tests of proper size asymptotically can be based on the χ^2 distribution using this form for $\hat{J}_n$ when m is chosen so that $\{ m_t^*, \mathcal{F}^t \}$ is a martingale difference sequence also, because this immediately implies that $\{ m_t^* - \nabla_\theta' \bar{M}_n^* A_n^{*-1} s_t^*, \mathcal{F}^t \}$ is a martingale difference sequence. For example, the choice $m_t = vec\ s_t\ s_{t-1}'$ discussed earlier has this martingale difference property when $\mathcal{M}$ is correctly specified for $\{ E(Y_t \mid \tilde{X}^{t-1}) \}$.

An advantage of the $\mathcal{M}_n$ statistic of Corollary 9.10(iii.a) is that it yields tests of proper size in the presence of neglected heterogeneity. Essentially, it embodies an analog of a heteroskedasticity-consistent covariance matrix estimator (White [1980b]) in forming $\mathcal{M}_n$, so that failure to model conditional variances correctly will not adversely affect the size of specification tests based on this choice for $\hat{J}_n$. The nR^2 statistic of (iii.b) shares this property, but can be conveniently computed from a simple artificial regression of the constant unity on the explanatory variables $\hat{\xi}_t'$.

In other words, the stochastic specification yielding $\hat{\theta}$ may suffer from distributional misspecification including neglected heterogeneity (so that in general $\hat{\theta}_n$ does not attain the minimum asymptotic variance bound), but one may nevertheless construct valid m-tests sensitive to other forms of misspecification, such as misspecification of the conditional mean or dynamic misspecification.

9.2 Some Simplifying Restrictions

Although the statistics of Corollary 9.10 are reasonably convenient computationally, further restriction of the model implicitly tested can yield further computational efficiencies. This restriction involves using an estimator for V_n^* that is consistent when $\hat{\theta}_n$ is asymptotically efficient, but is not necessarily consistent otherwise. We saw in Chapter 8 that the information matrix equality can be exploited to allow use of $\hat{B}_n = n^{-1} \sum_{t=1}^{n} \hat{s}_t \hat{s}_t'$ as a consistent estimator for $-A_n^*$. Use of $\hat{B}_n$ thus makes it possible to avoid calculating the second derivatives of $\log f_t$ appearing in $\hat{A}_n = n^{-1} \sum_{t=1}^{n} \nabla' \hat{s}_t = n^{-1} \sum_{t=1}^{n} \nabla^2 \log \hat{f}_t$. It turns out that an analogous computational saving can be achieved when m and $\hat{\theta}$ are properly chosen.

To investigate this possibility, suppose that m_t is chosen so that for each π in Π and all θ in Θ

$$\int_{S_{\theta,t}} m_t(x^t, \theta, \pi) f_t(x^t, \theta) \, d\zeta_t(y_t) = 0, \qquad t = 1, 2, \ldots,$$

i.e., $m_t(X^t, \theta, \pi)$ has (conditional) expectation zero given $\tilde{X}^{t-1}$ regardless of which $\theta \in \Theta$ may have generated the observed data, for any π in Π. If derivatives with respect to θ and integrals can be interchanged (as in Assumption 6.3), we have

$$\begin{aligned}
\nabla_\theta & \int_{S_{\theta,t}} m_t(x^t, \theta, \pi) f_t(x^t, \theta) \, d\zeta_t(y_t) \\
&= \int_{S_{\theta,t}} \nabla_\theta [m_t(x^t, \theta, \pi) f_t(x^t, \theta)] \, d\zeta_t(y_t) \\
&= \int_{S_{\theta,t}} \nabla_\theta \, m_t(x^t, \theta, \pi) f_t(x^t, \theta) \, d\zeta_t(y_t) \\
&\qquad + \int \nabla_\theta \log f_t(x^t, \theta) \, m_t(x^t, \theta, \pi)' \, f_t(x^t, \theta) \, d\zeta_t(y_t) \\
&= 0 .
\end{aligned}$$

With $\mathcal{S}$ correctly specified for $\{Y_t | \tilde{X}^{t-1}\}$, setting $\theta = \theta_o$ gives

$$E(\nabla_\theta' \, m_t(X^t, \theta_o, \pi) \mid \tilde{X}^{t-1}) = - E(m_t(X^t, \theta_o, \pi) \, s_t(X^t, \theta_o)' \mid \tilde{X}^{t-1})$$

for all π in Π. Taking expectations, setting $\pi = \pi_n^*$ and summing over n then gives

$$\nabla'_\theta \bar{M}_n^* = - G_n^* .$$

With the information matrix equality ensuing $A_n^* = - B_n^*$ (or $A_n^* + B_n^* \to 0$), we can write J_n^* as given in Corollary 9.10 as

$$J_n^* = K_n^* - \nabla'_\theta \bar{M}_n^* A_n^{*-1} G_n^{*\prime} - G_n^* A_n^{*-1\prime} \nabla_\theta \bar{M}_n^* + \nabla'_\theta \bar{M}_n^* A_n^{*-1} \bar{B}_n^* A_n^{*-1} \nabla_\theta \bar{M}$$

$$= K_n^* - G_n^* B_n^{*-1} G_n^{*\prime} - G_n^* B_n^{*-1} G_n^{*\prime} + G_n^* B_n^{*-1} G_n^{*\prime}$$

$$= K_n^* - G_n^* B_n^{*-1} G_n^{*\prime} ,$$

where we have used the martingale difference property to set $\bar{B}_n^* = B_n^*$ in the absence of dynamic misspecification.

This form for J_n^* suggests use of the estimator

$$\hat{J}_n = n^{-1} \sum_{t=1}^{n} \hat{m}_t \hat{m}_t' - (n^{-1} \sum_{t=1}^{n} \hat{m}_t \hat{s}_t')[n^{-1} \sum_{t=1}^{n} \hat{s}_t \hat{s}_t']^- (n^{-1} \sum_{t=1}^{n} \hat{s}_t \hat{m}_t') .$$

Our next result sets out the leading cases in which m-tests based on this choice have correct size asymptotically, and exploits the form of this choice for $\hat{J}_n$ to obtain a computationally straightforward test statistic.

COROLLARY 9.11: *(i) Given the conditions of Theorem 2.12 or 2.15 and Assumptions 2.4, 9.1(a) and 9.2(a)*

$$\{\hat{J}_n = n^{-1} \sum_{t=1}^{n} \hat{m}_t \hat{m}_t' - (n^{-1} \sum_{t=1}^{n} \hat{m}_t \hat{s}_t')[n^{-1} \sum_{t=1}^{n} \hat{s}_t \hat{s}_t']^- (n^{-1} \sum_{t=1}^{n} \hat{s}_t \hat{m}_t')\}$$

is a measurable sequence of symmetric positive semi-definite matrices.

(ii) If in addition the conditions of Theorem 3.5 or 3.10 and Assumptions 8.6, 9.2(b), 9.4 and 9.6 hold then $\hat{J}_n - J_n^* \to 0$ *prob* $- P_o$ *where*

$$J_n^* = K_n^* - G_n^* \bar{B}_n^{*-1} G_n^{*\prime} .$$

Further, $\{J_n^*\}$ *is* $O(1)$.

(iii) Suppose in addition $\{J_n^*\}$ *is uniformly positive definite and* $P_o \in \mathcal{P}_a^u$. *Then*

(a) Letting $\mathcal{M}_n = n\hat{M}_n' \hat{J}_n^- \hat{M}_n$ *for* $\hat{J}_n$ *as in (i),* $\mathcal{M}_n \overset{A}{\sim} N_2(a_n^*, V_n^*; J_n^{*-1})$, *and if* $P_o \in \mathcal{P}_o^i$, *then* $\mathcal{M}_n \overset{A}{\sim} \chi_q^2$, *where* $\mathcal{P}_o^i$ *is the model implicitly tested using* $\hat{J}_n$ *as given in (i).*

(b) Letting $\mathcal{M}_n' = nR^2$ *where* R^2 *is the (constant unadjusted) squared multiple correlation coefficient of the regression of the constant unity on the explanatory variables* $\hat{m}_t'$, $\hat{s}_t'$, $t = 1, 2, \ldots, n$, *it follows that* $\mathcal{M}_n - \mathcal{M}_n' \to 0$ *prob*$-P_o$ *and* $\mathcal{M}_n' \overset{A}{\sim} N_2(a_n^*, V_n^*; J_n^{*-1})$. *If* $P_o \in \mathcal{P}_o^i$, *then* $\mathcal{M}_n' \overset{A}{\sim} \chi_q^2$.

In particular, $\mathcal{P}_o^i$ *includes all elements of* $\mathcal{P}_o^u$ *for which* $\{s_t^*, \mathcal{F}^t\}$ *and* $\{m_t^*, \mathcal{F}^t\}$ *are martingale difference sequences, and either* $\{\nabla' s_t^* + s_t^* s_t^{*\prime}, \mathcal{F}^t\}$ *and* $\{\nabla_\theta' m_t^* + m_t^* s_t^{*\prime}, \mathcal{F}^t\}$ *are martingale difference sequences or* $\nabla_\theta' \bar{M}_n^* A_n^{*-1} - G_n^* B_n^{*-1} = 0$.

(iv) If $P_o \in \mathcal{P}_A^u$ *and, in addition to the conditions of (i) and (ii),* $\{J_n^*\}$ *is uniformly positive definite and Assumption 9.3 holds, then for* $\{k_n\} = o(n)$ *we have* $P_o[\mathcal{M}_n > k_n] \to 1$. *If in addition Assumption 3.2′ holds for the specification(s) generating the (2S)QMLE, then* $P_o[\mathcal{M}_n' > k_n] \to 1$. □

The nR^2 form for this test is quite convenient; it is analyzed by Newey [1985] for the case of i.i.d. observations and by White [1987] in a general context similar to that considered here.

The martingale difference conditions of part (iii) suffice to ensure that $\nabla_\theta' \bar{M}_n^* A_n^{*-1} - G_n^* B_n^{*-1} = 0$. Typically, these conditions hold when $\hat{\theta}_n$ attains the asymptotic variance bound. In other words, specification tests obtained from Corollary 9.11 have proper size when $\hat{\theta}_n$ is a minimum asymptotic variance estimator.

Other convenient regression-based tests are available in cases in which m_t and s_t are linear transformations of a generalized residual vector (recall Definition 6.8) as in the case of the linear exponential family. When $\nabla_\theta \bar{M}_n^* = 0$, it is only required that m_t be a linear transformation of a generalized residual. These generalized residuals need bear no direct relation to those admitted by the specification generating $\hat{\theta}$. We use the following condition.

ASSUMPTION 9.7: (a) There exist functions $v_t : \mathbb{R}^{vt} \times \Theta \to \mathbb{R}^{\bar{l}}$ and $j_t : \mathbb{R}^{vt-l} \times \Theta \times \Pi \to \mathbb{R}^{q \times \bar{l}}$ such that $v_t(\cdot, \theta)$ is measurable for each θ in Θ

and $v_t(X^t, \cdot)$ is continuous on Θ $a.s.-P_o$; $j_t(\cdot, \theta, \pi)$ is measurable for each (θ, π) in $\Theta \times \Pi$ and $j_t(\tilde{X}^{t-1}, \cdot, \cdot)$ is continuous on $\Theta \times \Pi$ $a.s.-P_o$; and $m_t(X^t, \theta, \pi) = j_t(\tilde{X}^{t-1}, \theta, \pi)\, v_t(X^t, \theta)$, $t = 1, 2, \ldots$;

(b) In addition, $v_t(X_t, \cdot)$ is continuously differentiable on Θ $a.s.-P_o$, and for each π in Π, $j_t(\tilde{X}^{t-1}, \cdot, \pi)$ is continuously differentiable on Θ $a.s.-P_o$, $t = 1, 2, \ldots$. □

In any particular application, there is usually a variety of ways to choose j_t and v_t to satisfy this assumption. The issue of which choice is most appropriate is resolved by part (iii) of Corollary 9.12 below, which establishes that the statistic of interest under Assumption 9.7 has the χ^2_q distribution asymptotically under the null hypothesis (as desired) provided that $E(v_t^* v_t^{*\prime} \mid \tilde{X}^{t-1}) = I_{\tilde{l}}$, $v_t^* \equiv v_t(X^t, \theta_n^*)$. This requires that v_t is standardized in such a way as to eliminate conditional heterogeneity. Note that at least for now we need not have $\tilde{l} = l$. This provides useful flexibility in certain applications.

The following conditions allow us to obtain a result analogous to Corollary 9.9.

ASSUMPTION 9.8: (a) The elements of $\ddot{J}_n$, $\ddot{J}_n \equiv n^{-1} \sum_{t=1}^n E(j_t(\tilde{X}^{t-1}, \cdot, \cdot)\, j_t(\tilde{X}^{t-1}, \cdot, \cdot)')$, are finite and continuous on $\Theta \times \Pi$ uniformly in $n = 1, 2, \ldots$;

(b) The elements of $\{ j_t(\tilde{X}^{t-1}, \theta, \pi) j_t(\tilde{X}^{t-1}, \theta, \pi)' \}$ obey the weak ULLN. □

ASSUMPTION 9.9: (a) The function σ_n^2, $\sigma_n^2 \equiv (n\tilde{l})^{-1} \sum_{t=1}^n \sum_{i=1}^{\tilde{l}} E(v_{ti}(X^t, \cdot)^2)$, is finite and continuous on Θ uniformly in $n = 1, 2, \ldots$; (b) $\{ v_{ti}(X^t, \theta)^2 \}$ obeys the weak ULLN, $i = 1, \ldots, \tilde{l}$. □

COROLLARY 9.12: *(i) Given the conditions of Theorem 2.12 or 2.15, Assumption 9.2(a), and Assumption 9.7(a), $\{\hat{J}_n = n^{-1} \sum_{t=1}^n \hat{j}_t \hat{j}_t'\}$ is a measurable sequence of symmetric positive semi-definite matrices, $\hat{j}_t \equiv j_t(\tilde{X}^{t-1}, \hat{\theta}_n, \hat{\pi}_n)$. Under the same conditions, $\{\hat{\sigma}_n^2 = (n\tilde{l})^{-1} \sum_{t=1}^n \sum_{i=1}^{\tilde{l}} \hat{v}_{ti}^2\}$ is a measurable sequence, $\hat{v}_{ti} = v_{ti}(X^t, \hat{\theta}_n)$.*

(ii) If in addition, the conditions of Theorem 3.5 or 3.10 hold and Assumptions 9.2(b) and 9.8 hold, then $\hat{J}_n - \ddot{J}_n^* \to 0$ $prob-P_o$, $\ddot{J}_n^* \equiv n^{-1} \sum_{t=1}^n E(j_t^* j_t^{*\prime})$, $j_t^* \equiv j_t(\tilde{X}^{t-1}, \theta_n^*, \pi_n^*)$. Further, $\ddot{J}_n^*$ is $O(1)$.

If Assumption 9.9 holds in place of 9.8, then $\hat{\sigma}_n^2 - \sigma_n^{*2} \to 0$ *prob* $- P_o$, $\sigma_n^{*2} \equiv (n\tilde{l})^{-1} \sum_{t=1}^{n} \sum_{i=1}^{\tilde{l}} E(v_{ti}^{*2})$, $v_{ti}^{*} = v_{ti}(X^t, \theta_n^*)$. *Further,* $\{\sigma_n^{*2}\}$ is $O(1)$.

(iii) If in addition Assumption 9.7(b) holds, $\sigma_n^{*2} > \varepsilon > 0$ *a. a. n,* $\{\ddot{J}_n^{*}\}$ *is uniformly positive definite, and* $P_o \in \mathcal{P}_a^u$, *then* $\ddot{\mathcal{M}}_n = n\tilde{l}\ R^2 \overset{A}{\sim} N_2(a_n^*,\ V_n^*;\ \ddot{J}_n^{*-1} / \sigma_n^{*2})$, *where* R^2 *is the squared multiple correlation coefficient (e.g. Theil [1971, p. 164]) for the regression of* $\hat{v}_{ti} = v_{ti}(X^t, \hat{\theta}_n)$ on the $1 \times q$ *vector* $\hat{j}_{ti}'$, $i = 1, \ldots, \tilde{l}$, $t = 1, \ldots, n$. *If* $P_o \in \mathcal{P}_o^i$, *the model implicitly tested using* $\hat{J}_n$, *then* $\ddot{\mathcal{M}}_n \overset{A}{\sim} \chi_q^2$.

In particular $\mathcal{P}_o^i$ *includes all elements of* $\mathcal{P}_o^u$ *for which* $\{m_t^*, \mathcal{F}^t\}$ *and* $\{v_t^*\ v_t^{*\prime} - \sigma_o^2\ I_{\tilde{l}},\ \tilde{\mathcal{F}}^t\}$ *are martingale difference sequences for some real constant* $\sigma_o^2 > 0$ *and either* $\{\nabla_\theta\ m_t^*, \mathcal{F}^t\}$ *is a martingale difference sequence or* $\nabla_\theta \bar{M}_n^* = 0$.

(iv) If $P_o \in \mathcal{P}_A^u$ *and, in addition to the conditions of (i) and (ii),* $\sigma_n^{*2} > \varepsilon > 0$ *a. a. n,* $\{\ddot{J}_n^{*}\}$ *is uniformly positive definite, and Assumption 9.3 holds, then for* $\{k_n\} = o(n)$, $P_o[\ddot{\mathcal{M}}_n > k_n] \to 1$. □

This result is quite convenient, as the $n\tilde{l}R^2$ statistic in (iii) is easy to compute; it also has an appealing interpretation. The test based on the χ_q^2 distribution has the correct size asymptotically provided that $\nabla_\theta\ \bar{M}_n^* = 0$, and also that v_t^* is conditionally homoskedastic. White's [1980b] $n\,R^2$ heteroskedasticity test is covered by this result. The homokurtosis assumption that appears in the assumptions for that test is an example of the homoskedasticity requirement for v_t^*.

When $\nabla_\theta\ \bar{M}_n^* \nrightarrow 0$, further structure is needed to obtain analogs of Corollary 9.11 that take advantage of the availability of generalized residuals u_t for the specification generating $\hat{\theta}$. As the next result shows, tests of proper size can be obtained, provided that $v_t = u_t$. The example with $m_t = vec\ s_t\ s_{t-1}'$ for the linear exponential family satisfies this assumption, with $s_t = i_t\ u_t$, $m_t = j_t\ u_t$, for

$$u_t = \nabla_\mu\ c_t^{1/2}\ (Y_t - \mu_t)\ ,$$

$$i_t = \nabla_\theta\ \mu_t\ \nabla_\mu\ c_t^{1/2}$$

and

$$j_t = [\nabla_\theta \mu_{t-1} \nabla_\mu c_{t-1}(Y_{t-1} - \mu_{t-1}) \otimes \nabla_\theta \mu_t] \nabla_\mu c_t^{1/2} .$$

To exploit fully the computational convenience afforded by the availability of generalized residuals, we require conditions analogous to Assumptions 9.4 and 9.6.

ASSUMPTION 9.10: (a) The elements of $E[n^{-1} \sum_{t=1}^{n} i_t(W_t, \cdot)\, i_t(W_t, \cdot)']$ and $E[n^{-1} \sum_{t=1}^{n} i_t(W_t, \cdot)\, j_t(\tilde{X}^{t-1}, \cdot, \cdot)']$ are finite and continuous on Θ and $\Theta \times \Pi$ respectively, uniformly in $n = 1, 2, \ldots$;

(b) The elements of $\{i_t(W_t, \theta)\, i_t(W_t, \theta)'\}$ and $\{i_t(W_t, \theta)\; j_t(\tilde{X}^{t-1}, \theta, \pi)'\}$ obey the weak ULLN. □

ASSUMPTION 9.11: Assumption 9.9 holds with u_{ti} replacing v_{ti}, $i = 1, \ldots, l$, $t = 1, \ldots, n$. □

The specification testing result for the case in which generalized residuals are available is the following.

COROLLARY 9.13: *Suppose that the specification $\mathcal{S}$ generating $\hat{\theta}$ admits generalized residuals $u = \{u_t\}$ with generalized instruments $i = \{i_t\}$.*

(i) Given the conditions of Theorem 2.12 or 2.15 and Assumptions 9.2(a) and 9.7(a) with $\tilde{l} = l$

$$\{\hat{J}_n = n^{-1} \sum_{t=1}^{n} \hat{j}_t\, \hat{j}_t' - (n^{-1} \sum_{t=1}^{n} \hat{j}_t\, \hat{i}_t')[n^{-1} \sum_{t=1}^{n} \hat{i}_t\, \hat{i}_t']^{-} (n^{-1} \sum_{t=1}^{n} \hat{i}_t\, \hat{j}_t')\}$$

is a measurable sequence of symmetric positive semi-definite matrices, with $\hat{i}_t \equiv i_t(W_t, \hat{\theta}_n)$. Under these conditions, $\{\hat{\sigma}_n^2 = (nl)^{-1} \sum_{t=1}^{n} \sum_{i=1}^{l} \hat{u}_{ti}^2\}$ is a measurable non-negative sequence, $\hat{u}_{ti} = u_{ti}(Y_t, W_t, \hat{\theta}_n)$.

(ii) If in addition the conditions of Theorem 3.5 or 3.10 hold and Assumptions 9.2(b), 9.8 and 9.10 hold, then $\hat{J}_n - \dddot{J}_n^{*} \to 0$ prob $- P_o$ where now

$$\dddot{J}_n^{*} = \ddot{K}_n^{*} - \ddot{G}_n^{*}\, \ddot{B}_n^{*-1}\, \ddot{G}_n^{*\prime}$$

and $\{J_n^*\}$ *is* $O(1)$, *with* $\ddot{K}_n^* = n^{-1}\sum_{t=1}^n E(j_t^*\, j_t^{*\prime})$, $\ddot{G}_n^* \equiv n^{-1}\sum_{t=1}^n E(j_t^*\, i_t^{*\prime})$ *and* $\ddot{B}_n^* \equiv n^{-1}\sum_{t=1}^n E(i_t^*\, i_t^{*\prime})$, $i_t^* = i_t(W_t, \theta_n^*)$.

If Assumption 9.11 holds in place of 9.8 and 9.10 then $\hat{\sigma}_n^2 - \sigma_n^{*2} \to 0$ *prob* $-P_o$, $\sigma_n^{*2} = (nl)^{-1}\sum_{t=1}^n \sum_{i=1}^l E(u_{ti}^{*2})$, $u_{ti}^* = u_{ti}(Y_t, W_t, \theta_n^*)$. *Further,* $\{\sigma_n^{*2}\}$ *is* $O(1)$.

(iii) Suppose in addition Assumption 9.7(b) holds, $\sigma_n^{*2} > \varepsilon > 0$ *a. a. n,* $\{J_n^*\}$ *is uniformly positive definite and* $P_o \in \mathcal{P}_a^u$. *Then*

(a) Letting $\ddot{\mathcal{M}}_n = n\,\hat{M}_n'\,\hat{J}_n^-\,\hat{M}_n/\hat{\sigma}_n^2$ *for* $\hat{J}_n$ *and* $\hat{\sigma}_n^2$ *as in (i),* $\ddot{\mathcal{M}}_n \overset{A}{\sim} N_2(a_n^*, V_n^*;\ \ddot{J}_n^{*-1}/\sigma_n^{*2})$ *and if* $P_o \in \mathcal{P}_o^i$, *then* $\ddot{\mathcal{M}}_n \overset{A}{\sim} \chi_q^2$, *where* $\mathcal{P}_o^i$ *is the model implicitly tested using* $\hat{\sigma}_n^2\,\hat{J}_n$.

(b) Letting $\ddot{\mathcal{M}}_n' = nlR^2$, *where* R^2 *is the (constant unadjusted) squared multiple correlation coefficient of the generalized residual* $\hat{u}_{ti}$ *on the explanatory variables* $\hat{j}_{ti}'$ $(1\times q)$, $\hat{i}_{ti}'$ $(1\times p)$, $i = 1,\ldots,l$, $t = 1,\ldots,n$, $\ddot{\mathcal{M}}_n - \ddot{\mathcal{M}}_n' \to 0$ *prob* $-P_o$ *and* $\ddot{\mathcal{M}}_n' \overset{A}{\sim} N_2(a_n^*,\ V_n^*;\ \ddot{J}_n^{*-1}/\sigma_n^{*2})$. *If* $P_o \in \mathcal{P}_o^i$, then $\ddot{\mathcal{M}}_n' \overset{A}{\sim} \chi_q^2$.

In particular, when $v_t = u_t$, $t = 1, 2, \ldots$, $\mathcal{P}_o^i$ *contains all elements of* $\mathcal{P}_o^u$ *for which* $\{u_t^*, \tilde{\mathcal{F}}^t\}$ *is a martingale difference sequence, and for some real constant* $\sigma_0^2 > 0$, $\{u_t^*\,u_t^{*\prime} - \sigma_0^2 I_l, \tilde{\mathcal{F}}^t\}$ *and* $\{i_t^* + \nabla_\theta u_t^*/\sigma_0^2, \tilde{\mathcal{F}}^t\}$ *are martingale difference sequences.*

(iv) If $P_o \in \mathcal{P}_A^u$ *and, in addition to the conditions of (i) and (ii),* $\sigma_n^{*2} > \varepsilon > 0$ *a. a. n,* $\{\ddot{J}_n^*\}$ *is uniformly positive definite and Assumption 9.3 holds, then for* $\{k_n\} = o(n)$ $P_o[\ddot{\mathcal{M}}_n > k_n] \to 1$. *If in addition Assumption 3.2′ holds for the specification(s) generating the (2S)QMLE, then* $P_o[\ddot{\mathcal{M}}_n' > k_n] \to 1$. □

Notice that the form given for this specification test statistic is identical to that of the Lagrange multiplier test for omitted variables $\hat{j}_{ti}$ in a linear regression that already includes variables $\hat{i}_{ti}$. (See Exercises 4.34 and 4.35 of White [1984a].)

Comparing Corollaries 9.11, 9.12 and 9.13, we see that each makes use of certain aspects of a specification yielding an efficient estimator under H_o. Corollaries 9.11 and 9.13 both make essential use of information equalities to deliver more easily computed statistics. However, Corollary 9.13 exploits hypothesized conditional homogeneity of generalized residuals to permit these residuals to be used as dependent variables in the artificial regression generating the test statistic. When this conditional homogeneity assumption is valid, the true distribution of the resulting statistic may be better approximated by its asymptotic distribution than would be the statistic of Corollary 9.11.

Corollary 9.12 also relies on conditional homogeneity to permit generalized residuals to be used in the artificial regression generating the specification test statistic. However, it does not rely to the same extent as the information matrix equalities exploited in Corollaries 9.11 and 9.13 because $\nabla_\theta \bar{M}_n^*$ is assumed to vanish.

Thus, the results of Theorem 9.5 and its corollaries provide useful specification tests with known size asymptotically for a variety of more or less restrictive models implicitly tested. The more restrictive the model implicitly tested, the more convenient the test statistic. However, distributional misspecification, neglected heterogeneity or dynamic misspecification generally invalidate use of the χ_q^2 distribution in forming critical values for the statistics of Corollaries 9.11-9.13. Corollary 9.10 allows nR^2 from a somewhat more complicated regression to be used as a χ_q^2 statistic despite the presence of distributional misspecification or neglected heterogeneity. Dynamic misspecification still invalidates use of the χ_q^2 distribution. A statistic with asymptotic size unaffected by dynamic misspecification can fairly generally be based on the Gallant-White estimator.

Although all of the test statistics just discussed have tractable asymptotic distributions under appropriate conditions, these asymptotic distributions need not provide very close approximations to the exact distribution of these statistics for finite samples. Statistics based on the Gallant-White estimator may require especially large samples in order to be well approximated by the χ_q^2 distribution. Furthermore, analytic results of Cavanagh [1985] and simulation results of Chesher and Spady [1986] show that the convenient nR^2 tests given in Corollaries 9.10-9.12 may be rather poorly approximated by the χ_q^2 distribution. Analysis of these issues is beyond the scope of our work here. However, the approach of Wooldridge mentioned above delivers as one of its benefits statistics that appear to be well approximated by their asymptotic distributions in samples of reasonable size. We now turn to a consideration of Wooldridge's approach.

9.3 Wooldridge's Modified m-Test

The tests of the Corollaries 9.11 and 9.13 essentially exploited the asymptotic efficiency of $\hat{\theta}_n$ under H_o to obtain convenient test statistics; the properties of the efficient estimator help in dealing with the difficulties created when $\nabla_\theta \bar{M}_n^* \nrightarrow 0$ for a given choice of indicator. Obtaining an efficient estimator under H_o is often an elaborate production. Wooldridge [1990] has proposed a clever modification to the indicators of m-tests that avoids the need for an efficient estimator by ensuring that $\nabla \bar{M}_n^* = 0$ for the modified indicators. Corollary 9.9 then applies, using any $\sqrt{n}$-consistent estimator for θ_o under H_o.

To describe Wooldridge's modification, suppose $m_t = j_t \, v_t$ as in Assumption 9.7, and suppose that

$$\underset{p \times \bar{l}}{\mathcal{V}_t} (\tilde{X}^{t-1}, \theta) \equiv E(\nabla_\theta v_t(X^t, \theta) \mid \tilde{X}^{t-1})$$

is of known form under H_o. Define

$$\underset{p \times q}{\gamma_n^*} \equiv [\, n^{-1} \sum_{t=1}^{n} E(\mathcal{V}_t^* \mathcal{V}_t^{*\prime}) \,]^{-1} \; n^{-1} \sum_{t=1}^{n} E(\mathcal{V}_t^* j_t^{*\prime}), \quad n = 1, 2, \ldots,$$

where $\mathcal{V}_t^* \equiv \mathcal{V}_t(\tilde{X}^{t-1}, \theta_n^*)$ (and $j_t^* \equiv j_t(\tilde{X}^{t-1}, \theta_n^*, \pi_n^*)$ as before). Wooldridge's modification puts

$$\underset{\sim}{m}_t(X^t, \theta, \underset{\sim}{\pi}) = [\, j_t(\tilde{X}^{t-1}, \theta, \pi) - \gamma' \mathcal{V}_t(\tilde{X}^{t-1}, \theta) \,] \, v_t(X_t, \theta),$$

where $\underset{\sim}{\pi} = (\pi', \gamma')'$ is an augmented vector of nuisance parameters. The modified indicators $\{ \underset{\sim}{m}_t \}$ now have the property that $\nabla_\theta \underset{\sim}{\bar{M}}_n^* = n^{-1} \Sigma_{t=1}^n E(\nabla_\theta \underset{\sim}{m}_t^*) = 0$ under H_o where $\nabla_\theta \underset{\sim t}{m}^* = \nabla_\theta \underset{\sim}{m}_t(X^t, \theta_n^*, \underset{\sim}{\pi}_n^*)$, $\underset{\sim}{\pi}_n^* = (\pi_n^{*\prime}, \gamma_n^{*\prime})'$ (and we have $\theta_n^* = \theta_o$ under H_o).

To see that this is so, observe that

$$\nabla_\theta' \underset{\sim}{m}_t = [\, j_t - \gamma' \mathcal{V}_t \,] \nabla_\theta' v_t + (v_t' \otimes I_q) \nabla_\theta' [\, j_t - \gamma' \mathcal{V}_t \,],$$

so that $E(v_t^* \mid \tilde{X}^{t-1}) = 0$ implies $E(\nabla_\theta' m_t^* \mid \tilde{X}^{t-1}) = [\, j_t^* - \gamma_n^{*\prime} \mathcal{V}_t^* \,] \mathcal{V}_t^{*\prime}$. Now the law of iterated expectations implies

$$\nabla_\theta \underset{\sim}{\bar{M}}_n^* = E(n^{-1} \sum_{t=1}^{n} E(\nabla_\theta \underset{\sim}{m}_t^* \mid \tilde{X}^{t-1}))$$

$$= n^{-1} \sum_{t=1}^{n} E(\mathcal{V}_t^* j_t^{*\prime}) - n^{-1} \sum_{t=1}^{n} E(\mathcal{V}_t^* \mathcal{V}_t^{*\prime}) \gamma_n^* .$$

If $n^{-1} \sum_{t=1}^{n} E(\mathcal{V}_t^* \mathcal{V}_t^{*\prime})$ is nonsingular, it follows that $\nabla_\theta \bar{\underset{\sim}{M}}_n^* = 0$ as claimed, by definition of γ_n^*. The effect of the modification, as noted by Wooldridge, is to purge j_t^* of components correlated with $\mathcal{V}_t^*$.

The result is a set of modified indicators $\underset{\sim}{m}_t = \underset{\sim}{j}_t\, v_t$ (with $\underset{\sim}{j}_t = j_t - \gamma' \mathcal{V}_t$) to which Corollary 9.9(iii) applies. Implementation of the m-test is now simple: given $\hat{\theta}_n$ and $\hat{\pi}_n$, one computes $\hat{\mathcal{V}}_t = \mathcal{V}_t(\tilde{X}^{t-1}, \hat{\theta}_n)$ and $\hat{j}_t = j_t(\tilde{X}^{t-1}, \hat{\theta}_n, \hat{\pi}_n)$. From this, one forms

$$\hat{\gamma}_n = (\sum_{t=1}^{n} \hat{\mathcal{V}}_t \hat{\mathcal{V}}_t')^{-} \sum_{t=1}^{n} \hat{\mathcal{V}}_t \hat{j}_t .$$

Finally, one computes $\hat{v}_t = v(X^t, \hat{\theta}_n)$ and $\hat{\underset{\sim}{m}}_t = [\hat{j}_t - \hat{\gamma}_n' \hat{\mathcal{V}}_t]\, \hat{v}_t$ and regresses the constant unity on $\hat{\underset{\sim}{m}}_t'$. $\mathcal{M}_n = n R^2$ from this regression is χ_q^2 under H_o provided the conditions of Corollary 9.9(iii) hold.

The following assumptions permit verification of these conditions, allowing us to state a formal result.

ASSUMPTION 9.12 (a) $\mathcal{V}_t(\tilde{X}^{t-1}, \cdot) \equiv E(\nabla_\theta v_t(X^t, \cdot) \mid \tilde{X}^{t-1})$ is continuous on Θ $a.s.-P_o$;

(b) $\mathcal{V}_t(\tilde{X}^{t-1}, \cdot)$ is continuously differentiable on Θ $a.s.-P_o$. □

ASSUMPTION 9.13 (a) The elements of $E[n^{-1} \Sigma_{t=1}^n \mathcal{V}_t(\tilde{X}^{t-1}, \cdot)\, \mathcal{V}_t(\tilde{X}^{t-1}, \cdot)']$ and $E[n^{-1} \Sigma_{t=1}^n \mathcal{V}_t(\tilde{X}^{t-1}, \cdot)\, j_t(\tilde{X}^{t-1}, \cdot, \cdot)']$ are finite and continuous on Θ and $\Theta \times \Pi$ respectively, uniformly in $n = 1, 2, \ldots$;

(b) The elements of $\{ \mathcal{V}_t(\tilde{X}^{t-1}, \theta)\, \mathcal{V}_t(\tilde{X}^{t-1}, \theta)' \}$ and $\{ \mathcal{V}_t(\tilde{X}^{t-1}, \theta)\, j_t(\tilde{X}^{t-1}, \theta, \pi)' \}$ obey the weak ULLN. □

ASSUMPTION 9.14: $\{E(n^{-1} \Sigma_{t=1}^n \mathcal{V}_t^* \mathcal{V}_t^{*\prime})\}$ is uniformly positive definite. □

These assumptions serve to ensure first that $\hat{\gamma}_n$ is measurable, and second that $\hat{\gamma}_n - \gamma_n^* = o_{P_o}(1)$.

Note that an alternative estimator for γ_n^* is available that does not require Assumption 9.12, namely

$$\tilde{\gamma}_n = [\sum_{t=1}^{n} \nabla_\theta \hat{v}_t \nabla_\theta' \hat{v}_t]^- \sum_{t=1}^{n} \nabla_\theta \hat{v}_t \hat{j}_t' ,$$

where $\nabla_\theta \hat{v}_t = \nabla_\theta v_t(X^t, \hat{\theta}_n)$. When using this estimator, $\nabla_\theta v_t$ replaces $\mathcal{V}_t$ in Assumptions 9.13 and 9.14. A knowledge of $\mathcal{V}_t$ is thus not needed to estimate γ_n^* consistently.

COROLLARY 9.14: *(i) Given the conditions of Theorem 2.12 or 2.15 and Assumptions 9.2(a), 9.7(a) and 9.12(a),* $\{ \hat{\underset{\sim}{K}}_n = n^{-1} \Sigma_{t=1}^n \hat{\underset{\sim}{m}}_t \hat{\underset{\sim}{m}}_t' \}$ *is a measurable sequence of symmetric positive semi-definite matrices, where* $\hat{\underset{\sim}{m}}_t = (\hat{j}_t - \hat{\gamma}_n' \hat{\mathcal{V}}_t) \hat{v}_t$.

(ii) If in addition the conditions of Theorem 3.5 or 3.10 hold, Assumptions 9.2(b), 9.13, 9.14 hold and Assumption 9.4 holds for $\underset{\sim}{m}_t = [j_t - \gamma' \mathcal{V}_t] v_t$, *then* $\hat{\underset{\sim}{K}}_n - \underset{\sim}{K}_n^* \to 0$ *prob* $-P_o$, $\underset{\sim}{K}_n^* \equiv n^{-1} \Sigma_{t=1}^n E(\underset{\sim}{m}_t^* \underset{\sim}{m}_t^{*\prime})$. *Further,* $\{ \underset{\sim}{K}_n^* \}$ *is* $O(1)$.

(iii) If in addition Assumptions 9.7(b) and 9.12(b) hold, $\{ \underset{\sim}{K}_n^* \}$ *is uniformly positive definite, and* $P_o \in \mathcal{P}_a^u$, *then* $\underset{\sim}{\mathcal{M}}_n = n \hat{\underset{\sim}{M}}_n' \hat{\underset{\sim}{K}}_n^- \hat{\underset{\sim}{M}}_n = n R^2 \overset{A}{\sim} N_2(a_n^*, V_n^*; K_n^{*-1})$, *where* R^2 *is the uncentered squared multiple regression coefficient for the regression of 1 on* $\hat{\underset{\sim}{m}}_t'$, *and if* $P_o \in \mathcal{P}_o^i$, *the model implicitly tested using* $\hat{\underset{\sim}{K}}_n$, then $\mathcal{M}_n \overset{A}{\sim} \chi_q^2$.

In particular, $\mathcal{P}_o^i$ *includes all elements of* $\mathcal{P}_o^u$ *for which* $\{ \underset{\sim}{m}_t^*, \mathcal{F}^t \}$ *is a martingale difference sequence.*

(iv) If $P_o \in \mathcal{P}_A^u$ *and, in addition to the conditions of (i) and (ii)* $\{ \underset{\sim}{K}_n^* \}$ *is uniformly positive definite and Assumption 9.3 holds for* $\underset{\sim}{m}_t$, *then for* $\{ k_n \} = o(n)$, $P_o[\underset{\sim}{\mathcal{M}}_n > k_n] \to 1$. □

Wooldridge's approach thus affords very convenient computation of the specification test statistic. Furthermore, as Wooldridge [1990, p. 31] points out, this statistic does exploit the presence of the generalized residual; for this and other reasons the finite sample distribution of this statistic may be better approximated by the asymptotic distribution given here than the statistics of Corollary 9.9 based on unmodified indicators.

The price paid for these potential benefits is that the sensitivity of this test differs from that of Corollary 9.9 using unmodified indicators. Specifically, misspecifications for which $n^{-1} \Sigma_{t=1}^{n} E(\mathcal{V}_t^* v_t^*) \nrightarrow 0$ will not be detectable using the modified indicators. To see this, observe that when $m_t = \mathcal{V}_t v_t$, the modification $\underset{\sim}{m}_t = (\mathcal{V}_t - \gamma' \mathcal{V}_t) v_t$ implies $\hat{\underset{\sim}{M}}_n \equiv 0$. If such misspecifications must be detected, Corollaries 9.10, 9.11 or 9.13 provide the needed tools.

Apart from the fact that Wooldridge's approach is based on availability of generalized residuals, the modification is limited in practice by the need to know the function $\mathcal{V}_t$. Wooldridge [1987] shows that $\mathcal{V}_t$ is always known under the relevant null hypothesis for conditional mean and conditional variance testing in the linear exponential family. Wooldridge [1990] also discusses many other cases in which $\mathcal{V}_t$ is known.

Even when $\mathcal{V}_t$ is not known, it appears possible to obtain a test statistic asymptotically equivalent to that of Corollary 9.14 based on a nonparametric estimator (say $\tilde{\mathcal{V}}_t$) of $E(\nabla_\theta v_t(X^t, \theta_o) \mid \tilde{X}^{t-1})$ that is consistent under H_o. Specifically, a modified indicator of the form $\underset{\sim}{\tilde{m}}_t = (\hat{j}_t - \tilde{\gamma}_n' \tilde{\mathcal{V}}_t) \hat{v}_t$ may be used in place of $\underset{\sim}{\hat{m}}_t$. The nonparametric estimator $\tilde{\mathcal{V}}_t$ can be obtained from nonparametric regression with $\nabla_\theta v_t(X^t, \hat{\theta}_n)$ serving as the dependent variable, and with conditioning variables $\tilde{X}^{t-1}$. Numerous delicate and/or complex issues arise in the analysis of tests based on $\underset{\sim}{\tilde{m}}_t$. We leave these for other work.

To conclude this section, we note that Wooldridge's approach is only apparently limited by reliance on generalized residuals. In fact, one may set $v_t(X^t, \theta) = m_t(X^t, \theta)$ (where π is absorbed into θ if necessary) and put $j_t(\tilde{X}^{t-1}, \theta, \pi) = I_q$. Corollary 9.14 applies with $\mathcal{V}_t(\tilde{X}^{t-1}, \theta) = E(\nabla_\theta m_t(X^t, \theta) \mid \tilde{X}^{t-1})$. The difficulty in applications arises because this choice for $\mathcal{V}_t$ may be unknown; however, the nonparametric approach of the preceding paragraph is again appropriate.

9.4 m-Tests as Lagrange Multiplier Tests

It has been suggested by White [1984c] that m-tests may be viewed as a particular form of Lagrange multiplier test. If this is so, it brings the theory of m-tests within the scope of Chapter 8 as well as permitting interpretation of m-tests within the classical hypothesis testing framework. In this section, we show by construction that m-tests are indeed a special case of the Lagrange multiplier test. This demonstration also highlights some of the differences inherent in the interpretation of specification tests and classical tests.

In order to motivate our construction, suppose we have the usual specification $\mathcal{S} = \{ f_t \}$, and partition θ as $\theta' = (\beta', \gamma')$. It is straightforward to show (see Section 10.1) that a Lagrange multiplier test of the hypothesis $H_o: \beta_o = 0$ corresponds to an m-test with

$$m_t(X^t, \hat{\theta}_n, \hat{\pi}_n) = \nabla^2_\beta \hat{L}_n^- \nabla_\beta \log f_t(X^t, 0, \hat{\gamma}_n),$$

where $\hat{\pi}_n = vech\, \nabla^2_\beta \hat{L}_n^-$, $\nabla^2_\beta \hat{L}_n \equiv n^{-1} \sum_{t=1}^n \nabla^2_\beta \log f(X^t, 0, \hat{\gamma}_n)$, and $\hat{\theta}_n$ corresponds to the (Q)MLE $\hat{\gamma}_n$,

$$\hat{\gamma}_n = \text{argmax}_{\gamma \in \Gamma} L_n(X^n, 0, \gamma).$$

Because $\nabla^2_\beta \hat{L}_n^-$ is nonsingular with probability approaching one under the null hypothesis and local alternatives, we can simplify the problem by dropping it, and considering the equivalent m-test based on

$$m_t(X^t, \hat{\theta}_n, \hat{\pi}_n) = \nabla_\beta \log f_t(X^t, 0, \hat{\gamma}_n),$$

where, for the time being, π is null. The significance of this equation is that not only does it imply that the Lagrange multiplier test is an m-test, but it also suggests that an m-test may be representable as a Lagrange multiplier test of the hypothesis that $\beta_o = 0$ for some properly chosen specification $\{ f_t \}$. The key to this representation is to demonstrate the existence of such a specification for arbitrary m_t. The result of this section shows that such specifications generally exist under plausible conditions.

Our proof is based on the following construction. Suppose we are given a specification $\mathcal{S}_1 = \{ f_{1t} \}$ with associated QMLE $\hat{\theta}$, and a sequence $\{ m_t : \mathbb{R}^{vt} \times \Theta \times \Pi \to \mathbb{R}^q \}$ such that for all $\tilde{x}^{t-1}$ in $\mathbb{R}^{vt-l}$ and all (θ, π) in $\Theta \times \Pi$

$$\int m_t(x^t, \theta, \pi) f_{1t}(x^t, \theta)\, d\zeta_t(y_t) = 0, \quad t = 1, 2, \ldots,$$

i.e. $E_\theta(m_t(X^t, \theta, \pi) \mid \tilde{X}^{t-1}) = 0$, where $E_\theta(\cdot \mid \cdot)$ denotes conditional expectation under an element of $\mathcal{S}_1$. Under appropriate conditions on υ_t, the functions $f_{2t} = (1 + \upsilon_t) f_{1t}$ also generate a specification satisfying appropriate regularity conditions. For our purposes, the following condition suffices.

ASSUMPTION 9.15: (a) The functions $\upsilon_t : \mathbb{R} \to [-1+\delta, \Delta]$, $0 < \delta \leq 1$, $\Delta < \infty$ are continuous on $\mathbb{R}$ with $\upsilon_t(0) = 0$, $t = 1, 2, \ldots$;

(b) υ_t has continuous derivative $\dot{\upsilon}_t$ bounded on $\mathbb{R}$ uniformly in t, with $\dot{\upsilon}_t(0) = 1$, $t = 1, 2, \ldots$. □

A simple example of a function satisfying this condition is $\upsilon_t(x) = (1-\delta)\sin[x/(1-\delta)]$, $x \in \mathbb{R}$, $0 < \delta < 1$. The presence of $\delta > 0$ allows us to avoid technicalities associated with division by zero.

We consider specifications of the form

$$f_{2t}(x^t, \beta, \theta, \pi) \equiv (1 + \upsilon_t[\beta' m_t(x^t, \theta, \pi)]) \times f_{1t}(x^t, \theta) / \mathcal{Y}_t(\tilde{x}^{t-1}, \beta, \theta, \pi),$$

$$\mathcal{Y}_t(\tilde{x}^{t-1}, \beta, \theta, \pi) \equiv \int (1 + \upsilon_t[\beta' m_t(x^t, \theta, \pi)])\, f_{1t}(x^t, \theta)\, d\zeta_t(y_t).$$

The conditions imposed on υ_t ensure that f_{2t} is nonnegative, and that the normalizing function $\mathcal{Y}_t$ is bounded above and away from zero, given that f_{1t} is a conditional density with respect to ζ_t.

It follows that f_{2t} provides the desired specification if it can be shown that

$$\nabla_\beta \log f_{2t}(X^t, 0, \hat{\theta}_n, \hat{\pi}_n) = m_t(X^t, \hat{\theta}_n, \hat{\pi}_n).$$

Now $\hat{\theta}_n$ is the QMLE generated by $\{ f_{2t} \}$ when $\beta = 0$, so it suffices to show that for all x^t in $\mathbb{R}^{vt}$ and (θ, π) in $\Theta \times \Pi$

$$\nabla_\beta \log f_{2t}(x^t, 0, \theta, \pi) = m_t(x^t, \theta, \pi).$$

By definition

$$\log f_{2t} = \log(1 + \upsilon_t) + \log f_{1t} - \log \mathcal{Y}_t .$$

Because f_{1t} doesn't depend on β,

$$\nabla_\beta \log f_{2t} = \nabla_\beta \log (1 + \upsilon_t) - \nabla_\beta \log \mathcal{Y}_t$$

$$= \nabla_\beta \upsilon_t / (1 + \upsilon_t) - \nabla_\beta \mathcal{Y}_t / \mathcal{Y}_t \, .$$

Also,

$$\nabla_\beta \upsilon_t = m_t \, \dot{\upsilon}_t \, , \qquad \nabla_\beta \mathcal{Y}_t = \int m_t \, \dot{\upsilon}_t \, f_{1t} \, d\zeta_t \, .$$

Evaluating these expressions at $\beta = 0$ gives

$$\nabla_\beta \upsilon_t(0) = m_t (x^t , \theta , \pi) \, \dot{\upsilon}_t(0) = m_t (x^t , \theta , \pi)$$

$$\nabla_\beta \mathcal{Y}_t (\tilde{x}^{t-1} , 0 , \theta , \pi) = \dot{\upsilon}_t(0) \int m_t (x^t , \theta , \pi) \, f_{1t} (x^t , \theta) \, d\zeta_t (y_t) = 0 \, .$$

Because $\upsilon_t(0) = 0$, $\dot{\upsilon}_t(0) = 1$ and $\mathcal{Y}_t (\tilde{x}^{t-1} , 0 , \theta , \pi) = 1$ we have

$$\nabla_\beta \log f_{2t} (x^t , 0 , \theta , \pi) = m_t (x^t , \theta , \pi) \, ,$$

as required. Regularity conditions that justify a rigorous version of the foregoing heuristics are given by the following assumption.

ASSUMPTION 9.16 (a) For each $\tilde{x}^{t-1} \in \mathbb{R}^{vt-l}$ and each (θ , π) in $\Theta \times \Pi$

$$\int | \, m_{ti} (x^t , \theta , \pi) \, | \, f_{1t} (x^t , \theta) \, d\zeta_t (y_t) < \infty \quad t = 1, 2, \ldots , \quad i = 1, \ldots , q \, ;$$

(b) For each $\tilde{x}^{t-1} \in \mathbb{R}^{vt-l}$ and each (θ , π) in $\Theta \times \Pi$

$$\int m_t (x^t , \theta , \pi) \, f_{1t}(x^t , \theta) \, d\zeta_t (y_t) = 0 \qquad t = 1, 2, \ldots . \ \square$$

The first of the two conditions ensures the differentiability of $\log \mathcal{Y}_t$ with respect to β. The second imposes the fundamental property required of m_t.

Stated formally, we have the following result.

THEOREM 9.15: *(i) Given Assumptions 2.1 and 2.2, suppose that Assumption 2.3 holds for $\mathcal{S}_1 = \{ f_{1t} \}$ and that $\mathcal{S}_1 = \{ f_{1t} \}$ specifies dependent variables $\{ Y_t \}$ with respect to $\{ \zeta_t \}$. Let Assumption 9.1(a) hold for $\{ m_t \}$, let Assumption 9.15(a) hold for $\{ \upsilon_t \}$, and define functions $\mathcal{Y}_t$ and f_{2t} such that for β in a compact neighborhood $\mathcal{B}$ of $0 \in \mathbb{R}^q$ with non-empty interior*

$$\mathcal{Y}_t(\tilde{x}^{t-1}, \beta, \pi) \equiv \int (1 + \upsilon_t [\beta' m_t(x^t, \theta, \pi)])\, f_{1t}(x^t, \theta)\, d\zeta_t(y_t)$$

and

$$f_{2t}(x^t, \beta, \theta, \pi)$$

$$\equiv (1 + \upsilon_t [\beta' m_t(x^t, \theta, \pi)])\, f_{1t}(x^t, \theta) / \mathcal{Y}_t(\tilde{x}^{t-1}, \beta, \theta, \pi).$$

Then Assumption 2.3 holds for $\mathcal{S}_2 = \{ f_{2t} \}$ and $\mathcal{S}_2$ specifies dependent variables $\{ Y_t \}$ with respect to $\{ \zeta_t \}$.

Further, if $\hat{\theta}_n$ is a measurable solution to $\max_\Theta L_{1n}(X^n, \theta) = n^{-1} \sum_{t=1}^n \log f_{1t}(X^t, \theta)$, *it is also a measurable solution to*

$$\max_\Theta L_{2n}(X^n, 0, \theta, \pi) = n^{-1} \sum_{t=1}^{n} \log f_{2t}(X^t, 0, \theta, \pi)$$

for each π in Π.

(ii) If Assumptions 9.15(b) and 9.16 also hold then for all $x^t \in \mathbb{R}^{vt}$ and (θ, π) in $\Theta \times \Pi$

$$\nabla_\beta \log f_{2t}(x^t, 0, \theta, \pi) = m_t(x^t, \theta, \pi).$$

Consequently, the Lagrange multiplier statistic for testing $H_o: \beta_o = 0$ vs. $H_a: \beta_o \neq 0$ in the specification $\mathcal{S}_2$ using covariance matrix estimator $\tilde{C}_n$ is numerically equivalent to the m-test statistic based on $\hat{M}_n$ using $\hat{J}_n = \tilde{C}_n$. □

This result implies a direct correspondence between any particular m-test and an entire family of stochastic specifications that yield Lagrange multiplier tests of a particular parametric restriction. The family arises because υ_t is not unique; indeed there are uncountably many υ_t satisfying Assumption 9.15. The present case illustrates the local equivalence property of Lagrange multiplier tests (observed in another context by Godfrey [1981]). In fact, Assumption 9.15 restricts υ_t more than necessary. If m_t is itself bounded, then one could choose $\upsilon_t(\,\cdot\,) = \exp(\,\cdot\,)$ (see, e.g., Pérez-Amaral [1989]) and obtain similar results.

Viewing m_t as the basis for a Lagrange multiplier test, one has available the results of Chapter 8, and in particular, results indicating parametric alternatives against which the m-test has power. Because of the somewhat artificial nature of the construction used here, specifications such as $f_{2t}(x^t, \beta, \theta, \pi) = (1 + (1-\delta)\sin[(1-\delta)^{-1}\ \beta' m_t(x^t, \theta, \pi)])\ f_{1t}(x^t, \theta) /\ \mathcal{Y}_t(\tilde{x}^{t-1}, \beta, \theta, \pi)$ need not be sensible directions in which to extend a given specification $\{f_{1t}\}$. On the other hand, they may well yield improved approximations to the data generation process g^n, as measured by the KLIC.

The availability of the results of Chapter 8 also implies the existence of Wald and Likelihood Ratio tests asymptotically equivalent to a given m-test. For example, a Wald test would compare the estimate $\hat{\beta}$ from $\mathcal{S}_2 = \{f_{2t}\}$ to zero. Theorems 8.9 to 8.10 are directly relevant for this test. We need only to ensure that conditions previously imposed for $\{f_t\}$ now hold for $\{f_{2t}\}$. Because non-nested hypothesis tests are m-tests (see section 10.4) this approach provides a potentially useful way to turn non-nested hypotheses into a form of nested hypothesis.

Finally, the fact that the statistic for the m-test is identical to the statistic for a particular Lagrange multiplier test indicates that the only difference between the two is in their interpretation. Within the classical hypothesis testing framework, the correctness of the specification of the probability model $\mathcal{P}$ (e.g. the probability model compatible with $\mathcal{S}_2$) which nests the model of the null hypothesis, $\mathcal{P}_o$ (the model compatible with $\mathcal{S}_1$), is never in doubt. If one rejects $\mathcal{P}_o$, then $\mathcal{P} - \mathcal{P}_o$ is still maintained. If one fails to reject $\mathcal{P}_o$, then elements of the implicit null hypothesis outside $\mathcal{P}$ are of no interest. In the specification testing framework, rejecting $\mathcal{P}_o^i$ (Definition 9.8) does not permit us to maintain $\mathcal{P} - \mathcal{P}_o^i$. Moreover, $\mathcal{P}_o^i$ explicitly contains elements of the implicit null hypothesis of $\mathcal{P}_o$.

9.5 Summary and Concluding Remarks

The m-testing framework provides flexible tools for detecting a variety of misspecifications. This chapter has provided some general theory. The next chapter discusses some specific examples.

A variety of forms for the test are available; the validity of each form depends on the extent to which various aspects of the specification generating $\hat{\theta}$ are exploited in constructing the test statistic. Heavier use of model features resulting in efficient estimators $\hat{\theta}_n$ generally leads to computationally simpler forms of the m-test, but control over the size of the test is sacrificed when these model features are misspecified (e.g., conditional error homogeneity is imposed by the model, but errors are not conditionally homogeneous).

An approach due to Wooldridge permits computationally simple m-testing, at the expense of insensitivity to a specific form of misspecification. The theories of hypothesis testing treated in Chapter 8 and m-testing are unified by the fact that every m-test is a version of a particular classical Lagrange multiplier test, as we saw in Section 9.4.

Finally, we mention one very useful feature of the m-tests. This is that m-tests lend themselves to combination or separation, thus increasing their potential for detecting specific misspecifications. In particular, if $\hat{M}_{1n}$ and $\hat{M}_{2n}$ form the basis for different m-tests then $\hat{M}_n{}' = (\hat{M}_{1n}{}', \hat{M}_{2n}{}')$ forms the basis for a combined (joint) m-test. This allows combination of (e.g.) Hausman tests and encompassing tests within a single joint test. In certain cases $\hat{M}_{1n}$ and $\hat{M}_{2n}$ are asymptotically independent, so that a joint test can be based on $\mathcal{M}_n = \mathcal{M}_{1n} + \mathcal{M}_{2n}$ (see, e.g. Bera and Jarque [1982]). When $\hat{M}_{1n}$ and $\hat{M}_{2n}$ are not asymptotically independent, Theorem 9.5 and its corollaries are still directly available for $\hat{M}_n$. Separation works in the reverse manner and may be useful for gaining insight into in which directions misspecifications detected by a joint m-test may lie.

MATHEMATICAL APPENDIX

PROOF OF THEOREM 9.2: (i) By assumption

$$\begin{aligned}\sqrt{n}\,\hat{M}_n &= \sqrt{n}\,M_n^* - G_n^*\,\sqrt{n}\,(\hat{\theta}_n - \theta_n^*) + o_P(1)\\ &= \sqrt{n}\,(M_n^* + G_n^*\,A_n^{*-1}\,\psi_n^*)\\ &\quad - G_n^*\,(\sqrt{n}\,(\hat{\theta}_n - \theta_n^*) + A_n^{*-1}\,\sqrt{n}\,\psi_n^*) + o_P(1)\,.\end{aligned}$$

But $\sqrt{n}\,(\hat{\theta}_n - \theta_n^*) + A_n^{*-1}\,\sqrt{n}\,\psi_n^* = o_P(1)$ by Theorem 6.10 and G_n^* is $O(1)$ by assumption, so that the second term above is $o_P(1)$. Consequently $\sqrt{n}\,\hat{M}_n = \sqrt{n}\,(M_n^* + G_n^*\,A_n^{*-1}\,\psi_n^*) + o_P(1)$.

(ii) It follows immediately from (i) and from Proposition 8.5 that $\sqrt{n}\,\hat{M}_n \overset{A}{\sim} N(a_n^*, V_n^*)$ given that $\sqrt{n}\,(M_n^* + G_n^*\,A_n^{*-1}\,\psi_n^*) \overset{A}{\sim} N(a_n^*, V_n^*)$, with $\{a_n^*\}$, $\{V_n^*\}$ $O(1)$, and $\{V_n^*\}$ uniformly positive definite.

(iii) This follows immediately from Theorem 8.6. □

PROOF OF THEOREM 9.5: It suffices to verify the conditions of Theorem 9.2 for P_o in $\mathcal{P}_a^u$. Because $P_o \in \mathcal{P}_a^u$, the conditions of Theorem 6.10 hold as verified in the proof of Theorem 6.11, and as can be analogously verified for Theorem 6.4. The measurability and convergence conditions for $\hat{\pi}_n$ are imposed by Assumption 9.2, while Assumption 9.1 ensures the measurability of $\{m_t\}$ by Lemma 2.15 of Stinchcombe and White [1992] and Theorem 13.1 of Billingsley [1979]. Because $P_o \in \mathcal{P}_a^u$ we have by 9.4(i) that $\sqrt{n}\,\hat{M}_n = \sqrt{n}\,M_n^* - G_n^*\,\sqrt{n}\,(\hat{\theta}_n - \theta_n^*) + o_{P_o}(1)$ with $\{G_n^* = -\nabla_\theta'\,\bar{M}_n^*\}$ a $O(1)$ sequence. Hence Theorem 9.2(i) applies. The conditions of 9.2(ii) hold by condition 9.4(ii), so Theorem 9.2(ii) applies. The assumed consistency of $\hat{J}_n$ for J_n^* posited in the statement of Theorem 9.5 ensures that Theorem 9.2(iii) applies, and the result follows. □

PROOF OF THEOREM 9.7: The argument is analogous to that of the proof of Theorem 8.16(i). Given Assumption 9.3 and the conditions of Definition 9.6, it follows from Corollary 3.8 that $\hat{M}_n'\,\hat{M}_n - \bar{M}_n^{*\prime}\,\bar{M}_n^* \to 0$ $prob - P_o$. Because $\bar{M}_n^{*\prime}\,\bar{M}_n^* > \varepsilon_o$ *a.a.n*, application of the implication rule gives $P_o\,[\hat{M}_n'\,\hat{M}_n > \varepsilon_o/2] \to 1$.

Given the conditions imposed on $\hat{J}_n$ and J_n^*, it now follows from Theorem 8.13 that $P_o[\mathcal{M}_n > k_n] \to 1$ for $\{k_n\} = o(n)$. □

PROOF OF COROLLARY 9.9: (i) By construction $\hat{K}_n = n^{-1} \sum_{t=1}^{n} \hat{m}_t \hat{m}_t'$ is a sequence of symmetric positive semi-definite matrices. For measurability, it suffices that $\hat{m}_t = m_t(X^t, \hat{\theta}_n, \hat{\pi}_n)$ is measurable. The function m_t is measurable in its arguments given Assumption 9.1(a), while X^t is measurable given Assumption 2.1, $\hat{\theta}_n$ is measurable from Theorem 2.12 or 2.15, and $\hat{\pi}_n$ is measurable by Assumption 9.2(a). Because compositions of measurable functions are measurable (Billingsley [1979, Theorem 3.1]), $\hat{m}_t$ and (therefore) $\hat{K}_n$ are measurable.

(ii) The result follows from Corollary 3.8 given that $\hat{\theta}_n - \theta_n^* \rightarrow 0$ $prob-P_o$ by Theorem 3.5 or 3.10, $\hat{\pi}_n - \pi_n^* \rightarrow 0$ $prob-P_o$ by Assumption 9.2(b), and the ULLN for $\{m_t\, m_t'\}$ (Assumption 9.4). Because K_n is finite and continuous uniformly in n on the compact set $\Theta \times \Pi$ it follows that the elements of $K_n(\theta, \pi)$ are uniformly bounded on $\Theta \times \Pi$ for all $n = 1, 2, \ldots$. In particular, $\{K_n^* \equiv K_n(\theta_n^*, \pi_n^*)\}$ is $O(1)$.

(iii) If $\{K_n^*\}$ is uniformly positive definite, then the conditions of Theorem 9.5 are satisfied for $\hat{K}_n$, and it follows immediately that $\mathcal{M}_n \overset{A}{\sim} N_2(a_n^*, V_n^*; K_n^{*-1})$ for $P_o \in \mathcal{P}_a^u$. If $P_o \in \mathcal{P}_o^i$, then $P_o \in \mathcal{P}_o^u$ and $K_n^* = V_n^*$ so that $\mathcal{M}_n \overset{A}{\sim} \chi_q^2$.

To verify that $\mathcal{P}_o^i$ contains all elements of $\mathcal{P}_o^u$ for which $\{m_t^*, \mathcal{F}^t\}$ is a martingale difference sequence and either $\{\nabla_\theta m_t^*, \mathcal{F}^t\}$ is a martingale difference sequence or $\nabla_\theta \bar{M}_n^* = 0$, it suffices to show that these conditions imply

$$V_n^* = \text{var}[n^{-1/2} \sum_{t=1}^{n} \xi_t^*] = K_n^*,$$

where $\xi_t^* = m_t^* - \nabla_\theta' \bar{M}_n^* A_n^{*-1} s_t^*$. If $\{\nabla_\theta m_t^*, \mathcal{F}^t\}$ is a martingale difference sequence, $\nabla_\theta \bar{M}_n^* = n^{-1} \sum_{t=1}^{n} E(\nabla_\theta m_t^*) = 0$. Therefore $V_n^* = \text{var}[n^{-1/2} \sum_{t=1}^{n} m_t^*]$. When $\{m_t^*, \mathcal{F}^t\}$ is a martingale difference sequence, then $\text{var}[n^{-1/2} \sum_{t=1}^{n} m_t^*] = n^{-1} \sum_{t=1}^{n} E(m_t^* m_t^{*\prime}) = K_n^*$, so that $V_n^* = K_n^*$ as desired.

(iv) The conditions of (i) and (ii), Assumption 9.3 and $\{K_n^*\}$ uniformly positive definite ensure that the conditions of Theorem 9.7 hold, so that if $P_o \in \mathcal{P}_A^u$, $P_o[\mathcal{M}_n > k_n] \rightarrow 1$ for $\{k_n\} = o(n)$. □

PROOF OF COROLLARY 9.10: (i) By construction $\hat{J}_n = n^{-1} \sum_{t=1}^{n} \hat{\xi}_t \hat{\xi}_t'$ is a sequence of symmetric positive semi-definite matrices. For measurability, it suffices that $\hat{\xi}_t = m_t(X^t, \hat{\theta}_n, \hat{\pi}_n) - \nabla_\theta' \hat{M}_n \hat{A}_n^- s_t(X^t, \hat{\theta}_n)$

is measurable. The functions s_t and $\nabla' s_t$ are measurable given Assumptions 2.3 and 3.6 while m_t and $\nabla'_\theta m_t$ are measurable given Assumption 9.1. Given Assumption 9.2 $\hat{\pi}_n$ is measurable and $\hat{\theta}_n$ is measurable by the appropriate existence theorem (Theorem 2.12 or 2.15). Because compositions of measurable functions are measurable (Billingsley [1979, Theorem 13.1]), $\hat{\xi}_t$ and (therefore) $\hat{J}_n$ are measurable.

(ii) Now consider the consistency of $\hat{J}_n$. We write

$$\hat{J}_n = \hat{K}_n - \nabla'_\theta \hat{M}_n \hat{A}_n^- \hat{G}_n' - \hat{G}_n \hat{A}_n^- \nabla_\theta \hat{M}_n + \nabla'_\theta \hat{M}_n \hat{A}_n^- \hat{B}_n \hat{A}_n^{-\prime} \nabla_\theta \hat{M}_n ,$$

where $\hat{K}_n \equiv n^{-1} \sum_{t=1}^n \hat{m}_t \hat{m}_t'$, $\hat{G}_n \equiv n^{-1} \sum_{t=1}^n \hat{m}_t \hat{s}_t'$, $\hat{B}_n \equiv n^{-1} \sum_{t=1}^n \hat{s}_t \hat{s}_t'$. For $\hat{J}_n - J_n^* \to 0$, $prob-P_o$, it suffices that $\hat{K}_n - K_n^* \to 0$ $prob-P_o$, $\nabla_\theta \hat{M}_n - \nabla_\theta \bar{M}_n^* \to 0$ $prob-P_o$, $\hat{A}_n - A_n^* \to 0$ $prob-P_o$, $\hat{G}_n - G_n^* \to 0$ $prob-P_o$, and $\hat{B}_n - \bar{B}_n^* \to 0$ $prob-P_o$. In each case, these convergences follow as a consequence of Corollary 3.8, given that $\hat{\pi}_n - \pi_n^* \to 0$ $prob-P_o$ (Assumption 9.2) and $\hat{\theta}_n - \theta_n^* \to 0$ $prob-P_o$ (Theorem 3.5 or 3.10), and that the uniform law of large numbers holds for $m_t\, m_t'$ (Assumption 9.4) $\nabla_\theta m_t$ (Assumption 9.5), $\nabla' s_t$ (Assumption 3.8), $m_t\, s_t'$ (Assumption 9.6) and $s_t\, s_t'$ (Assumption 8.6). Therefore $\hat{J}_n - J_n^* \to 0$ $prob-P_o$, with

$$J_n^* = K_n^* - \nabla'_\theta \bar{M}_n^* A_n^{*-1} G_n^{*\prime} - G_n^* A_n^{*-1} \nabla_\theta \bar{M}_n^* + \nabla'_\theta \bar{M}_n^* A_n^{*-1} \bar{B}_n^* A_n^{*-1\prime} \nabla_\theta \bar{M}_n^* .$$

J_n^* is $O(1)$ given that K_n^*, $\nabla_\theta \bar{M}_n^*$, A_n^{*-1}, G_n^* and $\bar{B}_n^*$ are $O(1)$. The relevant assumptions are Assumption 9.4(a) (K_n^*), Assumption 9.5(a) ($\nabla_\theta \bar{M}_n^*$), Assumption 3.9 ($A_n^{*-1}$), Assumption 9.6(a) ($G_n^*$) and Assumption 8.6(a) ($\bar{B}_n^*$) and the compactness of $\Theta \times \Pi$.

(iii) (a) If $\{J_n^*\}$ is uniformly positive definite, then the conditions of Theorem 9.5 are satisfied for $\hat{J}_n$, and it follows immediately that $\mathcal{M}_n \overset{A}{\sim} N_2(a_n^*, V_n^*; J_n^{*-1})$ for $P_o \in \mathcal{P}_a^u$. If $P_o \in \mathcal{P}_o^i$ then $P_o \in \mathcal{P}_o^u$ and $J_n^* = V_n^*$, so that $\mathcal{M}_n \overset{A}{\sim} \chi_q^2$.

(b) The (constant unadjusted) R^2 for the regression of the constant unity on the explanatory variables $\hat{\xi}_t'$ may be written

$$R^2 = \iota' \hat{\xi} [\hat{\xi}' \hat{\xi}]^- \hat{\xi}' \iota / n = n^{-2} \iota' \hat{\xi} \hat{J}_n^- \hat{\xi}' \iota ,$$

where ι is an $n \times 1$ vector of ones, and $\hat{\xi}$ is the $n \times q$ matrix with rows $\hat{\xi}_t'$ and we use the fact that $\hat{J}_n = \hat{\xi}'\hat{\xi} / n$. Consequently,

$$nR^2 = \mathcal{M}_n + n^{-1}\,\iota'\,\hat{m}\,\hat{J}_n^-\,(\hat{\xi} - \hat{m})'\iota + n^{-1}\,\iota'(\hat{\xi} - \hat{m})\,\hat{J}_n^-\,\hat{m}'\,\iota$$

$$+\, n^{-1}\,\iota'\,(\hat{\xi} - \hat{m})\,\hat{J}_n^-\,(\hat{\xi} - \hat{m})'\iota\,,$$

where $\hat{m}$ is the $n \times q$ matrix with rows $\hat{m}'_t$. Now

$$n^{-1}\,\iota'\,\hat{m}\,\hat{J}_n^-\,(\hat{\xi} - \hat{m})'\,\iota = -\,(n^{-1/2}\textstyle\sum_{t=1}^n \hat{m}_t)\,\hat{J}_n^-\,(n^{-1/2}\sum_{t=1}^n \nabla'_\theta\,\hat{M}_n\,\hat{A}_n^-\,\hat{s}_t)\,.$$

Because $P_o \in \mathcal{P}_a^u$, it follows that $(n^{-1/2}\sum_{t=1}^n \hat{m}_t) = \sqrt{n}\,\hat{M}_n$ is $O_{P_o}(1)$ by Theorem 9.5. Because $\hat{J}_n - J_n^* \to 0$ $prob-P_o$ with $\{J_n^*\}$ $O(1)$ and uniformly positive definite, $\hat{J}_n^- - J_n^{*-1} \to 0$ $prob-P_o$, with $\{J_n^{*-1}\}$ $O(1)$. Consequently $\hat{J}_n^-$ is $O_{P_o}(1)$. Now $n^{-1/2}\sum_{t=1}^n \nabla'_\theta\,\hat{M}_n\,\hat{A}_n^-\,\hat{s}_t = \nabla'_\theta\,\hat{M}_n\,\hat{A}_n^-\,n^{-1/2}\sum_{t=1}^n \hat{s}_t$, and $\nabla_\theta\,\hat{M}_n$ and $\hat{A}_n^-$ are $O_{P_o}(1)$ by reasoning similar to that for $\hat{J}_n^-$. Finally, $n^{-1/2}\sum_{t=1}^n \hat{s}_t = o_{P_o}(1)$ under the conditions of Theorem 6.4 or 6.11. It follows that $n^{-1}\,\iota'\,\hat{m}\,\hat{J}_n^-\,(\hat{\xi} - \hat{m})'\iota \to 0$ $prob-P_o$. Similar reasoning yields $n^{-1}\,\iota(\hat{\xi} - \hat{m})\,\hat{J}_n^-\,(\hat{\xi} - \hat{m})'\iota \to 0$ $prob-P_o$, so that if $P_o \in \mathcal{P}_a^u$

$$nR^2 = \mathcal{M}_n + o_{P_o}(1)\,.$$

It follows immediately from the asymptotic equivalence lemma (White [1984a, Lemma 4.7]) that $nR^2 \overset{A}{\sim} N_2(a_n^*, V_n^*; J_n^{*-1})$. Because $\mathcal{M}_n \overset{A}{\sim} \chi_q^2$ when $P_o \in \mathcal{P}_o^i$, the asymptotic equivalence lemma also implies $nR^2 \overset{A}{\sim} \chi_q^2$.

To verify the statement that $\mathcal{P}_o^i$ contains all elements of $\mathcal{P}_o^u$ for which $\{\xi_t^* \equiv m_t^* - \nabla'_\theta\,\bar{M}_n^*\,A_n^{*-1}\,s_t^*,\ \mathcal{F}^t\}$ is a martingale difference sequence, it suffices to show that

$$V_n^* \equiv \text{var}\,[n^{-1/2}\sum_{t=1}^n \xi_t^*] = J_n^*\,.$$

Because $\{\xi_t^*, \mathcal{F}^t\}$ is a martingale difference sequence

$$\text{var}\,[n^{-1/2}\sum_{t=1}^n \xi_t^*] = n^{-1}\sum_{t=1}^n E(\xi_t^*\,\xi_t^{*\prime})$$

$$= n^{-1} \sum_{t=1}^{n} E([m_t^* - \nabla'_\theta \bar{M}_n^* A_n^{*-1} s_t^*] [m_t^* - \nabla'_\theta \bar{M}_n^* A_n^{*-1} s_t^*]')$$

$$= J_n^* .$$

(iv) The conditions of (i) and (ii), Assumption 9.3 and $\{J_n^*\}$ uniformly positive definite ensure that the conditions of Theorem 9.7 hold for $\mathcal{M}_n$, so that if $P_o \in \mathcal{P}_A^u$, $P_o[\mathcal{M}_n > k_n] \to 1$ for $\{k_n\} = o(n)$.

To show the same conclusion for $\mathcal{M}_n'$, it suffices to show that $\mathcal{M}_n - \mathcal{M}_n' \to 0$ $prob - P_o$, as $\mathcal{M}_n > k_n + \varepsilon$ and $|\mathcal{M}_n - \mathcal{M}_n'| < \varepsilon$ imply $\mathcal{M}_n' > k_n$. We give explicit argument for the QMLE. From (iii.b) we have

$$\mathcal{M}_n - \mathcal{M}_n' = \hat{M}_n \hat{J}_n^- \nabla'_\theta \hat{M}_n \hat{A}_n^- (\sum_{t=1}^{n} \hat{s}_t) + (\sum_{t=1}^{n} \hat{s}_t') \hat{A}_n^{-\prime} \nabla_\theta \hat{M}_n \hat{J}_n^- \hat{M}_n'$$
$$- (\sum_{t=1}^{n} \hat{s}_t') \hat{A}_n^{-\prime} \nabla_\theta \hat{M}_n \hat{J}_n^- \nabla'_\theta \hat{M}_n \hat{A}_n^- (n^{-1} \sum_{t=1}^{n} \hat{s}_t) .$$

The conditions given ensure that $\hat{M}_n$, $\hat{J}_n^-$, $\nabla_\theta \hat{M}_n$ and $\hat{A}_n^-$ are $O_{P_o}(1)$. Thus, it suffices to establish that $\sum_{t=1}^{n} \hat{s}_t$ is $o_{P_o}(1)$.

Let $\{n'\}$ be an arbitrary sequence. Because $\hat{\theta}_n - \theta_n^* \to 0$ $prob - P_o$, it follows that there exists a further subsequence $\{n''\}$ such that $\hat{\theta}_{n''} - \theta_{n''}^* \to 0$ $a.s. - P_o$. Because $\theta_{n''}^*$ is interior to Θ uniformly in n'' given Assumption 3.2′, it follows that $\hat{\theta}_{n''}$ is interior to Θ $a.a.$ n'' $a.s. - P_o$. By definition, $\hat{\theta}_{n''}$ maximizes $L_{n''}(X^{n''}, \theta)$; interiority of $\hat{\theta}_{n''}$ implies $\nabla L_{n''}(X^{n''}, \hat{\theta}_{n''}) = n''^{-1} \sum_{t=1}^{n''} \hat{s}_t = 0$ $a.a. n''$ $a.s. - P_o$, or $\sum_{t=1}^{n''} \hat{s}_t = 0$ $a.a.$ n'' $a.s. - P_o$. Because $\{n'\}$ is an arbitrary subsequence, it follows from the subsequence theorem that $\sum_{t=1}^{n} \hat{s}_t \to 0$ $prob - P_o$, and the result follows.

An analogous argument holds for the 2SQMLE under Assumption 3.2′ for $\bar{L}_{1n}$ and $\bar{L}_{2n}$ as in Theorem 6.11. □

PROOF OF COROLLARY 9.11: (i) and (ii) The proof is analogous to that of Corollary 9.10(i, ii), except that we ignore $\nabla_\theta \hat{M}_n$ and $\hat{A}_n^-$, allowing us to dispense with Assumptions 9.1(b) and 9.5, Assumptions 3.8 and 3.9, and to replace Assumption 3.6 with Assumption 2.4.

(iii) (a) The result follows immediately from Theorem 9.5. (b) The argument is entirely analogous to that of Corollary 9.10(iii.b). For algebraic details, see the proof of Theorem 3.3 of White [1987].

To show that $\mathcal{P}_o^i$ includes all elements of $\mathcal{P}_o^u$ for which $\{s_t^*, \mathcal{F}^t\}$, $\{m_t^*, \mathcal{F}^t\}$, $\{\nabla' s_t^* + s_t^* s_t^{*\prime}, \mathcal{F}^t\}$ and $\{\nabla'_\theta m_t^* + m_t^* s_t^{*\prime}, \mathcal{F}^t\}$ are martingale difference sequences, it suffices to show that $V_n^* = K_n^* - G_n^* \bar{B}_n^{*-1} G_n^{*\prime}$.

As in the preceding result $\{\xi_t^* = m_t^* - \nabla'_\theta \bar{M}_n^* A_n^{*-1} s_t^*, \mathcal{F}^t\}$ is a martingale difference sequence, a fact ensured by the assumptions that $\{m_t^*, \mathcal{F}^t\}$ and $\{s_t^*, \mathcal{F}^t\}$ are martingale difference sequences. Again we have

$$V_n^* = K_n^* - \nabla'_\theta \bar{M}_n^* A_n^{*-1} G_n^{*\prime} - G_n^* A_n^{*-1\prime} \nabla_\theta \bar{M}_n^* + \nabla'_\theta \bar{M}_n^* A_n^{*-1} \bar{B}_n^* A_n^{*-1\prime} \nabla_\theta \bar{M}_n^*,$$

and the desired result follows if $\nabla'_\theta \bar{M}_n^* = -G_n^*$ and $A_n^* = -\bar{B}_n^*$.

By assumption, $E(\nabla'_\theta m_t^* + m_t^* s_t^{*\prime} \mid X^{t-1}) = 0$, so that

$$\begin{aligned}\nabla'_\theta \bar{M}_n^* &= n^{-1} \sum_{t=1}^{n} E(\nabla'_\theta m_t^*) = n^{-1} \sum_{t=1}^{n} E(E(\nabla'_\theta m_t^* \mid X^{t-1}) \\ &= -n^{-1} \sum_{t=1}^{n} E(E(m_t^* s_t^{*\prime} \mid X^{t-1})) = -n^{-1} \sum_{t=1}^{n} E(m_t^* s_t^{*\prime}) \\ &= -G_n^* .\end{aligned}$$

Similarly, $E(\nabla' s_t^* + s_t^* s_t^{*\prime} \mid X^{t-1}) = 0$, so that

$$\begin{aligned}A_n^* &= n^{-1} \sum_{t=1}^{n} E(\nabla' s_t^*) = -n^{-1} \sum_{t=1}^{n} E(s_t^* s_t^{*\prime}) \\ &= -\bar{B}_n^* .\end{aligned}$$

Substituting these equalities into the above expression for V_n^* gives $V_n^* = K_n^* - G_n^* \bar{B}_n^{*-1} G_n^{*\prime} = J_n^*$ as desired. The result for $\nabla'_\theta \bar{M}_n^* A_n^{*-1} = G_n^* B_n^{*-1}$ follows by direct substitution into the expression for V_n^*.

(iv) The argument is analogous to that of Corollary 9.10(iv). □

PROOF OF COROLLARY 9.12: (i, ii) The proof for $\hat{J}_n$ is identical to that of Corollary 9.9(i, ii) with $\hat{j}_t$ replacing $\hat{m}_t$. We use Assumption 9.7(a) in place of Assumption 9.1(a) and Assumption 9.8 in place of Assumption 9.4.

The proof for $\hat{\sigma}_n^2$ is also identical to that of Corollary 9.9(i, ii) with $\bar{l}^{-1} \sum_{i=1}^{\bar{l}} \hat{v}_{ti}$ replacing $\hat{m}_t$. Assumption 9.7(a) is used in place of Assumption 9.1(a) and Assumption 9.9 is used in place of Assumption 9.4.

(iii) The (constant unadjusted) R^2 for the regression of $\hat{v}_{ti}$ on $\hat{j}_{ti}'$ can be written

$$R^2 = \hat{v}' \hat{j}[\hat{j}'\hat{j}]^- \hat{j}'\hat{v} / \hat{v}'\hat{v}$$

where $\hat{v}$ is the $n\tilde{l} \times 1$ vector with elements $\hat{v}_{ti}$ and $\hat{j}$ is the $n\tilde{l} \times q$ matrix with rows $\hat{j}_{ti}'$ $(1 \times q)$, so that with $\hat{\sigma}_n^2 = \hat{v}'\hat{v} / n\tilde{l}$

$$n\tilde{l}\ R^2 = n\ \hat{M}_n'\ \hat{J}_n^-\ \hat{M}_n / \hat{\sigma}_n^2 .$$

This is of the form treated by Theorem 9.5, with $\hat{J}_n$ replaced with $\hat{\sigma}_n^2\ \hat{J}_n$. From (i) and (ii), this choice for $\hat{J}_n$ satisfies the conditions of Theorem 9.5, so that $\ddot{\mathcal{M}}_n = n\tilde{l}\ R^2 \overset{A}{\sim} N(a_n^*, V_n^*; \ddot{J}_n^{*-1} / \sigma_n^{*2})$ for $P_o \in \mathcal{P}_a^u$. If $P_o \in \mathcal{P}_o^i$, then $P_o \in \mathcal{P}_o^u$ and $V_n^* = \sigma_n^{*2}\ \ddot{J}_n^*$ so that $\ddot{\mathcal{M}}_n \overset{A}{\sim} \chi_q^2$.

To verify that $\mathcal{P}_o^i$ contains all elements of $\mathcal{P}_o^u$ for which $\{m_t^*, \mathcal{F}^t\}$ and $\{\nabla_\theta\, m_t^*, \mathcal{F}^t\}$ are martingale difference sequences and for some $\sigma_o^2 > 0$, $E(v_t^*\ v_t^{*\prime} \mid \tilde{X}^{t-1}) = \sigma_o^2\ I_{\tilde{l}}$, $t = 1, 2, \ldots$, it suffices to show that $V_n^* = \sigma_n^{*2}\ \ddot{J}_n^*$ under these conditions. As in the proof of Corollary 9.9(iii) we have that

$$V_n^* = n^{-1} \sum_{t=1}^{n} E(m_t^*\ m_t^{*\prime}) ,$$

given that $\{m_t^*, \mathcal{F}^t\}$ and $\{\nabla_\theta\, m_t^*, \mathcal{F}^t\}$ are martingale difference sequences. Given Assumption 9.7, $m_t^* = j_t^*\ v_t^*$ so that $V_n^* = n^{-1} \sum_{t=1}^{n} E(j_t^*\ v_t^*\ v_t^{*\prime}\ j_t^{*\prime})$. By the law of iterated expectations

$$\begin{aligned} E(j_t^*\ v_t^*\ v_t^{*\prime}\ j_t^{*\prime}) &= E(E(j_t^*\ v_t^*\ v_t^{*\prime}\ j_t^{*\prime} \mid \tilde{X}^{t-1})) \\ &= E(j_t^*\ E(v_t^*\ v_t^{*\prime} \mid \tilde{X}^{t-1})\ j_t^{*\prime}) \\ &= \sigma_o^2\ E(j_t^*\ j_t^{*\prime}) , \end{aligned}$$

where the last equality follows form the assumption that $E(v_t^*\ v_t^{*\prime} \mid \tilde{X}^{t-1}) = \sigma_o^2\ I_{\tilde{l}}$ for some $\sigma_o^2 > 0$. Hence

$$V_n^* = \sigma_o^2\ \ddot{J}_n^* .$$

The conclusion follows if $\sigma_n^{*2} = \sigma_o^2$. From (ii), $\sigma_n^{*2} = (n\tilde{l})^{-1} \sum_{t=1}^{n} \sum_{i=1}^{\tilde{l}} E(v_{ti}^{*2}) = (n\tilde{l})^{-1} \sum_{t=1}^{n} tr\, E(v_t^* v_t^{*\prime}) = (n\tilde{l})^{-1} \sum_{t=1}^{n} \sigma_o^2\, tr\, I_{\tilde{l}} = \sigma_o^2$ given that $E(v_t^* v_t^{*\prime} \mid \tilde{X}^{t-1}) = \sigma_o^2 I_{\tilde{l}}$. The result with $\nabla_\theta \bar{M}_n^* = 0$ follows similarly and the proof is complete.

(iv) The proof is identical to that of Corollary 9.9(iv). □

PROOF OF COROLLARY 9.13: (i, ii) The proof for $\hat{J}_n$ is analogous to that of Corollary 9.11(i, ii), with i_t replacing s_t and j_t replacing m_t. We use the definition of generalized residuals and Assumption 9.7(a) to establish measurability and Assumptions 9.8 and 9.10 in place of Assumptions 8.6, 9.4 and 9.6.

The proof for $\hat{\sigma}_n^2$ is identical to that of Corollary 9.11(i, ii) with the definition of generalized residual replacing Assumption 9.7 and Assumption 9.11 used in place of Assumption 9.9.

(iii) (a) If $\{\ddot{J}_n^*\}$ is uniformly positive definite and $\sigma_n^{*2} > \varepsilon > 0$ *a.a. n*, then $J_n^* = \sigma_n^{*2} \ddot{J}_n^*$ satisfies the conditions of Theorem 9.5, and it follows immediately that $\ddot{\mathcal{M}}_n \overset{A}{\sim} N_2(a_n^*, V_n^*; \ddot{J}_n^{*-1}/\sigma_n^{*2})$ if $P_o \in \mathcal{P}_a^u$, and $\ddot{\mathcal{M}}_n \overset{A}{\sim} \chi_q^2$ if $P_o \in \mathcal{P}_o^i$.

(b) The argument is entirely analogous to that of Corollary 9.11(iii.b), using algebraic details as given in the proof of Theorem 3.3 of White [1987].

To show that $\mathcal{P}_o^i$ contains all elements of $\mathcal{P}_o^u$ for which $\{u_t^*, \tilde{\mathcal{F}}^t\}$ is a martingale difference sequence and $u_t^* = v_t^*$, $E(u_t^* u_t^{*\prime} \mid \tilde{X}^{t-1}) = \sigma_o^2 I_l$ and $i_t^* = -E(\nabla_\theta u_t^* \mid \tilde{X}^{t-1})/\sigma_o^2$, $t = 1, 2, \ldots$, it suffices to show that $V_n^* = \sigma_n^{*2} \ddot{J}_n^*$. Now $\xi_t^* = m_t^* - \nabla_\theta' \bar{M}_n^* A_n^{*-1} s_t^* = (j_t^* - \nabla_\theta' \bar{M}_n^* A_n^{*-1} i_t^*) u_t^*$ given Assumption 9.7, and generalized residuals $u_t = v_t$. Because $\{u_t^*, \tilde{\mathcal{F}}^t\}$ is a martingale difference sequence, it follows that $\{\xi_t^*, \mathcal{F}^t\}$ is a martingale difference sequence. Consequently $V_n^* = n^{-1} \sum_{t=1}^{n} E(\xi_t^* \xi_t^{*\prime})$. Substituting for ξ_t^*, we have

$$V_n^* = n^{-1} \sum_{t=1}^{n} E((j_t^* - \nabla_\theta' \bar{M}_n^* A_n^{*-1} i_t^*) u_t^* u_t^{*\prime} (j_t^{*\prime} - i_t^{*\prime} A_n^{*-1\prime} \nabla_\theta \bar{M}_n^*)) .$$

Using the law of iterated expectations and the assumption that $E(u_t^* u_t^{*\prime} \mid \tilde{X}^{t-1}) = \sigma_o^2 I_l$, we may write

$$V_n^* = \sigma_o^2 (n^{-1} \sum_{t=1}^{n} E(j_t^* j_t^{*\prime}) - \nabla_\theta' \bar{M}_n^* A_n^{*-1} n^{-1} \sum_{t=1}^{n} E(i_t^* j_t^{*\prime})$$

$$- n^{-1} \sum_{t=1}^{n} E(j_t^* \, i_t^{*\prime}) \, A_n^{*-1\prime} \, \nabla_\theta \, \bar{M}_n^*$$

$$+ \nabla_\theta' \, \bar{M}_n^* \, A_n^{*-1} \, (n^{-1} \sum_{t=1}^{n} i_t^* \, i_t^{*\prime}) \, A_n^{*-1\prime} \, \nabla_\theta \, \bar{M}_n^*)$$

$$= \sigma_o^2 \, \ddot{K}_n^* - \nabla_\theta' \, \bar{M}_n^* \, A_n^{*-1} \, \sigma_o^2 \, \ddot{G}_n^{*\prime} - \sigma_o^2 \, \ddot{G}_n^* \, A_n^{*-1\prime} \, \nabla_\theta \, \bar{M}_n^*$$

$$+ \nabla_\theta' \, \bar{M}_n^* \, A_n^{*-1} \, \sigma_o^2 \, \ddot{B}_n^* \, A_n^{*-1\prime} \, \nabla_\theta \, \bar{M}_n^* \, .$$

The desired result follows if $\nabla_\theta' \, \bar{M}_n^* = - \sigma_o^2 \, \ddot{G}_n^*$ and $A_n^{*-1} = - \sigma_o^2 \, \ddot{B}_n^*$ under the conditions given, provided that $\sigma_n^{*2} = \sigma_o^2$. This last equality holds as in the proof of Corollary 9.12(iii).

Because $m_t = j_t u_t$, we have $\nabla_\theta' \, m_t = j_t \, \nabla_\theta' \, u_t + (u_t' \otimes I_q) \, \nabla_\theta' \, j_t$. Consequently, $E(\nabla_\theta' \, m_t^* \mid \tilde{X}^{t-1}) = j_t^* \, E(\nabla_\theta' \, u_t^* \mid \tilde{X}^{t-1})$, as

$$E((u_t^{*\prime} \otimes I_q) \, \nabla_\theta' \, j_t^* \mid \tilde{X}^{t-1}) = E(u_t^{*\prime} \otimes I_q \mid \tilde{X}^{t-1}) \, \nabla_\theta' \, j_t^* = 0 \, ,$$

given that $\{ u_t^* , \tilde{\mathcal{F}}^t \}$ is a martingale difference sequence. Given that $i_t^* = - E(\nabla_\theta \, u_t^* \mid \tilde{X}^{t-1}) / \sigma_o^2$, it follows that $E(\nabla_\theta' \, m_t^* \mid \tilde{X}^{t-1}) = - \sigma_o^2 \, j_t^* \, i_t^{*\prime}$, which implies

$$\nabla_\theta' \, \bar{M}_n^* = - \sigma_o^2 \, \ddot{G}_n^*$$

as desired, upon taking expectations and summing.

Similarly, because $s_t = i_t \, u_t$, we have $\nabla_\theta' \, s_t = i_t \, \nabla_\theta' \, u_t + (u_t' \otimes I_p) \, \nabla_\theta' \, i_t$, so that $E(\nabla_\theta' \, s_t^* \mid \tilde{X}^{t-1}) = i_t^* \, E(\nabla_\theta' \, u_t^* \mid \tilde{X}^{t-1}) = - \sigma_o^2 \, i_t^* \, i_t^{*\prime}$. Taking expectations and summing gives

$$A_n^* = - \sigma_o^2 \, \ddot{B}_n^*$$

as desired, and the proof is complete.

(iv) The proof is directly analogous to that of Corollary 9.9(iv) and Corollary 9.10(iv), with j_t replacing s_t and j_t replacing m_t. □

PROOF OF COROLLARY 9.14: We verify the conditions of Corollary 9.9 for $\underset{\sim}{m}_t = (j_t - \gamma' \mathcal{V}_t) \, v_t$.

(i) The conditions of Theorem 2.12 or 2.15 are assumed. The measurability and continuity conditions of Assumption 9.1(a) hold for $\underset{\sim}{m}_t$ given Assumptions 9.7(a) and 9.12(a) because sums and products of measurable or continuous functions are again measurable or continuous. Assumption 9.2(a) ensures the measurability of $\hat{\pi}_n$; the measurability of $\hat{\gamma}_n = [\Sigma_{t=1}^n \hat{\mathcal{V}}_t \hat{\mathcal{V}}_t']^- \Sigma_{t=1}^n \hat{\mathcal{V}}_t \hat{j}_t$ follows from the measurability of $\hat{\theta}_n$ (Theorem 2.12 or 2.15) and $\hat{\pi}_n$, the fact that compositions of measurable functions are measurable and the measurability of products and sums of measurable functions. Thus $\underset{\sim}{\hat{\pi}}_n = (\hat{\pi}_n', \hat{\gamma}_n')'$ is measurable, so that Assumption 9.2(a) holds for $\underset{\sim}{\hat{\pi}}_n$. The proof of (i) is complete.

(ii) The conditions of Theorem 3.5 or 3.10 are assumed. Assumption 9.2(b) ensures that $\hat{\pi}_n - \pi_n^* \to 0$ $prob - P_o$. Assumptions 9.13 and 9.14 suffice to establish $\hat{\gamma}_n - \gamma_n^* \to 0$ $prob - P_o$ via Corollary 3.8. Assumption 9.2(b) thus holds for $\underset{\sim}{\pi}_n^* = (\pi_n^{*\prime}, \gamma_n^{*\prime})'$. Assumption 9.4 is directly assumed for $\underset{\sim}{m}_t$, and the proof of (ii) is complete.

(iii) Assumptions 9.7(b) and 9.12(b) are easily seen to suffice for Assumption 9.1(b), and the other conditions are imposed directly. It is verified in the text that $\nabla_\theta \bar{M}_n^* = 0$, and the proof of (iii) is done.

(iv) The required conditions are imposed directly. □

PROOF OF THEOREM 9.15: (i) Given Assumptions 2.3, 9.1(a) and 9.15(a), it follows that $(1 + \upsilon_t) f_{1t}$ is measurable $- \mathcal{B}^{vt}$ for each (β, θ, π) in $\mathcal{B} \times \Theta \times \Pi$ (Theorem 13.1 of Billingsley [1979]) and continuous on $\mathcal{B} \times \Theta \times \Pi$ $a.s. - P_o$ (Theorems 20.6 and 20.8 of Bartle [1976], applied pointwise to each $x^t \in F_t \in \mathbb{B}^{vt}$, $P_o(F_t) = 1$). From Definition 4.3 and Assumption 9.15(a) $(1 + \upsilon_t) f_{1t}$ is integrable with respect to ζ_t, and for all (β, θ, π) in $\mathcal{B} \times \Theta \times \Pi$

$$\mathcal{Y}_t(\tilde{x}^{t-1}, \beta, \theta, \pi) \equiv \int (1 + \upsilon_t[\beta' m_t(x^t, \theta, \pi)]) \, f_{1t}(x^t, \theta) \, d\zeta_t(y_t)$$
$$\leq 1 + \Delta < \infty ,$$
$$\mathcal{Y}_t(\tilde{x}^{t-1}, \beta, \theta, \pi) \geq \delta, \qquad t = 1, 2, \ldots ,$$

because $\upsilon_t : \mathbb{R} \to [-1 + \delta, \Delta]$, $0 < \delta \leq 1$, $\Delta < \infty$ and $\int f_{1t}(x^t, \theta) \, d\zeta_t(y_t) = 1$ for all θ in Θ and $\tilde{x}^{t-1}$ in $\mathbb{R}^{vt-l}$.

For each (β, θ, π) in $\mathcal{B} \times \Theta \times \Pi$, it follows from Lemma 2.6 of Bartle [1966] that $f_{2t} = (1 + \upsilon_t) f_{1t} / \mathcal{Y}_t$ is measurable $- \mathcal{B}^{vt}$, and it follows from

Theorems 20.6 and 20.8 of Bartle [1976] that f_{2t} is continuous on $\mathcal{B} \times \Theta \times \Pi$ $a.s. - P_o$.

Because $\upsilon_t \geq -1 + \delta$ and $\mathcal{Y}_t \geq \delta$, it follows that $f_{2t} : \mathbb{R}^{vt} \times \mathcal{B} \times \Theta \times \Pi \to \mathbb{R}^+$, so that Assumption 2.3 is satisfied for f_{2t}.

To verify that $\mathcal{S}_2 = \{ f_{2t} \}$ specifies dependent variables $\{ Y_t \}$ with respect to $\{ \zeta_t \}$, we verify Definition 4.3 for f_{2t}. We have for all $\tilde{x}^{t-1}$ in $\mathbb{R}^{vt-l}$ and all (β, θ, π) in $\mathcal{B} \times \Theta \times \Pi$

$$\int_{\mathbb{R}^l} f_{2t}(x^t, \beta, \theta, \pi)\, d\zeta_t(y_t)$$

$$= \int (1 + \upsilon_t[\beta' m_t(x^t, \theta)])\, f_{1t}(x^t, \theta)\, d\zeta_t(y_t) / \mathcal{Y}_t(\tilde{x}^{t-1}, \beta, \theta, \pi)$$

$$= \mathcal{Y}_t(\tilde{x}^{t-1}, \beta, \theta, \pi) / \mathcal{Y}_t(\tilde{x}^{t-1}, \beta, \theta, \pi)$$
$$= 1 .$$

Setting $\beta = 0$ and using the facts that $\upsilon_t(0) = 0$, $\mathcal{Y}_t(\tilde{x}^{t-1}, 0, \theta, \pi) = 1$, we have for every measure $\tilde{\zeta}_t$ on $(\mathbb{R}^{\tilde{l}_t}, \mathbb{B}^{\tilde{l}_t})$ that

$$\int_{\mathbb{R}^{\tilde{l}_t}} f_{2t}(x^t, 0, \theta, \pi)\, d\tilde{\zeta}_t(\tilde{y}_t) = \int_{\mathbb{R}^{\tilde{l}_t}} f_{1t}(x^t, \theta)\, d\tilde{\zeta}_t(\tilde{y}_t)$$
$$\neq 1$$

for some θ in Θ or $\tilde{w}_t$ in $\mathbb{R}^{\tilde{k}_t}$ by Definition 4.3 for $\mathcal{S}_1$. Definition 4.3 thus holds for $\mathcal{S}_2$.

Because for all x^t in $\mathbb{R}^{vt}$

$$f_{2t}(x^t, 0, \theta, \pi) = (1 + \upsilon_t(0))\, f_{1t}(x^t, \theta) / \mathcal{Y}_t(\tilde{x}^{t-1}, 0, \theta, \pi)$$
$$= f_{1t}(x^t, \theta) ,$$

it follows immediately that $\hat{\theta}_n = \text{argmax}_\Theta\, L_{1n}(X^n, \theta) = n^{-1} \sum_{t=1}^n \log f_{1t}(X^t, \theta)$ is also the solution to the problem

$$\max_{\theta \in \Theta} L_{2n}(X^n, 0, \theta, \pi) = n^{-1} \sum_{t=1}^{n} \log f_{2t}(X^t, 0, \theta, \pi)$$

for all π in Π.

(ii) By definition, $\log f_{2t} = \log(1 + \upsilon_t) + \log f_{1t} - \log \mathcal{Y}_t$. Because f_{1t} doesn't depend on β, we have for all β in an open neighborhood of zero that

$$\nabla_\beta \log f_{2t}(x^t, \beta, \theta, \pi) = \nabla_\beta \log[1 + \upsilon_t(\beta' m_t(x^t, \theta, \pi))]$$

$$- \nabla_\beta \log \mathcal{Y}_t(\tilde{x}^{t-1}, \beta, \theta, \pi)$$

$$= m_t(x^t, \theta, \pi)\, \dot{\upsilon}_t(\beta' m_t(x^t, \theta, \pi)) / [1 + \upsilon_t(\beta' m_t(x^t, \theta, \pi))]$$

$$- \nabla_\beta \mathcal{Y}_t(\tilde{x}^{t-1}, \beta, \theta, \pi) / \mathcal{Y}(\tilde{x}^{t-1}, \beta, \theta, \pi)$$

for all x^t, θ and π (where $\dot{\upsilon}$ exists by Assumption 9.15(b)), provided that $\nabla_\beta \mathcal{Y}_t(\tilde{x}^{t-1}, \cdot, \theta, \pi)$ exists. By Theorem 16.8(ii) of Billingsley [1979], it suffices that there exists $\bar{d}_{ti}(x^t, \theta, \pi)$ such that $\int \bar{d}_{ti}(x^t, \theta, \pi)\, d\zeta_t < \infty$ and for all β in a neighborhood of zero $| m_{ti}(x^t, \theta, \pi)\, \dot{\upsilon}_t(\beta' m_t(x^t, \theta, \pi))\, f_{1t}(x^t, \theta) | < \bar{d}_{ti}(x^t, \theta, \pi)$, $i = 1, \ldots, q$. Because $\dot{\upsilon}_t$ is bounded on $\mathbb{R}$ uniformly in t, it suffices that $\int | m_{ti}(x^t, \theta, \pi) | f_{1t}(x^t, \theta)\, d\zeta_t(y_t) < \infty$, $i = 1, \ldots, q$. But this is Assumption 9.16(a), so by Billingsley [1979, Theorem 16.8(ii)] we have

$$\nabla_\beta \mathcal{Y}_t(\tilde{x}^{t-1}, \beta, \theta, \pi)$$

$$= \int m_t(x^t, \theta, \pi)\, \dot{\upsilon}_t(\beta' m_t(x^t, \theta, \pi))\, f_{1t}(x^t, \theta)\, d\zeta_t(y_t).$$

Because $\dot{\upsilon}_t(0) = 1$ and $\upsilon_t(0) = 0$ by Assumption 9.15, we have

$$\nabla_\beta \log f_{2t}(x^t, 0, \theta, \pi)$$

$$= m_t(x^t, \theta, \pi) - \int m_t(x^t, \theta, \pi)\, f_{1t}(x^t, \theta)\, d\zeta_t(y_t).$$

The second term vanishes given Assumption 9.16(b) so that

$$\nabla_\beta \log f_{2t}(x^t, 0, \theta, \pi) = m_t(x^t, \theta, \pi)$$

as claimed. The numerical equivalence of the Lagrange multiplier statistics follows immediately. □

CHAPTER 10

Applications of m-Testing

In this chapter we see how a number of leading specification testing procedures fall into the m-testing framework. These procedures are the Lagrange Multiplier test, Newey's [1985] conditional moment test, the Hausman [1978] test, Cox's [1961, 1962] test of non-nested hypotheses, and the encompassing tests (Hendry and Richard [1982], Mizon [1984] and Mizon and Richard [1986]). For each case we find indicators $\hat{M}_n = n^{-1} \sum_{t=1}^{n} m_t (X^t , \hat{\theta}_n , \hat{\pi}_n)$ and covariance matrix estimators $\hat{J}_n$ such that the test statistic of interest either equals or converges in probability to $\mathcal{M}_n = n \hat{M}'_n \hat{J}_n^- \hat{M}_n$.

Having identified the indicators $\{ m_t \}$ and the objects corresponding to $\hat{\theta}_n$ and $\hat{\pi}_n$, the theory of Chapter 9 applies immediately to establish asymptotic properties of those tests under the null and locally alternative hypotheses. Moreover, the results of Sections 9.2 and 9.3 provide results for a variety of alternative versions of the original tests.

To avoid getting bogged down in technicalities any more than necessary, the discussion of this chapter focuses mainly on heuristics and does not provide every last detail required for stating formal results.

10.1 The Lagrange Multiplier Test

The Lagrange multiplier test has been championed by Engle [1982b] and Bera and Jarque [1982], among others, as a general and powerful tool for detecting model misspecifications. The recent book of Godfrey [1988] gives an extensive treatment of the Lagrange multiplier approach to specification testing. To construct specification tests based on $\mathcal{LM}_n$, one treats the model to be tested as a restricted version of a broader parametric model that exhibits specific features absent in the restricted model.

For example, a regression model may be tested for the misspecification of neglected autocorrelation in the regression disturbances (a form of dynamic misspecification) by formulating a broader model that parameterizes the autocorrelation in a specific way, say as an ARMA(p, q) process. The absence of autocorrelation amounts to correct specification of the original model in this regard, expressible as a specific restriction on the parameters of the broader model, say $r(\theta_o) = 0$, where r selects the parameters appearing in the ARMA(p, q) structure. Lagrange multiplier tests constructed in this way have been discussed by Godfrey [1978a, b]. Another possibility is to test a regression model for neglected heteroskedasticity in the disturbances. As in the case of autocorrelation, a broader model is formulated that parameterizes the heteroskedasticity. The absence of heteroskedasticity (correct specification) can again be formulated as a specific restriction $r(\theta_o) = 0$ on the parameters of the broader model. This approach is taken by Breusch and Pagan [1979]. Yet another common use of $\mathcal{LM}_n$ is to test a regression model for the omission of relevant explanatory variables (e.g. variables in $\tilde{X}^{t-1}$ omitted from W_t). Again, a broader parametric model is specified that allows particular explanatory variables to enter the model. The absence of these variables (correct specification) is again a specific restriction of the form $r(\theta_o) = 0$. This case is discussed by Engle [1982b].

Engle [1982b], Bera and Jarque [1982], and Godfrey [1988] give numerous other applications of the $\mathcal{LM}_n$ statistic as a tool for detecting model misspecification. Among its primary advantages are its relative ease of computation, and the clear formulation of the alternative against which the test will have power (the nature of the contemplated misspecification).

To see how the $\mathcal{LM}_n$ statistic falls into the m-testing framework, recall that

$$\mathcal{M}_n \equiv n \nabla' \tilde{L}_n \nabla^2 \tilde{L}_n^- \tilde{R}_n' (\tilde{R}_n \tilde{C}_n \tilde{R}_n')^- \tilde{R}_n \nabla^2 \tilde{L}_n^- \nabla \tilde{L}_n .$$

Theorem 9.5 immediately suggests the correspondences

$$\hat{M}_n = \tilde{R}_n \nabla^2 \tilde{L}_n^- \nabla \tilde{L}_n$$

$$\hat{J}_n = \tilde{R}_n \tilde{C}_n \tilde{R}_n' .$$

Now $\nabla \tilde{L}_n = n^{-1} \sum_{t=1}^n s_t(X^t, \tilde{\theta}_n)$, so that

$$\hat{M}_n = n^{-1} \sum_{t=1}^{n} \tilde{R}_n \nabla^2 \tilde{L}_n^- s_t(X^t, \tilde{\theta}_n) .$$

Because $\hat{M}_n \equiv n^{-1} \sum_{t=1}^n m_t(X^t, \hat{\theta}_n, \hat{\pi}_n)$, we take $m_t(X^t, \hat{\theta}_n, \hat{\pi}_n)$ =

$\tilde{R}_n \nabla^2 \tilde{L}_n^- s_t(X^t, \tilde{\theta}_n)$. Obviously, X^t plays the identical role on either side of the equality. It is also straightforward to see that choosing $\hat{\pi}_n = vec\ \tilde{R}_n \nabla^2 \tilde{L}_n^-$ is consistent with Assumptions 9.1 and 9.2. It is then tempting to identify $\hat{\theta}_n$ with $\tilde{\theta}_n$, but this is inappropriate because $\tilde{\theta}_n$ is a constrained estimator with a degenerate asymptotic distribution. Instead, we use the fact that the constrained estimator can generally be represented as $\tilde{\theta}_n = d_n(\hat{\gamma}_n)$ for a suitable function d_n (see Chapter 7), where $\hat{\gamma}_n$ is an unconstrained QMLE obtained from a model that satisfies the relevant conditions of Definitions 9.3 and 9.4. Consequently, we identify $\hat{\theta}_n$ with $\hat{\gamma}_n$, and for clarity we write

$$m_t(X^t, \hat{\gamma}_n, \hat{\pi}_n) = \tilde{R}_n \nabla^2 \tilde{L}_n^- s_t(X^t, d_n(\hat{\gamma}_n))$$

with $\hat{\pi}_n = vec\ \tilde{R}_n \nabla^2 \tilde{L}_n^-$, $\hat{\theta}_n = \hat{\gamma}_n$. Note that the appearance of d_n in the arguments of s_t implies that m_t depends on n as well as t.

To apply Theorem 9.5 requires checking Assumptions 9.1 and 9.2 and the other conditions of Definitions 9.3 and 9.4. Our choice for m_t is measurable and continuously differentiable as required by Assumption 9.1 given Assumptions 2.3 and 3.6 (restricting s_t) and Assumption 7.1 (for d_n, uniformly in n). For Assumption 9.2 we require $\{\pi_n^*\}$ such that $\hat{\pi}_n - \pi_n^* \to 0$ $prob - P_o$. This is generally satisfied by $\pi_n^* = vec\ R_n^* \nabla^2 \bar{L}_n^{*-1}$, where $R_n^* = R_n(d_n(\gamma_n^*))$, $\nabla^2 \bar{L}_n^* = \nabla^2 \bar{L}_n(d_n(\gamma_n^*))$.

The role of conditions 9.3(i) and 9.3(ii), (9.4(i) and 9.4(ii)) is to specify the probability measures belonging to the null (local alternative) hypothesis associated with a particular m-test. The first requirement for either $P^o \in \mathcal{P}_o^u$ or $P^o \in \mathcal{P}_a^u$ is that

$$\sqrt{n}\, \hat{M}_n = n^{-1/2} \sum_{t=1}^{n} m_t^* + \nabla_\gamma' \bar{M}_n^* \sqrt{n}(\hat{\gamma}_n - \gamma_n^*) + o_{P^o}(1) .$$

Now, a mean value expansion of $\nabla \tilde{L}_n$ around γ_n^* gives

$$\sqrt{n}\, \tilde{R}_n \nabla^2 \tilde{L}_n^- \nabla \tilde{L}_n = \tilde{R}_n \nabla^2 \tilde{L}_n^- n^{-1/2} \sum_{t=1}^{n} s_t(X^t, d_n((\hat{\gamma}_n))$$

$$= \tilde{R}_n \nabla^2 \tilde{L}_n^- \left[n^{-1/2} \sum_{t=1}^{n} s_t(X^t, d_n(\gamma_n^*)) + \nabla^2 \ddot{L}_n \ddot{D}_n \sqrt{n}(\hat{\gamma}_n - \gamma_n^*) \right],$$

where $\nabla^2 \ddot{L}_n \ddot{D}_n$ is the $p \times c$ matrix $n^{-1} \sum_{t=1}^n \nabla' s_t(X^t, d_n(\gamma)) D_n(\gamma)$ with rows evaluated at mean values lying between $\hat{\gamma}_n$ and γ_n^*. (Recall $D_n(\gamma) \equiv \nabla_\gamma' d_n(\gamma)$.) Setting $D_n^* = D_n(\gamma_n^*)$ and adding and subtracting appropriate terms gives

$$\sqrt{n}\, \tilde{R}_n \nabla^2 \tilde{L}_n^- \nabla \tilde{L}_n$$

$$= R_n^* \nabla^2 \bar{L}_n^{*-1} n^{-1/2} \sum_{t=1}^{n} s_t(X^t, d_n(\gamma_n^*)) + R_n^* D_n^* \sqrt{n}(\hat{\gamma}_n - \gamma_n^*)$$

$$+ (\tilde{R}_n \nabla^2 \bar{L}_n^{-} - R_n^* \nabla^2 \bar{L}_n^{*-1}) n^{-1/2} \sum_{t=1}^{n} s_t(X^t, d_n(\gamma_n^*))$$

$$+ (\tilde{R}_n \nabla^2 \tilde{L}_n^{-} \nabla^2 \ddot{L}_n \ddot{D}_n - R_n^* D_n^*) \sqrt{n}(\hat{\gamma}_n - \gamma_n^*)$$

$$= n^{-1/2} \sum_{t=1}^{n} R_n^* \nabla^2 \bar{L}_n^{*-1} s_t(X^t, d_n(\gamma_n^*))$$

$$+ R_n^* D_n^* \sqrt{n}(\hat{\gamma}_n - \gamma_n^*) + o_{P^o}(1) .$$

The final equality gives us the desired result, and holds provided that $\tilde{R}_n - R_n^* \to 0$ $prob - P^o$, $\nabla^2 \tilde{L}_n - \nabla^2 \bar{L}_n^* \to 0$ $prob - P^o$, $\nabla^2 \ddot{L}_n - \nabla^2 \bar{L}_n^* \to 0$ $prob - P^o$, $\ddot{D}_n - D_n^* \to 0$ $prob - P^o$, $\sqrt{n}(\hat{\gamma}_n - \gamma_n^*) = O_{P^o}(1)$ and $n^{-1/2} \sum_{t=1}^{n} s_t(X^t, d_n(\gamma_n^*)) = O_{P^o}(1)$. All but the last condition hold generally; the last condition holds given the null hypothesis ($\sqrt{n}\, r_n(\theta_n^*) \to 0$) and Assumption 6.1. It also holds when $\sqrt{n}\, r_n(\theta_n^*)$ is $O(1)$, the case relevant for local alternatives. Note that we can identify $\nabla_\gamma' \bar{M}_n^*$ as $R_n^* D_n^*$ from the expression just obtained.

To examine the content of condition 9.3(ii) or 9.4(ii), we require the objects corresponding to s_n^* and A_n^*. Following the proof of Theorem 7.10, we have

$$\sqrt{n}(\hat{\gamma}_n - \gamma_n^*)$$

$$= - [D_n^{*\prime} \nabla^2 \bar{L}_n^* D_n + (\nabla' \bar{L}_n^* \otimes I_c) \nabla_\gamma^2 d_n^*]^{-1} n^{-1/2} \sum_{t=1}^{n} D_n^{*\prime} s_t(X^t, d_n(\gamma_n^*))$$

$$+ o_{P^o}(1) ,$$

where $\nabla \bar{L}_n^* = \nabla \bar{L}_n(d_n(\gamma_n^*))$ and $\nabla_\gamma^2 d_n^* = \nabla^2 d_n(\gamma_n^*)$. We see immediately that

$$A_n^* = D_n^{*\prime} \nabla^2 \bar{L}_n^* D_n^* + (\nabla' \bar{L}_n^* \otimes I_c) \nabla_\gamma^2 d_n^*$$

$$s_n^* = n^{-1} \sum_{t=1}^{n} D_n^{*\prime} s_t(X^t, d_n(\gamma_n^*)) .$$

Conditions 9.3(ii) or 9.4(ii) therefore require the asymptotic normality of

$$\sqrt{n}(M_n^* - \nabla_\theta' \bar{M}_n^* A_n^{*-1} s_n^*)$$

$$= (R_n^* \nabla^2 \bar{L}_n^{*-1} - R_n^* D_n [D_n^{*\prime} \nabla^2 \bar{L}_n^* D_n + (\nabla' \bar{L}_n^* \otimes I_c) \nabla_\gamma^2 d_n^*]^{-1} D_n^{*\prime})$$

$$\times n^{-1/2} \sum_{t=1}^{n} s_t (X^t , d_n (\gamma_n^*))$$
$$\equiv T_n^* \, n^{-1/2} \sum_{t=1}^{n} s_t (X^t , d_n (\gamma_n^*)) \, .$$

Thus, $\sqrt{n} \, (M_n^* - \nabla_\theta' \bar{M}_n^* \, A_n^{*-1} \, s_n^*)$ is simply a linear transformation of $n^{-1/2} \sum_{t=1}^{n} s_t (X^t , d_n (\gamma_n^*))$. When P^o is such that $\sqrt{n} \, r (\theta_n^*) \to 0$ so that $\theta_n^* = d_n (\gamma_n^*)$, Assumptions 3.2′ and 6.1 ensure that $n^{-1/2} \sum_{t=1}^{n} s_t (X^t , d_n (\gamma_n^*)) \overset{A}{\sim} N (0 , B_n^*)$. Under local alternatives ($\{ \sqrt{n} \, r_n (\theta_n^*) \} = O(1)$), we still have asymptotic normality, but with bounded mean. Because $\{ T_n^* \}$ is generally $O(1)$, such probability measures belong to $\mathcal{P}_o^u$ or $\mathcal{P}_a^u$.

Thus, we see that the Lagrange multiplier test is a particular m-test, and that the model underlying the test and the local alternatives are those probability measures for which regularity conditions hold and either $\sqrt{n} \, r_n (\theta_n^*) \to 0$ (null hypothesis) or $\{ \sqrt{n} \, r_n (\theta_n^*) \} = O(1)$ (local alternative). Theorem 9.5 thus delivers essentially the same result as Theorems 8.9(ii) and 8.10(ii). The results of Sections 9.2 and 9.3 provide further versions of the Lagrange Multiplier test. We leave investigation of these to the interested reader.

10.2 Newey's Conditional Moment Tests

In the case of independent $\{ X_t \}$ Newey [1985] observed that because $E (s_t (X_t , \theta_o) \mid Z_t) = 0$ under correct specification, it follows that $E (w_t (Z_t) \, s_t (X_t , \theta_o) \mid Z_t) = 0$ for any measurable $q \times p$ matrix function w_t (we follow Newey's notation here—the function w_t is not to be confused with the notation for a realization of W_t used elsewhere) under correct specification, so that $E (w_t (Z_t) \, s_t (X_t , \theta_o)) = 0$. This was extended to the dynamic case in White [1987], where entirely analogous reasoning implies that whenever $E (s_t^* \mid \tilde{X}^{t-1}) = 0$, then $E (w_t^* s_t^*) = 0$, where $w_t^* \equiv v_t (\tilde{X}^{t-1} , \theta_n^*, \pi_n^*)$, because by the law of iterated expectations,

$$\begin{aligned} E (w_t^* s_t^*) &= E (E (w_t^* s_t^* \mid \tilde{X}^{t-1})) \\ &= E (w_t^* \, E (s_t^* \mid \tilde{X}^{t-1})) \\ &= 0 \, . \end{aligned}$$

Here we take θ_n^* and π_n^* to be the stochastic limits of appropriate estimators $\hat{\theta}_n$ (the QMLE generated by $\mathcal{S} = \{ f_t \}$) and $\hat{\pi}_n$ (some nuisance parameter estimator). Thus, m_t has the form

$$m_t(X^t, \theta, \pi) = w_t(\tilde{X}^{t-1}, \theta, \pi) \cdot s_t(X^t, \theta),$$

because $E(m_t(X^t, \theta_n^*, \pi_n^*)) = 0$ whenever the model is correctly specified to the extent that $E(s_t^* \mid \tilde{X}^{t-1}) = 0$. (Recall that conditions for this are given in some detail in Chapter 6.)

Newey [1985] discusses a number of interesting applications of such conditional moment tests, including tests for heteroskedasticity, non-normality, simultaneity, and omitted variables in the probit model. The dynamic information matrix test introduced by White [1987] and treated in detail in the next chapter is also a conditional moment test.

We now investigate the conditions required by Theorem 9.5. The measurability, continuity, and differentiability conditions of Assumption 9.1 hold given those already available for s_t, together with conditions on w_t identical to those required of m_t in Assumption 9.1(a). Direct computation gives

$$\nabla'_\theta m_t = w_t \nabla'_\theta s_t + (s_t' \otimes I_q) \nabla'_\theta w_t$$

$$\nabla'_\pi m_t = (s_t' \otimes I_q) \nabla'_\pi w_t,$$

provided that w_t is differentiable in π as well. Assumption 9.2 is imposed directly, so $\hat{\pi}_n - \pi_n^* \to 0 \quad prob-P_o$.

To investigate the model underlying the test and the relevant local alternatives, we first investigate condition 9.3(i), i.e.

$$\sqrt{n}\, \hat{M}_n - n^{-1/2} \sum_{t=1}^{n} m_t^* - \nabla'_\theta \bar{M}_n^* \sqrt{n}\,(\hat{\theta}_n - \theta_n^*) \to 0 \qquad prob-P_o.$$

We take a mean value expansion of $\hat{M}_n = n^{-1} \sum_{t=1}^n \hat{w}_t\, \hat{s}_t$ ($\hat{w}_t \equiv w_t(\tilde{X}^{t-1}, \hat{\theta}_n, \hat{\pi}_n)$) around (θ_n^*, π_n^*) to obtain

$$n^{-1/2} \sum_{t=1}^{n} \hat{w}_t\, \hat{s}_t = n^{-1/2} \sum_{t=1}^{n} w_t^*\, s_t^* + \nabla'_\theta \ddot{M}_n \sqrt{n}\,(\hat{\theta}_n - \theta_n^*)$$
$$+ \nabla'_\pi \ddot{M}_n \sqrt{n}\,(\hat{\pi}_n - \pi_n^*),$$

where $\nabla'_\theta \ddot{M}_n$ and $\nabla'_\pi \ddot{M}_n$ represent the $q \times p$ and $q \times r$ submatrices of the Jacobian $\nabla' M_n$ for this choice of m. Provided that (say) $\nabla_\theta \ddot{M}_n - \nabla_\theta \bar{M}_n^* \to 0$ $prob-P^o$, P^o belongs to $\mathcal{P}_o^u$ or $\mathcal{P}_a^u$ if $\nabla'_\pi \ddot{M}_n \sqrt{n}\,(\hat{\pi}_n - \pi_n^*) \to 0$ $prob-P^o$. A leading case occurs when $\nabla_\pi \ddot{M}_n - \nabla_\pi \bar{M}_n^* \to 0$ $prob-P^o$ and $\sqrt{n}\,(\hat{\pi}_n - \pi_n^*) = O_{P^o}(1)$ (a strengthening of Assumption 9.2). In this case P^o belongs to $\mathcal{P}_o^u$ or $\mathcal{P}_a^u$ whenever $\nabla_\pi \bar{M}_n^* \to 0$. This holds whenever $E(s_t^* \mid \tilde{X}^{t-1}) = 0$ because $\nabla_\pi \bar{M}_n^* = n^{-1} \sum_{t=1}^n E(\nabla_\pi m_t^*)$ and

$$
\begin{aligned}
E(\nabla'_\pi m_t^*) &= E(E[\nabla'_\pi m_t^* \mid \tilde{X}^{t-1}]) \\
&= E(E[s_t^{*\prime} \otimes I_q \mid \tilde{X}^{t-1}]\, \nabla'_\pi w_t^*) \\
&= 0 .
\end{aligned}
$$

Such cases are associated with $\mathcal{P}_o^u$. Alternatively, it suffices that $n^{-1/2} \sum_{t=1}^n E(\nabla_\pi m_t^*) = O(1)$, as this implies $n^{-1} \sum_{t=1}^n E(\nabla_\pi m_t^*) \to 0$. This case is associated with $\mathcal{P}_a^u$.

In other cases, it happens that $\sqrt{n}\, \nabla_\pi \ddot{M}_n = O_{P^o}(1)$, in which case Assumption 9.2 ($\hat{\pi}_n - \pi_n^* \to 0$ $prob-P^o$) suffices for $\nabla'_\pi\, \ddot{M}_n \sqrt{n}\, (\hat{\pi}_n - \pi_n^*) \to 0$ $prob-P^o$. This occurs when $v_t(\tilde{X}^{t-1}, \theta, \pi)$ depends linearly on π. If nothing guarantees $\nabla'_\pi\, \ddot{M}_n \sqrt{n}\, (\hat{\pi}_n - \pi_n^*) \to 0$ $prob-P^o$, then the offending elements of $\hat{\pi}_n$ must be absorbed into $\hat{\theta}_n$.

Now consider conditions 9.3(ii) and 9.4(ii). For this we require the objects corresponding to s_n^* and A_n^*. Because $\hat{\theta}_n$ is the QMLE in this application, the correspondences are simply those of Theorem 6.4 or 6.11, i.e.,

$$
s_n^* = n^{-1} \sum_{t=1}^{n} s_t(X^t, \theta_n^*) \qquad \text{and} \qquad A_n^* = n^{-1} \sum_{t=1}^{n} E(\nabla' s_t^*) .
$$

Conditions 9.3(ii) or 9.4(ii) thus require the asymptotic normality of

$$
\begin{aligned}
&\sqrt{n}\,(M_n^* - \nabla'_\theta \bar{M}_n^*\, A_n^{*-1}\, s_n^*) \\
&= n^{-1/2} \sum_{t=1}^{n} (w_t^* - \nabla'_\theta \bar{M}_n^*\, A_n^{*-1})\, s_t^* .
\end{aligned}
$$

The model underlying the test $\mathcal{P}_o^u$ and the local alternative $\mathcal{P}_a^u$ therefore include all probability measures for which $(w_t^* - \nabla'_\theta \bar{M}_n^*\, A_n^{*-1})\, s_t^*$ obeys the central limit theorem, with bounded mean and variance. Because $n^{-1/2} \sum_{t=1}^n E(s_t^*) \to 0$ in general, $P_o \in \mathcal{P}_a^u$ when $n^{-1/2} \sum_{t=1}^n E(w_t^*\, s_t^*)$ is $O(1)$.

Just as the fact that $E(s_t^* \mid \tilde{X}^{t-1}) = 0$ under correct specification can be used in the manner proposed by Newey to generate conditional moment specification tests, one may use the fact

$$
E(\nabla' s_t^* + s_t^*\, s_t^{*\prime} \mid \tilde{X}^{t-1}) = 0
$$

under correct specification to generate conditional moment specification tests of what we shall call "order two." (Newey's tests are thus of "order one.") The simplest test of order two is the information matrix test of White

[1982], treated in the next chapter. This test involves setting

$$m_t = S \; vec \; [\, \nabla' \, s_t + s_t \, s_t{}' \,] \, ,$$

where S is some nonstochastic $q \times p^2$ selection matrix. The general conditional moment test of order two sets

$$m_t (X^t , \theta , \pi) = w_t \; (\tilde{X}^{t-1} , \theta , \pi)$$
$$\times S \; vec \; [\, \nabla' \, s_t (X^t , \theta) + s_t (X^t , \theta) \, s_t (X^t , \theta)' \,] \, .$$

The analysis for this case is entirely analogous to that given for conditional moment tests of order one, but with $S \; vec \; [\nabla' s_t + s_t \, s_t{}']$ replacing s_t.

Conditional moment tests of arbitrary order $i = 1, 2, \ldots$ may be generated as a consequence of the requirement that

$$\int_{S_{\theta,t}} \nabla^i \, f_t (x^t , \theta) \, d \, \zeta_t (y_t) = 0 \, .$$

For $i = 1$, we have Assumption 6.3(a), which implies $E (s_t^o \mid \tilde{X}^{t-1}) = 0$; $i = 2$ gives Assumption 6.3(b), which implies that $E (\nabla' \, s_t^o + s_t^o \, s_t^{o\prime} \mid \tilde{X}^{t-1}) = 0$ (under correct specification). For linear exponential family members, correct specification of conditional moments of successively higher orders suffices in place of correct distributional specification.

Another extension of Newey's tests involves replacing $\hat{\theta}_n$ generated by $\mathcal{S} = \{ f_t \}$ with $\tilde{\theta}_n$ generated by $\mathcal{S}_2 = \{ f_{2t} \}$ (say), where $\sqrt{n} \; (\tilde{\theta}_n \; - \; \theta_o) = O_{P^o} (1)$ under $\mathcal{P}_o^u$. We now put $s_{1t} = \nabla \log f_{1t}$, where $\hat{\theta}_n$ is generated by $\mathcal{S}_1 = \{ f_{1t} \}$. For this extension, we have

$$\hat{M}_n = n^{-1/2} \sum_{t=1}^{n} \tilde{w}_t \, \tilde{s}_{1t} \, ,$$

with $\tilde{w}_t = w_t (\tilde{X}^{t-1} , \tilde{\theta}_n , \hat{\pi}_n)$, $\tilde{s}_{1t} = s_{1t} (X^t , \tilde{\theta}_n)$. Analysis analogous to that just given proceeds by expanding $\hat{M}_n$ around $(\theta_{2n}^* , \pi_n^*)$ (where $\sqrt{n} \; (\tilde{\theta}_n - \theta_{2n}^*) = O_{P^o} (1)$ under $\mathcal{P}_a^u$), giving

$$n^{-1/2} \sum_{t=1}^{n} \tilde{w}_t \, \tilde{s}_{1t} = n^{-1/2} \sum_{t=1}^{n} \tilde{w}_t^* \, \tilde{s}_{1t}^* + \nabla_\theta' \, \ddot{M}_n \, \sqrt{n} \, (\tilde{\theta}_n - \theta_{2n}^*)$$
$$+ \nabla_\pi' \, \ddot{M}_n \, \sqrt{n} \, (\hat{\pi}_n - \pi_n^*) \, ,$$

where $\tilde{w}_t^* = w_t (\tilde{X}^{t-1} , \theta_{2n}^* , \pi_n^*)$ and $\tilde{s}_{1t}^* = s_{1t} (X^t , \theta_{2n}^* , \pi_n^*)$, and $\nabla_\theta \, \ddot{M}_n$ and $\nabla_\pi \, \ddot{M}_n$ are evaluated at mean values between $\tilde{\theta}_n$ and θ_{2n}^*. When $\nabla_\pi' \, \ddot{M}_n \, \sqrt{n} \, (\hat{\pi}_n - \pi_n^*) = o_{P^o} (1)$ and $\nabla_\theta \, \ddot{M}_n - \nabla_\theta \, \tilde{M}_n^* = o_{P^o} (1)$ (where $\nabla_\theta \, \tilde{M}_n^* = \nabla_\theta \, \bar{M}_n (\theta_{2n}^*))$, we have

$$n^{-1/2} \sum_{t=1}^{n} \tilde{w}_t \tilde{s}_{1t} = n^{-1/2} \sum_{t=1}^{n} \tilde{w}_t^* \tilde{s}_{1t}^* + \nabla_\theta' \tilde{M}_n^* \sqrt{n} (\tilde{\theta}_n - \theta_{2n}^*) + o_{P^o} (1) ,$$

so that condition 9.3(i) holds.

To investigate the elements of $\mathcal{P}_o^u$ and $\mathcal{P}_a^u$, we apply Theorem 6.4 or 6.11 to $\mathcal{S}_2$ to get $\sqrt{n} (\tilde{\theta}_n - \theta_{2n}^*) + A_{2n}^{*-1} n^{-1/2} \sum_{t=1}^n s_{2t}^* = o_{P^o} (1)$, with $s_{2t}^* = s_{2t} (X^t , \theta_{2n}^*)$. Expanding $n^{-1/2} \sum_{t=1}^n \tilde{w}_t^* \tilde{s}_{1t}^*$ around $(\theta_{1n}^* , \pi_n^*)$ (where $\sqrt{n} (\hat{\theta}_n - \theta_{1n}^*) = O_{P^o} (1))$ then yields

$$n^{-1/2} \sum_{t=1}^{n} \tilde{w}_t \tilde{s}_{1t} = n^{-1/2} \sum_{t=1}^{n} [w_t^* s_{1t}^* - \nabla_\theta' \tilde{M}_n^* A_{2n}^{*-1} s_{2t}^*]$$

$$+ \nabla_\theta' \bar{M}_n^* \sqrt{n} (\theta_{2n}^* - \theta_{1n}^*) + o_{P^o} (1) ,$$

where we have $\nabla_\theta' \bar{M}_n^* = \nabla_\theta' \bar{M}_n (\theta_{1n}^*)$ and use is made of the requirement that $\sqrt{n} (\theta_{2n}^* - \theta_{1n}^*) = O (1)$ under $\mathcal{P}_a^u$ in arriving at this expression.

Under $\mathcal{P}_o^u$, we have $\theta_{2n}^* = \theta_{1n}^*$, while $\sqrt{n} (\theta_{2n}^* - \theta_{1n}^*) = O (1)$ under $\mathcal{P}_a^u$, leading to $a_n^* = n^{-1/2} \sum_{t=1}^n E (w_t^* s_{1t}^*) + \nabla_\theta' \bar{M}_n^* \sqrt{n} (\theta_{2n}^* - \theta_{1n}^*)$, given that $n^{-1/2} \sum_{t=1}^n [w_t^* s_{1t}^* - E (w_t^* s_{1t}^*) - \nabla_\theta' \tilde{M}_n^* A_{2n}^{*-1} s_{2t}^*]$ will generally have a normal distribution asymptotically with mean zero under regularity conditions compatible with $\mathcal{P}_a^u$.

A special case of this extension is the Hausman test, which we now investigate in detail.

10.3 The Hausman Test

We saw in Chapters 4 and 5 that when a model is correctly specified to some extent, there generally exists a multitude of consistent asymptotically normal estimators for parameters θ_o with a probability or location interpretation. We also saw in Chapter 3 that parameter estimates obtained from misspecified models are generally sensitive to the specification adopted. This provides the motivation for the Hausman [1978] tests: under correct specification, two different consistent asymptotically normal estimators for θ_o, say $\hat{\theta}_n$ and $\tilde{\theta}_n$, should be close together. Equivalently, if $\hat{\theta}_n - \tilde{\theta}_n$ is not close to zero, then misspecification is evident. Hausman tests have power against alternatives for which $\hat{\theta}_n$ and $\tilde{\theta}_n$ generally diverge under misspecification.

We have already seen one particular instance of a Hausman test in Chapter 8. There, we compared a QMLE estimated subject to constraints $r_n (\theta) = 0$, denoted $\tilde{\theta}_n$, to a QMLE estimated without imposing such constraints, denoted $\hat{\theta}_n$. Theorems 8.9 and 8.10 described the properties of this Hausman test, which is based on $\hat{M}_n = \hat{R}_n (\hat{\theta}_n - \tilde{\theta}_n)$. Although Hausman tests are usually thought of as based strictly on a comparison of $\hat{\theta}_n$ and $\tilde{\theta}_n$ we consider a simple extension of the Hausman test. Specifically, we refer to any test based on or asymptotically equivalent to

$$\tilde{M}_n = \hat{S}_n (\hat{\theta}_n - \tilde{\theta}_n)$$

as a Hausman test, where $\hat{S}_n$ is a stochastic $q \times p$ matrix, $q \le p$. In the example just discussed, $\hat{S}_n = \hat{R}_n$. In the general case $\hat{S}_n$ serves to ensure that $\tilde{M}_n$ has a nondegenerate limiting distribution, as well as possibly acting to focus attention on particular elements or linear combinations of elements of $\hat{\theta}_n - \tilde{\theta}_n$ whose divergence from zero may be of interest.

We show that the Hausman test based on $\tilde{M}_n$ falls into the m-testing framework by showing that it is asymptotically equivalent to an m-test within a relevant collection of probability measures.

Specifically, let $\hat{\theta}$ be obtained from $\mathcal{S}_1 = \{ f_{1t} \}$ for which the assumptions of Theorem 6.4 or 6.11 hold, and for simplicity let $\tilde{\theta}$ be similarly obtained from $\mathcal{S}_2 = \{ f_{2t} \}$. Let θ^*_{1n} and θ^*_{2n} denote the probability limits of $\hat{\theta}_n$ and $\tilde{\theta}_n$ respectively, and let $\tilde{\mathcal{P}}^u_a$ denote the collection of probability measures P^o for which $\{\sqrt{n}\ (\theta^*_{1n}(P^o) - \theta^*_{2n}(P^o))\} = O(1)$. We follow White [1982] and consider

$$n^{-1/2} \sum_{t=1}^{n} s_{2t}(X^t, \hat{\theta}_n) = n^{-1/2} \sum_{t=1}^{n} s_{2t}(X^t, \tilde{\theta}_n) + \nabla^2 \ddot{L}_{2n} \sqrt{n}\ (\hat{\theta}_n - \tilde{\theta}_n)\,,$$

where $s_{2t} = \nabla \log f_{2t}$, and $\nabla^2 \ddot{L}_{2n}$ is the Hessian $n^{-1} \sum_{t=1}^{n} \nabla^2 \log f_{2t}$ with rows evaluated at mean values lying between $\hat{\theta}_n$ and $\tilde{\theta}_n$. Because $\tilde{\theta}_n$ is the QMLE generated by $\mathcal{S}_2$, we have $n^{-1/2} \sum_{t=1}^{n} s_{2t}(X^t, \tilde{\theta}_n) \to 0 \ \ prob - P^o$ generally, while

$$\nabla^2 \ddot{L}_{2n} \sqrt{n}(\hat{\theta}_n - \tilde{\theta}_n) - \nabla^2 \bar{L}^*_{2n} \sqrt{n}\ (\hat{\theta}_n - \tilde{\theta}_n) \to 0 \qquad prob - P^o$$

when $P^o \in \tilde{\mathcal{P}}^u_a$. The inclusion of P^o in $\tilde{\mathcal{P}}^u_a$ plays a crucial role. First, it ensures that

$$\sqrt{n}\,(\hat{\theta}_n - \tilde{\theta}_n) = \sqrt{n}\,(\hat{\theta}_n - \theta^*_{1n}) - \sqrt{n}\,(\tilde{\theta}_n - \theta^*_{2n}) - \sqrt{n}\ (\theta^*_{2n} - \theta^*_{1n})$$

is bounded in probability and the last term is bounded for P^o in $\tilde{\mathcal{P}}^u_a$. Second, because $\{\sqrt{n}\ (\theta^*_{1n} - \theta^*_{2n})\} = O(1)$, it follows that $\theta^*_{1n} - \theta^*_{2n} \to 0$, so that the mean values in $\nabla^2 \ddot{L}_{2n}$ converge in probability to θ^*_{2n}. Using Corollary 3.8 we then have $\nabla^2 \ddot{L}_{2n} - \nabla^2 \bar{L}^*_{2n} \to 0 \ prob - P^o$. Consequently, for $P^o \in \tilde{\mathcal{P}}^u_a$

$$n^{-1/2} \sum_{t=1}^{n} s_{2t}(X^t, \hat{\theta}_n) = \nabla^2 \bar{L}^*_{2n} \sqrt{n}\ (\hat{\theta}_n - \tilde{\theta}_n) + o_{P^o}(1)\,.$$

Because of the symmetry of the problem, we also have

$$n^{-1/2} \sum_{t=1}^{n} s_{1t}(X^t, \tilde{\theta}_n) = \nabla^2 \bar{L}_{1n}^* \sqrt{n}\, (\tilde{\theta}_n - \hat{\theta}_n) + o_{P^o}(1).$$

It follows that for $P^o \in \tilde{\mathcal{P}}_a^u$

$$\begin{aligned} \sqrt{n}\, \tilde{M}_n &= \hat{S}_n \sqrt{n}\, (\hat{\theta}_n - \tilde{\theta}_n) \\ &= \hat{S}_n \nabla^2 \bar{L}_{2n}^{*-1}\, n^{-1/2} \sum_{t=1}^{n} s_{2t}(X^t, \hat{\theta}_n) + o_{P^o}(1) \\ &= - \hat{S}_n \nabla^2 \bar{L}_{1n}^{*-1}\, n^{-1/2} \sum_{t=1}^{n} s_{1t}(X^t, \tilde{\theta}_n) + o_{P^o}(1). \end{aligned}$$

These expressions are not quite in the desired form because of the presence of the unknown quantities $\nabla^2 \bar{L}_{2n}^{*-1}$ or $\nabla^2 \bar{L}_{1n}^{*-1}$. However, these can be replaced by consistent estimators, say $\nabla^2 \hat{L}_{2n}^{-}$, $\nabla^2 \hat{L}_{2n} \equiv n^{-1} \sum_{t=1}^{n} \nabla^2 \log f_{2t}(X^t, \hat{\theta}_n)$, or $\nabla^2 \tilde{L}_{1n}^{-}$, $\nabla^2 \tilde{L}_{1n} \equiv n^{-1} \sum_{t=1}^{n} \nabla^2 \log f_{1t}(X^t, \tilde{\theta}_n)$. Because $n^{-1/2} \sum_{t=1}^{n} s_{2t}(X^t, \hat{\theta}_n)$ is $O_{P^o}(1)$ and $\nabla^2 \hat{L}_{2n}^{-} - \nabla^2 \bar{L}_{2n}^{*-1} \to 0$ $prob - P^o$ for $P^o \in \tilde{\mathcal{P}}_a^u$ or $n^{-1/2} \sum_{t=1}^{n} s_{1t}(X^t, \tilde{\theta}_n)$ is $O_{P^o}(1)$ and $\nabla^2 \tilde{L}_{1n}^{-} - \nabla^2 \bar{L}_{1n}^{*-1} \to 0$ $prob - P^o$ for $P^o \in \tilde{\mathcal{P}}_a^u$, we have for $P^o \in \tilde{\mathcal{P}}_a^u$

$$\begin{aligned} \sqrt{n}\, \tilde{M}_n &= \hat{S}_n \nabla^2 \hat{L}_{2n}^{-}\, n^{-1/2} \sum_{t=1}^{n} s_{2t}(X^t, \hat{\theta}_n) + o_{P^o}(1) \\ &= - \hat{S}_n \nabla^2 \tilde{L}_{1n}^{-}\, n^{-1/2} \sum_{t=1}^{n} s_{1t}(X^t, \tilde{\theta}_n) + o_{P^o}(1). \end{aligned}$$

Consequently, the theory of m-tests applies to Hausman tests either with

$$m_{1t}(X^t, \tilde{\theta}_n, \tilde{\pi}_n) = - \hat{S}_n \nabla^2 \tilde{L}_{1n}^{-}\, s_{1t}(X^t, \tilde{\theta}_n)$$

or

$$m_{2t}(X^t, \hat{\theta}_n, \hat{\pi}_n) = \hat{S}_n \nabla^2 \hat{L}_{2n}^{-}\, s_{2t}(X^t, \hat{\theta}_n),$$

where $\tilde{\pi}_n = vec - \hat{S}_n \nabla^2 \tilde{L}_{1n}^{-}$ and $\hat{\pi}_n = vec\, \hat{S}_n \nabla^2 \hat{L}_{2n}^{-}$. Observe that neither m_{1t} nor m_{2t} falls directly into Newey's conditional moment testing framework, because $\tilde{\theta}_n$ (generated by $\mathcal{S}_2$) appears in m_{1t} and $\hat{\theta}_n$ (generated by $\mathcal{S}_1$) appears in m_{2t}. However, the extension of Newey's framework discussed at the end of the previous section contains the Hausman test as the special case in which $vec\, w_t(\tilde{X}^{t-1}, \theta, \pi) = \pi$.

Note that Assumptions 2.3 and 3.6 for f_{1t} and f_{2t} ensure the validity of Assumption 9.1. To ensure the validity of Assumption 9.2, it suffices merely to assume that existence of $S_n^* = O(1)$ such that $\hat{S}_n - S_n^* \to 0$ $prob - P_o$.

The model underlying the test $\mathcal{P}_o^u$ and the local alternatives $\mathcal{P}_a^u$ are closely related to $\tilde{\mathcal{P}}_a^u$ discussed above. We discuss only the choice m_{2t} for brevity. The symmetry of the problem yields analogous results for m_{1t}.

A mean value expansion of $n^{-1/2} \sum_{t=1}^n s_{2t}(X^t, \hat{\theta}_n)$ around θ_{1n}^* yields

$$\begin{aligned}
\sqrt{n}\, \hat{M}_n &= \hat{S}_n \nabla^2 \hat{L}_{2n}^- n^{-1/2} \sum_{t=1}^n s_{2t}(X^t, \theta_{1n}^*) \\
&\quad + \hat{S}_n \nabla^2 \hat{L}_{2n}^- \nabla^2 \ddot{L}_{2n} \sqrt{n}\, (\hat{\theta}_n - \theta_{1n}^*) \\
&= S_n^* \nabla^2 \bar{L}_{2n}^{*-1} n^{-1/2} \sum_{t=1}^n s_{2t}(X^t, \theta_{1n}^*) + S_n^* \sqrt{n}\, (\hat{\theta}_n - \theta_{1n}^*) \\
&\quad + (\hat{S}_n \nabla^2 \hat{L}_{2n}^- - S_n^* \nabla^2 \bar{L}_{2n}^{*-1})\, n^{-1/2} \sum_{t=1}^n s_{2t}(X^t, \theta_{1n}^*) \\
&\quad + (\hat{S}_n \nabla^2 \hat{L}_{2n}^- \nabla^2 \ddot{L}_{2n} - S_n^*) \sqrt{n}\, (\hat{\theta}_n - \theta_{1n}^*) \\
&= n^{-1/2} \sum_{t=1}^n m_t^* + S_n^* \sqrt{n}\, (\hat{\theta}_n - \theta_{1n}^*) + o_{P^o}(1) ,
\end{aligned}$$

with $m_t^* = S_n^* \nabla^2 \bar{L}_{2n}^{*-1} s_{2t}^*$, $\nabla^2 \bar{L}_{2n}^* \equiv n^{-1} \sum_{t=1}^n E^o(\nabla^2 \log f_{2t}^*)$ and with $\nabla^2 \ddot{L}_{2n}$ denoting the Hessian of $L_{2n}(\theta)$ with rows evaluated at mean values lying between $\hat{\theta}_n$ and θ_{1n}^*, provided that

$$(\hat{S}_n \nabla^2 \hat{L}_{2n}^- - S_n^* \nabla^2 \bar{L}_{2n}^{*-1})\, n^{-1/2} \sum_{t=1}^n s_{2t}(X^t, \theta_{1n}^*) \to 0 \qquad prob - P^o$$

and

$$(\hat{S}_n \nabla^2 \hat{L}_{2n}^- \nabla^2 \ddot{L}_{2n} - S_n^*) \sqrt{n}\, (\hat{\theta}_n - \theta_{1n}^*) \to 0 \qquad prob - P^o .$$

This latter convergence generally holds, as $\sqrt{n}\, (\hat{\theta}_n - \theta_{1n}^*)$ is generally $O_{P^o}(1)$, while in general $\hat{S}_n - S_n^* \to 0$ $prob - P^o$ and $\nabla^2 \hat{L}_{2n}^- \nabla^2 \ddot{L}_{2n} - I_p \to 0$ $prob - P^o$ so that $\hat{S}_n \nabla^2 \hat{L}_{2n}^- \nabla^2 \ddot{L}_{2n} - S_n^* \to 0$ $prob - P^o$.

It is the former convergence that restricts $\mathcal{P}_o^u$ and $\mathcal{P}_a^u$. In general, we will have $\hat{S}_n \nabla^2 \hat{L}_{2n}^- - S_n^* \nabla^2 \bar{L}_{2n}^{*-1} \to 0$ $prob - P^o$ (a consequence of Corollary 3.8), so that the desired convergence follows when $n^{-1/2} \sum_{t=1}^n s_{2t}(X^t, \theta_{1n}^*)$ is $O_{P^o}(1)$. Taking a mean value expansion around θ_{2n}^* gives

$$n^{-1/2} \sum_{t=1}^n s_{2t}(X^t, \theta_{1n}^*) = n^{-1/2} \sum_{t=1}^n s_{2t}(X^t, \theta_{2n}^*) + \nabla^2 \ddot{L}_{2n} \sqrt{n}\, (\theta_{1n}^* - \theta_{2n}^*) .$$

The first term on the right is generally $O_{P^o}(1)$ (e.g. by Assumption 6.1), while the second term (with $\nabla^2 \ddot{L}_{2n}$ having rows evaluated at a mean value lying between θ^*_{1n} and θ^*_{2n}) is $O_{P^o}(1)$ under $\tilde{\mathcal{P}}^u_a$, but not necessarily otherwise. Because $S^*_n = \nabla'_\theta \bar{M}^*_n$ generally, we thus have condition 9.3(i) satisfied for P^o in $\tilde{\mathcal{P}}^u_a$.

Next consider conditions 9.3(ii) and 9.4(ii). Given our choice of $\hat{\theta}_n$, the choices $s^*_n = n^{-1} \sum_{t=1}^n s_{1t}(X^t, \theta^*_{1n})$ and $A^*_n = n^{-1} \sum_{t=1}^n E(\nabla^2 \log f_{1t}(X^t, \theta^*_{1n})) = \nabla^2 \bar{L}^*_{1n}$ are immediate. To belong to $\mathcal{P}^u_a$, it is thus necessary that

$$\sqrt{n}\,(M^*_n - \nabla'_\theta \bar{M}^*_n A^{*-1}_n s^*_n)$$

$$= S^*_n n^{-1/2} \sum_{t=1}^n [\nabla^2 \bar{L}^{*-1}_{2n} s_{2t}(X^t, \theta^*_{1n}) - \nabla^2 \bar{L}^{*-1}_{1n} s_{1t}(X^t, \theta^*_{1n})]$$

$$\overset{A^o}{\sim} N(a^*_n, V^*_n).$$

This requirement implies restrictions that may in some cases exclude certain elements of $\tilde{\mathcal{P}}^u_a$, as the requirement that $\nabla^2 \bar{L}^{*-1}_{2n} s_{2t}(X^t, \theta^*_{1n}) - \nabla^2 \bar{L}^{*-1}_{1n} s_{1t}(X^t, \theta^*_{1n})$ obeys a central limit theorem is not necessarily implied by the requirements that $s_{2t}(X^t, \theta^*_{1n})$ and $s_{1t}(X^t, \theta^*_{1n})$ each obey a central limit theorem individually. Nevertheless, most applications will generally possess enough structure to ensure that this is the case.

To investigate the elements of $\mathcal{P}^u_a$ a little further, we again make use of a mean value expansion of $n^{-1/2} \sum_{t=1}^n s_{2t}(X^t, \theta^*_{1n})$ around θ^*_{2n} to write

$$\sqrt{n}\,(M^*_n - \nabla'_\theta \bar{M}^*_n A^{*-1}_n s^*_n)$$

$$= S^*_n n^{-1/2} \sum_{t=1}^n [\nabla^2 \bar{L}^{*-1}_{2n} s_{2t}(X^t, \theta^*_{2n}) - \nabla^2 \bar{L}^{*-1}_{1n} s_{1t}(X^t, \theta^*_{1n})]$$

$$+ S^*_n \sqrt{n}\,(\theta^*_{2n} - \theta^*_{1n}) + o_{P^o}(1)$$

provided that $P^o \in \tilde{\mathcal{P}}^u_a$. Now we generally have $\nabla^2 \bar{L}^*_{2n} s_{2t}(X^t, \theta^*_{2n}) - \nabla^2 \bar{L}^{*-1}_{1n} s_{1t}(X^t, \theta^*_{1n})$ satisfying the central limit theorem with expectation zero, which allows us to identify $a^*_n = S^*_n \sqrt{n}\,(\theta^*_{2n} - \theta^*_{1n})$. Thus, $a^*_n = 0$ $(P^o \in \mathcal{P}^u_o)$ when $\sqrt{n}\,(\theta^*_{2n} - \theta^*_{1n}) \to 0$, but we may also have $a^*_n = 0$ for certain choices of S^*_n.

Thus, Theorem 9.5 and the results of Sections 9.2 and 9.3 give general results for m-tests asymptotically equivalent to (an extension of) the Hausman test. These tests are sensitive to misspecifications that result in the divergence of the stochastic limits of two estimators that would be consistent for the same value (θ^o) in the absence of misspecification.

As introduced by Hausman, and as often interpreted in the literature, a Hausman test involves a comparison of an efficient estimator with an inefficient estimator that retains consistency for θ_o despite misspecification of the model generating the efficient estimator. However, these restrictions are unnecessary. Efficiency only affects the possibility of exploiting covariance matrix simplifications in computing a Hausman test statistic; the effect is to restrict the model implicitly tested. Nor is there any necessity for either estimator to retain consistency in the presence of misspecification. Power is achieved because the estimators chosen have differing probability limits under misspecified alternatives. These alternatives necessarily go beyond those that allow one of the estimators to retain consistency for a certain parameter value.

Because Hausman tests based on either m_{1t} or m_{2t} are asymptotically equivalent under $\mathcal{P}_a^u$, choice between them must be based either on their finite sample properties or on the basis of computational convenience. Consideration of finite sample properties is beyond the scope of our treatment here, so we content ourselves with consideration of computational convenience. If neither $\mathcal{S}_1$ or $\mathcal{S}_2$ is assumed to yield an efficient estimator, the choice of m_{1t} over m_{2t} is dictated primarily by which of $\hat{\theta}_n$ or $\tilde{\theta}_n$ is easier to compute. For example, if $\tilde{\theta}_n$ is easier to compute (e.g., $\tilde{\theta}_n$ is unweighted nonlinear least squares, while $\hat{\theta}_n$ is weighted nonlinear least squares with weights depending on θ), then m_{1t} gives a simpler m-statistic. On the other hand, if one of $\mathcal{S}_1$ or $\mathcal{S}_2$ yields an efficient estimator, then the computational conveniences of Corollaries 9.11 or 9.13 may become available. If $\hat{\theta}_n$ is treated as efficient, then m_{2t} gives a simpler m-statistic. Additional convenience is possible using Wooldridge's [1990] approach.

10.4 Cox Tests of Non-Nested Hypotheses

10.4.a General Case

Cox's [1961, 1962] tests are useful in contexts in which one wishes to test the correctness of a given probability model, say $\mathcal{P}_1$, in such a way that the test is particularly powerful against elements of an alternative model $\mathcal{P}_2$ that does not contain $\mathcal{P}_1$. (If it did, the tests of Chapter 8 would be appropriate.)

The motivation for Cox's test is that when $\mathcal{P}_1$ is correctly specified, then

$$\hat{M}_n \equiv \hat{L}_{1n} - \hat{L}_{2n} - E_{\hat{\theta}_n}(\hat{L}_{1n} - \hat{L}_{2n})$$

should be close to zero, where $\hat{L}_{1n} = n^{-1} \sum_{t=1}^{n} \log f_{1t}(X^t, \hat{\theta}_n)$, $\hat{L}_{2n} = n^{-1} \sum_{t=1}^{n} \log f_{2t}(X^t, \hat{\pi}_n)$, and $f_{1t} : \mathbb{R}^{vt} \times \Theta \to \mathbb{R}^+$ and $f_{2t} : \mathbb{R}^{vt} \times \Pi \to \mathbb{R}^+$ are the conditional densities and $\hat{\theta}_n$ and $\hat{\pi}_n$ the QMLE's generated by the parametric probability models $\mathcal{P}_1$ and $\mathcal{P}_2$ respectively. The difference $\hat{L}_{1n} - \hat{L}_{2n}$ is the average log-likelihood ratio for model 1 relative to model 2, while

$$E_{\hat{\theta}_n}(\hat{L}_{1n} - \hat{L}_{2n}) \equiv n^{-1} \int (\log f_1{}^n(x^n, \hat{\theta}_n)$$

$$- \log f_2{}^n(x^n, \hat{\pi}_n)) f_1{}^n(x^n, \hat{\theta}_n)\, d\nu^n(x^n)$$

(with $f_1{}^n \equiv \Pi_{t=1}^n f_{1t}$) is an estimate of the expected value of this average log-likelihood ratio when $\mathcal{P}_1$ is correctly specified. When n is large and $\mathcal{P}_1$ is correctly specified, the law of large numbers generally ensures that $\hat{L}_{1n} - \hat{L}_{2n}$ and (an appropriate estimate of) its expectation will be close to each other, so that $\hat{M}_n$ should indeed be close to zero.

The question of how far from zero is too far for $\hat{M}_n$ to be consonant with the correct specification of $\mathcal{P}_1$ can be answered approximately using the asymptotic distribution of $\hat{M}_n$. This distribution can be obtained straightforwardly by showing that $\hat{M}_n$ is in a form treated by Theorem 9.5 and its corollaries.

Substituting appropriately, we have

$$(9.1) \qquad \hat{M}_n = n^{-1} \sum_{t=1}^{n} (\log f_{1t}(X^t, \hat{\theta}_n) - \log f_{2t}(X^t, \hat{\pi}_n))$$

$$- \int (n^{-1} \sum_{t=1}^{n} [\log f_{1t}(x^t, \hat{\theta}_n) - \log f_{2t}(x^t, \hat{\pi}_n)])$$

$$\times \prod_{t=1}^{n} f_{1t}(x^t, \hat{\theta}_n)\, d\nu^n(x^n)$$

$$= n^{-1} \sum_{t=1}^{n} [(\log f_{1t}(x^t, \hat{\theta}_n) - \log f_{2t}(x^t, \hat{\pi}_n)$$

$$- \int (\log f_{1t}(x^t, \hat{\theta}_n) - \log f_{2t}(x^t, \hat{\pi}_n))\, f_1{}^t(x^t, \hat{\theta}_n)\, d\nu^t(x^t)] .$$

The second equality follows by "integrating out" appropriate terms in the integral in the first equation and collecting terms. From the second equation, we see that this gives an m-statistic using indicators

$$m_t(x^t, \theta, \pi) = \log f_{1t}(x^t, \theta) - \log f_{2t}(x^t, \pi)$$

$$- \int (\log f_{1t}(x^t, \theta) - \log f_{2t}(x^t, \pi))\, f_1{}^t(x^t, \theta)\, d\nu^t(x^t)\,.$$

This choice for m_t can be shown to satisfy Assumption 9.1 and the other conditions of Definition 9.3 under appropriate primitive conditions on f_{1t} and f_{2t}. However, some potentially severe computational difficulties arise from the νt-fold integration. In the case studied by Cox [1961, 1962], the observations are assumed independent. In that case, the integral above becomes the ν-fold integral

$$\int (\log f_{1t}(x_t, \theta) - \log f_{2t}(x_t, \pi))\, f_{1t}(x_t, \theta)\, d\nu_t(x_t)\,.$$

Although this is much more tractable, significant analytical and/or computational effort may still be required. Note also that the models treat the entire vector X_t as dependent, thus not allowing particular variables to be treated as exogenous.

These difficulties can be avoided by instead using indicators

$$m_t(x^t, \theta, \pi) = \log f_{1t}(x^t, \theta) - \log f_{2t}(x^t, \pi)$$

$$- \int (\log f_{1t}(x^t, \theta) - \log f_{2t}(x^t, \pi))\, f_{1t}(x^t, \theta)\, d\zeta_t(y_t)\,,$$

where now f_{1t} and f_{2t} are conditional densities of Y_t given W_t. Now the integral to be calculated is now only l-fold ($l \leq \nu$). This choice retains the spirit of Cox's approach because when $\mathcal{S}_1 = \{ f_{1t} \}$ is correctly specified for $\{ Y_t \mid W_t \}$ we have

$$E(m_t(X^t, \theta_o, \pi_n^*) \mid W_t)$$

$$= E\,(\log f_{1t}(X^t, \theta_o) - \log f_{2t}(X^t, \pi_n^*) \mid W_t)$$

$$- \int (\log f_{1t}(y_t, \tilde{X}^{t-1}, \theta_o) - \log f_t(y_t, \tilde{X}^{t-1}, \pi_n^*))$$

$$\times f_{1t}(y_t, \tilde{X}^{t-1}, \theta_o)\, d\zeta_t(y_t)$$

$$= 0\,.$$

Comparing

$$\hat{M}_n = n^{-1} \sum_{t=1}^{n} m_t(X^t, \hat{\theta}_n, \hat{\pi}_n)$$

$$= n^{-1} \sum_{t=1}^{n} [\log f_{1t}(X^t, \hat{\theta}_n) - \log f_{2t}(X^t, \hat{\pi}_n)]$$

$$\times n^{-1} \sum_{t=1}^{n} \int (\log f_{1t}(y_t, \tilde{X}^{t-1}, \hat{\theta}_n)$$

$$- \log f_{2t}(y_t, \tilde{X}^{t-1}, \hat{\pi}_n))\, f_{1t}(y_t, \tilde{X}^{t-1}, \hat{\theta}_n)\, d\zeta_t(y_t)$$

with equation (9.1), we see that the present expression effectively uses the sample to average over $\tilde{X}^{t-1}$ (W_t) in the second term, while the integral in (9.1) uses the model to average over $\tilde{X}^{t-1}$.

The asymptotic distribution of $\hat{M}_n$ may now be found by verifying the conditions of Theorem 9.5. Before doing this, we note that because $\hat{M}_n$ is a scalar in the present case, convenient tests can be based either on the χ_1^2 distribution (as have all tests discussed so far) or on the standard normal distribution. Indeed, as originally given, Cox's test is based on the normal distribution, and is proposed as a *one-tailed* test, with large negative values leading to rejection of the correctness of $\mathcal{P}_1$ $(\mathcal{S}_1)$ (Cox [1961, p. 114]). While large negative values are in fact to be expected when $\mathcal{P}_2$ $(\mathcal{S}_2)$ indeed contains the data generation process, it is nevertheless possible for $\hat{M}_n$ to take excessively large positive values when neither specification is correct. Because (as Cox [1962, p. 407] explicitly states) the hypotheses $P_o \in \mathcal{P}_1$ and $P_o \in \mathcal{P}_2$ are not the only possibilities (i.e., neither model need be correctly specified), the problem addressed by Cox's test is one of "significance testing," rather than model selection. For this reason, it is desirable to conduct two-tailed tests using the normal distribution, or, equivalently, tests based on the upper tail of the χ_1^2 distribution. However, the sign of $\hat{M}_n$ may contain potentially useful information.

Now consider the requirements of Assumptions 9.1, 9.2 and the other conditions of Definition 9.3 for m_t. It is convenient to consider the terms $\log f_{1t}(X^t, \theta) - \log f_{2t}(X^t, \pi)$ and

$$\mu_{12t}(w_t, \theta, \pi) \equiv \int (\log f_{1t}(x^t, \theta) - \log f_{2t}(x^t, \pi))\, f_{1t}(x^t, \theta)\, d\zeta_t(y_t)$$

separately.

Measurability, continuity and differentiability conditions hold for log

$f_{1t} - \log f_{2t}$ given analogous conditions separately for $\log f_{1t}$ and $\log f_{2t}$. Only f_{1t} contributes to $\nabla_\theta\, m_t$ from $\log f_{1t} - \log f_{2t}$.

Additional conditions are needed to ensure that μ_{12t} is properly behaved. Specifically, measurability will follow by Fubini's theorem (Billingsley [1979, Theorem 18.3]) given the integrability of $[\log f_{1t}(x^t, \theta)]\, f_{1t}(x^t, \theta)$ and $\log f_{2t}(x^t, \pi)\, f_{1t}(x^t, \theta)$ with respect to ζ_t *a.e.*-$\tilde{\nu}^{t-1}$ for each θ in Θ and (θ, π) in $\Theta \times \Pi$ respectively. This condition requires careful verification in applications. It fails for example when f_{1t} is a (conditional) Cauchy density and f_{2t} is a (conditional) normal density. Next, continuity and differentiability ($a.s.-P_o$) can be ensured as consequences of the Lebesgue dominated convergence theorem (e.g. Theorem 16.8 of Billingsley [1979]). For this, appropriate domination conditions on $[\log f_{1t}(x^t, \theta)]\, f_{1t}(x^t, \theta)$, $[\log f_{2t}(x^t, \pi)]\, f_{1t}(x^t, \theta)$ and the derivatives of these with respect to θ will suffice. Domination conditions on the derivatives of $[\log f_{2t}(x^t, \pi)]\, f_{1t}(x^t, \theta)$ with respect to π will also be useful in permitting a mean value expansion useful in verifying condition 9.3(i). Thus, verifying Assumption 9.1 for μ_{12t} requires a little care.

Assumption 9.2 requires an appropriate limit π_n^* for $\hat{\pi}_n$. Because $\hat{\pi}_n$ is the QMLE generated by $\mathcal{S}_2$, any relevant consistency result of Chapters 3 through 5 can be used to provide appropriate conditions.

Now consider the requirements of Definition 9.3. A mean value expansion of $\hat{M}_n$ around $(\hat{\theta}_n, \hat{\pi}_n)$ gives

$$\begin{aligned}
\sqrt{n}\, \hat{M}_n &= n^{-1/2} \sum_{t=1}^{n} \log \hat{f}_{1t} - \log \hat{f}_{2t} - \hat{\mu}_{12t} \\
&= n^{-1/2} \sum_{t=1}^{n} \log f_{1t}^* - \log f_{2t}^* - \mu_{12t}^* \\
&\quad + (\nabla_\theta' \ddot{L}_{1n} - \nabla_\theta' \ddot{\mu}_{12n})\, \sqrt{n}\, (\hat{\theta}_n - \theta_n^*) \\
&\quad - (\nabla_\pi' \ddot{L}_{2n} + \nabla_\pi' \ddot{\mu}_{12n})\, \sqrt{n}\, (\hat{\pi}_n - \pi_n^*)\,,
\end{aligned}$$

where $\hat{f}_{1t} \equiv f_{1t}(X^t, \hat{\theta}_n)$, $\hat{f}_{2t} \equiv f_{2t}(X^t, \hat{\pi}_n)$, $\hat{\mu}_{12t} = \mu_{12t}(W_t, \hat{\theta}_n, \hat{\pi}_n)$, $f_{1t}^* \equiv f_{2t}(X^t, \theta_n^*)$, $f_{2t}^* \equiv f_{2t}(X^t, \pi_n^*)$, $\mu_{12t}^* \equiv \mu_{12t}(W_t, \theta_n^*, \pi_n^*)$ and $\nabla_\theta \ddot{L}_{1n}$, $\nabla_\pi \ddot{L}_{2n}$, $\nabla_\theta \ddot{\mu}_{12n}$ and $\nabla_\pi \ddot{\mu}_{12n}$ represent the gradients of L_{1n}, L_{2n}, and $n^{-1} \sum_{t=1}^n \mu_{12t}$ with respect to θ and π as indicated, evaluated at mean values lying between $(\hat{\theta}_n, \hat{\pi}_n)$ and (θ_n^*, π_n^*). Adding and subtracting appropriate terms gives

$$\sqrt{n}\,\hat{M}_n = n^{-1/2} \sum_{t=1}^{n} \log f_{1t}^* - \log f_{2t}^* - \mu_{12t}^*$$

$$+ (\nabla_\theta' \bar{L}_{1n}^* - \nabla_\theta' \bar{\mu}_{12n}^*) \sqrt{n}\,(\hat{\theta}_n - \theta_n^*)$$

$$- (\nabla_\pi' \bar{L}_{2n}^* + \nabla_\pi' \bar{\mu}_{12n}^*) \sqrt{n}\,(\hat{\pi}_n - \pi_n^*)$$

$$+ (\nabla_\theta' \ddot{L}_{1n} - \nabla_\theta' \ddot{\mu}_{12n} - \nabla_\theta' \bar{L}_{1n}^* + \nabla_\theta' \bar{\mu}_{12n}^*) \sqrt{n}\,(\hat{\theta}_n - \theta_n^*)$$

$$- (\nabla_\pi' \ddot{L}_{2n} + \nabla_\pi' \ddot{\mu}_{12n} - \nabla_\pi' \bar{L}_{2n}^* - \nabla_\pi' \bar{\mu}_{12n}^*) \sqrt{n}\,(\hat{\pi}_n - \pi_n^*),$$

where $\nabla_\theta \bar{L}_{1n}^*$, $\nabla_\theta \bar{\mu}_{12n}^*$, $\nabla_\pi \bar{L}_{2n}^*$, $\nabla_\pi \bar{\mu}_{12n}^*$ will be explicitly given shortly. Now in general $\sqrt{n}\,(\hat{\theta}_n - \theta_n^*)$ and $\sqrt{n}\,(\hat{\pi}_n - \pi_n^*)$ are $O_{P_o}(1)$. The last two terms vanish provided that $\nabla_\theta \ddot{L}_{1n} - \nabla_\theta \bar{L}_{1n}^* \to 0$ $prob-P_o$, $\nabla_\theta \ddot{\mu}_{12n} - \nabla_\theta \bar{\mu}_{12n}^* \to 0$ $prob-P_o$, $\nabla_\pi \ddot{L}_{2n} - \nabla_\pi \bar{L}_{2n}^* \to 0$ $prob-P_o$ and $\nabla_\pi \ddot{\mu}_{12n} - \nabla_\pi \bar{\mu}_{12n}^* \to 0$ $prob-P_o$. These follow as a consequence of Corollary 3.8 given the consistency of $\hat{\theta}_n$ for θ_n^* and $\hat{\pi}_n$ for π_n^*, together with a uniform law of large numbers for $\{s_{1t}(X^t, \theta)\}$, $\{\nabla_\theta \mu_{12t}(W_t, \theta, \pi)\}$, $\{s_{2t}(X^t, \theta)\}$ and $\{\nabla_\pi \mu_{12t}(W_t, \theta, \pi)\}$, with $\nabla_\theta \bar{L}_{1n}^* = n^{-1} \sum_{t=1}^n E(s_{1t}^*)$, $\nabla_\theta \bar{\mu}_{12n}^* = n^{-1} \sum_{t=1}^n E(\nabla_\theta \mu_{12t}^*)$, $\nabla_\pi \bar{L}_{2n}^* = n^{-1} \sum_{t=1}^n E(s_{2t}^*)$, $\nabla_\pi \bar{\mu}_{12n}^* = n^{-1} \sum_{t=1}^n E(\nabla_\pi \mu_{12t}^*)$, where $\nabla_\theta \mu_{12t}^* \equiv \nabla_\theta \mu_{12t}(W_t, \theta_n^*, \pi_n^*)$ and $\nabla_\pi \mu_{12t}^* \equiv \nabla_\pi \mu_{12t}(W_t, \theta_n^*, \pi_n^*)$.

Setting $m_t^* = \log f_{1t}^* - \log f_{2t}^* - \mu_{12t}^*$ and $\nabla_\theta \bar{M}_n^* = \nabla_\theta \bar{L}_{1n}^* - \nabla_\theta \bar{\mu}_{12n}^*$, we have

$$\sqrt{n}\,\hat{M}_n = n^{-1/2} \sum_{t=1}^{n} m_t^* + \nabla_\theta' \bar{M}_n^* \sqrt{n}\,(\hat{\theta}_n - \theta_n^*) + o_{P_o}(1)$$

as desired, provided that

$$(\nabla_\pi' \bar{L}_{2n}^* + \nabla_\pi' \bar{\mu}_{12n}^*) \sqrt{n}\,(\hat{\pi}_n - \pi_n^*) \to 0 \quad prob-P_o\,.$$

Because $\sqrt{n}\,(\hat{\pi}_n - \pi_n^*)$ is $O_{P_o}(1)$, it suffices that $\nabla_\pi \bar{L}_{2n}^* + \nabla_\pi \bar{\mu}_{12n}^* \to 0$. Now $\nabla_\pi \bar{L}_{2n}^* = 0$, because π_n^* maximizes $\bar{L}_{2n}$ interior to Π, so it remains to establish $\nabla_\pi \bar{\mu}_{12n}^* \to 0$. Consider

$$E(\nabla_\pi \mu^*_{12t}) = \int [\nabla_\pi \int \log f_{2t}(x^t, \pi^*_n) f_{1t}(x^t, \theta^*_n) d\zeta_t(y_t)] \ddot{g}_t(w_t) d\ddot{\nu}_t(w_t)$$

$$= \int\int \nabla_\pi \log f_{2t}(x^t, \pi^*_n) f_{1t}(x^t, \theta^*_n) \ddot{g}_t(w_t) d\zeta_t(y_t) d\ddot{\nu}_t(w_t)$$

where $\ddot{g}_t$ is the probability density for W_t, and the second equality follows when the interchange of derivative and integral is allowed. If S_1 is correct for $\{Y_t \mid W_t\}$ then $\theta^*_n = \theta_o$ and $f_{1t}(x^t, \theta_o)\, \ddot{g}_t(w_t) = \ddot{g}_t(y_t, w_t)$, the joint probability density for Y_t, W_t. It follows that

$$E(\nabla_\pi \mu^*_{12t}) = E(\nabla_\pi \log f_{2t}(X^t, \pi^*_n)) = E(s^*_{2t}),$$

which implies that $\nabla_\pi \bar{\mu}^*_{12n} = n^{-1} \sum_{t=1}^n E(\nabla_\pi \mu^*_{12t}) = n^{-1} \sum_{t=1}^n E(s^*_{2t}) = \nabla_\pi \bar{L}^*_{2n} = 0$, as desired.

For the case of local alternatives, it suffices that $\{f_{1t}\}$ is locally misspecified in such a way that $\sqrt{n}\, \nabla_\pi \bar{\mu}^*_{12n}$ is $O(1)$, in which case we still have $\nabla_\pi \bar{\mu}^*_{12n} \to 0$. Such local misspecifications can be constructed as $f_{1t} = (1 + \upsilon_t/\sqrt{n})\, f^o_{1t}$, where f^o_{1t} is correctly specified for $\{Y_t \mid W_t\}$ and $\upsilon_t : \mathbb{R}^{vt} \times \Theta \to \mathbb{R}$ is properly chosen.

This establishes that condition 9.3(i) holds generally for correctly specified and locally misspecified $\{f_{1t}\}$. To examine condition 9.3(ii) and 9.4(ii), we need to determine A^*_n and s^*_n. Because $\hat{\theta}_n$ is the QMLE in this application, the required forms for A^*_n and s^*_n are given by any relevant result of Chapter 6. For concreteness, put $A^*_n = \nabla^2 \bar{L}^*_{1n}$ and $s^*_n = n^{-1} \sum_{t=1}^n s^*_t$, $s^*_t = \nabla \log f^*_{1t}$. Conditions 9.3(ii) or 9.4(ii) then require the asymptotic normality of

$$n^{-1/2} \sum_{t=1}^{n} m^*_t - \nabla'_\theta \bar{M}^*_n A^{*-1}_n s^*_t$$

$$= n^{-1/2} \sum_{t=1}^{n} [\log f^*_{1t} - \log f^*_{2t} - \mu^*_{12t} - \nabla'_\theta \bar{\mu}^*_{12n} \nabla^2 \bar{L}^{*-1}_{1n} \nabla \log f^*_{1t}].$$

An appropriate central limit theorem will guarantee this provided (among other things) that the expectation of the quantity above is bounded. For the null hypothesis, this includes cases in which $E(\log f^*_{1t} - \log f^*_{2t} - \mu^*_{12t}) = 0$. This occurs when the model is correctly specified, by arguments similar to those used to examine $E(\nabla_\pi \mu^*_{12t})$. Local alternatives arise when $n^{-1/2} \sum_{t=1}^n m^*_t$ is $O_p(1)$. Again, this occurs for locally misspecified $\{f_{1t}\}$.

The results of Sections 9.2 and 9.3 provide a variety of different versions of the Cox test. As before, we leave investigation of these as an exercise for the reader.

10.4.b Linear Exponential Family

Now consider the Cox test that arises when $\mathcal{S}_1$ and $\mathcal{S}_2$ specify members of the (extended) linear exponential family (Assumptions 5.3 or 6.7). Put

$$f_{1t}(Y_t, W_t, \theta) = \exp \phi_{1t}(Y_t, \mu_{1t}(W_t, \beta), \kappa_{1t}(W_t, \alpha))$$

and

$$f_{2t}(Y_t, W_t, \pi) = \exp \phi_{2t}(Y_t, \mu_{2t}(W_t, \delta), \kappa_{2t}(W_t, \gamma)),$$

where

$$\phi_{1t}(y, \mu, \kappa) = a_{1t}(\mu, \kappa) + b_{1t}(y, \kappa) + y' c_{1t}(\mu, \kappa)$$

$$\phi_{2t}(y, \mu, \kappa) = a_{2t}(\mu, \kappa) + b_{2t}(y, \kappa) + y' c_{2t}(\mu, \kappa)$$

as in Assumption 6.7. This family is closely related to the Koopmans-Darmois family discussed by Cox [1961].

A leading case is the multivariate normal with mean μ and covariance matrix Σ. In this case, set $\kappa = \textit{vech}\ \Sigma^{-1}$ and

$$a(\mu, \kappa) = -\mu' \Sigma^{-1} \mu/2 + (1/2) \log \det \Sigma^{-1}$$

$$b(y, \kappa) = -y' \Sigma^{-1} y/2 - (1/2) \log 2\pi$$

$$c(\mu, \kappa) = \Sigma^{-1} \mu .$$

These choices for a, b, and c are particularly useful for testing non-nested hypotheses involving conditional means and/or conditional variances. Testing non-nested hypotheses about conditional means has been a major focus of interest in econometrics since the influential work of Pesaran and Deaton [1978] (see the survey by MacKinnon [1983]). Testing non-nested hypotheses about conditional variances has been approached somewhat differently by King and his colleagues (King [1985], Evans and King [1985]). Dastoor and Fisher [1988] provide an interpretation of King's approach within the context of Cox tests.

Returning to the general linear exponential family, let

$$\hat{\mu}_{1t} = \mu_{1t}(W_t, \hat{\beta}_n), \hat{\kappa}_{1t} = \kappa_{1t}(W_t, \hat{\alpha}_n),$$

$$\hat{\mu}_{2t} = \mu_{2t}(W_t, \hat{\delta}_n), \; \hat{\kappa}_{2t} = \kappa_{2t}(W_t, \hat{\gamma}_n),$$

and define $\hat{a}_{1t}$, $\hat{a}_{2t}$, $\hat{b}_{1t}$, $\hat{b}_{2t}$, $\hat{c}_{1t}$ and $\hat{c}_{2t}$ in the obvious manner. Then

$$\hat{M}_n = n^{-1} \sum_{t=1}^{n} \log \hat{f}_{1t} - \log \hat{f}_{2t} - \hat{\mu}_{12t}$$

$$= n^{-1} \sum_{t=1}^{n} (\hat{a}_{1t} - \hat{a}_{2t}) + (\hat{b}_{1t} - \hat{b}_{2t}) + Y_t'(\hat{c}_{1t} - \hat{c}_{2t}) - \hat{\mu}_{12t}.$$

Now

$$\hat{\mu}_{12t} \equiv \int [(\hat{a}_{1t} - \hat{a}_{2t}) + (\hat{b}_{1t} - \hat{b}_{2t}) + y_t'(\hat{c}_{1t} - \hat{c}_{2t})$$

$$\times \qquad \exp \phi_{1t}(y_t, \hat{\mu}_{1t}, \hat{\kappa}_{1t}) \, d\zeta_t(y_t)$$

$$= (\hat{a}_{1t} - \hat{a}_{2t}) + \int (\hat{b}_{1t} - \hat{b}_{2t}) \exp \hat{\phi}_{1t} \, d\zeta_t + \hat{\mu}_{1t}'(\hat{c}_{1t} - \hat{c}_{2t}),$$

where we have written $\hat{\phi}_{1t} = \phi_{1t}(y, \hat{\mu}_{1t}, \hat{\kappa}_{1t})$ and made use of Assumption 6.7. Consequently,

$$\hat{M}_n = [n^{-1} \sum_{t=1}^{n} (\hat{a}_{1t} - \hat{a}_{2t}) - \int (\hat{b}_{1t} - \hat{b}_{2t}) \exp \hat{\phi}_{1t} \, d\zeta_t]$$

$$+ n^{-1} \sum_{t=1}^{n} (Y_t - \hat{\mu}_{1t})'(\hat{c}_{1t} - \hat{c}_{2t}).$$

This statistic splits into two parts. The second is sensitive to departures of the conditional mean from μ_{1t} in the direction of μ_{2t}; the first part essentially allows detection of misspecification of conditional dispersion as specified by ϕ_{1t} in the direction specified by ϕ_{2t}.

To see this more clearly, suppose first that both specifications posit multivariate normality with $\Sigma = I_l$, so that $\hat{\beta}_n$ and $\hat{\delta}_n$ are (nonlinear multivariate) least squares estimators for the models $\mathcal{M}_1 = \{\mu_{1t}\}$ and $\mathcal{M}_2 = \{\mu_{2t}\}$. Then $b_{1t}(y, \hat{\kappa}_{1t}) = b_{2t}(y, \hat{\kappa}_{2t})$, $\hat{c}_{1t} = \hat{\mu}_{1t}$ and $\hat{c}_{2t} = \hat{\mu}_{2t}$, so that

$$\hat{M}_n = n^{-1} \sum_{t=1}^{n} (\hat{\mu}_{1t} - \hat{\mu}_{2t})'(Y_t - \hat{\mu}_{1t}).$$

Note that the form of $\hat{m}_t = (\hat{\mu}_{1t} - \hat{\mu}_{2t})' \, (Y_t - \hat{\mu}_{1t})$ and $\hat{s}_t = \nabla_\beta \, \hat{\mu}_{1t} \, \nabla_\mu \, \hat{c}_{1t} \, (Y_t - \hat{\mu}_{1t})$ implies the potential applicability of Corollary 9.13 for this case.

Next, suppose that both specifications posit multivariate normality with $\mu_{1t} = \mu_{2t}$, but with κ_{1t} and κ_{2t} non-nested. In this case, tedious algebra yields

$$\hat{M}_n = tr\, n^{-1} \sum_{t=1}^{n} (\hat{\Sigma}_{2t}^{-1} - \hat{\Sigma}_{1t}^{-1}) \, [(Y_t - \hat{\mu}_{1t}) \, (Y_t - \hat{\mu}_{1t})' - \hat{\Sigma}_{1t}] \, ,$$

where $\hat{\Sigma}_{1t}$ and $\hat{\Sigma}_{2t}$ are the estimated conditional covariances associated with $\mathcal{S}_1$ and $\mathcal{S}_2$ respectively. Note that the form of $\hat{M}_n$ in this case is analogous to that obtained in the case of non-nested models of conditional mean.

The general case in which models for the conditional mean and conditional variance are both non-nested can be handled similarly. The form of $\hat{M}_n$ can be shown to be

$$\hat{M}_n = tr\, n^{-1} \sum_{t=1}^{n} (\hat{\Sigma}_{2t}^{-1} - \hat{\Sigma}_{1t}^{-1}) \, [(Y_t - \hat{\mu}_{1t}) \, (Y_t - \hat{\mu}_{1t})' - \hat{\Sigma}_{1t}]$$

$$+ \, n^{-1} \sum_{t=1}^{n} (\hat{\mu}_{1t} - \hat{\mu}_{2t})' \, \hat{\Sigma}_{2t}^{-1} \, (Y_t - \hat{\mu}_{1t}) \, .$$

This expression contains two terms, one for the conditional variance identical to that given above, and the other for the conditional mean, analogous to that given earlier.

The theory of the m-test easily allows for consideration of any finite number of non-nested alternatives, as advocated by Davidson and MacKinnon [1981]. To treat more than one alternative, one stacks $\hat{M}_n$ for each non-nested alternative into a vector. For example, a least squares based test of the correctness of $\mathcal{M}_1 = \{ \mu_{1t} \}$ using Cox tests against non-nested alternatives $\mathcal{M}_2 = \{ \mu_{2t} \}$ and $\mathcal{M}_3 = \{ \mu_{3t} \}$ can be based on

$$\hat{M}_n' = n^{-1} \sum_{t=1}^{n} [(\hat{\mu}_{1t} - \hat{\mu}_{2t})' \, (Y_t - \hat{\mu}_{1t}), \, (\hat{\mu}_{1t} - \hat{\mu}_{3t})' \, (Y_t - \hat{\mu}_{1t})] \, .$$

The theory of the m-test applies straightforwardly to this statistic.

10.5 Encompassing Tests

The encompassing principle is a general model evaluation principle developed by Hendry, Mizon and Richard, among others (Hendry and Richard [1982], Mizon [1984], Mizon and Richard [1986]). The essential concept underlying the encompassing approach is simple, but of fundamental importance to the investigation of any empirical phenomenon. This is that any correctly specified model must be capable of explaining (or predicting) the statistical results obtained from any other (possibly misspecified) model of the same phenomenon. We saw in Chapter 3 that the QMLE tends to a limit that depends on both the model specification and on the underlying data generation process. This dependence is the basis for using a correctly specified model to explain the statistical results of any competitor.

10.5.a Complete Parametric Encompassing

Notions of encompassing split into two convenient subcategories, "complete parametric encompassing" (CPE) and "incomplete parametric encompassing" (IPE).

To motivate CPE, let $\mathcal{P} = \{ f_1{}^n(\cdot, \alpha) : \alpha \in \mathrm{A} \}$ be a parametric probability model, correctly specified in its entirety, and let $\mathcal{S} = \{ f_{2t}(\cdot, \delta) : \delta \in \Delta \}$ be any alternative specification, not necessarily compatible with $\mathcal{P}$. Let the QMLE generated by $\mathcal{S}$ be denoted $\tilde{\delta}_n$. Then the conditions of Theorem 3.5 (for example) ensure that $\tilde{\delta}_n - \delta_n^* \to 0$ *a.s.* $- P_o$ (*prob* $- P_o$), where

$$\delta_n^* = \operatorname{argmax}_\Delta \bar{L}_{2n}(\delta) = n^{-1} \sum_{t=1}^{n} E(\log f_{2t}(X^t, \delta))$$
$$= \operatorname{argmax}_\Delta \int [n^{-1} \sum_{t=1}^{n} \log f_{2t}(x^t, \delta)] f_1{}^n(x^n, \alpha_o)\, d\nu^n(x^n).$$

The second equality holds when $\mathcal{P}$ is correctly specified, with $dP_o^n / d\nu^n = f_1{}^n(\cdot, \alpha_o)$. Now let α_o vary over $\mathcal{A}$. When $f_1{}^n$ and $f_2{}^n = \Pi_{t=1}^n f_{2t}$ are appropriately regular, the theorem of the maximum (e.g. Varian [1984, pp. 326–327]) ensures that the function

$$\delta_n(\alpha) \equiv \operatorname{argmax}_\Delta \int [n^{-1} \sum_{t=1}^{n} \log f_{2t}(x^t, \delta)]\, f_1{}^n(x^n, \alpha)\, d\nu^n(x^n)$$

is smooth in α. For present purposes, it suffices that $\delta_n : \mathcal{A} \to \Delta$ is continuously differentiable.

When $\mathcal{P}$ is correctly specified, it follows that $\delta_n^* = \delta_n(\alpha_o)$. In the terminology of Mizon [1984] and Mizon and Richard [1986], it is said that $\mathcal{P}$ has the property of complete parametric encompassing of $\mathcal{S}$. A definition somewhat more specific than that of Mizon and Richard [1986, Definition 3] is the following.

DEFINITION 10.1: Given Assumption 2.1, let $\mathcal{S}_1 = \{ f_{1t} : \mathbb{R}^{vt} \times \mathcal{A} \to \mathbb{R}^+ \}$ and $\mathcal{S}_2 = \{ f_{2t} : \mathbb{R}^{vt} \times \Delta \to \mathbb{R}^+ \}$ be specifications such that Assumptions 2.3 and 3.2 hold for $\mathcal{S}_1$, generating dependent variables $\{ Y_t \}$ and explanatory variables $\{ W_{1t} \}$ with respect to $\{ \zeta_t \}$, and suppose Assumptions 2.3 and 3.2 hold for $\mathcal{S}_2$. Define

$$\alpha_n^* = \text{argmax}_{\mathcal{A}} \, \bar{L}_{1n}(\alpha) \equiv n^{-1} \sum_{t=1}^{n} E(\log f_{1t}(X^t, \alpha))$$

$$\delta_n^* = \text{argmax}_{\Delta} \, \bar{L}_{2n}(\delta) \equiv n^{-1} \sum_{t=1}^{n} E(\log f_{2t}(X^t, \delta))$$

and suppose that $\mathcal{S}_1$ and $\mathcal{S}_2$ ensure the existence and finiteness of the functions

$$\delta_n(\alpha) =$$

$$\text{argmax}_{\Delta} \, n^{-1} \sum_{t=1}^{n} E\left[\int \log f_{2t}(y_t, \tilde{X}^{t-1}; \delta) f_{1t}(y_t, \tilde{X}^{t-1}; \alpha) \, d\zeta_t(y_t) \right]$$

$n = 1, 2, \ldots$. Then $\mathcal{S}_1$ has the property of *complete parametric encompassing (CPE) of $\mathcal{S}_2$ to order $\sqrt{n}$ under P_o* if $\{ \sqrt{n}\,(\delta_n^* - \delta_n(\alpha_n^*)) \} = O(1)$. □

We impose the requirement $\{ \sqrt{n}\,(\delta_n^* - \delta_n(\alpha_n^*)) \} = O(1)$ to aid in investigating $\mathcal{P}_a^u$. This requirement implies $\delta_n^* - \delta_n(\alpha_n^*) \to 0$, and holds when $\delta_n^* = \delta_n(\alpha_n^*)$ *a.a.n.* For brevity we shall say "$\mathcal{S}_1$ parametrically encompasses $\mathcal{S}_2$ completely." Thus, complete parametric encompassing is a property of the joint relation of $\mathcal{S}_1$ and $\mathcal{S}_2$ to P_o. It does not necessarily require the correctness of $\mathcal{S}_1$. It is nevertheless an important fact that the correctness of $\mathcal{S}_1$ for $\{ Y_t \mid W_{1t} \}$ is sufficient for CPE as the following result establishes.

THEOREM 10.2: *Given Assumption 2.1, let $\mathcal{S}_1$ and $\mathcal{S}_2$ satisfy the conditions of Definition 10.1. Suppose also that for all $\delta \in \Delta$, $f_{2t}(X^t, \delta)$ is measurable $-\sigma(Y_t, W_{2t})$, $t = 1, 2, \ldots$.*

(i) if $\mathcal{S}_1$ is correctly specified for $\{ Y_t \mid W_{1t} \}$, $\sigma(W_{2t}) \subseteq \sigma(W_{1t})$, then $\mathcal{S}_1$ parametrically encompasses $\mathcal{S}_2$ completely.

(ii) Suppose Assumption 5.1 and either Assumption 5.3 or 6.7 hold so that $\mathcal{S}_1 = \{ \exp \phi_{1t} \}$ is based on $\mathcal{M}_1 = \{ \mu_{1t} \}$ and $\mathcal{S}_2 = \{ \exp \phi_{2t} \}$ is based on $\mathcal{M}_2 = \{ \mu_{2t} \}$. If $\mathcal{M}_1$ is correctly specified for $\{ E(Y_t \mid W_{1t}) \}$, $\sigma(W_{2t}) \subseteq \sigma(W_{1t})$, then $\mathcal{S}_1$ parametrically encompasses $\mathcal{S}_2$ completely. □

Note that $\mathcal{S}_2$ need not generate the same dependent variables as $\mathcal{S}_1$. Also note that while $\mathcal{S}_1$ may be correctly specified for $\{ Y_t \mid W_{1t} \}$, it may be misspecified for $\{ Y_t \mid \tilde{X}^{t-1} \}$, i.e. there may be dynamic misspecification. CPE nevertheless holds.

This result forms the basis for encompassing tests based on a comparison of $\tilde{\delta}_n$ (generated by $\mathcal{S}_2$) and $\hat{\delta}_n = \delta_n(\hat{\alpha}_n)$, where $\hat{\alpha}_n$ is generated by $\mathcal{S}_1$. If $\mathcal{S}_1$ is correctly specified to some extent, then $\tilde{\delta}_n - \hat{\delta}_n$ should be close to zero. If not, then one has evidence of model misspecification. Mizon and Richard [1986] derive the asymptotic distribution of $\sqrt{n}\,(\tilde{\delta}_n - \hat{\delta}_n)$ under the hypothesis of correct specification of $\mathcal{S}_1$, and obtain a Wald Encompassing Test (WET) and a Score Encompassing Test (SET). As may be expected, $\sqrt{n}\,(\tilde{\delta}_n - \hat{\delta}_n) \overset{A}{\sim} N(0, J_n^*)$ under the null hypothesis for a covariance matrix J_n^* consistently estimated by $\hat{J}_n$, say. This yields a WET of the form $n\,(\tilde{\delta}_n - \hat{\delta}_n)'\,\hat{J}_n^-\,(\tilde{\delta}_n - \hat{\delta}_n)$. For now, we focus on the WET. In the present context, the SET is asymptotically equivalent under CPE.

Our goal here is to show that the WET falls into the m-testing framework. Unlike Mizon and Richard [1986] we do not assume that $\mathcal{S}_1$ is correctly specified; our theory holds under Definition 10.1. We show that the WET statistic is asymptotically equivalent to an m-statistic. For this it suffices to show that $\sqrt{n}\,(\tilde{\delta}_n - \hat{\delta}_n)$ is asymptotically equivalent to $\sqrt{n}\,\hat{M}_n$ for suitable choice of $\hat{M}_n$ under CPE.

Consider the collection $\tilde{\mathcal{P}}_a^u$ of probability measures P^o such that $\{\sqrt{n}\,(\delta_n^* - \delta_n(\alpha_n^*))\}$ is $O(1)$. We take a mean value expansion of $n^{-1/2}\sum_{t=1}^n s_{2t}(X^t, \hat{\delta}_n)$ around $\tilde{\delta}_n$ to get

$$n^{-1/2}\sum_{t=1}^{n} s_{2t}(X^t, \hat{\delta}_n) = n^{-1/2}\sum_{t=1}^{n} s_{2t}(X^t, \tilde{\delta}_n) + \nabla_\delta^2 \ddot{L}_{2n}\,\sqrt{n}\,(\hat{\delta}_n - \tilde{\delta}_n)\,,$$

where $\nabla_\delta^2 \ddot{L}_{2n}$ is the Hessian of $L_{2n}(X^n, \delta)$ with rows evaluated at mean values lying between $\hat{\delta}_n$ and $\tilde{\delta}_n$. In general, we have $n^{-1/2}\sum_{t=1}^n s_{2t}(X^t, \tilde{\delta}_n) \to 0$ $prob-P^o$. Let $\nabla_\delta^2 \hat{L}_{2n} \equiv n^{-1}\sum_{t=1}^n \nabla_\delta^2 \log f_{2t}(X^t, \hat{\delta}_n)$. Then

$$n^{-1/2}\sum_{t=1}^{n} s_{2t}(X^t, \hat{\delta}_n) = \nabla_\delta^2 \hat{L}_{2n}\;\sqrt{n}\,(\hat{\delta}_n - \tilde{\delta}_n) + (\nabla_\delta^2 \ddot{L}_{2n} - \nabla_\delta^2 \hat{L}_{2n})$$
$$\times\sqrt{n}\,(\hat{\delta}_n - \tilde{\delta}_n) + o_{P^o}(1)$$

$$= \nabla_\delta^2 \hat{L}_{2n}\,\sqrt{n}\,(\hat{\delta}_n - \tilde{\delta}_n) + o_{P^o}(1)\,.$$

The term $(\nabla_\delta^2 \ddot{L}_{2n} - \nabla_\delta^2 \hat{L}_{2n}) \sqrt{n}\,(\hat{\delta}_n - \tilde{\delta}_n) \to 0$ $prob-P^o$ under $\tilde{\mathcal{P}}_a^u$ because $\sqrt{n}\,(\hat{\delta}_n - \tilde{\delta}_n) = \sqrt{n}\,(\hat{\delta}_n - \delta_n(\alpha_n^*)) + \sqrt{n}\,(\tilde{\delta}_n - \delta_n^*) + \sqrt{n}\,(\delta_n(\alpha_n^*) - \delta_n^*)$ is $O_{P^o}(1)$ when $\sqrt{n}\,(\delta_n^* - \delta_n(\alpha_n^*))$ is $O(1)$, generally, and because $\nabla_\delta^2 \ddot{L}_{2n} - \nabla_\delta^2 \hat{L}_{2n} \to 0$ $prob-P^o$ as a consequence of the uniform law of large numbers and the facts that $\tilde{\delta}_n - \delta_n^* \to 0$ $prob-P^o$, $\hat{\delta}_n - \delta_n(\alpha_n^*) \to 0$ $prob-P^o$ and $\delta_n^* - \delta_n(\alpha_n^*) \to 0$ (applying Corollary 3.8). From this it follows that

$$\sqrt{n}\,(\hat{\delta}_n - \tilde{\delta}_n) = \nabla_\delta^2 \hat{L}_{2n}^- \, n^{-1/2} \sum_{t=1}^{n} s_{2t}(X^t, \delta_n(\hat{\alpha}_n)) + o_{P^o}(1),$$

which allows us to specify

$$m_t(X^t, \hat{\theta}_n, \hat{\pi}_n) = \nabla_\delta^2 \hat{L}_{2n}^- \, s_{2t}(X^t, \delta_n(\hat{\alpha}_n)).$$

Here, $\hat{\theta}_n = \hat{\alpha}_n$ and $\hat{\pi}_n = vec\, \nabla_\delta^2 \hat{L}_{2n}^-$. Note the implicit dependence of m_t on n.

As with the Hausman test, it is often convenient to premultiply $\sqrt{n}\,(\hat{\delta}_n - \tilde{\delta}_n)$ by a (possibly) stochastic matrix $\hat{S}_n$. Thus, we consider

$$m_t(X^t, \hat{\theta}_n, \hat{\pi}_n) = \hat{S}_n \, \nabla_\delta^2 \hat{L}_{2n}^- \, s_{2t}(X^t, \delta_n(\hat{\alpha}_n))$$

so that now $\hat{\pi}_n = vec\, \hat{S}_n \nabla^2 \hat{L}_{2n}^-$, and when $\hat{S}_n$ is $O_{P^o}(1)$, we have for this choice of m_t

$$\sqrt{n}\, \hat{S}_n (\hat{\delta}_n - \tilde{\delta}_n) = \sqrt{n}\, \hat{M}_n + o_{P^o}(1)$$

when P^o belongs to $\tilde{\mathcal{P}}_a^u$.

Thus, Theorem 9.5 applies to the WET. Measurability and differentiability conditions on f_{2t}, together with conditions ensuring that $\delta_n : A \to \Delta$ is continuously differentiable uniformly in n will ensure the validity of Assumption 9.1, while Assumption 9.2 holds by assuming the existence of $\{S_n^*\} = O(1)$ such that $\hat{S}_n - S_n^* \to 0$ $prob-P_o$, and ensuring that $\nabla_\delta^2 \hat{L}_{2n} - \nabla_\delta^2 \bar{L}_{2n}^* \to 0$ $prob-P_o$.

It remains to investigate the other conditions of Definitions 9.3 and 9.4. As with the Hausman test, $\mathcal{P}_o^u$ and $\mathcal{P}_a^u$ are closely related to $\tilde{\mathcal{P}}_a^u$. For condition 9.3(i), take a mean value expansion of $n^{-1/2} \sum_{t=1}^{n} s_{2t}(X^t, \delta_n(\hat{\alpha}_n))$ around α_n^* to obtain

$$n^{-1/2} \sum_{t=1}^{n} s_{2t}(X^t, \delta_n(\hat{\alpha}_n)) = n^{-1/2} \sum_{t=1}^{n} s_{2t}(X^t, \delta_n(\alpha_n^*))$$
$$+ \nabla_\delta^2 \ddot{L}_{2n} \nabla_\alpha' \ddot{\delta}_n \sqrt{n}\,(\hat{\alpha}_n - \alpha_n^*),$$

where $\nabla_\delta^2 \ddot{L}_{2n} \nabla'_\alpha \ddot{\delta}_n$ represents the matrix $\nabla_\delta^2 L_{2n}(X^n, \delta_n(\alpha)) \nabla'_\alpha \delta_n(\alpha)$ with rows evaluated at a mean value lying between $\hat{\alpha}_n$ and α_n^*. Therefore

$$\sqrt{n}\, \hat{M}_n = S_n^* \nabla_\delta^2 \bar{L}_{2n}^{*-1} n^{-1/2} \sum_{t=1}^{n} s_{2t}(X^t, \delta_n(\alpha_n^*))$$

$$+ S_n^* \nabla'_\alpha \delta_n^* \sqrt{n}(\hat{\alpha}_n - \alpha_n^*)$$

$$+ (\hat{S}_n \nabla_\delta^2 \hat{L}_{2n}^- - S_n^* \nabla_\delta^2 \bar{L}_{2n}^{*-1})\, n^{-1/2} \sum_{t=1}^{n} s_{2t}(X^t, \delta_n(\alpha_n^*))$$

$$+ (\hat{S}_n \nabla_\delta^2 \hat{L}_{2n}^- \nabla_\delta^2 \ddot{L}_{2n} \nabla'_\alpha \ddot{\delta}_n - S_n^* \nabla'_\alpha \delta_n^*) \sqrt{n}\, (\hat{\alpha}_n - \alpha_n^*)$$

$$= n^{-1/2} \textstyle\sum_{t=1}^{n} m_t^* + \nabla'_\theta \bar{M}_n^* \sqrt{n}\, (\hat{\theta}_n - \theta_n^*) + o_{P^o}(1)$$

with $\nabla_\alpha \delta_n^* \equiv \nabla_\alpha \delta_n(\alpha_n^*)$ and $m_t^* \equiv S_n^* \nabla_\delta^2 \bar{L}_{2n}^{*-1} s_{2t}(X^t, \delta_n(\alpha_n^*))$, provided that the second and third terms in the first of the two equalities above vanish in probability and that $\nabla'_\theta \bar{M}_n^* = S_n^* \nabla'_\alpha \delta_n^*$. The last equality is readily verified. To establish the desired convergence in probability, we have $\hat{S}_n \nabla_\delta^2 \hat{L}_{2n}^- - S_n^* \nabla_\delta^2 \bar{L}_{2n}^{*-1} \to 0$ $prob - P^o$ as a consequence of Corollary 3.8, so that the second term vanishes in probability if $n^{-1/2} \sum_{t=1}^{n} s_{2t}(X^t, \delta_n(\alpha_n^*))$ is $O_{P^o}(1)$. This holds under $\tilde{\mathcal{P}}_a^u$; to see this, take a mean value expansion around δ_n^* to obtain

$$n^{-1/2} \sum_{t=1}^{n} s_{2t}(X^t, \delta_n(\alpha_n^*))$$

$$= n^{-1/2} \sum_{t=1}^{n} s_{2t}(X^t, \delta_n^*) + \nabla_\delta^2 \ddot{L}_{2n} \sqrt{n}\, (\delta_n^* - \delta_n(\alpha_n^*)) .$$

The first term is generally $O_{P^o}(1)$, while the second term is $O(1)$ under $\tilde{\mathcal{P}}_a^u$, which ensures $\sqrt{n}\, (\delta_n^* - \delta_n(\alpha_n^*))$ is $O(1)$. Hence

$$(\hat{S}_n \nabla^2 \hat{L}_{2n}^- - S_n^* \nabla_\delta^2 \bar{L}_{2n}^{*-1})\, n^{-1/2} \textstyle\sum_{t=1}^{n} s_{2t}(X^t, \delta_n(\alpha_n^*)) \to 0 \quad prob - P^o$$

under $\tilde{\mathcal{P}}_a^u$.

Because $\sqrt{n}\, (\hat{\alpha}_n - \alpha_n^*)$ is generally $O_{P^o}(1)$ and $\hat{S}_n \nabla_\delta^2 \hat{L}_{2n}^- \nabla_\delta^2 \ddot{L}_{2n} \nabla'_\alpha \ddot{\delta}_n - S_n^* \nabla'_\alpha \delta_n^* \to 0$ $prob - P^o$ generally, the third term in the expansion for $\sqrt{n}\, \hat{M}_n$ vanishes in probability. Condition 9.3(i) thus holds for those P^o in $\tilde{\mathcal{P}}_a^u$ satisfying the usual regularity conditions.

To investigate conditions 9.3(ii) and 9.4(ii), we must specify s_n^* and A_n^*. Given our choice of $\hat{\theta}_n = \hat{\alpha}_n$, the correspondences $s_n^* = n^{-1} \sum_{t=1}^n s_{1t}(X^t, \alpha_n^*)$ and $A_n^* = \nabla_\alpha^2 \bar{L}_{1n}^*$ are immediate. Condition 9.4(ii) thus requires the asymptotic normality of

$$\sqrt{n}\,(M_n^* - \nabla_\theta' \bar{M}_n^* A_n^{*-1} s_n^*)$$

$$= n^{-1/2} \sum_{t=1}^{n} S_n^* [\nabla_\delta^2 \bar{L}_{2n}^{*-1} s_{2t}(X^t, \delta_n(\alpha_n^*)) - \nabla_\alpha' \delta_n^* \nabla_\alpha^2 \bar{L}_{1n}^{*-1} s_{1t}(X^t, \alpha_n^*)]\,.$$

Using the mean value expansion for $n^{-1/2} \sum_{t=1}^n s_{2t}(X^t, \delta_n(\alpha_n^*))$ above, we have

$$\sqrt{n}\,(M_n^* - \nabla_\theta' \bar{M}_n^* A_n^{*-1} s_n^*)$$

$$= n^{-1/2} \sum_{t=1}^{n} S_n^* [\nabla_\delta^2 \bar{L}_{2n}^{*-1} s_{2t}(X^t, \delta_n^*) - \nabla_\alpha' \delta_n^* \nabla_\alpha^2 \bar{L}_{1n}^{*-1} s_{1t}(X^t, \alpha_n^*)]$$

$$+ S_n^* \sqrt{n}(\delta_n^* - \delta_n(\alpha_n^*)) + (S_n^* \nabla_\delta^2 \bar{L}_{2n}^{*-1} \nabla_\delta^2 \ddot{L}_{2n} - S_n^*)\sqrt{n}(\delta_n^* - \delta_n(\alpha_n^*))$$

$$= n^{-1/2} \sum_{t=1}^{n} S_n^* [\nabla_\delta^2 \bar{L}_{2n}^{*-1} s_{2t}(X^t, \delta_n^*) - \nabla_\alpha' \delta_n^* \nabla_\alpha^2 \bar{L}_{1n}^{*-1} s_{1t}(X^t, \alpha_n^*)]$$

$$+ S_n^* \sqrt{n}\,(\delta_n^* - \delta_n(\alpha_n^*)) + o_{P^o}(1)\,,$$

where the $o_{P^o}(1)$ is valid under $\tilde{\mathcal{P}}_a^u$, for reasons by now familiar.

The usual regularity conditions (which thus restrict $\mathcal{P}_a^u$) ensure the asymptotic normality with mean zero of the sum above, so that we may identify a_n^* in 9.4(ii) with $S_n^* \sqrt{n}\,(\delta_n^* - \delta_n(\alpha_n^*)) = O(1)$ under $\tilde{\mathcal{P}}_a^u$. Thus $a_n^* = 0$ (*i.e.*, $P^o \in \mathcal{P}_o^u$) when $\sqrt{n}\,(\delta_n^* - \delta_n(\alpha_n^*)) \to 0$ but we may also have $a_n^* = 0$ for certain choices of S_n^*.

It is important to realize that when *either* $\mathcal{S}_1$ or $\mathcal{S}_2$ is not correctly specified for $\{Y_t \mid \tilde{X}^{t-1}\}$ (the typical case), then the summands $S_n^* [\nabla_\delta^2 \bar{L}_{2n}^* s_{2t}(X^t, \delta_n^*) - \nabla_\alpha' \delta_n^* \nabla_\delta^2 \bar{L}_{1n}^{*-1} s_{1t}(X^t, \alpha_n^*)]$ will not be martingale difference sequences. This necessitates the use of a dependent central limit theorem, such as that of Wooldridge [1986]. For consistent estimation of V_n^*, it also necessitates use of an autocorrelation/misspecification-consistent covariance matrix estimator (e.g. Gallant and White [1988, Ch. 6]). This fact constitutes a nontrivial challenge to application of dynamic encompassing tests, as only modest experience with such estimators has accumulated; they can be quite badly behaved.

Thus Theorem 9.5 and the results of Sections 9.2 and 9.3 yield general results asymptotically equivalent to the WET of Mizon and Richard [1986].

Because of the nature of $\mathcal{P}_a^u$, the test is sensitive to failure of CPE. Because correct specification implies CPE, a rejection based on the various versions of the WET is evidence of model misspecification. However, failure to reject does not imply the correctness of $\mathcal{S}_1$; *CPE* can occur even under misspecification of $\mathcal{S}_1$. Thus we view tests of CPE as specification tests, and not as a model selection criterion.

Mizon [1984] and Mizon and Richard [1986] give numerous examples of the WET and show how a multitude of testing procedures amount to special cases of the WET or an extension of it to be discussed shortly. In particular, the Lagrange Multiplier test can be viewed as a test of CPE, so the theory of Section 9.5 permits interpretation of m-tests generally as tests of CPE.

Although the function δ_n can often be obtained with modest analytical effort, as attested by the numerous examples given by Mizon [1984] and Mizon and Richard [1986], this is by no means generally so. When analytic derivation of δ_n is intractable, it is possible to replace $\delta_n(\hat{\alpha}_n)$ with an m-estimator $\hat{\delta}_n$ chosen so that

$$\hat{\delta}_n = \text{argmax}_\Delta\; n^{-1} \sum_{t=1}^{n} \int \log f_{2t}(y_t, \tilde{X}^{t-1}; \delta)\, f_{1t}(y_t, \tilde{X}^{t-1}; \hat{\alpha}_n)\, d\zeta_t(y_t)\,.$$

This is a 2SQMLE that can be treated using Theorem 6.10. We do not pursue this here. Some care may be needed to ensure that $\sqrt{n}\,(\hat{\delta}_n - \delta_n(\hat{\alpha}_n)) \to 0$ $prob-P^o$ under $\mathcal{P}_a^u$. When this is the case, the discussion above immediately applies. Theorem 9.5 and some of its corollaries will require an estimate of $\nabla_\alpha\, \delta_n^*$. This can be obtained by numerical methods. However, the need for this can be avoided by use of Corollary 9.11 or 9.13.

10.5.b Incomplete Encompassing

A more general formulation of the encompassing test is based on the requirement that $\mathcal{S}_1$ be capable of explaining not merely any statistic that can be expressed solely as a function of $\tilde{\delta}_n$, but any statistic expressible as a function of $\tilde{\delta}_n$ and of the data, X^n. A formal definition appropriate in our context is the following.

DEFINITION 10.3: Given Assumption 2.1, suppose that the conditions of Definition 10.1 hold and that $b = \{ b_t : \mathbb{R}^{vt} \times \mathcal{A} \times \Delta \to \mathbb{R}^q \}$ is a sequence of measurable functions such that for each (α, δ) in $\mathcal{A} \times \Delta$ we have $E[\int b_t(y_t, \tilde{X}^{t-1}; \alpha, \delta)\, f_{1t}(y_t, \tilde{X}^{t-1}, \alpha)\, d\zeta_t(y_t)] < \infty$. Then $\mathcal{S}_1$

encompasses $\mathcal{S}_2$ *with respect to b under* P_o *to order* $\sqrt{n}$ if

$$\{ n^{-1/2} \sum_{t=1}^{n} E[b_t (X^t , \alpha_n^* , \delta_n^*)] - n^{-1/2} \sum_{t=1}^{n} E[\int b_t (y_t , \tilde{X}^{t-1} ; \alpha_n^* , \delta_n (\alpha_n^*)) \times f_{1t} (y_t , \tilde{X}^{t-1} , \alpha_n^*) \, d \zeta_t (y_t)] \}$$

$$= O(1) .$$ □

The function b_t in this definition is not to be confused with b_t appearing in our formulation of the linear exponential family, but is chosen for correspondence with the encompassing literature. This definition is more precise and somewhat narrower than the definition of "incomplete encompassing" given in Mizon and Richard [1986, Definition 1]. There Mizon and Richard consider any statistic $\tilde{b}_n$ obtained as a function of the data and $\tilde{\delta}_n$. Here, we limit attention to statistics of the form $\tilde{b}_n = n^{-1} \sum_{t=1}^{n} b_t (X^t , \hat{\alpha}_n , \tilde{\delta}_n)$, restricting the manner in which $\tilde{b}_n$ is allowed to depend on the data. The advantage of this is that it allows straightforward treatment of encompassing tests using existing techniques. We could also allow b_t to depend on other nuisance parameters, say $\hat{\gamma}_n$, so that $\tilde{b}_n = n^{-1/2} \sum_{t=1}^{n} b_t (X^t , \hat{\alpha}_n, \tilde{\delta}_n, \hat{\gamma}_n)$ but do not make this explicit for notational economy.

To interpret the requirements of encompassing with respect to b, notice first that if $b_t (X^t , \alpha , \delta) = \delta$, the requirement of the definition reduces to $\{ \sqrt{n} (\delta_n^* - \delta_n (\alpha_n^*)) \} = O (1)$, so that complete parametric encompassing is a special case. Encompassing with respect to b may be viewed as an extension of the non-nested hypothesis testing approach of Cox [1961, 1962] discussed in the previous section. In the Cox test, $b_t (X^t , \alpha , \delta) = \log f_{1t} (X^t , \alpha) - \log f_{2t} (X^t , \delta)$.

As with CPE, correct specification of $\mathcal{S}_1$ implies incomplete parametric encompassing.

THEOREM 10.4: *Given Assumption 2.1, let* $\mathcal{S}_1$, $\mathcal{S}_2$ *and* $b = \{ b_t \}$ *satisfy the conditions of Definition 10.3. Suppose also that for all* $\delta \in \Delta$, $f_{2t} (X^t , \delta)$ *is measurable* $- \sigma (Y_t , W_{2t})$, $t = 1, 2, \ldots$ *and for all* $(\alpha , \delta) \in A \times \Delta$, $b_t (X^t , \alpha, \delta)$ *is measurable* $- \sigma (Y_t, W_{1t})$, $t = 1, 2, \ldots$.

(i) If $\mathcal{S}_1$ *is correctly specified for* $\{ Y_t \mid W_{1t} \}$, $\sigma (W_{2t}) \subseteq \sigma (W_{1t})$, *then* $\mathcal{S}_1$ *encompasses* $\mathcal{S}_2$ *with respect to b.*

(ii) Suppose Assumption 5.1 and either Assumption 5.3 or 6.7 hold so that $\mathcal{S}_1 = \{ \exp \phi_{1t} \}$ *is based on* $\mathcal{M}_1 = \{ \mu_{1t} \}$ *and* $\mathcal{S}_2 = \{ \exp \phi_{2t} \}$ *is based on* $\mathcal{M}_2 = \{ \mu_{2t} \}$. *If* $\mathcal{M}_1$ *is correctly specified for* $\{ E (Y_t \mid W_{1t}) \}$,

$\sigma(W_{2t}) \subseteq \sigma(W_{1t})$, *then* $\mathcal{S}_1$ *encompasses* $\mathcal{S}_2$ *with respect to* b. □

As for the Cox test, it is analytically and computationally simpler to compare the average of the difference between $b_t(X^t, \alpha_n^*, \delta_n^*)$ to its conditional expectation under $\mathcal{S}_1$ instead of comparing the average of $b_t(X^t, \alpha_n^*, \delta_n^*)$ to its unconditional expectation under a parametric probability model. The incomplete encompassing test of Mizon and Richard [1986] is thus based on

$$\hat{M}_n = \tilde{b}_n - n^{-1} \sum_{t=1}^{n} \int b_t(y_t, \tilde{X}^{t-1}; \hat{\alpha}_n, \hat{\delta}_n) f_{1t}(y_t, \tilde{X}^{t-1}, \hat{\alpha}_n)\, d\zeta_t(y_t)$$

$$= n^{-1} \sum_{t=1}^{n} [b_t(X^t, \hat{\alpha}_n, \tilde{\delta}_n)$$

$$- \int b_t(y_t, \tilde{X}^{t-1}; \hat{\alpha}_n, \hat{\delta}_n) f_{1t}(y_t, \tilde{X}^{t-1}, \hat{\alpha}_n)\, d\zeta_t(y_t)],$$

where $\hat{\delta}_n \equiv \delta_n(\hat{\alpha}_n)$. With this choice for $\hat{M}_n$, we evidently have

$$m_t(x^t, \theta, \pi) = b_t(x^t, \alpha, \delta) - \int b_t(x^t, a, \delta_n(\alpha)) f_{1t}(x^t, \alpha)\, d\zeta_t(y_t).$$

In the case of Cox's test, we identify θ with α and π with δ so that $\hat{\theta}_n = \hat{\alpha}_n$ and $\hat{\pi}_n = \tilde{\delta}_n$. This is not generally appropriate. If we don't identify π with δ, we may always let π be null and identify θ with (α, δ). We investigate this further below.

Now consider the requirements of Theorem 9.5. To satisfy the conditions of Assumption 9.1, b_t must satisfy the conditions imposed there on m_t, as must $\int b_t(y_t, \tilde{X}^{t-1}; \alpha, \delta)\, f_{1t}(y_t, \tilde{X}^{t-1}, \alpha)\, d\zeta_t(y_t)$. The Lebesgue dominated convergence theorem plays a role for this integral analogous to its role in the Cox test, so that domination conditions on b_t f_{1t} and its derivatives with respect to α and δ will play useful roles. When $\pi = \delta$, Assumption 9.2 is satisfied by conditions on $\tilde{\delta}_n$ ensuring that $\tilde{\delta}_n - \delta_n^* \to 0$ $prob - P_o$.

To investigate condition 9.3(i), we take a mean value expansion of $\sqrt{n}\,\hat{M}_n$ around (α_n^*, δ_n^*). This gives

$$\sqrt{n}\,\hat{M}_n = n^{-1/2} \sum_{t=1}^{n} (b_t^* - \mu_{bt}^*) + (\nabla_\alpha' \ddot{b}_n - \nabla_\alpha' \ddot{\mu}_{bn})$$

$$\times \sqrt{n}\,(\hat{\alpha}_n - \alpha_n^*) + \nabla_\delta' \ddot{b}_n \sqrt{n}\,(\tilde{\delta}_n - \delta_n^*),$$

where $b_t^* \equiv b_t(X^t, \alpha_n^*, \delta_n^*)$, $\mu_{bt}^* \equiv \int b_t(y_t, \tilde{X}^{t-1}; \alpha_n^*, \delta_n(\alpha_n^*)) f_{1t}(y_t, \tilde{X}^{t-1}, \alpha_n^*) \, d\zeta_t(y)$ and $\nabla_\delta \ddot{b}_n$, $\nabla_\alpha \ddot{b}_n$ and $\nabla_\alpha \ddot{\mu}_{bn}$ represent the gradients of $n^{-1}\sum_{t=1}^n b_t$ and $\mu_{bn} \equiv n^{-1}\sum_{t=1}^n \int b_t f_{1t} \, d\zeta_t$ with respect to δ and α as indicated, evaluated at mean values lying between $(\hat{\alpha}_n, \tilde{\delta}_n)$ and (α_n^*, δ_n^*). Adding and subtracting appropriate terms gives

$$\sqrt{n}\,\hat{M}_n = n^{-1/2}\sum_{t=1}^{n}(b_t^* - \mu_{bt}^*) + (\nabla_\alpha' \bar{b}_n^* - \nabla_\alpha' \bar{\mu}_{bn}^*)\sqrt{n}(\hat{\alpha}_n - \alpha_n^*)$$

$$+ \nabla_\delta' \bar{b}_n^* \sqrt{n}(\tilde{\delta}_n - \delta_n^*)$$

$$- (\nabla_\alpha' \bar{b}_n^* - \nabla_\alpha' \bar{\mu}_{bn}^* - \nabla_\alpha' \ddot{b}_n + \nabla_\alpha' \ddot{\mu}_{bn})\sqrt{n}(\hat{\alpha}_n - \alpha_n^*)$$

$$- (\nabla_\delta' \bar{b}_n^* - \nabla_\delta' \ddot{b}_n)\sqrt{n}(\tilde{\delta}_n - \delta_n^*)\,.$$

For appropriate choice of $\nabla_\alpha \bar{\mu}_{bn}^*$, $\nabla_\alpha \bar{b}_n^*$ and $\nabla_\delta \bar{b}_n^*$, the last two terms generally vanish in probability $-P^o$, because $\sqrt{n}(\hat{\alpha}_n - \alpha_n^*) = O_{P^o}(1)$ and $\sqrt{n}(\tilde{\delta}_n - \delta_n^*) = O_{P^o}(1)$, while the uniform law of the large numbers will ensure that $\nabla_\alpha \mu_{bn}(\alpha) - E(\nabla_\alpha \mu_{bn}(\alpha)) \to 0 \;\; prob - P^o$ uniformly on $\mathcal{A}$, $\nabla_\alpha b_n(\alpha, \delta) - E(\nabla_\alpha b_n(\alpha, \delta)) \to 0 \; prob - P^o$ uniformly on $\mathcal{A} \times \Delta$ and $\nabla_\delta b_n(\alpha, \delta) - E(\nabla_\delta b_n(\alpha, \delta)) \to 0 \; prob - P^o$ uniformly on $\mathcal{A} \times \Delta$. Letting $\nabla_\alpha \bar{\mu}_{bn}^* \equiv E[\nabla_\alpha \mu_{bn}(\alpha_n^*)]$, $\nabla_\alpha \bar{b}_n^* \equiv E[\nabla_\alpha b_n(\alpha_n^*, \delta_n^*)]$ and $\nabla_\delta \bar{b}_n^* \equiv E[\nabla_\delta b_n(\alpha_n^*, \delta_n^*)]$, Corollary 3.8 implies that in general $(\nabla_\alpha \bar{b}_n^* - \nabla_\alpha \bar{\mu}_{bn}^* - \nabla_\alpha \ddot{b}_n + \nabla_\alpha \ddot{\mu}_{bn}) \to 0 \; prob - P^o$ and $\nabla_\delta \bar{b}_n^* - \nabla_\delta \ddot{b}_n \to 0 \; prob - P^o$, in which case

$$\sqrt{n}\,\hat{M}_n = n^{-1/2}\sum_{t=1}^{n}(b_t^* - \mu_{bt}^*) + (\nabla_\alpha' \bar{b}_n^* - \nabla_\alpha' \bar{\mu}_{bn}^*)\sqrt{n}(\hat{\alpha}_n - \alpha_n^*)$$

$$+ \nabla_\delta' \bar{b}_n^* \sqrt{n}(\tilde{\delta}_n - \delta_n^*) + o_{P^o}(1)\,.$$

With θ identified with α and π identified with δ, we see that this has the form required by condition 9.3(i), provided that $\nabla_\delta \bar{b}_n^* = n^{-1}\sum_{t=1}^n E(\nabla_\delta b_t(X^t, \alpha_n^*, \delta_n^*)) \to 0$. In the case of the Cox test, this is guaranteed because $\nabla_\delta b_t(X^t, \alpha, \delta) = s_{2t}(X^t, \delta)$, and $n^{-1}\sum_{t=1}^n E(s_{2t}^*) = 0$ necessarily. (In this case, $\nabla_\alpha \bar{b}_n^* = 0$ also). When we do not have $\nabla_\delta \bar{b}_n^* \to 0$, we let π be null, and identify θ in m_t with (α, δ) in $b_t - \int b_t f_{1t} \, d\zeta_t$.

We note a useful computational convenience that arises in the special case $\nabla_\delta \bar{b}_n^* \to 0$, explicitly taken advantage of in the Cox test. This is the replacement of $\hat{\delta}_n = \delta_n(\hat{\alpha}_n)$ with $\tilde{\delta}_n$ in the second term of $\hat{M}_n$, thus eliminating the need to calculate the potentially troublesome $\delta_n(\hat{\alpha}_n)$. A heuristic justification for this is given in the appendix.

Finally, we investigate the requirements of conditions 9.3(ii) and 9.4(ii). When $\nabla_\delta \bar{b}_n^* \to 0$, we may set $\hat{\theta}_n = \hat{\alpha}_n$, so that $s_n^* = n^{-1} \sum_{t=1}^n s_{1t}^*$ and $A_n^* = n^{-1} \sum_{t=1}^n E(\nabla_\delta^2 \log f_{1t}^*)$. Otherwise, we set $\hat{\theta}_n{}' = (\hat{\alpha}_n{}', \tilde{\delta}_n{}')$ and use the structure of Theorem 6.11 for the 2SQMLE to justify the choice $s_n^{*\prime} = n^{-1} \sum_{t=1}^n (s_{1t}^{*\prime}, s_{2t}^{*\prime})$ and

$$A_n^* = \begin{bmatrix} n^{-1} \sum_{t=1}^n E(\nabla_\delta^2 \log f_{1t}^*) & 0 \\ 0 & n^{-1} \sum_{t=1}^n E(\nabla_\delta^2 \log f_{2t}^*) \end{bmatrix}.$$

The zero elements off the diagonal arise because of the assumed absence of dependence of f_{2t} on α or f_{1t} on δ. These are convenient assumptions, but their failure poses no particular challenge. In such cases, either Theorem 6.10 or 6.11 applies. For simplicity, we do not pursue this here.

Condition 9.4(ii) requires the asymptotic normality of

$$\begin{aligned} &\sqrt{n}\,(M_n^* - \nabla_\theta' \bar{M}_n^* A_n^{*-1} s_n^*) \\ &\quad = n^{-1/2} \sum_{t=1}^n b_t^* - \mu_{bt}^* - (\nabla_\alpha' \bar{b}_n^* - \nabla_\alpha' \bar{\mu}_{bn}^*) \nabla_\alpha^2 \bar{L}_{1n}^{*-1} s_{1t}^* \\ &\qquad - \nabla_\delta' \bar{b}_n^* \nabla_\delta^2 \bar{L}_{2n}^{*-1} s_{2t}^* . \end{aligned}$$

Thus, it suffices that a central limit theorem applies to

$$b_t^* - \mu_{bt}^* - (\nabla_\alpha' \bar{b}_n^* - \nabla_\alpha' \bar{\mu}_{bn}^*) \nabla_\alpha^2 \bar{L}_{1n}^{*-1} s_{1t}^* - \nabla_\delta' \bar{b}_n^* \nabla_\delta^2 \bar{L}_n^{*-1} s_{2t}^* .$$

The terms involving s_{1t}^* and s_{2t}^* generally contribute nothing to the expectation of $\sqrt{n}\,(M_n^* - \nabla_\theta' \bar{M}_n^* A_n^{*-1} s_n^*)$, so that $E(\sqrt{n}\,(M_n^* - \nabla_\theta' \bar{M}_n^* A_n^{*-1} s_n^*)) = n^{-1/2} \sum_{t=1}^n E(b_t^* - \mu_{bt}^*)$. But this summation is $O(1)$ under Definition 10.3, so a central limit theorem will be generally available with $a_n^* = n^{-1/2} \sum_{t-1}^n E(b_t^* - \mu_{bt}^*)$.

As before, the summands above will generally not be martingale difference sequences, presenting challenges for tests of incomplete encompassing in the dynamic context comparable to those met for tests of CPE.

Again, we see that Theorem 9.5 and its corollaries apply. We leave as an exercise for the reader investigation of details.

10.6 SUMMARY

In this chapter we have seen how a variety of leading specification testing procedures fit into the m-testing framework. The Lagrange Multiplier, conditional moment, Hausman, Cox, and encompassing tests all have interpretations as m-tests for which the theory of Chapter 9 applies. Many other specification testing procedures can be similarly treated. The various methods used in handling the special cases considered here provide a body of technique for putting specification testing procedures into the convenient format treated by the theory of Chapter 9. Related theory and technique useful for analyzing specification testing procedures such as those discussed in this chapter is provided by Gourieroux, Monfort and Trognon [1983], whose comprehensive work antedates the m-testing approach.

One class of specification tests not treated in this chapter is the class of information matrix tests mentioned briefly in our discussion of conditional moment tests. These are the subject of our next chapter.

MATHEMATICAL APPENDIX

PROOF OF THEOREM 10.2: (i) It suffices to show that $\delta_n^* = \delta_n(\alpha_n^*)$, $n = 1, 2, \ldots$. By definition of $\delta_n(\alpha_n^*)$,

$$n^{-1} \sum_{t=1}^{n} E\left[\int \log f_{2t}(y_t, \tilde{X}^{t-1};\ \delta_n(\alpha_n^*))\, f_{1t}(y_t, \tilde{X}^{t-1};\ \alpha_n^*)\, d\zeta_t(y_t) \right]$$

$$\geq n^{-1} \sum_{t=1}^{n} E\left[\int \log f_{2t}(y_t, \tilde{X}^{t-1};\ \delta)\, f_{1t}(y_t, \tilde{X}^{t-1};\ \alpha_n^*)\, d\zeta_t(y_t) \right]$$

for all $\delta \in \Delta$. When $\mathcal{S}_1$ is correctly specified for $\{Y_t \mid W_{1t}\}$, it follows that $\alpha_n^* = \alpha_o$ with $f_{1t}(x^t, \alpha_o) = h_t(y_t, w_{1t})$, where h_t is the conditional density function of Y_t given W_{1t} implied by P_o. Consequently,

$$n^{-1} \sum_{t-1}^{n} E\left[\int \log f_{2t}(y_t, \tilde{X}^{t-1};\ \delta)\, f_{1t}(y_t, \tilde{X}^{t-1};\ \alpha_n^*)\, d\zeta_t(y_t) \right]$$

$$= n^{-1} \sum_{t=1}^{n} E\left[\int \log f_{2t}(y_t, \tilde{X}^{t-1};\ \delta)\, h_t(y_t, W_{1t})\, d\zeta_t(y_t) \right]$$

$$= n^{-1} \sum_{t=1}^{n} E(\log f_{2t}(X^t, \delta)) .$$

The last equality holds given the measurability conditions imposed on $f_{2t}(X^t, \delta)$. Therefore

$$n^{-1} \sum_{t=1}^{n} E\left[\int \log f_{2t}(y_t, \tilde{X}^{t-1};\ \delta_n(\alpha_n^*))\, f_{1t}(y_t, \tilde{X}^{t-1};\ \alpha_n^*)\, d\zeta_t(y_t) \right]$$

$$= n^{-1} \sum_{t=1}^{n} E(\log f_{2t}(X^t, \delta_n(\alpha_n^*)))$$

$$\geq n^{-1} \sum_{t=1}^{n} E(\log f_{2t}(X^t, \delta_n^*)) = \bar{L}_{2n}(\delta_n^*) .$$

But δ_n^* is the identifiably unique maximizer of $\bar{L}_{2n}$ so $\delta_n(\alpha_n^*) = \delta_n^*$, $n = 1, 2, \ldots$.

(ii) Again we show that $\delta_n^* = \delta_n(\alpha_n^*)$, $n = 1, 2, \ldots$. By definition of $\delta_n(\alpha_n^*)$ and the choices $f_{1t} = \exp \phi_{1t}$, $f_{2t} = \exp \phi_{2t}$

$$n^{-1} \sum_{t=1}^{n} E\left[\int [\, a_{2t}(\mu_{2t}(W_{2t}, \delta_n(\alpha_n^*)), \kappa_{2t}^*) + b_{2t}(y_t, \kappa_{2t}^*) \right.$$

$$+ \; y_t' c_{2t}(\mu_{2t}(W_{2t}, \delta_n(\alpha_n^*)), \kappa_{2t}^*)] \, f_{1t}(y_t, \tilde{X}^{t-1}, \alpha_n^*) \, d\zeta_t(y_t) \Big]$$

$$\geq n^{-1} \sum_{t=1}^{n} E\Big[\int [\, a_{2t}(\mu_{2t}(W_{2t}, \delta), \kappa_{2t}^*) + b_{2t}(y_t, \kappa_{2t}^*)$$

$$+ \; y_t' c_{2t}(\mu_{2t}(W_{2t}, \delta), \kappa_{2t}^*)] \, f_{1t}(y_t, \tilde{X}^{t-1}, \alpha_n^*) \, d\zeta_t(y_t) \Big]$$

for all $\delta \in \Delta$, where κ_{2t}^* is any random vector measurable $-\sigma(W_{2t})$. When $\mathcal{M}_1$ is correctly specified for $\{ E(Y_t \mid W_{1t}) \}$, it follows that $\alpha_n^* = \alpha_o$, where $\mu_{1t}(W_{1t}, \alpha_o) \equiv \int y_t f_{1t}(y_t, \tilde{X}^{t-1}, \alpha_o) \, d\zeta_t(y_t) = E(Y_t \mid W_{1t})$, so that when $\sigma(W_{2t}) \subseteq \sigma(W_{1t})$ the law of iterated expectations gives

$$n^{-1} \sum_{t=1}^{n} E[\, a_{2t}(\mu_{2t}(W_{2t}, \delta_n(\alpha_n^*)), \kappa_{2t}^*)$$

$$+ E(Y_t' \mid W_{1t}) \, c_{2t}(\mu_{2t}(W_{2t}, \delta(\alpha_n^*)), \kappa_{2t}^*)]$$

$$= n^{-1} \sum_{t=1}^{n} E[\, a_{2t}(\mu_{2t}(W_{2t}, \delta_n(\alpha_n^*)), \kappa_{2t}^*)$$

$$+ Y_t' \, c_{2t}(\mu_{2t}(W_{2t}, \delta_n(\alpha_n^*)), \kappa_{2t}^*)]$$

$$\geq n^{-1} \sum_{t=1}^{n} E[\, a_{2t}(\mu_{2t}(W_{2t}, \delta), \kappa_{2t}^*)$$

$$+ Y_t' \, c_{2t}(\mu_{2t}(W_{2t}, \delta), \kappa_{2t}^*)]$$

for all $\delta \in \Delta$. The final term differs from $\bar{L}_{2n}(\delta)$ by a constant, and is therefore (identifiably) uniquely maximized by δ_n^*. Thus $\delta_n(\alpha_n^*) = \delta_n^*$, $n = 1, 2, \ldots$. □

PROOF OF THEOREM 10.4: (i) From Theorem 10.2 we have that $\delta_n^* = \delta_n(\alpha_n^*)$, $n = 1, 2, \ldots$ given correct specification, so that

$$E[\, b_t(X^t, \alpha_n^*, \delta_n^*)]$$

$$- E\Big[\int b_t(y_t, \tilde{X}^{t-1}; \alpha_n^*, \delta_n(\alpha_n^*)) \, f_{1t}(y_t, \tilde{X}^{t-1}, \alpha_n^*) \, d\zeta_t(y_t) \Big]$$

$$= E[\, b_t(X^t, \alpha_n^*, \delta_n^*)]$$

$$- E\Big[\int b_t(y_t, \tilde{X}^{t-1}; \alpha_n^*, \delta_n^*) \, f_{1t}(y_t, \tilde{X}^{t-1}, \alpha_n^*) \, d\zeta_t(y_t) \Big].$$

Correct specification also implies that $f_{1t}(y_t, \tilde{X}^{t-1}, \alpha_n^*) = h_t(y_t, W_{1t})$ for all t and n, so that

$$E\left[\int b_t(y_t, \tilde{X}^{t-1};\ \alpha_n^*, \delta_n^*)\, f_{1t}(y_t, \tilde{X}^{t-1}, \alpha_n^*)\, d\zeta_t(y_t)\right]$$

$$= E\left[\int b_t(y_t;\ \tilde{X}^{t-1};\ \alpha_n^*, \delta_n^*)\, h_t(y_t, W_{1t})\, d\zeta_t(y_t)\right]$$

$$= E\,[\,E(b_t(Y_t, \tilde{X}^{t-1};\ \alpha_n^*, \delta_n^*) \mid W_{1t})\,]$$

$$= E\,[\,b_t(X^t, \alpha_n^*, \delta_n^*)\,]\,,$$

where the second equality follows given the measurability conditions on b_t.

It follows immediately that

$$n^{-1/2} \sum_{t=1}^{n} E\,[\,b_t(X^t, \alpha_n^*, \delta_n^*)\,] -$$

$$n^{-1/2} \sum_{t=1}^{n} E\left[\int b_t(y_t, \tilde{X}^{t-1};\ \alpha_n^*, \delta_n(\alpha_n^*))\, f_{1t}(y_t, \tilde{X}^{t-1}, \alpha_n^*)\, d\zeta_t(y_t)\right]$$

$$= 0\,.$$

Definition 10.3 is therefore satisfied, and the proof is complete.

(ii) This is analogous to part (i) of Theorem 10.2, and is left as an exercise for the reader.

SKETCH OF SIMPLIFICATION FOR COX ENCOMPASSING TEST

We consider the conditions required for $\sqrt{n}\,(\hat{M}_n - \tilde{M}_n) \to 0 \quad prob-P^o$, where $\tilde{M}_n$ is the statistic used in the Cox test,

$$\tilde{M}_n \equiv n^{-1} \sum_{t=1}^{n} [\,b_t(X^t, \hat{\alpha}_n, \tilde{\delta}_n) - \int b_t(y_t, \tilde{X}^{t-1}; \hat{\alpha}_n, \tilde{\delta}_n)$$

$$\times f_{1t}(y_t, \tilde{X}^{t-1}, \hat{\alpha}_n)\, d\zeta_t(y_t)\,]\,.$$

Note that if b_t depends only on (α, δ), or, more generally, $b_t(X^t, \alpha, \delta)$ is measurable $-\sigma(V_t)$ for all (α, δ) in $\mathcal{A} \times \Delta$ while $f_{1t}(X^t, \alpha)$ is measurable $-\sigma(Y_t, W_t)$ for all α in $\mathcal{A}$ (recall $\sigma(X^t) = \sigma(Y_t, W_t, V_t)$, $\sigma(Y_t, W_t) \wedge \sigma(V_t) = \{\Omega, \varnothing\}$), then $\tilde{M}_n = 0$ for all $(\hat{\alpha}_n, \tilde{\delta}_n)$ and the test is void. Thus, we rule out this case in what follows.

Because $\tilde{b}_n \equiv n^{-1} \sum_{t=1}^{n} b_t(X^t, \hat{\alpha}_n, \tilde{\delta}_n)$ appears in both $\tilde{M}_n$ and $\hat{M}_n$, it suffices to consider

$$\sqrt{n}\ (\hat{\mu}_{bn} - \tilde{\mu}_{bn}) \equiv n^{-1/2} \sum_{t=1}^{n} \int b_t(y_t, \tilde{X}^{t-1}; \hat{\alpha}_n, \delta_n(\hat{\alpha}_n))$$

$$\times f_{1t}(y_t, \tilde{X}^{t-1}, \hat{\alpha}_n)\, d\zeta_t(y_t)$$

$$- n^{-1/2} \sum_{t=1}^{n} \int b_t(y_t, \tilde{X}^{t-1}; \hat{\alpha}_n, \tilde{\delta}_n)\, f_{1t}(y_t, \tilde{X}^{t-1}, \hat{\alpha}_n)\, d\zeta_t(y_t)\,.$$

Taking a mean value expansion of the first term around $(\hat{\alpha}_n, \tilde{\delta}_n)$ gives

$$\sqrt{n}\ (\hat{\mu}_{bn} - \tilde{\mu}_{bn}) = \nabla_\delta'\, \ddot{\mu}_{bn}\, \sqrt{n}\ (\delta_n(\hat{\alpha}_n) - \tilde{\delta}_n)\,,$$

where $\nabla_\delta\, \ddot{\mu}_{bn}$ is the gradient of μ_{bn} evaluated at a mean value lying between $(\hat{\alpha}_n, \delta_n(\hat{\alpha}_n))$ and $(\hat{\alpha}_n, \tilde{\delta}_n)$. Under *CPE*, we have that $\sqrt{n}\ (\delta_n(\hat{\alpha}_n) - \tilde{\delta}_n) = \sqrt{n}\ (\delta_n(\hat{\alpha}_n) - \delta_n(\alpha_n^*)) + \sqrt{n}\ (\delta_n^* - \tilde{\delta}_n) + \sqrt{n}\ (\delta_n(\alpha_n^*) - \delta_n^*) = O_{P^o}(1)$, as the first two terms are generally $O_{P^o}(1)$, while the third is $O_{P^o}(1)$ under *CPE*. In general, we will also have $\nabla_\delta\, \ddot{\mu}_{bn} - \nabla_\delta\, \bar{\mu}_{bn}^* \to 0$ prob $- P^o$ by a uniform law of large numbers and Corollary 3.8 where

$$\nabla_\delta\, \bar{\mu}_{bn}^* = n^{-1} \sum_{t=1}^{n} E\Big[\int \nabla_\delta\, b_t(y_t, \tilde{X}^{t-1}; \alpha_n^*, \delta_n^*)\, f_{1t}(y_t, \tilde{X}^{t-1}, \alpha_n^*)\, d\zeta_t(y_t) \Big].$$

When $\mathcal{S}_1$ is correctly specified for $\{Y_t \mid \tilde{X}^{t-1}\}$ under P^o, it follows that

$$\nabla_\delta\, \bar{\mu}_{bn}^* = n^{-1} \textstyle\sum_{t=1}^{n} E(\nabla_\delta\, b_t(X^t; \alpha^o, \delta_n^*)) \equiv \nabla_\delta\, \bar{b}_n^* = 0\,.$$

Consequently, for correctly specified $\mathcal{S}_1$

$$\sqrt{n}\ (\hat{\mu}_{bn} - \tilde{\mu}_{bn}) \to 0 \quad prob - P^o\,,$$

implying that $\sqrt{n}\ (\hat{M}_n - \tilde{M}_n) \to 0$ $prob - P^o$, so that $\tilde{\delta}_n$ can be used in place of $\delta_n(\hat{\alpha}_n)$ in conducting the encompassing test. This remains valid under local alternatives for which $\sqrt{n}\ (\nabla_\delta\, \bar{\mu}_{bn}^* - \nabla_\delta\, \bar{b}_n^*)$ is $O(1)$.

CHAPTER 11

Information Matrix Testing

In Chapters 6 through 9 we have repeatedly observed the useful role played by the information matrix equality in simplifying the computation of hypothesis and specification test statistics, and in ensuring attainment of the minimum asymptotic variance bound. In this chapter we examine a number of specification tests designed to detect particular failures of the information matrix equality: the original information matrix test introduced by White [1982], the dynamic information matrix test of White [1987], and a new form of information matrix test, the "cross-information matrix" test. The theoretical results are obtained in a particularly straightforward manner by exploiting the m-testing framework of Chapter 9. We illustrate the application of these tests to simple dynamic linear regression models.

11.1 General Theory of the Information Matrix Test

We say that the "information matrix equality holds" for a given specification $\mathcal{S}$ whenever $A_n^* + B_n^* = 0$ or $A_n^* + B_n^* \to 0$.

As we saw in Chapter 7, this equality (or convergence) plays a key role in the attainment of the minimum asymptotic variance bound. Specifications for which the information matrix equality fails ($A_n^* + B_n^* \not\to 0$) generally do not attain the asymptotic bound. Therefore, evidence of failure of the information matrix equality indicates that the precision of estimation and the power of hypothesis tests can be improved by the use of some other estimator.

In Chapter 8, we saw that the information matrix equality plays a key role in ensuring the consistency of the classical asymptotic covariance matrix estimators used in constructing the Wald, Lagrange multiplier and Hausman tests of parametric constraints. When the information matrix equality fails, the "usual" asymptotic standard error estimates for the parameter estimates are inconsistent, and the test statistics just mentioned, as well as the likelihood ratio statistic, no longer have the χ^2 distribution asymptotically under the null hypothesis. Tests of incorrect size result if the χ^2 distribution is used in the standard way to determine critical values. Therefore, evidence of the failure of the information matrix equality indicates that the usual asymptotic covariance matrix estimators (those of Theorem 8.24 or 8.26) are inappropriate, and that a more sophisticated estimator must be used to conduct valid hypothesis tests (e.g., the Gallant-White [1988] estimator or the estimator of Corollary 8.28).

The failure of the information matrix equality may also indicate the misspecification of $\mathcal{S}$ for $\{Y_t \mid W_t\}$ or of $\mathcal{M}$ for $\{E(Y_t \mid W_t)\}$, as the correctness of $\mathcal{S}$ or $\mathcal{M}$ is typically one of the assumptions used in establishing the theoretical validity of the information matrix equality (viz., Theorems 6.5, 6.6, 6.9 and 6.13). Evidence of failure of the information matrix equality thus suggests the usefulness of investigating the possible misspecification of $\mathcal{S}$ or $\mathcal{M}$ using further specification tests, such as those of Chapter 10.

In Chapter 9 the information matrix equality played a role in helping to ensure the availability of computationally convenient test statistics for conducting m-tests (Corollaries 9.11 and 9.13). There, more than the information matrix equality was used: we required $\nabla'_\theta \bar{M}_n^* A_n^{*-1} - G_n^* B_n^{*-1} \rightarrow 0$. The information matrix equality ensures $A_n^* + B_n^* \rightarrow 0$. What we shall call the "cross-information matrix equality" ensures that $\nabla'_\theta \bar{M}_n^* + G_n^* \rightarrow 0$. The failure of either the information matrix equality or the cross-information matrix equality thus indicates the advisability of using one of the more generally valid m-tests of Chapter 9.

We now turn our attention to the details of specific tests designed to detect failures of the information or cross-information matrix equality.

11.1.a Dynamic (First Order) Information Matrix Tests

As we saw in Chapter 6, the information matrix equality can usefully be broken into two parts: $A_n^* + \bar{B}_n^* \rightarrow 0$ and $B_n^* - \bar{B}_n^* \rightarrow 0$. Dynamic (first order) information matrix tests focus on the second of these parts, $B_n^* - \bar{B}_n^* \rightarrow 0$, i.e.,

$$\text{var}\, [\, n^{-1/2} \sum_{t=1}^{n} s_t^*] = n^{-1} \sum_{t=1}^{n} \text{var}\; s_t^* + o(1)\,.$$

A sufficient (but not necessary) condition for this is that $E(s_t^*) = 0$ and $E(s_t^*\, s_{t-\tau}^{*\prime}) = 0$, $t = 1, 2, \ldots, \tau = 1, \ldots, t$. For this, it suffices that $\{s_t^*, \mathcal{F}^t\}$ is a martingale difference sequence, as ensured by Assumption 6.3(a) with a specification correct for $\{Y_t \mid \tilde{X}^{t-1}\}$. (The terminology "first order" is intended to suggest such a condition, involving the first derivatives of f_t.)

Neither the martingale difference condition nor $E(s_t^* \, s_{t-\tau}^{*\prime}) = 0$ is needed to have $B_n^* - \bar{B}_n^* \to 0$; however, cases in which $B_n^* - \bar{B}_n^* \to 0$ despite $E(s_t^* \, s_{t-\tau}^{*\prime}) \neq 0$ for all t, τ are sufficiently pathological that little will be lost (and much analytical and computational convenience will be gained) by ignoring such cases.

For simplicity, we shall only examine whether a finite number of elements of $\{E(s_t^* \, s_{t-\tau}^{*\prime})\}$ are zero. Thus, we base the dynamic information matrix test on the following "dynamic information matrix indicators"

$$m_t(X^t, \theta, \pi) = S \; vec \; s_t(X^t, \theta)[s_{t-1}(X^{t-1}, \theta)', \ldots, s_{t-\lambda}(X^{t-\lambda}, \theta)']$$

where $\lambda \geq 1$ is a prespecified integer that determines the maximum autocorrelation of s_t^* to be examined, and S is a nonstochastic $q \times \lambda p^2$ selection (or other fixed) matrix that can be used to focus attention on particular elements (or linear combinations) of $s_t[s_{t-1}', \ldots, s_{t-\lambda}']$. Later we examine the consequences of particular choices for S and λ.

In this section, we choose $\hat{\theta}$ to be the QMLE obtained from a specification $\mathcal{S}$ to which Theorem 6.4 applies, so that π is null. We consider the modifications necessary to treat the case in which $\hat{\theta}$ is a 2SQMLE in a subsequent section. It is possible to construct information matrix tests using a QMLE $\hat{\theta}$ associated with $\mathcal{S}_2$ (say) different than $\mathcal{S} = \{f_t\}$, but we shall not take up this possibility here.

Observe that the dynamic information matrix indicators give a special case of Newey's conditional moment test of first order, as the formula $vec \; ABC = (C' \otimes A) \; vec \; B$ implies

$$\begin{aligned} m_t &= S([\, s_{t-1}', \ldots, s_{t-\lambda}' \,]' \otimes I_p) \; s_t \\ &= w_t \; s_t \, , \end{aligned}$$

where $w_t \equiv S([\, s_{t-1}', \ldots, s_{t-\lambda}' \,]' \otimes I_p)$.

Now that we have specified m_t and with $\hat{\theta}$ taken as a QMLE to which Theorem 6.4 applies, it is a straightforward exercise to obtain conditions ensuring the applicability of Theorem 9.5 and its corollaries. We simply verify that conditions already in place ensure the conditions of Theorem 9.5 and its corollaries, or add additional assumptions ensuring the desired condition(s).

For Assumption 9.1, Assumptions 2.3 and 3.6 already suffice. For condition 9.3(i) or 9.4(i), the following assumption suffices.

ASSUMPTION 11.1:

(a) For $\tau = 1, \ldots, \lambda$, $\lambda \in I\!N$, the elements of $n^{-1} \sum_{t=1}^{n} E[s_t(X^t, \cdot)\,(vec\ \nabla' s_{t-\tau}(X^{t-\tau}, \cdot))']$ and $n^{-1} \sum_{t=1}^{n} E[s_{t-\tau}(X^{t-\tau}, \cdot)\ (vec\ \nabla' s_t(X^t, \cdot))']$ are finite and continuous on Θ uniformly in $n = 1, 2, \ldots$;

(b) For $\tau = \pm 1, \ldots, \pm\lambda$, $\lambda \in I\!N$, the elements of $\{s_t(X^t, \theta)\ (vec\ \nabla' s_{t-\tau}(X^{t-\tau}, \theta))'\}$ obey the weak ULLN. □

Because π is null, Assumption 9.2 is irrelevant.

Now consider the requirements of condition 9.3(i), i.e.,

$$\sqrt{n}\ \hat{M}_n = n^{-1/2} \sum_{t=1}^{n} m_t^* + \nabla'_\theta\ \bar{M}_n^*\ \sqrt{n}\ (\hat{\theta}_n - \theta_n^*) + o_{P^o}(1)\ ,$$

with $\nabla_\theta\ \bar{M}_n^* \equiv n^{-1} \sum_{t=1}^{n} E(\nabla_\theta\ m_t^*)$. When π is null, the conditions already given allow this to be verified immediately, as a mean value expansion gives

$$\sqrt{n}\ \hat{M}_n = n^{-1/2} \sum_{t=1}^{n} m_t^* + \nabla'_\theta\ \bar{M}_n^*\ \sqrt{n}\ (\hat{\theta}_n - \theta_n^*)$$

$$+ (\nabla'_\theta\ \ddot{M}_n - \nabla'_\theta\ \bar{M}_n^*)\ \sqrt{n}\ (\hat{\theta}_n - \theta_n^*)\ ,$$

with $(\nabla'_\theta\ \ddot{M}_n - \nabla'_\theta\ \bar{M}_n^*)\ \sqrt{n}\ (\hat{\theta}_n - \theta_n^*) = o_{P^o}(1)$ given that $\sqrt{n}\ (\hat{\theta}_n - \theta_n^*)$ is $O_{P^o}(1)$ and that $\nabla'_\theta\ \ddot{M}_n - \nabla'_\theta\ \bar{M}_n^* \to 0\ \ prob - P^o$ by Corollary 3.8 given $\hat{\theta}_n - \theta_n^* \to 0\ \ prob - P^o$ and Assumption 11.1.

Given our choice for $\hat{\theta}$, the following condition is useful in verifying conditions 9.3(ii) and 9.4(ii).

ASSUMPTION 11.2: $\{n^{-1/2}\,(w_t^* - \nabla'_\theta\ \bar{M}_n^*\ A_n^{*-1})\ s_t^*\}$ obeys the central limit theorem, with covariance matrix $\{V_n^*\}$ ($O(1)$ and uniformly positive definite), and with $w_t^* = w_t(X^{t-1}, \theta_n^*)$ for w_t as previously given. □

Note that this assumption places no restrictions on $a_n^* \equiv n^{-1/2} \sum_{t=1}^{n} E(w_t^*\ s_t^*)$ beyond a requirement that a_n^* is $O(1)$ (recall Definition 6.1). It is the behavior of a_n^* that determines whether P_o belongs to $\mathcal{P}_o^u$ ($a_n^* \to 0$) or to $\mathcal{P}_a^u$ ($\{a_n^*\} = O(1)$). Cases falling into the global alternative do not require Assumption 11.2. Instead, the following condition is relevant.

ASSUMPTION 11.3:

(a) For $\tau = 1, \ldots, \lambda$, $\lambda \in I\!N$, the elements of $n^{-1} \sum_{t=1}^{n} E(s_t(X^t, \theta) s_{t-\tau}(X^{t-\tau}, \theta)')$ are finite and continuous on Θ uniformly in n;

(b) For $\tau = 1, \ldots, \lambda$, $\lambda \in I\!N$, the elements of $\{s_t(X^t, \theta)\, s_{t-\tau}(X^{t-\tau}, \theta)'\}$ obey the weak ULLN. □

Conditions that imply Assumptions 8.6(a) and (b) will also generally ensure that Assumptions 11.3(a) and (b) also hold.

Theorems 9.5 and 9.7 apply immediately to establish the following result.

THEOREM 11.1: *Let $\{\hat{J}_n\}$ be a sequence of measurable symmetric positive semi-definite $q \times q$ matrices such that $\hat{J}_n - J_n^* \to 0$ prob $- P_o$ where $\{J_n^*\}$ is a sequence of nonstochastic symmetric $q \times q$ matrices, $O(1)$ and uniformly positive definite.*

(i) Suppose the conditions of Theorem 6.4 hold, together with Assumptions 11.1 and 11.2, and let $\mathcal{M}_n = n\hat{M}_n{}' \hat{J}_n^- \hat{M}_n$, with

$$\hat{M}_n = n^{-1} \sum_{t=1}^{n} \hat{m}_t, \quad \hat{m}_t = S \text{ vec } \hat{s}_t\, [\hat{s}_{t-1}{}', \ldots, \hat{s}_{t-\lambda}{}'],$$

where S is a nonstochastic $q \times \lambda p^2$ matrix, $\hat{s}_t = s_t(X^t, \hat{\theta}_n)\, 1[t > 0]$ and $\lambda \in I\!N$ is given. Then $\mathcal{M}_n \overset{A}{\sim} N_2(a_n^*, V_n^*; J_n^{*-1})$, where $a_n^* \equiv n^{-1/2} \sum_{t=1}^{n} E(w_t^*\, s_t^*)$.

In particular, if $a_n^* \to 0$ and $J_n^* = V_n^*$, then $\mathcal{M}_n \overset{A}{\sim} \chi_q^2$.

(ii) Suppose instead that the conditions of Theorem 3.5 hold, together with Assumptions 2.4 and 11.3. If $\bar{M}_n^{*\prime} \bar{M}_n^* > \varepsilon > 0$ a.a. n, then for $\{k_n\} = o(n)$, $P_o[\mathcal{M}_n > k_n] \to 1$. □

The statistic given in this theorem is called a "dynamic information matrix test statistic."

The first result indicates that a test of $a_n^* \to 0$ at the asymptotic level α can be performed by comparing $\mathcal{M}_n$ to $\chi^2_{q,1-\alpha}$, and rejecting $a_n^* \to 0$ if

$\mathcal{M}_n > \chi^2_{q,1-\alpha}$. The test has local power against alternatives for which $\{a_n^*\}$ is $O(1)$. It has global power against alternatives for which $\bar{M}_n^{*\prime} \bar{M}_n^* > \varepsilon > 0$. Essentially, the test will detect any autocorrelation in the elements of s_t^* of order up to λ not specifically excluded by the form of S.

When such autocorrelations exist, we generally do not have $B_n^* - \bar{B}_n^* \to 0$, so that even if $A_n^* + \bar{B}_n^* \to 0$ we do not have $A_n^* + B_n^* \to 0$, thus indicating the failure of the information matrix equality, with the resulting adverse consequences for attainment of the minimum asymptotic variance bound and the consistency of the classical parameter covariance matrix estimators.

The detection of autocorrelation in s_t^* also signals directly the failure of the martingale difference property. This implies either a dynamic misspecification in $\mathcal{S}$ or $\mathcal{M}$ (i.e., the distribution (conditional expectation) of Y_t given $\tilde{X}^{t-1}$ differs from that of Y_t given W_t) or the fundamental misspecification of $\mathcal{S}$ for $\{Y_t \mid W_t\}$ or $\mathcal{M}$ for $\{E(Y_t \mid W_t)\}$. If desired, which possibility is the case can be investigated by further specification testing using the methods of the previous two chapters.

Because the role played by the martingale difference property is so fundamental to the interpretation of results and the availability of computationally convenient test statistics, the dynamic information matrix test is perhaps the single most informative and useful specification test available in a dynamic context.

Simplified versions of the dynamic information matrix test can be constructed using the results of Sections 9.2 and 9.3, recognizing that in general we have $E(\nabla_\theta m_t^* \mid X^{t-1}) \neq 0$. The analysis is straightforward, so we leave it to the interested reader (see White [1988, ch. 10]). However, when the specification admits a generalized residual (recall Definition 6.8), a particularly appealing form for the dynamic information matrix test is available, which we now discuss. We apply Corollary 9.13 and impose the following condition.

ASSUMPTION 11.4: (a) Assumption 9.8 holds for $j_t \equiv w_t\, i_t$, $t = 1, 2, \ldots$, where i_t are the generalized instruments, $s_t = i_t\, u_t$;

(b) Assumption 9.10 holds for i_t and j_t; $t = 1, 2, \ldots$;

(c) Assumption 9.9 holds for u_t, $t = 1, 2, \ldots$. □

The application of Corollary 9.13 immediately yields the following result. We set $\hat{i}_t = i_t(\tilde{X}^{t-1}, \hat{\theta}_n)$, $\hat{j}_t = \hat{w}_t\, \hat{i}_t$.

COROLLARY 11.2: *Suppose the specification $\mathcal{S}$ generating $\hat{\theta}$ admits generalized residuals u with generalized instruments i.*

(i) Given Assumptions 2.1, 2.3 and 2.4

$$\hat{J}_n = n^{-1} \sum_{t=1}^{n} \hat{j}_t \hat{j}_t' - (n^{-1} \sum_{t=1}^{n} \hat{j}_t \hat{i}_t')[n^{-1} \sum_{t=1}^{n} \hat{i}_t \hat{i}_t']^{-} (n^{-1} \sum_{t=1}^{n} \hat{i}_t \hat{j}_t'), \; n = 1, 2, \ldots$$

defines a sequence $\{\hat{J}_n\}$ of measurable nonnegative symmetric positive semi-definite matrices. Under the same conditions $\{\hat{\sigma}_n^2 = (nl)^{-1} \sum_{t=1}^{n} \sum_{i=1}^{l} \hat{u}_{ti}^2\}$ is a measurable nonnegative sequence.

(ii) If Assumptions 3.1, 3.2 and 11.4 also hold, then $\hat{J}_n - \ddot{J}_n^* \to 0$ prob $- P_o$, where $\ddot{J}_n^*$ is as in Corollary 9.13, with $j_t^* = w_t^* i_t^*$ and $i_t^* = i_t(W_t, \theta_n^*)$. Further, $\{\ddot{J}_n^*\}$ is $O(1)$. Under the same conditions $\hat{\sigma}_n^2 - \sigma_n^{*2} \to 0$ prob $- P_o$, $\sigma_n^{*2} \equiv (nl)^{-1} \sum_{t=1}^{n} \sum_{i=1}^{l} E(u_{ti}^{*2})$. Further, $\{\sigma_n^{*2}\}$ is $O(1)$.

(iii) Suppose in addition that $\{a_n^* = n^{-1/2} \sum_{t=1}^{n} E(v_t^* s_t^*)\}$ is $O(1)$, that Assumptions 3.2′, 3.7(a), 3.8, 3.9, 6.1, 11.1 and 11.2 hold, that $\{J_n^*\}$ is uniformly positive definite, and that $\sigma_n^{*2} > \varepsilon > 0$ a. a. n..

(a) Letting $\mathcal{M}_n = n \hat{M}_n' \hat{J}_n^{-} \hat{M}_n / \hat{\sigma}_n^2$ for $\hat{J}_n$ and $\hat{\sigma}_n^2$ as in (i), we have $\mathcal{M}_n \overset{A}{\sim} N_2(a_n^*, V_n^*; \ddot{J}_n^{*-1} / \sigma_n^{*2})$.

(b) Letting $\mathcal{M}_n' = nlR^2$, where R^2 is the (constant unadjusted) squared multiple correlation coefficient from the regression of the generalized residual $\hat{u}_{ti}$ on explanatory variables $\hat{j}_{ti}'$ $(1 \times q)$, $\hat{i}_{ti}'$ $(1 \times p)$, $i = 1, \ldots, l$, $t = 1, \ldots, n$, we have that $\mathcal{M}_n - \mathcal{M}_n' \to 0$ prob $- P_o$ and $\mathcal{M}_n' \overset{A}{\sim} N_2$ $(a_n^*, V_n^*; \ddot{J}_n^{*-1} / \sigma_n^{*2})$.

In particular, if $\{u_t^*, \tilde{\mathcal{F}}^t\}$ is a martingale difference sequence and for some real constant $\sigma_o^2 > 0$, we have $E(u_t^* u_t^{*\prime} \mid \tilde{W}_t) = \sigma_o^2 I_l$ and $i_t^* = - E(\nabla_\theta u_t^* \mid W_t) / \sigma_o^2$, $t = 1, 2, \ldots$, then $\mathcal{M}_n \overset{A}{\sim} \chi_q^2$ and $\mathcal{M}_n' \overset{A}{\sim} \chi_q^2$, where $\sigma(\tilde{W}_t) = \vee_{\tau=0}^{\lambda} \sigma(W_{t-\tau})$.

(iv) In addition to the conditions of (i) and (ii), suppose that Assumption 11.3 also holds, $\{J_n^*\}$ is uniformly positive definite, and $\sigma_n^{*2} > \varepsilon > 0$ a.a. n. If $\bar{M}_n^{*\prime} \bar{M}_n^* > \varepsilon > 0$ a.a. n then for $\{k_n\} = o(n)$, $P_o[\mathcal{M}_n > k_n] \to 1$. If in addition Assumption 3.2′ holds $P_o[\mathcal{M}_n' > k_n] \to 1$. □

This result contains as special cases a considerable variety of interesting specification tests that can be conducted by regressing a generalized residual on its lagged value(s) and on products of its lagged value(s) with functions of predetermined variables. We examine specific forms of several such tests in more detail in the following section.

Note that the requirements that $E(u_t^* \, u_t^{*\prime} \mid \tilde{W}_t) = \sigma_o^2 \, I_l$ and $i_t^* = - E(\nabla_\theta u_t^* \mid W_t)/\sigma_o^2$ are very stringent. The condition on the conditional covariance matrix of u_t^* can be satisfied by using (a correctly specified model of) the conditional covariance matrix to transform generalized residuals that otherwise would exhibit conditional heteroskedasticity. Thus, neglected conditional heteroskedasticity (e.g. neglected ARCH) would lead to tests of incorrect size. The generalized instruments i_t^* are also severely restricted; essentially they must be such that $\hat{\theta}$ attains the minimum asymptotic variance bound (see Bates and White [1988]). Failure of $\hat{\theta}$ to attain this bound thus generally yields tests of incorrect size when the χ_q^2 distribution is used with the statistics of this result.

In all of the dynamic specification tests discussed in this section, we have set $s_t^* = s_t(X^t, \theta_n^*) \, 1[t > 0]$ and constructed statistics as n times R^2 from an appropriate regression. This is done for the sake of convenience, and to provide maximum analogy with the previous chapter. However, it may be preferable in practice to set $s_t^* = s_t(X^t, \theta_n^*)$, $t = 1, 2, \ldots$ as usual, perform regressions (or form $\hat{M}_n$) using observations $t = \lambda + 1, \lambda + 2, \ldots, n$ and replace nR^2 by $(n - \lambda)R^2$. All of the results in this section apply equally to either formulation.

11.1.b (Second Order) Information Matrix Tests

In this section we consider tests sensitive to failure of the information matrix equality $A_n^* + \overline{B}_n^* = 0$ (or $A_n^* + \overline{B}_n^* \to 0$). Here we call such tests "second order information matrix tests" to distinguish them from dynamic (first order) information matrix tests. The tests we consider are versions of the test originally proposed by White [1982], who considered only the case of i.i.d. observations. Versions of some of the tests discussed in this section are given under mixing conditions by White [1987].

In Chapter 6 we gave several results that provide conditions ensuring $A_n^* + \overline{B}_n^* = 0$, i.e.,

$$n^{-1} \sum_{t=1}^{n} E(\nabla' s_t^*) + n^{-1} \sum_{t=1}^{n} E(s_t^* \, s_t^{*\prime}) = 0 \qquad n = 1, 2, \ldots$$

(see Theorems 6.5, 6.6, 6.9 and 6.13). To focus attention on this equality, we consider m-tests based on

$$m_t(x^t, \theta) = S \; vec \; [\nabla' s_t(x^t, \theta) + s_t(x^t, \theta) \; s_t(x^t, \theta)'] \, ,$$

where S is again a selection (or other fixed) matrix of dimension $q \times p^2$. Because $\nabla' s_t + s_t \; s_t'$ is a symmetric matrix, S need only select elements of the lower triangle of $\nabla' s_t + s_t \; s_t'$ to yield a test with power against any failure of the information matrix equality. It will be assumed throughout this section that S is of such form.

As in the previous section, we choose $\hat{\theta}$ to be the QMLE generated by specification $\mathcal{S}$ to which Theorem 6.4 applies, so that π is null.

To ensure that the conditions of Theorem 9.5 hold, we require the differentiability of m_t in Assumption 9.1. We make the following assumption.

ASSUMPTION 11.5: $f_t(X^t, \cdot\,)$ is continuously differentiable of order 3 on Θ $a.s.$–P_o, $t = 1, 2, \ldots$. □

With this assumption we have $\nabla' m_t = S[\nabla^2 \, s_t + [(s_t \otimes I_p) + (I_p \otimes s_t)] \; \nabla' s_t]$ where $\nabla^2 \, s_t \equiv \nabla' \, \nabla s_t$ is the $p^2 \times p$ Hessian matrix of s. (We exploit the symmetry of $\nabla' s$ here.) We further impose

ASSUMPTION 11.6:

(a) The elements of $n^{-1} \sum_{t=1}^n E(\nabla^2 \, s_t(X^t, \cdot\,))$ and $n^{-1} \sum_{t=1}^n E[[(s_t(X^t, \cdot\,) \otimes I_p) \; \nabla' s_t(X^t, \cdot\,)]$ are finite and continuous on Θ uniformly in $n = 1, 2, \ldots$;

(b) The elements of $\{\nabla^2 \, s_t(X^t, \theta)\}$ and $\{(s_t(X^t, \theta) \otimes I_p) \; \nabla' s_t(X^t, \theta)\}$ obey the weak ULLN. □

Note that $(s_t \otimes I_p) \; \nabla' \, s_t$ involves all cross-products of elements of s_t and $\nabla' \, s_t$, so separate conditions for $(I_p \otimes s_t) \; \nabla' \, s_t$ are not needed.

As with the dynamic information matrix test, Assumption 11.6 generally ensures that

$$\sqrt{n} \, \hat{M}_n = n^{-1/2} \sum_{t=1}^{n} m_t^* + \nabla'_\theta \, \bar{M}_n^* \, \sqrt{n} \, (\hat{\theta}_n - \theta_n^*) + o_{P_o}(1) \, .$$

To verify condition 9.3(ii) or 9.4(ii), we use the following assumption.

ASSUMPTION 11.7: For given nonstochastic $q \times p^2$ matrix S, $\{n^{-1/2} (S\ vec\ [\nabla' s_t^* + s_t^* s_t^{*\prime}] - \nabla_\theta' \bar{M}_n^* A_n^{*-1} s_t^*)\}$ obeys the central limit theorem, with covariance matrix $\{V_n^*\}$ $O(1)$ and uniformly positive definite. □

As with the dynamic information matrix test, P_o belongs to $\mathcal{P}_o^u$ when

$$a_n^* = n^{-1/2} \sum_{t=1}^n S\ vec\ E(\nabla' s_t^* + s_t^* s_t^{*\prime}) \to 0$$

and belongs to $\mathcal{P}_a^u$ when $\{a_n^*\}$ is $O(1)$. Cases belonging to the global alternative do not require Assumption 11.7; instead Assumptions 3.8 and 8.6 are relevant.

The result for the (second order) information matrix test is obtained directly from Theorem 9.5.

THEOREM 11.3: *Let $\{\hat{J}_n\}$ be a sequence of measurable symmetric positive semi-definite $q \times q$ matrices such that $\hat{J}_n - J_n^* \to 0$ prob $- P_o$, where $\{J_n^*\}$ is a sequence of non-stochastic symmetric $q \times q$ matrices, $O(1)$ and uniformly positive definite.*

(i) Suppose the conditions of Theorem 6.4 hold, together with Assumptions 11.6 and 11.7 and let $\mathcal{M}_n = n \hat{M}_n' \hat{J}_n^- \hat{M}_n$ with

$$\hat{M}_n = n^{-1} \sum_{t=1}^{n} \hat{m}_t, \quad \hat{m}_t = S\ vec\ [\nabla' \hat{s}_t + \hat{s}_t \hat{s}_t'],$$

where S is a nonstochastic $q \times p^2$ real matrix.

If $\{a_n^* \equiv n^{-1/2} \sum_{t=1}^n S\ vec\ E(\nabla' s_t^* + s_t^* s_t^{*\prime}) = S \sqrt{n}\ vec\ (A_n^* + \bar{B}_n^*)\}$ is $O(1)$, then $\mathcal{M}_n \overset{A}{\sim} N_2(a_n^*, V_n^*; J_n^{*-1})$.

In particular, if $a_n^* \to 0$ and $J_n^* = V_n^*$, then $\mathcal{M}_n \overset{A}{\sim} \chi_q^2$.

(ii) Suppose instead that the conditions of Theorem 3.5 hold, together with Assumptions 3.6, 3.8 and 8.6. If $\bar{M}_n^{*\prime} \bar{M}_n^* > \varepsilon > 0$ a.a. n, then for $\{k_n\} = o(n)$, $P_o[\mathcal{M}_n > k_n] \to 1$. □

Thus the (second order) information matrix test is consistent against alternatives for which the information matrix equality fails in the directions determined by S; it can be based on the χ_q^2 distribution asymptotically, provided that $\hat{J}_n$ is chosen appropriately.

Failure of $A_n^* + \bar{B}_n^* \to 0$ implies that $\hat{\theta}$ generally doesn't attain the minimum asymptotic variance bound, and that the classical parameter covariance matrix estimators and associated test statistics do not behave in the desired manner.

The (second order) information matrix test is not necessarily sensitive to dynamic misspecification (although it sometimes can be), but is generally sensitive to neglected heterogeneity, signaling the failure of $\mathcal{S}$ to be correct for $\{Y_t \mid W_t\}$. This information matrix statistic may also signal the failure of the correctness of $\mathcal{M}$ for $\{E(Y_t \mid W_t)\}$. If desired, this possibility can be investigated more directly using tests of the previous chapter.

Application of Corollary 9.9 is possible when $\nabla_\theta \bar{M}_n^* = 0$. This occurs in certain important special cases, such as the linear regression model (e.g. White [1980b]) when S does not select elements of $\nabla' s_t^* + s_t\, s_t'$ involving variance parameters. We investigate the specifics in Section 11.3 below. For now it suffices to remark that $\nabla_\theta \bar{M}_n^* = 0$ in this case as the relevant elements of $\nabla^2 s_t$ vanish identically, while $\nabla' s_t^*$ is measurable $-\mathcal{F}^{\,t-1}$, so that $E([(s_t^* \otimes I_p) + (I_p \otimes s_t^*)]\, \nabla' s_t^* \mid X^{t-1}) = 0$.

We obtain a convenient statistic for this case from Corollary 9.9. For simplicity we impose the needed condition in the following way:

ASSUMPTION 11.8: Assumption 9.4 holds for $m_t = S\ vec\ (\nabla'\, s_t + s_t\, s_t')$.□

COROLLARY 11.4: *(i) Given Assumptions 2.1, 2.3 and 3.6,* $\{\hat{K}_n = n^{-1} \sum_{t=1}^n \hat{m}_t\, \hat{m}_t'\}$ *is a measurable sequence of symmetric positive semi-definite matrices,* $\hat{m}_t = S\ vec\ (\nabla' \hat{s}_t + \hat{s}_t\, \hat{s}_t')$.

(ii) If Assumptions 3.1, 3.2 and 11.8 also hold, then $\hat{K}_n - K_n^* \to 0$ $prob - P_o$, $K_n^* \equiv n^{-1} \sum_{t=1}^n E(m_t^*\, m_t^{*\prime})$. *Further* $\{K_n^*\}$ *is* $O(1)$.

(iii) Suppose in addition that $\{a_n^* = \sqrt{n}\ S\ vec\ (A_n^* + \bar{B}_n^*)\}$ *is* $O(1)$, *that Assumptions 3.2′, 3.7(a), 3.8, 3.9, 6.1, 11.6 and 11.7 hold and that* $\{K_n^*\}$ *is uniformly positive definite. Then* $\mathcal{M}_n = n\, \hat{M}_n'\, \hat{K}_n^-\, \hat{M}_n = n\, R^2 \overset{A}{\sim} N_2\, (a_n^*, V_n^*\,;\, K_n^{*-1})$, *where* R^2 *is the constant-unadjusted squared multiple correlation coefficient of the constant unity on the explanatory variables* $\hat{m}_t'$, $t = 1, \ldots, n$.

In particular, if $\{m_t^*, \mathcal{F}^{\,t}\}$ *and* $\{\nabla_\theta\, m_t^*, \mathcal{F}^{\,t}\}$ *are martingale difference* *sequences, then* $\mathcal{M}_n \overset{A}{\sim} \chi^2_q$.

(iv) In addition to the conditions of (i) and (ii) suppose that Assumptions 3.8 and 8.6 hold and that $\{K_n^*\}$ *is uniformly positive definite. If* $\bar{M}_n' \bar{M}_n^* > \varepsilon > 0$ *a.a. n, then for* $\{k_n\} = o(n)$, $P_o[\mathcal{M}_n > k_n] \to 1$. □

Even if $\{\nabla_\theta m_t^*, \mathcal{F}^t\}$ is not a martingale difference sequence, convenient test statistics can be obtained from Corollary 9.10 when $\{s_t^*, \mathcal{F}^t\}$ and $\{\nabla' s_t^* + s_t^* s_t^{*\prime}, \mathcal{F}^t\}$ are martingale difference sequences. The test statistic is formed by regressing $\hat{\xi}_t \equiv \hat{m}_t - \nabla_\theta' \hat{M}_n \hat{A}_n^- \hat{s}_t$ on the constant unity and computing nR^2 from this regression. We leave the details to the interested reader (see White [1988, ch.10]).

Now consider the situation in which the specification admits a generalized residual. Letting $\nabla' i_t^* = \nabla' i_t(W_t, \theta_n^*)$ denote the $lp \times p$ Jacobian matrix of the generalized instruments, we have

$$\nabla' s_t^* = i_t^* \nabla' u_t^* + (u_t^{*\prime} \otimes I_p) \nabla' i_t^*$$

$$s_t^* s_t^{*\prime} = i_t^* u_t^* u_t^{*\prime} i_t^{*\prime}$$

so that

$$m_t^* = S \, vec \, [i_t^* \nabla' u_t^* + (u_t^{*\prime} \otimes I_p) \nabla' i_t^* + i_t^* u_t^* u_t^{*\prime} i_t^{*\prime}] \, .$$

Evidently, this is not in the form treated by either Corollary 9.12 or 9.13, so a statistic analogous to that of Corollary 11.2 is not available. A "partial" information matrix test obtained from Corollary 9.12 could be conducted using $(u_t^{*\prime} \otimes I_p) \nabla' i_t^*$. However, this would yield a test sensitive to the failure of $\{u_t^*, \tilde{\mathcal{F}}^t\}$ to be a martingale difference sequence; the dynamic information matrix tests are more convenient for testing this. Although there may certainly be circumstances in which we would want to base tests on elements of $(u_t^{*\prime} \otimes I_p) \nabla' i_t^*$, we do not give a formal treatment.

It is also possible to base information matrix tests on $i_t^* \nabla' u_t^* + i_t^* u_t^* u_t^{*\prime} i_t^{*\prime}$ (set $m_t = S \, vec \, (i_t \nabla' u_t + i_t u_t u_t' i_t')$. Essentially this takes $\{u_t^*, \tilde{\mathcal{F}}^t\}$ to be a martingale difference sequence, and focuses attention on the designated indicators. The preceding results of this section have analogs that can be based on this choice of m_t rather than that explicitly considered. Note the computational advantage gained by not having to compute ∇i_t.

Tests based on such a choice for m_t can be conducted using regressions with generalized residuals as the dependent variables, provided that $E(u_t^* u_t^{*\prime} \mid W_t) = I_l$ and that $i_t^* = -E(\nabla u_t^* \mid W_t)$, $t = 1, 2, \ldots$. To proceed, we let $\nabla \tilde{u}_t^* = E(\nabla u_t^* \mid W_t)$, and set $m_t^* = S \; vec \;\; i_t^* \; \nabla' \tilde{u}_t^* + i_t^* \; u_t^* \; u_t^{*\prime} \; i_t^{*\prime}$, so that we have replaced ∇u_t^* with $\nabla \tilde{u}_t^*$. Under the assumptions just given,

$$\begin{aligned} E(m_t^* \mid W_t) &= S \; vec \; [E(i_t^* \; \nabla' \tilde{u}_t^* \mid W_t) + E(i_t^* \; u_t^* \; u_t^{*\prime} \; i_t^{*\prime} \mid W_t)] \\ &= S \; vec \; [- i_t^* \; i_t^{*\prime} + i_t^* \; E(u_t^* \; u_t^{*\prime} \mid W_t) \; i_t^{*\prime}] \\ &= S \; vec \; [- i_t^* \; i_t^{*\prime} + i_t^* \; i_t^{*\prime}] \\ &= 0 \, . \end{aligned}$$

This shows that replacing ∇u_t^* with $\nabla \tilde{u}_t^*$ allows us to test the same null hypothesis. Convenience is afforded by the fact that with $\nabla \tilde{u}_t^* = - i_t^{*\prime}$, we can write $m_t^* = S \; vec \; [i_t^* \; u_t^* \; u_t^{*\prime} \; i_t^{*\prime} - i_t^* \; i_t^{*\prime}] = S \, (i_t^* \otimes i_t^*) \; vec \; (u_t^* \; u_t^{*\prime} - I_l)$. This suggests choosing

$$\begin{aligned} m_t &= S \, (i_t \otimes i_t) \; vec \; (u_t \; u_t' - I_l) \\ &= j_t \; v_t \, , \end{aligned}$$

with $j_t = S \, (i_t \otimes i_t)$ and $v_t = vec \; (u_t \; u_t' - I_l)$. Note that here the dimension of v_t, denoted $\tilde{l}$, is given by $\tilde{l} = l^2$.

The possibility of representing m_t as $m_t = j_t \; v_t$ raises the possibility of applying Corollary 9.12. To obtain a test of proper size from this result, we will rely on the assumption that $\{m_t^* , \mathcal{F}^t \}$ and $\{\nabla_\theta \; m_t^* , \mathcal{F}^t \}$ are martingale difference sequences.

In order that $\{m_t^* , \mathcal{F}^t \}$ be a martingale difference sequence, it suffices that $W_t = \tilde{X}^{t-1}$, as we saw above that $E(m_t^* \mid W_t) = 0$. Thus, we rely on the assumptions that $E(u_t^* \; u_t^{*\prime} \mid \tilde{X}^{t-1}) = I_l$ (absence of conditional heteroskedasticity) and $i_t^* = - \, E(\nabla_\theta \; u_t^* \mid \tilde{X}^{t-1})$ (optimal generalized instruments).

The requirement that $\{\nabla_\theta \; m_t^* , \mathcal{F}^t \}$ be a martingale difference sequence is also straightforward. Because $m_t = j_t \; v_t$, we have

$$\nabla'_\theta \; m_t^* = j_t^* \; \nabla'_\theta \; v_t^* + (v_t^{*\prime} \otimes I_q) \; \nabla'_\theta \; j_t^* \, .$$

By assumptions, $E(v_t^* \mid \tilde{X}^{t-1}) = 0$, so we are left with $E(\nabla'_\theta \; m_t^* \mid \tilde{X}^{t-1}) = j_t^* \; E(\nabla'_\theta \; v_t^* \mid \tilde{X}^{t-1})$. Now $\nabla'_\theta \; v_t = [(u_t \otimes I_l) + (I_l \otimes u_t)] \; \nabla'_\theta \; u_t$. Typically $\nabla_\theta \; u_t^*$ is measurable with respect to $\tilde{X}^{t-1}$, so that

$$\begin{aligned} E(\nabla'_\theta \; v_t^* \mid \tilde{X}^{t-1}) &= E([(u_t^* \otimes I_l) + (I_l \otimes u_t^*)] \mid \tilde{X}^{t-1}) \; \nabla'_\theta \; u_t^* \\ &= 0 \, , \end{aligned}$$

provided that $E(u_t^* \mid \tilde{X}^{t-1}) = 0$. With these conditions $E(\nabla_\theta m_t^* \mid \tilde{X}^{t-1}) = 0$, so that $\{\nabla_\theta m_t^*, \mathcal{F}^t\}$ is a martingale difference sequence, as desired.

This discussion motivates a straightforward corollary to Corollary 9.12. We use the following condition.

ASSUMPTION 11.9: When $\hat{\theta}$ is generated by a specification $\mathcal{S}$ admitting generalized residuals $u = \{u_t\}$ and generalized instruments $i = \{i_t\}$, Assumption 9.8 holds for $\{j_t = S(i_t \otimes i_t)\}$ and Assumption 9.9 holds for $\{v_t = (vec\,(u_t\, u_t' - I_l))\}$. □

COROLLARY 11.5: *Suppose that the specification $\mathcal{S}$ generating $\hat{\theta}$ admits generalized residuals $u = \{u_t\}$ with generalized instruments $i = \{i_t\}$, define $j_t \equiv S\,(i_t \otimes i_t)$ for given nonstochastic $q \times p^2$ matrix S and define $v_t \equiv vec(u_t\, u_t' - I_l)$, so that j_t* is *$q \times l^2$ and v_t* is *$l^2 \times 1$, $t = 1, 2, \ldots$.*

(i) Given Assumptions 2.1 and 2.3, $\hat{J}_n = n^{-1} \sum_{t=1}^n \hat{j}_t\, \hat{j}_t'$, $n = 1, 2, \ldots$ defines a sequence $\{\hat{J}_n\}$ of measurable symmetric positive semi-definite matrices. Under the same conditions, $\{\hat{\sigma}_n^2 = (nl^2)^{-1} \sum_{t=1}^n \sum_{i=1}^{l^2} \hat{v}_{ti}^2\}$ is a measurable non-negative sequence.

(ii) If Assumptions 3.1, 3.2 and 11.9 also hold, then $\hat{J}_n - \ddot{J}_n^* \to 0$ prob$-P_o$ and $\hat{\sigma}_n^2 - \sigma_n^{*2} \to 0$ prob$-P_o$ where $\ddot{J}_n \equiv n^{-1} \sum_{t=1}^n E(j_t^*\, j_t^{*\prime})$, $\sigma_n^{*2} = (nl^2)^{-1} \sum_{t=1}^n \sum_{i=1}^{l^2} E(v_{ti}^{*2})$. Further $\{\ddot{J}_n^*\}$ and $\{\sigma_n^{*2}\}$ are $O(1)$.

(iii) Suppose in addition that $\{a_n^* = \sqrt{n}\, S\, vec\,(A_n^* + \bar{B}_n^*)\}$ is *$O(1)$, that Assumptions 3.2′, 3.6, 3.7(a), 3.8, 3.9, 6.1, 11.6 and 11.7 hold, that $\sigma_n^{*2} > \varepsilon > 0$ a.a. n, and that $\{\ddot{J}_n^*\}$ is uniformly positive definite. Then $\ddot{\mathcal{M}}_n = nl^2\, R^2 \overset{A}{\sim} N_2(a_n^*, V_n^*;\ \ddot{J}_n^{*-1} / \sigma_n^{*2})$, where R^2 is the squared multiple correlation coefficient for the regression of $\hat{v}_{ti}$ on the $1 \times q$* vector *$\hat{j}_{ti}'$, $i = 1, \ldots, l^2$, $t = 1, \ldots, n$.*

In particular, if $\{u_t^*, \tilde{\mathcal{F}}^t\}$, $\{u_t^*\, u_t^{*\prime} - I_l,\ \tilde{\mathcal{F}}^t\}$, $\{i_t^* + \nabla u_t^*,\ \tilde{\mathcal{F}}^t\}$, $\{j_t^*\, \nabla'_\theta v_t^*,\ \tilde{\mathcal{F}}^t\}$, and $\{v_t^*\, v_t^{*\prime} - \sigma_o^2\, I_{l^2},\ \tilde{\mathcal{F}}^t\}$ are martingale difference sequences for some real constant $\sigma_o^2 > 0$, then $\ddot{\mathcal{M}}_n \overset{A}{\sim} \chi_q^2$.

(iv) In addition to the conditions of (i) and (ii), suppose that Assumptions 3.8 and 8.6 hold and that $\sigma_n^{*2} > \varepsilon > 0$ a.a. n, and $\{\ddot{J}_n^*\}$ is uniformly positive definite. If $\bar{M}_n^{*\prime}\, \bar{M}_n^* > \varepsilon > 0$ a.a. n, then for $\{k_n\} = o(n)$, $P_o\,[\ddot{\mathcal{M}}_n > k_n] \to 1$. □

This result is a substantial generalization of a result of White [1980b], who provides an information matrix test for heteroskedasticity in the linear regression model. There, one regresses the squared residuals from a linear regression on (selected) squares and cross-products of the regressors. Here one regresses squares and cross-products of generalized residuals from a multivariate quasi-likelihood specification on (selected) squares and cross-products ($S(\hat{i}_t \otimes \hat{i}_t)$) of generalized instruments. The underlying heuristics are the same in both cases, however. We discuss the linear regression case in somewhat more detail in Section 11.3.b below.

Because it generally will not be possible to have $v_t = u_t$ as Corollary 9.13 requires in order to form a test of proper size asymptotically, we do not use Corollary 9.13 to try to obtain a (second order) information matrix test.

11.1.c The Cross-Information Matrix Test

In numerous instances the validity of the cross-information matrix equality ($\nabla'_\theta \bar{M}_n^* + G_n^* \to 0$) permits considerable simplification of the computations needed to construct particular specification test statistics. In some circumstances, we may wish to test the validity of the cross-information matrix equality. When it fails, specification tests of proper size cannot be based on Corollaries 9.10, 9.11 or 9.13. Furthermore, failure of the cross-information matrix equality generally indicates the failure of the QMLE generated by $\mathcal{S}$ to attain the asymptotic minimum variance bound.

A test of the cross-information matrix equality can be cast as an m-test by choosing indicators to be of the form

$$m_t(X^t, \theta) = S\ vec\ [\nabla' \lambda_t(X^t, \theta) + \lambda_t(X^t, \theta)\ s_t(X^t, \theta)'\ ],$$

where λ_t is a given (vector) function determining the direction(s) in which the test is desired to have power. Now λ_t corresponds to the choice of m_t explicit in earlier discussion of m tests, but we reserve the notation m_t for the function forming the basis for the m-test at hand. Observe that the (second order) information matrix test arises as the special case of the cross-information matrix test in which $\lambda_t = s_t$. For this reason our treatment of the cross-information matrix test is entirely parallel to that of the (second order) information matrix test.

Again we take $\hat{\theta}$ to be the QMLE generated by a specification $\mathcal{S}$ to which Theorem 6.4 applies, so that π is null. To ensure that the present choice of m_t satisfies Assumption 9.1, we impose the following condition.

ASSUMPTION 11.10: The functions $\lambda_t : \mathbb{R}^{vt} \times \Theta \to \mathbb{R}^c$, $c \in \mathbb{N}$, are such that $\lambda_t(\cdot, \theta)$ is measurable -$\mathbb{B}^{vt}$ for each θ in Θ, and $\lambda_t(X^t, \cdot)$ is continuously differentiable of order two on Θ $a.s. - P_o$. □

With this condition, we have $\nabla' m_t = S\ (\nabla^2 \lambda_t + (s_t \otimes I_c)\ \nabla' \lambda_t + (I_p \otimes \lambda_t)\ \nabla' s_t)$, where we abuse notation for convenience and write $\nabla^2 \lambda_t \equiv \nabla'(\nabla' \lambda_t)$, a $cp \times p$ matrix.

The uniform continuity and the uniform law of large numbers that help ensure the validity of Condition 9.3(i) are imposed by the next assumption.

ASSUMPTION 11.11:
(a) The elements of $n^{-1}\sum_{t=1}^{n} E(\nabla^2 \lambda_t(X^t, \cdot))$, $n^{-1}\sum_{t=1}^{n} E[(s_t(X^t, \theta) \otimes I_c)\nabla' \lambda_t(X^t, \cdot)]$ and $n^{-1}\sum_{t=1}^{n} E[(I_p \otimes \lambda_t(X^t, \cdot))\nabla' s_t(X^t, \cdot)]$ are finite and continuous on Θ uniformly in $n = 1, 2, \ldots$;
(b) The elements of $\{\nabla^2 \lambda_t(X^t, \theta)\}$, $\{(s_t(X^t, \theta) \otimes I_c)\nabla' \lambda_t(X^t, \theta)\}$ and $\{(I_p \otimes \lambda_t(X^t, \theta))\nabla' s_t(X^t, \theta)\}$ obey the weak ULLN. □

The following assumption helps in verifying condition 9.3(ii) or 9.4(ii). We set $\lambda_t^* \equiv \lambda_t(X^t, \theta_n^*)$.

ASSUMPTION 11.12: For given nonstochastic $q \times cp$ matrix S, $\{n^{-1/2}(S\, vec[\nabla'\lambda_t^* + \lambda_t^* s_t^{*\prime}] - \nabla'_\theta \bar{M}_n^* A_n^{*-1} s_t^*)\}$ obeys the central limit theorem, with covariance matrix $\{V_n^*\}$ $O(1)$ and uniformly positive definite. □

The DGP P_o belongs to $\mathcal{P}_o^u$ when $a_n^* = n^{-1/2}\sum_{t=1}^{n} S\, vec[E(\nabla'\lambda_t^* + \lambda_t^* s_t^{*\prime})] \to 0$, and belongs to $\mathcal{P}_a^u$ when $\{a_n^*\}$ is $O(1)$. Cases belonging to the global alternative do not require Assumption 11.12. Instead, the following assumption suffices.

ASSUMPTION 11.13:
(a) The elements of $n^{-1}\sum_{t=1}^{n} E(\nabla\lambda_t(X^t, \theta))$ and $n^{-1}\sum_{t=1}^{n} E(\lambda_t(X^t, \theta) s_t(X^t, \theta)')$ are finite and continuous on Θ uniformly in $n = 1, 2, \ldots$;
(b) The elements of $\{\nabla\lambda_t(X^t, \theta)\}$ and $\{\lambda_t(X^t, \theta)s_t(X^t, \theta)'\}$ obey the weak ULLN. □

The properties of the cross-information matrix test statistic now follow directly from Theorem 9.5.

THEOREM 11.6: *Let $\{\hat{J}_n\}$ be a sequence of measurable symmetric positive semi-definite $q \times q$ matrices such that $\hat{J}_n - J_n^* \to 0$ prob $- P_o$, where $\{J_n^*\}$ is a sequence of nonstochastic symmetric $q \times q$ matrices, $O(1)$ and uniformly positive definite.*
(i) Suppose the conditions of Theorem 6.4 hold, together with

Assumptions 11.10–11.12, and let $\mathcal{M}_n = n\, \hat{M}_n{}'\, \hat{J}_n^{-}\, \hat{M}_n$, *with*

$$\hat{M}_n = n^{-1} \sum_{t=1}^{n} \hat{m}_t\,, \quad \hat{m}_t = S\ vec\,[\nabla'\hat{\lambda}_t + \hat{\lambda}_t \hat{s}_t{}']\,,$$

where S *is a nonstochastic* $q \times cp$ *real matrix,* $\nabla\hat{\lambda}_t \equiv \nabla\, \lambda_t(X^t\,, \hat{\theta}_n)$, $\hat{\lambda}_t \equiv \lambda_t(X^t\,, \hat{\theta}_n)$. *If* $\{a_n^* = \sqrt{n}\, \bar{M}_n^*\}$ *is* $O(1)$, *then* $\mathcal{M}_n \overset{A}{\sim} N_2(a_n^*\,, V_n^*\,;\, J_n^{*-1})$.

In particular, if $a_n^* \to 0$ *and* $J_n^* = V_n^*$, *then* $\mathcal{M}_n \overset{A}{\sim} \chi_q^2$.

(ii) Suppose instead that the conditions of Theorem 3.5 hold, together with Assumptions 11.10 and 11.13. If $\bar{M}_n^{*\prime}\, \bar{M}_n^* > \varepsilon > 0$ *a.a.* n *then for* $\{k_n\} = o(n)$, $P_o[\mathcal{M}_n > k_n] \to 1$. □

Part (i) ensures that the test can be based on the χ_q^2 distribution when $\hat{J}_n$ is chosen appropriately. Rejection of the cross-information matrix equality indicates the failure of $\hat{\theta}$ to attain the minimum asymptotic variance bound, and the inappropriateness of the χ_q^2 distribution as an approximation to the null distributions of the more computationally convenient versions of m-tests based on λ_t. Rejection may also signal the misspecification of $\mathcal{S}$ for $\{Y_t \mid W_t\}$ or of $\mathcal{M}$ for $\{E(Y_t \mid W_t)\}$. Part (ii) guarantees that the cross-information matrix test is consistent against alternatives for which the cross-information matrix equality fails.

As with the (second order) information matrix test, it happens in special cases that $\nabla_\theta\, \bar{M}_n^* = 0$. The following condition allows statement of a corollary to Corollary 9.9.

ASSUMPTION 11.14: Assumption 9.4 holds for $m_t = S\ vec\,(\nabla'\, \lambda_t + \lambda_t\, s_t{}')$. □

COROLLARY 11.7:*(i) Given Assumptions 2.1, 2.3, 2.4 and 11.10,* $\{\hat{K}_n = n^{-1} \sum_{t=1}^{n} \hat{m}_t\, \hat{m}_t{}'\}$ *is a measurable sequence of symmetric positive semi-definite matrices, where* $\hat{m}_t = S\ vec\,(\nabla'\, \hat{\lambda}_t + \hat{\lambda}_t\, \hat{s}_t{}')$.

(ii) If Assumptions 3.1, 3.2 and 11.13 also hold, then $\hat{K}_n - K_n^* \to 0$ *prob* $- P_o$, $K_n^* \equiv n^{-1} \sum_{t=1}^{n} E(m_t^*\, m_t^{*\prime})$. *Further* $\{K_n^*\}$ is $O(1)$.

(iii) Suppose in addition that $\{\, a_n^* = \sqrt{n}\, \bar{M}_n^* = n^{-1/2} \sum_{t=1}^{n} S\, E\,(vec\,(\nabla'\, \lambda_t^* + \lambda_t^*\, s_t^{*\prime}))\}$ *is* $O(1)$, *that Assumptions 3.2′, 3.6, 3.7(a), 3.8, 3.9, 6.1, 11.11 and 11.12 hold, and that* $\{K_n^*\}$ *is uniformly positive definite. Then*

$\mathcal{M}_n = n\, \hat{M}_n'\, \hat{K}_n^-\, \hat{M}_n = n\, R^2 \overset{A}{\sim} N_2(a_n^*, V_n^*; K_n^{*-1})$, where R^2 is the constant unadjusted squared multiple correlation coefficient of the constant unity on the explanatory variables $\hat{m}_t'$, $t = 1, \ldots, n$.

In particular, if $\{m_t^*, \mathcal{F}^t\}$, and $\{\nabla_\theta\, m_t^*, \mathcal{F}^t\}$ are martingale difference sequences, then $\mathcal{M}_n \overset{A}{\sim} \chi_q^2$.

(iv) In addition to the conditions of (i) and (ii) suppose that Assumption 11.13 holds and that $\{K_n^*\}$ is uniformly positive definite. If $\bar{M}_n^{*\prime}\, \bar{M}_n^* > \varepsilon > 0$ a.a. n, then for $\{k_n\} = o(n)$, $P_o[\mathcal{M}_n > k_n] \to 1$. □

Even if $\{\nabla_\theta\, m_t^*, \mathcal{F}^t\}$ is not a martingale difference sequence, convenient test statistics can be obtained from Corollary 9.10, provided that $\{s_t^*, \mathcal{F}^t\}$ and $\{\nabla'\lambda_t^* + \lambda_t^*\, s_t^{*\prime}, \mathcal{F}^t\}$ are martingale difference sequences. The test is based on regressing unity on $\hat{\xi}_t' = (\hat{m}_t - \nabla_\theta'\, \hat{M}_n\, \hat{A}_n^-\, \hat{s}_t)'$ and forming nR^2.

An even simpler test can be constructed as a consequence of Corollary 9.11, based on a regression of unity on $\hat{m}_t'$ and $\hat{s}_t'$ and forming nR^2. We leave the details to the interested reader.

Finally, we consider situations in which the specification admits a generalized residual. The possibilities for taking advantage of Corollary 9.12 depend on the form of λ_t. The simplest situation arises when for some κ_t, $\lambda_t = \kappa_t u_t$. Then

$$\nabla'\lambda_t^* + \lambda_t^* s_t^{*\prime} = \kappa_t^* \nabla' u_t^* + (u_t^{*\prime} \otimes I_c)\, \nabla'\kappa_t^* + \kappa_t^* u_t^*\, u_t^{*\prime *}\, i_t^{*\prime},$$

a direct generalization of the situation $\lambda_t = s_t$, considered in the previous subsection. As before, we disregard the term $(u_t^{*\prime} \otimes I_c)\ \nabla'\kappa_t^*$, set $i_t^* = -\nabla\, \tilde{u}_t^*$, and consider tests based on

$$\begin{aligned} &\kappa_t^*\ \nabla'\tilde{u}_t^* + \kappa_t^* u_t^*\, u_t^{*\prime}\, i_t^{*\prime} \\ &= \kappa_t^*\, (u_t^*\, u_t^{*\prime} - I_l)\, i_t^{*\prime}\,. \end{aligned}$$

Specifically, we let

$$\begin{aligned} m_t &= S(i_t \otimes \kappa_t)\ vec\ (u_t\, u_t' - I_l) \\ &= j_t\, v_t\,, \end{aligned}$$

where now $j_t = S(i_t \otimes \kappa_t)$ and $v_t = vec\ (u_t\, u_t' - I_l)$ as before.

To ensure a straightforward application of Corollary 9.12, we impose the following condition.

ASSUMPTION 11.15: When $\hat{\theta}$ is generated by a specification $\mathcal{S}$ admitting generalized residuals $u = \{u_t\}$ and generalized instruments $i = \{i_t\}$,

(a) There exist functions $\kappa_t : \mathbb{R}^{k_t} \times \Theta \to \mathbb{R}^{c \times l}$ is such that $\kappa_t(\cdot, \theta)$ is measurable for each θ in Θ, $\kappa_t(W_t, \cdot)$ is continuously differentiable on Θ $a.s. - P_o$, and $\lambda_t(X^t, \theta) = \kappa_t(W_t, \theta)\, u_t(X^t, \theta)$, $t = 1, 2, \ldots$,

(b) Assumption 9.8 holds for $\{j_t = S(i_t \otimes \kappa_t)\}$ and Assumption 9.9 holds for $\{v_t = (vec\ (u_t\, u_t' - I_l))\}$. □

COROLLARY 11.8: *Suppose that the specification $\mathcal{S}$ generating $\hat{\theta}$ admits generalized residuals $u = \{u_t\}$ and generalized instruments $i = \{i_t\}$, let Assumption 11.15(a) hold, define $j_t \equiv S(i_t \otimes \kappa_t)$ for given nonstochastic $q \times cp$ matrix S and define $v_t = vec\ (u_t\, u_t' - I_l)$, so that j_t is $q \times l^2$ and v_t is $l^2 \times 1$, $t = 1, 2, \ldots$.*

(i) Given Assumptions 2.1 and 2.3, $\hat{J}_n = n^{-1} \sum_{t=1}^{n} \hat{j}_t\, \hat{j}_t'$ $n = 1, 2, \ldots$ defines a sequence $\{\hat{J}_n\}$ of measurable non-negative symmetric positive semi-definite matrices. Under the same condition, $\{\hat{\sigma}_n^2 = (nl^2)^{-1} \sum_{t=1}^{n} \sum_{i=1}^{l^2} \hat{v}_{ti}^2\}$ is a measurable nonnegative sequence.

(ii) If Assumptions 3.1, 3.2 and 11.15(b) also hold, then $\hat{J}_n - \ddot{J}_n^* \to 0$ prob $- P_o$ and $\hat{\sigma}_n^2 - \sigma_n^{*2} \to 0$ prob $- P_o$ where

$$\ddot{J}_n^* \equiv n^{-1} \sum_{t=1}^{n} E(j_t^*\, j_t^{*\prime}),\ \sigma_n^{*2} \equiv (nl^2)^{-1} \sum_{t=1}^{n} \sum_{i=1}^{l^2} E(v_{ti}^{*2})\,.$$

Further $\{\ddot{J}_n^*\}$ and $\{\sigma_n^{*2}\}$ are $O(1)$.

(iii) Suppose in addition that $\{a_n^* = \sqrt{n}\, \bar{M}_n^*\}$ is $O(1)$, that Assumptions 3.2′, 3.6, 3.7(a), 3.8, 3.9, 6.1, 11.11 and 11.12 hold, and that $\sigma_n^{*2} > \varepsilon > 0$ a.a. n and $\{\ddot{J}_n^*\}$ is uniformly positive definite. Then $\ddot{\mathcal{M}}_n = nl^2 R^2 \overset{A}{\sim} N_2(a_n^*, V_n^*; \ddot{J}_n^{*-1})$, where R^2 is the squared multiple correlation coefficient for the regression of $\hat{v}_{ti}^2$ on the $1 \times q$ vector $\hat{j}_{ti}'$, $i = 1, \ldots, l^2$, $t = 1, \ldots, n$.

In particular, if $\{u_t^*, \tilde{\mathcal{F}}^t\}$, $\{i_t^* + \nabla u_t^*, \tilde{\mathcal{F}}^t\}$, $\{j_t^*\, \nabla'_\theta v_t^*, \tilde{\mathcal{F}}^t\}$ and $\{v_t^*\, v_t^{*\prime} - \sigma_o^2 I_{l^2}, \tilde{\mathcal{F}}^t\}$ are martingale difference sequences for some real constant $\sigma_o^2 > 0$, then $\ddot{\mathcal{M}}_n \overset{A}{\sim} \chi_q^2$.

(iv) In addition to the conditions of (i) and (ii), suppose that Assumption 11.13 holds, that $\sigma_n^{*2} > \varepsilon > 0$ a.a. n and $\{\ddot{J}_n^*\}$ is uniformly positive definite. Then for $\{k_n\} = o(n)$, $P_o[\ddot{\mathcal{M}}_n > k_n] \to 1$. □

The cross information matrix test is therefore conducted by regressing squares and cross-products of u_t^* on (selected) cross products of $\hat{\iota}_t$ and $\hat{\kappa}_t$, generalizing the test of Corollary 11.5 in an appealing way. As should be expected, this test has proper size only under rather stringent conditions.

11.2 Information Matrix Tests with a 2SQMLE

In this section we consider the modifications or reinterpretations of the results of the previous section needed to apply them using a 2SQMLE. Although we give some consideration to the case of members of the linear exponential family satisfying Assumptions 6.7 and 6.8, detailed discussion of this case is deferred to Section 11.3.

11.2.a Dynamic Information Matrix Tests

In constructing m_t for the dynamic information matrix test using a 2SQMLE, the focus of interest is typically on the properties of $s_{2t}^* = \nabla_\beta \log f_{2t}^*$. Hence, we construct m_t as

$$m_t = S\ vec\ s_{2t}[s_{2t-1}', \ldots, s_{2t-\lambda}'] ,$$

so that Assumption 11.1 holds with s_{2t} replacing s_t and with $\Theta = \mathcal{A} \times \mathcal{B}$. As in the foregoing section, π is null. Because we now have $\hat{\theta}_n' = (\hat{\alpha}_n', \hat{\beta}_n')$, Assumption 11.2 is modified by specifying that A_n^{*-1} and s_t^* be defined in accordance with Theorem 6.11, i.e., $s_t^{*\prime} = (s_{1t}^{*\prime}, s_{2t}^{*\prime})$ and

$$A_n^* = \begin{bmatrix} A_{11n}^* & 0 \\ A_{21n}^* & A_{22n}^* \end{bmatrix},$$

so that Assumption 11.2 requires $\{n^{-1/2}[w_{2t}^* s_{2t}^* - \nabla_\theta' \bar{M}_n^* A_n^{*-1} s_t^*]\}$ to satisfy the central limit theorem, where

$$w_{2t}^* = S([s_{2t-1}^{*\prime}, \ldots, s_{2t-\lambda}^{*\prime}]' \otimes I_p) .$$

Assumption 11.3 holds with s_{2t} replacing s_t.

With these minor modifications, Theorem 11.1 translates directly. We leave details of replacement of specific assumptions to the reader. Conditions of Theorem 3.5 are replaced by those of Theorem 3.10 and those of Theorem 6.4 by those of Theorem 6.11.

Translation of Corollary 11.2 requires that Assumption 11.4 be modified so that both $\mathcal{S}_1 = \{f_{1t}\}$ and $\mathcal{S}_2 = \{f_{2t}\}$ admit generalized residuals such that $u_{1t}^* = u_{2t}^* = u_t^*$ (say) with generalized instruments i_1 and i_2, say. Whether or not this is possible must be checked in each application; it is quite a stringent condition. Assumption 11.5 is modified by requiring Assumption 9.6 to hold for i_1, i_2 and $j = \{j_t\}$, $j_t = w_{2t}\, i_{2t}$, $t = 1, 2, \ldots$.

Calculating $\hat{J}_n$ in Corollary 11.2 with $\hat{j}_t = \hat{w}_{2t}\hat{i}_{2t}$ and $\hat{i}_t{}' = (\hat{i}_{1t}{}', \hat{i}_{2t}{}')$, we can obtain a straightforward translation of the results found there. In particular, $nlR^2 \overset{A}{\sim} \chi_q^2$ with R^2 obtained from the regression of $\hat{u}_t$ on explanatory variables $\hat{j}_{ti}{}'\ (1 \times q)$, $\hat{i}_{ti}{}' = (\hat{i}_{1ti}{}', \hat{i}_{2ti}{}')$, $i = 1, \ldots, l$, $t = 1, \ldots, n$ given that $\{u_t^*, \tilde{\mathcal{F}}^t\}$, $\{\nabla_\alpha{}' u_{1t}^* + u_{1t}^* s_{1t}^{*}{}', \ \tilde{\mathcal{F}}^t\}$, and $\{\nabla'_\beta u_{2t}^* + u_{2t}^*\, s_{2t}^{*}{}', \ \tilde{\mathcal{F}}^t\}$ are martingale difference sequences, and $A_{21n}^* = 0$. Because of the stringency of the conditions required, this analog of Corollary 11.2 is unlikely to be generally available.

It is worthwhile to observe that application of these results using the 2SQMLE of the linear exponential family requires us to be much more specific about the first stage estimator $\hat{\alpha}_n$ than has previously been required. Before, we only required that $\sqrt{n}(\hat{\alpha}_n - \alpha_n^*)$ be $O_{P_o}(1)$ (Assumption 6.6). Now we essentially require $\hat{\alpha}_n$ to be a specific and appropriately regular QMLE. However, certain choices for m and $\mathcal{S}$ possess a joint structure that can be exploited to simplify the requirements placed on $\hat{\alpha}_n$, and that lead to computationally simpler analogs of our specification tests. This structure essentially allows $\hat{\alpha}_n$ to be treated as a nuisance parameter, thus playing the role of π in the treatment of Chapter 9.

For simplicity, consider the case $m_t = S\ vec\ s_{2t} s_{2t-1}{}'$. A mean value expansion of $\hat{M}_n$ around $\theta_n^{*}{}' = (\alpha_n^{*}{}', \beta_n^{*}{}')$ gives

$$\sqrt{n}\ \hat{M}_n = n^{-1/2} \sum_{t=1}^{n} m_t^* + \nabla_\beta{}'\ \ddot{M}_n\ \sqrt{n}(\hat{\beta}_n - \beta_n^*) + \nabla_\alpha{}'\ \ddot{M}_n\ \sqrt{n}(\hat{\alpha}_n - \alpha_n^*),$$

where $\nabla_\beta{}'\ \ddot{M}_n$ is the Jacobian of M_n with respect to β with rows evaluated at mean values lying between $\theta_n{}' = (\hat{\alpha}_n{}', \hat{\beta}_n{}')$ and $\theta_n^{*}{}' = (\alpha_n^{*}{}', \beta_n^{*}{}')$, and $\nabla_\alpha{}'\ \ddot{M}_n$ is defined similarly for α. At issue here is the behavior of $\nabla_\alpha{}'\ \ddot{M}_n\ \sqrt{n}(\hat{\alpha}_n - \alpha_n^*)$. To identify π with α, it suffices that $\nabla_\alpha \ddot{M}_n \to 0$ $prob - P_o$, as we generally assume $\sqrt{n}(\hat{\alpha}_n - \alpha_n^*)$ is $O_{P_o}(1)$.

Now

$$\begin{aligned}\nabla'_\alpha M_n &= n^{-1} \sum_{t=1}^{n} \nabla'_\alpha\ m_t = n^{-1} \sum_{t=1}^{n} S\ \nabla'_\alpha\ vec\ s_{2t} s'_{2,t-1} \\ &= n^{-1} \sum_{t=1}^{n} S[(s_{2,t-1} \otimes I_p)\ \nabla'_\alpha\ s_{2,t} + (I_p \otimes s_{2t})\ \nabla'_\alpha\ s_{2,t-1}]\ .\end{aligned}$$

When a uniform law of large numbers holds for $\{(s_{2,t-1} \otimes I_p)\, \nabla'_\alpha\, s_{2t}\}$ and $\{I_p \otimes s_{2t})\, \nabla'_\alpha s_{2,t-1}\}$ (cf. Assumption 11.1), and given $\hat{\theta}_n - \theta_n^* \to 0$ *prob* $- P_o$, it follows from Corollary 3.8 that $\nabla_\alpha\, \ddot{M}_n - \nabla_\alpha \bar{M}_n^* \to 0$ *prob* $- P_o$, where

$$\nabla'_\alpha \bar{M}_n^* = n^{-1} \sum_{t=1}^{n} S\; E[(I_p \otimes s_{2t}^*)\, \nabla'_\alpha s_{2,t-1}^* + (s_{2,t-1}^* \otimes I_p)\, \nabla'_\alpha s_{2t}^*\,] \,.$$

When $\{s_{2t}^*, \mathcal{F}^{\,t}\}$ is a martingale difference sequence, we have

$$E((I_p \otimes s_{2t}^*)\, \nabla'_\alpha s_{2,t-1}^*) = E(E[(I_p \otimes s_{2t}^*)\, \nabla'_\alpha s_{2,t-1}^* \mid X^{t-1}])$$

$$= E(E[(I_p \otimes s_{2t}^*) \mid X^{t-1})]\, \nabla'_\alpha s_{2t-1}^*) = 0\,.$$

It follows that $\nabla_\alpha \bar{M}_n^*$ vanishes as desired if

$$E[(s_{2,t-1}^* \otimes I_p)\, \nabla'_\alpha s_{2t}^*\,] = 0\,.$$

For the linear exponential family, recall that

$$s_{2t} = \nabla_\beta\, \mu_t\, c_t\, u_t$$

so that

$$\nabla'_\alpha s_{2t} = (u_t' \otimes \nabla_\beta\, \mu_t)\, \nabla'_\alpha\, (\nabla_\mu\, c_t)\,,$$

because only c_t depends on α (through $\kappa_t(W_t, \alpha)$). When $\{u_t^*, \tilde{\mathcal{F}}^t\}$ is a martingale difference sequence, it follows that $E(\nabla'_\alpha s_{2t}^* \mid \tilde{X}^{t-1}) = 0$, which implies that

$$E[(s_{2,t-1}^* \otimes I_p)\, \nabla'_\alpha s_{2t}^*\,] = E(E[(s_{2,t-1}^* \otimes I_p)\, \nabla'_\alpha s_{2t}^* \mid \tilde{X}^{t-1})$$

$$= E((s_{2,t-1}^* \otimes I_p)\, E\,(\nabla'_\alpha s_{2t}^* \mid \tilde{X}^{t-1}))$$

$$= 0\,.$$

This implies that $\nabla_\alpha \ddot{M}_n \to 0$ *prob* $- P_o$, so that when $\sqrt{n}(\hat{\alpha}_n - \alpha_n^*)$ is $O_{P_o}(1)$ we have $\nabla_\alpha' \ddot{M}_n\, \sqrt{n}(\hat{\alpha}_n - \alpha_n^*) \to 0$ *prob* $- P_o$. Thus we can ignore the contribution to the asymptotic distribution of $\hat{M}_n$ resulting from the presence of $\hat{\alpha}_n$. We have shown that this occurs when $\{u_t^*, \tilde{\mathcal{F}}^t\}$ is a martingale difference sequence with a linear exponential specification; similar arguments apply under local alternatives to ensure that $\nabla \bar{M}_n^* \to 0$. Consequently, $\hat{\alpha}_n$ acts as a nuisance parameter under the null hypothesis and local alternatives; this fact can be used to simplify information matrix testing procedures in the linear exponential family.

11.2.b (Second Order) Information Matrix Tests

In this subsection, we consider the translations required to test the information matrix equality for the model of the second stage, $\mathcal{S}_2 = \{f_{2t}\}$. As in the previous subsection we have $\Theta = \mathcal{A} \times \mathcal{B}$, so that $\theta' = (\alpha', \beta')$. We choose m so that

$$m_t = S \; vec \; [\nabla'_\beta s_{2t} + s_{2t} s_{2t}{}']$$

where $s_{2t} = \nabla_\beta \log f_{2t}$ as before. Again π is null.

Assumption 11.5 holds with f_t replaced by f_{2t}, while Assumption 11.6 holds with $\nabla_\theta(\nabla'_\beta s_{2t})$ replacing $\nabla^2 \; s_t$ and $(s_{2t} \otimes I_{p+r}) \; \nabla^2_\theta \log f_{2t}$ replacing $(s_t \otimes I_p) \; \nabla' s_t$. In Assumption 11.7, we impose the asymptotic normality of $\{n^{-1/2}(S \; vec \; [\nabla'_\beta s^*_{2t} + s^*_{2t} s^*_{2t}{}'] - \nabla'_\theta \bar{M}^*_n A^{*-1}_n s^*_t)\}$, where $s^{*\prime}_t = (s^{*\prime}_{1t}, s^{*\prime}_{2t})$ and

$$A^*_n = \begin{bmatrix} A^*_{11n} & 0 \\ A^*_{21n} & A^*_{22n} \end{bmatrix}$$

as in the preceding subsection.

With these changes, and with the conditions of Theorems 3.10 and 6.11 replacing those of Theorems 3.5 and 6.4 respectively, Theorem 11.3 translates directly.

A translation of Corollary 11.4 is available with

$$m_t = S \; vec \; [\nabla'_\beta s_{2t} + s_{2t} s_{2t}{}'] \, ,$$

in Assumption 11.8. The nR^2 statistic has the χ^2_q distribution asymptotically provided that $\{m^*_t, \mathcal{F}^t\}$, $\{\nabla_\alpha \, m^*_t, \mathcal{F}^t\}$ $\{\nabla_\beta \, m^*_t, \mathcal{F}^t\}$ are martingale difference sequences.

A translation of Corollary 11.5 obtains by replacing u_t with u_{2t} and i_t with i_{2t} (now $s_{2t} = i_{2t} \, u_{2t}$), and defining j_t as $S(i_{2t} \otimes i_{2t})$ and v_t as $vec \; (u_{2t} \, u_{2t}{}' - I_l)$ in Assumption 11.9 and the initial conditions of Corollary 11.5. Now we have $nl^2 \, R^2 \overset{A}{\sim} \chi^2_q$, where R^2 is obtained from the regression of $\hat{v}_{ti}$ on $\hat{j}_{ti}{}'$, $i = 1, \ldots, l^2$, $t = 1, \ldots, n$, provided that $\{u^*_{2t}, \tilde{\mathcal{F}}^t\}$, $\{u^*_{2t} \, u^*_{2t}{}' - I_l, \tilde{\mathcal{F}}^t\}$, $\{i^*_{2t} + \nabla_\beta \, u^*_{2t}, \tilde{\mathcal{F}}^t\}$, $\{j^*_t \, \nabla'_\theta \, v^*_t, \tilde{\mathcal{F}}^t\}$ and $\{v^*_t \, v^{*\prime}_t - \sigma^2_o \, I_{l^2}, \tilde{\mathcal{F}}^t\}$ are martingale difference sequences for some real constant $\sigma^2_o > 0$. The considerations regarding $\nabla'_\theta \, v^*_t$ are the same as discussed prior to Corollary 11.5.

11.2.c Cross Information Matrix Tests

Now we consider the modifications required to translate the cross-information matrix tests of Section 11.1.c when the QMLE is replaced by the 2SQMLE $\hat{\theta}_n' = (\hat{\alpha}_n', \hat{\beta}_n')$. Because the m-tests for which the cross-information matrix test is relevant generally depend on $\theta' = (\alpha', \beta')$ and not just β (despite two-stage estimation) the appropriate choice for m_t in the present context is

$$m_t = S\; vec\,(\nabla'_\theta\, \lambda_t + \lambda_t\, s_t')\,,$$

where $\lambda_t : \mathbb{R}^{vt} \times \Theta \rightarrow \mathbb{R}^c$, $c \in \mathbb{N}$ and $s_t' = (s_{1t}', s_{2t}')$. Theorems 11.6 and Corollary 11.7 translate in the obvious manner with

$$A_n^* = \begin{bmatrix} A_{11n}^* & 0 \\ A_{21n}^* & A_{22n}^* \end{bmatrix} \qquad \hat{A}_n = \begin{bmatrix} \hat{A}_{11n} & 0 \\ \hat{A}_{21n} & \hat{A}_{22n} \end{bmatrix}.$$

Because the translations are essentially immediate, we do not go into detail. As before, conditions of Theorem 3.10 and 6.11 replace those of Theorems 3.5 and 6.4. Translation of Corollary 11.8 is also immediate, where in Assumption 11.15 and the initial conditions of the Corollary u_t and i_t are replaced by u_{2t} and i_{2t} ($s_{2t} = i_{2t}\, u_{2t}$) and λ_t is replaced by λ_{2t} which is of the form $\lambda_{2t} = \kappa_{2t}\, u_{2t}$. Now $j_t = S\,(i_{2t} \otimes \kappa_{2t})$ and $v_t = vec\,(u_{2t}\, u_{2t}' - I_l)$.

11.3 Information Matrix Tests for the Linear Regression Model

In this section we illustrate the application of the information matrix tests with a discussion of information matrix tests for the linear regression model. Although we consider only the simplest models, the discussion reveals many essential features of the general situation, especially for members of the linear exponential family. Even so, our discussion only barely scratches the surface of the insights available from information matrix testing.

For simplicity, our discussion will treat $\{X_t\}$ as if it were a stationary process; nothing essential changes, and all the insights remain valid when $\{X_t\}$ is a heterogeneous process.

11.3.a Dynamic (First Order) Information Matrix Tests

A very simple model of the behavior of a scalar sequence $\{X_t\}$ is

$$X_t \mid X^{t-1} \sim N(\theta, 1) \qquad \theta \in \Theta\,,$$

where Θ is a compact interval in $\mathbb{R}$. The log-likelihood for this model is

$$\log f_t(X^t, \theta) = -\,.5 \log 2\pi - (X_t - \theta)^2 / 2$$

so that

$$s_t(X^t, \theta) = (X_t - \theta) \equiv u_t(\theta) ,$$

$$\nabla' s_t(X^t, \theta) = -1 .$$

This specification yields the QMLE $\hat{\theta}_n = n^{-1} \sum_{t=1}^{n} X_t$, and it follows easily that $\hat{\theta}_n - \theta_o \to 0$ $prob-P_o$, where $\theta_o = \theta_n^* \equiv n^{-1} \sum_{t=1}^{n} E(X_t)$, under general conditions (the first equality follows from stationarity).

Recall that the general form of m_t for the dynamic information matrix test is $m_t = S\ vec\ [s_t(s_{t-1}', \ldots, s_{t-\lambda}')]$. For simplicity set $S = I_\lambda$, so that in the present case

$$m_t' = u_t(u_{t-1}, \ldots, u_{t-\lambda}) .$$

First, set $\lambda = 1$. This implies $m_t = u_t u_{t-1}$, so that

$$\nabla_\theta M_n = n^{-1} \sum_{t=1}^{n} u_t \nabla u_{t-1} + u_{t-1} \nabla u_t$$

$$= -n^{-1} \sum_{t=1}^{n} (u_t + u_{t-1}) .$$

For simplicity, set $u_t = 0$ for $t \leq 0$. Because $\nabla_\theta \bar{M}_n^* = 0$ in general, we take $\nabla_\theta \hat{M}_n = 0$.

Corollary 9.9 can be applied here, so with $\hat{u}_t = X_t - \hat{\theta}_n$, we obtain a dynamic information matrix test statistic by regressing 1 on $\hat{u}_t \hat{u}_{t-1}$. When $\{s_t^*, \mathcal{F}^t\} = \{X_t - \theta_o, \mathcal{F}^t\}$ is a martingale difference sequence, then nR^2 from this regression is χ_1^2. The test is consistent for cases in which $|n^{-1} \sum_{t=1}^{n} E(u_t^* u_{t-1}^*)| = |E(u_t^* u_{t-1}^*)| > \varepsilon > 0$ (equality arises from stationarity), i.e. for cases in which X_t exhibits non-zero first order autocorrelation.

Such autocorrelation does not adversely affect the consistency of $\hat{\theta}_n$ for θ_o, but it does affect its efficiency and the consistency of the standard parameter covariance matrix estimator.

Now consider the application of Corollary 11.2. In the present case we have $s_t = i_t u_t$ with $i_t(X^t, \theta) = 1$ for all (X^t, θ). As we also have $w_t = u_{t-1}$, it follows that $j_t = w_t i_t = u_{t-1}$. This implies

$$\ddot{G}_n^* = n^{-1} \sum_{t=1}^{n} E(j_t^* i_t^{*\prime}) = n^{-1} \sum_{t=1}^{n} E(u_{t-1}^*) = 0$$

under general conditions. For this reason, we may replace $(n^{-1} \sum_{t=1}^{n} \hat{j}_t \hat{i}_t')$ with zero in Corollary 11.2 and conduct a test based on $\hat{J}_n = n^{-1} \sum_{t=1}^{n} \hat{j}_t \hat{j}_t'$.

For the regression form of the test, one computes nR^2 from the regression of $\hat{u}_t$ on $\hat{u}_{t-1}(=\hat{j}_t)$. This yields a test of correct size asymptotically, using the χ_1^2 distribution, provided that $\{u_t^*, \mathcal{F}^t\}$ is a martingale difference sequence and that $E(u_t^{*2}) = \sigma_o^2$. The requirement that $i_t^* = -E(\nabla_\theta u_t^* \mid W_t)/\sigma_o^2$ is irrelevant, as $\nabla_\theta \bar{M}_n^* = 0$.

Note that the specification of the model imposes $E(u_t^{*2} \mid X^{t-1}) = 1$, but this need not be true for the data generation process. The nR^2 test only requires that $E(u_t^{*2}) = \sigma_o^2$, so that the size of the nR^2 test will not be affected by model misspecification resulting in $E(u_t^{*2} \mid X^{t-1}) \neq 1$.

Next, set $\lambda = 2$. Now $m_t' = (u_t u_{t-1}, u_t u_{t-2})$, so that

$$\nabla_\theta M_n = \begin{bmatrix} n^{-1} \sum_{t=1}^{n} u_t + u_{t-1} \\ n^{-1} \sum_{t=1}^{n} u_t + u_{t-2} \end{bmatrix}$$

and again $\nabla_\theta \bar{M}_n^* = 0$, so we take $\nabla_\theta \hat{M}_n = 0$. Applying Corollary 9.9 with $\hat{m}_t = (\hat{u}_t \hat{u}_{t-1}, \hat{u}_t \hat{u}_{t-2})'$ yields a dynamic information matrix test statistic as nR^2 from the regression of 1 on $\hat{u}_t\hat{u}_{t-1}, \hat{u}_t\hat{u}_{t-2}$. When $\{u_t^*, \mathcal{F}^t\}$ is a martingale difference sequence, $nR^2 \overset{A}{\sim} \chi_2^2$. Similarly, with $\lambda = 3$ we regress 1 on $\hat{u}_t\hat{u}_{t-1}, \hat{u}_t\hat{u}_{t-2}, \hat{u}_t\hat{u}_{t-3}$ to get $n^2R^2 \overset{A}{\sim} \chi_3^2$ and similarly for $\lambda = 4, 5, \ldots$. Using the matrix S we can select any desired subset or linear combination of $u_t u_{t-1}, u_t u_{t-2}, \ldots, u_t u_{t-\lambda}$ to obtain a dynamic information matrix test statistic. Each of these will be consistent against the alternative of nonzero autocorrelation at (any of) the selected lags.

Tests based on regressions of generalized residuals are conducted analogously. For $\lambda = 2$, we regress $\hat{u}_t$ on $\hat{u}_{t-1}$ and $\hat{u}_{t-2}$. When $\{u_t^*, \mathcal{F}^t\}$ is a martingale difference sequence and when $E(u_t^{*2} \mid X^{t-1}) = \sigma_o^2$, $t = 1, 2, \ldots$, then $nR^2 \overset{A}{\sim} \chi_2^2$. For $\lambda = 3$, regress $\hat{u}_t$ on $\hat{u}_{t-1}, \hat{u}_{t-2}$ and $\hat{u}_{t-3}$ to get $nR^2 \overset{A}{\sim} \chi_3^2$. In these cases, failure of $E(u_t^{*2} \mid X^{t-1}) = \sigma_o^2$ may give a test of incorrect size.

These generalized residual dynamic information matrix tests are quite similar to the Lagrange multiplier test for serial correlation of Godfrey [1978a, b]. In fact, Godfrey's tests can be interpreted directly as dynamic information matrix tests. Any hypothesis test based on the dynamic information matrix indicators $m_t = S \; vec \; s_t(s_{t-1}', \ldots, s_{t-\lambda}')$ can be interpreted as a dynamic information matrix test, regardless of the statistic used to conduct the test.

Now suppose we elaborate the model by no longer imposing our "knowledge" that $E(u_t^{*2}|X^{t-1}) = 1$ and instead posit that $X_t|X^{t-1} \sim N(\mu, \sigma^2)$ where now $\theta' = (\mu, \sigma)$. For this model

$$\log f_t(X^t, \theta) = -.5 \log 2\pi - \log \sigma - (X_t - \mu)^2 / 2\sigma^2$$

so that with $u_t(\theta) = (X_t - \mu) / \sigma$

$$s_t(X^t, \theta)' = [u_t(\theta)/\sigma \quad (u_t(\theta)^2 - 1)/\sigma]$$

$$\nabla' s_t(X^t, \theta) = -\sigma^{-2} \begin{bmatrix} 1 & 2u_t(\theta) \\ 2u_t(\theta) & 3u_t(\theta)^2 - 1 \end{bmatrix}.$$

For this specification, $\hat{\theta}_n' = (\hat{\mu}_n, \hat{\sigma}_n)$, with

$$\hat{\mu}_n = n^{-1} \sum_{t=1}^{n} X_t, \quad \hat{\sigma}_n = (n^{-1} \sum_{t=1}^{n} X_t^2 - \hat{\mu}_n^2)^{1/2}.$$

Now set $\lambda = 1$ and consider

$$m_t = S \; vec \; s_t s'_{t-1}$$

$$= S \; vec \; \sigma^{-2} \begin{bmatrix} u_t(\theta) u_{t-1}(\theta) & u_t(\theta)(u_{t-1}(\theta)^2 - 1) \\ (u_t(\theta)^2 - 1) u_{t-1}(\theta) & (u_t(\theta)^2 - 1)(u_{t-1}(\theta)^2 - 1) \end{bmatrix}.$$

We see here quite clearly how choice of S determines the directions in which given tests have power. If S selects the (1, 1) element of $s_t s'_{t-1}$, we obtain tests sensitive to the failure of $E(u_t^* u_{t-1}^*) = 0$, as in the first test considered in this section. If S selects the (2,2) element of $s_t s'_{t-1}$, we obtain tests sensitive to the failure of $E[(u_t^{*2} - 1)(u_{t-1}^{*2} - 1)] = 0$. This failure occurs in the presence of autoregressive conditional heteroskedasticity (ARCH), proposed by Engle [1982a].

When S selects the (1, 2) element of $s_t s'_{t-1}$ we obtain tests sensitive to the failure of $E(u_t^* (u_{t-1}^{*2} - 1)) = 0$. This indicates dynamic misspecification of the conditional mean, such as that which arises when X_t is generated by an ARCH-in-mean process (Engle, Lilien, and Robins [1987]). When S selects the (2,1) element of $s_t s'_{t-1}$, we obtain tests sensitive to the failure of $E((u_t^{*2} - 1) u_{t-1}^*) = 0$. This indicates dynamic misspecification of the conditional variance.

Because

$$\nabla' \; vec \; s_t s'_{t-1} = (I_2 \otimes s_t) \nabla' s_{t-1} + (s_{t-1} \otimes I_2) \nabla' s_t,$$

we have

$$-\sigma^3 \nabla' \, vec \; s_t s'_{t-1} =$$

$$\begin{bmatrix} u_t + u_{t-1} & 4u_t u_{t-1} \\ (u_t^2 - 1) + 2u_{t-1}u_t & 2u_{t-1}(u_t^2 - 1) + u_{t-1}(3u_t^2 - 1) \\ 2u_{t-1}u_t + (u_{t-1}^2 - 1) & u_t(3u_{t-1}^2 - 1) + 2u_t(u_{t-1}^2 - 1) \\ 2u_{t-1}(u_t^2 - 61) + 2u_t(u_{t-1}^2 - 1) & (u_t^2 - 1)(3u_{t-1}^2 - 1) + (u_{t-1}^2 - 1)(3u_t^2 - 1) \end{bmatrix}.$$

Examination of $E(\nabla'_\theta m_t^*) = S\, E[\nabla' \, vec \; s_t^* s_{t-1}^{*\prime}]$ allows us to investigate circumstances under which $\nabla_\theta \bar{M}_n^*$ can be estimated in more or less computationally convenient ways.

For simplicity, and because it illustrates the issues involved, let S select the (2, 2) element of $s_t s'_{t-1}$, i.e. $S = (0, 0, 0, 1)$. Hence we consider the dynamic information matrix test sensitive to conditional heteroskedasticity. Letting $\sigma_o^2 = E(u_t^{*2})$, we have

$$E(\nabla'_\theta m_t^*) = -\sigma_o^{-3}(2E[u_{t-1}^*(u_t^{*2} - 1) + u_t^*(u_{t-1}^{*2} - 1)]\,,$$

$$E[\,(u_t^{*2} - 1)(3u_{t-1}^{*2} - 1) + (u_{t-1}^{*2} - 1)(3u_t^{*2} - 1)]) \,.$$

When $\{s_t^* = (u_t^* / \sigma_o \,, (u_t^{*2} - 1)/\sigma_o)' \,, \mathcal{F}^t\}$ is a martingale difference sequence, we can use the law of iterated expectations to obtain

$$\begin{aligned} E(\nabla'_\theta m_t^*) &= -\sigma_0^{-3}\,(0, E\,[\,E((3u_t^{*2} - 1) \mid X^{t-1})(u_{t-1}^{*2} - 1)]) \\ &= -\sigma_o^3\,(0, 2E(u_{t-1}^{*2} - 1)) \\ &= (0\,, 0)\,. \end{aligned}$$

As in the previous case, setting $\nabla_\theta \hat{M}_n = 0$ will therefore not affect the model implicitly tested too severely.

This implies that the nR^2 form of the dynamic information matrix test implied by Corollary 9.9 can be constructed from the regression of 1 on $(\hat{u}_t^2 - 1)(\hat{u}_{t-1}^2 - 1)/\hat{\sigma}_n^2$. (The division by $\hat{\sigma}_n^2$ can be dropped, as this leaves R^2 unaffected.) When $\{s_t^*, \mathcal{F}^t\}$ is a martingale difference sequence, $nR^2 \overset{A}{\sim} \chi_1^2$. The test has particular power against (autoregressive) conditional heteroskedasticity.

Because conditional heteroskedasticity can appear to exist when $\{u_t^*, \mathcal{F}^t\}$ fails to be a martingale difference sequence (with possible adverse consequences for the size of the foregoing test), it is useful to test the (1,1) and (2,2) elements of $s_t s'_{t-1}$ jointly. For this we specify

$$S = \begin{bmatrix} 1 & 0 & 0 & 0 \\ 0 & 0 & 0 & 1 \end{bmatrix},$$

so that

$$E(\nabla'_\theta m_t^*) = -\sigma_o^{-3} \begin{bmatrix} E(u_t^* + u_{t-1}^*) & 4E(u_t^* u_{t-1}^*) \\ E[2u_{t-1}^*(u_t^{*2} - 1) & E[(u_t^{*2} - 1)(3u_{t-1}^{*2} - 1) \\ \quad + 2u_t^*(u_{t-1}^{*2} - 1)] & \quad + (u_{t-1}^{*2} - 1)(3u_t^{*2} - 1)] \end{bmatrix}.$$

Again, when $\{s_t^*, \mathcal{F}^t\}$ is a martingale difference sequence $\nabla_\theta \bar{M}_n^* = 0$, so that $\nabla_\theta \hat{M}_n = 0$ is an appropriate choice.

The nR^2 form of the dynamic information matrix test implied by Corollary 9.9 can therefore be constructed from the regression of 1 on $\hat{u}_t \hat{u}_{t-1} / \hat{\sigma}_n^2$ and $(\hat{u}_t^2 - 1)(\hat{u}_{t-1}^2 - 1)/\hat{\sigma}_n^2$. (Again, division by $\hat{\sigma}_n^2$ can be dropped.) When $\{s_t^*, \mathcal{F}^t\}$ is a martingale difference sequence, then $nR^2 \overset{A}{\sim} \chi_2^2$. The test has power jointly against autocorrelation or (autoregressive) conditional heteroskedasticity in X_t.

At first sight, it might appear that tests based on generalized residuals are not applicable because the model does not admit a generalized residual. That is, we cannot write $s'_t = [u_t/\sigma, (u_t^2 - 1)/\sigma]$ as $s_t = i_t u_t$ where i_t does not depend on X_t, essentially because of the presence of u_t^2. However, by treating the problem in the context of the 2SQMLE, it is indeed possible to obtain a test based on generalized residuals.

To put the problem in the context of the 2SQMLE, we treat μ as a nuisance parameter (corresponding to α) estimated in a first stage by $\hat{\mu}_n = n^{-1} \Sigma_{t=1}^n X_t$ (e.g. using the model $X_t | X^{t-1} \sim N(\mu, 1)$) and treat $\hat{\sigma}_n$ as the solution to the problem

$$\max_\sigma L_{2n}(X^n, \sigma, \hat{\mu}_n) = -.5 \log 2\pi - \log \sigma - n^{-1} \sum_{t=1}^n (X_t - \hat{\mu}_n)^2 / 2\sigma^2,$$

where $\log f_{2t} = \log f_t$ with f_t as given above, so that now

$$s_{2t} = \nabla_\sigma \log f_{2t} = (u_t^2 - 1)/\sigma.$$

Now let $v_t = u_t^2 - 1$ be the generalized residual. With this choice, $i_t = 1/\sigma$. As long as m_t involves only linear combinations of v_t, Corollary 9.9 applies. In the present case, take $m_t = v_t v_{t-1}/\sigma^2$, which yields tests sensitive to (autoregressive) conditional heteroskedasticity. When $\{s_t^* = (s_{1t}^*, s_{2t}^*)', \mathcal{F}^t\}$ (with $s_{1t}^* = X_t - \mu_n^*$) is a martingale difference sequence, then $\nabla_\theta m_t^* = 0$ as before, so that $\nabla_\theta \hat{M}_n = 0$ is appropriate. The 2SQMLE analog of Corollary 9.9 justifies construction of a dynamic information matrix test based on nR^2 from the regression of $\hat{v}_t = (\hat{u}_t^2 - 1)$ on $\hat{v}_{t-1} = (\hat{u}_{t-1}^2 - 1)$. We have $nR^2 \overset{A}{\sim} \chi_1^2$ provided that $\{s_t^*, \mathcal{F}^t\}$ and $\{v_t^{*2} - \sigma_o^2, \mathcal{F}^t\}$ are martingale difference sequences.

Tests based on the (2, 1) element of $s_t s'_{t-1}$ can also be based on regressions involving the generalized residuals v_t. Analogous treatment with the roles of $\hat{\sigma}_n^2$ and $\hat{\mu}_n$ reversed yield dynamic information matrix tests of the (1,1) or (1,2) elements of $s_t s'_{t-1}$ using generalized residuals $\hat{u}_t$.

Now consider the effects of elaborating the dynamic specification by specifying the model

$$X_t \mid X^{t-1} \sim N(\alpha + \rho X_{t-1}, 1) .$$

For this case, $\theta' = (\alpha, \rho)$, and

$$\log f_t(X^t, \theta) = -.5 \log 2\pi - (X_t - \alpha - \rho X_{t-1})^2 / 2 .$$

Letting $u_t(\theta) = X_t - \alpha - \rho X_{t-1}$, we have

$$s_t(X^t, \theta)' = [u_t(\theta) , X_{t-1} u_t(\theta)]$$

$$\nabla' s_t(X^t, \theta) = -\begin{bmatrix} 1 & X_{t-1} \\ X_{t-1} & X_{t-1}^2 \end{bmatrix} .$$

With this specification, the QMLE delivers the usual least squares estimators

$$\hat{\rho}_n = [n^{-1} \sum_{t=1}^n X_{t-1}^2 - (n^{-1} \sum_{t=1}^n X_{t-1})^2]^{-1} [n^{-1} \sum_{t=1}^n X_{t-1} X_t - (n^{-1} \sum_{t=1}^n X_{t-1})(n^{-1} \sum_{t=1}^n X_t)]$$

$$\hat{\alpha}_n = n^{-1} \sum_{t=1}^n X_t - \hat{\rho}_n n^{-1} \sum_{t=1}^n X_{t-1} .$$

Set $\lambda = 1$ and consider

$$m_t = S \; vec \; s_t s'_{t-1}$$

$$= S \; vec \begin{bmatrix} u_t u_{t-1} & X_{t-2} u_t u_{t-1} \\ X_{t-1} u_t u_{t-1} & X_{t-1} X_{t-2} u_t u_{t-1} \end{bmatrix} .$$

When S selects the (1,1) element of $s_t s'_{t-1}$, we obtain tests sensitive to the failure of $E(u_t^* u_{t-1}^*) = 0$, as before. Tests in new directions arise for other choices of S. When S selects the (1, 2) element, we obtain tests sensitive to the failure of $E(X_{t-2} u_t^* u_{t-1}^*) = 0$, while selecting the (2, 1) and (2, 2) elements leads to tests sensitive to failures of $E(X_{t-1} u_t^* u_{t-1}^*) = 0$ and $E(X_{t-1} X_{t-2} u_t^* u_{t-1}^*) = 0$, respectively. Each of these indicate particular forms of dynamic misspecification, arising either because $E(X_t | X^{t-1})$ is not measurable - $\sigma(X_{t-1})$ as the model assumes (here $W_t = X_{t-1}$) (i.e., omission of Granger-causal variables from the model of the conditional mean) or because even if it is measurable - $\sigma(X_{t-1})$, it is not of the form $\alpha + \rho X_{t-1}$ (e.g., neglected nonlinearity).

To investigate $\nabla_\theta m_t$, we again use $\nabla' \, vec \; s_t s'_{t-1} = (I_p \otimes s_t) \nabla' s_{t-1} + (s_{t-1} \otimes I_p) \nabla' s_t$ to write

$$\nabla' \, vec \; s_t s'_{t-1}$$
$$= - \begin{bmatrix} u_t + u_{t-1} & X_{t-2} u_t + X_{t-1} u_{t-1} \\ X_{t-1} u_t + X_{t-1} u_{t-1} & X_{t-1} X_{t-2} u_t + X_{t-1}^2 u_{t-1} \\ X_{t-2} u_t + X_{t-2} u_{t-1} & X_{t-2}^2 u_t + X_{t-2} X_{t-1} u_{t-1} \\ X_{t-1} X_{t-2} u_t + X_{t-1} X_{t-2} u_{t-1} & X_{t-1} X_{t-2}^2 u_t + X_{t-2} X_{t-1}^2 u_{t-1} \end{bmatrix} .$$

Again, examination of $E(\nabla_\theta m_t^*) = S \; E(\nabla_\theta \; vec \; s_t s'_{t-1})$ allows us to investigate circumstances in which $\nabla_\theta \bar{M}_n^*$ can be estimated in more or less computationally convenient ways.

First, let $S = (1, 0, 0, 0)$, so that $m_t = u_t u_{t-1}$, the indicator for simple autocorrelation. In this case we have

$$E(\nabla'_\theta m_t^*) = - \, [E(u_t^* + u_{t-1}^*) \, , \, E(X_{t-2} u_t^* + X_{t-1} u_{t-1}^*)] \, .$$

Unlike the previous examples, this generally does not vanish under the null hypothesis of correct specification. For example, suppose the data are generated as $X_t = \alpha_o + \rho_o \, X_{t-1} + \varepsilon_t$, where ε_t is i.i.d with $E(\varepsilon_t) = 0$, $E(\varepsilon_t^2) = 1$. Then we have $u_{t-1}^* = \varepsilon_{t-1}$ and $E(X_{t-1} u_{t-1}^*) = 1$, so that $E(\nabla'_\theta \; m_t^*) = (0, -1)$. Although we can set $\nabla' \hat{M}_n = (0, -1)$ in such circumstances, Corollary 9.10 nevertheless yields a somewhat cumbersome test statistic.

Instead, consider what is required to apply Corollary 9.11. For this, we require that $\{s_t^*, \mathcal{F}^t\}$ and $\{\nabla' s_t^* + s_t^* s_t^{*\prime}, \mathcal{F}^t\}$ be martingale difference sequences. The hypothesis implicitly tested is restricted by the latter requirement. Now

$$\nabla' s_t + s_t s_t{}' = -\begin{bmatrix} 1 & X_{t-1} \\ X_{t-1} & X_{t-1}^2 \end{bmatrix} + \begin{bmatrix} u_t^2 & X_{t-1} u_t^2 \\ X_{t-1} u_t^2 & X_{t-1}^2 u_t^2 \end{bmatrix},$$

so that

$$E(\nabla' s_t^* + s_t^* s_t^{*\prime} | X^{t-1}) = \begin{bmatrix} 1 & X_{t-1} \\ X_{t-1} & X_{t-1}^2 \end{bmatrix} E(u_t^{*2} - 1 | X^{t-1}).$$

Consequently, $\{\nabla' s_t^* + s_t^* s_t^{*\prime}, \mathcal{F}^t\}$ is a martingale difference sequence when $E(u_t^{*2} | X^{t-1}) = 1$, as the model specifies. When the model is misspecified in this respect, then the χ_q^2 distribution cannot be used to obtain a test of proper size based on the statistics of Corollary 9.11.

In particular, a test for departures from $E(u_t^* u_{t-1}^*) = 0$ can be obtained from Corollary 9.11 (iii) as nR^2 from the regression of the constant unity on $\hat{u}_t \hat{u}_{t-1}$ and $\hat{s}_t{}' = (\hat{u}_t, X_{t-1} \hat{u}_t)$. The χ_1^2 distribution can be used to obtain critical values yielding a test of proper size when $E(u_t^{*2} | X^{t-1}) = 1$, but generally not otherwise. This is an analogue of Durbin's [1970] h-test for autocorrelation in the presence of a lagged dependent variable.

Corollary 11.2 also yields useful test statistics under somewhat restrictive conditions. Because $s_t{}' = (1, X_{t-1})\, u_t$, the model admits generalized residuals with $i_t{}' = (1, X_{t-1})$. When $m_t = u_t u_{t-1}$ so that $j_t = u_{t-1}$, Corollary 11.2 gives conditions ensuring that $nR^2 \overset{A}{\sim} \chi_1^2$, where R^2 is obtained from the regression of $\hat{u}_t$ on $\hat{u}_{t-1}, 1, X_{t-1}$. In this case, it suffices that $E(u_t^{*2} | X^{t-1}) = \sigma_o^2$, as this ensures also that $i_t^* = -E(\nabla_\theta u_t^* \mid X^{t-1}) / \sigma_o^2$. Again, the presence of autoregressive conditional heteroskedasticity may adversely affect the size of tests based on this analog of Durbin's h-test statistic.

By making different choices for S, we obtain dynamic specification tests sensitive to a variety of other possible misspecifications. Any or all of these may be appropriate for investigation in particular applications. For example, a test sensitive to failures of $E(X_{t-1} u_t^* u_{t-1}^*) = 0$ is obtained setting $S = (0, 1, 0, 0)$. From Corollary 11.2 a convenient test statistic is nR^2 from the regression of $\hat{u}_t$ on $X_{t-1} \hat{u}_{t-1}, 1, X_{t-1}$. For the model implicitly tested we have $nR^2 \overset{A}{\sim} \chi_1^2$. A joint test for failure of $E(u_t^* u_{t-1}^*) = 0$ and $E(X_{t-1} u_t^* u_{t-1}^*) = 0$ is obtained by regressing $\hat{u}_t$ on $\hat{u}_{t-1}, X_{t-1} \hat{u}_t$, 1, and X_{t-1}. Under the model implicitly tested, nR^2 from this regression is distributed asymptotically as χ_2^2.

We leave as an exercise for the reader investigation of the dynamic information matrix tests for the model

$$X_t | X^{t-1} \sim N(\alpha + \rho X_{t-1}, \sigma^2) .$$

These are discussed briefly by White [1987].

Dynamic information matrix tests for the ARCH models of Engle [1982a] can be similarly obtained by considering models of the form

$$X_t | X^{t-1} \sim N(\alpha + \rho X_{t-1}, \sigma^2 + \gamma (X_{t-1} - \alpha - \rho X_{t-2})^2) .$$

We leave these to other work.

11.3.b (Second Order) Information Matrix Tests

Although even simpler models can yield useful insights, we begin by considering the model

$$X_t \mid X^{t-1} \sim N(\mu, \sigma^2) .$$

With $\theta' = (\mu, \sigma)$, we again have

$$\log f_t(X^t, \theta) = -.5 \log 2\pi - \log \sigma - (X_t - \mu)^2 / 2\sigma^2$$

$$s_t(X^t, \theta)' = [u_t(\theta)/\sigma, \ (u_t(\theta)^2 - 1)/\sigma]$$

$$\nabla' s_t(X^t, \theta) = -\sigma^{-2} \begin{bmatrix} 1 & 2u_t(\theta) \\ 2u_t(\theta) & 3u_t(\theta)^2 - 1 \end{bmatrix},$$

where $u_t(\theta) = (X_t - \mu)/\sigma$ as before. Again $\hat{\mu}_n = n^{-1} \sum_{t=1}^{n} X_t$ and $\hat{\sigma}_n = (n^{-1} \sum_{t=1}^{n} X_t^2 - \hat{\mu}_n^2)^{1/2}$.

In the present case, the information matrix indicators are given by $m_t = S \, vec \, (\nabla' s_t + s_t s_t')$

$$= S \, vec \, \sigma^{-2} \begin{bmatrix} u_t^2 - 1 & u_t^3 - 3u_t \\ u_t^3 - 3u_t & u_t^4 - 5u_t^2 + 2 \end{bmatrix}.$$

As before, different choices for S give tests with power in different directions. When S selects the (1, 1) element of $\nabla' s_t + s_t s_t'$, the resulting test has no power, as the normalization by $1/\sigma$ in u_t^2 ensures that $E(u_t^{*2}) = 1$. Consequently, interesting tests are those based on the (2, 1) and/or (2, 2) elements of $\nabla' s_t + s_t s_t'$. Tests based on the (2, 1) element are sensitive to departures from $E(u_t^{*3} - 3u_t^*) = E(u_t^{*3}) = 0$, i.e. skewness, and tests based on the (2, 2) element are sensitive to departures from $E(u_t^{*4} - 5u_t^{*2} + 2) = E(u_t^{*4} - 3) = 0$, i.e., kurtosis.

To investigate circumstances in which the information matrix tests can be conveniently computed, we examine $\nabla' m_t = S\, \nabla'\, vec\, (\nabla'\, s_t + s_t s_t{}')$. Now

$$\nabla'\, vec(\nabla' s_t + s_t s_t{}') = -\,\sigma^{-3} \begin{bmatrix} 2u_t & 4u_t^2 - 2 \\ 3u_t^2 - 3 & 5u_t^3 - 9u_t \\ 3u_t^2 - 3 & 5u_t^3 - 9u_t \\ 4u_t^3 - 10u_t & 6u_t^4 - 20u_t^2 + 4 \end{bmatrix}.$$

The tests of interest are those for which $S = (0, 0, 1, 0)$ (skewness) or $S = (0, 0, 0, 1)$ (kurtosis).

With $S = (0, 0, 1, 0)$, we have

$$E(\nabla_\theta' m_t^*) = -\,\sigma_o^{-3}[E(3u_t^{*2} - 3),\, E(5u_t^{*3} - 9u_t^*)].$$

When $E(u_t^{*3}) = 0$, as occurs when $\{s_t^*, \mathcal{F}^t\}$ and $\{\nabla' s_t^* + s_t^* s_t^{*\prime}, \mathcal{F}^t\}$ are martingale difference sequences, we have $E(\nabla_\theta m_t^*) = 0$. Consequently, we may set $\nabla_\theta \hat{M}_n = 0$ and apply Corollary 11.4. Thus we obtain an information matrix test statistic sensitive to skewness by regressing 1 on $(\hat{u}_t^3 - 3\hat{u}_t)/\hat{\sigma}_n^2$ and computing nR^2. When $\{s_t^*, \mathcal{F}^t\}$ and $\{\nabla' s_t^* + s_t^* s_t^{*\prime}, \mathcal{F}\}$ are martingale difference sequences, then $nR^2 \overset{A}{\sim} \chi_1^2$. (Note that the regression may also be conducted using regressors $\hat{u}_t^3 - 3\hat{u}_t$ as the division by $\hat{\sigma}_n^2$ leaves R^2 unaffected.)

Because of the special structure of the present example, tests based on generalized residuals can be obtained by regressing $\hat{u}_t^3$ on the constant 1, i.e. simply averaging $\hat{u}_t^3$. The statistic nR^2 from this regression is χ_1^2 under the same conditions as the previous test.

With $S = (0, 0, 0, 1)$, we have

$$E(\nabla'_\theta m_t^*) = -\,\sigma_o^{-3}(E(4u_t^{*3} - 10u_t^*),\, E(6u_t^{*4} - 20u_t^{*2} + 4)).$$

When $\{s_t^*, \mathcal{F}^t\}$ and $\{\nabla' s_t^* + s_t^* s_t^{*\prime}, \mathcal{F}^t\}$ are martingale difference sequences we have $E(u_t^{*4}) = 3$, $E(u_t^{*3}) = 0$, $E(u_t^{*2}) = 1$, $E(u_t^*) = 0$, so that

$$E(\nabla'_\theta m_t^*) = -\,\sigma_o^{-3}(0, 2).$$

This does not vanish, so that Corollary 9.10 applies, but this gives a somewhat cumbersome test statistic. Consequently, we consider the statistic arising from Corollary 9.11. For this it suffices that $E(\nabla'_\theta m_t^*) = -E(m_t^* s_t^{*\prime})$. In the present case,

$$m_t\ s_t' = \sigma^{-2}(u_t^4 - 5u_t^2 + 2)[u_t/\sigma\,,\,(u_t^2 - 1)/\sigma\,]$$
$$= [(u_t^5 - 5u_t^3 + 2u_t)/\sigma^3\,,\,(u_t^6 - 6u_t^4 + 7u_t^2 - 2)/\sigma^3]\,.$$

When $E(u_t^{*5}) = 0$ and $E(u_t^{*6}) = 15$ (in addition to the other moment equalities given above), we have that $E(m_t^* s_t^{*\prime}) = \sigma_o^{-3}(0\,,2) = -\,E(\nabla'_\theta m_t^*)$, so that the statistics of Corollary 9.10 yield tests of proper size when the χ_1^2 distribution is used to obtain critical values. Note that the conditions $E(u_t^{*5}) = 0$ and $E(u_t^{*6}) = 15$ hold for the normal distribution. To this extent, normality is needed to ensure that tests have proper size. Specifically, when $\{s_t^*\,,\mathcal{F}^{\,t}\}$ and $\{\nabla' s_t^* + s_t^* s_t^{*\prime}\,,\mathcal{F}^{\,t}\}$ are martingale difference sequences and when $E(u_t^{*5}) = 0$ and $E(u_t^{*6}) = 15$, then $nR^2 \overset{A}{\sim} \chi_1^2$, where R^2 is obtained from the regression of 1 on $(\hat{u}_t^4 - 5\hat{u}_t^2 + 2)/\hat{\sigma}_n^2$ and $\hat{s}_t' = (\hat{u}_t/\hat{\sigma}_n\,,\,(\hat{u}_t^2 - 1)/\hat{\sigma}_n)$ (or equivalently on $(\hat{u}_t^4 - 5\hat{u}_t^2 + 2)$, $\hat{u}_t$, and $(\hat{u}_t^2 - 1)$).

Now consider information matrix tests for models with a lagged dependent variable, e.g.

$$X_t \,|\, X^{t-1} \sim N(\alpha + \rho X_{t-1}\,,\sigma^2)\,.$$

With $\theta' = (\alpha\,,\rho\,,\sigma)$ we have

$$\log f_t = -.5\,\log 2\pi - \log\sigma - (X_t - \alpha - \rho X_{t-1})^2/2\sigma^2$$

$$s_t(X^t\,,\theta) = [u_t(\theta)/\sigma\,,\,X_{t-1}u_t(\theta)/\sigma\,,\,(u_t(\theta)^2 - 1)/\sigma]'$$

$$\nabla' s_t(X^t\,,\theta) = -\,\sigma^{-2}\begin{bmatrix} 1 & X_{t-1} & 2u_t(\theta) \\ X_{t-1} & X_{t-1}^2 & 2X_{t-1}u_t(\theta) \\ 2u_t(\theta) & 2X_{t-1}u_t(\theta) & (3u_t\,(\theta)^2 - 1) \end{bmatrix},$$

where now $u_t(\theta) = (X_t - \alpha - \rho X_{t-1})/\sigma$. This model generates the usual least squares estimates $\hat{\alpha}_n$ and $\hat{\rho}_n$. We also have $\hat{\sigma}_n = (n^{-1}\sum_{t=1}^{n}(X_t - \hat{\alpha}_n - \hat{\rho}_n X_{t-1})^2)^{1/2}$.

The information matrix indicators are

$$m_t = S\ vec\ (\nabla' s_t + s_t s_t')$$

$$= \sigma^{-2}\ S\ vec\begin{bmatrix} (u_t^2 - 1) & X_{t-1}(u_t^2 - 1) & (u_t^3 - 3u_t) \\ X_{t-1}(u_t^2 - 1) & X_{t-1}^2(u_t^2 - 1) & X_{t-1}(u_t^3 - 3u_t) \\ (u_t^3 - 3u_t) & X_{t-1}(u_t^3 - 3u_t) & (u_t^4 - 5u_t^2 + 2) \end{bmatrix}.$$

When S selects the (1 , 1), (3, 1) or (3, 3) elements of $\nabla' s_t + s_t s_t'$ we obtain tests essentially identical to those just considered. The new information matrix indicators are those appearing in the second row. Tests based on the (2, 1) or (2, 2) element are sensitive to failures of $E(X_{t-1}(u_t^{*2} - 1)) = 0$ or $E(X_{t-1}^2(u_t^{*2} - 1)) = 0$, which can occur in the presence of conditional heteroskedasticity, or when $\mathcal{M} = \{\alpha + \rho X_{t-1}\}$ is misspecified for $\{E(X_t \mid X^{t-1})\}$. Tests based on the (2, 3) element are sensitive to failures of $E(X_{t-1}(u_t^{*3} - 3u_t^*)) = 0$, which can occur in the presence of conditional skewness or when $\mathcal{M}$ is misspecified for $\{E(X_t \mid X^{t-1})\}$.

To investigate circumstances in which the information matrix tests can be conveniently computed, we examine $\nabla'_\theta m_t = S\, \nabla' (vec\ \nabla' s_t + s_t s_t')$. To avoid redundancy, we consider only the elements of $\nabla' s_t + s_t s_t'$ that are new here; this is accomplished by setting

$$S = \begin{bmatrix} 0 & 0 & 0 & 1 & 0 & 0 & 0 & 0 & 0 \\ 0 & 0 & 0 & 0 & 1 & 0 & 0 & 0 & 0 \\ 0 & 0 & 0 & 0 & 0 & 1 & 0 & 0 & 0 \end{bmatrix}.$$

With this choice of S we have

$$\nabla'_\theta m_t = -\sigma^{-3} \begin{bmatrix} 2X_{t-1}u_t & 2X_{t-1}^2 u_t & X_{t-1}(4u_t^2 - 2) \\ 2X_{t-1}^2 u_t & 2X_{t-1}^3 u_t & X_{t-1}^2(4u_t^2 - 2) \\ 3X_{t-1}(u_t^2 - 1) & 3X_{t-1}^2(u_t^2 - 1) & X_{t-1}(5u_t^3 - 9u_t) \end{bmatrix}.$$

We first consider the heteroskedasticity test based on the (2, 2) element of $\nabla' s_t + s_t s_t'$ obtained by setting $S = (0 , 0 , 0 , 0 , 1 , 0 , 0 , 0 , 0)$. In this case we have

$$E(\nabla'_\theta m_t^*) = -\sigma_o^{-3}[(2E(X_{t-1}^2 u_t^*),\ 2E(X_{t-1}^3 u_t^*),\ E(X_{t-1}^2(4u_t^{*2} - 2))] .$$

When $\{s_t^*, \mathcal{F}^t\}$ is a martingale difference sequence, we have that $E(u_t^* \mid X^{t-1}) = 0$, which implies that the first two terms vanish. The last term does not vanish, however. When $\{\nabla' s_t^* + s_t^* s_t^{*\prime}, \mathcal{F}^t\}$ is a martingale difference sequence we have $E(u_t^{*2} \mid X^{t-1}) = 1$, so that

$$E(X_{t-1}^2(4u_t^{*2} - 2)) = E(E(X_{t-1}^2(4u_t^{*2} - 2) \mid X^{t-1}))$$
$$= E(X_{t-1}^2\ E(4u_t^{*2} - 2 \mid X^{t-1})) = 2E(X_{t-1}^2) .$$

Consequently,

$$E(\nabla'_\theta m_t^*) = (0 , 0 , -2E(X_{t-1}^2)/\sigma_o^3).$$

The test obtained from Corollary 9.10 applies, but is not very convenient.

Tests of proper size can be straightforwardly obtained when $E(m_t^* s_t^{*\prime}) = -E(\nabla'_\theta m_t^*)$, using Corollary 9.11. In the present case

$$\begin{aligned} m_t s_t' &= \sigma^{-3} X_{t-1}^2 (u_t^2 - 1)[u_t, X_{t-1} u_t, (u_t^2 - 1)] \\ &= \sigma^{-3} [X_{t-1}^2 (u_t^3 - u_t), X_{t-1}^3 (u_t^3 - u_t), X_{t-1}^2 (u_t^2 - 1)^2], \end{aligned}$$

so that

$$E(m_t^* s_t^{*\prime}) = (0, 0, E(X_{t-1}^2 E(u_t^{*4} - 2u_t^{*2} + 1 \mid X^{t-1})) / \sigma_o^3).$$

When $\{\nabla' s_t^* + s_t^* s_t^{*\prime}, \mathcal{F}^t\}$ is a martingale difference sequence, we have $E(u_t^{*4} \mid X^{t-1}) = 3$, $E(u_t^{*2} \mid X^{t-1}) = 1$, so that $E(u_t^{*4} - 2u_t^{*2} + 1 \mid X^{t-1}) = 2$, and

$$E(m_t^* s_t^{*\prime}) = (0, 0, 2E(X_{t-1}{}^2) / \sigma_o^3) = -E(\nabla'_\theta m_t^*)$$

as desired.

Corollary 9.11 then gives the result that $nR^2 \overset{A}{\sim} \chi_1^2$ when $\{s_t^*, \mathcal{F}^t\}$ and $\{\nabla' s_t^* + s_t^* s_t^{*\prime}, \mathcal{F}^t\}$ are martingale difference sequences and R^2 is obtained from the regression of a constant on $\hat{m}_t = X_{t-1}^2 (\hat{u}_t^2 - 1) / \hat{\sigma}_n^2$ and $\hat{s}_t' = (\hat{u}_t / \hat{\sigma}_n, X_{t-1} \hat{u}_t / \hat{\sigma}_n, (\hat{u}_t^2 - 1) / \hat{\sigma}_n)$. Because R^2 is unaffected, divisions by $\hat{\sigma}_n^2$ and $\hat{\sigma}_n$ can be omitted.

Tests based on generalized residuals are available in the present case by taking advantage of the particular structure of the problem at hand. The facts that $n^{-1} \Sigma_{t=1}^n \hat{m}_t \hat{s}_t' \to (0, 0, 2E(X_{t-1}^2) / \sigma_o^3)$ $prob - P_o$ and that $n^{-1} \Sigma_{t=1}^n \hat{s}_t \hat{s}_t'$ converges in probability to a block diagonal 3×3 matrix with sole non-zero element in the third row and column (given the validity of the information matrix equalities) imply that a test asymptotically equivalent to that of Corollary 9.11 just given can be obtained from the regression of a constant on $X_{t-1}^2 (\hat{u}_t^2 - 1)$ and $(\hat{u}_t^2 - 1)$. The statistic nR^2 from this regression is also χ_1^2 when $\{s_t^*, \mathcal{F}^t\}$ and $\{\nabla' s_t^* + s_t^* s_t^{*\prime}, \mathcal{F}^t\}$ are martingale difference sequences.

Application of Corollary 11.5 yields tests based on generalized residuals, conducted by regressing $\hat{u}_t^2 - 1$ on $X_{t-1}^2 / \hat{\sigma}_n^2$ and $1 / \hat{\sigma}_n$, or, equivalently, regressing $\hat{u}_t^2$ on X_{t-1}^2 and a constant. When $E(u_t^{*4} \mid X^{t-1})$ is a constant (conditional homokurtosis) nR^2 (constant *adjusted*) from this regression is distributed asymptotically as χ_1^2. This is a generalization of the heteroskedasticity test of White [1980b] to the time series context with lagged dependent variables present in the regression.

When S picks both the (2,1) and (2,2) elements of $\nabla' s_t + s_t\, s_t'$, a (second order) information matrix test can be obtained by regressing $\hat{u}_t^2$ on X_{t-1}, X_{t-1}^2, and a constant. When $\{s_t^*, \mathcal{F}^t\}$ and $\{\nabla' s_t^* + s_t^* s_t^{*\prime}, \mathcal{F}^t\}$ are martingale difference sequences, then $nR^2 \overset{A}{\sim} \chi_2^2$ (R^2 constant *adjusted*). This jointly tests for departures from $E(X_{t-1}(u_t^{*2} - 1)) = 0$ and $E(X_{t-1}^2\, (u_t^{*2} - 1)) = 0$.

Lastly, consider the case $S = (0, 0, 0, 0, 0, 1, 0, 0, 0)$, which yields tests sensitive to departures from $E(X_{t-1}(u_t^{*3} - 3u_t^*)) = 0$. This equality may fail either because of dynamic misspecification ($E(X_{t-1}u_t^*) \neq 0$) or because of conditional skewness ($E(X_{t-1}u_t^{*3}) \neq 0$). Examining the appropriate row of $\nabla'_\theta\, m_t$, we see that for this choice of S,

$$
\begin{aligned}
E(\nabla'_\theta\, m_t^*) = -\,\sigma_o^{-3}[&3E(X_{t-1}(u_t^{*2} - 1)),\, 3E(X_{t-1}^2(u_t^{*2} - 1)),\\
&E(X_{t-1}(5u_t^{*3} - 9u_t^*))]\\
= 0,&
\end{aligned}
$$

when $\{s_t^*, \mathcal{F}^t\}$ and $\{\nabla' s_t^* + s_t^* s_t^{*\prime}, \mathcal{F}^t\}$ are martingale difference sequences.

Consequently, a convenient test can be obtained from Corollary 11.4. From this we have that $nR^2 \overset{A}{\sim} \chi_1^2$, where R^2 is obtained from the regression of 1 on $X_{t-1}(\hat{u}_t^3 - 3\hat{u}_t)$, provided that $\{s_t^*, \mathcal{F}^t\}$ and $\{\nabla' s_t^* + s_t^* s_t^{*\prime}, \mathcal{F}^t\}$ are martingale difference sequences. A test based on generalized residuals is available from the regression of $\hat{u}_t^3 - 3\hat{u}_t$ on X_{t-1}. When $E(u_t^{*6} \mid X_{t-1})$ is constant and $\{s_t^*, \mathcal{F}^t\}$ and $\{\nabla s_t^{*\prime} + s_t^* s_t^{*\prime}, \mathcal{F}^t\}$ are martingale difference sequences, then $nR^2 \overset{A}{\sim} \chi_1^2$, with R^2 from this regression.

11.3.c A Cross Information Matrix Test

To illustrate application of the cross information matrix test, consider the cross-information matrix equality that arises in conducting a Hausman test based on a comparison of $\hat{\rho}_n$, the QMLE from the simple ARCH model

$$X_t \mid X^{t-1} \sim N(\rho X_{t-1},\, \sigma^2 + \gamma\,(X_{t-1} - \rho X_{t-2})^2)\,,$$

with $\tilde{\rho}_n$, the QMLE from the AR model

$$X_t \mid X^{t-1} \sim N(\rho X_{t-1},\, 1)\,.$$

The heuristics underlying the Hausman test are that when the first model is correctly specified, both $\hat{\rho}_n$ and $\tilde{\rho}_n$ will consistently estimate the "true parameter," say ρ_o, while if it is misspecified, then $\hat{\rho}_n$ and $\tilde{\rho}_n$ will diverge (say $\hat{\rho}_n \to \rho_1^*$, $\tilde{\rho}_n \to \rho_2^*$ $prob - P_o$, $\rho_1^* \neq \rho_2^*$).

As we saw in Chapter 10, there are two m-tests asymptotically equivalent to the Hausman test based on $\hat{\rho}_n - \tilde{\rho}_n$. For simplicity, we consider the test based on

$$\lambda_t(X^t, \rho, \pi) = \pi s_{2t}(X^t, \rho)$$
$$= \pi X_{t-1}(X_t - \rho X_{t-1}).$$

In the present case, we have $\hat{\pi}_n = -(n^{-1}\sum_{t=1}^n X_{t-1}^2)^-$; when the law of large numbers holds in the presence of stationarity (ergodicity suffices) $\hat{\pi}_n \to \pi_o \equiv -E(X_{t-1}^2)^{-1}$ $prob - P_o$. Note that $E(\nabla'_\rho \lambda_t^*) = -[E(X_{t-1}^2)]^{-1} X_{t-1}^2$, so that the cross-information matrix equality is potentially useful.

Thus, our focus is on the validity of the cross information matrix equality, which in the present instance amounts to $-E(\nabla'_\rho \lambda_t^*) = E(\lambda_t^* s_{11t}^{*\prime})$, where $s_{11t} = \nabla_\rho \log f_{1t}$, where $\log f_{1t}$ is the log - likelihood associated with the ARCH model

$$\log f_{1t}(X^t, \theta) = -.5 \log 2\pi - .5 \log[\sigma^2 + \gamma (X_{t-1} - \rho X_{t-2})^2]$$
$$- (X_t - \rho X_{t-1})^2 / 2[\sigma^2 + \gamma (X_{t-1} - \rho X_{t-2})^2].$$

Now

$$s_{11t}(X^t, \theta) = \gamma X_{t-2}(X_{t-1} - \rho X_{t-2}) / [\sigma^2 + \gamma (X_{t-1} - \rho X_{t-2})^2]$$
$$+ X_{t-1}(X_t - \rho X_{t-1}) / [\sigma^2 + \gamma (X_{t-1} - \rho X_{t-2})^2]$$
$$- \gamma X_{t-2}(X_{t-1} - \rho X_{t-2})(X_t - 6\rho X_{t-1})^2 / [\sigma^2 + \gamma (X_{t-1} - \rho X_{t-2})^2]^2,$$

which implies that

$$E(\lambda_t^* s_{11t}^{*\prime}) = \gamma_o \pi_o E(u_t^* u_{t-1}^* X_{t-1} X_{t-2} / [\sigma_o^2 + \gamma_o u_{t-1}^{*2}])$$
$$+ \pi_o E(u_t^{*2} X_{t-1}^2 / [\sigma_o^2 + \gamma_o u_{t-1}^{*2}])$$
$$- \gamma_o \pi_o E(u_t^{*3} u_{t-1}^* X_{t-1} X_{t-2} / [\sigma_o^2 + \gamma_o u_{t-1}^{*2}]^2),$$

where $u_t^* = X_t - \rho_1^* X_{t-1}$.

It follows that the cross information matrix test based on $m_t = \nabla'_\rho \lambda_t + \lambda_t s'_{11t}$ will be sensitive to departures from $E(m_t^*) = E(\nabla'_\rho \lambda_t^*) + E(\lambda_t^* s_{11t}^{*\prime}) = 0$, i.e. to failures of

$$\gamma_o \pi_o E(u_t^* u_{t-1}^* X_{t-1} X_{t-2} / [\sigma_o^2 + \gamma_o u_{t-1}^{*2}])$$

$$+ \pi_o \, E((u_t^{*2} - [\sigma_o^2 + \gamma_o \, u_{t-1}^{*2}])X_{t-1}^2 / [\sigma_o^2 + \gamma_o \, u_{t-1}^{*2}])$$
$$- \gamma_o \, \pi_o \, E(u_t^{*3} u_{t-1}^{*} X_{t-1} X_{t-2} / [\sigma_o^2 + \gamma_o \, u_{t-1}^{*2}]^2)$$
$$= 0.$$

The first term is sensitive to failure of $E(u_t^* \mid X^{t-1}) = 0$, the second term to failure of $E(u_t^{*2} \mid X^{t-1}) = \sigma_o^2 + \gamma_o \, u_{t-1}^{*2}$, and the third term to failure of $E(u_t^{*3} \mid X^{t-1}) = 0$.

The cross information matrix test thus functions as an omnibus test for misspecification of the simple ARCH model under consideration, and is for this reason of interest in its own right. It is in particular sensitive to departures from correct specification that would lead to tests of incorrect size for a Hausman test based on the statistics of Corollary 9.11.

Proceeding in the usual way, we investigate $E(\nabla_\theta m_t^*)$, where $\theta = (\rho, \gamma, \sigma)'$. Now

$$\nabla'_\theta \, m_t = \nabla'_\theta \, (\nabla'_\rho \lambda_t) + \lambda_t \, \nabla'_\theta \, s'_{11t} + s_{11t} \, \nabla'_\theta \, \lambda_t$$
$$= \lambda_t \, \nabla'_\theta \, s_{11t} + (s_{11t} \nabla'_\rho \lambda_t \, , 0 \, , 0) \, ,$$

because $\nabla'_\theta \, (\nabla'_\rho \lambda_t) = 0 \, , \nabla_\gamma \, \lambda_t = 0$ and $\nabla_\sigma \lambda_t = 0$. Tedious algebra reveals that generally $E(\nabla_\theta m_t^*) \neq 0$, so that the statistics of Corollary 11.7 are not computationally convenient. However, convenient statistics can be obtained from Corollary 9.11 when $E(\nabla'_\theta \, m_t^* + m_t^* s_{1t}^{*\prime} \mid X^{t-1}) = 0$, where $s_{1t} = \nabla_\theta \log f_{1t}$. Letting $s_{12t} = \nabla_\gamma \log f_{1t}$, and $s_{13t} = \nabla_\sigma \log f_{1t}$, we have

$$m_t \;\; s_{1t}' = (\nabla_\rho{}' \lambda_t + \lambda_t s_{11t}{}')(s_{11t} \, , s_{12t} \, , s_{13t})$$
$$= \lambda_t (s_{11t}^2 \, , s_{11t} s_{12t} \, , s_{11t} s_{13t})$$
$$+ (s_{11t} \nabla_\rho{}' \lambda_t \, , s_{12t} \nabla_\rho{}' \lambda_t \, , s_{13t} \, \nabla_\rho{}' \, \lambda_t \,) \, .$$

From the expressions for $\nabla_\theta m_t$ and $m_t s_{1t}'$, it is clear that $E \; (\nabla'_\theta \; m_t^* + m_t^* s_{1t}^{*\prime} \mid X^{t-1}) = 0$ when

$$E(\nabla'_\theta s_{11t}^* \mid X^{t-1}) + E(s_{11t}^{*2} \, , s_{11t}^* s_{12t}^* \, , s_{11t}^* s_{13t}^* \mid X^{t-1}) = 0 \, ,$$

and

$$E(s_{1t}^* \nabla'_\rho \lambda_t^* \mid X^{t-1}) = 0 \, .$$

The first of these equalities holds when the information matrix equality holds for $\mathcal{S} = \{f_{1t}\}$, i.e. when $\{\nabla'_\theta \, s_{1t}^* + s_{1t}^* s_{1t}^{*\prime} \, , \mathcal{F}^t \}$ is a martingale difference sequence. Because $\nabla'_\rho \lambda_t^* = - \pi_o X_{t-1}^2$, the second equality follows when $\{s_{1t}^* \, , \mathcal{F}^t\}$ is a martingale difference sequence. Thus, the cross-information matrix equality holds for the cross information matrix test indicators considered here when $\{s_{1t}^*, \mathcal{F}^t\}$ and $\{\nabla'_\theta s_{1t}^* + s_{1t}^* s_{1t}^{*\prime}, \mathcal{F}^t\}$ are martingale difference sequences.

It follows from Corollary 9.11 that a cross - information matrix test statistic can be constructed as nR^2 from the regression of a constant on the cross-information matrix indicators $\hat{m}_t = \hat{\pi}_n(X_{t-1}^2 + X_{t-1}\hat{u}_t\hat{s}_{11t})$ and on $\hat{s}_{1t}'$. Because R^2 is unaffected by multiplication of any regressor by a constant, the regression can be conducted equivalently by regressing 1 on $X_{t-1}^2 + X_{t-1}\hat{u}_t\hat{s}_{11t}$ and $\hat{s}_{1t}'$. When $\{s_{1t}^*, \mathcal{F}^t\}$ and $\{\nabla'_\theta s_{1t}^* + s_{1t}^* s_{1t}^{*\prime}, \mathcal{F}^t\}$ are martingale difference sequences, then $nR^2 \overset{A}{\sim} \chi_1^2$.

11.4 Summary

This chapter explores specification tests based on the first order, second order and cross-information matrix equalities. We use the m-testing framework to characterize the asymptotic distributions of a variety of more or less computationally convenient forms of these tests. In the third section we illustrate application of these results to obtain dynamic information matrix tests, (second order) information matrix tests and cross-information matrix tests for simple dynamic linear regression models. We saw there that these tests are sensitive to a variety of potentially serious misspecifications: dynamic information matrix tests are sensitive to autocorrelation, dynamic misspecification and/or functional misspecification of conditional means, as well as autoregressive conditional heteroskedasticity (ARCH), dynamic misspecification and/or functional misspecification of conditional variances; (second order) information matrix tests are sensitive to conditional heteroskedasticity, (conditional) skewness, (conditional) kurtosis, and, in particular cases, dynamic misspecification; cross-information matrix tests can function as omnibus tests for misspecification, particularly sensitive to misspecifications that adversely affect the size of specific underlying m-tests.

Whenever misspecification is detected by the information matrix tests, appropriate corrective measures are indicated. Use of misspecification consistent covariance matrix estimators such as those given in Chapter 8 is immediately indicated; furthermore, one may wish to respecify the model to eliminate possible sources of detected misspecification.

Finally, it must be emphasized that it is the misspecification indicator vector m_t that defines a particular information matrix test, through the null hypothesis $E(m_t^*) = 0$, rather than any specific statistic. The statistics discussed here have been chosen for their analytical tractability and computational convenience, not because their distributions can be expected to be well approximated by their asymptotic distributions. Finite sample performance of certain information matrix test statistics can be quite bad, as reported by Kennan and Neumann [1988], Orme [1990] and Chesher and Spady [1991]. An important direction for present and future work is the exploration of modifications of test statistics or the approximating distributions for the tests discussed here that can yield more accurate control over size in samples of realistic size. Useful work in this direction is that of Kennan and Neumann [1988], Davidson and MacKinnon [1988] and Chesher and Spady [1991].

MATHEMATICAL APPENDIX

PROOF OF THEOREM 11.1: We verify the conditions of Theorem 9.5. The conditions required for $\{ \hat{J}_n \}$ and $\{ J_n^* \}$ are imposed directly. Assumptions 2.3 and 3.6 ensure that Assumption 9.1 holds for $m_t = w_t \, s_t'$, and the nullity of π renders Assumption 9.2 irrelevant. With Assumption 11.1 and the conditions of Theorem 6.4, it follows easily that $\sqrt{n}\, \hat{M}_n = \sqrt{n}\, M_n^* + \nabla_\theta' \bar{M}_n^* \sqrt{n}\,(\hat{\theta}_n - \theta_n^*) + o_{P_o}(1)$. Assumption 11.2 ensures the asymptotic normality required in condition 9.4(ii). Because $\{a_n^* = \sqrt{n}\, E(M_n^*)\}$ is $O(1)$ by assumption, it follows that $P_o \in \mathcal{P}_a^u$. hence, by Theorem 9.5, $\mathcal{M}_n \overset{A}{\sim} N_2(a_n^*, V_n^*; J_n^{*-1})$.

When $a_n^* \to 0$ and $J_n^* = V_n^*$, we immediately have $P_o \in \mathcal{P}_o^i$, so that $\mathcal{M}_n \overset{A}{\sim} \chi_q^2$.

(ii) We verify the conditions of Theorem 9.7. The condition on $\{\hat{J}_n\}$ and $\{J_n^*\}$ are directly imposed. Verifying the conditions of Definition 9.6, we have the conditions of Theorem 3.5 imposed directly; the measurability and integrability conditions of Definition 9.1(ii) are ensured by Assumption 2.4 and 11.3(a); Assumption 9.2 is irrelevant as π is null; and $\bar{M}_n^{*\prime} \bar{M}_n^* > \varepsilon > 0$ *a.a. n* by assumption. Hence $P_o \in \mathcal{P}_A^u$. Assumption 9.3 holds given Assumption 11.3, so that the required conditions for application of Theorem 9.7 are met. Consequently, for $\{k_n\} = o(n)$, $P_o[\mathcal{M}_n > k_n] \to 1$. □

PROOF OF COROLLARY 11.2: The proof is obtained by verifying the conditions of Corollary 9.13 in a straightforward manner. Note that because $m_t = w_t \, s_t' = w_t \, i_t, u_t = j_t \, u_t$, we have immediately that $u_t = v_t$ as required for $P_o \in \mathcal{P}_o^i$. □

PROOF OF THEOREM 11.3: (i) We verify the conditions of Theorem 9.5. The conditions required for $\{\hat{J}_n\}$ and $\{J_n^*\}$ are imposed directly. Assumptions 2.3 and 11.5 ensure that Assumption 9.1 holds for $m_t = S \, vec \, \nabla' s_t + s_t \, s_t'$, and the nullity of π renders Assumption 9.2 irrelevant. With Assumption 11.6 and the conditions of Theorem 6.4, it follows easily that $\sqrt{n}\, \hat{M}_n = \sqrt{n}\, M_n^* + \nabla_\theta' \bar{M}_n^* \sqrt{n}\,(\hat{\theta}_n - \theta_n^*) + o_{P_o}(1)$. Assumption 11.7 ensures the asymptotic normality required in Condition 9.4(ii). Because $\{a_n^*\}$ is $O(1)$ by assumption, it follows that $P_o \in \mathcal{P}_a^u$. Hence, by Theorem 9.5, $\mathcal{M}_n \overset{A}{\sim} N_2(a_n^*, V_n^*; J_n^{*-1})$.

When $a_n^* \to 0$ and $J_n^* = V_n^*$, we immediately have $P_o \in \mathcal{P}_o^i$, so that $\mathcal{M}_n \overset{A}{\sim} \chi_q^2$.

(ii) We verify the conditions of Theorem 9.7. The conditions on $\{\hat{J}_n\}$ and $\{J_n^*\}$ are directly imposed. Verifying the conditions of Definition 9.6, we have the conditions of Theorem 3.5 imposed directly; the measurability and integrability conditions of Definition 9.1(ii) are ensured by Assumptions 3.8 and 8.6; Assumption 9.2 is irrelevant as π is null; and $\bar{M}_n^{*\prime} \bar{M}_n^* > \varepsilon > 0$ $a.a.n$ by assumption. Hence $P_o \in \mathcal{P}_A^u$. Assumption 9.3 holds given Assumptions 3.8 and 8.6, so that Theorem 9.7 applies. Consequently, for $\{k_n\} = o(n)$, $P_o[\mathcal{M}_n > k_n] \to 1$. □

PROOF OF COROLLARY 11.4: We verify the conditions of Corollary 9.9.

(i) The conditions of Theorem 2.15 are assumed directly, and condition 9.1 holds given Assumptions 2.3 and 3.6. The result follows from Corollary 9.9(i).

(ii) The conditions of Theorem 3.5 are assumed directly, and Assumption 9.4 holds under Assumption 11.8. The result follows from Corollary 9.9(ii).

(iii) As in the proof of Theorem 11.3(iii), $P_o \in \mathcal{P}_a^u$. Assumptions 11.6 and 11.7 are imposed directly so that $\mathcal{M}_n \overset{A}{\sim} N_2(a_n^*, V_n^*; K_n^{*-1})$ by Corollary 9.9(iii). When $\{m_t^*, \mathcal{F}^t\}$ and $\{\nabla_\theta\, m_t^*, \mathcal{F}^t\}$ are martingale difference sequences, then $P_o \in \mathcal{P}_o^i$ and $\mathcal{M}_n \overset{A}{\sim} \chi_q^2$.

(iv) Assumptions 3.8 and 8.6 ensures that Assumption 9.3 holds. The other conditions are assumed directly, so that the result follows from Corollary 9.9(iv). □

PROOF OF COROLLARY 11.5: The proof is obtained by verifying the conditions of Corollary 9.12 in a straightforward manner. The argument given in the text can be trivially modified to show that $P_o \in \mathcal{P}_o^i$ under the conditions given. □

PROOF OF THEOREM 11.6: The proof is identical to that of Theorem 11.3 with $\nabla' \lambda_t + \lambda_t\, s_t'$ replacing $\nabla' s_t + s_t\, s_t'$. Assumption 11.10 ensures the measurability and continuous differentiability previously ensured by Assumption 3.6, and Assumptions 11.11 and 11.12 replace Assumptions 11.6 and 11.7. Assumption 11.13 is applied in place of Assumptions 3.8 and

8.6 in verifying (ii). □

PROOF OF COROLLARY 11.7: The proof is identical to that of Corollary 11.4, with modifications analogous to those in Theorem 11.6. Assumption 11.14 replaces Assumption 11.8. □

PROOF OF COROLLARY 11.8: The proof is identical to that of Corollary 11.5, with modification analogous to those in the proof of Theorem 11.6. Assumption 11.15 replaces Assumption 11.9. □

CHAPTER 12

Conclusion

The results of the foregoing chapters are intended to provide empirical researchers with an appreciation of the dangers of taking one's explanatory models too literally, and with tools for coping with the necessity of using models, which by their very nature as human artifacts, may be misspecified to greater or lesser extent.

Chapter 2 of this book motivates use of the method of maximum likelihood in the presence of misspecification and establishes the existence of the quasi-maximum likelihood estimator. We see in Chapter 3 how misspecification can cause quasi-maximum likelihood estimators to fail to be consistent for parameters of interest, but that the QMLE $\hat{\theta}$ generally retains an information theoretic interpretation: it is consistent for a parameter vector θ^* that minimizes Kullback-Leibler information. As such, θ^* depends generally on the specification generating $\hat{\theta}$ as well as on the data generation process. In Chapters 4 and 5 we see that in certain special cases, specification correct to a limited extent can allow consistent estimation of parameters of interest. For example, use of exponential family quasi-likelihood functions yields consistent estimators for the parameters of a correctly specified model of the conditional expectation of the dependent variables given the explanatory variables.

The results of Chapter 6 establish that the QMLE generally retains the property of asymptotic normality despite misspecification, but that the parameter covariance matrix is of a form that differs from the classical expression. We observe the crucial role played by the information matrix equality in ensuring the validity of classical expressions and provide conditions ensuring the validity of the information matrix equality. Generally, these conditions require the model to be correctly specified to a considerable extent: no dynamic misspecification, and correct specification of conditional mean and variance, at the least.

Misspecification generally affects adversely the efficiency of the QMLE, as we see in Chapter 7. Even if a QMLE retains consistency for parameters of interest, failure of the information matrix equality leads to a larger asymptotic covariance matrix than would otherwise be the case. Certain forms of misspecification do not have this effect: neglecting to model the distribution of variables uninformative for the parameters of interest ("exogenous" variables) does not affect efficiency adversely. Also, efficiency within more limited classes of estimators is possible, as when the conditional mean and variance are correctly specified within a linear exponential quasi-likelihood.

The form of the asymptotic covariance matrix affects the statistics used to test hypotheses, and the possibility of misspecification affects the interpretation of the null and alternative hypotheses, as we show in Chapter 8. Generally useful statistics for performing hypothesis tests are available, provided that a consistent estimator for the asymptotic covariance matrix can be found. We find that consistent estimators are available in particular circumstances, but that this is by no means guaranteed. Consistent estimators may fail to exist for dynamically misspecified models of dependent heterogeneous processes.

A multitude of methods is available for detecting the presence of various forms of misspecification. As we see in Chapters 9 and 10, the m-testing approach unifies a broad array of specification testing procedures, and makes clear the relation between the hypotheses tested by the extensions of classical procedures given in Chapter 8 and the hypotheses tested by specification tests. Specification tests that may prove particularly useful are the information matrix tests examined at length in Chapter 11.

Thus, the collection of results given in this book can be viewed as providing a fairly coherent theoretical basis for a general econometric methodology along the lines of the progressive research strategy outlined by Hendry and Richard [1982] (inspired by Popper [1962]). To implement this methodology in the present context, the researcher should clearly define the phenomenon of interest, and justify the relation of that phenomenon to observables $\{X_t\}$ and to any partition of X_t into "dependent" variables Y_t and "explanatory" variables Z_t (as in the discussion of Chapters 1 and 4). At the same time, the researcher should clearly enunciate the ultimate goal of the research, e.g., arriving at a sufficiently well-specified model or arriving at a KLIC-optimal model (as in a forecasting exercise). The appropriate procedures of Chapters 8-11 can be applied if the ultimate research goal is either of these objectives. (See White [1990] for a further discussion of issues arising in selecting a sufficiently well-specified model.)

In many cases, the goal of empirical economic research is to test hypotheses about parameters to which one wishes to attribute economic meaning. It is our view that this is inappropriate and unjustified without first establishing that the model within which the hypotheses are being tested is correctly specified to at least some extent. Otherwise, one may only have confidence that one is testing hypotheses about θ^*; the economic interpretation desired is untenable.

In arriving at a sufficiently well-specified model, the researcher should be quite clear about the specification requirements used and the specification tests by which these requirements were investigated. The importance of this arises from the necessity of other researchers being able to replicate results, and from the possible sensitivity of the conclusions drawn to the methods used to obtain them.

Nonparametric techniques (or variants of them, such as "semi-nonparametric" techniques) are rapidly gaining adherents in econometrics, precisely because of the potential for avoiding the potentially calamitous effects of misspecification. (A unified treatment of nonparametric methods is given by Stone [1985]; a review of econometric work in nonparametrics is given by Robinson [1988]; other econometric work in the area is contained in a volume of the *Journal of Econometrics*, edited by Duncan [1986] and in the volume edited by Barnett, Powell and Tauchen [1991].) While it is certain that nonparametric techniques offer great potential for advances in both applied and theoretical econometrics, parametric approaches are not likely to be abandoned. Indeed, many nonparametric methods arise from a sequence of parametric solutions to a particular estimation problem (e.g., the method of sieves proposed by Grenander [1981]; (see also Geman and Hwang [1982] and White and Wooldridge [1991]). In such cases, the present results afford some useful interpretations.

A serious limitation of the theory given here (as well as most of the theory in nonparametric estimation) is that the results are asymptotic, holding only as approximations for n "sufficiently large." We make no apologies for this, as asymptotic results are a useful first step in any econometric or statistical analysis: when we set out on a journey, it is helpful to know where we are going. However, the investigator must be emphatically warned that the operating characteristics of the various statistics and tests given here are not well known for samples of the size usually encountered in economics (a few hundred or perhaps a few thousand observations). Monte Carlo evidence suggests that asymptotic approximations can sometimes be quite bad, and that judicious modification of statistics such as those given here can often yield dramatic improvements in finite sample performance. Finite sample investigation of the methods proposed here and of appropriate modifications is thus an important research priority.

The results of this book have been purposely formulated to apply to a wide range of the stochastic processes encountered in economics. Our results apply to i.i.d. processes as well as to dependent heterogeneous processes. Although this covers quite a bit, our results typically do not treat explosive or trending processes, except perhaps after some stabilizing transformation. We have not attempted to treat unstabilized processes, in order to keep the task at hand manageable; they have certainly not been neglected because they are in any way unimportant. Maximum likelihood methods are directly relevant to such processes, and have been studied among others by Weiss [1971, 1973] and Crowder [1976]. Work of Wooldridge [1986] indicates that the approach taken in this monograph extends in certain ways to allow treatment of such processes, yielding an analogous theory of estimation, inference and specification analysis for certain explosive or trending processes ("non-stationary" in common parlance).

Throughout we have made relatively strong assumptions on the stochastic specifications $\mathcal{S}$ for the sake of convenience, such as assuming the existence of two or even three derivatives for $\log f_t$. Such conditions rule out treatment of the asymptotic normality of least absolute deviations estimators, for example. Nevertheless, well known methods (e.g., Huber [1967]) can be used to relax these assumptions. Some work along these lines in a context similar to that considered here has also been done by Wooldridge [1986].

The present work has many other limitations that the reader will no doubt have discovered for herself or himself. I hope that these limitations will not completely preclude the beneficial use of the methods discussed here. I hope also that these limitations will provide an inspiration to further progress in understanding and coping with the consequences of model misspecification, and ultimately, to progress in understanding empirical phenomena.

APPENDIX 1

Elementary Concepts of Measure Theory and the Radon-Nikodým Theorem

This appendix presents some elementary measure theoretic concepts extensively used in the text, together with a statement of the Radon-Nikodým Theorem.

DEFINITION A.1.1 (*σ-field*): Let Ω be any set, and let $\mathcal{F}$ be a collection of subsets of Ω. $\mathcal{F}$ is a *σ-field* (*σ-algebra*) if:

(i) Ω belongs to $\mathcal{F}$;

(ii) If $F \in \mathcal{F}$, then $F^c \in \mathcal{F}$;

(iii) If $F_n \in \mathcal{F}$, $n = 1, 2, \ldots$, then $\cup_{n=1}^{\infty} F_n \in \mathcal{F}$. □

When $\mathcal{F}$ is a σ-field, we call the pair $(\Omega, \mathcal{F})$ a *measurable space*.

DEFINITION A.1.2 (*Borel σ-field* $\mathcal{B}^{\nu}$): The *Borel σ-field* $\mathcal{B}^{\nu}$ is the smallest collection of subsets of $\mathbb{R}^{\nu}$, $\nu \in \mathbb{N}$, that includes

(i) all open sets of $\mathbb{R}^{\nu}$;

(ii) the complement B^c of any set $B \in \mathcal{B}^{\nu}$;

(iii) the union $\cup_{n=1}^{\infty} B_n$ of any sequence $\{B_n\}$ in $\mathcal{B}^{\nu}$. □

$\mathcal{B}^{\nu}$ is called "the Borel σ-field generated by the open sets of $\mathbb{R}^{\nu}$."

DEFINITION A.1.3 (*Borel σ-field* $\mathcal{B}^{\nu\infty}$): The Borel σ-field $\mathcal{B}^{\nu\infty}$ is the smallest collection of subsets of $\mathbb{R}^{\nu\infty} \equiv \times_{n=1}^{\infty} \mathbb{R}^{\nu}$ that includes:

(i) all sets of the form $\times_{n=1}^{\infty} B_n$, where each $B_n \in \mathcal{B}^{\nu}$ and $B_n = \mathbb{R}^{\nu}$ except for finitely many n;

(ii) the complement A^c of any set A in $\mathcal{B}^{\nu\infty}$;

(iii) the union $\cup_{n=1}^{\infty} A_n$ of any sequence $\{A_n\}$ in $\mathcal{B}^{\nu\infty}$. □

$\mathcal{B}^{\nu\infty}$ is called "the Borel σ-field generated by the measurable finite dimensional product cylinders."

DEFINITION A.1.4 (*Measurable function*): A function $g : \Omega \to \boldsymbol{R}$ is measurable-$\mathcal{F}$ if for every $a \in \boldsymbol{R}$ the set $[\omega \in \Omega : g(\omega) \le a]$ belongs to $\mathcal{F}$. □

Measurable functions correspond directly to the "random variables" of probability theory. A vector function $g : \Omega \to \boldsymbol{R}^q$ is measurable-$\mathcal{F}$ if it is measurable component by component.

DEFINITION A.1.5 (*Measure*): Let $(\Omega, \mathcal{F})$ be a measurable space. A function $\mu : \mathcal{F} \to \bar{\boldsymbol{R}}^+$ is a *measure* on $(\Omega, \mathcal{F})$ if:

(i) $\mu(\varnothing) = 0$;

(ii) $\mu(F) \ge 0$ for all $F \in \mathcal{F}$;

(iii) μ is *countably additive*, i.e., $\mu(\cup_{n=1}^{\infty} F_n) = \sum_{n=1}^{\infty} \mu(F_n)$ for any disjoint sequence $\{F_n\}$ of sets in $\mathcal{F}$. □

When μ is a measure on $(\Omega, \mathcal{F})$, we call the triple $(\Omega, \mathcal{F}, \mu)$ a *measure space*.

DEFINITION A.1.6 (*Probability, finite and σ-finite measures*): Let $(\Omega, \mathcal{F}, \mu)$ be a measure space. If $\mu(\Omega) = 1$, then μ is a *probability measure*. If $\mu(\Omega) < \infty$, then μ is a *finite measure*. If there exists a sequence $\{F_n\}$ of sets in $\mathcal{F}$ such that $\cup_{n=1}^{\infty} F_n = \Omega$ and $\mu(F_n) < \infty$, $n = 1, 2, \ldots$, then μ is a *σ-finite measure*. □

When μ is a probability measure, we call $(\Omega, \mathcal{F}, \mu)$ a *probability space*.

DEFINITION A.1.7 (*Complete measure space*): The measure space $(\Omega, \mathcal{F}, \mu)$ is *complete* whenever $G \subset F$, $F \in \mathcal{F}$ and $\mu(F) = 0$, then $G \in \mathcal{F}$. □

DEFINITION A.1.8 (*Absolute continuity*): Let μ and ν be measures on $(\Omega, \mathcal{F})$. ν is absolutely continuous with respect to μ, denoted $\nu \ll \mu$, if $\mu(F) = 0$ implies $\nu(F) = 0$ for each $F \in \mathcal{F}$. □

THEOREM A.1.9 (*Radon Nikodým Theorem*): Let μ and ν be σ-finite measures on $(\Omega, \mathcal{F})$ and suppose that $\nu \ll \mu$. Then there exists $g : \Omega \to \boldsymbol{R}^+$ measurable-$\mathcal{F}$ such that

$$\nu(F) = \int_F g(\omega)\, d\mu(\omega) \quad \text{for all} \quad F \in \mathcal{F}.$$

Further, g is uniquely determined except on a set of μ-measure zero. □

We call $g = d\nu/d\mu$ the *Radon-Nikodým density* of ν with respect to μ.

For useful treatment of measure theory, the reader is referred to Bartle [1966] and Billingsley [1979].

APPENDIX 2

Uniform Laws of Large Numbers

This appendix collects together a number of strong and weak uniform laws of large numbers suitable for application in a variety of model and data generation contexts.

THEOREM A.2.1 (Jennrich [1969, *Theorem 2*]): Let X_t, $t = 1, 2, \ldots$ be an i.i.d sequence of random $k \times 1$ vectors, with common cumulative distribution function F.

Let Θ be a compact subset of $\mathbb{R}^p$, $p \in \mathbb{N}$, and let $q : \mathbb{R}^k \times \Theta \to \mathbb{R}$ be a function such that $q(\cdot, \theta)$ is measurable-$\mathcal{B}^k$ for each θ in Θ and $q(x, \cdot)$ is continuous on Θ for each x in $\mathbb{R}^k$.

Suppose there exists $D : \mathbb{R}^k \to \mathbb{R}^+$ measurable-$\mathcal{B}^k$ such that $|q(x, \theta)| \leq D(x)$ for all θ in Θ and x in $X = supp\ F$ (the support of F, i.e., the smallest Borel set containing X_1 with probability 1) and $E(D(X_t)) = \int_{\mathbb{R}^k} D(x)dF(x) < \infty$.

Then:

(i) $\bar{Q}(\theta) = E(q(X_t, \theta))$ is continuous on Θ; and

(ii) $Q_n(\theta) - \bar{Q}(\theta) \to 0$ as $n \to \infty$ $a.s.$ uniformly on Θ, where $Q_n(\theta) \equiv n^{-1} \sum_{t=1}^{n} q(X_t, \theta)$. □

A ULLN for stationary ergodic processes is the following.

THEOREM A.2.2 (Ranga Rao [1962]): Let $(\Omega, \mathcal{F}, P)$ be a probability space, and let $T: \Omega \to \Omega$ be a one-to-one measure preserving transformation.

Let Θ be a compact subset of $\mathbb{R}^P$, $p \in \mathbb{N}$, and let $q : \Omega \times \Theta \to \mathbb{R}$ be a function such that $q(\cdot, \theta)$ is measurable-$\mathcal{F}$ for each θ in Θ and $q(\omega, \cdot)$ is continuous on Θ for each ω in Ω.

Suppose there exists $D : \Omega \to \mathbb{R}^+$ measurable-$\mathcal{F}$ such that $|q(\omega, \theta)| \leq D(\omega)$ for all θ in Θ and ω in Ω, and $E(D) \equiv \int_\Omega DdP < \infty$.

If for each θ in Θ $q_t(\theta) \equiv q(T^t\omega, \theta)$ is ergodic, then

(i) $\bar{Q}(\theta) = E(q_t(\theta))$ is continuous on Θ; and

(ii) $Q_n(\theta) - \bar{Q}(\theta) \to 0$ as $n \to \infty$ $a.s.-P$ uniformly on Θ, where $Q_n(\theta) \equiv n^{-1} \sum_{t=1}^{n} q_t(\theta)$. □

In order to treat heterogeneous processes and double arrays, we modify some results of Andrews [1987] along the lines of results given by Gallant and White [1988, Ch. 3]. For convenience, we state results only for convergence in probability for double arrays. Related results hold for almost sure convergence of single arrays, but we do not give them explicitly. The interested reader is referred to Gallant and White [1988, Ch. 3].

We use the following definition.

DEFINITION A.2.3 (*Lipshitz-L_1 a.s.*): Let $(\Omega, \mathcal{F}, P)$ be a probability space, and let (Θ, ρ) be a separable metric space. The double array $\{q_{nt} : \Omega \times \Theta \to \mathbb{R},\ n, t = 1, 2, \ldots\}$ is defined to be *Lipschitz-L_1 a.s. on* Θ if $q_{nt}(\cdot, \theta)$ is measurable-$\mathcal{F}$ for each θ in Θ, $n, t = 1, 2, \ldots$ and for each θ^o in Θ there exist a constant $\delta^o > 0$, functions $L_{nt}^o : \Omega \to \mathbb{R}^+$ measurable-$\mathcal{F}$ and functions $a_{nt}^o : \mathbb{R}^+ \to \mathbb{R}^+$, $a_{nt}^o(\delta) \downarrow 0$ as $\delta \to 0$, $n, t = 1, 2, \ldots$ such that either

(i) $\bar{a}^o(\delta) \equiv \sup_n \sup_t a_{nt}^o(\delta) < \infty$ for all $0 < \delta \le \delta^o$, $\bar{a}^o(\delta) \downarrow 0$ as $\delta \to 0$, and $\{n^{-1} \sum_{t=1}^{n} E(L_{nt}^o)\}$ is $O(1)$; or

(ii) For some $p > 1$, $\bar{a}^o(\delta) \equiv \sup_n [n^{-1} \sum_{t=1}^{n} a_{nt}^o(\delta)^p]^{1/p} < \infty$ for all $0 < \delta \le \delta^o$, $\bar{a}^o(\delta) \downarrow 0$ as $\delta \to 0$ and $\{n^{-1} \sum_{t=1}^{n} (E[L_{nt}^o])^{p/(p-1)}\}$ is $O(1)$; and for all θ in $\bar{\eta}^o(\delta^o) \equiv \{\theta \in \Theta : \rho(\theta, \theta^o) \le \delta^o\}$

$$|q_{nt}(\theta) - q_{nt}(\theta^o)| \le L_{nt}^o\, a_{nt}^o[\rho(\theta, \theta^o)] \quad a.s.-P \quad n, t = 1, 2, \ldots.$$ □

DEFINITION A.2.4 (*Weak Law of Large Numbers Locally*): Let $(\Omega, \mathcal{F}, P)$ be a probability space, and let (Θ, ρ) be a separable metric space. Let $\{q_{nt} : \Omega \times \Theta \to \mathbb{R},\ n, t = 1, 2, \ldots\}$ be a sequence of random functions continuous on Θ $a.s.-P$. For given θ^o in Θ and $\delta > 0$ define the random variables

$$\bar{q}_{nt}^o(\delta) \equiv \sup_{\eta^o(\delta)} q_{nt}(\theta) \quad \text{and} \quad \underline{q}_{nt}^o(\delta) = \inf_{\eta^o(\delta)} q_{nt}(\theta),$$

where $\eta^o(\delta) \equiv \{\theta \in \Theta : \rho(\theta, \theta^o) < \delta\}$.

We say that $\{\bar{q}_{nt}^o(\delta)\}$ *obeys the weak law of large numbers locally at* θ^o if there exists $\delta^o > 0$ (depending on θ^o) such that for all $0 < \delta \le \delta^o$, $n^{-1} \sum_{t=1}^{n} [\bar{q}_{nt}^o(\delta) - E(\bar{q}_{nt}^o(\delta))] \to 0$ *prob* $- P$, and similarly for $\{\underline{q}_{nt}^o(\delta)\}$. □

The definition also applies to single arrays, and satisfies the "*strong* law of large numbers locally" if the convergence is almost surely -P rather than in probability. Strong convergence for double arrays is only known to occur under strong assumptions (e.g., Teicher [1985]). We do not treat this case.

A generic weak uniform law of large numbers which is only a slight extension of one given by Andrews [1987] is the following:

THEOREM A.2.5: Let $(\Omega, \mathcal{F}\ P)$ be a complete probability space, and let (Θ, ρ) be a compact metric space. Suppose

(a) $\{q_{nt}\}$ is Lipschitz-L_1 *a.s.* on Θ; and

(b) $\{\overline{q}_{nt}^{\,o}(\delta)\}$ and $\{\underline{q}_{nt}^{\,o}(\delta)\}$ obey the weak law of large numbers locally at θ^o for all θ^o in Θ.

Then

(i) $\bar{Q}_n(\cdot) \equiv n^{-1} \sum_{t=1}^{n} E(q_{nt}(\cdot)) : \Theta \to \mathbb{R}$ is continuous on Θ uniformly in n; and

(ii) $Q_n(\theta) - \bar{Q}_n(\theta) \to 0$ *prob* $-P$ uniformly on Θ, $Q_n(\theta) \equiv n^{-1} \sum_{t=1}^{n} q_{nt}(\theta)$. □

Gallant and White [1988, Ch. 3] establish this result for single arrays under strong convergence. The proof of the present result follows from their argument, replacing the single index t with the double index n, t and invoking weak convergence instead of strong convergence.

Although condition (a) is a natural primitive condition to impose in specific contexts, condition (b) is usually too abstract. Fortunately, a law of large numbers can usually be applied under reasonable primitive conditions that will ensure that condition (b) holds. A weak law of large numbers by Andrews [1988] for dependent heterogeneous processes is useful in this regard.

Andrews [1988] introduces the following definition, a generalization of the mixingale concept of McLeish [1975]:

DEFINITION A.2.6 (L_p*–mixingale*): Let $(\Omega, \mathcal{F}, P)$ be a probability space, let $X_{nt} : \Omega \to \mathbb{R}$ be measurable-$\mathcal{F}$, $t = 1, \ldots, k_n$, $n = 1, 2, \ldots$ and let $\mathcal{F}_{nt} \subset \mathcal{F}_{n,t+1} \subset \mathcal{F}$, $t = 1, \ldots, k_{n-1}$, $n = 1, 2, \ldots$. For $p \in \mathbb{R}^+$, the triangular array $\{X_{nt}, \mathcal{F}_{nt}\}$ is an L_p*-mixingale* if $\| X_{nt} \|_p < \infty$, $t = 1, \ldots, k_n$, $n = 1, 2, \ldots$, and there exist real non-negative constants $\{c_{nt} : t = 1, \ldots, k_n, n = 1, 2, \ldots\}$ and $\{\psi_m : m = 0, 1, 2, \ldots\}$ such that $\psi_m \to 0$ as $m \to \infty$, and for all $t = 1, \ldots, k_n$, $n = 1, 2, \ldots$ and $m = 0, 1, \ldots$

(a) $\| E(X_{nt} \mid \mathcal{F}_{n,t-m}) \|_p \le c_{nt}\, \psi_m$; and

(b) $\| X_{nt} - E(X_{nt} \mid \mathcal{F}_{n,t+m}) \|_p \le c_{nt}\, \psi_{m+1}$. □

Here and elsewhere $\| \cdot \|_p$ denotes the L_p- norm. In particular $\| X \|_1 = E \mid X \mid$.

Andrews gives examples of L_1 –mixingales, including independent sequences, martingale difference sequences, m –dependent sequences, stationary mean zero Gaussian processes with continuous non-zero spectrum, ϕ–, α–, and ρ –mixing processes (see McLeish [1975] and Herrndorf [1984] for definitions), general infinite moving averages of independent or martingale difference sequences, generalizations of near epoch dependent (NED) sequences, (Billingsley [1968], McLeish [1975], Gallant and White [1988]), and McLeish's original (L_2–) mixingales. Such processes cover a wide range of possibilities for dependence, while imposing relatively little in the way of restrictions on allowable heterogeneity. Andrews [1988, Theorem 2(b)] gives the following useful result.

THEOREM A.2.7: If $\{X_{nt}, \mathcal{F}_{nt}\}$ is a uniformly integrable L_1-mixingale with $c_{nt} = \| X_{nt} \|_1$, then $E \mid n^{-1} \sum_{t=1}^{n} X_{nt} \mid \to 0$ as $n \to \infty$, so that $n^{-1} \sum_{t=1}^{n} X_{nt} \to 0 \ prob - P$. □

Unlike the strong ULLN of McLeish, no rates are required for the convergence of ψ_m to zero. Heterogeneity is restricted by the mild requirement that $\{X_{nt}\}$ be uniformly integrable. This is also a mild moment requirement. For this it is sufficient but not necessary that $E \mid X_{nt} \mid^{1+\delta} < \Delta < \infty$ for some $\delta > 0$, $t = 1, 2, \ldots, n$, $n = 1, 2, \ldots$.

We exploit this result by adopting the following definition for a random function continuous on Θ to be an L_1 –mixingale.

DEFINITION A.2.8 (*Uniformly Integrable L_1 –mixingale on* (Θ, ρ)): Let $(\Omega, \mathcal{F}, P)$ be a probability space and let (Θ, ρ) be a separable metric space. Suppose $q_{nt} : \Omega \times \Theta \to \mathbb{R}$ are random functions continuous on Θ $a.s.-P$, $t = 1, \ldots, n$, $n = 1, 2, \ldots$, and let $\mathcal{F}_{n,t-1} \subset \mathcal{F}_{n,t} \subset \mathcal{F}$, $t = 1, \ldots, n$, $n = 1, 2, \ldots$. The double array $\{q_{nt}, \mathcal{F}_{nt}\}$ is a *uniformly integrable* L_1 *–mixingale on* (Θ, ρ) if and only if for each θ^o in Θ there exists $\delta^o > 0$ such that the double arrays $\{\overset{o}{\bar{q}}_{nt}(\delta) - E(\overset{o}{\bar{q}}_{nt}(\delta)), \mathcal{F}_{nt}\}$ and $\{\overset{o}{\underline{q}}_{nt}(\delta) - E(\overset{o}{\underline{q}}_{nt}(\theta)), \mathcal{F}_{nt}\}$ are L_1 –mixingales for all $0 < \delta \le \delta^o$, with $\{c^o_{nt}(\delta) = 2 \max(\| \overset{o}{\bar{q}}_{nt}(\delta) \|_1, \| \underline{q}^o_{nt}(\delta) \|_1)\}$ uniformly integrable. □

The uniform integrability condition typically holds under mild domination conditions, e.g., $E[(\sup_\Theta \mid q_{nt}(\theta) \mid)^{1+\delta}] < \Delta$, for some $\delta > 0$, $t = 1, \ldots, n$, $n = 1, 2, \ldots$. The L_1 –mixingale condition is usually straightforward to verify. For example, if for each θ in Θ $q_{nt}(\cdot, \theta)$ is a function measurable with respect to a finite number of lags of an independent process or of a $\phi-$, $\alpha-$, or ρ –mixing process, then so must be $\overline{q}^o_{nt}(\delta)$ and $\underline{q}^o_{nt}(\delta)$, ensuring that they are L_1 –mixingales. NED functions of mixing processes can also be verified to be L_1 –mixingales using Lipschitz conditions as in Andrews [1988], or techniques analogous to those of Gallant and White [1988, Chapter 4]. Thus the conditions of Definition A.2.8 are appropriately primitive conditions useful in stating a weak ULLN.

From Theorem A.2.7, uniformly integrable L_1 –mixingales obey the weak law of large numbers locally for each θ^o in Θ. This allows statement of the following rather general weak uniform law of large numbers.

THEOREM A.2.9: Let $(\Omega, \mathcal{F}, P)$ be a complete probability space, let $\mathcal{F}_{nt-1} \subset \mathcal{F}_{nt} \subset \mathcal{F}$, $t = 1, \ldots, n$, $n = 1, 2, \ldots$, and let (Θ, ρ) be a compact metric space. Suppose

(a) $\{q_{nt} : \Omega \times \Theta \to \mathbb{R}\}$ is Lipschitz-L_1 $a.s.$ on Θ; and

(b) $\{q_{nt}, \mathcal{F}_{nt}\}$ is a uniformly integrable L_1 –mixingale on (Θ, ρ).

Then

(i) $\bar{Q}_n(\cdot) \equiv n^{-1} \sum_{t=1}^n E(q_{nt}(\cdot)) : \Theta \to \mathbb{R}$ is continuous on Θ uniformly in n; and

(ii) $Q_n(\theta) - \bar{Q}_n(\theta) \to 0$ $prob-P$ uniformly on Θ. □

PROOF: The result follows immediately from Theorem A.2.5 and Theorem A.2.7. □

Because of the relatively mild conditions it imposes, this result can be applied in many commonly encountered situations. As should already be evident, it delivers results immediately for cases involving q_{nt} measurable with respect to a finite number of independent or mixing processes under mild domination conditions. A little more work is required to obtain results for NED functions of an underlying mixing process. We leave the straightforward details to the interested reader.

Besides the references already given, the interested reader may wish to consult Hoadley [1971], Bierens [1981, 1982], Pollard [1984] and Pötscher and Prucha [1989] for related results.

APPENDIX 3

Central Limit Theorems

This appendix collects together a number of useful central limit theorems.

THEOREM A.3.1 (*Lindeberg-Lévy*): Let $\{X_t\}$ be a sequence of i.i.d random scalars. If var $X_t \equiv \sigma^2 < \infty$, $\sigma^2 \neq 0$, then $n^{-1/2} \Sigma_{t=1}^{n} (X_t - \mu) / \sigma \overset{A}{\sim} N(0, 1)$, where $\mu \equiv E(X_1)$. □

THEOREM A.3.2: Let $\{X_t, \mathcal{F}_t, t = 0, \pm 1, \pm 2, \ldots\}$ be an adapted stochastic sequence such that $\{X_t\}$ is stationary and ergodic with $E(X_t^2) < \infty$. Suppose that $E(X_0 \mid \mathcal{F}_{-m}) \overset{qm}{\rightarrow} 0$ as $m \rightarrow \infty$ and $\Sigma_{j=0}^{\infty}$ (var $R_{0j})^{1/2} < \infty$, $R_{0j} \equiv E(X_0 \mid \mathcal{F}_{-j}) - E(X_0 \mid \mathcal{F}_{-j-1})$. Let $\bar{\sigma}_n^2 \equiv n\, E[(n^{-1} \Sigma_{t=1}^{n} X_t)^2]$. Then there exists $\bar{\sigma}^2 < \infty$ such that $\bar{\sigma}_n^2 \rightarrow \bar{\sigma}^2$ as $n \rightarrow \infty$, and if $\bar{\sigma}^2 > 0$, $n^{-1/2} \Sigma_{t=1}^{n} (X_t / \bar{\sigma}) \overset{A}{\sim} N(0, 1)$. □

In this result, note that the condition $E(X_0 \mid \mathcal{F}_{-m}) \overset{qm}{\rightarrow} 0$ implies $E(X_0) = 0$ (e.g. White [1984a, Lemma 5.14]). (The notation $\overset{qm}{\rightarrow}$ denotes convergence in quadratic mean.) More general results are given by Gordin [1969] and Hannan [1973].

THEOREM A.3.3: Let $\{X_{nt}\}$ be a double array of independent random scalars such that $\mu_{nt} \equiv E(X_{nt}) < \infty$ and $E \mid X_{nt} - \mu_{nt} \mid^{2+\delta} < \Delta$ for some $\delta > 0$, $\Delta < \infty$, $t = 1, \ldots, n$, $n = 1, 2, \ldots$. Let $\bar{\sigma}_n^2 \equiv n^{-1} \Sigma_{t=1}^{n} \sigma_{nt}^2$, with $\sigma_{nt}^2 \equiv$ var X_{nt}. If $\bar{\sigma}_n^2 > \delta' > 0$ $a.a.n$, then $n^{-1/2} \Sigma_{t=1}^{n} (X_{nt} - \mu_{nt}) / \bar{\sigma}_n \overset{A}{\sim} N(0, 1)$. □

THEOREM A.3.4: Let $\{X_{nt}, \mathcal{F}_{nt}\}$ be a scalar martingale difference sequence such that $E \mid X_{nt} \mid^{2+\delta} < \Delta$ for some $\delta > 0$, $\Delta < \infty$, $t = 1, \ldots, n$, $n = 1, 2, \ldots$. Let $\bar{\sigma}_n^2 \equiv n^{-1} \Sigma_{t=1}^n \sigma_{nt}^2$, with $\sigma_{nt}^2 \equiv \text{var } X_{nt}$. If $\bar{\sigma}_n^2 > \delta' > 0$ $a.a.n$ and if $\{X_{nt}^2 - E(X_{nt}^2), \mathcal{F}_{nt}\}$ is an L_1-mixingale then $n^{-1/2} \Sigma_{t=1}^n X_{nt} / \bar{\sigma}_n \overset{A}{\sim} N(0, 1)$. □

In the preceding result, the assumption that $\{X_{nt}^2 - E(X_{nt}^2), \mathcal{F}_{nt}\}$ is an L_1-mixingale and the uniform integrability of $\{X_{nt}^2\}$ (a consequence of $E \mid X_{nt}^2 \mid^{1+\delta/2} = E \mid X_{nt} \mid^{2+\delta} < \Delta$) imply by Andrews' WLLN ([1988, Theorem A.2.7]) that $n^{-1} \Sigma_{t=1}^n X_{nt}^2 - \bar{\sigma}_n^2 \to 0$ $prob - P$. (See White [1984a, Corollary 5.25].)

A central limit theorem related to results of Withers [1981] valid for general dependent heterogeneous double arrays has been given by Wooldridge [1986]. Wooldridge's result applies to near epoch dependent functions of mixing processes. To state the conditions of Wooldridge's central limit theorem, we use the following definitions.

DEFINITION A.3.5 (*Mixing*): Let $\{V_t\}$ be a sequence of random vectors, let $\mathcal{F}_\tau^t \equiv \sigma(V_\tau, \ldots, V_t)$ and for each $m = 0, 1, 2, \ldots$ define the *mixing coefficients*

$$\phi_m \equiv \sup_\tau \sup_{\{F \in \mathcal{F}_{-\infty}^\tau, G \in \mathcal{F}_{\tau+m}^\infty : P(F>0)\}} \mid P(G \mid F) - P(G) \mid ,$$

$$\alpha_m \equiv \sup_\tau \sup_{\{F \in \mathcal{F}_{-\infty}^\tau, G \in \mathcal{F}_{\tau+m}^\infty\}} \mid P(G \cap F) - P(G)P(F) \mid .$$

If $\phi_m \to 0$ ($\alpha_m \to 0$) as $m \to \infty$ then we say that $\{V_t\}$ is a ϕ-*mixing* (α-*mixing*) sequence. If $\phi_m = O(m^\lambda)$ for some $\lambda < -a$, then ϕ_m is said to be *of size* -a, and similarly for α_m. □

DEFINITION A.3.6 (*Near Epoch Dependence*): Let $\{X_{nt}\}$ be a double array of random variables with $E(X_{nt}^2) < \infty$, $n, t = 1, 2, \ldots$, and let $\{V_t\}$ be a sequence of random variables. Let $E_{t-m}^{t+m}(\cdot) \equiv E(\cdot \mid \mathcal{F}_{t-m}^{t+m})$, $\mathcal{F}_{t-m}^{t+m} = \sigma(V_{t-m}, \ldots, V_{t+m})$. Then $\{X_{nt}\}$ is *near epoch dependent on* $\{V_t\}$ *of size* -a if

$$\nu_m \equiv \sup_n \sup_t \| X_{nt} - E_{t-m}^{t+m}(X_{nt}) \|_2$$

is of size -a. □

See Gallant and White [1988] for a discussion of near epoch dependence. We can now state the central limit result of Wooldridge [1986].

THEOREM A.3.7: Let $\{X_{nt}\}$ be a double array such that $\| X_{nt} \|_r \leq \Delta < \infty$ for some $r > 2$, $E(X_{nt}) = 0$, n, $t = 1, 2, \ldots$, and $\{X_{nt}\}$ is near epoch dependent on $\{V_t\}$ of size -1, where $\{V_t\}$ is a mixing process with ϕ_m of size $-r/(r-1)$ or α_m of size $-2r/(r-2)$. Define $\sigma_n^2 \equiv \text{var}\,(\Sigma_{t=1}^n X_{nt})$ and suppose that σ_n^{-2} is $O(n^{-1})$. Then $\sigma_n^{-1} \sum_{t=1}^n X_{nt} \overset{A}{\sim} N\,(0\,,1)$. □

Although all of the foregoing results apply to scalar sequences, results for vector sequences follow from the preceding results upon application of the well known Cramér-Wold device.

THEOREM A.3.8 (*Cramér-Wold Device*): Let $\{Z_n\}$ be a sequence of random $p \times 1$ vectors and suppose that for any real $p \times 1$ vector λ, $\lambda'\lambda = 1$, $\lambda' Z_n \overset{A}{\sim} \lambda' Z$, where Z is a $p \times 1$ random vector with joint distribution function F. Then the limiting distribution function of Z_n exists and equals F, i.e. $Z_n \overset{A}{\sim} F$. □

For some further discussion of the central limit theorem in econometric contexts, see White [1984a, Ch. 5].

References

Aitcheson J. and S.D. Silvey [1958]: "Estimation Subject to Restraints," *Annals of Mathematical Statistics* 29, 813–828.

Akaike, H. [1973]: "Information Theory and an Extension of the Likelihood Principle," in B.N. Petrov and F. Csáki, eds., *Proceedings of the Second International Symposium on Information Theory*. Budapest: Akadémiai Kiado, 267–281.

Amemiya, T. [1966]: "Specification Analysis in the Estimation of Parameters of a Simultaneous Equation Model with Autoregressive Errors," *Econometrica* 34, 283–306.

Amemiya, T. [1977]: "The Maximum Likelihood and the Nonlinear Three-Stage Least Squares Estimator in the General Nonlinear Simultaneous Equation Model," *Econometrica* 45, 955–968.

Andersen, E.B. [1970]: "Asymptotic Properties of Conditional Maximum Likelihood Estimators," *Journal of the Royal Statistical Society* B 32, 283–301.

Anderson, T.W. and H. Rubin [1949]: "Estimation of the Parameters of a Single Equation in a Complete System of Stochastic Equations," *Annals of Mathematical Statistics* 20, 46–63.

Andrews, D.W.K. [1987]: "Consistency in Nonlinear Econometric Models: A Generic Uniform Law of Large Numbers," *Econometrica* 55, 1465–1472.

Andrews, D.W.K. [1988]: "Laws of Large Numbers for Dependent Non-identically Distributed Random Variables," *Econometric Theory* 4, 458–467.

Andrews, D.W.K. [1991]: "Heteroskedasticity and Autocorrelation Consistent Covariance Matrix Estimation," *Econometrica* 59, 817–858.

Apostol, T.M. [1957]: *Mathematical Analysis*. Reading, MA: Addison Wesley.

Bahadur, R.R. [1964]: "On Fisher's Bound for Asymptotic Variances," *Annals of Mathematical Statistics* 35, 1545–52.

Baldessari, B. [1969]: "The Distribution of a Quadratic Form of Normal Random Variables," *Annals of Mathematical Statistics*, 1700–1704.

Barnett, W., J. Powell and G. Tauchen [1991]: *Nonparametric and Semiparametric Methods in Econometrics and Statistics*. New York: Cambridge University Press.

Bartle, R. [1966]: *The Elements of Integration*. New York: Wiley.

Bartle, R. [1976]: *The Elements of Real Analysis*. New York: Wiley.

Bates, C. and H. White [1985]: "A Unified Theory of Consistent Estimation for Parametric Models," *Econometric Theory* 1, 151–178.

Bates, C. and H. White [1988]: "Efficient Instrumental Variables Estimation of Systems of Implicit Heterogeneous Nonlinear Dynamic Equations With Nonspherical Errors," in W.A. Barnett, E.R. Berndt and H. White, eds., *Proceedings of the Third International Symposium in Economy Theory and Econometrics*, pp. 3–26.

Bates, C. and H. White [1990]: "Determination of Estimators with Minimum Asymptotic Covariance Matrices," UCSD Department of Economics Discussion Paper.

Bera, A.K. and C.M. Jarque [1982]: "Model Specification Tests: A Simultaneous Approach," *Journal of Econometrics* 20, 59–82.

Beran, R. [1977]: "Minimum Hellinger Distance Estimates for Parametric Models," *Annals of Statistics* 5, 445–463.

Beran, R. [1980]: "Asymptotic Lower Bounds for Risk in Robust Estimation," *Annals of Statistics* 8, 1252–1264.

Berk, R.H. [1966]: "Limiting Behavior of Posterior Distributions When the Model is Incorrect," *Annals of Mathematical Statistics* 37, 51–58.

Berk, R.H. [1970]: "Consistency A Posteriori," *Annals of Mathematical Statistics* 41, 894–906.

Berndt, E.R., B.H. Hall, R.E. Hall and J.A. Hausman [1974]: "Estimation and Inference in Nonlinear Structural Models," *Annals of Economic and Social Measurement* 3, 653–666.

Bierens, H. [1981]: *Robust Methods and Asymptotic Theory in Nonlinear Econometrics*. New York: Springer-Verlag.

Bierens, H. [1982]: "A Uniform Weak Law of Large Numbers Under ϕ-mixing with Application to Nonlinear Least Squares Estimation," *Statistica Neerlandica* 36, 81–86.

Bierens, H.J. [1990]: "A Consistent Conditional Moment Test of Functional Forms," *Econometrica* 58, 1443–1458.

Bildikar, S. and G.P. Patil [1968]: "Multivariate Exponential-Type Distributions," *Annals of Mathematical Statistics* 39, 1316–1326.

Billingsley, P. [1968]: *Convergence of Probability Measures*. New York: Wiley.

Billingsley, P. [1979]: *Probability and Measure*. New York: Wiley.

Billingsley, P. [1986]: *Probability and Measure*, second edition. New York: Wiley.

Border, K. [1984]: "Measurability of Restricted Two-Step Estimators," California Institute of Technology Working Paper.

Breusch, T.S. and A.R. Pagan [1979]: "A Simple Test for Heteroscedasticity and Random Coefficient Variation," *Econometrica* 50, 987–1007.

Burguete, J.F., A.R. Gallant and G. Souza [1982]: "On Unification of the Asymptotic Theory of Nonlinear Econometric Models," *Econometric Reviews* 1, 151–190.

Cavanagh, C.L. [1985]: "Second Order Admissibility of Likelihood Based Tests," Harvard Institute for Economic Research Discussion Paper 1148.

Charnes, A., E.L. Frome and P. L. Yu, [1976]: "The Equivalence of Generalized Least Squares and Maximum Likelihood Estimates in the Exponential Family," *Journal of the American Statistical Association* 71, 169–171.

Chesher, A. and R. Spady [1986]: "The Finite Sample Properties of the Information Matrix Test," Bell Communications Research mimeo.

Chesher, A. and R. Spady [1991]: "Asymptotic Expansions of the Information Test Statistic," *Econometrica* 59, 787–815.

Chow, G.C. [1981]: "Selection of Models by the Information Criterion," in E.G. Charatsis, ed., *Proceedings of the Econometric Society European Meeting 1979*. Amsterdam: North Holland.

Cox, D.R. [1961]: "Tests of Separate Families of Hypotheses," in *Proceedings of the Fourth Berkeley Symposium on Mathematical Statistics and Probability*, Vol. 1. Berkeley: University of California Press, 105–123.

Cox, D.R. [1962]: "Further Results on Tests of Separate Families of Hypotheses," *Journal of the Royal Statistical Society* B, 406–424.

Cox, D.R. and E.J. Snell [1968]: "A General Definition of Residuals," *Journal of the Royal Statistical Society* B 30, 248–265.

Cramér, H. [1946]: *Mathematical Methods of Statistics*. Princeton: Princeton University Press.

Crowder, M. [1976]: "Maximum Likelihood Estimation for Dependent Observations," *Journal of the Royal Statistical Society* B38, 45–53.

Darmois, G. [1945]: "Sur le Lois Limites de la Dispersion de Certaines Estimations," *Review of the Institute of the International Statistical Society* 13, 9–15.

Dastoor, N.K. and G. Fisher [1988]: "On Point-Optimal Cox Tests," *Econometric Theory* 4, in press.

Davidson, R. and J.G. MacKinnon [1981]: "Several Tests for Model Misspecification in the Presence of Alternative Hypotheses," *Econometrica* 49, 781–793.

Davidson, R. and J.G. MacKinnon [1988]: "A New Form of the Information Matrix Test," Queen's University Department of Economics Discussion Paper #724.

Debreu, G. [1967]: "Integration of Correspondences," in *Proceedings of the Fifth Berkeley Symposium on Mathematical Statistics and Probability*, Vol II-1. Berkeley: University of California Press, 351–372.

Domowitz, I. and H. White [1982]: "Misspecified Models with Dependent Observations," *Journal of Econometrics* 20, 35–58.

Duncan, G.M. (ed.) [1986]: "Continuous/Discrete Econometric Models with Unspecified Error Distribution," *Journal of Econometrics* 32.

Durbin, J. [1970]: "Testing for Serial Correlation in Least Squares Regression When Some of the Regressors are Lagged Dependent Variables," *Econometrica* 38, 410–421.

Efron, B. [1982]: *The Jackknife, the Bootstrap and Other Resampling Plans*. Philadelphia: Society for Industrial and Applied Mathematics.

Engle, R.F. [1982a]: "Autoregressive Conditional Heteroskedasticity with Estimates of the Variance of United Kingdom Inflations," *Econometrica* 50, 987–1008.

Engle, R.F. [1982b]: "A General Approach to Lagrange Multiplier Model Diagnostics," *Journal of Econometrics* 20, 83–104.

Engle, R.F., D.F. Hendry and J.F. Richard [1983]: "Exogeneity," *Econometrica* 51, 277–304.

Engle, R.F., D.M. Lilien and R.P. Robins [1987]: "Estimating Time-Varying Risk Premia in the Term Structure: The ARCH-M Model," *Econometrica* 55, 391–407.

Evans, M.A. and M. King [1985]: "A Point Optimal Test for Heteroskedastic Disturbances," *Journal of Econometrics* 27, 163–178.

Florens, J.-P. and M. Mouchart [1980]: "Initial and Sequential Reduction of Bayesian Experiments," Université Catholique de Louvain CORE Discussion Paper 8015.

Foutz, R.V. [1977]: "On the Unique Consistent Solution to the Likelihood Equations," *Journal of the American Statistical Association* 72, 147–148.

Foutz, R.V. and R.C. Srivastava [1977]: "The Performance of the Likelihood Ratio Test When the Model is Incorrect," *Annals of Statistics* 5, 1183–1194.

Frechet, M. [1943]: "Sur l'Extension de Certaines Evaluations Statistiques de Petits Echantillons," *Review of the Institute of the International Statistical Society* 1943, 182–205.

Freedman, D.A. and P. Diaconis [1982]: "On Inconsistent M-Estimators," *Annals of Statistics* 10, 454–461.

Gallant, A.R. and D. Jorgenson [1979]: "Statistical Inference for a System of Simultaneous, Nonlinear Implicit Equations in the Context of Instrumental Variables Estimation," *Journal of Econometrics* 11, 275–302.

Gallant, A.R. and H. White [1988]: *A Unified Theory of Estimation and Inference for Nonlinear Dynamic Models*. Oxford: Basil Blackwell.

Geman, S. and C.H. Hwang [1982]: "Nonparametric Maximum Likelihood Estimation by the Method of Sieves," *Annals of Statistics* 10, 401–414.

Geweke, J. [1978]: "Testing the Exogeneity Specification in the Complete Dynamic Simultaneous Equations Model," *Journal of Econometrics* 7, 163–185.

Geweke, J. [1982]: "Causality, Exogeneity and Inference," in W. Hildenbrand ed., *Advances in Econometrics*. New York: Cambridge University Press, 209–236.

Godfrey, L.G. [1978a]: "Testing Against General Autoregressive and Moving Average Error Models when the Regressors Include Lagged Dependent Variables," *Econometrica* 46, 1293–1302.

Godfrey, L.G. [1978b]: "Testing for Higher Order Serial Correlation in Regression Equations when the Regressors Include Lagged Dependent Variables," *Econometrica* 46, 1303–1310.

Godfrey, L.G. [1981]: "On the Invariance of the Lagrange Multiplier Test with Respect to Certain Changes in the Alternative Hypothesis," *Econometrica* 49, 1443–1456.

Godfrey, L.G. [1988]: *Misspecification Tests in Econometrics: The LM Principle and Other Approaches*. New York: Cambridge University Press.

Goldberger, A. [1981]: "Linear Regression after Selection," *Journal of Econometrics* 15, 357–366.

Gordin, M.I. [1969]: "The Central Limit Theorem for Stationary Processes," *Soviet Mathematics Doklady* 10, 1174–1176.

Gourieroux, C. and A. Monfort [1985]: "A General Theory for Asymptotic Tests," INSEE Document de Travail 8509.

Gourieroux, C., A. Monfort and A. Trognon [1983]: "Testing Nested or Nonnested Hypotheses," *Journal of Econometrics* 21, 83–116.

Gourieroux, C., A. Monfort and A. Trognon [1984]: "Pseudo-Maximum Likelihood Methods: Theory," *Econometrica* 681–700.

Gourieroux, C., A. Monfort and A. Trognon [1985]: "A General Approach to Serial Correlation," *Econometric Theory* 1, 315–340.

Granger, C.W.J. [1969]: "Investigating Causal Relations by Econometric Models and Cross-Spectral Methods," *Econometrica* 37, 424–438.

Granger, C.W.J. and P. Newbold [1986]: *Forecasting Economic Time Series*, 2nd ed. Orlando: Academic Press.

Greene, W. [1981]: "On the Asymptotic Bias of the Ordinary Least Squares Estimator of the Tobit Model," *Econometrica* 49, 505–514.

Grenander, U. [1981]: *Abstract Inference*. New York: Wiley.

Haavelmo, T. [1944]: "The Probability Approach in Econometrics," *Econometrica* 12, supplement.

Hannan, E.J. [1973]: "Central Limit Theorems for Time Series Regression," *Zeitschrift für Wahrscheinlichkeitstheorie und Verwandete Gebiete* 26, 157–170.

Hansen, L. [1982]: "Large Sample Properties of Generalized Method of Moments Estimators," *Econometrica* 50, 1029–1054.

Hausman, J.A. [1978]: "Specification Tests in Econometrics," *Econometrica* 46, 1251–1272.

Heckman, J. [1974]: "Shadow Prices, Market Wages and Labor Supply," *Econometrica* 42, 679–694.

Hendry, D.F. [1976]: "The Structure of Simultaneous Equations Estimators," *Journal of Econometrics* 4, 51–88.

Hendry, D.F. and J.-F. Richard [1982]: "On the Formulation of Empirical Models in Dynamic Econometrics," *Journal of Econometrics* 20, 3–34.

Herrndorf, N. [1984]: "An Invariance Principle for Weakly Dependent Sequences of Random Variables," *Annals of Probability* 12, 141–153.

Hildenbrand, W. [1974]: *Core and Equilibria of a Large Economy*. Princeton: Princeton University Press.

Hoadley, B. [1971]: "Asymptotic Properties of Estimators for the Independent Not Identically Distributed Case," *Annals of Mathematical Statistics* 42, 1977–1991.

Holly, A. [1982]: "A Remark on Hausman's Specification Test," *Econometrica* 50, 749–760.

Huber, P. [1964]: "Robust Estimation of a Location Parameter," *Annals of Mathematical Statistics* 35, 73–101.

Huber, P. [1967]: "The Behavior of Maximum Likelihood Estimates Under Nonstandard Conditions," in *Proceedings of the Fifth Berkeley Symposium in Mathematical Statistics and Probability*, Vol. 1, Berkeley: University of California Press.

Ibragimov, I.A. and R.Z. Has'minskii [1981]: *Statistical Estimation: Asymptotic Theory*. New York: Springer-Verlag.

Jennrich, R.I. [1969]: "Asymptotic Properties of Nonlinear Least Squares Estimators," *Annals of Mathematical Statistics* 40, 633–643.

Johnson, N.L. and S. Kotz [1970]: *Continuous Univariate Distributions-1*. New York: Houghton-Mifflin.

Kennan, J. and G. Neumann [1988]: "Why Does the Information Matrix Test Reject Too Often? A Diagnosis of Some Monte Carlo Symptoms," University of Iowa, Department of Economics Discussion Paper.

Kent, J.T. [1982]: "Robust Properties of Likelihood Ratio Tests," *Biometrika* 69, 19–27.

King, M. [1985]: "A Point Optimal Test for Autoregressive Disturbances," *Journal of Econometrics* 27, 21–38.

Klein, E. and A. Thompson [1984]: *Theory of Correspondences*. New York: Wiley.

Koenker, R. and G. Bassett [1978]: "Regression Quantiles," *Econometrica* 46, 33–50.

Koopmans, T.C. [1950]: "When is an Equation System Complete for Statistical Purposes?" in T.C. Koopmans, ed. *Statistical Inference in Dynamic Economic Models*. New York: Wiley.

Kullback, L. and R.A. Leibler [1951]: "On Information and Sufficiency," *Annals of Mathematical Statistics* 22, 79–86.

Lancaster, T. [1984]: "The Covariance Matrix of the Information Matrix Test," *Econometrica* 52, 1051–1054.

Le Cam, L. [1953]: "On Some Asymptotic Properties of the Maximum Likelihood Estimates and Related Bayes' Estimates," *University of California Publications in Statistics*, 277–329.

Le Cam, L. [1956]: "On the Asymptotic Theory of Estimation and Testing Hypotheses," *Proceedings of the Third Berkeley Symposium on Mathematical Statistics and Probability* 1, 129–56.

Le Cam, L. [1960]: "Locally Asymptotically Normal Families of Distributions," *University of California Publications in Statistics* 3, 37–98.

Le Cam, L. [1986]: *Asymptotic Methods in Statistical Decision Theory*. New York: Springer-Verlag.

Le Cam, L. and E.L. Lehmann [1974]: "J. Neyman - On the Occasion of His 80th Birthday," *Annals of Statistics* 2, vii-xiii.

Lehmann, E. [1983]: *Theory of Point Estimation*. New York: Wiley.

Levine, D. [1983]: "A Remark on Serial Correlation in Maximum Likelihood," *Journal of Econometrics* 23, 337–342.

Ljung, L. [1987]: *Systems Identification: Theory for the User*. Englewood Cliffs: Prentice Hall.

Lucas, R.E., Jr. [1976]: "Econometric Policy Evaluation: A Critique," in K. Brunner and A.H. Meltzer (eds.) *The Phillips Curve and Labor Markets*. Carnegie-Rochester Conference Series on Public Policy, Vol. 1. Amsterdam: North Holland.

Lukacs, E. [1975]: *Stochastic Convergence*. New York: Academic Press.

MacKinnon, J.G. [1983]: "Model Specification Tests Against Non-nested Alternatives," *Econometric Reviews* 2, 85–110.

MacKinnon, J.G. and H. White [1985]: "Some Heteroskedasticity Consistent Covariance Matrix Estimators with Improved Finite Sample Properties," *Journal of Econometrics* 29, 305–326.

Magnus, Jan R. and Heinz Neudecker [1988]: *Matrix Differential Calculus with Applications in Statistics and Econometrics*. New York: Wiley.

Marschak, J. [1953]: "Economic Measurements for Policy and Prediction," in W.C. Hood and T.C. Koopman, eds. *Studies in Econometric Method*. New Haven: Yale University Press.

McLeish, D.L. [1975]: "A Maximal Inequality and Dependent Strong Laws," *Annals of Probability* 3, 826–836.

Mizon, G. [1984]: "The Encompassing Approach in Econometrics," in D.F. Hendry and K.F. Wallis, eds., *Econometrics and Quantitative Economics*. Oxford: Basil Blackwell.

Mizon, G. and J.-F. Richard [1986]: "The Encompassing Principle and its Application to Testing Non-nested Hypotheses," *Econometrica* 54, 657–678.

Newey, W.K. [1985]: "Maximum Likelihood Specification Testing and Conditional Moment Tests," *Econometrica* 53, 1047–1070.

Newey, W. and K. West [1987]: "A Simple Positive Semi-Definite Heteroskedasticity and Autocorrelation Consistent Covariance Matrix," *Econometrica* 55, 703–708.

Neyman, J. [1937]: "'Smooth' test for goodness of fit," *Skandinavisk Aktuarietiskrift* 20, 149–199.

Neyman, J. and E.S. Pearson [1933]: "On the Problem of the Most Efficient Tests of Statistical Hypotheses," *Philosophical Transactions of the Royal Society* A 236, 333–380.

Oberhofer, W. [1982]: "The Consistency of the Nonlinear Regression Minimizing the L-Norm," *Annals of Statistics* 10, 316–319.

Orcutt, G.H. [1952]: "Toward a Partial Re-direction of Econometrics," *Review of Economics and Statistics* 34, 195–213.

Orme, C. [1990]: "The Small-Sample Performance of the Information Matrix Test," *Journal of Econometrics* 46, 309–331.

Parzen, E. [1954]: "On Uniform Convergence of Families of Distributions," *University of California Publications in Statistics* 3, 37–98.

Perez-Amaral, T.F. [1989]: "Dynamic Information Matrix Tests and m-Tests: New

Results, Simulations and an Application," University of California San Diego Department of Economics Doctoral Dissertation.

Pesaran, H. and A. Deaton [1978]: "Testing Non-nested Nonlinear Regression Models," *Econometrica* 46, 677–694.

Pitman, E.G. [1949]: *Lecture Notes on Nonparametric Inference*, Columbia University, New York (unpublished).

Pitman, E.J.G. [1979]: *Some Basic Theory for Statistical Inference*. London: Chapman and Hall.

Phillips, A.W. [1956]: "Some Notes on the Estimation of Time-Forms of Reactions in Interdependent Dynamic Systems," *Economica* 23, 99–113.

Phillips, P.C.B. [1982]: "On the Consistency of Nonlinear FIML," *Econometrica* 50, 1307–1324.

Poirier, D.J. and P.A. Ruud [1988]: "Probit with Dependent Observations," *Review of Economic Studies*, 54, 593–614.

Pollard, D.B. [1984]: *Convergence of Stochastic Processes*. New York: Springer-Verlag.

Popper, K. [1962]: *Conjectures and Refutations: The Growth of Scientific Knowledge*. London: Routledge and Paul.

Pötscher, B. and I. Prucha [1989]: "A Uniform Law of Large Numbers for Dependent and Heterogeneous Data Processes," *Econometrica* 57, 675–684.

Ranga Rao, R. [1962]: "Relations Between Weak and Uniform Convergence of Measures with Applications," *Annals of Mathematical Statistics* 33, 659–680.

Rao, C.R. [1945]: "Information and Accuracy Attainable in the Estimation of Statistical Parameters," *Bulletin of the Calcutta Mathematical Society* 37, 81–91.

Rao, C.R. [1947]: "Large Sample Tests of Statistical Hypotheses Concerning Several Parameters with Applications to Problems of Estimation," *Proceedings of the Cambridge Philosophical Society* 44, 50–57.

Rao, C.R. [1963]: "Criteria of Estimation in Large Samples," *Sankhyā* A 25, 189–206.

Rao, C.R. [1973]: *Linear Statistical Inference and Its Applications*. New York: Wiley.

Renyi, A. [1961]: "On Measures of Entropy and Information," in *Proceedings of the Fourth Berkeley Symposium in Mathematical Statistics*. Berkeley: University of California Press.

Renyi, A. [1970]: *Probability Theory*. Amsterdam: North Holland.

Richard, J.F. [1979]: "Exogeneity, Inference and Prediction in so-called Incomplete Dynamic Simultaneous Equation Models," Université Catholique de Louvain CORE Discussion Paper 7922.

Robinson, P.J. [1988]: "Semiparametric Econometrics: A Survey," *Journal of Applied Econometrics*.

Robinson, P.M. [1982]: "On the Asymptotic Properties of Estimators of Models Containing Limited Dependent Variables," *Econometrica* 50, 27–42.

Rockafellar, R.T. [1970]: *Convex Analysis*. Princeton: Princeton University Press.

Rothenberg, T. [1973]: *Efficient Estimation with a Priori Information*. New Haven: Yale University Press.

Roussas, G. [1972]: *Contiguity of Probability Measures: Some Applications in Statistics*. Cambridge: Cambridge University Press.

Rudin, W. [1964]: *Principles of Mathematical Analysis*. New York: McGraw-Hill.

Rumelhart, D. and J. McClelland [1986]: *Parallel Distributed Processing: Explorations in the Microstructures of Cognition*, Vol. 1. Cambridge: MIT Press.

Ruud, P.A. [1983]: "Sufficient Conditions for the Consistency of Maximum Likelihood Estimation Despite Misspecification of Distribution," *Econometrica* 51, 225–228.

Ruud, P.A. [1986]: "Consistent Estimation of Limited Dependent Variable Models Despite Misspecification of Distribution," *Journal of Econometrics* 32, 157–187.

Sargan, D. [1958]: "The Estimation of Economic Relationships Using Instrumental Variables," *Econometrica* 26, 393–415.

Sims, C.A. [1972]: "Money, Income and Causality," *American Economic Review* 62, 540–552.

Sims, C.A. [1977]: "Exogeneity and Causal Ordering in Macroeconomic Models," in C.A. Sims, ed., *New Methods in Business Cycle Research: Proceedings from a Conference*. Minneapolis: Federal Reserve Bank of Minneapolis.

Stinchcombe, M. and H. White [1992]: "Some Measurability Results for Extrema of Random Functions Over Random Sets," *Review of Economic Studies*, forthcoming.

Stone, C.J. [1985]: "Additive Regression and Other Nonparametric Models," *Annals of Statistics* 13, 689–705.

Tauchen, G. [1985]: "Diagnostic Testing and Evaluation of Maximum Likelihood Models," *Journal of Econometrics* 30, 415–444.

Teicher, H. [1985]: "Almost Certain Convergence in Double Arrays," *Zeitschrift für Wahrscheinlichkeitstheorie und Verwandete Gebiete* 69, 331–345.

Theil, H. [1953]: "Repeated Least-Squares Applied to Complete Equation Systems," The Hague: Central Planning Bureau (mimeo).

Theil, H. [1961]: *Economic Forecasts and Policy*, second edition. Amsterdam: North-Holland.

Theil, H. [1971]: *Principles of Econometrics*. New York: Wiley.

Varian, H. [1984]: *Microeconomic Analysis*. New York: Norton.

Vuong, Q. [1983]: "Misspecification and Conditional Maximum Likelihood Estimation," California Institute of Technology Working Paper.

Vuong, Q. [1984]: "Two Stage Conditional Maximum Likelihood Estimation of Econometric Models," California Institute of Technology Division of Humanities and Social Sciences mimeo.

Vuong, Q. [1986]: "Cramer-Rao Bounds for Misspecified Models," California Institute of Technology Working Paper.

Wald, A. [1943]: "Tests of Statistical Hypotheses Concerning Several Parameters when the Number of Observations is Large," *Transactions of the American Mathematial Society* 54, 426–482.

Weiss, L. [1971]: "Asymptotic Properties of Maximum Likelihood Estimators in Some Nonstandard Cases," *Journal of the American Statistical Association* 66, 345–350.

Weiss, L. [1973]: "Asymptotic Properties of Maximum Likelihood Estimators in Some Nonstandard Cases, II," *Journal of the American Statistical Society* 68, 428–430.

White, H. [1980a]: "A Note on Normality and the Consistency of the Nonlinear Simultaneous Equations Maximum Likelihood Estimator," UCSD Department of Economics mimeo.

White, H. [1980b]: "A Heteroskedasticity-Consistent Covariance Matrix Estimator and a Direct Test for Heteroskedasticity," *Econometrica* 48, 817–838.

White, H. [1981]: "Consequences and Detection of Misspecified Nonlinear Regression Models," *Journal of the American Statistical Association* 76, 419–433.

White, H. [1982]: "Maximum Likelihood Estimation of Misspecified Models," *Econometrica* 50, 1–25.

White, H. [1984a]: *Asymptotic Theory for Econometricians.* Orlando: Academic Press.

White, H. [1984b]: "Maximum Likelihood Estimation of Misspecified Dynamic Models," in T.K. Dijkstra, ed., *Misspecification Analysis.* New York: Springer-Verlag.

White, H. [1984c]: "Comment on 'Tests of Specification in Econometrics' by Paul A. Ruud," *Econometric Reviews* 3, 261–267.

White, H. [1987]: "Specification Testing in Dynamic Models," in T. Bewley, ed., *Advances in Econometrics - Fifth World Congress*, Vol. 1. New York: Cambridge University Press, 1–58.

White, H. [1988]: *Estimation, Inference and Specification Analysis.* Manuscript, The Department of Economics, University of California San Diego.

White, H. [1989]: "Learning in Artificial Neural Networks: A Statistical Perspective," *Neural Computation* 1, 425–464.

White, H. [1990]: "A Consistent Model Selection Procedure Based on *m*-Testing," in C.W.J. Granger, ed., *Modelling Economic Series: Readings in Econometric Methodology.* Oxford: Oxford University Press, pp. 369–383.

White, H. and J. Wooldridge [1991]: "Sieve Estimation with Dependent Observations," in W. Barnett, J. Powell and G. Tauchen, eds., *Nonparametric and Semi-Parametric Methods in Econometrics and Statistics.* New York: Cambridge University Press, pp. 459–493.

Widder, D.V. [1946]: *The Laplace Transform.* Princeton: Princeton University Press.

Withers, C.S. [1981]: "Central Limit Theorems for Dependent Variables I," *Zeitschrift für Wahrscheinlichkeitstheorie und Verwandete Gebiete* 57, 509–534.

Wooldridge, J. [1986]: "Asymptotic Properties of Econometric Estimators," University of California San Diego Department of Economics Doctoral Dissertation.

Wooldridge, J. [1987]: "Specification Testing and Quasi-Maximum Likelihood Estimation," MIT Department of Economics Working Paper No. 479.

Wooldridge, J. [1990]: "A Unified Approach to Robust, Regression-based Specification Tests," *Econometric Theory* 6, 17–43.

Zellner, A. [1962]: "An Efficient Method of Estimating Seemingly Unrelated Regressions and Tests for Aggregation Bias," *Journal of the American Statistical Association* 57, 348–368.

Zellner, A. and H. Theil [1962]: "Three-Stage Least Squares: Simultaneous Estimation of Simultaneous Equations," *Econometrica* 30, 54–78.

ASSUMPTION INDEX

For ease of reference, this index lists all of the labeled assumptions given in the text in the order in which they are introduced. The assumptions and their various subparts are not in force before the indicated page.

DEFINITION, LEMMA, PROPOSITION, THEOREM AND COROLLARY INDEX

For ease of reference, this index lists all of the labeled definitions, lemmas, propositions and theorems given in the text in the order in which they are introduced.

INFERENCE INDEX